CONTENTS

Learning the Special Techniques

Test Yourself

OVERVIEW

Introduction

■ DO I REALLY NEED TO STUDY?

If you want a realistic chance to get a good job with the United States Postal Service (USPS), the answer is—YES! Just examine these figures.

In 1992, approximately 500,000 persons, nationwide, applied to take the various Postal Service examinations. In 1998, 550,000 turned out. The great majority of them were seeking the most popular jobs: postal clerk, letter carrier, and mail handler. The 1994 460/470 exam, attracted 158,000 people for jobs in only two of New York City's five boroughs!

The picture is not complete, however, unless we also know how many job openings there were. Several year ago, in Chicago, 39,000 people signed up for the mail handler test—but there were only 300 jobs available. A test given in St. Louis for postal clerk carrier drew 8,000 candidates for about 50 job openings. In 1998, when filing for the 460/470 test was due to open, a USPS official estimated that there would be 2,000 job openings. But, based on the experience in 1994 and other years, there could easily be 200,000 people filing. When you examine these and other records, it appears that only 1 percent of those who file actually end up with a job. Obviously the competition is stiff, but you can turn the odds in your favor, if *you prepare for the test*.

Exactly why is the competition so great? It's because these Postal Service jobs are extremely desirable in terms of salary, opportunity for advancement, and a broad range of other job benefits. (The *staring* salary of a full-time, regular letter carrier, for instance, is now over $25,000 per year.) Undoubtedly, the size of these turnouts is also a reflection of a growing decline in the number of good entry-level jobs. Persistently high levels of unemployment in many parts of the country also play a part. Regardless of the times, however, a job with the Postal Service is quite a good one. It offers a career opportunity with salary and fringe benefits that match or exceed those in many other private agencies and the public sector. In Chapter 1, you will get specific information on salaries, benefits, and the work itself.

Right now, the most important point to consider about the above statistics is the best way to overcome the competition. Obviously, not everyone who applies and passes will be appointed because the number of vacancies is limited. Those who pass will be considered for a job appointment in accordance with their score placements, and veteran status. The higher your test score, the higher your standing on the placement list and the better your chance for early appointment. Even *one* extra point can boost you hundreds of places on the job appointment list. This, of course, means hard, cold (and welcome) money to you.

Numerous studies and firsthand experience show that those who prepare for this test have a tremendous advantage over those who take the test "cold." This book is *dedicated to helping you gain that advantage*.

Another perhaps more vivid way to answer the question, "Do I really need to study?" comes from the author's personal experience taking many Postal Service exams.

I make it a point to meet and talk firsthand with several test takers, before and after the test. Most people appear nervous and anxious about taking the test but, all in all, the mood is upbeat. Most of them confess that they have prepared very little, if at all, for it. They say they've heard that the questions just call for "common sense." There is tension in the air but at the same time a lot of chatter and laughter.

But *after the test*, the picture is quite different. Many people register shock, disappointment, and amazement over the rigorousness of the exam. The general mood is subdued; there is very little of the laughter and chatter there was before. Some are openly downcast about their performance and their prospects of getting called for a job. They regret their lost opportunity and vow that they will really prepare of the next exam. *But that may not be held for another three years!*

■ WHAT THIS BOOK IS ALL ABOUT

Coming out high on the eligible list is what this book is "all about." This book had its origin in a series of exam preparation courses attended by several thousand candidates for the most recent Postal Service tests. The courses taught these men and women techniques for taking the test that were based on the author's years of successful test preparation experience. Special research was done to develop the best methods for taking this examination. The end result—success on the actual test—has been the final and best way known to show the value of these mentioned and the courses.

Now, all of this knowledge had been combined with his *personal* experiences taking the U.S. Postal Service Test Battery Series 460/470. This *one* test is now used to fill *all* these eight entry-level positions: Postal Clerk, City/Rural Mail Carriers, Machine Distribution Clerk, Mail Handler, Mail Processor, Mark-Up Clerk, and Flat-Sorting Machine Operator. This new exam selects portions of the separate exams formerly given for these titles and combine them into one test, They are: Address Checking, Memory for Addresses, Number Series, and Following Oral Directions.

Accordingly, this one book combines all of the invaluable test strategies and techniques, drills, self-study exercises, practice tests, and visual aids formerly contained in our separate books.

Use this book at home to help you pass—and *pass high*—when you take your examination. It will provide practical information on the following:

- How and when to apply

- Eligibility requirements

- Why and what you should study

- What the U.S. Postal Service Battery Test Series 460/470* is like

- Complete test-taking strategies and techniques

- How to study and to apply what you've learned

The format is simple. First, you will be given a clear description of the application and testing procedures. Sample questions will show you exactly what the real test consists of. Then you will take a Diagnostic Practice Test modeled after the actual examination to help you evaluate your present strengths and weaknesses. The strategies and techniques used to score high on these questions will be clearly explained, step by step. Throughout the book, you will be working on timed practice drills and examinations that show how to apply these techniques under realistic test conditions. Throughout your work, you will follow a diagnostic system whereby you can keep track of your progress. If you study and practice the way this book directs, you will master the kinds of questions that appear on the real test.

---

* Throughout the remainder of this book, instead of using this rather long title, the test will be referred to merely as Test 460/470 or the new postal exam.

Moreover you will find that the abilities you develop as you use this book are transferable to your job in the Postal Service and to your everyday life. Improving your reading ability, memory, and listening skills will help you to become a better worker because these abilities, for which the examination tests, are directly related to learning and performing various Postal Service jobs. In addition, becoming a faster, more accurate reader, acquiring a better memory, and becoming a good listener are assets that can enlarge the personal, educational, and social aspects of your life.

HOW TO USE THIS BOOK

Chapter 1 includes important background information on eligibility and application for the test. Be sure to review the test description and do the sample questions.

Chapter 2 answers the question, "Why apply to the Postal Service?" by providing detailed information on its background and programs, and on the salaries, benefits, and duties of the various jobs you might be eligible for.

You will then be ready to take the Diagnostic Practice Test in **Chapter 3.** Your results on this test will help you to see where your present strengths and weaknesses lie. Record these results on the Personal Progress Cards and on the special Diagnostic Charts that accompany each Practice Test chapter. With these in hand, you can effectively plan your study program and evaluate your progress as you go along.

Chapters 4 through 9 are designed to help you to develop the four basic skills that these examinations have tested for. The test strategies and techniques presented in these chapters are related specifically to the kind of questions that you will face. Each method is fully explained and illustrated.

If you wish, you may proceed to the appropriate part of each practice test in Chapters 10 through 15 immediately after reading the corresponding chapters above. Many readers prefer to complete each practice test as a whole. It really doesn't matter which way you work, but, whatever method you select, allow some time between practice tests for reviewing and drilling.

The final section of this book, **Chapters 10 through 15,** is composed of six complete practice tests, each containing questions on Address Checking, Memory for Addresses, Number series, and Following Oral Directions. As you complete each chapter, enter the results in the Diagnostic Charts within the chapter, and the Personal Progress Record on pages 439–440. Note any special areas of weakness and reread the appropriate sections in Chapters 4 through 9. Do additional drilling as necessary before proceeding with the next practice test.

Note that the drills, as well as the practice tests, may be taken several times. The Personal Progress Record also has space to record scores for three trials. You should see progress as you continue practicing. Be sure to read the important guidelines and summaries that appear in Chapters 9 and 10, and at the beginning of Chapter 12 before you take Practice Tests 1 and 3.

It is recommended that you begin your study program *now.* You cannot be certain when the registration will open, and when it does, you may have only a few weeks' notice. The *skills and techniques you learn now will not be lost over the passage of time.* Then, when you are given the exact test date, a brief rereading of the test and the summaries on pages 223 to 227 will bring you back to peak performance.

THE 460/470 TEST FORMAT

Part	Description	Number of Questions	Time Allowed
A	Address Checking	95	6 minutes
B	Memory for Addresses	88	5 minutes
C	Number Series	24	20 minutes
D	Following Oral Directions	25 to 30	25 minutes

This time allowance is for the time spent on the *rated* part of the test. You can, however, expect to spend approximately 2½ hours in the examination room. See Chapter 1, page 6 for complete details.

Application and Testing Procedures

■ HOW AND WHEN TO APPLY

Your first step is to keep informed of Postal Service job opportunities so that you don't miss taking the next examination that is offered. Often, local radio stations and newspapers, job referral centers, and government personnel offices publicize forthcoming exams. However, the best way to be certain about postal job opportunities is to visit your local post office or local Federal Job Information Center to find out if it is accepting applications. If so, you will be given the proper application form to fill out. At the same time, you should read the official test announcement, which contains specific, current information on such things as the test-filing period (*which may last only one week*), eligibility requirements, salary, job location, job duties, and the tests you must pass in order to be appointed.

If your local post office is not accepting applications at this time, don't give up. Examinations are not held at the same time for the same job titles for all post offices in a region—especially when it is densely populated. Rather, tests are scheduled to meet the staffing needs of *local* post offices in a particular postal district or "sector." This means that the tests you are interested in may very well be due soon for another post office not too far away. What you should decide on at this point is how anxious you are to get into the Postal Service and how far from home you are willing to travel. Then, check the Post Office Directory at your local post office, and list the postal centers you would consider. Visit them personally. Try to speak to the most knowledgeable persons, such as the postmaster, his assistant, or someone in the personnel department. Get as much information as you can on the tests you are interested in, especially when they were last held and when the next ones are due. Ask for the telephone number of the Postal Job Information Hotline that some districts have. By calling this number, an automated voice will give you the locations of those post offices in the district where jobs exist or for which a test filing may soon open. Keep track of these visits and follow up on them frequently. You don't want to miss out when registration finally opens up! Exams under the traditional system are usually scheduled *only once every two or three years*.

At some post offices, a different registration system called OPTEX (Open Testing Exam System) is used. Under this system, the filing period is much longer than in the traditional system described above. Registration may be open many weeks; sometimes it stays open indefinitely. The applications that come in during this time are put in a computer file. Then, based on anticipated hiring needs, a percentage of these applications is randomly selected by the computer to be scheduled for examination. The good news about this system is that, although fewer names are called, exams are held more frequently. If you are lucky, your name will be selected early in the process and you won't have to wait for years to take the test. On the other hand, the luck of the draw may leave your application untouched for a long time.

When you visit the various post offices ask about which system is used. If it is OPTEX, find out how long your name will be held in the pool of applicants.

ANSWERS TO FREQUENTLY ASKED QUESTIONS ABOUT ELIGIBILITY FOR THE TEST BATTERY 460/470

Here are some highlights summarized from the most recent official test announcement and other official sources that answer the most frequently asked questions about applying for the Test 460/470:

What are the educational and experience qualifications?
No experience is required; no minimum education is required.

Must I be a U.S. citizen?
You must be a U.S. citizen, or owe allegiance to the United States, or have been granted permanent resident alien status in the United States.

Are there any residence requirements?
There are no residence requirements.

How old must I be to be appointed?
The general minimum age for positions in the Postal Service is 18 at the time of appointment. For high school graduates or persons certified by local school authorities as having terminated formal education for adequate reasons, the minimum age is 16. Applicants who are less than 18 years of age, who are high school graduates, and who have not terminated formal education may participate in the examination if they will reach the age of 18 within two years from the date of examination. There is no maximum age limit.

Are there any physical requirements?
You must be physically able to perform the duties of the position. Physical, medical, and vision examinations are required before appointment as well as a urinalysis to detect drug use.

How is salary determined?
Salary is determined from collective bargaining agreements. (At the time of publication, those appointed as part-time, flexible-schedule clerks will start at a salary of $13.61 per hour with a maximum of $18.92 per hour, including cost of living adjustments, after eight years. Such employees are converted to Regular Status according to seniority and openings, at an annual salary range of between $25,647 and $40,206 including COLA [Cost of Living Adjustment].)

Are there any special requirements for carrier positions?
City and rural carrier applicants must have a valid state driver's license and are required to have a safe driving record. You must also pass a special Postal Service road test before appointment.

How are job vacancies filled?
The examination will be used to establish a register of eligibles or to expand the current register of eligibles from which future vacancies will be filled. Separate registers are prepared according to the different job categories.

Are there any special provisions for veterans?

Absolutely. Once they have passed the test, qualified veterans are eligible to have points added to their basic rating. Depending on your veteran status, you may receive 5 or even 10 points extra; however, you must attain the passing score of 70 before these extra points will be added. Disabled veterans who qualify may also receive absolute priority in hiring. Certain family members of such veterans may also be entitled to these benefits. A reminder: To secure these benefits, you must claim them on your application.

Are there any other policies that govern employment?

If you pass the written and physical tests, you will be required to complete a comprehensive employment application and attend a personal interview, including physical agility and drug tests. The Postal Service utilizes these means to further assess your suitability for the job in terms of character, qualifications, and employment record. See the Appendix pages 435–438 for a facsimile of the official Employment Application PS 2591.)

You will find two more important policy statements in the official test announcement and on the employment application:

1. The U.S. Postal Service is an Equal Opportunity Employer.

2. THE LAW (39 U.S. CODE 1002) PROHIBITS POLITICAL AND CERTAIN OTHER RECOMMENDATIONS FOR APPOINTMENTS, PROMOTIONS, ASSIGNMENTS, TRANSFERS, OR DESIGNATIONS OF PERSONS IN THE POSTAL SERVICE. Statements relating solely to character and residence are permitted, but every other kind of statement or recommendation is prohibited unless it is either requested by the Postal Service and consists solely of an evaluation of the work performance, ability, aptitude, and general qualifications of an individual or is requested by a government representative investigating the individual's loyalty, suitability, and character. Anyone who requests or solicits a prohibited statement or recommendation is subject to disqualification from the Postal Service, and anyone in the Postal Service who accepts such a statement may be suspended from office.

What kind of a test is this?

Test 460/470 is a written, multiple-choice test designed to test aptitude for learning and performing the duties of these positions. It has four parts described and illustrated on pages 6 to 15. Everyone must achieve a minimum score of 70.

The official test announcement will contain current information on all the topics discussed above. Make sure to read it when it comes out.

How many times may I take this test?

You may take a test for a specific title, e.g., Postal Clerk, more than once, provided you are not retaking the same test used to establish a register at a particular postal installation. Otherwise it is advised that you take as many tests for as many titles as you feel you are eligible for. It is to your advantage to get a place on as many different registers as possible.

◼ FILING THE APPLICATION

Once you have read the official test announcement and have received the application card (see Figure 1 and 2), be very careful to fill it out legibly, accurately, and completely. Otherwise, it may be rejected. Then return the entire card (without separating the two parts) *within the time period specified in the announcement.* (It is recommended that you hand it in personally.) You must file your application on time in order to receive your admission card. Without the admission card, you will not be allowed to take the test.

A facsimile of the front of the application form, which consists of two parts—the application card and the admission card—appears on page 5:

The admission card will be returned to you later, advising you when and where to report for the test. With it will come a packet of information specifying what you must bring with you on test day, including Applicant Instructions, Sample Questions and Answers, a Sample Answer Sheet, and so on. (See Appendix, pages 427–433.)

BEFORE THE TEST—REMINDERS

- Get a good night's rest. Wake up in time to eat a sensible breakfast.

- Wear comfortable clothes. Include a sweater or light jacket that can be added or removed according to room temperature.

- Gather your supplies. Do not forget to bring your admission card, the completed Sample Answer Sheet, two properly prepared #2 lead pencils (see page 79) with erasers, and personal identification bearing your picture or description. The identification will be checked, and a fingerprint or signature specimen may be required.

- Come early. If you are not certain about how to get to the test location or how long the trip will take, check these things out as soon as you get your admission card. If you have to rush into the test, worried and out of breath, you will not be in the best condition to take the examination. If you come late, you will not be admitted.

- By coming early, you have a better chance to select a good seat. Pick one where you can see and hear the person conducting the test. Avoid seats where you'll be subject to hot radiators, drafts, or street noise. Stay away from people who might disturb you: loud talkers, coughers, and restless people who drum their fingers or pencils on the table.

- If you're having a problem of any kind, raise your hand and ask one of the monitors to help you. They are there for that purpose. They are supposed to make sure that everyone has a chance to take the test fairly under the best possible conditions.

- *Carefully* complete the Sample Answer Sheet that you will receive along with your admission card. In the exam room, there will be only 15 minutes to copy your work from the Sample Answer Sheet to the Official Answer Sheet. You will not have enough time in the exam room to gather information and dates you may not remember, such as veteran status, Social Security, and disability.

It is particularly important for you to have decided on which post offices you want to work in and on what jobs you want most. (In the packet of information you receive will be a list of post offices—"installations"—and the types of jobs available at each.) *Once you make your choices, you cannot later change them.* Now is the time to take the advice given you on page 1. Visit the locations listed, check on convenience of travel from your home, find out, if you can, how many openings exist at each of those you're interested in. Most of all, decide on the kind of work you'd like best, i.e., carrier, clerk, mail handler, and so on.

APPLICATION CARD

ADMISSION CARD
Do Not Write In This Space

Title of Examination

Social Security No. ___ - __ - ____

Date of Birth	Today's Date	Post Office Applied For

If you have performed active duty in the Armed Forces of the United States and were separated under honorable conditions indicate periods of service
From (Mo., Day, Yr.) ___ to (Mo., Day, Yr.) ___

DO YOU CLAIM VETERAN PREFERENCE? ☐ NO   ☐ YES. IF YES, BASED ON
☐ (1) Active duty in the Armed Forces of the U.S. during World War I or the period December 7, 1941, through July 1, 1955, or the period beginning June 27, 1950, and ending January 31, 1955
☐ (2) More than 180 consecutive days of active duty (other than for training), in the Armed Forces of the U.S. any part of which occurred between Jan. 31, 1955 and Oct. 14, 1976, or (3) Award of a campaign badge or service medal
☐ Your status as (1) a disabled veteran or a veteran who was awarded the purple heart for wounds or injuries received in action, (2) a veteran's widow who has not remarried, (3) the wife of an ex serviceman who has a service connected disability which disqualifies him for civil service appointment, or (4) the widowed, divorced or separated mother of an ex-service son or daughter who died in action or who is totally and permanently disabled

**Print or Type
Your Name
and Address**

Name (First, Middle, Last)

Address (House, Apt. No. & Street)

City, State, ZIP Code (ZIP Code must be included)

PS Form 2479-B, April 1987

This card will be returned to you. Bring it, along with personal identification bearing your picture or description, with you when you report for the test. ID's will be checked, and a fingerprint or signature specimen may be required.

APPLICATION CARD

Name (Last, First, Middle Initial)

Address (House/Apt. No. & Street)

City, State, ZIP Code

Do Not Write In This Space

Birthdate (Month, Date, Year)		Today's Date
Telephone Number		

Title of Examination

Post Office Applied For

PS Form 2479-A, April 1987

Figure 1

Instructions to Applicants

Furnish all the information requested on these cards. The attached card will be returned to you with sample questions and necessary instructions, including the time and place of the written test.

TYPEWRITE OR PRINT IN INK. DO NOT SEPARATE THESE CARDS. FOLD ONLY AT PERFORATION.

Mail or Take This Form—Both Parts—to The Postmaster of the Post Office Where You Wish to Be Employed.

PS Form 2479-A, April 1987 (Reverse)

Final Eligibility in This Examination is Subject to Suitability Determination

The collection of information on this form is authorized by 39 U.S.C. 401.1001; completion of this form is voluntary. This information will be used to determine qualification, suitability, and availability of applicants for USPS employment, and may be disclosed to relevant Federal Agencies regarding eligibility and suitability for employment, law enforcement activities when there is an indication of a potential violation of law, in connection with private relief legislation (to Office of Management and Budget); to a congressional office at your request, to a labor organization as required by the NLRA, and where pertinent, in a legal proceeding to which the Postal Service is a party. If this information is not provided, you may not receive full consideration for a position.

Disclosure by you of your Social Security Number (SSN) is mandatory to obtain the services, benefits, or processes that you are seeking. Solicitation of the SSN by the United States Postal Service is authorized under provisions of Executive Order 9397, dated November 22, 1943. The information gathered through the use of the number will be used only as necessary in authorized personnel administration processes.

Political Recommendations Prohibited

The law (39 U.S. Code 1002) prohibits political and certain other recommendations for appointments, promotions, assignments, transfers, or designations of persons in the Postal Service. Statements relating solely to character and residence are permitted, but every other kind of statement or recommendation is prohibited unless it either is requested by the Postal Service and consists solely of an evaluation of the work performance, ability, aptitude, and general qualifications of an individual or is requested by a Government representative investigating the individual's loyalty, suitability, and character. Anyone who requests or solicits a prohibited statement or recommendation is subject to disqualification from the Postal Service and anyone in the Postal Service who accepts such a statement may be suspended or removed from office.

Applicant	Fingerprint
Make no marks on this side of the card unless so instructed by examiner.	
Signature of Applicant	

PS Form 2479-B, April 1987 (Reverse)

Have You Answered All Questions on the Reverse of This Form?   ★ U.S. GPO: 1993-342-723-83796

Figure 2

In any case, exercise your full choice. (You probably will be given several to pick from.) It is advised that you include post offices that have openings in several titles. That way you may be considered for as many as eight different positions (see page 64 on scoring) and your prospects for an early appointment will be increased.

The test you take will be used to fill the available job positions. Be aware, however, that not all positions are available at every location. The Postal Service will provide you with additional information before you take the exam, specifying which positions exist in the post offices that will use the area register.

WHAT IT'S LIKE AT THE TEST—SOME THINGS TO REMEMBER

When you receive your admission card, it will be accompanied by a few sample questions like the ones you will take on the test. These are extremely useful. Later, you will see what these questions look like. First, to complete the picture of what the testing procedure is like, the following describes what you may experience during the test itself as well as what happens afterward.

On the day of the test, you will be one of a group of other test candidates assembled in a room. The exact number of test takers will depend on many things. The staffing needs of the post offices that are to be served by the exam and the employment situation in the area are two important deciding factors. Often, these tests are held in large public places, such as halls and schools, so that all those who want to take the examination can be accommodated. You may, therefore, find yourself to be one of 300 to 400 persons seated in small groups around tables placed throughout the room. Your identification and admission cards will be checked by Postal Service employees who act as test monitors. The monitor in charge of administering the test will direct you in filling out a form containing questions on your job preference, veteran's status, date of birth, and so on. You must indicate your answers by darkening the boxes on the form. (This is similar to the way you will indicate your answers on the test. In Chapters 3, 10, 11, 12, 13, 14, and 15, you will see and use this kind of answer sheet.) The monitor will also explain the test procedure fully and will emphasize that the various parts of the test are carefully timed. Follow these directions exactly. If you are not sure of something, ask for clarification. *The monitors are extremely strict. It is emphasized repeatedly that failure to follow any directive given by an examiner may be grounds for disqualification.*

The test and the completion of related forms will require approximately 2½ hours.

THE TEST ITSELF—SAMPLE QUESTIONS

As the official announcement indicates, this Postal Service examination is definitely job related. You will be able to see how true this is when you go over some of the sample questions recently sent to test applicants.

Part A—Address Checking

In Part A you will have to decide whether two addresses are alike or different. This kind of question is included in the test because every member of the Postal Service staff is responsible for seeing that each piece of mail arrives at the right destination as quickly as possible. If addresses are misread, delays in delivery will result. In spite of various new developments in sorting and handling the mail that use electronic and computerized devices, the human element is crucial in providing fast and efficient service. Here are the instructions and the sample questions that go with them.

Questions

If the two addresses are alike in every way, darken space Ⓐ for the question. If the two addresses are different in any way, darken space Ⓓ for the question. Mark your answers to these questions in the grids provided.

1.	2134 S 20th St	2134 S 20th St	1 ⒶⒹ
2.	4608 N Warnock St	4806 N Warnock St	2 ⒶⒹ
3.	1202 W Girard Dr	1202 W Girard Rd	3 ⒶⒹ
4.	Chappaqua NY 10514	Chappaqua NY 10514	4 ⒶⒹ
5.	2207 Markland Ave	2207 Markham Ave	5 ⒶⒹ

Answers

1. **A**   2. **D**   3. **D**   4. **A**   5. **D**

The questions seem easy, but the test itself is not. At least, it's not easy if you want to score higher than your many competitors. In the latest test, candidates were given *95* pairs of addresses to compare in *6* minutes.

To pass with high scores, test takers had to work as fast and accurately as possible. They knew that every extra point they made meant they would be that much higher on the list for job appointment. When a list has thousands of names, *one* extra point may make a difference of *hundreds* of places on the list. Also, when there are a limited number of job openings, list position can mean the difference between getting a job or "dying" on the list. That is why merely passing is not good enough. In the next chapters, you will learn exactly what to do to earn those extra points.

Part B—Memory for Addresses

The majority of postal clerks work behind the scenes sorting and distributing mail. They must be able to remember sorting schemes by which mail is organized for delivery. Carriers need to have good memories too. One of a carrier's responsibilities is to arrange mail according to the delivery route he or she will follow on a particular day. For this reason carriers must be able to learn and remember the streets and building addresses on their routes. Now you know why memory questions appear on this exam. Here are some sample questions and instructions for answering them:

Questions

In this test, you will have to memorize the locations (A, B, C, D, or E) of 25 addresses shown in five boxes below. For example, "Sardis" is in Box C, and 5600–6499 West is in Box A.

Study the locations of the addresses for *5 minutes*. As you study, sound them to yourself. Then cover the boxes and try to answer the questions below. Mark your answer for each question by darkening the space in the grids provided, as was done for questions 1 and 2.

A	B	C	D	E
4700–5599 Table	6800–6999 Table	5600–6499 Table	6500–6799 Table	4400–4699 Table
Belmore	Kelford	Joel	Tatum	Rusken
5600–6499 West	6500–6799 West	6800–6999 West	4400–4699 West	4700–5599 West
Hesper	Musella	Sardis	Porter	Nathan
4400–4699 Blake	5600–6499 Blake	6500–6799 Blake	4700–5599 Blake	6800–6999 Blake

1. Musella   1 Ⓐ●ⒸⒹⒺ
2. 4700–5599 Blake   2 ⒶⒷⒸ●Ⓔ
3. 4700–5599 Table   3 ⒶⒷⒸⒹⒺ
4. Tatum   4 ⒶⒷⒸⒹⒺ
5. 4400–4699 Blake   5 ⒶⒷⒸⒹⒺ
6. Hesper   6 ⒶⒷⒸⒹⒺ
7. Kelford   7 ⒶⒷⒸⒹⒺ
8. Nathan   8 ⒶⒷⒸⒹⒺ
9. 6500–6799 Blake   9 ⒶⒷⒸⒹⒺ
10. Joel   10 ⒶⒷⒸⒹⒺ
11. 4400–4699 Blake   11 ⒶⒷⒸⒹⒺ
12. 6500–6799 West   12 ⒶⒷⒸⒹⒺ
13. Porter   13 ⒶⒷⒸⒹⒺ
14. 5600–6499 Table   14 ⒶⒷⒸⒹⒺ

Answers

1. **B**	5. **A**	9. **C**	13. **D**
2. **D**	6. **A**	10. **C**	14. **C**
3. **A**	7. **B**	11. **A**	
4. **D**	8. **E**	12. **B**	

Now imagine a test situation where you are given a total of *5* minutes to answer *88* questions! This is what the memory test will be like. Very few people feel that this test is easy. But don't be like those who immediately give up on the memory part by saying, "Either you've got it or you don't." The implication is that nothing can be done to improve memory performance. This belief is not accurate. There are definite methods, universally recognized, that are used for memory improvement. The most helpful and practical of these methods have been selected and refined for your use on the Memory for Addresses section of the Test 460/470. You will be happily surprised at how good your memorization capabilities really are!

Part C—Number Series

The Number Series part of the test is intended to gauge your reasoning ability and your aptitude for working with machines. Because you may be working on a letter sorting machine and possibly other kinds of machines, this part of the test is relevant to your job duties.

Questions

For each Number Series question, there is at the left a series of numbers that follows some definite order and at the right five sets of two numbers each. You are to look at the numbers in the series at the left and find out what order they follow. Then decide what the next two numbers in that series would be if the same order were continued. Mark your answers to these questions by darkening the proper space in the grids provided. (To help you get started, the answers and explanations for the first five questions are given directly below each question.)

1. 1 2 3 4 5 6 7 __ __

  A) 1 2   B) 5 6   C) 8 9   D) 4 5   E) 7 8

  The correct answer is C. The numbers in this series are increasing by 1. If the series were continued for two more numbers, it would read: 1 2 3 4 5 6 7 8 9. Therefore, the correct answer is C) 8 and 9.

2. 15 14 13 12 11 10 9 __ __

  A) 2 1   B) 17 16 C) 8 9   D) 8 7   E) 9 8

  The correct answer is D. The numbers in this series are decreasing by 1. If the series were continued for two more numbers, it would read: 15 14 13 12 11 10 9 8 7. Therefore, the correct answer is 8 and 7 and you should have darkened D for this question.

3. 20 20 21 21 22 22 23 __ __

  A) 23 23 B) 23 24 C) 19 19 D) 22 23 E) 21 22

  The correct answer is B. Each number in this series is repeated and then increased by 1. If the series were continued for two or more numbers, it would read: 20 20 21 21 22 22 23 23 24. Therefore, the correct answer is 23 and 24.

4. 17 3 17 4 17 5 17 __ __

  A) 6 17   B) 6 7   C) 17 6   D) 5 6   E) 17 7

The correct answer is A. In this series the number 17 is separated by numbers increasing by 1, beginning with the number 3. If the series were continued for two more numbers, it would read: 17 3 17 4 17 5 17 6 17. Therefore, the correct answer is 6 and 17, and you should have darkened A.

5. 1 2 4 5 7 8 10 __ __
    A) 11 12   B) 12 14   C) 10 13   D) 12 13   E) 11 13

The correct answer is E. The numbers in this series are increasing first by 1 (plus 1) and then by 2 (plus 2). If the series were continued for two more numbers, it would read: 1 2 4 5 7 8 10 (plus 1) 11 (plus 2) 13. Therefore, the correct answer is 11 and 13, and you should have darkened E.

Questions

Now try sample questions 6 through 10, and mark your answers in the grid provided.

6. 21 21 20 20 19 19 18 __ __
    A) 18 18   B) 18 17   C) 17 18   D) 17 17   E) 18 19

                                                            6 Ⓐ Ⓑ Ⓒ Ⓓ Ⓔ

7. 1 22 1 23 1 24 1 __ __
    A) 26 1   B) 25 26   C) 25 1   D) 1 26   E) 1 25

                                                            7 Ⓐ Ⓑ Ⓒ Ⓓ Ⓔ

8. 1 20 3 19 5 18 7 __ __
    A) 8 9   B) 8 17   C) 17 10   D) 17 9   E) 9 18

                                                            8 Ⓐ Ⓑ Ⓒ Ⓓ Ⓔ

9. 4 7 10 13 16 19 22 __ __
    A) 23 26   B) 25 27   C) 25 25   D) 25 28   E) 24 27

                                                            9 Ⓐ Ⓑ Ⓒ Ⓓ Ⓔ

10. 30 2 28 4 26 6 24 __ __
    A) 23 9   B) 26 8   C) 8 9   D) 26 22   E) 8 22

                                                          10 Ⓐ Ⓑ Ⓒ Ⓓ Ⓔ

Answers

  6. **B**   7. **C**   8. **D**   9. **D**   10. **E**

Part D—Following Oral Directions

This part of the test gauges your ability to understand and carry out spoken instructions *exactly* as they are given to you. On the "real-life" job, your supervisor will frequently give you oral instructions and expect you to listen carefully and to comply swiftly and correctly. You may be sure that your future boss will appreciate it if you are able to get a message straight the first time you hear it, without the need for repetition. This test assesses how well you will be able to measure up to these requirements.

In order to answer the sample items on the next page, here is what you should do:

1. Find a quiet comfortable place to practice; it should be that way in the room where you take the actual Postal Service exam. (Remember, talking among the test takers is *not* allowed by the test examiners.)

2. Enlist the help of a friend who will be the "reader." He/she will read aloud a series of directions that you are to follow exactly. The reader will need a watch that displays seconds because the directions must be given at the correct speed.

3. Tear out page 13. This is the worksheet you should have in front of you as you follow the directions for Sample 1 through Sample 5.

4. *Now, hand this entire book to the reader.* Ask him/her to review the section on page 15 headed *"Instructions to the Reader,"* which explains exactly how to proceed. When the reader is ready, he/she will begin reading the directions to you. YOU ARE NOT TO READ THESE. If you do, you will lose the benefit of this sample exercise.

5. Listen carefully to the instructions for each sample question. Use the blank answer grid at the bottom of the worksheet for your answers. Darken the appropriate spaces in accordance with the directions the reader gives you.

Worksheet for the Sample Test

Sample 1.   5 ___

Sample 2.   1   6   4   3   7

Sample 3.   D   B   A   E   C

Sample 4.   8 ___   5 ___   2 ___   9 ___   10 ___

Sample 5.   7 ___   6 ___   1 ___   12 ___

Answer Grid

1 Ⓐ Ⓑ Ⓒ Ⓓ Ⓔ	10 Ⓐ Ⓑ Ⓒ Ⓓ Ⓔ
2 Ⓐ Ⓑ Ⓒ Ⓓ Ⓔ	11 Ⓐ Ⓑ Ⓒ Ⓓ Ⓔ
3 Ⓐ Ⓑ Ⓒ Ⓓ Ⓔ	12 Ⓐ Ⓑ Ⓒ Ⓓ Ⓔ
4 Ⓐ Ⓑ Ⓒ Ⓓ Ⓔ	13 Ⓐ Ⓑ Ⓒ Ⓓ Ⓔ
5 Ⓐ Ⓑ Ⓒ Ⓓ Ⓔ	14 Ⓐ Ⓑ Ⓒ Ⓓ Ⓔ
6 Ⓐ Ⓑ Ⓒ Ⓓ Ⓔ	15 Ⓐ Ⓑ Ⓒ Ⓓ Ⓔ
7 Ⓐ Ⓑ Ⓒ Ⓓ Ⓔ	16 Ⓐ Ⓑ Ⓒ Ⓓ Ⓔ
8 Ⓐ Ⓑ Ⓒ Ⓓ Ⓔ	17 Ⓐ Ⓑ Ⓒ Ⓓ Ⓔ
9 Ⓐ Ⓑ Ⓒ Ⓓ Ⓔ	18 Ⓐ Ⓑ Ⓒ Ⓓ Ⓔ

Remove by cutting on dotted line.

Instructions to the "Reader"

The directions should be read at about 80 words per minute. Practice reading aloud the material in the box below until you can do it in exactly 1 minute. The number of words in the passage and the natural pauses described below will give you a good feel for the rate of speed and the way you should read the test questions.

1-MINUTE PRACTICE

(This is for practice in reading aloud. It is not part of the sample test.)

> Look at line 20 on your worksheet. There are two circles and two boxes of different sizes with numbers in them. If 7 if less than 3 and if 2 is smaller than 4, write a C in the larger circle. Otherwise write B as in *baker* in the smaller box. Now on your answer sheet darken the space for the number-letter combination in the box or circle.

As you read the directions (below) you will see words in parentheses. These words should *not* be read aloud. They are there to tell you how long you should pause at the various spots. You should time the pauses using a watch with a second hand The instruction "Pause slightly" means that you should stop long enough to take a breath.

Do not repeat any directions or any of the questions.

The Test Begins Now

Directions to be read: You are to follow the instructions that I read to you. I cannot repeat them.

Look at the samples. Sample 1 has a number and a line beside it. (Pause slightly.) On the line write an A. (Pause 2 seconds.) Now, on the answer grid, find number 5 (pause 2 seconds) and darken the space for the letter you just wrote on the line. (Pause 5 seconds.)

Look at Sample 2. (Pause slightly.) Draw a line under the third number. (Pause 2 seconds.) Now, on the answer grid, find the number under which you just drew a line and darken space B as in *baker* for that number. (Pause 5 seconds.)

Look at the letters in Sample 3. (Pause slightly.) Draw a line under the third letter in the line. (Pause 2 seconds.) Now, on the answer grid, find number 9 (pause 2 seconds) and darken the space for the letter under which you drew a line. (Pause 5 seconds.)

Look at the five circles in Sample 4. (Pause slightly.) Each circle has a number and a line in it. Write D as in *dog* on the line in the last circle. (Pause 2 seconds.) Now, on the answer grid, darken the space for the number-letter combination that is in the circle you just wrote in. (Pause 5 seconds.)

Look at Sample 5. (Pause slightly.) There are two circles and two boxes of different sizes with numbers in them. (Pause slightly.) If 4 is more than 2 and if 5 is less than 3, write A in the smaller circle. (Pause slightly.) Otherwise write C in the larger box. (Pause 2 seconds.) Now, on the answer grid, darken the space for the number-letter combination that is in the box or circle you just wrote in. (Pause 5 seconds.)

Now look at the answer grid. (Pause slightly.) You should have darkened spaces 4B, 5A, 9A, 10D, and 12C.

AFTER THE TEST

The answer sheets are sent to a special division of the Postal Service that prepares and rates examinations. After the papers have been scored and the registers (lists) established, you will receive a Notice of Rating by mail in about 8 weeks. (The register is established in the order of the scores on the test, subject to veterans preference. If you request and are entitled to veterans preference, you will receive extra points on your rating.) If you have passed, the Notice of Rating will also indicate on which post office registers your name has been placed and the date on which this was done. These locations are the ones you *should notify in writing* if you: (1) change your address, (2) have any change in your availability, (3) have any inquiries, (4) want to extend your eligibility. This last point is particularly important because it gives you an opportunity to remain on the list for an extra year. Normally, eligibility is good for two years only. However, you may receive an extension of your eligibility for an additional year if you send in a written request. Send your request in 18 months from the date on which your name was placed on the register (unless, of course, you have been appointed in the interim). The maximum length of eligibility is three years.

Keep the Notice of Rating in a safe place—you will need it some day. At some point, when your name is reached on the list, you will receive a longer, more detailed "Application for Employment" to fill out. Just as for the yellow, short-form Application Card, it is most important that you answer every question legibly, truthfully, and completely. Usually, this Application for Employment is accompanied by a sheet of instructions. In the Appendix, both the application (pages 427 to 433) and a typical set of instructions have been reproduced.

It is worthwhile for you to assemble all the information required now, ready to submit when you are asked for it. All this information and the documents you submit form the basis for a background investigation, your personal interview, a drug test and, at a later time, a medical exam.

Until this process is completed, you will not be offered a job, so do not quit your present job, change your permanent residence or take any irreversible action on the basis of the prospects of getting hired. Also, remember that all new career employees are hired on a probationary basis for their first 90 days of employment.

Chapter 2

The United States Postal Service: Background, Benefits, and the Future

■ BACKGROUND

Organization

The United States Postal Service (USPS) had its origin as part of the federal government shortly before the American Revolution, when it was called the Post Office Department. Its principal mandate was—and still is—to provide prompt and efficient postal service to all communities throughout the country. The importance of this role becomes obvious when one examines the scope and size of its mail delivery system (following).

In 1969, however, responding to widespread complaints about the way it was doing the job—waste, poor service, mismanagement, and enormous dollar losses—Congress passed the Postal Reorganization Act that established the USPS as we know it today. It is now an independent, self-supporting public corporation whose policies and operations are administered by an 11-member Board of Governors. Nine of them are appointed by the President. Postage rates and categories are continually studied by a 5-member Postal Rate Commission, which makes recommendations for needed changes, subject to approval by the Board of Governors. We all experienced just such a change, when the price of a first-class stamp was raised by 1 cent.

Although the mission of the USPS remains the same as in 1775 and 1969, enormous changes in our society have magnified the challenges, responsibilities *and* opportunities confronting the Postal Service. A part of this entire picture can be seen if one looks, first, at the size and scope of its operation.

Scope and Size

When you are hired by the Postal Service, you will be working for an employer that does things in a big way. It is the world's largest postal system, delivering 41 percent of the world's mail; next comes Japan with just 6 percent. For the 12 months ending September 30, 1998, it processed over 198 billion pieces of mail. To do that required the services of about 792,000 career employees working in over 38,000 postal stations and branches. They rode in a fleet of approximately 200,000 vehicles belonging to the Postal Service. These properties and other assets totaled to $54 billion on the USPS balance sheet. If it were listed in the Fortune 500 survey, the Postal Service would appear as the nation's tenth largest corporation.

Lots of money was spent during all this and more; operating expenses came to $57.7 billion—three quarters of which went to pay salaries and benefits. Please note that under the

Postal Act, the USPS is required to pay its own way. Taxes are not raised to make up income in years when there is a deficit. For the last four years in a row, the budget figures showed a positive net income; for 1998 it came to $550 million.

Challenges and Responses

The preceding statistics are staggering, yet they show only part of the picture. Our society is changing rapidly and the USPS has been moving on a widespread front to respond to the challenges and opportunities that come with change.

- Our growth in population and mail volume

- The exploration of new technologies for transmitting and processing information

- The demands by the general public and private business for additional and faster services

- The growth of aggressive competition by private carriers

- Greater cost consciousness on the part of just about everyone

- An increased awareness of the need for protecting the environment

This list could go on and on but because this book's primary intention is to help you enter the postal system by passing high on the next 460/470 exam, this chapter will give you only a little information on some of the programs that the USPS now has, or will soon put in place, to meet these changes.*

Programs

Customer Perfect

The USPS has committed itself to improving its understanding and response to the needs of its customers. This effort is part of an approach called *Customer Perfect*—a catchy slogan you'll see at many postal installations.

It uses information gathered through Postal Customer Councils (meetings between postal officials and local customers throughout the country), visits to individual business customers by an Operation Mail Team, plus various surveys, studies, and suggestions by its own employees.

The results can be seen in a variety of innovations to improve and extend services.

- Acceptance of *credit/debit (ATM) cards* for window retail purchases

- Plans to establish six *National Service Centers* that customers may call, 24 hours a day, to receive *line* answers to postal questions

- A *Priority Mail Processing* network to improve package delivery service

---

* After you become a career employee whose livelihood rests with the postal system, you can readily obtain more information about what's happening from the many articles that frequently appear in newspapers and magazines (see *Postal Life* and *Update*—USPS employee publications). Just as important, you may be meeting the public, and if you are aiming to reach a higher position in the postal system, appearing more knowledgeable and professional about the postal affairs will stand you in good stead.

- *Mobile Post Offices* that provide window services to senior communities and elsewhere

- The *Easy Stamps Program*, which offers Stamps by Mail, *Stamps by Phone*, Stamps on Consignment, and Stamps by Prodigy

- An *Operation Mail Team* that visits individual businesses to study and make recommendations for reducing costs through improved package design and mailing methods (e.g., it helped a Phoenix-based company called Express-A-Cake meet its special requirements for shipping its cheesecakes and carrot cakes across the country, so that they arrived at their destination fresh and whole)

- A *Postal Service Website* at *www.urs.gov* that offers an array of business-related services where customers can track Express Mail packages, order supplies, and calculate rates

High Tech

E-mail and enhanced fax services have reduced the USPS's share of business and personal correspondence. The Postal Service, however, is also using this technology and other advances in computerization, automation, and (soon-to-be) robotics. These will assist in meeting the growth of mail volume, the request for additional services, and the demands for increased productivity.

Here are some examples of mind-boggling technology at work.

- A special bar coding machine at a computerized command center in Washington, DC processed 30,000 pieces of mail in one hour—on the busiest day of the year!

- The Morgan Station in New York City, a 10-story fortress, handled 2½ million letters during the Christmas rush.

- High-speed bar-code scanners can spot bar codes in large-size mail such as catalogs, magazines, and envelopes regardless of where the code has been put on the piece.

- Optical Character Readers (OCRs) have been developed that can read handwritten addresses—even ones that have been scribbled. When necessary, such mail is automatically handled by a remote bar coding system (RBCS), thus permitting decentralization of operations.

- A special bar code containing a fluorescent ID tag is used to facilitate mail sorting. In the future, it will be used to identify, track, and trace all classes of mail.

Today, the USPS, thanks to the uses of technology illustrated above, is the most highly automated postal system in the world, resulting in a tremendous reduction in costs. Automated mail handling is more than ten times faster than manual operations. A recent estimate concluded that it costs about $40 to process 1,000 letters by manual sorting and $18 by mechanized equipment, but only $4 by automation.

Relationships with Customers, the General Public, and Its Employees

The USPS is very, very aware of the importance of maintaining a favorable image in the eyes of its publics. To do that, it has gone beyond increasing the speed, efficiency, and number of its postal services. It has acted in many additional ways to enhance its reputation in the hope of attracting more business and support from the general public.

Customers

The postal service literally has embraced a New Look. Its logo, featuring a dark blue eagle ready for flight, has been given a sleeker, more modern look. Post office lobbies have been painted and decorated to make them look warmer and more inviting. Recently, original WPA murals painted during the Great Depression of the 1920s and 1930s have been uncovered and restored on the walls and ceilings of some of the older, larger post offices throughout the country.

It has made history come alive by issuing a series of beautiful, commemorative stamps dedicated to legendary personalities in film (Marilyn Monroe, James Dean, Alfred Hitchcock), historical events and places like the California Gold Rush, Irish immigration, and Mount Vernon, and holidays such as Kwanza and Christmas. Soon to be issued is a new series of 150 stamps called Celebrate the Century. Special postal stamps have been issued to raise public awareness of health and social concerns including drug abuse, AIDS, and environmental protection. The net proceeds of some of them, like the Breast Cancer Research Stamp, will go to fund the fight against an affliction.

In 1993, The Smithsonian Institution in Washington, DC established a National Postal Museum to add to its other 15 museums and galleries. This was done in recognition of what the Postal Service has done to tie our country together. The museum will include one of the largest and most important philatelic collections in the world.

The Local Community and General Public

The cooperation of its employees and their unions has been the key to make possible a host of other programs that serve the local community and the general public, nationwide:

- *Carrier Alert.* An example of this spirit of cooperation is Carrier Alert, a joint program by the Postal Service and the National Association of Letter Carriers (NALC). Under this program, letter carriers keep alert to indications of problems facing elderly and infirm residents on their routes. They watch for accumulated mail and other signs of distress, and they notify the proper authorities to secure help. The Postal Service widely publicizes the numerous instances where its employees act resourcefully and often heroically through its Postal Achievement Awards. Press releases of such newsworthy events are sent to local newspapers.

    There are other indications that the Postal Service tries to be responsive to the changing times and needs of society.

- As a humanitarian gesture, the Postal Service, a few years ago, offered a low-cost "airlift" to send aid packages to the Baltic nations and the Soviet Republics. A 5-pound airlift package was sent for only $17.85 instead of the $40.30 required for regular airmail at that time.

- In an effort to support literacy throughout the country, local post offices have joined with area elementary schools in a venture called "Wee Deliver." Children perform all the duties of a local post office and in the process learn the reading and writing skills required to address and sort mail.

- *National Food Drive.* Again, the NALC in partnership with the Postal Service has mounted a national food drive gathering nonperishables during postal routes and delivering them to area food banks.

- *"Delivering the Gift of Life"* began in August 1997. This unique campaign encourages all Postal Service employees in 12 cities to become volunteer marrow donors.

By the end of 1998, 6,855 postal employees were added to the National Registry of unrelated marrow donors.

- *Charitable Donations.* Postal Service employees pledged over $117 million, allocated from a percentage of their paychecks to charities of their choice.

- *The Postal Inspection Service.* In addition to its other functions, it has devoted much time and staff to combating the use of the mail to send drugs such as cocaine, heroin, and LSD. In cooperation with local police and agents of the Drug Enforcement Agency (DEA), the number of drug-related arrests has risen sharply. In 1996, the postal inspectors working with government agents helped close down a major child pornography ring run by Americans based in Mexico. Fifty-six persons were arrested.

  - *Speaking of Image Building!* In 1998, *The Inspectors*, a movie about the exciting adventures of these inspectors, was independently produced and shown on Showtime. It received the highest rating for any original film in that channel's history. Four more movies about these adventures have been contracted for by the producer, Showtime, and the Postal Service. They will be publicized through poster displays in its lobbies, commemorative envelopes, and messages on the Postal Service Web site.

- *Environmental Activities.* The Postal Service has been active in attempts to reduce pollution through recycling waste, using recycled material to make its products, using rerefined oil and retreaded tires, and by continuing to add to its fleet of electric and gas-powered vehicles.

Now, let's take a look to see what the results have been of all these programs combined. Several years ago, a Customer Satisfaction index was developed to measure overall customer perception of the Postal Service. In 1998, a survey by the PEW Research Center, an independent research group, reported that nine out of ten Americans gave the USPS the highest favorability rating of any federal agency. It also showed that 78 percent of Americans have a highly or moderately favorable opinion of the Postal Service, putting it at the top of a list of 15 federal agencies.

Independent surveys such as these, are planned for the coming years. They will continue to serve to identify and correct the customer dissatisfactions that obviously still remain.

Employees

One of the most important aspects of the Postal Service's "new look" involves its personnel policies and practices. These are of direct concern to you as a future employee.

Since its reorganization, two major events have occurred. First, in 1971, the Postal Service signed a historic agreement with employee unions, the first labor contract in the history of the federal government to be achieved through the collective bargaining process. Negotiations with the four major labor organizations representing the various postal employee groups determine wages and working conditions. Most postal clerks and carriers are members of the American Postal Workers Union and the National Association of Letter Carriers.

Second, the Postal Service abolished political patronage in selecting postmasters and rural carriers. It adopted a merit system that is used to select these and all other positions. (That's how the test you're going to take, and scores of others, came to be.)

All does not run perfectly smooth, however. The Postal Service, in response to a series of adverse incidents and employee complaints, instituted two major employee opinion surveys. These showed that although the majority of its employees favorably rated the categories of pay, benefits, and job security, they also indicated the need to improve working conditions and employee cooperation, and to recognize quality performance. Recently, Congress released its own study confirming the need for change in the workplace culture. The General Accounting Office (GAO), which is an arm of the legislative branch of the federal government, audited the Postal Service a couple of years ago and issued a report that stated, in part, "persistent labor problems have generally contributed to tense working conditions in postal facilities . . ."

The Postal Service, recognizing the need to improve some work methods and supervisory practices, began by allowing employees to rate their bosses' "people skills." It has revised the training courses that managers and supervisors attend, to focus on incorporating desirable change into its daily operations. It has created a leadership team composed of some of its key officials and the presidents of the seven major unions and employee associations to set up similar local leadership teams to adopt new performance-based pay systems, improve teamwork, and gain cooperation throughout the system.

Their corporate policies regarding its employees and their importance may be seen in an official statement recently released:

"Employee satisfaction and customer satisfaction are inextricably linked. That's why the Postal Service is focused on creating an environment that promotes fairness and opportunities, instills pride, and enhances safety in the workplace. In 1998, we established a corporate policy on diversity and an Office of Workplace Environment to ensure that these values are put into practice throughout the Postal Service.

"Management is listening more closely to employees, finding new ways to resolve conflicts, and promoting communication at every level of the organization. In 1998, the Postal Service introduced a new employee opinion survey—part of a broader initiative called Voice of the Employee—to gather input from employees and track improvements in the culture, environment, and working conditions. It's all part of an effort to make the Postal Service a better place to work."

A summary of some benefits that can affect you as an employee is given below. (Unless otherwise specified, all figures apply to full-time regular employees.)

▰ BENEFITS*

Work Schedules, Wage Scales, and Leave Provisions

Postal clerks and carriers are classified as *casual, part-time flexible, part-time regular,* or *full-time.* Casual workers are not career employees but are hired to help process mail during peak mailing or vacation periods. Part-time flexible workers are career employees who work as the need arises and usually work less than 40 hours per week. Part-time regulars have a set work schedule (for example, 4 hours a day). Full-time employees work a 40-hour week over five days. All new career employees work on a probationary basis for their first 90 days of employment.

---

* The various salary schedules, leave provisions, and other program descriptions currently in effect will change as new policies are adopted by the Postal Service and as new contracts are negotiated between it and the several unions that represent its employees. We suggest that you inquire, at the time you are being interviewed, as to the current status of the benefits and programs important to you.

As employees build seniority, they may request transfer to more desirable or convenient shifts and locations. In order to be considered for such reassignments when they arise, employees prepare written "bids." The bidder with the most seniority gets the job, provided that he or she meets all other qualifications.

Annual Leave

Annual leave includes leave for vacations, personal and emergency purposes, and so on. The amount of paid leave you receive depends upon length of service (as an employee and in military service).

Length of Service	Leave Days per Year
Less than 3 years	13 days
3 to 15 years	20 days
Over 15 years	26 days

Sick Leave

You are permitted 13 days of sick leave per year.

Base Wage Scale (Including COLA)
(effective as of 1/1/99)

It is likely that you will begin your career as a part-time flexible worker. The hourly rate varies according to title:

	START	MAXIMUM
Postal Clerk, City Mail Carrier, Machine Distribution Clerk Flat-Sorting Machine Operator	$13.61/hr	$18.92/hr
Mail Processor, Mark-Up Clerk	13.16/hr	18.88/hr
Mail Handler	11.90/hr	18.44/hr

The maximum rate is reached through a series of graded increases over a 12-year period. Of course, you may get appointed as a "regular" after a time at which point your salary will be converted to a different scale.

Currently, the maximum salary for a full-time regular clerk exceeds $40,000 per year.

COLA

COLA stands for Cost of Living Adjustment. These adjustments are pay increases that are based on the Consumer Price Indexes for March and September of each year. If they rise, your pay increases too, according to a special formula.

Special Pay Provisions

1. *Overtime.* This is paid at time-and-a-half your base hourly straight-time rate, after 8 hours in a day, or 40 hours in a week.

2. *Night pay.* A premium of 10 percent of your base hourly rate is paid for work done between 6 P.M. and 6 A.M.

Holidays

Regular employees receive 10 paid holidays a year.

Free Life Insurance

You will receive regular life insurance coverage of approximately one year's salary plus an equivalent amount of accidental death and dismemberment insurance. As your base pay increases, your insurance coverage will rise to a maximum of $60,000.

Workers' Compensation

When postal employees are injured on the job, they are entitled to workers' compensation benefits. The Postal Service pays for lost wages and medical bills related to their on-the-job injuries out of its own funds.

Retirement

As a new employee, you will automatically be covered by the new Federal Employees Retirement System (FERS). This is one of the most important benefit programs you receive as a federal employee since it is designed to help provide financial security for you and your family on your retirement.

The FERS has three components:

Social Security benefits

Basic benefit plan

Savings plan

Many of its features are "portable" so that, if you leave federal employment, you may still qualify for the benefits. Moreover, PERS is flexible and allows you to choose what is best for your situation. Because of this flexibility and the various retirement options available, it is not feasible to go into detail here regarding the kinds and amounts of benefits you may receive. These benefits depend on many factors such as length of service, earnings, family composition, age at retirement, and the Consumer Price Index.

The Postal Service will help guide you to the various sources you need to answer any questions you have about FERS.

Low-Cost Health Insurance

The Postal Service pays 89 percent of the cost.

Program of Cash Awards for Suggestions

The Postal Service has a sliding scale of awards for employees who suggest improvements in procedures, equipment, scheduling, and so on. Recently, an employee in St. Louis was awarded $35,000 for her idea on eliminating duplicate payments for replacement money orders.

Training and Development

The Postal Service places a premium on developing a well-trained and committed career work force. It believes that its investment of time and money to do this is essential to its present good health and to its future success. Now that more and more automated and complex equipment is in use, and changes in technology are increasing, proper training of postal employees is a high priority.

Hand in hand with this concern is the Postal Service's adherence to policies that give its employees the opportunity to advance within the organization. Once you have been working for the USPS for at least a year, you are eligible to take the entrance examination for any position, enabling you to change careers if you wish and advance accordingly. For example, you may become an initial-level supervisor (see following).

Several of the key programs offered by the Postal System will help you get the education and experience to qualify, as described below.

1. *New Employee Training (NET).*

   This provides training and support over the entire 90 days of an employee's probationary period. Orientation and job skills are taught by local supervisors with the assistance of experienced workers who coach and "break in" new workers.

   Within the larger cities, there are designated academies that can accommodate the larger groups of new hirees; e.g., there are two district academies in Brooklyn and Queens given the task of preparing 400 new carriers appointed from the test register cited on page xi.

2. *Postal Employee Development Centers (PEDCs).*

   A national network of over 200 centers helps current workers upgrade their skills and knowledge. These centers play a key part in preparing craft employees to operate and repair automation equipment as it comes on line. A great variety of training courses are developed and offered each year through the PEDCs, which are the principal vehicle for employee development. These programs make it possible for a postal worker to learn new skills and eventually qualify for a career change to a higher skilled, better paying job within the Postal Service.

3. *Advancement to Initial-Level Supervisor.*

   About 8,000 postal employees are promoted into supervisory jobs each year. This opportunity is open to all employees with one year of career employment. Interested individuals nominate themselves and are then evaluated by their supervisor. They must also take a test designed to measure their supervisory aptitude. A review panel looks over the nominations and makes its recommendations to the officials responsible for selection.

4. *Technical Training Center (TTC).*

   A 29,000-square-foot complex situated in Norman, Oklahoma, trains almost 20,000 employees a year in the maintenance and repair of high-technology systems, equipment, vehicles, and facilities.

5. *Nontechnical Training.*

   Courses and workshops to develop management and supervisory skills are held in a center in Chicago, Illinois. Training is offered on conflict resolution, team building, and communication skills. One of these programs, called Advanced Leadership offers training designed to build leadership skills to employees who manage large groups. A special fast-track management program is offered to qualified employees.

   Both centers also use learning devices such as satellite and audio tele-training networks to reach distant locations. Through a new agreement with PBS's, The Business Channel, the Postal Service now offers an additional 1,200 hours of live satellite seminars. On-site training gives employees all across the country a chance to learn and grow without leaving home.

Special Programs

Diversity Development

In 1992, a diversity development unit was created to ensure that the Postal Service recognizes and appreciates the needs of all members of this culturally diverse society. It serves the needs of the employees and customers of the Postal Service by assisting affirmative action, customer relations, and vendor programs. It helps design and analyze the Employee Opinion Survey and tries to increase the awareness and appreciation for ethnic and cultural diversity both in the postal workplace and among customers.

A profile of the workforce for 1993 shows that Blacks, Hispanics, and other minority groups comprise 38 percent of the workforce. About 33 percent of its employees are women, who now constitute 23 percent of the management and supervisory staff.

Employee Assistance Program (EAP)

This program provides confidential, prepaid counseling to employees and family members on a wide range of job-related problems, including sexual harassment, equal opportunity, emotional, personal, and stress issues. It seeks also to rehabilitate employees who have alcohol- and drug-related habits. Its services are provided 24 hours a day, free of charge, by licensed professional counselors who are not employed by the Postal Service.

How Much Are These Benefits Worth?

It has been estimated* that for a postal employee earning $29,700 a year, the annual contributions by the U.S. Postal Service toward these benefits can easily be worth $10,000. This figure does not include the value of annual leave and sick leave, which in this case amounts to $1,713.

Job Duties and Conditions

The test you take will be used to fill the job positions described below. Be aware, however, that not all positions are available at every location. The Postal Service will provide you with additional information before you take the exam, specifying which positions exist in the post offices that will use the area register.

Postal Clerks

Most people are familiar with the post office window clerk who sells stamps and accepts parcel post. Window clerks also weigh packages to determine postage and suitability for mailing. They register, certify, and insure mail, and answer questions about postage rates, mailing restrictions, and other postal matters. Occasionally they may help a customer file a claim for a damaged package.

Most postal clerks, however, are distribution clerks who sort incoming and outgoing mail in workrooms out of public view. Distribution clerks work at local post offices or at large mail-processing facilities. Clerks at local post offices sort local mail for delivery to individual customers. Incoming mail gathered from collection boxes is forwarded to the nearest mail processing center, where clerks sort and prepare the mail for delivery.

---

* Taken from *Postal Life*, May–June 1990

WORKING CONDITIONS

Working conditions for clerks differ according to the work assignment and the type of labor-saving machinery available. In small post offices, clerks may use a hand truck to move mail sacks from one part of the building to another and may sort mail by hand. In large post offices and mail processing centers, chutes and conveyors move the mail, and much of the sorting is done with machines. When they are not operating a letter-sorting machine, clerks are usually on their feet reaching for sacks and trays of mail and placing packages and bundles into sacks and trays. (Some of these may weigh as much as 70 pounds.)

Mail Carriers—City/Rural

Most mail carriers travel planned routes delivering and collecting mail. Carriers start work at the post office early in the morning, where they spend a few hours arranging their mail for delivery and taking care of other details.

A carrier may cover the route on foot, by vehicle, or by a combination of both. Foot carriers use a satchel or cart to deliver their mail. In some areas, a car or small truck is used to deliver mail. Carriers serving residential areas cover their routes only once a day, but some carriers assigned to a business district may make two trips a day. Deliveries are made door-to-door, to curbside or roadside mailboxes, to neighborhood delivery and collection boxes, to office buildings, and to apartment houses which have all the mailboxes located in the lobby

Besides delivering and collecting mail, carriers collect money for postage-due and C.O.D. items and obtain signed receipts for registered, certified, and insured mail. If a customer is not home, the carrier leaves a notice that tells what the item is and where it is being held.

After completing their routes, carriers return to the post office with mail gathered from street collection boxes, homes, and business places. They turn in their delivery receipts and money collected during the day, and separate the letters and large flats they collected for further processing by clerks.

Many city carriers have more specialized duties. Some deliver only parcel post while others collect mail from street boxes and receiving boxes in office buildings. In contrast, rural carriers provide a wide variety of postal services. In addition to delivering and picking up mail, they sell stamps and money orders and accept parcels, letters, and items to be registered, certified, or insured.

All carriers answer customers questions about postal regulations and services, and provide change-of-address cards and other postal forms upon request.

WORKING CONDITIONS

Most carriers begin work early in the morning, some as early as 4 A.M. if they have routes in the business district. Carriers spend most of their time outdoors in all kinds of weather delivering mail. Even those who drive often must walk when making deliveries and must lift sacks of parcel post when loading their vehicles.

The job, however, has its advantages. Carriers who begin work early in the morning are through by early afternoon.

Mail Handler

The mail handler is not as visible to the public as the window clerk in an average post office. However, you can get a glimpse of one if you pass the loading platform at the side or rear of a post office. Part of the mail handlers' job is done here, where these workers load and unload trucks carrying sacks of mail, cartons, and pallets from other cities and from airports. They place the sacks onto carts and wheel them to conveyor belts and sorting tables. There they empty the sacks and separate (cull) the contents into various categories, such as newspapers, books, airmail parcels, and oversized mail. Depending on the post office, mail handlers may also be assigned other tasks, for example, working on stamp cancellation machines or operating addressograph or mimeograph machines. Their duties may also include rewrapping parcels, placing outgoing parcels and packages into pouches, and even operating forklift trucks.

WORKING CONDITIONS

Like most other vocations, the mail handler job has its advantages and disadvantages. There is no doubt that this job is more strenuous. and dirtier than that of the clerk who sorts mail or sells money orders. Mail handlers have to repeatedly lift up to 70 pounds. Then, too, the mail handler may be exposed to inclement weather while working on a loading platform. In some offices, mail handlers work at night and on weekends.

On the other hand, the mail handler may very well enjoy the fresh air, particularly on nice days. Also, because the mail handler shuttles between various workstations, performing a variety of tasks, the job is less routine and more interesting than that of a letter-sorting machine operator, who does a repetitious job all day long.

Mail Processor

The mail processor title is a relatively new one in the Postal Service. The duties of the job include:

1. Starting and stopping a variety of mail-processing equipment such as bar-code sorters and optical bar-code readers.

2. Clearing jams that do not require hand tools.

3. Sweeping mail from bins, tying it into bundles as necessary, and placing the bundles into trays; pulling out nonprocessible items.

4. Loading mail onto transport units.

5. Performing other job-related tasks.

The mail processor's work is performed in large mail-processing facilities in an industrial environment. These employees are required to stand for long periods of time loading and unloading mail on a variety of automated mail-processing equipment. Mail processors normally work nights and weekends. Although the job does involve standing and lifting, it is not as strenuous as that of the mail handler. For this reason, the pay scale is slightly lower.

Machine Distribution Clerks

Machine distribution clerks, operating electronic letter-sorting machines, quickly scan the addresses on the mail that passes before them. Working at the rate of about one letter per second, they sort letters automatically by entering the proper sorting code on a specially developed keyboard. The machine then drops each letter into the proper slot. Needless to say, the letter-sorting machine clerk must have the ability to read addresses quickly and accurately, and to be able to remember and select the appropriate codes and sorting schemes. Operators are required to maintain an average keying accuracy of 98 percent. When they are not operating a letter-sorting machine, clerks are usually on their feet reaching for sacks and trays of mail and placing packages and bundles into sacks and trays.

WORKING CONDITIONS

The machine distribution clerk must cope with a certain amount of monotony and noise that is inherent in the job. The environment is more akin to a factory or warehouse than an office, with various pieces of machinery and rolling stock in view.

Individuals must have the willingness to maintain close visual attention for sustained periods and must be able to meet performance standards.

Some of the tedium of the job is overcome by the rotation of tasks and by work breaks. Many of the operators listen to music through headphones while they work. It can be an easy job for the right person. These employees usually work at night and on weekends.

The machine distribution clerk is compensated in other ways, too. He or she is slotted at a higher grade than regular clerks and thereby earns more money. Also, chances for advancement and development may be greater because the Postal Service is increasingly committed to the mechanization of mail processing. Greater employment opportunities can be expected by those willing and able to learn how to operate new and sophisticated equipment.

Flat-Sorting Machine Operator

The flat-sorting machine operator's job is very similar to that of the machine distribution clerk. These employees also operate a machine from memory or by using a zip code. Their machine, however, is called a flat sorter and is used to sort oversized letters, magazines, and so on using a special purpose keypad to distribute these flats at the rate of 45 per minute while maintaining an accuracy rate of 98 percent. They, too, must have an ability to maintain close visual attention for long periods of time. These operators usually work at nights and on weekends.

Mark-Up Clerks

Mark-up clerks work indoors entering change of address data into a computer database. They also process mail and perform other clerical functions. They operate a keyboard in order to process these changes and are therefore expected to have some experience with office machines.

Applicants for mark-up clerk must have good data entry skills and are required to pass a typing test. They may work at night and on weekends.

The Future—Job Outlook

In the last five years there has been an increase in the total number of career Postal System employees from 720,000 in 1994 to 792,000 in 1998. The USPS appears to be meeting the challenges to its market position with the responses described previously. Not only that—it is working aggressively to increase its share of business in all areas; for example, it has plans to catch up with the International Mail market and become the leading supplier of direct marketing and package delivery to its business customers worldwide. It will invest $4.4 billion on its Capital Improvement Plan (new post offices, equipment, technology, repairs, vehicles) and a total of $17 billion through the year 2002.

All these figures mean that in spite of reductions in certain job categories there will continue to be career opportunities and examinations will be offered by the Postal Service to replace some of the workers who are promoted, who transfer to other occupations, or who retire each year. Openings will arise also as a result of growth in the volume of mail handled by the Postal Service, reflecting the expanding economy, the rising population, and the increased emphasis on marketing and customer service. Openings will be most frequent in areas with rapid population growth. Although the Postal Service's policy of increasing mechanization and automation works to decrease the number of clerks needed to process a given volume of mail, it also results in additional opportunities for clerks who wish to learn how to operate the new machines and to transfer to new opportunities within the Postal Service. Employees who plan to continue or expand their education should be aware that there will be a growing need for computer specialists and for electronics, electrical, and mechanical maintenance technicians as more and more sophisticated equipment is used to process the mail. The job outlook for certain other positions such as mail handler and mail processor should be more stable. There seems to be no way to substitute machines for human beings to do these jobs.

The tremendous number of job titles in the USPS including Craft, Professional, and Management positions, together with the opportunities for career advancement and job security, makes the goal of entering the Postal System seem entirely worthwhile.

■ A FINAL WORD

You now have a good picture of most matters connected with the Test 460/470—before, during, and after. You will be able to act in your best interests in regard to applying, job choice, retaining eligibility, obtaining information, and so on. You should also have gained a certain amount of confidence in knowing why and how certain things happen. Now we've come to building the best confidence of all, the confidence you feel when you're thoroughly prepared to do well on the test itself. It is that thorough preparation to which the rest of this book is dedicated.

DIAGNOSING YOUR SKILLS

Answer Sheet—Diagnostic Practice Test

Part A—Address Checking

1 Ⓐⓓ	25 Ⓐⓓ	49 Ⓐⓓ	73 Ⓐⓓ
2 Ⓐⓓ	26 Ⓐⓓ	50 Ⓐⓓ	74 Ⓐⓓ
3 Ⓐⓓ	27 Ⓐⓓ	51 Ⓐⓓ	75 Ⓐⓓ
4 Ⓐⓓ	28 Ⓐⓓ	52 Ⓐⓓ	76 Ⓐⓓ
5 Ⓐⓓ	29 Ⓐⓓ	53 Ⓐⓓ	77 Ⓐⓓ
6 Ⓐⓓ	30 Ⓐⓓ	54 Ⓐⓓ	78 Ⓐⓓ
7 Ⓐⓓ	31 Ⓐⓓ	55 Ⓐⓓ	79 Ⓐⓓ
8 Ⓐⓓ	32 Ⓐⓓ	56 Ⓐⓓ	80 Ⓐⓓ
9 Ⓐⓓ	33 Ⓐⓓ	57 Ⓐⓓ	81 Ⓐⓓ
10 Ⓐⓓ	34 Ⓐⓓ	58 Ⓐⓓ	82 Ⓐⓓ
11 Ⓐⓓ	35 Ⓐⓓ	59 Ⓐⓓ	83 Ⓐⓓ
12 Ⓐⓓ	36 Ⓐⓓ	60 Ⓐⓓ	84 Ⓐⓓ
13 Ⓐⓓ	37 Ⓐⓓ	61 Ⓐⓓ	85 Ⓐⓓ
14 Ⓐⓓ	38 Ⓐⓓ	62 Ⓐⓓ	86 Ⓐⓓ
15 Ⓐⓓ	39 Ⓐⓓ	63 Ⓐⓓ	87 Ⓐⓓ
16 Ⓐⓓ	40 Ⓐⓓ	64 Ⓐⓓ	88 Ⓐⓓ
17 Ⓐⓓ	41 Ⓐⓓ	65 Ⓐⓓ	89 Ⓐⓓ
18 Ⓐⓓ	42 Ⓐⓓ	66 Ⓐⓓ	90 Ⓐⓓ
19 Ⓐⓓ	43 Ⓐⓓ	67 Ⓐⓓ	91 Ⓐⓓ
20 Ⓐⓓ	44 Ⓐⓓ	68 Ⓐⓓ	92 Ⓐⓓ
21 Ⓐⓓ	45 Ⓐⓓ	69 Ⓐⓓ	93 Ⓐⓓ
22 Ⓐⓓ	46 Ⓐⓓ	70 Ⓐⓓ	94 Ⓐⓓ
23 Ⓐⓓ	47 Ⓐⓓ	71 Ⓐⓓ	95 Ⓐⓓ
24 Ⓐⓓ	48 Ⓐⓓ	72 Ⓐⓓ	

Remove by cutting on dotted line.

Part B – Memory for Addresses—List 1

1 Ⓐ Ⓑ Ⓒ Ⓓ Ⓔ	19 Ⓐ Ⓑ Ⓒ Ⓓ Ⓔ	37 Ⓐ Ⓑ Ⓒ Ⓓ Ⓔ	55 Ⓐ Ⓑ Ⓒ Ⓓ Ⓔ	73 Ⓐ Ⓑ Ⓒ Ⓓ Ⓔ
2 Ⓐ Ⓑ Ⓒ Ⓓ Ⓔ	20 Ⓐ Ⓑ Ⓒ Ⓓ Ⓔ	38 Ⓐ Ⓑ Ⓒ Ⓓ Ⓔ	56 Ⓐ Ⓑ Ⓒ Ⓓ Ⓔ	74 Ⓐ Ⓑ Ⓒ Ⓓ Ⓔ
3 Ⓐ Ⓑ Ⓒ Ⓓ Ⓔ	21 Ⓐ Ⓑ Ⓒ Ⓓ Ⓔ	39 Ⓐ Ⓑ Ⓒ Ⓓ Ⓔ	57 Ⓐ Ⓑ Ⓒ Ⓓ Ⓔ	75 Ⓐ Ⓑ Ⓒ Ⓓ Ⓔ
4 Ⓐ Ⓑ Ⓒ Ⓓ Ⓔ	22 Ⓐ Ⓑ Ⓒ Ⓓ Ⓔ	40 Ⓐ Ⓑ Ⓒ Ⓓ Ⓔ	58 Ⓐ Ⓑ Ⓒ Ⓓ Ⓔ	76 Ⓐ Ⓑ Ⓒ Ⓓ Ⓔ
5 Ⓐ Ⓑ Ⓒ Ⓓ Ⓔ	23 Ⓐ Ⓑ Ⓒ Ⓓ Ⓔ	41 Ⓐ Ⓑ Ⓒ Ⓓ Ⓔ	59 Ⓐ Ⓑ Ⓒ Ⓓ Ⓔ	77 Ⓐ Ⓑ Ⓒ Ⓓ Ⓔ
6 Ⓐ Ⓑ Ⓒ Ⓓ Ⓔ	24 Ⓐ Ⓑ Ⓒ Ⓓ Ⓔ	42 Ⓐ Ⓑ Ⓒ Ⓓ Ⓔ	60 Ⓐ Ⓑ Ⓒ Ⓓ Ⓔ	78 Ⓐ Ⓑ Ⓒ Ⓓ Ⓔ
7 Ⓐ Ⓑ Ⓒ Ⓓ Ⓔ	25 Ⓐ Ⓑ Ⓒ Ⓓ Ⓔ	43 Ⓐ Ⓑ Ⓒ Ⓓ Ⓔ	61 Ⓐ Ⓑ Ⓒ Ⓓ Ⓔ	79 Ⓐ Ⓑ Ⓒ Ⓓ Ⓔ
8 Ⓐ Ⓑ Ⓒ Ⓓ Ⓔ	26 Ⓐ Ⓑ Ⓒ Ⓓ Ⓔ	44 Ⓐ Ⓑ Ⓒ Ⓓ Ⓔ	62 Ⓐ Ⓑ Ⓒ Ⓓ Ⓔ	80 Ⓐ Ⓑ Ⓒ Ⓓ Ⓔ
9 Ⓐ Ⓑ Ⓒ Ⓓ Ⓔ	27 Ⓐ Ⓑ Ⓒ Ⓓ Ⓔ	45 Ⓐ Ⓑ Ⓒ Ⓓ Ⓔ	63 Ⓐ Ⓑ Ⓒ Ⓓ Ⓔ	81 Ⓐ Ⓑ Ⓒ Ⓓ Ⓔ
10 Ⓐ Ⓑ Ⓒ Ⓓ Ⓔ	28 Ⓐ Ⓑ Ⓒ Ⓓ Ⓔ	46 Ⓐ Ⓑ Ⓒ Ⓓ Ⓔ	64 Ⓐ Ⓑ Ⓒ Ⓓ Ⓔ	82 Ⓐ Ⓑ Ⓒ Ⓓ Ⓔ
11 Ⓐ Ⓑ Ⓒ Ⓓ Ⓔ	29 Ⓐ Ⓑ Ⓒ Ⓓ Ⓔ	47 Ⓐ Ⓑ Ⓒ Ⓓ Ⓔ	65 Ⓐ Ⓑ Ⓒ Ⓓ Ⓔ	83 Ⓐ Ⓑ Ⓒ Ⓓ Ⓔ
12 Ⓐ Ⓑ Ⓒ Ⓓ Ⓔ	30 Ⓐ Ⓑ Ⓒ Ⓓ Ⓔ	48 Ⓐ Ⓑ Ⓒ Ⓓ Ⓔ	66 Ⓐ Ⓑ Ⓒ Ⓓ Ⓔ	84 Ⓐ Ⓑ Ⓒ Ⓓ Ⓔ
13 Ⓐ Ⓑ Ⓒ Ⓓ Ⓔ	31 Ⓐ Ⓑ Ⓒ Ⓓ Ⓔ	49 Ⓐ Ⓑ Ⓒ Ⓓ Ⓔ	67 Ⓐ Ⓑ Ⓒ Ⓓ Ⓔ	85 Ⓐ Ⓑ Ⓒ Ⓓ Ⓔ
14 Ⓐ Ⓑ Ⓒ Ⓓ Ⓔ	32 Ⓐ Ⓑ Ⓒ Ⓓ Ⓔ	50 Ⓐ Ⓑ Ⓒ Ⓓ Ⓔ	68 Ⓐ Ⓑ Ⓒ Ⓓ Ⓔ	86 Ⓐ Ⓑ Ⓒ Ⓓ Ⓔ
15 Ⓐ Ⓑ Ⓒ Ⓓ Ⓔ	33 Ⓐ Ⓑ Ⓒ Ⓓ Ⓔ	51 Ⓐ Ⓑ Ⓒ Ⓓ Ⓔ	69 Ⓐ Ⓑ Ⓒ Ⓓ Ⓔ	87 Ⓐ Ⓑ Ⓒ Ⓓ Ⓔ
16 Ⓐ Ⓑ Ⓒ Ⓓ Ⓔ	34 Ⓐ Ⓑ Ⓒ Ⓓ Ⓔ	52 Ⓐ Ⓑ Ⓒ Ⓓ Ⓔ	70 Ⓐ Ⓑ Ⓒ Ⓓ Ⓔ	88 Ⓐ Ⓑ Ⓒ Ⓓ Ⓔ
17 Ⓐ Ⓑ Ⓒ Ⓓ Ⓔ	35 Ⓐ Ⓑ Ⓒ Ⓓ Ⓔ	53 Ⓐ Ⓑ Ⓒ Ⓓ Ⓔ	71 Ⓐ Ⓑ Ⓒ Ⓓ Ⓔ	
18 Ⓐ Ⓑ Ⓒ Ⓓ Ⓔ	36 Ⓐ Ⓑ Ⓒ Ⓓ Ⓔ	54 Ⓐ Ⓑ Ⓒ Ⓓ Ⓔ	72 Ⓐ Ⓑ Ⓒ Ⓓ Ⓔ	

Part B – Memory for Addresses—List 2

1 Ⓐ Ⓑ Ⓒ Ⓓ Ⓔ	19 Ⓐ Ⓑ Ⓒ Ⓓ Ⓔ	37 Ⓐ Ⓑ Ⓒ Ⓓ Ⓔ	55 Ⓐ Ⓑ Ⓒ Ⓓ Ⓔ	73 Ⓐ Ⓑ Ⓒ Ⓓ Ⓔ
2 Ⓐ Ⓑ Ⓒ Ⓓ Ⓔ	20 Ⓐ Ⓑ Ⓒ Ⓓ Ⓔ	38 Ⓐ Ⓑ Ⓒ Ⓓ Ⓔ	56 Ⓐ Ⓑ Ⓒ Ⓓ Ⓔ	74 Ⓐ Ⓑ Ⓒ Ⓓ Ⓔ
3 Ⓐ Ⓑ Ⓒ Ⓓ Ⓔ	21 Ⓐ Ⓑ Ⓒ Ⓓ Ⓔ	39 Ⓐ Ⓑ Ⓒ Ⓓ Ⓔ	57 Ⓐ Ⓑ Ⓒ Ⓓ Ⓔ	75 Ⓐ Ⓑ Ⓒ Ⓓ Ⓔ
4 Ⓐ Ⓑ Ⓒ Ⓓ Ⓔ	22 Ⓐ Ⓑ Ⓒ Ⓓ Ⓔ	40 Ⓐ Ⓑ Ⓒ Ⓓ Ⓔ	58 Ⓐ Ⓑ Ⓒ Ⓓ Ⓔ	76 Ⓐ Ⓑ Ⓒ Ⓓ Ⓔ
5 Ⓐ Ⓑ Ⓒ Ⓓ Ⓔ	23 Ⓐ Ⓑ Ⓒ Ⓓ Ⓔ	41 Ⓐ Ⓑ Ⓒ Ⓓ Ⓔ	59 Ⓐ Ⓑ Ⓒ Ⓓ Ⓔ	77 Ⓐ Ⓑ Ⓒ Ⓓ Ⓔ
6 Ⓐ Ⓑ Ⓒ Ⓓ Ⓔ	24 Ⓐ Ⓑ Ⓒ Ⓓ Ⓔ	42 Ⓐ Ⓑ Ⓒ Ⓓ Ⓔ	60 Ⓐ Ⓑ Ⓒ Ⓓ Ⓔ	78 Ⓐ Ⓑ Ⓒ Ⓓ Ⓔ
7 Ⓐ Ⓑ Ⓒ Ⓓ Ⓔ	25 Ⓐ Ⓑ Ⓒ Ⓓ Ⓔ	43 Ⓐ Ⓑ Ⓒ Ⓓ Ⓔ	61 Ⓐ Ⓑ Ⓒ Ⓓ Ⓔ	79 Ⓐ Ⓑ Ⓒ Ⓓ Ⓔ
8 Ⓐ Ⓑ Ⓒ Ⓓ Ⓔ	26 Ⓐ Ⓑ Ⓒ Ⓓ Ⓔ	44 Ⓐ Ⓑ Ⓒ Ⓓ Ⓔ	62 Ⓐ Ⓑ Ⓒ Ⓓ Ⓔ	80 Ⓐ Ⓑ Ⓒ Ⓓ Ⓔ
9 Ⓐ Ⓑ Ⓒ Ⓓ Ⓔ	27 Ⓐ Ⓑ Ⓒ Ⓓ Ⓔ	45 Ⓐ Ⓑ Ⓒ Ⓓ Ⓔ	63 Ⓐ Ⓑ Ⓒ Ⓓ Ⓔ	81 Ⓐ Ⓑ Ⓒ Ⓓ Ⓔ
10 Ⓐ Ⓑ Ⓒ Ⓓ Ⓔ	28 Ⓐ Ⓑ Ⓒ Ⓓ Ⓔ	46 Ⓐ Ⓑ Ⓒ Ⓓ Ⓔ	64 Ⓐ Ⓑ Ⓒ Ⓓ Ⓔ	82 Ⓐ Ⓑ Ⓒ Ⓓ Ⓔ
11 Ⓐ Ⓑ Ⓒ Ⓓ Ⓔ	29 Ⓐ Ⓑ Ⓒ Ⓓ Ⓔ	47 Ⓐ Ⓑ Ⓒ Ⓓ Ⓔ	65 Ⓐ Ⓑ Ⓒ Ⓓ Ⓔ	83 Ⓐ Ⓑ Ⓒ Ⓓ Ⓔ
12 Ⓐ Ⓑ Ⓒ Ⓓ Ⓔ	30 Ⓐ Ⓑ Ⓒ Ⓓ Ⓔ	48 Ⓐ Ⓑ Ⓒ Ⓓ Ⓔ	66 Ⓐ Ⓑ Ⓒ Ⓓ Ⓔ	84 Ⓐ Ⓑ Ⓒ Ⓓ Ⓔ
13 Ⓐ Ⓑ Ⓒ Ⓓ Ⓔ	31 Ⓐ Ⓑ Ⓒ Ⓓ Ⓔ	49 Ⓐ Ⓑ Ⓒ Ⓓ Ⓔ	67 Ⓐ Ⓑ Ⓒ Ⓓ Ⓔ	85 Ⓐ Ⓑ Ⓒ Ⓓ Ⓔ
14 Ⓐ Ⓑ Ⓒ Ⓓ Ⓔ	32 Ⓐ Ⓑ Ⓒ Ⓓ Ⓔ	50 Ⓐ Ⓑ Ⓒ Ⓓ Ⓔ	68 Ⓐ Ⓑ Ⓒ Ⓓ Ⓔ	86 Ⓐ Ⓑ Ⓒ Ⓓ Ⓔ
15 Ⓐ Ⓑ Ⓒ Ⓓ Ⓔ	33 Ⓐ Ⓑ Ⓒ Ⓓ Ⓔ	51 Ⓐ Ⓑ Ⓒ Ⓓ Ⓔ	69 Ⓐ Ⓑ Ⓒ Ⓓ Ⓔ	87 Ⓐ Ⓑ Ⓒ Ⓓ Ⓔ
16 Ⓐ Ⓑ Ⓒ Ⓓ Ⓔ	34 Ⓐ Ⓑ Ⓒ Ⓓ Ⓔ	52 Ⓐ Ⓑ Ⓒ Ⓓ Ⓔ	70 Ⓐ Ⓑ Ⓒ Ⓓ Ⓔ	88 Ⓐ Ⓑ Ⓒ Ⓓ Ⓔ
17 Ⓐ Ⓑ Ⓒ Ⓓ Ⓔ	35 Ⓐ Ⓑ Ⓒ Ⓓ Ⓔ	53 Ⓐ Ⓑ Ⓒ Ⓓ Ⓔ	71 Ⓐ Ⓑ Ⓒ Ⓓ Ⓔ	
18 Ⓐ Ⓑ Ⓒ Ⓓ Ⓔ	36 Ⓐ Ⓑ Ⓒ Ⓓ Ⓔ	54 Ⓐ Ⓑ Ⓒ Ⓓ Ⓔ	72 Ⓐ Ⓑ Ⓒ Ⓓ Ⓔ	

Remove by cutting on dotted line.

Part B – Memory for Addresses—List 3

1 Ⓐ Ⓑ Ⓒ Ⓓ Ⓔ	19 Ⓐ Ⓑ Ⓒ Ⓓ Ⓔ	37 Ⓐ Ⓑ Ⓒ Ⓓ Ⓔ	55 Ⓐ Ⓑ Ⓒ Ⓓ Ⓔ	73 Ⓐ Ⓑ Ⓒ Ⓓ Ⓔ
2 Ⓐ Ⓑ Ⓒ Ⓓ Ⓔ	20 Ⓐ Ⓑ Ⓒ Ⓓ Ⓔ	38 Ⓐ Ⓑ Ⓒ Ⓓ Ⓔ	56 Ⓐ Ⓑ Ⓒ Ⓓ Ⓔ	74 Ⓐ Ⓑ Ⓒ Ⓓ Ⓔ
3 Ⓐ Ⓑ Ⓒ Ⓓ Ⓔ	21 Ⓐ Ⓑ Ⓒ Ⓓ Ⓔ	39 Ⓐ Ⓑ Ⓒ Ⓓ Ⓔ	57 Ⓐ Ⓑ Ⓒ Ⓓ Ⓔ	75 Ⓐ Ⓑ Ⓒ Ⓓ Ⓔ
4 Ⓐ Ⓑ Ⓒ Ⓓ Ⓔ	22 Ⓐ Ⓑ Ⓒ Ⓓ Ⓔ	40 Ⓐ Ⓑ Ⓒ Ⓓ Ⓔ	58 Ⓐ Ⓑ Ⓒ Ⓓ Ⓔ	76 Ⓐ Ⓑ Ⓒ Ⓓ Ⓔ
5 Ⓐ Ⓑ Ⓒ Ⓓ Ⓔ	23 Ⓐ Ⓑ Ⓒ Ⓓ Ⓔ	41 Ⓐ Ⓑ Ⓒ Ⓓ Ⓔ	59 Ⓐ Ⓑ Ⓒ Ⓓ Ⓔ	77 Ⓐ Ⓑ Ⓒ Ⓓ Ⓔ
6 Ⓐ Ⓑ Ⓒ Ⓓ Ⓔ	24 Ⓐ Ⓑ Ⓒ Ⓓ Ⓔ	42 Ⓐ Ⓑ Ⓒ Ⓓ Ⓔ	60 Ⓐ Ⓑ Ⓒ Ⓓ Ⓔ	78 Ⓐ Ⓑ Ⓒ Ⓓ Ⓔ
7 Ⓐ Ⓑ Ⓒ Ⓓ Ⓔ	25 Ⓐ Ⓑ Ⓒ Ⓓ Ⓔ	43 Ⓐ Ⓑ Ⓒ Ⓓ Ⓔ	61 Ⓐ Ⓑ Ⓒ Ⓓ Ⓔ	79 Ⓐ Ⓑ Ⓒ Ⓓ Ⓔ
8 Ⓐ Ⓑ Ⓒ Ⓓ Ⓔ	26 Ⓐ Ⓑ Ⓒ Ⓓ Ⓔ	44 Ⓐ Ⓑ Ⓒ Ⓓ Ⓔ	62 Ⓐ Ⓑ Ⓒ Ⓓ Ⓔ	80 Ⓐ Ⓑ Ⓒ Ⓓ Ⓔ
9 Ⓐ Ⓑ Ⓒ Ⓓ Ⓔ	27 Ⓐ Ⓑ Ⓒ Ⓓ Ⓔ	45 Ⓐ Ⓑ Ⓒ Ⓓ Ⓔ	63 Ⓐ Ⓑ Ⓒ Ⓓ Ⓔ	81 Ⓐ Ⓑ Ⓒ Ⓓ Ⓔ
10 Ⓐ Ⓑ Ⓒ Ⓓ Ⓔ	28 Ⓐ Ⓑ Ⓒ Ⓓ Ⓔ	46 Ⓐ Ⓑ Ⓒ Ⓓ Ⓔ	64 Ⓐ Ⓑ Ⓒ Ⓓ Ⓔ	82 Ⓐ Ⓑ Ⓒ Ⓓ Ⓔ
11 Ⓐ Ⓑ Ⓒ Ⓓ Ⓔ	29 Ⓐ Ⓑ Ⓒ Ⓓ Ⓔ	47 Ⓐ Ⓑ Ⓒ Ⓓ Ⓔ	65 Ⓐ Ⓑ Ⓒ Ⓓ Ⓔ	83 Ⓐ Ⓑ Ⓒ Ⓓ Ⓔ
12 Ⓐ Ⓑ Ⓒ Ⓓ Ⓔ	30 Ⓐ Ⓑ Ⓒ Ⓓ Ⓔ	48 Ⓐ Ⓑ Ⓒ Ⓓ Ⓔ	66 Ⓐ Ⓑ Ⓒ Ⓓ Ⓔ	84 Ⓐ Ⓑ Ⓒ Ⓓ Ⓔ
13 Ⓐ Ⓑ Ⓒ Ⓓ Ⓔ	31 Ⓐ Ⓑ Ⓒ Ⓓ Ⓔ	49 Ⓐ Ⓑ Ⓒ Ⓓ Ⓔ	67 Ⓐ Ⓑ Ⓒ Ⓓ Ⓔ	85 Ⓐ Ⓑ Ⓒ Ⓓ Ⓔ
14 Ⓐ Ⓑ Ⓒ Ⓓ Ⓔ	32 Ⓐ Ⓑ Ⓒ Ⓓ Ⓔ	50 Ⓐ Ⓑ Ⓒ Ⓓ Ⓔ	68 Ⓐ Ⓑ Ⓒ Ⓓ Ⓔ	86 Ⓐ Ⓑ Ⓒ Ⓓ Ⓔ
15 Ⓐ Ⓑ Ⓒ Ⓓ Ⓔ	33 Ⓐ Ⓑ Ⓒ Ⓓ Ⓔ	51 Ⓐ Ⓑ Ⓒ Ⓓ Ⓔ	69 Ⓐ Ⓑ Ⓒ Ⓓ Ⓔ	87 Ⓐ Ⓑ Ⓒ Ⓓ Ⓔ
16 Ⓐ Ⓑ Ⓒ Ⓓ Ⓔ	34 Ⓐ Ⓑ Ⓒ Ⓓ Ⓔ	52 Ⓐ Ⓑ Ⓒ Ⓓ Ⓔ	70 Ⓐ Ⓑ Ⓒ Ⓓ Ⓔ	88 Ⓐ Ⓑ Ⓒ Ⓓ Ⓔ
17 Ⓐ Ⓑ Ⓒ Ⓓ Ⓔ	35 Ⓐ Ⓑ Ⓒ Ⓓ Ⓔ	53 Ⓐ Ⓑ Ⓒ Ⓓ Ⓔ	71 Ⓐ Ⓑ Ⓒ Ⓓ Ⓔ	
18 Ⓐ Ⓑ Ⓒ Ⓓ Ⓔ	36 Ⓐ Ⓑ Ⓒ Ⓓ Ⓔ	54 Ⓐ Ⓑ Ⓒ Ⓓ Ⓔ	72 Ⓐ Ⓑ Ⓒ Ⓓ Ⓔ	

Part C – Number Series

1 Ⓐ Ⓑ Ⓒ Ⓓ Ⓔ	6 Ⓐ Ⓑ Ⓒ Ⓓ Ⓔ	11 Ⓐ Ⓑ Ⓒ Ⓓ Ⓔ	16 Ⓐ Ⓑ Ⓒ Ⓓ Ⓔ	21 Ⓐ Ⓑ Ⓒ Ⓓ Ⓔ
2 Ⓐ Ⓑ Ⓒ Ⓓ Ⓔ	7 Ⓐ Ⓑ Ⓒ Ⓓ Ⓔ	12 Ⓐ Ⓑ Ⓒ Ⓓ Ⓔ	17 Ⓐ Ⓑ Ⓒ Ⓓ Ⓔ	22 Ⓐ Ⓑ Ⓒ Ⓓ Ⓔ
3 Ⓐ Ⓑ Ⓒ Ⓓ Ⓔ	8 Ⓐ Ⓑ Ⓒ Ⓓ Ⓔ	13 Ⓐ Ⓑ Ⓒ Ⓓ Ⓔ	18 Ⓐ Ⓑ Ⓒ Ⓓ Ⓔ	23 Ⓐ Ⓑ Ⓒ Ⓓ Ⓔ
4 Ⓐ Ⓑ Ⓒ Ⓓ Ⓔ	9 Ⓐ Ⓑ Ⓒ Ⓓ Ⓔ	14 Ⓐ Ⓑ Ⓒ Ⓓ Ⓔ	19 Ⓐ Ⓑ Ⓒ Ⓓ Ⓔ	24 Ⓐ Ⓑ Ⓒ Ⓓ Ⓔ
5 Ⓐ Ⓑ Ⓒ Ⓓ Ⓔ	10 Ⓐ Ⓑ Ⓒ Ⓓ Ⓔ	15 Ⓐ Ⓑ Ⓒ Ⓓ Ⓔ	20 Ⓐ Ⓑ Ⓒ Ⓓ Ⓔ	

Part D – Following Oral Directions

1 Ⓐ Ⓑ Ⓒ Ⓓ Ⓔ	19 Ⓐ Ⓑ Ⓒ Ⓓ Ⓔ	37 Ⓐ Ⓑ Ⓒ Ⓓ Ⓔ	55 Ⓐ Ⓑ Ⓒ Ⓓ Ⓔ	73 Ⓐ Ⓑ Ⓒ Ⓓ Ⓔ
2 Ⓐ Ⓑ Ⓒ Ⓓ Ⓔ	20 Ⓐ Ⓑ Ⓒ Ⓓ Ⓔ	38 Ⓐ Ⓑ Ⓒ Ⓓ Ⓔ	56 Ⓐ Ⓑ Ⓒ Ⓓ Ⓔ	74 Ⓐ Ⓑ Ⓒ Ⓓ Ⓔ
3 Ⓐ Ⓑ Ⓒ Ⓓ Ⓔ	21 Ⓐ Ⓑ Ⓒ Ⓓ Ⓔ	39 Ⓐ Ⓑ Ⓒ Ⓓ Ⓔ	57 Ⓐ Ⓑ Ⓒ Ⓓ Ⓔ	75 Ⓐ Ⓑ Ⓒ Ⓓ Ⓔ
4 Ⓐ Ⓑ Ⓒ Ⓓ Ⓔ	22 Ⓐ Ⓑ Ⓒ Ⓓ Ⓔ	40 Ⓐ Ⓑ Ⓒ Ⓓ Ⓔ	58 Ⓐ Ⓑ Ⓒ Ⓓ Ⓔ	76 Ⓐ Ⓑ Ⓒ Ⓓ Ⓔ
5 Ⓐ Ⓑ Ⓒ Ⓓ Ⓔ	23 Ⓐ Ⓑ Ⓒ Ⓓ Ⓔ	41 Ⓐ Ⓑ Ⓒ Ⓓ Ⓔ	59 Ⓐ Ⓑ Ⓒ Ⓓ Ⓔ	77 Ⓐ Ⓑ Ⓒ Ⓓ Ⓔ
6 Ⓐ Ⓑ Ⓒ Ⓓ Ⓔ	24 Ⓐ Ⓑ Ⓒ Ⓓ Ⓔ	42 Ⓐ Ⓑ Ⓒ Ⓓ Ⓔ	60 Ⓐ Ⓑ Ⓒ Ⓓ Ⓔ	78 Ⓐ Ⓑ Ⓒ Ⓓ Ⓔ
7 Ⓐ Ⓑ Ⓒ Ⓓ Ⓔ	25 Ⓐ Ⓑ Ⓒ Ⓓ Ⓔ	43 Ⓐ Ⓑ Ⓒ Ⓓ Ⓔ	61 Ⓐ Ⓑ Ⓒ Ⓓ Ⓔ	79 Ⓐ Ⓑ Ⓒ Ⓓ Ⓔ
8 Ⓐ Ⓑ Ⓒ Ⓓ Ⓔ	26 Ⓐ Ⓑ Ⓒ Ⓓ Ⓔ	44 Ⓐ Ⓑ Ⓒ Ⓓ Ⓔ	62 Ⓐ Ⓑ Ⓒ Ⓓ Ⓔ	80 Ⓐ Ⓑ Ⓒ Ⓓ Ⓔ
9 Ⓐ Ⓑ Ⓒ Ⓓ Ⓔ	27 Ⓐ Ⓑ Ⓒ Ⓓ Ⓔ	45 Ⓐ Ⓑ Ⓒ Ⓓ Ⓔ	63 Ⓐ Ⓑ Ⓒ Ⓓ Ⓔ	81 Ⓐ Ⓑ Ⓒ Ⓓ Ⓔ
10 Ⓐ Ⓑ Ⓒ Ⓓ Ⓔ	28 Ⓐ Ⓑ Ⓒ Ⓓ Ⓔ	46 Ⓐ Ⓑ Ⓒ Ⓓ Ⓔ	64 Ⓐ Ⓑ Ⓒ Ⓓ Ⓔ	82 Ⓐ Ⓑ Ⓒ Ⓓ Ⓔ
11 Ⓐ Ⓑ Ⓒ Ⓓ Ⓔ	29 Ⓐ Ⓑ Ⓒ Ⓓ Ⓔ	47 Ⓐ Ⓑ Ⓒ Ⓓ Ⓔ	65 Ⓐ Ⓑ Ⓒ Ⓓ Ⓔ	83 Ⓐ Ⓑ Ⓒ Ⓓ Ⓔ
12 Ⓐ Ⓑ Ⓒ Ⓓ Ⓔ	30 Ⓐ Ⓑ Ⓒ Ⓓ Ⓔ	48 Ⓐ Ⓑ Ⓒ Ⓓ Ⓔ	66 Ⓐ Ⓑ Ⓒ Ⓓ Ⓔ	84 Ⓐ Ⓑ Ⓒ Ⓓ Ⓔ
13 Ⓐ Ⓑ Ⓒ Ⓓ Ⓔ	31 Ⓐ Ⓑ Ⓒ Ⓓ Ⓔ	49 Ⓐ Ⓑ Ⓒ Ⓓ Ⓔ	67 Ⓐ Ⓑ Ⓒ Ⓓ Ⓔ	85 Ⓐ Ⓑ Ⓒ Ⓓ Ⓔ
14 Ⓐ Ⓑ Ⓒ Ⓓ Ⓔ	32 Ⓐ Ⓑ Ⓒ Ⓓ Ⓔ	50 Ⓐ Ⓑ Ⓒ Ⓓ Ⓔ	68 Ⓐ Ⓑ Ⓒ Ⓓ Ⓔ	86 Ⓐ Ⓑ Ⓒ Ⓓ Ⓔ
15 Ⓐ Ⓑ Ⓒ Ⓓ Ⓔ	33 Ⓐ Ⓑ Ⓒ Ⓓ Ⓔ	51 Ⓐ Ⓑ Ⓒ Ⓓ Ⓔ	69 Ⓐ Ⓑ Ⓒ Ⓓ Ⓔ	87 Ⓐ Ⓑ Ⓒ Ⓓ Ⓔ
16 Ⓐ Ⓑ Ⓒ Ⓓ Ⓔ	34 Ⓐ Ⓑ Ⓒ Ⓓ Ⓔ	52 Ⓐ Ⓑ Ⓒ Ⓓ Ⓔ	70 Ⓐ Ⓑ Ⓒ Ⓓ Ⓔ	88 Ⓐ Ⓑ Ⓒ Ⓓ Ⓔ
17 Ⓐ Ⓑ Ⓒ Ⓓ Ⓔ	35 Ⓐ Ⓑ Ⓒ Ⓓ Ⓔ	53 Ⓐ Ⓑ Ⓒ Ⓓ Ⓔ	71 Ⓐ Ⓑ Ⓒ Ⓓ Ⓔ	
18 Ⓐ Ⓑ Ⓒ Ⓓ Ⓔ	36 Ⓐ Ⓑ Ⓒ Ⓓ Ⓔ	54 Ⓐ Ⓑ Ⓒ Ⓓ Ⓔ	72 Ⓐ Ⓑ Ⓒ Ⓓ Ⓔ	

Chapter 3

Diagnostic Practice Test

One of the first questions that you may be asking yourself is, What kind of test score could I make right now? Where would I stand in relation to others taking the same test?

To help answer these questions, it is suggested that you take the following Diagnostic Practice Test, which is modeled after actual Postal Service tests. After you have taken the test, you will be shown how to score it and how that score might compare with the scores of typical test candidates. By knowing your present level of achievement and your strengths and weaknesses, you will be able to direct your improvement efforts. You will know exactly *what* and *how much* to study and practice. You will have a starting point against which to measure the progress you make as you go through this book. The satisfaction you get from seeing your score improve is the best motivating force we know.

These test questions and many additional examples will be used to illustrate certain techniques and strategies given in Chapters 4 through 9 Before you begin, read the section below:

◼ TIMING METHODS FOR PRACTICE TESTS AND DRILLS

The best method for timing your practice tests and drills is to have someone else do it for you. In that way, you will be free from the distraction and loss of time involved in looking at a timepiece. Also, you will be less likely to lose your rhythm or your place on the question and answer sheets. (On the actual test, one of the monitors directs all the timing.)

If you cannot get someone to time you, you can minimize the disadvantages of working alone by following some of these suggestions:

1. Use a count down timer that can be preset so that, when the time is up for a particular study or practice period, an alarm sounds or flashes to alert you.

2. Use an ordinary wall clock, with a face large enough for you to see the numerals clearly from your seat. Mount it at eye level, in a position where you can see it without moving your head or searching for it. It must have a sweep second-hand or a continuous digital readout in seconds. Clocks without this feature allow too much margin for error.

3. Use a wristwatch, taking it off your wrist and setting it in front of you before you begin work. It, too, must show the passage of seconds as well as minutes, and have a clear, easy-to-read display.

4. Use a stopwatch or chronometer that can be preset for an exact time period. It ensures extreme accuracy.

5. Use a metronome for the drills and practice tests on address checking. You can develop a rhythm for working that will help you move along at a consistent pace. (See pages 85 to 86.)

6. Do *not* use egg timers or spring-wound kitchen timers. They do not keep time accurately and consistently. Being even a few seconds off can make an appreciable difference in your final score.

■ DIAGNOSTIC PRACTICE TEST

Part A — Address Checking

Work—6 minutes

In this test you are to decide whether two addresses are alike or different. If the two addresses are *exactly alike in every way*, darken space Ⓐ. If they are *different in any way*, darken space Ⓓ.

Mark your answers on the Answer Sheet for Address Checking at the beginning of this section. Tear it out, put today's date on it, and place it next to the questions.

Use any of the timing methods described in this chapter, pages 37 to 38, but remember to allow yourself *exactly 6 minutes* to do as many of the 95 questions as you can. If you finish before the time is up, check your answers.

1.	3043 Pickfair Dr	3043 Pickford Rd
2.	2124 Van Nostrand Ct	2124 Van Nostrand Ct
3.	2041 S Conestoga St	2041 S Conestoga St
4.	6374 W Tomlinson Blvd	6374 W Tomlinsun Blvd
5.	203 Martin Luther King Hwy N	203 Martin Luther King Hwy S
6.	164 Calle De la Fuente	164 Calle De la Fuente
7.	4958 E Grosvenor St	4957 E Grosvenor St
8.	341 White Sage Ln	341 White Cage Ln
9.	Senoia GA 32076	Senoia GA 32076
10.	877 1st Ave	877 1st Ave
11.	5156 S Janesville Ct	5156 S Jonesville Ct
12.	4456 Bloomington Ave W	4456 Bloomingtown Ave W
13.	2989 Von Felcher Rd	2989 Von Felcher Rd
14.	4941 Borealis Ln	4914 Borealis Ln
15.	6840 Furmanville Ave	6840 Furmanview Ave
16.	6005 Forshey Ln	6005 Farshey Ln
17.	Hagerman NM	Haberman NM
18.	112 Fergus St NE	112 Fergus St NE
19.	9916 W Feathercock Blvd	9913 W Feathercock Blvd
20.	Lawton OK 73507	Lawton OK 73507
21.	9603 Druim Moir Ct	9603 Druim Moir Ct
22.	5831 Edgelake Rd W	5831 Edgelake Rd N
23.	Norwalk CT 06850	Norfalk CT 06850
24.	1601 S 117 Rd	1601 E 117 Rd

25.	9945 Leverington Ave SE	9945 Leverington Ave SE
26.	91 University Oaks Ln	91 University Oaks Ln
27.	1983 Earhart Blvd	1983 Earhart Blvd
28.	609 Laguna Seca Ct	609 Laguna Seca Ct
29.	Frederica DE 19946	Frederica DE 19846
30.	5190 Wayman Branch Rd	5190 Wayman Branch Rd
31.	1412 83 St Ter	1412 88 St Ter
32.	656 Friar Tuck Dr	656 Friar Tuck Dr
33.	6223 W Techahanny Blvd	6223 W Techahanny Blvd
34.	7978 W Overton Brooks Cir	7978 W Overtown Brooks Cir
35.	1601 S Avante Ln	1601 N Avante Ln
36.	5601 MacTibby Pl SW	5601 McTibby Pl SW
37.	Shreveport LA	Shreveport AL
38.	18012 Wyckwood Rd S	18012 Wickward Rd S
39.	2981 Dorgenois St	2981 Dorgenois St
40.	1706 Caminito Del Marfil	1706 Caminito Del Marfil
41.	50 Aqua Mansa Rd	50 Aqua Mansa Dr
42.	5119 S Dorchester Blvd	5119 S Dorchester Blvd
43.	6391 N Chaffe St	6391 N Chaffee St
44.	5545 Cherokee Trl	5545 Cherokee Trl
45.	6441 Yerda Anita Ln	6441 Yerda Anita Ln
46.	3130 Casimire Dr	3130 Casimira Dr
47.	1088 Hanford St	1088 Hanford Ct
48.	7885 Amundson Ave	7885 Amundson Ave
49.	1336 W Pohakupuna St	1336 W Pohakupuna St
50.	3309 S Paguera Ter	3309 S Paduera Ter
51.	18903 Valle Contento Dr	18903 Valle Contento Dr
52.	6325 Illinois Blvd N	6325 Illinois Blvd N
53.	1064 W Earlham St	1064 W Earlheim St
54.	1880 W Shagbark Ln	1808 W Shagbark Ln
55.	951 Pinehurst Ave	951 Pinehurst Ave
56.	Traverse MI 49684	Traverse MI 49684
57.	353 Ilex Cir	353 Ilex Cir
58.	6336 Verveleen Pl E	6336 Varveleeen Pl E
59.	5161 Emerick Pl	5161 Ewerick Pl
60.	8303 Forsyth St	8303 Forsyth Ave

61.	11843 Zea St	11843 Zea St
62.	1101 E Village Square Cir	1101 E Village Square Cir
63.	3551 N Deckbar Ave	3551 N Deckbar Ave
64.	Ladoga IN 47954	Ladoga IN 7954
65.	41 Jerome Rd	41 Gerome Rd
66.	32 Lake La Belle Cir	32 Lake La Belle Cir
67.	8986 Gerhard St NE	8986 Gerhard St NE
68.	5050 W Annsbury St	5050 W Annsdury St
69.	3402 E Stonehaven Ave	3402 E Stonehaven Ave
70.	6234 S Jewett Pky	6234 S Jemett Pky
71.	3604 Ursulines Ave	3640 Ursulines Ave
72.	6448 Depue Pl	6448 Depue Pl
73.	Aripeka FL	Apireka FL
74.	498 9 St	498 19 St
75.	4002 Depeyster St	4002 Depeyster St
76.	Kimmswick MO 63053	Kimmswick MD 63053
77.	2706 Oakridge Park Dr	2706 Oakridge Park Dr
78.	1187 Hartkopf Ln	1187 Hartkopf Ln
79.	Union Center NJ 07083	Union Center NJ 07803
80.	581 N Nicollet Ave	581 N Nicollet St
81.	2776 Negundo Ave	2776 Segundo Ave
82.	Trezevant TN	Trezevant TX
83.	5117 Skycroft Path	5117 Skycroft Path
84.	1121 Algeciras St E	1121 Algeciras St E
85.	501 Ealing on Duxbury St	501 Ealing on Duxbury St
86.	4869 Broadway Ter	4869 Broadway Ter
87.	Wynot NE 68792	Wynot NE 68792
88.	Box 97001 Saint Paul MN	Box 97001 Saint Paul MS
89.	7908 N Meandro Ln	7980 N Meandro Ln
90.	10 W Appaloosa Ave	10 E Appaloosa Ave
91.	3271 San Nicolo Blvd	3271 San Nicolo Ave
92.	8102 S Demont Luzin St	8102 S Demont Luzin St
93.	34416 Wiscassett Blvd SW	34461 Wiscassett Blvd SW
94.	1223 Hackberry Ct SE	1223 Hackberry Ct SE
95.	4710 E Higgs Beach St	4710 E Higgs Beach St

STOP.
If you finish before the time is up, go back and check
the questions in this section of the test only.

Part B — Memory for Addresses

In this test you will have five boxes labeled A, B, C, D, and E. Each box contains five addresses. Three of the five are groups of street addresses, such as 2100–2799 Mall, 4800–4999 Cliff, and 1900–2299 Laurel; and two are names of places. The addresses are different in each box.

There will be several opportunities to study the addresses and the boxes they are in. You will also be given three lists of 88 questions each, and the task of deciding where each address belongs. In some cases, you will have the list *and* the boxes in front of you at the same time; in others you will not. List 1 and List 2 are for warm-up practice. List 3 is the *real* one that will be scored.

Make sure you understand the format by examining the pretest samples below.

Pretest Samples

A	B	C	D	E
2100–2799 Mall	3900–4399 Mall	4400–4599 Mall	3400–3899 Mall	2800–3399 Mall
Ceres	Cedar	Niles	Cicero	Delhi
4800–4999 Cliff	4000–4299 Cliff	3300–3999 Cliff	4500–4799 Cliff	4300–4499 Cliff
Natoma	Foster	Dexter	Pearl	Magnet
1900–2299 Laurel	2300–2999 Laurel	3200–3799 Laurel	3000–3199 Laurel	1500–1899 Laurel

Questions

Questions 1 through 7 show the way the questions look. You have to decide in which lettered box (A, B, C, D, or E) the address belongs and then mark your answer by darkening the appropriate space in the answer grid.

1. 3300–3999 Cliff   1 Ⓐ Ⓑ Ⓒ Ⓓ Ⓔ

2. Natoma   2 Ⓐ Ⓑ Ⓒ Ⓓ Ⓔ

3. Foster   3 Ⓐ Ⓑ Ⓒ Ⓓ Ⓔ

4. 1500–1899 Laurel   4 Ⓐ Ⓑ Ⓒ Ⓓ Ⓔ

5. 3900–4399 Mall   5 Ⓐ Ⓑ Ⓒ Ⓓ Ⓔ

6. Pearl   6 Ⓐ Ⓑ Ⓒ Ⓓ Ⓔ

7. 3200–3799 Laurel   7 Ⓐ Ⓑ Ⓒ Ⓓ Ⓔ

Answers

1. **C**   2. **A**   3. **B**   4. **E**   5. **B**   6. **D**   7. **C**

Now that you know what to do, you can begin Part B of the Diagnostic Test. To get the most out of it and the other six practice tests in this book, follow the directions and timing *exactly*. Follow each phase of Part B of this Diagnostic Test, page by page, until you've completed List 3. It is modeled on the way the Postal Service actually conducts its tests.

Turn to the next page to begin.

Study—3 minutes

You will be given 3 minutes to spend memorizing the addresses in the boxes. *They are exactly the same ones that will be used for all three tests.* Try to memorize as many as you can. When the 3 minutes are up, turn to the next page and read the instructions for *List 1*.

A	B	C	D	E
2100–2799 Mall	3900–4399 Mall	4400–4599 Mall	3400–3899 Mall	2800–3399 Mall
Ceres	Cedar	Niles	Cicero	Delhi
4800–4999 Cliff	4000–4299 Cliff	3300–3999 Cliff	4500–4799 Cliff	4300–4499 Cliff
Natoma	Foster	Dexter	Pearl	Magnet
1900–2299 Laurel	2300–2999 Laurel	3200–3799 Laurel	3000–3199 Laurel	1500–1899 Laurel

List 1

Work—3 minutes

Tear out the Answer Sheet for Memory for Addresses for List 1. For each question, mark the answer sheet to show the letter of the box in which the address belongs. Try to remember the locations of as many addresses as you can. *You will now have 3 minutes to complete List 1*. If you are not sure of an answer, you should guess.

A	B	C	D	E
2100–2799 Mall	3900–4399 Mall	4400–4599 Mall	3400–3899 Mall	2800–3399 Mall
Ceres	Cedar	Niles	Cicero	Delhi
4800–4999 Cliff	4000–4299 Cliff	3300–3999 Cliff	4500–4799 Cliff	4300–4499 Cliff
Natoma	Foster	Dexter	Pearl	Magnet
1900–2299 Laurel	2300–2999 Laurel	3200–3799 Laurel	3000–3199 Laurel	1500–1899 Laurel

1. Magnet
2. Niles
3. 3400–3899 Mall
4. 1900–2299 Laurel
5. Cicero
6. Dexter
7. 2300–2999 Laurel
8. 3300–3999 Cliff
9. 3200–3799 Laurel
10. 2100–2799 Mall
11. Pearl

12. 3200–3799 Laurel
13. Ceres
14. 4500–4799 Cliff
15. 3900–4399 Mall
16. Delhi
17. 4300–4499 Cliff
18. 3000–3199 Laurel
19. Ceres
20. Foster
21. Natoma
22. 4400–4599 Mall

23. Cedar
24. 2300–2999 Laurel
25. 1500–1899 Laurel
26. 4000–4299 Cliff
27. Dexter
28. Magnet
29. 3300–3999 Cliff
30. 3400–3899 Mall
31. Niles
32. 2100–2799 Mall
33. 1900–2299 Laurel

34. Cedar
35. Pearl
36. 2800–3399 Mall
37. 4800–4999 Cliff
38. 3900–4399 Mall
39. Foster
40. 3000–3199 Laurel
41. Ceres
42. Niles
43. 3400–3899 Mall
44. Delhi

45. 2300–2999 Laurel
46. 4500–4799 Cliff
47. Dexter
48. Magnet
49. 3300–3999 Cliff
50. Cicero
51. 4300–4499 Cliff
52. 3900–4399 Mall
53. Natoma
54. 3200–3799 Laurel
55. Pearl

56. 4000–4299 Cliff
57. 4500–4799 Cliff
58. 2100–2799 Mall
59. Foster
60. 4400–4599 Mall
61. 4800–4999 Cliff
62. Ceres
63. 2800–3399 Mall
64. 1500–1899 Laurel
65. Natoma
66. 3000–3199 Laurel

67. 4000–4299 Cliff
68. Niles
69. 2300–2999 Laurel
70. Magnet
71. Delhi
72. 4400–4599 Mall
73. Cicero
74. Cedar
75. 2800–3399 Mall
76. 1900–2299 Laurel
77. Dexter

78. Pearl
79. 4300–4499 Cliff
80. 3900–4399 Mall
81. Foster
82. 4800–4999 Cliff
83. Delhi
84. Ceres
85. 1500–1899 Laurel
86. Natoma
87. 2800–3399 Mall
88. Niles

STOP.
**If you finish before the time is up, go back and check
the questions in this section of the test only.**

List 2

Work—3 minutes

Do these questions *without* looking back at the boxes. For each question, mark your answer on the Answer Sheet for List 2. If you are not sure of an answer, guess.

1.	Cedar	23.	3900–4399 Mall
2.	4300–4499 Cliff	24.	Natoma
3.	4400–4599 Mall	25.	4800–4999 Cliff
4.	Natoma	26.	1500–1899 Laurel
5.	2300–2999 Laurel	27.	Cedar
6.	4500–4799 Cliff	28.	4400–4599 Mall
7.	Ceres	29.	4500–4799 Cliff
8.	3400–3899 Mall	30.	Dexter
9.	Delhi	31.	3000–3199 Laurel
10.	Dexter	32.	Niles
11.	1900–2299 Laurel	33.	Delhi
12.	3300–3999 Cliff	34.	3900–4399 Mall
13.	Cicero	35.	Cicero
14.	4000–4299 Cliff	36.	Dexter
15.	2100–2799 Mall	37.	4800–4999 Cliff
16.	Foster	38.	2300–2999 Laurel
17.	Magnet	39.	2100–2799 Mall
18.	Ceres	40.	3300–3999 Cliff
19.	2800–3399 Mall	41.	3400–3899 Mall
20.	3200–3799 Laurel	42.	4300–4499 Cliff
21.	4300–4499 Cliff	43.	Ceres
22.	Pearl	44.	Foster

45. Magnet
46. 3200–3799 Laurel
47. Pearl
48. 1500– 1899 Laurel
49. 4500–4799 Cliff
50. 1900–2299 Laurel
51. Niles
52. 3300–3999 Cliff
53. 2800–3399 Mall
54. Cicero
55. Delhi

56. 4000–4299 Cliff
57. Dexter
58. Magnet
59. 3000–3199 Laurel
60. 3900–4399 Mall
61. Natoma
62. 3000–3199 Laurel
63. 4300–4499 Cliff
64. Cedar
65. 4400–4599 Mall
66. 1500–1899 Laurel

67. 4800–4999 Cliff
68. Delhi
69. Pearl
70. 2300–2999 Laurel
71. 4500–4799 Cliff
72. Niles
73. 4000–4299 Cliff
74. 3400–3899 Mall
75. 1900–2299 Laurel
76. 2800–3399 Mall
77. Ceres

78. Magnet
79. Cicero
80. 3200–3799 Laurel
81. 3000–3199 Laurel
82. 3900–4399 Mall
83. Natoma
84. 3300–3999 Cliff
85. 3400–3899 Mall
86. Foster
87. 2100–2799 Mall
88. 4300–4499 Cliff

STOP.
If you finish before the time is up, go back and check
the questions in this section of the test only.

List 3

Study—5 minutes

You are now about to take the test using List 3. *(This is the test that counts!)*

Turn back to page 44 and study the boxes again. *You have 5 minutes to restudy the addresses.* When the time is up, tear out the Answer Sheet for List 3. Use it for the test.

Work—5 minutes

For each question, mark the Answer Sheet to show the letter of the box in which the address belongs. You have exactly 5 minutes to do the test. During these 5 minutes, *do not* turn to any other page.

1.	Foster	23.	Pearl
2.	Ceres	24.	4300–4499 Cliff
3.	4300–4499 Cliff	25.	3200–3799 Laurel
4.	3400–3899 Mall	26.	2800–3399 Mall
5.	3300–3999 Cliff	27.	Ceres
6.	Magnet	28.	Magnet
7.	2300–2999 Laurel	29.	Foster
8.	4800–4999 Cliff	30.	2100–2799 Mall
9.	Dexter	31.	4000–4299 Cliff
10.	Cicero	32.	Cicero
11.	3900–4399 Mall	33.	3300–3999 Cliff
12.	Delhi	34.	1900–2299 Laurel
13.	Niles	35.	Dexter
14.	3000–3199 Laurel	36.	Delhi
15.	Dexter	37.	3400–3899 Mall
16.	4500–4799 Cliff	38.	Ceres
17.	4400–4599 Mall	39.	4500–4799 Cliff
18.	Cedar	40.	2300–2999 Laurel
19.	1500–1899 Laurel	41.	Natoma
20.	4800–4999 Cliff	42.	4400–4599 Mall
21.	Natoma	43.	4300–4599 Cliff
22.	3900–4399 Mall	44.	Cedar

45. 4300–4499 Cliff
46. 2100–2799 Mall
47. Foster
48. 3400–3899 Mall
49. 3300–3999 Cliff
50. Natoma
51. 3900–4399 Mall
52. 3000–3199 Laurel
53. 3200–3799 Laurel
54. Cicero
55. Magnet

56. Ceres
57. 2800–3399 Mall
58. 1900–2299 Laurel
59. 3400–3899 Mall
60. 4000–4299 Cliff
61. Niles
62. 4500–4799 Cliff
63. 2300–2999 Laurel
64. Pearl
65. Delhi
66. 4800–4999 Cliff

67. 1500–1899 Laurel
68. 4400–4599 Mall
69. Cedar
70. 4300–4499 Cliff
71. 3000–3199 Laurel
72. Natoma
73. 3900–4399 Mall
74. 3000–3199 Laurel
75. Magnet
76. Dexter
77. 4000–4299 Cliff

78. Delhi
79. Cicero
80. 2800–3399 Mall
81. 3300–3999 Cliff
82. Niles
83. 1900–2299 Laurel
84. 4500–4799 Cliff
85. 1500–1899 Laurel
86. Pearl
87. 3200–3799 Laurel
88. Magnet

STOP.
If you finish before the time is up, go back and check
the questions in this section of the test only.

Part C — Number Series

Work—20 minutes

For each Number Series question, there is at the left, a series of numbers that follows some definite order, and below each, five sets of two numbers each. You are to look at the numbers in the series at the left and find out what order they follow. Then decide what the next two numbers in that series would be if the same order were continued. Mark your choice of answers on the Answer Sheet for Number Series at the beginning of this section. Tear it out, put today's date on it, and place it next to the questions.

You have 20 minutes to complete this part of the test. If you finish before the time is up, check your answers. The correct answers and answer explanations are given at the end of the test on pages 61 to 63.

QUESTIONS

1. 12 10 15 13 18 16 21 __ __
   A) 19 24   B) 17 19   C) 19 20   D) 26 24   E) 21 23

2. 8 11 14 10 13 16 12 __ __
   A) 15 14   B) 15 11   C) 14 16   D) 11 8   E) 15 18

3. 15 16 17 15 16 17 15 __ __
   A) 15 16   B) 16 17   C) 16 15   D) 17 15   E) 15 17

4. 3 4 6 9 13 18 24 __ __
   A) 30 37   B) 31 38   C) 32 40   D) 29 35   E) 31 39

5. 7 7 8 9 9 10 11 __ __
   A) 11 12   B) 12 13   C) 13 13   D) 11 11   E) 10 11

6. 10 6 6 10 7 7 10 __ __
   A) 10 10   B) 8 10   C) 10 8   D) 8 8   E) 8 9

7. 18 9 17 10 16 11 15 __ __
   A) 13 14   B) 14 13   C) 12 14   D) 14 12   E) 12 13

8. 7 8 16 9 10 15 11 __ __
   A) 14 10   B) 13 12   C) 13 14   D) 15 13   E) 12 14

9. 4 9 8 13 12 17 16 __ __
   A) 18 19   B) 20 21   C) 21 19   D) 21 20   E) 18 21

10. 1 2 2 4 4 8 8 16 __ __
     A) 16 16   B) 16 32   C) 32 18   D) 12 32   E) 20 36

11. 6 9 10 7 11 12 8 __ __
     A) 9 10   B) 9 13   C) 16 14   D) 13 14   E) 14 15

12. 7 5 3 9 7 5 11 __ __
     A) 13 12   B) 7 5   C) 9 7   D) 13 7   E) 9 9

13. 7 9 18 10 12 18 13 __ __
     A) 18 14   B) 15 18   C) 14 15   D) 15 14   E) 14 18

14. 40 10 39 12 37 14 34 16 __ __
     A) 18 33   B) 28 20   C) 30 18   D) 29 18   E) 16 31

15. 7 9 12 14 17 19 22 __ __
     A) 25 27   B) 23 24   C) 23 25   D) 24 27   E) 26 27

16. 3 23 5 25 7 27 9 __ __
     A) 10 11   B) 27 29   C) 29 11   D) 11 28   E) 28 10

17. 18 17 16 14 13 12 10 __ __
     A) 9 8   B) 6 7   C) 8 6   D) 8 7   E) 10 9

18. 13 12 18 13 13 19 13 14 __ __
     A) 15 20   B) 17 13   C) 19 23   D) 13 18   E) 20 13

19. 28 27 25 24 22 21 19 __ __
     A) 18 16   B) 17 16   C) 18 17   D) 17 15   E) 20 18

20. 2 2 4 6 6 8 10 __ __
     A) 12 12   B) 12 14   C) 10 10   D) 10 8   E) 10 12

21. 2 7 3 8 4 9 5 __ __
     A) 6 7   B) 10 6   C) 6 10   D) 10 11   E) 5 10

22. 1 4 5 9 14 23 37 __ __
     A) 52 67   B) 63 17   C) 60 97   D) 73 105   E) 49 84

23. 3 5 7 7 4 6 8 8 5 7 9 __ __

  A) 9 6   B) 6 6   C) 6 9   D) 10 8   E) 8 10

24. 15 26 24 16 21 19 17 16 14 18 __ __

  A) 17 15   B) 11 9   C) 15 14   D) 17 16   E) 11 10

STOP.
**If you finish before the time is up, go back and check
the questions in this section of the test only.**

Part D — Following Oral Directions

This part of the test gauges your ability to understand and carry out spoken directions *exactly* as they are given to you.

In order to prepare to take Part D of the test, follow the steps below:

1. Enlist the help of a friend (the "reader") whose job it will be to read aloud a series of directions that you are to follow *exactly*. The reader will need a watch that displays seconds, because the directions must be read at the correct speed.

2. Tear out pages 55 and 56. These are the worksheets you should have in front of you as you listen to the directions given by the reader, who will tell you to do certain things with the items on each line on the worksheets.

3. Tear out the Answer Sheet for Following Oral Directions on page 35, and insert today's date. You will darken the appropriate spaces in accordance with the directions given by the reader.

4. *Now hand this entire book to the reader.* Ask him/her to review the section on page 57 headed "Instructions to the Reader." It explains exactly how the reader is to proceed.

When you and the reader are ready to start this part of the Diagnostic Practice Test, he/she will begin reading to you the section marked "Directions." YOU ARE NOT TO READ THESE AT ANY TIME BEFORE OR DURING THE TEST. If you do, you will lose the benefit of this part of the Diagnostic Practice Test.

Diagnostic Practice Test—Worksheet 1
Part D—Following Oral Directions

1.   33   49   68   22   8

2.   E   B   D   E   C   A   B

3.   30 ___   18 ___   5 ___   14 ___   7 ___

4.   29 ___   16 ___   23 ___   22 ___   27 ___

5.   33 ___   34 ___   48 ___   39 ___

6.   80 ___   65 ___   42 ___

7.   4 ___   1 ___   6 ___   7 ___   19 ___

8.   71 ___   59 ___

9.   57   43   61   38   50   52   45   40   39

10.   65   80   73   64   76   66   78   75   69

11.   9:32 ___ A   9:28 ___ B   9:24 ___ C   9:11 ___ D   9:31 ___ E

Diagnostic Practice Test—Worksheet 2
Part D—Following Oral Directions

12. 87___   70___   81___   92___   85___

13. ___A   ___B   ___C   ___D   ___E

14. 3___   32___   20___   10___

15. 53___   79___   67___   ABLE   EASY   DESK

16. X X O X O O O X O X X O X X

17. 22___   3___   21___   28___

18. 91___   82___   79___   61___

19.
3
DETROIT
HARTFORD
___

26
ST. LOUIS
CLEVELAND
___

Instructions to the "Reader"

These directions should be read at about 80 words per minute. You should practice reading the material in the box until you can do it in exactly 1 minute. The number of words in the passage and the natural pauses described below will give you a good feel for the rate of speed and the way you should read the test questions.

1-MINUTE PRACTICE

> Look at line 17 on your worksheet. There are two circles and two boxes of different sizes with numbers in them. If 7 is less than 3 and if 2 is smaller than 4, write C in the larger circle. Otherwise write B as in *baker* in the smaller box. Now, on your answer sheet darken the space for the number-letter combination in the box or circle.

You should read the entire test aloud before you read it to the person taking the test, in order to thoroughly acquaint yourself with the procedure and the desired rate of reading.

Read slowly, but at a natural pace. In other words, do not space the words so that there are unnaturally long pauses between them. The instruction "Pause slightly" indicates only enough time to take a breath. The other instructions for pauses give the recommended length for each. If possible, use a watch with a second hand.

All the material that follows, except the words in parentheses, is to be read aloud. Now start reading the directions. *Do not repeat any of the directions or any of the questions.*

The Test Begins Now

Directions: In this test, I will read instructions to you. You are to mark your worksheets according to the instructions that I read. After each set of instructions, I'll give you time to record your answers on your answer sheet.

Try to understand the instructions as I read them; I cannot repeat them. Do not ask any questions from now on.

If, when you go to darken a space for a number, you find that you have already darkened another space for that number, either (1) erase the first mark and darken the space for your new choice, or (2) let the first mark stay and do not darken any other space. When you finish, you should have no more than one space darkened for each number.

Turn to Worksheet 1.

Look at line 1 on your worksheet. (Pause slightly.) Draw a line under the fourth number in the line. (Pause 2 seconds.) Now, on your answer sheet, find the number under which you just drew the line and darken space A for that number. (Pause 5 seconds.)

Look at the letters in line 2 on your worksheet again. (Pause slightly.) Now draw two lines under the third letter in the line. (Pause 2 seconds.) Now, on your answer sheet, find number 52 (pause 2 seconds) and darken the space for the letter under which you drew two lines. (Pause 5 seconds.)

Look at line 3 on your worksheet. (Pause slightly.) Write an E in the last box. (Pause 2 seconds.) Now, on your answer sheet, find the number in that box and darken space E for that number. (Pause 5 seconds.)

Look at line 3 again. (Pause slightly.) Write an A in the first box. (Pause 2 seconds.) Now, on your answer sheet, find the number in that box and darken space A for that number. (Pause 5 seconds.)

Look at line 4. The number in each circle is the number of packages in a mail sack. In the circle for the sack holding the largest number of packages, write a B as in *baker*. (Pause 2 seconds.) Now, on your answer sheet, darken the space for the number-letter combination that is in the circle you just wrote in. (Pause 5 seconds.)

Look at line 4 again. In the circle for the sack holding the smallest number of packages, write an E. (Pause 2 seconds.) Now, on your answer sheet, darken the space for the number-letter combination that is in the circle you just wrote in. (Pause 5 seconds.)

Look at the drawings on line 5 on your worksheet. The four boxes are trucks for carrying mail. (Pause slightly.) The truck with the highest number is to be loaded first. Write B as in *baker* on the line beside the highest number. (Pause 2 seconds.) Now, on your answer sheet, darken the space for the number-letter combination that is in the box you just wrote in. (Pause 5 seconds.)

Look at line 6 on your worksheet. (Pause slightly.) Next to the middle number write the letter D as in *dog*. (Pause 2 seconds.) Now, on your answer sheet, find the number beside which you wrote and darken space D as in *dog* for that number. (Pause 5 seconds.)

Look at the five circles on line 7 on your worksheet. (Pause slightly.) Write B as in *baker* on the blank in the second circle. (Pause 2 seconds.) Now, on your answer sheet, darken the space for the number-letter combination that is in the circle you just wrote in. (Pause 5 seconds.)

Look at line 7 again. (Pause slightly.) Write C on the blank in the third circle on line 7. (Pause 2 seconds.) Now, on your answer sheet, darken the space for the number-letter combination that is in the circle you just wrote in. (Pause 5 seconds.)

Look at line 8 on your worksheet. (Pause slightly.) Write A on the line next to the right-hand number. (Pause 2 seconds.) Now, on your answer sheet, find the number beside which you wrote, and darken space A. (Pause 5 seconds.)

Look at line 9 on your worksheet. (Pause slightly.) Draw a line under every number that is more than 40 but less than 50. (Pause 12 seconds.) Now, on your answer sheet, for each number that you drew a line under, darken space C. (Pause 25 seconds.)

Look at line 10 in your worksheet. (Pause slightly.) Draw a line under every number that is more than 65 but less than 75. (Pause 10 seconds.) Now, on your answer sheet, for each number you drew a line under, darken space D as in *dog*. (Pause 25 seconds.)

Look at line 11 on your worksheet. (Pause slightly.) In each circle there is a time when the mail must leave. In the circle for the latest time, write on the line the last two figures of the time. (Pause 5 seconds.) Now, on your answer sheet, darken the space for the number-letter combination that is in the circle you just wrote in. (Pause 5 seconds.)

Now turn to Worksheet 2.

Look at the five boxes in line 12 on your worksheet. (Pause slightly.) If 6 is less than 3, put an E in the fourth box. (Pause slightly.) If 6 is not less than 3, put a B as in *baker* in the first box. (Pause 5 seconds.) Now, on your answer sheet, darken the space for the number-letter combination that is in the box you just wrote in. (Pause 5 seconds.)

Now look at line 13 in your test booklet. (Pause slightly.) There are 5 circles. Each circle has a letter. (Pause slightly.) In the second circle, write the answer to this question: Which of the following numbers is smallest: 83, 71, 90, 82, 77? (Pause 5 seconds.) Now, on your answer sheet, darken the space for the number-letter combination that is in the circle you just wrote in. (Pause 5 seconds.)

In the third circle on the same line, write 38. (Pause 2 seconds.) Now, on your answer sheet, darken the space for the number-letter combination that is in the circle you just wrote in. (Pause 5 seconds.)

In the fourth circle do nothing. In the fifth circle write the answer to this question: How many months are there in a year? (Pause 2 seconds.) Now, on your answer sheet, darken the space for the number-letter combination that is in the circle you just wrote in. (Pause 5 seconds.)

Look at line 14 on your worksheet. (Pause slightly.) There are two circles and two boxes of different sizes with numbers in them. (Pause slightly.) If 2 is smaller than 4 and if 7 is less than 3, write A in the larger circle. (Pause slightly.) Otherwise write B as in *baker* in the smaller box. (Pause 2 seconds.) Now, on your answer sheet, darken the space for the number-letter combination that is in the box or circle you just wrote in. (Pause 5 seconds.)

Look at the boxes and words in line 15 on your worksheet. (Pause slightly.) Write the second letter of the first word in the third box. (Pause 2 seconds.) Write the first letter of the second word in the first box. (Pause 2 seconds.) Write the first letter of the third word in the second box. (Pause 2 seconds.) Now, on your answer sheet, darken the spaces for the number-letter combinations that are in the three boxes you just wrote in. (Pause 10 seconds.)

Look at line 16 on your worksheet. (Pause slightly.) Draw a line under every "O" in the line. (Pause 5 seconds.) Count the number of lines that you have drawn, subtract 2, and write that number at the end of the line. (Pause 5 seconds.) Now, on your answer sheet, find that number and darken space D as in *dog* for that number. (Pause 5 seconds.)

Look at line 17 on your worksheet. (Pause slightly.) If the number in the left-hand circle is smaller than the number in the right-hand circle, add 2 to the number in the left-hand circle, and change the number in that circle to this number. (Pause 8 seconds.) Then write B as in *baker* next to the new number. (Pause slightly.) Otherwise write E next to the number in the smaller box. (Pause 3 seconds.) Then, on your answer sheet, darken the space for the number-letter combination that is in the box or circle you just wrote in. (Pause 5 seconds.)

Look at line 18 on your worksheet. (Pause slightly.) If in a year January comes before February, write A in the box with the smallest number. (Pause slightly.) If it does not, write C in the box with the largest number. (Pause 3 seconds.) Now, on your answer sheet, darken the space for the number-letter combination that is in the box you just wrote in. (Pause 5 seconds.)

Look at line 19 on your worksheet. (Pause slightly.) Mail for Detroit and Hartford is to be put in box 3. (Pause slightly.) Mail for Cleveland and St. Louis is to be put in box 26. (Pause slightly.) Write C in the box in which you put mail for St. Louis. Now, on your answer sheet, darken the space for the number-letter combination that is in the box you just wrote in. (Pause 5 seconds.)

END OF EXAMINATION.
If you finish before the time is up, go back and check
the questions in this section of the test only.

■ ANSWER KEY

Part A—Address Checking

1. D	11. D	21. A	31. D	41. D	51. A	61. A	71. D	81. D	91. D
2. A	12. D	22. D	32. A	42. A	52. A	62. A	72. A	82. D	92. A
3. A	13. A	23. D	33. A	43. A	53. D	63. A	73. D	83. A	93. D
4. D	14. D	24. D	34. D	44. A	54. D	64. D	74. D	84. A	94. A
5. D	15. D	25. A	35. D	45. A	55. A	65. D	75. D	85. A	95. A
6. A	16. D	26. A	36. D	46. D	56. A	66. A	76. D	86. A	
7. D	17. D	27. A	37. D	47. D	57. A	67. A	77. A	87. A	
8. D	18. A	28. A	38. D	48. A	58. D	68. D	78. A	88. D	
9. A	19. D	29. D	39. A	49. A	59. D	69. A	79. D	89. D	
10. A	20. A	30. A	40. A	50. D	60. D	70. D	80. D	90. D	

Part B—Memory for Addresses

List 1

1. E	10. A	19. A	28. E	37. A	46. D	55. D	64. E	73. D	82. A
2. C	11. D	20. B	29. C	38. B	47. C	56. B	65. A	74. B	83. E
3. D	12. C	21. A	30. D	39. B	48. E	57. D	66. D	75. E	84. A
4. A	13. A	22. C	31. C	40. D	49. C	58. A	67. B	76. A	85. E
5. D	14. D	23. B	32. A	41. A	50. D	59. B	68. C	77. C	86. A
6. C	15. B	24. B	33. A	42. C	51. E	60. C	69. B	78. D	87. E
7. B	16. E	25. E	34. B	43. D	52. B	61. A	70. E	79. E	88. C
8. C	17. E	26. B	35. D	44. E	53. A	62. A	71. E	80. B	
9. C	18. D	27. C	36. E	45. B	54. C	63. E	72. C	81. B	

List 2

1. B	10. C	19. E	28. C	37. A	46. C	55. E	64. B	73. B	82. B
2. E	11. A	20. C	29. D	38. B	47. D	56. B	65. C	74. D	83. A
3. C	12. C	21. E	30. C	39. A	48. E	57. C	66. E	75. A	84. C
4. A	13. D	22. D	31. D	40. C	49. D	58. E	67. A	76. E	85. D
5. B	14. B	23. B	32. C	41. D	50. A	59. D	68. E	77. A	86. B
6. D	15. A	24. A	33. E	42. E	51. C	60. B	69. D	78. E	87. A
7. A	16. B	25. A	34. B	43. A	52. C	61. A	70. B	79. D	88. E
8. D	17. E	26. E	35. D	44. B	53. E	62. D	71. D	80. C	
9. E	18. A	27. B	36. C	45. E	54. D	63. E	72. C	81. D	

List 3

1. B	10. D	19. E	28. E	37. D	46. A	55. E	64. D	73. B	82. C
2. A	11. B	20. A	29. B	38. A	47. B	56. A	65. E	74. D	83. A
3. E	12. E	21. A	30. A	39. D	48. D	57. E	66. A	75. E	84. D
4. D	13. C	22. B	31. B	40. B	49. C	58. A	67. E	76. C	85. E
5. C	14. D	23. D	32. D	41. A	50. A	59. D	68. C	77. B	86. D
6. E	15. C	24. E	33. C	42. C	51. B	60. B	69. B	78. E	87. C
7. B	16. D	25. C	34. A	43. E	52. D	61. C	70. E	79. D	88. E
8. A	17. C	26. E	35. C	44. B	53. C	62. D	71. D	80. E	
9. C	18. B	27. A	36. E	45. E	54. D	63. B	72. A	81. C	

Part C—Number Series

1. A	4. E	7. C	10. B	13. B	16. C	19. A	22. C
2. E	5. A	8. E	11. D	14. C	17. A	20. E	23. A
3. B	6. D	9. D	12. C	15. D	18. E	21. B	24. B

Part D—Following Oral Directions

1. B	12. E	24. B	32. A	48. B	61. A	69. D	87. B
4. D	16. E	26. C	38. C	52. D	65. D	71. B	
6. C	20. B	29. B	43. C	53. E	66. D	73. D	
7. E	22. A	30. A	45. C	59. A	67. B	79. D	

ANSWER EXPLANATIONS FOR PART C— NUMBER SERIES

1. **A** A loop diagram clearly shows the rule for this series

$$\overset{-2}{\frown}\overset{+5}{\frown}\overset{-2}{\frown}\overset{+5}{\frown}\overset{-2}{\frown}\overset{+5}{\frown}\overset{-2}{\frown}\overset{+5}{\frown}$$
$$12 \quad 10 \quad 15 \quad 13 \quad 18 \quad 16 \quad 21 \ldots 19 \; 24$$

2. **E** The rule for progressing from one number to the next is a little more complex, but again, the loop diagram will make it clear

$$\overset{+3}{\frown}\overset{+3}{\frown}\overset{-4}{\frown}\overset{+3}{\frown}\overset{+3}{\frown}\overset{-4}{\frown}\overset{+3}{\frown}\overset{+3}{\frown}$$
$$8 \quad 11 \quad 14 \quad 10 \quad 13 \quad 16 \quad 12 \ldots 15 \; 18$$

3. **B** This series is simply a repetition of three numbers: 15 16 17
4. **E** The difference between each number keeps increasing by 1.

$$\overset{+1}{\frown}\overset{+2}{\frown}\overset{+3}{\frown}\overset{+4}{\frown}\overset{+5}{\frown}\overset{+6}{\frown}\overset{+7}{\frown}\overset{+8}{\frown}$$
$$3 \quad 4 \quad 6 \quad 9 \quad 13 \quad 18 \quad 24 \ldots 31 \; 39$$

5. **A** In this series the numbers are increasing by 1, with every second number being repeated before it increases.
6. **D** This time you have the number 10 interrupting a sequence of numbers that go up by 1 after each has been repeated. (This rule is not easy to understand if it is *stated* or *written*. That is why it is strongly urged to use diagrams and other techniques you'll read about in Chapter 7.) Look at how readily the pattern shows up when properly diagrammed:

$$\overset{+0}{\frown}\overset{+1}{\frown}\overset{+0}{\frown}\overset{+1}{\frown}\overset{+0}{\frown}$$
$$\boxed{10} \quad 6 \quad 6 \quad \boxed{10} \quad 7 \quad 7 \quad \boxed{10} \ldots 8 \; 8$$

7. **C** The rule for this series is easy to follow if you consider it to be composed of two alternating series

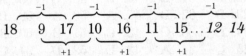

$$18 \quad 9 \quad 17 \quad 10 \quad 16 \quad 11 \quad 15 \ldots 12 \; 14$$

One series begins with 18 and decreases by *1*. The other begins with 9 and increases by 1.

8. **E** This is another example of alternating series, one going up by 1, the other going down by 1. In this case however, the series that is increasing continues for two numbers before it is interrupted by the other.

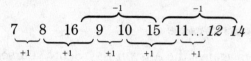

Most of the foregoing examples were diagrammed as well as explained to help you get started. The examples on the next page will not be diagrammed. You may do that now or after you've read Chapter 7.

9. **D** The rule here is +5, –1; +5, –1; etc.

10. **B** In this series multiplication by 2 is used to connect the numbers. After each multiplication the new number is repeated once and then the process continues.

11. **D** This series of numbers can be considered to be composed of *three* alternating series—one increasing by +1; two increasing by +2. If you wish, you can see them connected one to the other by this rule: +3, +1, –3; +4, +1, –4; . . . +5, +1

12. **C** This series follows the rule: –2, –2, +6.

13. **B** Basically, this is a series that increases according to this rule: +2, +1; +2, +1; . . . It is interrupted after every two numbers by the number 18.

14. **C** Here again are two alternating series. One decreases by ever increasing amounts –1, –2, –3 . . . etc. The other increases by +2.

15. **D** The rule is: +2, +3; +2, +3 . . .

16. **C** There are two alternating series here: one increases by +2. The alternate series also increases by +2

17. **A** This series follows the rule: –1, –1, –2; –1, –1, –2, etc.

18. **E** This series can be quite confusing until you realize that the number 13 interrupts the series by appearing every *third* number. With that fact accounted for, we have a series that follows the rule: +6, –5; +6, –5 . . .

19. **A** The series follows the pattern: –1, –2; –1, –2 . . .

20. **E** In this series the numbers are increasing by 2. Every other number is repeated before it increases.

21. **B** You can view this as two alternating series, each of which increases by +1. If you wish, you may connect them by the rule: +5, – 4; +5, – 4; +5, – 4 . . .

22. **C** Each number is obtained by adding together the two preceding numbers; that is, 1 + 4 = 5; 4 + 5 = 9; 5 + 9 = 14; 9 + 14 = 23; 14 + 23 = 37; 23 + 37; = 60; 37 + 60 = 97

23. **A** These numbers follow a complex set of rules. They may be viewed either as groups of 3 number "mini-series"—that is, 3 5 7; 4 6 8; 5 7 9, each of which increases by +2. Or they may be seen as three alternating series. In either case, the last number of the group is repeated once. In Chapter 7 you will see how to diagram and identify this series either way.

24. **B** This too is made of two alternating series: one is increasing by + 1 (see 15 . . . 16 . . . 17 . . .); the other follows the rule –2, –3; –2, –3 (see 26 . . . 24 . . . 21 . . . 19 . . .) and is interrupted after every two numbers by one member of the first series.

■ EVALUATING YOUR PROGRESS*

Part A—Address Checking

Computing Your Score

Check your answers against the Answer Key. Score yourself by using this formula:

Number right
− Number wrong

YOUR SCORE

For example, if you completed 52 questions and got 8 wrong,

Number right	=	44
− Number wrong	=	− 8
Your score	=	36

Notice that you do *not* figure in the questions that you did not answer.

Guidelines

How good is the score you just made?

52 or higher . . . . Good

Between 32 and 52 . . . . Fair

Below 32 . . . . You need to improve.

These are commonly accepted figures. However, you should not be satisfied with anything *less* than 52. In training many people to prepare for this test, it has been shown that most serious test candidates who use the preparation program described in this book (Chapter 4 covers Address Checking) will be able to raise their score to the upper sixties, seventies, or eighties.

Personal Progress Record

One of the most satisfying things that can happen while you are working toward a goal is to see signs of progress. The improvement you make on Address Checking can readily be seen by examining the scores you make on the practice tests and exercises in this book. You can keep track of your growing skill by using the Personal Progress Record, furnished for your use on page 439.

The following is a sample of this Personal Progress Record to familiarize you with it. The entries on this sample are based on the example above.

Furthermore, even though you take one test, your final score will vary depending on the title. For example, your rating on the Mail Handler register may very well be different

---

* Please note that the scores you obtain by following the computation instructions for the various parts of this test are "raw" scores. The Postal Service combines and converts the raw scores for the various parts of the test into a scaled score obtained by using special conversion formulas that are kept confidential. This scaled score (plus any veteran's credits to which you are entitled) forms the basis for your final rating and your standing on the list. This final rating will be sent to you after the tests have been marked.

from your rating on the Postal Clerk-Carrier register. Apparently, the relative rating given to each part of the test varies according to title. This is another argument for taking as many tests in as many titles as possible, as suggested on page 1.

You are encouraged to calculate your raw scores because they furnish a realistic and convenient way for you to keep track of your relative performance and progress as you work your way through this book.

PERSONAL PROGRESS RECORD—SAMPLE

ADDRESS CHECKING									
Initial Tests							**Repeated Tests**		
Date	Test	Number Completed	Number Correct −	Number Wrong =	Score	Date	Score	Date	Score
5/15	Diagnostic Practice Test	52	44 −	8 =	36				
5/16	Practice Test 1	64	54 −	10 =	44				
5/18	Practice Test 2	66	57 −	9 =	48				
5/20	Practice Test 3	70	60 −	10 =	50				
	Practice Test 4		−	=					
	Practice Test 5		−	=					
	Practice Test 6		−	=					

Now turn to page 439. In the table entitled "Personal Progress Record–Address Checking," make the proper entries on the line for the Diagnostic Practice Test you just took. This table will help you record your progress as you take additional practice tests.

Part B—Memory for Addresses

Computing Your Score

Check the answers on your answer sheet against the Answer Key. Calculate your score by using these four steps:
1. Enter the name of answers you got right . . . . _____
2. Enter the number of answers you got wrong. . . . . _____
3. Divide the number wrong by 4 (or multiply by ¼) . . . . − _____
4. Subtract Line 3 from Line 1 . . . . YOUR SCORE = _____

Follow this example to make sure that you have figured your score correctly. Assume that you have completed 32 questions, of which you got 24 right and 8 wrong.

Line 1 . . . Number right.   24

Line 2 . . . Number wrong. 8

Line 3 . . . ¼ of line 2 = ¼ × 8. . . .   −2

Line 4 . . . 24 − 2   YOUR SCORE =   22

Notice that, just as for Address Checking, questions that are not answered are *not* taken into account.

Guidelines

How good is the score you just made?

> 44 or more .... Good
>
> 26 to 43 .... Fair
>
> 25 or less .... You need to improve.

If your score on this test was low, don't be discouraged. *Just about everyone who takes this memory test "cold" has the same experience.* Yet, most persons go on to make a vast improvement in their score after they have studied Chapters 5 and 6. If you are like the average person, and are willing to invest a little time in study and practice, you can confidently set your sights on a mark well above 44. In fact, scores of 70 and above are attainable by those who prepare thoroughly.

Personal Progress Record

Turn to page 439. Use the table entitled "Personal Progress—Memory for Addresses" to keep a permanent record of your scores on List 3 of the practice tests. A sample is printed below to familiarize you with it. The entries are based on the preceding example:

PERSONAL PROGRESS RECORD—SAMPLE

		MEMORY FOR ADDRESSES								
		Initial Tests							Repeated Tests	
Date	Test	Number Completed	Number Correct A	Number Wrong	$\times \frac{1}{4} =$	Points off B	Score (A − B)	Date	Score	Date	Score
5/15	Diagnostic Practice Test	32	24	8	$\times \frac{1}{4} =$	2	22				
5/16	Practice Test 1	46	38	8	$\times \frac{1}{4} =$	2	36				
5/18	Practice Test 2	58	52	6	$\times \frac{1}{4} =$	1½	50½				
5/20	Practice Test 3	64	60	4	$\times \frac{1}{4} =$	1	59				
	Practice Test 4				$\times \frac{1}{4} =$						
	Practice Test 5				$\times \frac{1}{4} =$						
	Practice Test 6				$\times \frac{1}{4} =$						

Make the proper entries on the record on page 439 for the Diagnostic Practice Test that you just took. You should be pleasantly surprised at how much higher your next entry on this table will be.

Part C—Number Series

Computing Your Score

Check the answers on your Answer Sheet against the Answer Key. Calculate your score by adding up the number of correct answers you have. You *do not* lose any credit for wrong answers or for questions you don't answer. For example, on a test having 24 questions, if you had 5 correct, 3 incorrect, and omitted 16, your score would be 5.

Guidelines

How good is the score you just made?

> 17 or higher . . . . Good
>
> Between 12 and 16 . . . . Fair
>
> Below 12. . . . . You need to improve

Once you have mastered the techniques explained in this book, you should routinely be scoring 20 to 24 correct.

Personal Progress Record

One of the most satisfying things that can happen while you are working toward a goal is to see signs of progress. The improvement you make by studying and practicing can readily be seen by examining the scores you make on the practice tests and exercises in this book. You can keep track of your increasing skill on the Personal Progress Record, furnished for your use on page 440.

The following is a sample of this Personal Progress Record to familiarize you with it. The entries on this sample are based on the example above.

PERSONAL PROGRESS RECORD—SAMPLE

NUMBER SERIES							
Initial Tests				**Repeated Tests**			
Date	Test	Number Completed	Number Correct (Your Score)	Date	Score	Date	Score
5/15	Diagnostic Practice Test	8	5				
5/16	Practice Test 1	15	11				
5/18	Practice Test 2	17	15				
5/20	Practice Test 3	20	19				
	Practice Test 4						
	Practice Test 5						
	Practice Test 6						

Now turn to page 440. Look at the table entitled "Personal Progress Record— Number Series." Make the proper entries on the line for the Diagnostic Practice Test you just took. This table will help you record your progress as you take additional practice tests.

Part D—Following Oral Directions

Computing Your Score

Check your answers against the Answer Key. Calculate your score as you did for the Number Series by adding up the number of correct answers you have. You do *not* lose any credit for wrong answers or for questions you don't answer. For example, on a test having 30 questions, if you had 17 correct and 6 incorrect, and omitted 7, your score would be 17.

Guidelines

How good is the score you just made?

> 28 or higher . . . . Good
>
> Between 24 and 27 . . . . Fair
>
> Below 24. . . . . You need to improve.

Once you have mastered the techniques explained in this book (Chapter 8 covers Following Oral Directions), you should routinely score 28 to 30 correct.

Personal Progress Record

Now turn to page 440. In the table entitled "Personal Progress Record—Following Oral Directions," make the proper entries on the line for the Diagnostic Practice Test you just took. This table will help you record your progress as you take additional practice tests. A sample is printed below to familiarize you with it. The first entry is based on the preceding example.

PERSONAL PROGRESS RECORD—SAMPLE

FOLLOWING ORAL DIRECTIONS							
Initial Tests				Repeated Tests			
Date	Test	Number Completed	Number Correct (Your Score)	Date	Score	Date	Score
5/15	Diagnostic Practice Test	23	17				
5/16	Practice Test 1	23	19				
5/18	Practice Test 2	27	25				
5/20	Practice Test 3	29	28				
	Practice Test 4						
	Practice Test 5						
	Practice Test 6						

How Addresses May Differ

Now that you have completed the Diagnostic Practice Test and checked your answers, you can see that the differences between address pairs fall into four main categories.

1. Number Differences. In a street address or a zip code number, numbers may be:

a. *Transposed.*

> 635 La Calle Mayor *versus* 653 La Calle Mayor

b. *Changed.*

> Washington DC 20013 *versus* Washington DC 20018

c. *Omitted.*

> 10476 Eastern Avenue *versus* 1047 Eastern Avenue

2. Directional Differences. These can occur *before* or *after* the street name.

> 1166 N Beaumont Dr *versus* 1166 S Beaumont Dr
>
> 758 Los Arboles Ave SE *versus* 758 Los Arboles Ave SW

3. Abbreviation Differences

a. *Streets, Drives, Avenues, etc.*

> 2560 Lansford Pl *versus* 2560 Lansford St
>
> 6434 E Pulaski St *versus* 6434 E Pulaski Ct

b. *States.*

These abbreviations are particularly important now that the new two-letter abbreviations of state names are replacing many of the longer, easy-to-distinguish ones. For example, the *Postal Service Directory* abbreviates California as CA, *not* CAL or CALIF. The abbreviation for Minnesota is MN, *not* MINN. Because many states now have two-letter abbreviations beginning or ending with the same letter, there is a greater chance to overlook the differences if they appear on the test. For example:

> Sparta GA *versus* Sparta VA
>
> Shreveport LA *versus* Shreveport IA
>
> Portland OR *versus* Portland OH

(A complete list of the two-letter state abbreviations, with which you may practice, appears on page 425.)

4. Spelling Differences

a. *Single letters may be added, transposed, or changed.*

> 22 Sagnaw Pkwy *versus* 22 Saganaw Pkwy
>
> 3302 W Avalon Rd *versus* 3302 W Alavon Rd
>
> 8406 La Casa St *versus* 8406 La Cosa St

b. *Small groups of letters may be changed.*

3282 E Downington St *versus* 3282 Dunnington St

565 Greenville Blvd SE *versus* 565 Greenview Blvd SE

(Very often these are groups that look or sound somewhat alike. A brief list of such groups is given in the table on page 426.)

DIAGNOSTIC CHARTS

The following charts will help pinpoint your weaknesses by making it easy for you to determine what particular type of question in each part of the test is most difficult for you.

Part A—Address Checking

Type of Difference	"D" Questions	Number of "D" Questions Wrong		
		Trial 1	Trial 2	Trial 3
Numbers: transposed	14, 54, 71, 79, 89, 93			
changed	7, 19, 29, 31			
omitted	64, 74			
Directions	5, 22, 24, 35, 90			

Abbreviations:
    streets, roads,
        avenues, etc.
	41, 47, 60, 80, 91			

states	37, 76, 82, 88			
Spelling: single letters	4, 8, 11, 16, 17, 23, 36, 46, 50, 58, 59, 65, 68, 76, 81			
groups of letters	1, 12, 15, 34, 38, 53, 73			
Total Number of All Types	48			
	Use the columns on the right to enter the question numbers of "A" items you marked "D."			

This chart will help you to pinpoint the kinds of errors you made on the Practice Test. Use it as directed below after you have taken and marked the test.

The first column on the left, "Type of Difference," contains the categories whereby addresses may differ (see pages 69 to 70). On the same line across, the second column gives the numbers of the questions that fall within each category. In the third column, you are to enter the numbers of any "A" questions you answered as "D." Do not include questions that you did not do. Checking the addresses you got wrong may reveal a problem on which you will want to work.

After you have made all the entries, you will be able to see the areas in which you need to improve. Then turn to the appropriate parts of Chapter 4: Address Checking—How to Improve Your Score, read them, and practice the drills that can help. For example, if you find you have been making too many errors picking out number differences, read page 94 and do Drills 18 through 21. If you have a problem with single letters because of reversals like *b* and *d*, or if you have been overlooking the differences between *a*, *e*, and *o*, read page 91. Examine the table and work on Drills 10 and 11 if the problem persists.

Remember that this chart is designed for diagnostic purposes and guidance on further practice. It has been drawn so that you can enter the results each time you retake a practice test. In this way you will be able to see how you are progressing. It is not necessary to record your scores here. That is best done by using the Personal Progress Record Card.

Part B—Memory for Addresses

Kind of Address		Number of Questions	Number Wrong		
			Trial 1	Trial 2	Trial 3
Direct:	List 1	40			
	List 2	36			
	List 3	37			
Numbered:	List 1	48			
	List 2	52			
	List 3	51			

The purpose of this chart is to help you evaluate your performance on the two kinds of memory questions that appear in the Diagnostic Practice Test—the questions on the direct (name) addresses and the questions on the numbered addresses. Use the chart as directed below after you have taken and marked the entire test.

The first column on the left, "Kind of Address," is divided by category into "Direct Address" versus "Numbered Address." The second column gives the number of questions in each category on List 1, List 2, and List 3. Use the third column to enter the total number of questions in each category that you answered incorrectly. There is room for you to make additional entries if you take the Diagnostic Practice Test more than once.

At a glance, you will be able to see which area you need to concentrate on and how well you are progressing as you take repeat trials. Use Chapter 5 and the drills in it to improve your memory for the direct addresses. Use Chapter 6 for the numbered addresses.

Remember to use the Personal Progress Record Card (Memory for Addresses) on page 439 to keep track of your actual scores as you keep studying and practicing.

Part C—Number Series and Part D—Following Oral Directions

Because of the nature of the questions in these tests, Diagnostic Charts for them have not been provided. If you find that you made many errors on these tests, study the techniques suggested in Chapters 7 and 8.

LEARNING THE SPECIAL TECHNIQUES

Chapter 4

Address Checking—How to Improve Your Score

■ TEST STRATEGY

Before specific ways to increase speed and accuracy are considered, test strategy should be discussed. One definition of strategy is "a plan, method, or series of maneuvers for obtaining a specific goal or result." You can see the importance of effective strategy everywhere. Effective strategy makes the difference between champions and also-rans in every field of human endeavor—from fighting a war to managing a baseball team. The reason why great big-league managers earn so much is that they have been known to take teams that ranked in fifth or sixth place under former managers and mold them into league champions. How? By using ways to make the most of the team's ability. Using *your* ability to the best advantage is what effective test strategy is all about. This is what we will now discuss.

Don't Go for 100 Percent

On the Address Checking test, your goal is, of course, to get the highest score you can. It is to your advantage to work as quickly and accurately as possible since the test score is based on the number of wrong answers as well as the number of right answers. The problem for most of us is that the faster we work, the more errors we make. But everyone is different in his or her speed and skills. Therefore, each of us has to know what combination of speed and accuracy will yield the best results. Practice, including trial and error, will determine the correct combination for *you*. To illustrate these ideas, here are a couple of examples:

> Joe Smith is preparing to take a U.S. Postal Service examination. He decides to work very carefully, as he did in school, and to avoid any errors. After taking the test, his results on the Address Checking part show that he completed 32 questions and got only 2 wrong. If he were graded the way he used to be in school, he would have a score of 94 percent!

But that's not the way this test is actually scored. Joe's true score (see page 64 will be calculated by the formula you saw before:

$$
\begin{array}{r}
30 \ \text{Right} \\
- \ 2 \ \text{Wrong} \\
\hline
28 = \text{Joe Smith's Score}
\end{array}
$$

This score is definitely too low according to the criteria on page 64.

A few years later, Joe has another opportunity to take a similar Postal Service examination. This time he prepares for it, and he rethinks his test strategy. He decides to push on a bit faster, even though he is not sure whether he can be as accurate as before.

Here is what happened:

He answered 44 questions and got 5 wrong.
His percentage score = 88 percent, quite a drop; *but . . .*
his actual test score = 34 (39 – 5).

Joe's new strategy paid off—he raised his score from 28 (below par) to 34 (fair) even though he got more than twice as many wrong!

Don't Guess Wildly

This discussion of test strategy wouldn't be complete without discussing the matter of guessing. After all, why not raise the number of possible right answers by making sure you've answered all 95 questions even if you have to guess blindly at the last 20 or 30? Guessing is *not* advisable if you consider the odds involved. You have a 50-50 chance on each question. If you guess, you will probably get as many wrong as you get right. The net result is zero—nothing gained. You might even be unlucky and get more wrong than right. In that case, you would be penalized because each wrong answer would deduct a point from your score. You would also stand to lose time better spent working at your usual pace, which you *know* would net you a few extra points.

Because everyone is different, you, the reader, will need to work out your individual test strategy on this and other parts of the test. You will learn how fast you can proceed while still maintaining reasonable accuracy. If you study and practice the techniques described in the following pages, you will increase speed and accuracy and keep raising your score. Use the Personal Progress Record on page 439 to help you see what your optimum speed is to yield the best score.

As was mentioned before, it is within the realm of possibility to score in the high eighties or above on this section of the test. The wonderful thing about this program is that *you are in charge* of your progress—you can go as fast and as far as your ability and persistence allow.

Don't Do More Than You Have To

Remember that the test directions specify, "If they [the two addresses] are *different in any way*, darken space D." This means that, just as soon as you have found a *single* difference between the addresses in a pair, you should immediately mark answer D. There is no point to checking the address any further. You are just wasting time you could be using to answer the next question. (For more on double-checking, see pages 83 and 84.)

■ TECHNIQUES FOR INCREASING YOUR ADDRESS CHECKING SKILLS

In any activity requiring skill, whether bowling, chess, or typing, the key to success is knowing the correct techniques and then practicing them. A good example of what proper technique and training can accomplish is seen in the advances that have been made in track and field sports.

Barely 50 years ago, a world record of 4 minutes and 6.2 seconds for the one-mile run was set by the "Flying Swede," Gunder Haegg. Running experts at that time were sure it would never be broken. The 4-minute mile wasn't even on the horizon. But things have certainly changed. Recently, 7 out of 11 runners competing in a one-mile race broke the once-invincible 4-minute barrier! What happened to explain this phenomenal performance? For one thing, the sport was scientifically studied to learn more about running techniques and training methods. Everything was scrutinized, including length of stride, recovery time, track shoe design, pacing, diet, and the psychology of running. Anything and everything, no matter how minute, was considered, as long as it led to faster time. Then, too, increased interest and participation in running led athletes to start their careers and training at an earlier age. Athletes trained longer and harder. Sports medicine used scientific methods to establish the best training regimens. You can see how the two factors—correct technique and diligent practice (see page 142) have paid dividends.

The TV game show *Jeopardy* seen around the world, although very different from running a marathon or taking the U.S. Postal exam, has great similarities to both in terms of strategy, technique, and motivation. *Jeopardy* seems simple—those who know more about many subjects will always win. *Wrong!* The next time you watch it, notice these elements:

Motivation—all three situations are highly competitive, Those "playing" have a lot riding on winning, in terms of money, careers, and personal status. Controlling emotions is important!

Preparation—interviews with winners confirm the importance of practice, study, and advance planning. They all prepared!

Guessing—knowing when and when not to guess, and when to pass.

Betting—knowing *how much* to bet and *timing* your bets.

Opponents—sizing up and assessing *their* background and their stance on betting, and guessing.

Correct technique and diligent practice are also the basis for this book. Every technique that can help you raise your score has been carefully considered and explained. Learn and practice each of them. Remember: when you raise your speed record, you get that much closer to a job appointment.

(Incidentally, the present world record is 3 minutes and 43.13 seconds, and no one talks about limits too much any more.)

Use Both Hands Properly

When you take the Postal Service test, you will find that the questions are printed on a separate page from the answer sheet (as has been done in this book). Nevertheless, many candidates lose time by not using their hands correctly. The most common error is to leave one or both hands idle and out of position while reading each address line. When the candidates have decided on Ⓐ or Ⓓ, they then have to bring their pencils up to the correct line on the answer sheet. Valuable fractions of a second are lost performing this movement. Sometimes the test taker loses his or her place on the question sheet or on the answer sheet. This wastes more time and may even result in putting an answer on the wrong line, a mistake that could lead to disaster. Every succeeding answer will then appear on the wrong line.

The remedy is simply to *keep both hands in the correct position relative to the question and answer sheets.* Assuming you are right-handed,* you should keep your left hand

---

* *Note for left-handed test takers:* The illustrations show a right-handed test taker. If you are left-handed, you will, of course, be placing the answer sheet on your left and the question page on the right. Be prepared, however, for the possibility that, on the Postal Service exam, the question page and the answer sheet may be bound together in a booklet *with the answer sheet on the right.* With a little practice ahead of time, you should be able to use your right hand to fill in the spaces just as speedily as your left.

on the question sheet as a guide, slowly moving it down for each question. Or else, use a second pencil as a guide across each line. Your right hand, holding the pencil, should be poised on the corresponding question number on the answer sheet. Keep both hands working together in this way as you take the test.

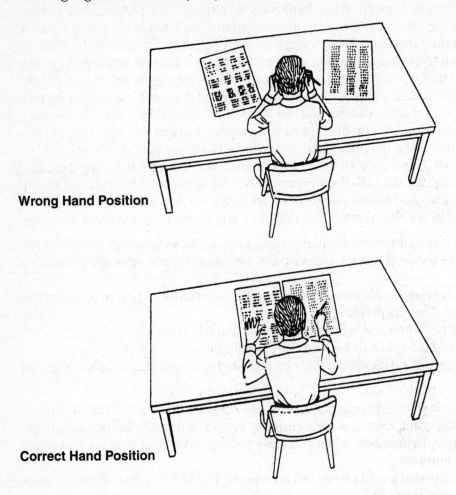

Wrong Hand Position

Correct Hand Position

Make Your Mark Neatly and Clearly

The instructions you receive at the time of the official test will include directions on how to fill out the answer sheet. Make sure you follow these directions, but be careful that you don't misinterpret them and do what is unnecessary and time-wasteful.

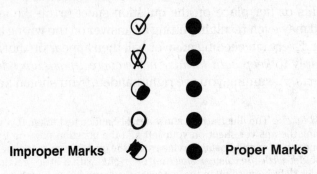

Improper Marks   **Proper Marks**

In referring to the way you are supposed to mark the answer sheet, you are instructed to darken completely the answer space that you have selected. You must keep your mark neat and stay within the circle.

On the other hand, some test candidates spend as much time carefully outlining and darkening the spaces as they did in examining the question and in deciding on the answer! This test is *not* an artistic competition. Don't waste time! You could be completing perhaps 50 to 100 percent more questions using the time wasted making beautiful marks.

Preparing Your Pencil

Prepare your pencil point so that the tip is angled, flat, and shaped like an oval about ⅛ inch long. An easy way to do this is by holding a regularly sharpened pencil point at a 45° angle to a piece of scrap paper and rubbing it back and forth until you get the desired size and shape. Your goal is to be able to darken an answer space with *one* circular rotation of your pencil instead of the half-dozen or more rotations you may have been making. (See pages 87 to 90 for practice in marking answers clearly and quickly.)

Prepare three or four pencils, with erasers, to take to the examination room. Incidentally, when you buy your pencils, tell the clerk at the store what they will be used for; they are supposed to leave a very dark mark without smearing. If the examiners require you to use pencils that they supply, all is not lost. You can readily prepare the points right there and then, using the method described above.

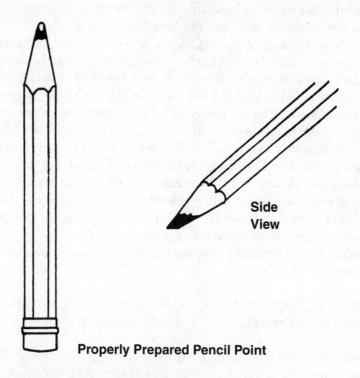

Side View

Properly Prepared Pencil Point

More Tips on Marking Your Answers

- *Remember that only one answer is allowed per question.* The machine that "reads" your answer sheet will mark you wrong if it picks up more than one answer.

- *Keep erasing to a minimum,* especially when speed is absolutely essential (Address Checking). You will probably lose more points than you gain if you stop to reexamine a question, erase the previous answer, and enter a new one. (Read the paragraphs on guessing in the Test Strategy sections at the beginning of Chapters 4, 5, and 6.)

- *Know when erasing is advisable;* if you notice smudges and extraneous pencil marks near the answer spaces; if you have blackened two answer spaces for one question; after you've completed all the questions in one part of the test and you are reviewing your answers to earlier questions. (You can speed up this review process by placing a check mark in the question booklet next to each question you aren't sure of.)

- *If you must erase an answer, do so completely.* The machine may read smudges and incomplete erasures as second answers.

- *Don't write words or anything else on the answer sheet.* The machine understands nothing but blackened spaces.

Use a Different Kind of "Reading"

Notice that this test is called "Address Checking." *Checking* is not the same as ordinary reading. For example, you can check a letter to see whether it has a return address without reading the address if it's there. Similarly, you can quickly check a "Help Wanted" column to see if there are any job openings for "receptionists" or "engineers" without reading the details in the ads. Did you ever have the experience of driving a car and suddenly realizing that, for a few minutes, you have not been aware of driving? Yet the car and you were still in one piece. Obviously, you had seen, heard, and reacted to the traffic about you, but in a special way. In other words, there are differences in the amount and quality of what you see and how it registers, depending upon the kind of "looking" you are doing.

In the first illustration, what you did is to look at the envelope just long enough and hard enough to *perceive* an address. You could not tell what the address was in terms of name, number, and so on, because you had not focused your understanding on it. You did not really *read* it—you just *scanned* it. This difference is of major importance to you in a test situation such as Address Checking, where speed is important. Reading for comprehension would slow you down, and it is not necessary for this type of test. Your brain would need time to translate the written symbols into meaningful words. You would not be able to read faster than you think. The remedy? Do *not* read for comprehension. Just scan the addresses to perceive any difference between the two.

To see how a slowdown caused by reading for comprehension can occur, check these two pairs of addresses:

2461 Cherry St., Springfield	2461 Sherry St., Springfield	Ⓐ Ⓓ
195 Vloovook, La Canton	195 Vloovool, La Canton	Ⓐ Ⓓ

The first pair of addresses has familiar words, especially Cherry and Sherry. If you let yourself visualize Cherry as a bunch of fruit and Sherry as a bottle of wine, you have attached meaning to these words. The momentary mental pause for recognition slowed you down. Your job was only to see that <u>C</u>herry was different from <u>S</u>herry and to mark choice Ⓓ.

When you looked at the second pair, you may have fallen into *two* time-consuming traps. First, you may have allowed yourself to reflect momentarily on that weird, unusual name—Vloovook. Maybe you tried to connect it to something or someplace you have heard of . . . Eskimos, perhaps?

Second, you may have sounded it out. Whether you whispered it aloud or to yourself, you lost time. Sounding it out lowered your speed of perception to that of your oral reading speed, which is far slower than your silent speed. Many people who read this way are largely unaware that they do so. To make sure that you are not moving your lips or subvocalizing, conduct this simple test. As you read, put your fingers gently alongside your lips and throat. You will feel a slight muscle movement or vibration if you are vocalizing. The cure lies first in becoming aware of the habit. Then, you must keep trying to let your brain register what your eyes see, in an instantaneous flash of recognition. Keep your lips still. Don't even think about how the words sound. Try keeping a pencil clenched between your teeth when you do the practice exercises in this book or whenever you read anything.

To summarize, your task is to compare Vloovook with Vloovool and to notice the difference between *k* and *l*. You must be able to perceive distinctions in shape,* spacing, and position, whether in letters, numbers, or names, as quickly as you can. That's all! Many test takers prepare themselves mentally for address checking by imagining that their eyes are picking up images the way a camera or an optical scanner does. It may seem silly, but for the purpose of this test, say to yourself, *"I am a camera."*

Use the exercises on pages 92 through 95 to develop your perceptual speed and accuracy. Here's one to try right now: Quickly read the sentence below, keeping track of the number of "t's" you see.

Two trees on the left and one shrub standing in between are attractive.

Now count the *t's* in the sentence *one time*—don't go back to check. Write the number here _____. The answer is nine *t's*. Did you get it right?

Widen Your Eye Span

To see how this important technique can help, imagine that you are timing two test candidates, Tom and Barbara, as they check these addresses on their test:

1462 Church Av Eaton Ill   1462 Church Av Eaton Ind

Results: Both candidates correctly selected choice Ⓓ.

Tom took a total of 6 seconds to come up with the answer; Barbara took only 4 seconds.

Although both of them got the right answer, Barbara worked 50 percent faster than Tom. At that rate, she could answer 75 questions in the same time it would take Tom to do 50! Her test score would then be in the upper ranks, whereas Tom's would be far, far behind.

---

* NOTE: Certain letters and letter combinations may cause perceptual problems. For example, the letters *b* and *d* are often mistaken for each other by people who reverse them. Reversal can occur vertically with the letters *m* and *w*. Errors may occur with words or parts of words, for example, "was" versus "saw." Some people are more prone to these difficulties than others. If you find you have this kind of problem, spend extra time practicing the letters and words that cause you trouble. Use the table "Some Common Perception Errors Made in Reading" page 9, which has a sampling of commonly confused letters, groups of letters, and words.

One of the factors working in Barbara's favor may have been her wider eye span, that is, her ability to perceive more at a glance than Tom could. To understand what eye span, or *span of perception*, really means, it is necessary to examine how the eye works.

The eyes are controlled by six tiny muscles as they move along a line of print. This eye movement is not smooth; it is more like a series of jumps and stops. It is during these stops, called *fixations*, that one actually perceives words. The units of type (numbers, letters, and spaces) the eyes pick up at each stop is called *eye span*. The wider your eye span, the faster you can go. To illustrate, note how Barbara and Tom each read the line below:

BARBARA

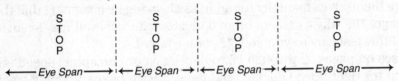

Notice that when Barbara reads this sentence, she stops four times. At each stop or fixation, her eye has spanned an average of three words.

Tom has not developed his eye span sufficiently. He reads the same line this way:

TOM

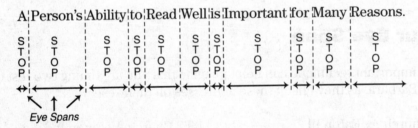

Tom has stopped for a fixation on every word. His average eye span is only *one* word. The result? He has read the line far slower than Barbara.

Word-by-word reading, with its greater number of fixations, slows a reader down dramatically. (On page 81 it was noted that "sounding out" words can be another reason for reading words in a sentence one at a time.) What makes matters worse is that many people who read this way are unaware of it. Now that it has been established that Tom is one of these people, compare the way Tom and Barbara read the address on page 81: In the samples that follow, dots (•) have been used to indicate points above which the eye focuses at each fixation; a solid line underscores the width of the eye span. Eye span width is measured by counting the units of type, including the spaces between words, in each fixation.

TOM

1462 Church Av Eaton III   1462 Church Av Eaton Ind
•   •   •   •   •   •   •   •   •   •

Number of fixations = 5 per side.
Average eye span = 5 type units.

BARBARA

1462 Church Av Eaton III   1462 Church Av Eaton Ind
•   •   •   •   •   •

Number of fixations = 3 per side.
Average eye span = 8 type units.

These diagrams clearly show the reason why Barbara is going 50 percent faster than Tom. But even Barbara's performance can be improved! It is possible to see each side in two, or in even in *one*, fixation if you train yourself to widen your eye span. You can learn to use your peripheral vision to widen your perception span to its maximum by using the exercises given on pages 100 through 105. As your eyes become able to grasp larger and larger "bunches" of each address at a time, your checking speed will increase.

There is still another benefit that comes with increased eye span. You save extra time because your eyes move back and forth fewer times as you compare the two addresses. If Barbara's eye movements could be seen as they sweep back and forth between the left- and right-hand columns, their path would look like this:

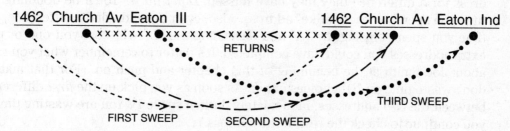

BARBARA

1462 Church Av Eaton III   1462 Church Av Eaton Ind

FIRST SWEEP   SECOND SWEEP   THIRD SWEEP   RETURNS

(The loops have been exaggerated to make the diagram clearer.)

Barbara made three "eye sweeps" going from the left side to the right side (plus the returns). She compared the "eyeful" gathered during each fixation on the left with the corresponding part of the address on the right. If Tom worked the same way, he would need more time because his eyes would have to make five sweeps (one for each fixation).

There is still room for improvement! Barbara could work even faster if she checked the entire address on the left side and then compared the mental images of the three fixations with the corresponding parts of the address line on the right.

Don't Go Back—Don't Regress

One day, a student who had just begun one of the exam preparation classes took the Address Checking portion of the Diagnostic Practice Test and scored only 15. When it was asked if he would describe any special difficulty he was having, he shamefacedly said, "I really feel awful about my score. If anything, I should have come out higher than most. After all, I work for a printer as a proofreader!" He was asked a few more questions about his job, and the reason for his troubles became clear. He had formed a tendency, reinforced by years of proofreading, to scrutinize all printed matter with the utmost care so that absolutely no errors appeared in the magazines his firm published. He developed into a perfectionist as far as catching errors in his on-the-job reading matter. Sad to say, he carried these proofreading habits over to *everything* he read, including the addresses on the Postal Service test. As a result, his test score was drastically low. On pages 75 through 76 test strategy was discussed and the reasons why absolute perfectionism is *not* a good idea. The proofreader's case makes the point perfectly. Others whose occupations may lead them into the same problem include stenographer-typists, file clerks, and accountants.

If you find yourself rereading work or pausing over an item in an address for too long a time, you can end the habit by (1) rereading the explanation on test strategy and (2) pushing yourself ahead to greater and greater speeds by using the special exercises at the end of this chapter.

There are still other reasons for regression:

1. Some adults carry over habits formed in school when they read and studied for exams. When people are reading difficult material that they must remember and understand thoroughly, they naturally read at a slower pace. There is often a need to reread and reflect until the material sinks in. Obviously, address checking involves a completely different kind of reading. So why not change your reading style to fit the task at hand?

2. Many people regress because they feel they have missed something, and they must look back to make sure they didn't. This is especially true for some people after they have chosen "A" for a particular address. They feel a need to check the address for a difference they may have missed. *Don't do it!* You'll be doubling the time you spend on each "alike" address. Also, even if you do find a difference, the time you spend erasing the "A" and darkening the "D" will cost you one or two extra addresses you could have completed. It's better to remember what you read about Joe Smith at the beginning of this chapter and push on. (For that matter, don't waste time on "D" choices either. As soon as you pick up the *first* difference between the two addresses, immediately darken space D. You are wasting time if you continue to check the rest of the address.)

3. Most people don't concentrate effectively. They daydream or let outside thoughts enter their consciousness. At that point, their work suffers. They may slow up. They may *really* miss seeing words. How can you learn to concentrate better? The secret is to focus your attention and not allow internal or external distractions to intrude. Become a machine! Pretend nothing can stop you—that you're an electronic scanning device passing over a succession of word and number images. (See Chapter 8 for more on putting yourself into the proper mental state.)

   Regardless of the reason, you can stop yourself from regressing. Each time you catch yourself ready to look back—force yourself to go on! Psych yourself into believing that you are really not going to miss much or make many errors, if you keep on going. To help you build that kind of confidence, special exercises have been provided that are aimed at overcoming regression. Turn to page 106 of this chapter for directions.

Work Rhythmically

As you do the practice tests and drills in this book, you should carefully time yourself. Soon you will get the feel of how fast you are going without looking at a clock. You will know when you are going at a pace that balances speed and accuracy for best results. Learn to feel that pace in your bones. Translate it into a rhythm, as your eyes sweep from one address to the other. If you keep the rhythm without letting regression or distractions get the better of you, you will *consistently* complete a certain number of lines in a given time. (This is one of the reasons why you are advised against stopping to erase in order to change an answer.)

To help you visualize how to go about finding, feeling, and using rhythm on the test, another illustration can be used. Assume that Tom becomes able to check an address in two fixations. He now needs only two eye sweeps to complete a typical address like this:

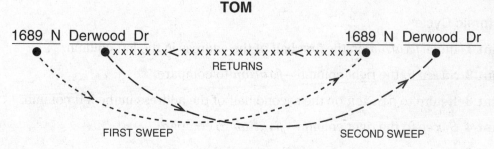

(The loops have been exaggerated to make the diagram clearer.)

Furthermore, assume that he has learned how to work at a rhythmic pace.

Tom then takes another practice test, completes 70 of the 95 questions, and gets 10 percent of his answers wrong. His score is: 63 right − 7 wrong = 56. Rhythm cannot be discussed without mentioning time, so calculate how long it took him to do *one* line. Divide 6 minutes (360 seconds) by 70. This works out to approximately 5 seconds per line (including the time needed for Tom to mark down his answer and move to the next line).

Because Tom has been practicing, he can really feel what a 5-second period is like. It is as though he has a mental metronome keeping time for him. His brain, eye movements, and hands all work together at the right rhythm to drive him along at the rate of 5 seconds per line.

How about you? Do you know what a 5-second period of time feels like? Or a 4-second period of time? Try this experiment:

Assume you are working to reach a 4-second-per-line speed. First, practice getting the feel of 4 seconds and the right rhythm by counting off 4 seconds as you look at a sweep second watch face. Do that several times. Then, chant out loud a few times " 1 - 2 - 3 - 4," etc. Now, chant mentally. When you think you've got the feel of a 4-second time period, check the addresses below. Fit your movements into that 4-second time slot. Establish the right rhythm. Try to move smoothly.

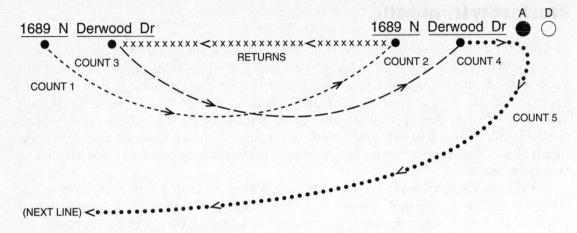

(The loops have been exaggerated to make the diagram clearer.)

Rhythmic Cycle

Count 1 Initial *fixation* on the first half of the address in the left column.

Count 2 *Sweep* to the right column—*fixation* to compare.

Count 3 Return to *fixation* on the second half of the address in the left column.

Count 4 *Sweep* to the right column—*fixation* to compare.

Count 5 Mark answer and *sweep* to the next line.

Repeat this cycle a few times. This experiment was intended only to illustrate the technique of working in rhythm. The 4-second cycle is probably too fast for you . . . *now*. Only you will be able to feel what is right for you at this stage. Experiment with the various practice tests in this book.

SPECIAL EXERCISES FOR BUILDING ADDRESS CHECKING SKILLS

You now have the "tools." You have learned the strategies and techniques that make a high score possible. Now you must be certain that you can apply them at test time. That means practice.

This section contains various exercises and drills. They will help you to eliminate any bad habits that you may have and to build the address checking skills you need. Work on them as needed. As you practice, remember that your progress may not be steady. Dramatic improvements are often followed by plateaus, times when your scores level off for a while. Sometimes there are even dips. These variations are perfectly natural and occur in all skills training. Just keep on practicing in the sure knowledge that your scores must rise. (Remember that 4-minute mile!)

Note that an Answer Key may be found on pages 112 to 113. In order to check your progress, since you may wish to take a number of exercises more than once, refer to the Drill Record Charts on pages 441 to 442 to record your scores.

Increasing Speed in Marking Answers

Drills 1–9

Use pages 88 through 90 to develop speed. There are nine answer drills with 95 answer lines in each. Four of the drills are laid out horizontally; five are laid out vertically. On the test, the answer sheets may be laid out either way. Prepare your pencil properly. Darken *one* space on each line, either box A or D. Pick boxes at random; it doesn't matter which you select. The idea is to practice making the entries cleanly and quickly. Time yourself. Practice until you can make 95 entries in one minute.

Answer Sheet—Drills 1–9

Drill 1

1 Ⓐ Ⓓ	2 Ⓐ Ⓓ	3 Ⓐ Ⓓ	4 Ⓐ Ⓓ	5 Ⓐ Ⓓ	6 Ⓐ Ⓓ	7 Ⓐ Ⓓ	8 Ⓐ Ⓓ	9 Ⓐ Ⓓ
10 Ⓐ Ⓓ	11 Ⓐ Ⓓ	12 Ⓐ Ⓓ	13 Ⓐ Ⓓ	14 Ⓐ Ⓓ	15 Ⓐ Ⓓ	16 Ⓐ Ⓓ	17 Ⓐ Ⓓ	18 Ⓐ Ⓓ
19 Ⓐ Ⓓ	20 Ⓐ Ⓓ	21 Ⓐ Ⓓ	22 Ⓐ Ⓓ	23 Ⓐ Ⓓ	24 Ⓐ Ⓓ	25 Ⓐ Ⓓ	26 Ⓐ Ⓓ	27 Ⓐ Ⓓ
28 Ⓐ Ⓓ	29 Ⓐ Ⓓ	30 Ⓐ Ⓓ	31 Ⓐ Ⓓ	32 Ⓐ Ⓓ	33 Ⓐ Ⓓ	34 Ⓐ Ⓓ	35 Ⓐ Ⓓ	36 Ⓐ Ⓓ
37 Ⓐ Ⓓ	38 Ⓐ Ⓓ	39 Ⓐ Ⓓ	40 Ⓐ Ⓓ	41 Ⓐ Ⓓ	42 Ⓐ Ⓓ	43 Ⓐ Ⓓ	44 Ⓐ Ⓓ	45 Ⓐ Ⓓ
46 Ⓐ Ⓓ	47 Ⓐ Ⓓ	48 Ⓐ Ⓓ	49 Ⓐ Ⓓ	50 Ⓐ Ⓓ	51 Ⓐ Ⓓ	52 Ⓐ Ⓓ	53 Ⓐ Ⓓ	54 Ⓐ Ⓓ
55 Ⓐ Ⓓ	56 Ⓐ Ⓓ	57 Ⓐ Ⓓ	58 Ⓐ Ⓓ	59 Ⓐ Ⓓ	60 Ⓐ Ⓓ	61 Ⓐ Ⓓ	62 Ⓐ Ⓓ	63 Ⓐ Ⓓ
64 Ⓐ Ⓓ	65 Ⓐ Ⓓ	66 Ⓐ Ⓓ	67 Ⓐ Ⓓ	68 Ⓐ Ⓓ	69 Ⓐ Ⓓ	70 Ⓐ Ⓓ	71 Ⓐ Ⓓ	72 Ⓐ Ⓓ
73 Ⓐ Ⓓ	74 Ⓐ Ⓓ	75 Ⓐ Ⓓ	76 Ⓐ Ⓓ	77 Ⓐ Ⓓ	78 Ⓐ Ⓓ	79 Ⓐ Ⓓ	80 Ⓐ Ⓓ	81 Ⓐ Ⓓ
82 Ⓐ Ⓓ	83 Ⓐ Ⓓ	84 Ⓐ Ⓓ	85 Ⓐ Ⓓ	86 Ⓐ Ⓓ	87 Ⓐ Ⓓ	88 Ⓐ Ⓓ	89 Ⓐ Ⓓ	90 Ⓐ Ⓓ
91 Ⓐ Ⓓ	92 Ⓐ Ⓓ	93 Ⓐ Ⓓ	94 Ⓐ Ⓓ	95 Ⓐ Ⓓ				

Drill 2

1 Ⓐ Ⓓ	2 Ⓐ Ⓓ	3 Ⓐ Ⓓ	4 Ⓐ Ⓓ	5 Ⓐ Ⓓ	6 Ⓐ Ⓓ	7 Ⓐ Ⓓ	8 Ⓐ Ⓓ	9 Ⓐ Ⓓ
10 Ⓐ Ⓓ	11 Ⓐ Ⓓ	12 Ⓐ Ⓓ	13 Ⓐ Ⓓ	14 Ⓐ Ⓓ	15 Ⓐ Ⓓ	16 Ⓐ Ⓓ	17 Ⓐ Ⓓ	18 Ⓐ Ⓓ
19 Ⓐ Ⓓ	20 Ⓐ Ⓓ	21 Ⓐ Ⓓ	22 Ⓐ Ⓓ	23 Ⓐ Ⓓ	24 Ⓐ Ⓓ	25 Ⓐ Ⓓ	26 Ⓐ Ⓓ	27 Ⓐ Ⓓ
28 Ⓐ Ⓓ	29 Ⓐ Ⓓ	30 Ⓐ Ⓓ	31 Ⓐ Ⓓ	32 Ⓐ Ⓓ	33 Ⓐ Ⓓ	34 Ⓐ Ⓓ	35 Ⓐ Ⓓ	36 Ⓐ Ⓓ
37 Ⓐ Ⓓ	38 Ⓐ Ⓓ	39 Ⓐ Ⓓ	40 Ⓐ Ⓓ	41 Ⓐ Ⓓ	42 Ⓐ Ⓓ	43 Ⓐ Ⓓ	44 Ⓐ Ⓓ	45 Ⓐ Ⓓ
46 Ⓐ Ⓓ	47 Ⓐ Ⓓ	48 Ⓐ Ⓓ	49 Ⓐ Ⓓ	50 Ⓐ Ⓓ	51 Ⓐ Ⓓ	52 Ⓐ Ⓓ	53 Ⓐ Ⓓ	54 Ⓐ Ⓓ
55 Ⓐ Ⓓ	56 Ⓐ Ⓓ	57 Ⓐ Ⓓ	58 Ⓐ Ⓓ	59 Ⓐ Ⓓ	60 Ⓐ Ⓓ	61 Ⓐ Ⓓ	62 Ⓐ Ⓓ	63 Ⓐ Ⓓ
64 Ⓐ Ⓓ	65 Ⓐ Ⓓ	66 Ⓐ Ⓓ	67 Ⓐ Ⓓ	68 Ⓐ Ⓓ	69 Ⓐ Ⓓ	70 Ⓐ Ⓓ	71 Ⓐ Ⓓ	72 Ⓐ Ⓓ
73 Ⓐ Ⓓ	74 Ⓐ Ⓓ	75 Ⓐ Ⓓ	76 Ⓐ Ⓓ	77 Ⓐ Ⓓ	78 Ⓐ Ⓓ	79 Ⓐ Ⓓ	80 Ⓐ Ⓓ	81 Ⓐ Ⓓ
82 Ⓐ Ⓓ	83 Ⓐ Ⓓ	84 Ⓐ Ⓓ	85 Ⓐ Ⓓ	86 Ⓐ Ⓓ	87 Ⓐ Ⓓ	88 Ⓐ Ⓓ	89 Ⓐ Ⓓ	90 Ⓐ Ⓓ
91 Ⓐ Ⓓ	92 Ⓐ Ⓓ	93 Ⓐ Ⓓ	94 Ⓐ Ⓓ	95 Ⓐ Ⓓ				

Drill 3

1 Ⓐ Ⓓ	2 Ⓐ Ⓓ	3 Ⓐ Ⓓ	4 Ⓐ Ⓓ	5 Ⓐ Ⓓ	6 Ⓐ Ⓓ	7 Ⓐ Ⓓ	8 Ⓐ Ⓓ	9 Ⓐ Ⓓ
10 Ⓐ Ⓓ	11 Ⓐ Ⓓ	12 Ⓐ Ⓓ	13 Ⓐ Ⓓ	14 Ⓐ Ⓓ	15 Ⓐ Ⓓ	16 Ⓐ Ⓓ	17 Ⓐ Ⓓ	18 Ⓐ Ⓓ
19 Ⓐ Ⓓ	20 Ⓐ Ⓓ	21 Ⓐ Ⓓ	22 Ⓐ Ⓓ	23 Ⓐ Ⓓ	24 Ⓐ Ⓓ	25 Ⓐ Ⓓ	26 Ⓐ Ⓓ	27 Ⓐ Ⓓ
28 Ⓐ Ⓓ	29 Ⓐ Ⓓ	30 Ⓐ Ⓓ	31 Ⓐ Ⓓ	32 Ⓐ Ⓓ	33 Ⓐ Ⓓ	34 Ⓐ Ⓓ	35 Ⓐ Ⓓ	36 Ⓐ Ⓓ
37 Ⓐ Ⓓ	38 Ⓐ Ⓓ	39 Ⓐ Ⓓ	40 Ⓐ Ⓓ	41 Ⓐ Ⓓ	42 Ⓐ Ⓓ	43 Ⓐ Ⓓ	44 Ⓐ Ⓓ	45 Ⓐ Ⓓ
46 Ⓐ Ⓓ	47 Ⓐ Ⓓ	48 Ⓐ Ⓓ	49 Ⓐ Ⓓ	50 Ⓐ Ⓓ	51 Ⓐ Ⓓ	52 Ⓐ Ⓓ	53 Ⓐ Ⓓ	54 Ⓐ Ⓓ
55 Ⓐ Ⓓ	56 Ⓐ Ⓓ	57 Ⓐ Ⓓ	58 Ⓐ Ⓓ	59 Ⓐ Ⓓ	60 Ⓐ Ⓓ	61 Ⓐ Ⓓ	62 Ⓐ Ⓓ	63 Ⓐ Ⓓ
64 Ⓐ Ⓓ	65 Ⓐ Ⓓ	66 Ⓐ Ⓓ	67 Ⓐ Ⓓ	68 Ⓐ Ⓓ	69 Ⓐ Ⓓ	70 Ⓐ Ⓓ	71 Ⓐ Ⓓ	72 Ⓐ Ⓓ
73 Ⓐ Ⓓ	74 Ⓐ Ⓓ	75 Ⓐ Ⓓ	76 Ⓐ Ⓓ	77 Ⓐ Ⓓ	78 Ⓐ Ⓓ	79 Ⓐ Ⓓ	80 Ⓐ Ⓓ	81 Ⓐ Ⓓ
82 Ⓐ Ⓓ	83 Ⓐ Ⓓ	84 Ⓐ Ⓓ	85 Ⓐ Ⓓ	86 Ⓐ Ⓓ	87 Ⓐ Ⓓ	88 Ⓐ Ⓓ	89 Ⓐ Ⓓ	90 Ⓐ Ⓓ
91 Ⓐ Ⓓ	92 Ⓐ Ⓓ	93 Ⓐ Ⓓ	94 Ⓐ Ⓓ	95 Ⓐ Ⓓ				

Drill 4

1 Ⓐ Ⓓ	2 Ⓐ Ⓓ	3 Ⓐ Ⓓ	4 Ⓐ Ⓓ	5 Ⓐ Ⓓ	6 Ⓐ Ⓓ	7 Ⓐ Ⓓ	8 Ⓐ Ⓓ	9 Ⓐ Ⓓ
10 Ⓐ Ⓓ	11 Ⓐ Ⓓ	12 Ⓐ Ⓓ	13 Ⓐ Ⓓ	14 Ⓐ Ⓓ	15 Ⓐ Ⓓ	16 Ⓐ Ⓓ	17 Ⓐ Ⓓ	18 Ⓐ Ⓓ
19 Ⓐ Ⓓ	20 Ⓐ Ⓓ	21 Ⓐ Ⓓ	22 Ⓐ Ⓓ	23 Ⓐ Ⓓ	24 Ⓐ Ⓓ	25 Ⓐ Ⓓ	26 Ⓐ Ⓓ	27 Ⓐ Ⓓ
28 Ⓐ Ⓓ	29 Ⓐ Ⓓ	30 Ⓐ Ⓓ	31 Ⓐ Ⓓ	32 Ⓐ Ⓓ	33 Ⓐ Ⓓ	34 Ⓐ Ⓓ	35 Ⓐ Ⓓ	36 Ⓐ Ⓓ
37 Ⓐ Ⓓ	38 Ⓐ Ⓓ	39 Ⓐ Ⓓ	40 Ⓐ Ⓓ	41 Ⓐ Ⓓ	42 Ⓐ Ⓓ	43 Ⓐ Ⓓ	44 Ⓐ Ⓓ	45 Ⓐ Ⓓ
46 Ⓐ Ⓓ	47 Ⓐ Ⓓ	48 Ⓐ Ⓓ	49 Ⓐ Ⓓ	50 Ⓐ Ⓓ	51 Ⓐ Ⓓ	52 Ⓐ Ⓓ	53 Ⓐ Ⓓ	54 Ⓐ Ⓓ
55 Ⓐ Ⓓ	56 Ⓐ Ⓓ	57 Ⓐ Ⓓ	58 Ⓐ Ⓓ	59 Ⓐ Ⓓ	60 Ⓐ Ⓓ	61 Ⓐ Ⓓ	62 Ⓐ Ⓓ	63 Ⓐ Ⓓ
64 Ⓐ Ⓓ	65 Ⓐ Ⓓ	66 Ⓐ Ⓓ	67 Ⓐ Ⓓ	68 Ⓐ Ⓓ	69 Ⓐ Ⓓ	70 Ⓐ Ⓓ	71 Ⓐ Ⓓ	72 Ⓐ Ⓓ
73 Ⓐ Ⓓ	74 Ⓐ Ⓓ	75 Ⓐ Ⓓ	76 Ⓐ Ⓓ	77 Ⓐ Ⓓ	78 Ⓐ Ⓓ	79 Ⓐ Ⓓ	80 Ⓐ Ⓓ	81 Ⓐ Ⓓ
82 Ⓐ Ⓓ	83 Ⓐ Ⓓ	84 Ⓐ Ⓓ	85 Ⓐ Ⓓ	86 Ⓐ Ⓓ	87 Ⓐ Ⓓ	88 Ⓐ Ⓓ	89 Ⓐ Ⓓ	90 Ⓐ Ⓓ
91 Ⓐ Ⓓ	92 Ⓐ Ⓓ	93 Ⓐ Ⓓ	94 Ⓐ Ⓓ	95 Ⓐ Ⓓ				

Drill 5

1 Ⓐ Ⓓ	49 Ⓐ Ⓓ		
2 Ⓐ Ⓓ	50 Ⓐ Ⓓ		
3 Ⓐ Ⓓ	51 Ⓐ Ⓓ		
4 Ⓐ Ⓓ	52 Ⓐ Ⓓ		
5 Ⓐ Ⓓ	53 Ⓐ Ⓓ		
6 Ⓐ Ⓓ	54 Ⓐ Ⓓ		
7 Ⓐ Ⓓ	55 Ⓐ Ⓓ		
8 Ⓐ Ⓓ	56 Ⓐ Ⓓ		
9 Ⓐ Ⓓ	57 Ⓐ Ⓓ		
10 Ⓐ Ⓓ	58 Ⓐ Ⓓ		
11 Ⓐ Ⓓ	59 Ⓐ Ⓓ		
12 Ⓐ Ⓓ	60 Ⓐ Ⓓ		
13 Ⓐ Ⓓ	61 Ⓐ Ⓓ		
14 Ⓐ Ⓓ	62 Ⓐ Ⓓ		
15 Ⓐ Ⓓ	63 Ⓐ Ⓓ		
16 Ⓐ Ⓓ	64 Ⓐ Ⓓ		
17 Ⓐ Ⓓ	65 Ⓐ Ⓓ		
18 Ⓐ Ⓓ	66 Ⓐ Ⓓ		
19 Ⓐ Ⓓ	67 Ⓐ Ⓓ		
20 Ⓐ Ⓓ	68 Ⓐ Ⓓ		
21 Ⓐ Ⓓ	69 Ⓐ Ⓓ		
22 Ⓐ Ⓓ	70 Ⓐ Ⓓ		
23 Ⓐ Ⓓ	71 Ⓐ Ⓓ		
24 Ⓐ Ⓓ	72 Ⓐ Ⓓ		
25 Ⓐ Ⓓ	73 Ⓐ Ⓓ		
26 Ⓐ Ⓓ	74 Ⓐ Ⓓ		
27 Ⓐ Ⓓ	75 Ⓐ Ⓓ		
28 Ⓐ Ⓓ	76 Ⓐ Ⓓ		
29 Ⓐ Ⓓ	77 Ⓐ Ⓓ		
30 Ⓐ Ⓓ	78 Ⓐ Ⓓ		
31 Ⓐ Ⓓ	79 Ⓐ Ⓓ		
32 Ⓐ Ⓓ	80 Ⓐ Ⓓ		
33 Ⓐ Ⓓ	81 Ⓐ Ⓓ		
34 Ⓐ Ⓓ	82 Ⓐ Ⓓ		
35 Ⓐ Ⓓ	83 Ⓐ Ⓓ		
36 Ⓐ Ⓓ	84 Ⓐ Ⓓ		
37 Ⓐ Ⓓ	85 Ⓐ Ⓓ		
38 Ⓐ Ⓓ	86 Ⓐ Ⓓ		
39 Ⓐ Ⓓ	87 Ⓐ Ⓓ		
40 Ⓐ Ⓓ	88 Ⓐ Ⓓ		
41 Ⓐ Ⓓ	89 Ⓐ Ⓓ		
42 Ⓐ Ⓓ	90 Ⓐ Ⓓ		
43 Ⓐ Ⓓ	91 Ⓐ Ⓓ		
44 Ⓐ Ⓓ	92 Ⓐ Ⓓ		
45 Ⓐ Ⓓ	93 Ⓐ Ⓓ		
46 Ⓐ Ⓓ	94 Ⓐ Ⓓ		
47 Ⓐ Ⓓ	95 Ⓐ Ⓓ		
48 Ⓐ Ⓓ			

Drill 6

1 Ⓐ Ⓓ	49 Ⓐ Ⓓ
2 Ⓐ Ⓓ	50 Ⓐ Ⓓ
3 Ⓐ Ⓓ	51 Ⓐ Ⓓ
4 Ⓐ Ⓓ	52 Ⓐ Ⓓ
5 Ⓐ Ⓓ	53 Ⓐ Ⓓ
6 Ⓐ Ⓓ	54 Ⓐ Ⓓ
7 Ⓐ Ⓓ	55 Ⓐ Ⓓ
8 Ⓐ Ⓓ	56 Ⓐ Ⓓ
9 Ⓐ Ⓓ	57 Ⓐ Ⓓ
10 Ⓐ Ⓓ	58 Ⓐ Ⓓ
11 Ⓐ Ⓓ	59 Ⓐ Ⓓ
12 Ⓐ Ⓓ	60 Ⓐ Ⓓ
13 Ⓐ Ⓓ	61 Ⓐ Ⓓ
14 Ⓐ Ⓓ	62 Ⓐ Ⓓ
15 Ⓐ Ⓓ	63 Ⓐ Ⓓ
16 Ⓐ Ⓓ	64 Ⓐ Ⓓ
17 Ⓐ Ⓓ	65 Ⓐ Ⓓ
18 Ⓐ Ⓓ	66 Ⓐ Ⓓ
19 Ⓐ Ⓓ	67 Ⓐ Ⓓ
20 Ⓐ Ⓓ	68 Ⓐ Ⓓ
21 Ⓐ Ⓓ	69 Ⓐ Ⓓ
22 Ⓐ Ⓓ	70 Ⓐ Ⓓ
23 Ⓐ Ⓓ	71 Ⓐ Ⓓ
24 Ⓐ Ⓓ	72 Ⓐ Ⓓ
25 Ⓐ Ⓓ	73 Ⓐ Ⓓ
26 Ⓐ Ⓓ	74 Ⓐ Ⓓ
27 Ⓐ Ⓓ	75 Ⓐ Ⓓ
28 Ⓐ Ⓓ	76 Ⓐ Ⓓ
29 Ⓐ Ⓓ	77 Ⓐ Ⓓ
30 Ⓐ Ⓓ	78 Ⓐ Ⓓ
31 Ⓐ Ⓓ	79 Ⓐ Ⓓ
32 Ⓐ Ⓓ	80 Ⓐ Ⓓ
33 Ⓐ Ⓓ	81 Ⓐ Ⓓ
34 Ⓐ Ⓓ	82 Ⓐ Ⓓ
35 Ⓐ Ⓓ	83 Ⓐ Ⓓ
36 Ⓐ Ⓓ	84 Ⓐ Ⓓ
37 Ⓐ Ⓓ	85 Ⓐ Ⓓ
38 Ⓐ Ⓓ	86 Ⓐ Ⓓ
39 Ⓐ Ⓓ	87 Ⓐ Ⓓ
40 Ⓐ Ⓓ	88 Ⓐ Ⓓ
41 Ⓐ Ⓓ	89 Ⓐ Ⓓ
42 Ⓐ Ⓓ	90 Ⓐ Ⓓ
43 Ⓐ Ⓓ	91 Ⓐ Ⓓ
44 Ⓐ Ⓓ	92 Ⓐ Ⓓ
45 Ⓐ Ⓓ	93 Ⓐ Ⓓ
46 Ⓐ Ⓓ	94 Ⓐ Ⓓ
47 Ⓐ Ⓓ	95 Ⓐ Ⓓ
48 Ⓐ Ⓓ	

Drill 7

1 Ⓐ Ⓓ	49 Ⓐ Ⓓ
2 Ⓐ Ⓓ	50 Ⓐ Ⓓ
3 Ⓐ Ⓓ	51 Ⓐ Ⓓ
4 Ⓐ Ⓓ	52 Ⓐ Ⓓ
5 Ⓐ Ⓓ	53 Ⓐ Ⓓ
6 Ⓐ Ⓓ	54 Ⓐ Ⓓ
7 Ⓐ Ⓓ	55 Ⓐ Ⓓ
8 Ⓐ Ⓓ	56 Ⓐ Ⓓ
9 Ⓐ Ⓓ	57 Ⓐ Ⓓ
10 Ⓐ Ⓓ	58 Ⓐ Ⓓ
11 Ⓐ Ⓓ	59 Ⓐ Ⓓ
12 Ⓐ Ⓓ	60 Ⓐ Ⓓ
13 Ⓐ Ⓓ	61 Ⓐ Ⓓ
14 Ⓐ Ⓓ	62 Ⓐ Ⓓ
15 Ⓐ Ⓓ	63 Ⓐ Ⓓ
16 Ⓐ Ⓓ	64 Ⓐ Ⓓ
17 Ⓐ Ⓓ	65 Ⓐ Ⓓ
18 Ⓐ Ⓓ	66 Ⓐ Ⓓ
19 Ⓐ Ⓓ	67 Ⓐ Ⓓ
20 Ⓐ Ⓓ	68 Ⓐ Ⓓ
21 Ⓐ Ⓓ	69 Ⓐ Ⓓ
22 Ⓐ Ⓓ	70 Ⓐ Ⓓ
23 Ⓐ Ⓓ	71 Ⓐ Ⓓ
24 Ⓐ Ⓓ	72 Ⓐ Ⓓ
25 Ⓐ Ⓓ	73 Ⓐ Ⓓ
26 Ⓐ Ⓓ	74 Ⓐ Ⓓ
27 Ⓐ Ⓓ	75 Ⓐ Ⓓ
28 Ⓐ Ⓓ	76 Ⓐ Ⓓ
29 Ⓐ Ⓓ	77 Ⓐ Ⓓ
30 Ⓐ Ⓓ	78 Ⓐ Ⓓ
31 Ⓐ Ⓓ	79 Ⓐ Ⓓ
32 Ⓐ Ⓓ	80 Ⓐ Ⓓ
33 Ⓐ Ⓓ	81 Ⓐ Ⓓ
34 Ⓐ Ⓓ	82 Ⓐ Ⓓ
35 Ⓐ Ⓓ	83 Ⓐ Ⓓ
36 Ⓐ Ⓓ	84 Ⓐ Ⓓ
37 Ⓐ Ⓓ	85 Ⓐ Ⓓ
38 Ⓐ Ⓓ	86 Ⓐ Ⓓ
39 Ⓐ Ⓓ	87 Ⓐ Ⓓ
40 Ⓐ Ⓓ	88 Ⓐ Ⓓ
41 Ⓐ Ⓓ	89 Ⓐ Ⓓ
42 Ⓐ Ⓓ	90 Ⓐ Ⓓ
43 Ⓐ Ⓓ	91 Ⓐ Ⓓ
44 Ⓐ Ⓓ	92 Ⓐ Ⓓ
45 Ⓐ Ⓓ	93 Ⓐ Ⓓ
46 Ⓐ Ⓓ	94 Ⓐ Ⓓ
47 Ⓐ Ⓓ	95 Ⓐ Ⓓ
48 Ⓐ Ⓓ	

Drill 8

1 Ⓐⓓ	49 Ⓐⓓ
2 Ⓐⓓ	50 Ⓐⓓ
3 Ⓐⓓ	51 Ⓐⓓ
4 Ⓐⓓ	52 Ⓐⓓ
5 Ⓐⓓ	53 Ⓐⓓ
6 Ⓐⓓ	54 Ⓐⓓ
7 Ⓐⓓ	55 Ⓐⓓ
8 Ⓐⓓ	56 Ⓐⓓ
9 Ⓐⓓ	57 Ⓐⓓ
10 Ⓐⓓ	58 Ⓐⓓ
11 Ⓐⓓ	59 Ⓐⓓ
12 Ⓐⓓ	60 Ⓐⓓ
13 Ⓐⓓ	61 Ⓐⓓ
14 Ⓐⓓ	62 Ⓐⓓ
15 Ⓐⓓ	63 Ⓐⓓ
16 Ⓐⓓ	64 Ⓐⓓ
17 Ⓐⓓ	65 Ⓐⓓ
18 Ⓐⓓ	66 Ⓐⓓ
19 Ⓐⓓ	67 Ⓐⓓ
20 Ⓐⓓ	68 Ⓐⓓ
21 Ⓐⓓ	69 Ⓐⓓ
22 Ⓐⓓ	70 Ⓐⓓ
23 Ⓐⓓ	71 Ⓐⓓ
24 Ⓐⓓ	72 Ⓐⓓ
25 Ⓐⓓ	73 Ⓐⓓ
26 Ⓐⓓ	74 Ⓐⓓ
27 Ⓐⓓ	75 Ⓐⓓ
28 Ⓐⓓ	76 Ⓐⓓ
29 Ⓐⓓ	77 Ⓐⓓ
30 Ⓐⓓ	78 Ⓐⓓ
31 Ⓐⓓ	79 Ⓐⓓ
32 Ⓐⓓ	80 Ⓐⓓ
33 Ⓐⓓ	81 Ⓐⓓ
34 Ⓐⓓ	82 Ⓐⓓ
35 Ⓐⓓ	83 Ⓐⓓ
36 Ⓐⓓ	84 Ⓐⓓ
37 Ⓐⓓ	85 Ⓐⓓ
38 Ⓐⓓ	86 Ⓐⓓ
39 Ⓐⓓ	87 Ⓐⓓ
40 Ⓐⓓ	88 Ⓐⓓ
41 Ⓐⓓ	89 Ⓐⓓ
42 Ⓐⓓ	90 Ⓐⓓ
43 Ⓐⓓ	91 Ⓐⓓ
44 Ⓐⓓ	92 Ⓐⓓ
45 Ⓐⓓ	93 Ⓐⓓ
46 Ⓐⓓ	94 Ⓐⓓ
47 Ⓐⓓ	95 Ⓐⓓ
48 Ⓐⓓ	

Drill 9

1 Ⓐⓓ	49 Ⓐⓓ
2 Ⓐⓓ	50 Ⓐⓓ
3 Ⓐⓓ	51 Ⓐⓓ
4 Ⓐⓓ	52 Ⓐⓓ
5 Ⓐⓓ	53 Ⓐⓓ
6 Ⓐⓓ	54 Ⓐⓓ
7 Ⓐⓓ	55 Ⓐⓓ
8 Ⓐⓓ	56 Ⓐⓓ
9 Ⓐⓓ	57 Ⓐⓓ
10 Ⓐⓓ	58 Ⓐⓓ
11 Ⓐⓓ	59 Ⓐⓓ
12 Ⓐⓓ	60 Ⓐⓓ
13 Ⓐⓓ	61 Ⓐⓓ
14 Ⓐⓓ	62 Ⓐⓓ
15 Ⓐⓓ	63 Ⓐⓓ
16 Ⓐⓓ	64 Ⓐⓓ
17 Ⓐⓓ	65 Ⓐⓓ
18 Ⓐⓓ	66 Ⓐⓓ
19 Ⓐⓓ	67 Ⓐⓓ
20 Ⓐⓓ	68 Ⓐⓓ
21 Ⓐⓓ	69 Ⓐⓓ
22 Ⓐⓓ	70 Ⓐⓓ
23 Ⓐⓓ	71 Ⓐⓓ
24 Ⓐⓓ	72 Ⓐⓓ
25 Ⓐⓓ	73 Ⓐⓓ
26 Ⓐⓓ	74 Ⓐⓓ
27 Ⓐⓓ	75 Ⓐⓓ
28 Ⓐⓓ	76 Ⓐⓓ
29 Ⓐⓓ	77 Ⓐⓓ
30 Ⓐⓓ	78 Ⓐⓓ
31 Ⓐⓓ	79 Ⓐⓓ
32 Ⓐⓓ	80 Ⓐⓓ
33 Ⓐⓓ	81 Ⓐⓓ
34 Ⓐⓓ	82 Ⓐⓓ
35 Ⓐⓓ	83 Ⓐⓓ
36 Ⓐⓓ	84 Ⓐⓓ
37 Ⓐⓓ	85 Ⓐⓓ
38 Ⓐⓓ	86 Ⓐⓓ
39 Ⓐⓓ	87 Ⓐⓓ
40 Ⓐⓓ	88 Ⓐⓓ
41 Ⓐⓓ	89 Ⓐⓓ
42 Ⓐⓓ	90 Ⓐⓓ
43 Ⓐⓓ	91 Ⓐⓓ
44 Ⓐⓓ	92 Ⓐⓓ
45 Ⓐⓓ	93 Ⓐⓓ
46 Ⓐⓓ	94 Ⓐⓓ
47 Ⓐⓓ	95 Ⓐⓓ
48 Ⓐⓓ	

Overcoming Reversal Errors

Drills 10–12

The following table shows errors made when individual letters, groups of letters, or entire words are somehow reversed, or otherwise changed, in our perception. Check the questions you had wrong on the Address Checking portion of the Diagnostic Practice Test. Pick out any errors showing this kind of mistake.

SOME COMMON PERCEPTION ERRORS MADE IN READING

Letters	Letter Groups	Words
b–d	ton–town	on–no
p–d	ville–view	top–pot
q–d	lawn–land	cite–ten
p–q	man–mon	never–ever
u–n	la–al	not–ton
u–v	le–el	pat–tap
n–m	ry–rey	saw–was
m–w	berg–burg	own–won
a–e	mont–mount	mar–arm
a–o	ham–heim	mint–tin

The three drills explained below may be used to remedy this situation. It is assumed, for the sake of illustration, that you are confusing b and d.

Drill 10

Write the letters b and d side by side.

b–d

1. _____ 3. _____ 5. _____ 7. _____ 9. _____
2. _____ 4. _____ 6. _____ 8. _____ 10. _____

Reverse their order and write them again.

d–b

1. _____ 3. _____ 5. _____ 7. _____ 9. _____
2. _____ 4. _____ 6. _____ 8. _____ 10. _____

Immediately after you write each pair, look away and picture the letters mentally. Write each pair ten times at each drill. Do this with other reversals with which you are having a problem.

Drill 11

On one side of a 3" × 5" card, write the letter b about one inch high. Write d on the other side. You have just made a flash card. Have a friend (or do it yourself) flash one side before you for the briefest instant. Call out what you see. Jot it down. Either side should be flashed at random. Each drill need last only 1 or 2 minutes. Do this with other reversals with which you are having a problem.

━━━━━━━━━━━━━ **Drill 12** ━━━━━━━━━━━━━

Take 3 seconds to check the line below to see how many *b*'s there are. Now check it for the number of *d*'s. Jot down the figures (the answer is at the end of this chapter).

b b d b d d d b d d

Number of *b*'s	Number of *d*'s
____	____

You or a friend can prepare similar lines consisting of the letters or groups of letters causing difficulty. Make certain that the number of items on each line varies. Drill several different lines each time.

Developing Speed and Accuracy With Names

Directions for Drills 13 through 17

A word or name is presented in Column 1. This word is not always a real one. Look at it once and then compare it to the words in Column 2. As your eyes sweep along these words, pick out the ones that are *exactly* the same as the one in Column 1. In the answer column, jot down the number of times you saw the original word repeated.

Example

Column 1	Column 2	Answers
heater	heaten heated heater beater heater heated	2

Do the following drills. The answer column has a space for you to repeat each drill three times. (Cover the column of answers you have already done so they do not influence you.) Keep a record in the space at the bottom of the answer column of the time (in seconds) and the number of correct answers. The object is to build required speed and accuracy. Do at least one drill a day. The answers to these drills are on page 112. Mark your progress on the Drill Record Chart on page 441.

━━━━━━━━━━━━━ **Drill 13** ━━━━━━━━━━━━━

			Answers		
Column 1	Column 2	Trials	3	2	1
1. Fishkill	Fishkill Dishkill Fisskill Fishkill Fishkill				
2. Ankava	Ankava Ankara Ankaqe Ankare Ankara Emkara Ankara				
3. Ellville	Ellvile Ellvalle Elville Ellview Elville Ellville				
4. Shepherd	Shepherd Shepherd Sheepherd Shepard Shepherd Shephard				
5. Seminary	Seminary Seminary Suminary Seminary Seminary				
6. Wallaby	Wallaby Wallbye Wallabey Wallaby Wallaby Wallaby				
7. Palmtry	Palmtree Palmitry Palmtry Palmtrey Palmtry Palmtry				
8. Overview	Overview Ovarview Ovarview Overville				
9. Lansdale	Lawnsdale Lansdale Landale Landsdale Lamdale				
10. Rottal	Rottal Rottel Rottal Rottel Rattal Rattle				
		Number Right			
		Time			

Drill 14

Column 1	Column 2	Trials	3	2	1
1. Acom	Acor Acom Acorn Acern Acem Acom				
2. Gardiner	Garpiner Gordoner Gardiner Gardinier Guardiner				
3. Milltown	Hilltown Miltown Millton Milltown Milldown				
4. Baxton	Baxten Boxton Baxton Baxtown Bixtown				
5. Quail	Quail Quill Kaill Quail Quail				
6. Marie	Marri Marry Mary Marei Mazie				
7. York	Yark York York Cork Yort				
8. Hardon	Hardon Hardly Mardon Hordon Harrton				
9. Polrey	Poulrey Paltry Porley Pulrey Polrey				
10. Dalland	Dalland Palland Dallawn Halland Dalland				

Number Right
Time

Drill 15

Column 1	Column 2	Trials	3	2	1
1. Connover	Connhaver Connover Commoner Connover Comnover				
2. Keswick	Kesvick Kaswick Keswick Koswick Keswwick				
3. Guerad	Gerard Gelard Geminar Guerad Jerrard				
4. Bumpers	Bumpers Bampers Pumpers Bowpers Bompers				
5. Lockridge	Lockruage Lockridge Lockridge Lockridge Leckridge				
6. Ronde	Romde Round Ronde Rondie Ronde Ronque				
7. Foulle	Fulle Foull Fully Foule Foulle Foully				
8. Fairfield	Fairview Firefield Fairfield Fairchild Fairfiel				
9. Winston	Vinston Wonston Minston Wintam Winstan				
10. Jemma	Jemma Jema Jenna Jamma Emma Jomma				

Number Right
Time

Drill 16

Column 1	Column 2	Trials	3	2	1
1. Angor	Anger Angor Anchor Angor Ankor Emgor Angor				
2. Restown	Reston Creston Reston Restown Reston Restown				
3. Calvin	Calvan Clavin Calvin Colvin Calwin Callin				
4. Tren	Tren Trend Ternd Tenn Tend Tren				
5. Vladek	Valdek Waldek Vlodek Vladek Valdek Vladeck				
6. Easton	Eston Easton Eastown Eastern Eeston Weston				
7. Wohlheim	Wahlheim Wohlham Wohlheim Valheim Wohlheim				
8. Mosley	Nosley Moslee Moslea Mosley Moseley				
9. Kile	Kile Kale Kill Kull Kile Kale Kile				
10. Glover	Glower Golver Grover Grower Glover Golver				

Number Right
Time

Drill 17

Column 1	Column 2	Trials	3	2	1
		Answers			
1. Hobart	Habart Hobard Habort Hobart Habort Hobart Habart				
2. Mainly	Mainley Mainly Manley Mairly Manly Mainly				
3. Pinelawn	Pinalawn Pinlawn Pinelaun Pineland				
4. Wood	Wood Wode Wood Wood Mood Woode				
5. Purton	Purtem Purdom Pumtom Partom Purdam				
6. Dumont	Dumont Dumomt Dumount Dummon Dumuumt Dumont				
7. Clover	Clover Claver Clovar Glover Clever				
8. Dunville	Duval Dunville Deville Duville Duvalle				
9. Logan	Logan Logan Locan Logan Locan Logam				
10. Mounte	Momte Montey Mounty Monte Mounte Mounty				
	Number Right				
	Time				

Developing Speed and Accuracy With Numbers

Directions for Drills 18 through 21

A number is printed in Column 1. Look at it once and then compare it to the numbers in Column 2. As your eyes sweep along these numbers pick out the ones that are *exactly* the same as the one in Column 1. In the answer column jot down the number of times you saw the original number repeated.

Example

Column 1	Column 2	Answers
11240	11240 12140 12104 11240 11240 21240 11204	3

Do the four drills on these pages. The answer column has a space for you to repeat each drill three times. (Cover the column of answers you have already done so they do not influence you.) Keep a record in the space at the bottom of the answer column of the time (in seconds) and the number of correct answers. The object is speed and accuracy. Do one drill a day. See page 112 for the answers.

Drill 18

Column 1	Column 2	Trials	3	2	1
		Answers			
1. 651	651 561 651 615 156 516 651 651				
2. 938	389 983 938 398 893 938 938 983				
3. 449	449 494 494 944 449 449 944 494				
4. 890	809 908 890 809 980 980 890 908				
5. 637	637 376 623 736 736 637 367 637				
6. 723	273 723 723 327 732 237 732 723				
7. 364	346 643 364 643 634 346 364 364				
8. 758	785 857 758 785 587 578 758 875				
9. 409	904 409 940 490 940 409 904 402				
10. 213	132 213 321 213 213 132 321 312				
	Number Right				
	Time				

Drill 19

Column 1	Column 2						Trials	3	2	1
1. 9601	9601 9016 6910 9601 6109 1960									
2. 2477	2747 2477 7427 2747 2477 7472									
3. 5308	7803 5308 8305 8530 3580 3508 5308									
4. 8119	8191 8911 8119 8119 9811 9118 1891									
5. 4047	4704 4047 4047 7440 7044 4047 4407									
6. 6238	6238 6328 6823 6238 6328 3862 2386									
7. 3879	8379 8793 3789 3879 3978 3789 3879									
8. 5234	2543 5342 5243 5234 4523 4235 5334									
9. 4261	4162 4621 4126 6241 6142 4261 4621									
10. 0542	0245 0524 5024 5420 0542 0254 0524									

Number Right
Time

Drill 20

Column 1	Column 2						Trials	3	2	1
1. 46342	46342 46324 46224 46342 46324 46342 43642									
2. 96114	96141 91614 96114 96141 96114									
3. 97423	79423 97432 97243 97433 97723 94732									
4. 59340	59304 59344 59840 95840 95340 95430									
5. 39045	30945 39044 39045 39054 39045 39044									
6. 42566	42566 42565 45266 46256 42666 42555									
7. 28683	28683 28688 28683 23683 23683 23688 28683									
8. 98337	97833 98373 98387 98337 68337 98333 98331									
9. 04567	04567 04568 04561 40516 4061 04576 04596									
10. 70634	70634 70634 70634 79634 70684 70674									

Number Right
Time

Drill 21

Column 1	Column 2						Trials	3	2	1
1. 50401	54010 50901 50401 50410 50410 50410 50140									
2. 28013	28031 82013 28113 28018 28310									
3. 90551	95051 90551 90515 90551 99551 90515 90551									
4. 52045	52045 52545 25452 50245 52095									
5. 75923	79523 75923 75923 75924 75932 75932									
6. 10458	14058 10458 10458 10485 10458 10458 10458 10458									
7. 11762	17162 11726 17162 11726 11762 11762									
8. 41097	41097 41097 40197 41097 41079 41094 41097									
9. 23819	32819 23819 28819 28819 23819 28819 28819									
10. 55710	57510 55710 55701 55701 55710 55107 55017 55017									

Number Right
Time

▬ USING THE EYE SPAN SELECTOR

Drills to Widen Your Eye Span

Directions for Drills 22–29

Here are several methods to increase eye span. All of them work, but for the sake of variety you may wish to alternate their use from day to day.

Method A: The Pyramid

Twenty-five addresses and parts of addresses are printed on separate lines on pages 97 and 98. They form a pyramid as the lines get successively wider toward the bottom of the page. Try to read each line with one fixation at its midpoint. The midpoint is indicated by a dot immediately above the line. Use your peripheral vision to make out the letters or numbers at the beginning and end of each line. Do not shift or slide your eyes. With practice you will be able to grasp (perceive) larger and larger pieces of each address. The width of each line is measured by the number of type units it includes: letters, numbers, and spaces in between. That number is printed near the right margin. Drill daily until you can span at least 15 units at one fixation. This span will enable you to check half of any address that you are likely to encounter on the test. Eventually, you can develop your eye span to take in a *long* address (22–25 type units) at one fixation.

Two full-scale drills are on the next two pages. Before you work on them, try this little drill. Do it before each of your practice sessions.

•
I
•
am
•
sure
•
to see
•
increases
•
in my span
•
if I practice
•
keeping my eyes
•
focused on the spot
•
at the middle of the line

Drill 22

	Type Units
Pl	2
840	3
Peal	4
11762	5
Dayton	6
Beagley	7
Old Town	8
Park St E	9
833 Cruger	10
136 Simpson	11
East Kantell	12
Morris Hts Pl	13
Caroline Dr SE	14
Copperburg Mass	15
13 West Broadway	16
Mauritania Centre	17
50 Eastern Parkway	18
7610 Lakeshore Terr	19
8130 Cold Spring Plz	20
Martin Luther King Rd	21
2940 Grand Concourse N	22
Springfield Gardens Ter	23
Calle De Las Vecinos Trl	24
625 Lake Charles LA 79701	25
Cambridge Springs PA 16043	26

Drill 23

	Type Units
46	2
NYC	3
Ohio	4
37142	5
Oak St	6
W Drive	7
276 Pear	8
El Centro	9
Paducah KY	10
394 E Apple	11
10 Orange Dr	12
Beaverkill NY	13
1004 Pitkim Av	14
795 N Jefferson	15
2 Brentwood Lane	16
Creelling Av W VA	17
98 S 132 Dr Joliet	18
4 Haring Zemba Kans	19
West Philadelphia PA	20
Jameville Calif 96114	21
5504 Caroline St Miami	22
Small Point Maine 04567	23
East Falmouth Mass 02536	24
158 St Massapequa Park NY	25

Method B: Using the Eye Span Selector

Two Eye Span Selectors are printed on the detachable page at the back of the book. These Selectors have been designed to help you gradually develop a greater eye span. Together, the Selectors have 15 slot windows ranging in size from 4 to 32 type units. The greater the number of type units, the wider the eye span you will need to see them all at one fixation. The middle slot on Selector II, which is 32 type units wide, enables you to see even the longest address at one glance. Use the Selectors to check the address pairs in Drills 24 through 29.

How to Use the Eye Span Selector in the Following Drills

1. Detach the page at the back of the book containing both Selectors. Next, cut around the perimeter of each in order to separate Selector I and Selector II. Now, cut out each blackened slot window.

2. Select a slot window that just about matches your present eye span, or is even a trifle wider.

3. Place the window over the first address line so that the beginning of the address and the left edge of the slot line up.

4. You should now see part of the address framed in the slot. Notice that a small arrow indicates the middle of the slot.

5. Quickly scan the part of the address you see. Use your peripheral vision to see the beginning and ending letters or numbers. Remember: your task is to compare whatever you see with the line below.

6. Make the comparison of the address either by (a) moving the Selector back and forth from the top line to the one below until you have scanned the entire address, or (b) moving the Selector horizontally along each part of the entire address and then checking what you saw against each part of the line below.

7. In either case, write in your answer choice, A (alike) or D (different), in the spaces available. (Cover the column of answers you have already completed so that they do not influence you on your second and third trials.)

8. If you wish, you may use the "guidelines" scribed along the side, top, and bottom edges of the Selectors. The space between each pair of lines corresponds exactly in width to the slot adjoining it. The center of each width is indicated by an arrow. The "guidelines" may be used for exactly the same purpose as the window slots. Which method you use is strictly a matter of preference. Incidentally, the Selectors may be used for practice when you are reading *any* printed matter—your favorite newspaper, magazine, or book.

9. The important thing is to keep drilling until you've mastered a certain width. Then move on to the next larger size. Keep increasing the size of the slots until you reach one that brings you consistently good results. You will, therefore, progress from Selector I to Selector II.

10. Do away with the Selector as soon as you can. It is only a tool designed to help develop new habits. At every opportunity drill for awhile *without* it. Soon, you will find your new skills are a natural part of the way you read.

Drill 24

To complete this exercise, follow the directions for using the Eye Span Selector on the detachable page at the back of the book.

		Answers		
	Trials	3	2	1
1. 5100 E Madeline St 5100 E Madeline St				
2. Gaithersburg MD 20879 Gaithersburg MD 20879				
3. 4001 Virginia Ave 4010 Virginia Ave				
4. 2104 Illinois Ave 2014 Illinois Ave				
5. 1899 7 Mile Rd W 1899 7 Mile Rd E				
6. 5713 Eastlawn St 5713 Eastland St				
7. 16473 Fairfield St 16473 Fiarfield St				
8. 7465 Navarro Pl 7465 Nauarro Pl				
9. 4817 W Yupon St 4817 W Yupon St				
10. 4010 Saint Charles Rd 4010 Saint Charles Ln				
11. 2908 Jane Rd 2908 Janet Rd				
12. 6453 Twin Hill Blvd 6543 Twin Hill Blvd				
13. 841 Quebec Pl 841 Quebec Pl				
14. 5927 Carnahan St 5927 Caravan St				
15. 12 James Ave S 12 James Ave S				
16. 5201 North Riverview Ln 5201 North Riverview Ln				
17. 7619 Dancaster Rd SW 7619 Dancaster Rd SE				
18. 2015 King Oak Ter 2015 Kings Oak Ter				
19. 17046 U.S. Highway 60 17046 U.S. Highway 60				
20. Lowell MA 01850 Lowell MO 01850				
	Number Right			
	Time			

Drill 25

To complete this exercise, follow the directions for using the Eye Span Selector on the detachable page at the back of the book.

Answers

Trials	3	2	1
1. Dagsbord DE Dagsburg DE			
2. Shreveport LA 71129 Shreveport LA 71129			
3. 1117 N Marvine St 1117 N Marvine St			
4. 4754 All Spice St 4574 All Spice St			
5. 431 Gansevoort Rd 431 Gannsevoort Rd			
6. 7196 E Leighton Dr 7196 W Leighton Dr			
7. 32 Lochloy Dr 32 Lochley Dr			
8. Blakeslee Ct Blakeslee Ct			
9. Hopkins MN 55343 Hopkins MN 55348			
10. 4334 Rockrose Pl 4334 Rockroll Pl			
11. 6230 Pillsbury Ave 6230 Pillsbury Blvd			
12. 1011 Mavelle Ln 1011 Mabelle Ln			
13. Viewcrest Terr S Viewcroft Terr S			
14. Kansas City MO 63303 Kansas City MO 63303			
15. 426 W 148 St 426 E 148 St			
16. 5674 Encinitas Ave S 5674 Encanitas Ave S			
17. 2914 Woodmasten Pl SW 2914 Woodmaster Pl SW			
18. Rickard Rd NE Richard Rd NE			
19. 5091 E Cottoncreek Path 5019 E Cottoncreek Path			
20. Briarwood GA Briarwood GA			
Number Right			
Time			

Drill 26

To complete this exercise, follow the directions for using the Eye Span Selector on the detachable page at the back of the book.

		Answers		
	Trials	**3**	**2**	**1**
1. 3786 N Dunton Ave 3786 N Dunton Ave				
2. 1702 S Merrick Ave 1702 S Herrick Ave				
3. Tennessee SC Tennessee NC				
4. 13135 Laburnum Ave 13375 Laburnum Ave				
5. 20 E 97 St 20 E 97 St				
6. 1604 S Chadbourne Dr 1604 W Chadbourne Dr				
7. Costa Mesa CA 92628 Costa Mesa CA 92628				
8. 106 Chestnut Hill Ave 106 Chestnut Hill Ter				
9. 606 N 55 St 606 N 65 St				
10. 2981 Charleston Pkwy N 2981 Charleston Path N				
11. 819 East Clark Pl 819 East Clark Pl				
12. Vancleve KY 41385 Vancleve KY 51385				
13. 53 Dean St SW 53 Dean St NW				
14. 100 W 304 St 100 W 340 St				
15. Pomonok NY 11275 Pomonok NY 11275				
16. 6005 Las Animas Way 6005 Las Animals Way				
17. 340 SE Park Plz 340 NE Park Plz				
18. 7843 Yukon Cir 7843 Yukon Ter				
19. 892 NE Holly Beach Blvd 892 NE Holly Beach Blvd				
20. 447 Apostolic Sq 447 Apostolic Sq				
Number Right				
Time				

Drill 27

To complete this exercise, follow the directions for using the Eye Span Selector on the detachable page at the back of the book.

Trials	3	2	1
1. 6789 Rutherglen Ave S 6798 Rutherglen Ave S			
2. 7307 Sunnymeade Path 7037 Synnymeade Path			
3. 2781 E Rapadan Ln 2781 E Ramadan Ln			
4. 3898 N 14th Ave 3898 N 14th Ave			
5. Huntsville AL 35805 Huntsville AR 35805			
6. 3803 W Abercorn St 3803 W Abercorn St			
7. 4947 Braxfield Dr NE 4947 Braxfield Dr NE			
8. 6412 N Parkchester Blvd 6419 N Parkchester Blvd			
9. 1681 Quincy Ct S 1681 Quince Ct S			
10. 17094 Highway North Ext 17094 Highway North Ext			
11. Jackson MI 49203 Jackson ME 49203			
12. 1514 Grand Gorge Pkwy 1514 Grand Groge Pkwy			
13. 252 S Andrea Rd 252 S Angrea Rd			
14. 7603 S Garahime Ave 7603 S Garaheim Ave			
15. 8124 E Hickory Dr 8124 E Hickory Dr			
16. Camino CA 95709 Camina CA 95709			
17. 2504 S 114th Pl 2504 S 114th Pl			
18. 5288 Riverview Walk SW 5288 Riverview Walk SW			
19. 50 Buena Vista Trailer Ct 50 Buena Vista Trailer Ct			
20. Jeffersonville NY 12748 Jeffersonville NY 12747			
Number Right			
Time			

Answers

Drill 28

To complete this exercise, follow the directions for using the Eye Span Selector on the detachable page at the back of the book.

	Answers		
Trials	3	2	1
1. 9664 W Oahu Ave 9664 W Oahu Ave			
2. 7793 S Glastonbury Ave 7793 S Glastonbury Ave			
3. Burbank CA 91505 Burbank CO 91505			
4. 6167 E 217th Ter 6167 E 216th Ter			
5. 1514 Sewickley Way SE 1514 Sweickley Way SE			
6. 29418 W Main St 29418 W Main St			
7. 3712 E Jewell Ave 3712 E Jewett Ave			
8. 6036 W Yolande St 6036 W Yolande Ct			
9. Scottsdale AZ 85257 Scottsdale AZ 85257			
10. Rhoadesville VA 22542 Rhoadesville VA 22542			
11. 7453 E Athlone Ave 7453 E Athbone Ave			
12. 3816 McCollough Ct NW 3816 McCullough Ct NW			
13. Marengo IN 47140 Marango IN 47140			
14. 1614 S 161st Pl 1614 S 161st Pl			
15. 1705 Forest Isle Ct W 1705 Forest Isle Ct W			
16. 8067 N Trimbach Ln 8067 N Trimback Ln			
17. 4134 Nottingham Park Pl 4143 Nottingham Park Pl			
18. Woodbridge VA Woodridge VA			
19. 6491 S Burntwood Cir 6491 N Burntwood Cir			
20. 4849 Summitville View Walk 4849 Summitville View Walk			
Number Right			
Time			

Drill 29

To complete this exercise, follow the directions for using the Eye Span Selector on the detachable page at the back of the book.

		Answers	
Trials	**3**	**2**	**1**
1. 4198 109th Ave NE 4198 109th Ave NE			
2. 5771 S Newell St 5771 S Nevell St			
3. Glendale AZ 85304 Glendale AZ 85304			
4. 7061 S 20th Cir 7061 S 20th Ct			
5. 1352 Johanna Ave SW 1352 Johanna Ave SE			
6. 20739 Back River Neck Rd 20739 Back River Neck Rd			
7. 86 Fair Meadows Pl 86 Fair Meadows Pl			
8. 1440 W Platten Dr 1440 W Platte Dr			
9. 282 McDuffie Ln S 282 MacDuffie Ln S			
10. 5753 Oakcrest Pl 5735 Oakcrest Pl			
11. 9367 E Pohick Ln 9367 E Potick Ln			
12. 135 San Carlos Ct 135 San Carlas Ct			
13. 2031 Spotted Jack Loop 2031 Spotted Jack Loop			
14. 8043 Shasta Blvd S 8043 Shanta Blvd S			
15. Port Neches TX 77651 Port Neches TX 77651			
16. 6457 N Penelope Cir 6457 N Penelope Cir			
17. 89 S Mescolero Dr 89 S Mescolera Dr			
18. 4172 E Compere Blvd 4171 E Compere Blvd			
19. 100 La Salle Ridge Rd 100 La Salle Ridge Rd			
20. 5307 W 104th St 5307 W 104th St			
Number Right			
Time			

Drills to Prevent Regression

Drills 30 and 31

There are several methods to use to help break yourself of the habit of rereading an address.

1. Use the top edge of the Eye Span Selector or of any small index card to block off each line after you have checked it. In that way you won't be able to look back even if you want to. Keep moving the card down the page, line by line, as rapidly as you can. This method may be used with any of the practice tests or drills in this book.

2. You may find that you are looking back at *parts* of an address instead of moving ahead to scan the rest of the line. The Eye Span Selector has a simple, yet effective design feature to help overcome that practice. Use it to check the addresses on the next drills. (See the figures below and on the next page on "Using the Selector for Regressions" and the instructions that follow.)

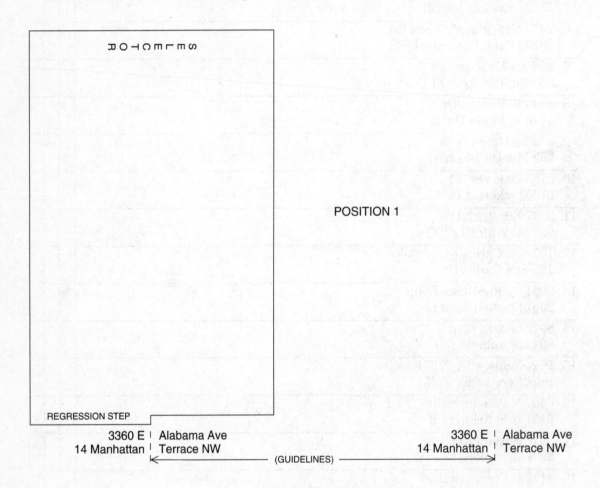

SELECTOR

POSITION 1

REGRESSION STEP

3360 E ¦ Alabama Ave
14 Manhattan ¦ Terrace NW
←——————— (GUIDELINES) ———————→

3360 E ¦ Alabama Ave
14 Manhattan ¦ Terrace NW

Using the Selector for Regressions

(position 2 on next page)

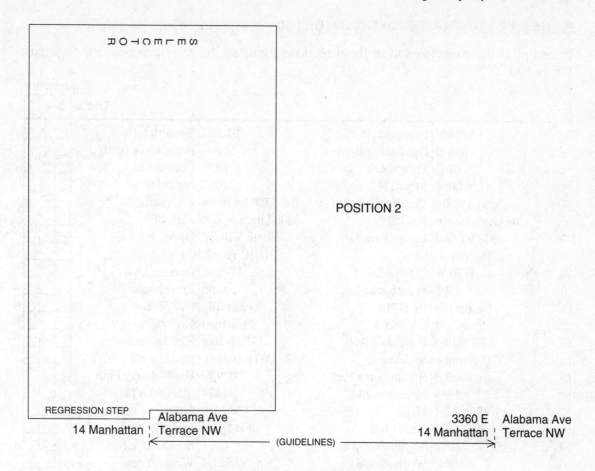

POSITION 2

SELECTOR

REGRESSION STEP

	Alabama Ave		3360 E	Alabama Ave
14 Manhattan	Terrace NW		14 Manhattan	Terrace NW

←———————————— (GUIDELINES) ————————————→

Using the Selector for Regressions

How to Use the Selector to Prevent Regression in the Following Drills

Assuming that you will be checking each address using two fixations, use the following procedure.

1. Hold the Selector *above the first line of addresses* on the page. Line up the edge of the little "STEP" with the dotted guide line (see Position 1). Scan the left half of the address in Column 1. Compare it with the left half of the address in Column 2 while moving the Selector down one line to Position 2.

2. Scan the *remaining portion of the address* in Column 1 and compare it to the remaining portion in Column 2. Now write your answer as to whether the items are A (alike) or D (different).

3. The Selector is now in the correct position for you to begin checking the *next line*. Now repeat steps 1 and 2 above.

Drill 30

To complete this exercise, follow the directions for using the Eye Span Selector on pages 106 and 107.

			Answers		
		Trials	**3**	**2**	**1**
1.	9194 N Giegerich Pl	9194 S Giegerich Pl			
2.	398 N Banklicker Blvd	398 N Banklicker Blvd			
3.	61 E Phoenix St	61 E Phoenix St			
4.	2003 Algard St	2003 Algard St			
5.	8325 La Belle Cherie St	8325 La Belle Chevrie St			
6.	3305 Lindamoore Path SW	3305 Lindamoore Path SE			
7.	4948 Willard Haven Park Dr	4948 Willard Haven Park Dr			
8.	5102 Yukoh Ct S	5012 Yukoh Ct S			
9.	1770 W Queens Ln	1770 W Queens Ln			
10.	1308 Fronthenac Ln	1308 Fronthenac St			
11.	Evansville IN 47715	Evansville IN 87715			
12.	Stratford CA 93266	Stratford CA 93266			
13.	7767 S Bay Highlands Ave	7767 S Bay Highlands Ave			
14.	9711 Avenue St. John St	9911 Avenue St. John St			
15.	2020 E Huckleberry Path	2020 W Huckleberry Path			
16.	1485 Macombs Pl	1484 Macombs Pl			
17.	Whiteford MD	Whitford MD			
18.	804 Lynis Falls Blvd	804 Lynis Falls Path			
19.	5921 Southlawn Ave	5921 Southdawn Ave			
20.	6882 E Wyckoff Ave	6882 E Wyckoff Ave			
21.	6300 S F Dr	6300 S P Dr			
22.	431 E Macalaster St	431 N Macalaster St			
23.	2323 Williamette Blvd SW	2323 Williamette Blvd SW			
24.	1131 University Mew Street	1131 University Mew Street			
25.	2353 S Baxter St	2353 S Baxter St			
26.	Palatka FL 32077	Palatka FL 32707			
27.	8101 E Stafford Pl	8101 E Stanford Pl			
28.	22003 N Chadwick St	22003 N Chadwick St			
29.	601 D St	601 P St			
30.	Everett PA 15537	Everett PA 15537			
31.	19031 S Saint Quen St	19031 W Saint Quen St			
32.	14344 McDevitt St NW	14344 McDevitt Dr NW			
33.	101 N Union St	101 N Union St			
34.	3707 Marlborough St	3707 Marlborough St			
35.	Otterbien OH 45036	Otterbien OK 45036			
36.	685 W Guacmayo Ct	685 E Guacmayo Ct			
37.	100 E Krewstown Rd	100 E Krewstown Rd			
38.	291 Huff Blvd	291 Haff Blvd			
39.	70139 Zimple Aly	70139 Zimple Aly			
40.	3666 Tecolote Rd NE	3666 Tecoloti Rd NE			
41.	43 E Lipscomb Rd	43 S Lipscomb Rd			
42.	20 East Hampton Blvd	20 East Hampton Blvd			
43.	4791 W Chittenden Pl	4791 W Chittenden Pl			
44.	Oriskanny VA	Oriskanny MA			

					Trials 3 2 1
45.	1905 W	Arrowwood Cir	1905 W	Arrowwood Ter	
46.	364 Villa	Rose Ln	364 Villa	Rose Ln	
47.	1221	27 St	1221	29 St	
48.	Reading, MI	49274	Reading, MN	49274	
49.	2771	Crescent Pl E	2771	Crescent Rd E	
50.	7162 SW	Reckinger Ave	7162 SW	Reckinger Ave	
51.	404	Jacaranda Ct	404	Jacarandi Ct	
52.	191	Picayune Pl	191	Picayune Pl	
53.	Gloucester	VA 23061	Gloucester	VA 23061	
54.	3992 S	Bass Creek Ave	3992 S	Boss Creek Ave	
55.	283 West	Seven Ridge Rd	283 West	Seven Ridge Rd	
56.	1823 Brandick	Cir S	1832 Brandick	Cir S	
57.	2023 W	Ferrare Cir	2023 W	Ferrare Cir	
58.	1201	Barton St	1201	Bartow St	
59.	Longmire	WA	Longmire	VA	
60.	1398 W	241 Ave	1398 W	214 Ave	

Number Right
Time

Drill 31

To complete this exercise, follow the directions for using the Eye Span Selector on pages 106 and 107.

Answers

					Trials	3	2	1
1.	1913 Via	Las Cumbres	1913 Via	Las Combres				
2.	3731	Temescal Ter	3731	Tenescal Ter				
3.	8108	Rutland Dr	8108	Rutland Dr				
4.	6761	Powhattan Ln	6761	Powhattan Ln				
5.	324 S	Miramar St	324 S	Mirimar St				
6.	1534 S	112 Pl	1534 E	112 Pl				
7.	9413 S	Blazewood Pl	9413 S	Blakewood Pl				
8.	Holladay	Vt 84117	Holliday	Vt 84117				
9.	200 E	Angelucci Way	200 E	Andelucci Way				
10.	734 Quantico	Ave S	734 Quantico	Ave S				
11.	7748 Quesada	Path S	7748 Quesada	Path S				
12.	7008 Yuerba	Buena Rd	7008 Yuerba	Buena Rd				
13.	6281 Point	Loma Ct NE	6281 Point	Loma Ct NE				
14.	Arlington Heights	IL 60004	Arlington Heights	IL 60004				
15.	3650	Baccus Ct	3650	Baccus Ct				
16.	5936	Frobisher Cir	5936	Frobisher Cir				
17.	2870 Stockton	Pl E	2870 Stockton	Pl E				
18.	4473	Viewbridge Pl	4473	Viewridge Pl				
19.	17 Kandace	Villa Ln	17 Kandace	Villa Pl				
20.	West Ossipee	NH 03890	West Ossipee	NH 03890				
21.	17981	Ashford Ave	17931	Ashford Ave				
22.	647 West	Portal St	647 West	Portol St				
23.	7200 Hempstead	Cir S	7200 Hempstead	Cir S				
24.	8483	Isleta Ave	8483	Isleta Cir				

25.	Vestaburg	PA 15368	Vestaburg	PA 15368					
26.	6011 N	Gabarda Rd	6011 S	Gabarda Rd					
27.	2587 Leicester	Way NW	2587 Leicester	Way SW					
28.	17045 Kelloch	Ave NE	17405 Kelloch	Ave NE					
29.	1617 Alta	Vista Way	1617 Alta	Vista Way					
30.	4025	Urbano Dr	4025	Urbano Dr					
31.	Kenosha	WI 53142	Kenosha	WI 53132					
32.	9724 Junipero	Serra Blvd	9724 Jupitero	Serra Blvd					
33.	8293 N	Idora Ave	8293 N	Idopa Ave					
34.	8039 S	Revelstoke Ter	8039 S	Bevelstore Ter					
35.	5732 O'Farrell	St SE	5732 O'Farrell	St SE					
36.	7012 W	Hamerton Ave	7012 W	Hammerton Ave					
37.	4712 Fratessa	Ct S	4712 Fratessa	Ct S					
38.	2751	Triton Blvd	2751	Triton Blvd					
39.	Sturdivant	MO 64782	Sturdivant	MO 63782					
40.	9658 South	Van Ness Ave	9658 South	Van Ness Ave					
41.	Alvaton	KY 42122	Alvaton	KS 42122					
42.	481 Bernal	Heights Blvd	481 Bernal	Heights Blvd					
43.	Cecilton	MD 21913	Cecilton	MD 21913					
44.	Wynantkill	NY 12198	Wynantrill	NY 12198					
45.	5908 W	Wayland Ave	5908 W	Wayland Ave					
46.	4360 New	Salem Ter	4360 New	Salem Ter					
47.	4289	Cale Nobleza	4289	Cale Nobleza					
48.	5527	El Mirasol	5572 El	Mirasol Pl					
49.	6349 Grand	View Ter	6349 Grand	View Trl					
50.	9112	Jocatal St	9112	Jocatal St					
51.	Yacima	WA 98902	Yakima	WA 98902					
52.	3712 Upshur	St W	3712 Upshur	St E					
53.	3597	Mariposa St	3597	Mariposo St					
54.	5051	Orleck Pl	5015	Orleck Pl					
55.	2580 W	234 Dr	2580 W	234 Dr					
56.	4745 Nob	Hill Cir	4745 Knob	Hill Cir					
57.	9401	Sabina Rd	9401	Sabrina Rd					
58.	85 Zircon	Ln SW	85 Zircon	Ln SW					
59.	5053	Zagala Ln	5053	Zacala Ln					
60.	3089 E	Codman Pl	3089 E	Cadman Pl					

Number Right

Time

Miscellaneous Drills

There are opportunities all around you for practicing address checking skills. When walking down the street, quickly scan license plates, street signs, and posters. Look away and attempt to repeat them. Try to read the quickly moving screen credits shown on television and in the movies. Practice using the Eye Span Selector or index card on the books, newspapers, and magazines you normally read. Use wider and wider slots to increase your eye span.

Also, have a friend help you play the following game. Your friend should checkmark, at random, a few names, telephone numbers, or addresses on different pages of an old phone book or catalog, making notes of the page numbers. You are to turn to each of these pages, scan the checkmarked item as fast as you can, and jot it down immediately. Then compare it with the book to see how accurate you are.

Or, have someone (or do it yourself) prepare 3" × 5" flash cards (see page 91), with the same address on either side. Make some exactly the same—Ⓐ, and others different—Ⓓ. After you have a stack of 20 or more cards, shuffle them and flash each side of each card before your eyes as quickly as you can. See how well you pick out the Ⓐ's and Ⓓ's.

The possibilities for practice are endless. Just use your imagination.

ANSWER KEY FOR DRILLS

Drills 1–11, not applicable

Drill 12, page 92

4 *b*'s
6 *d*'s

Drill 13, page 92

| 1. 3 | 2. 1 | 3. 1 | 4. 3 | 5. 4 | 6. 4 | 7. 3 | 8. 1 | 9. 1 | 10. 2 |

Drill 14, page 93

| 1. 2 | 2. 1 | 3. 1 | 4. 1 | 5. 3 | 6. 0 | 7. 2 | 8. 1 | 9. 1 | 10. 2 |

Drill 15, page 93

| 1. 2 | 2. 1 | 3. 1 | 4. 1 | 5. 3 | 6. 2 | 7. 1 | 8. 1 | 9. 0 | 10. 1 |

Drill 16, page 93

| 1. 3 | 2. 2 | 3. 1 | 4. 2 | 5. 2 | 6. 1 | 7. 2 | 8. 1 | 9. 3 | 10. 1 |

Drill 17, page 94

| 1. 2 | 2. 2 | 3. 0 | 4. 3 | 5. 0 | 6. 2 | 7. 1 | 8. 1 | 9. 3 | 10. 1 |

Drill 18, page 94

| 1. 4 | 2. 3 | 3. 3 | 4. 2 | 5. 3 | 6. 3 | 7. 3 | 8. 2 | 9. 2 | 10. 3 |

Drill 19, page 95

| 1. 2 | 2. 2 | 3. 2 | 4. 2 | 5. 3 | 6. 2 | 7. 2 | 8. 1 | 9. 1 | 10. 1 |

Drill 20, page 95

| 1. 3 | 2. 2 | 3. 0 | 4. 0 | 5. 2 | 6. 1 | 7. 3 | 8. 1 | 9. 1 | 10. 3 |

Drill 21, page 95

| 1. 1 | 2. 0 | 3. 3 | 4. 1 | 5. 2 | 6. 6 | 7. 2 | 8. 4 | 9. 2 | 10. 2 |

Drills 22–23, not applicable

Drill 24, page 100

| 1. A | 3. D | 5. D | 7. D | 9. A | 11. D | 13. A | 15. A | 17. D | 19. A |
| 2. A | 4. D | 6. D | 8. D | 10. D | 12. D | 14. D | 16. A | 18. D | 20. D |

Drill 25, page 101

| 1. D | 3. A | 5. D | 7. D | 9. D | 11. D | 13. D | 15. D | 17. D | 19. D |
| 2. A | 4. D | 6. D | 8. A | 10. D | 12. D | 14. A | 16. D | 18. D | 20. A |

Drill 26, page 102

| 1. A | 3. D | 5. A | 7. A | 9. D | 11. A | 13. D | 15. A | 17. D | 19. A |
| 2. D | 4. D | 6. D | 8. D | 10. D | 12. D | 14. D | 16. D | 18. D | 20. A |

Drill 27, page 103

| 1. D | 3. D | 5. D | 7. A | 9. D | 11. D | 13. D | 15. A | 17. A | 19. A |
| 2. D | 4. A | 6. A | 8. D | 10. A | 12. D | 14. D | 16. D | 18. A | 20. D |

Drill 28, page 104

| 1. A | 3. D | 5. D | 7. D | 9. A | 11. D | 13. D | 15. A | 17. D | 19. D |
| 2. A | 4. D | 6. A | 8. D | 10. A | 12. D | 14. A | 16. D | 18. D | 20. A |

Drill 29, page 105

| 1. A | 3. A | 5. D | 7. A | 9. D | 11. D | 13. A | 15. A | 17. D | 19. A |
| 2. D | 4. D | 6. A | 8. D | 10. D | 12. D | 14. D | 16. A | 18. D | 20. A |

Drill 30, page 108

1. D	7. A	13. A	19. D	25. A	31. D	37. A	43. A	49. D	55. A
2. A	8. D	14. D	20. A	26. D	32. D	38. D	44. D	50. A	56. D
3. A	9. A	15. D	21. D	27. D	33. D	39. A	45. D	51. D	57. A
4. A	10. D	16. D	22. D	28. A	34. A	40. D	46. A	52. A	58. D
5. D	11. D	17. D	23. A	29. D	35. D	41. D	47. D	53. A	59. D
6. D	12. A	18. D	24. A	30. A	36. D	42. A	48. D	54. D	60. D

Drill 31, pages 109 and 110

1. D	7. D	13. A	19. D	25. A	31. D	37. A	43. A	49. D	55. A
2. D	8. D	14. A	20. A	26. D	32. D	38. A	44. D	50. A	56. D
3. A	9. D	15. A	21. D	27. D	33. D	39. D	45. A	51. D	57. D
4. A	10. A	16. A	22. D	28. D	34. D	40. A	46. A	52. D	58. A
5. D	11. A	17. A	23. A	29. A	35. A	41. D	47. A	53. D	59. D
6. D	12. A	18. D	24. D	30. A	36. D	42. A	48. D	54. D	60. D

Chapter 5

Memory for *Direct* (Name) Addresses—How to Improve Your Score

◼ TEST STRATEGY

You have seen how important good test strategy is in taking the Address Checking part of the Test 460/470. You will be even more impressed by what an effective strategy can mean to your score on the Memory for Addresses part. Three major suggestions should be considered.

Use Some Practice Time for Studying

On the actual test, after you have completed Part A, you will be given a preliminary period of time to review the test directions for Part B and to do some sample questions. The purpose is to make certain that the test takers understand what the exam is all about—what is wanted, and where and how the answers should be indicated. *But you already know all of that.* The Diagnostic Practice Test you took used the same format that has appeared on prior examinations. Furthermore, if there should be any change in the type of question or in the format, you will know about it ahead of time. (All test candidates receive, before the test, a description of the test and several sample questions.) So why spend time rereading the same directions and doing samples? *Instead, use this time to memorize the addresses in the boxes.*

   After reviewing the directions and the pre-test sample questions (see p. 42), you will be given several trial tests, preceded by brief study periods. On some of these tests you must answer the questions from memory. But for the other trial tests, the boxes with the addresses will be in view as you answer the questions. You may then proceed to answer the questions from memory in the regular way. On the other hand, you may decide to spend the allotted time *studying* the addresses in the boxes instead. It is believed, for most people, time is better spent studying the boxes rather than answering the pre-test sample questions or the questions on List 1 and List 2. It is true that there is a benefit in answering the warm-up questions by memory and then discovering what you don't know. On the other hand, comparatively little *new* learning takes place. The majority of students report far better results by spending almost all the available time studying and remembering the addresses.

   In the past, the time *designated* for study totaled 8 minutes. A test candidate who followed the suggestions above and took advantage of all the time *available* for study might easily have doubled that amount. In this book, an effort has been made to be conservative by estimating that a total of 14 minutes will be available for study. Rather than being overly optimistic, it is better to be trained and ready to meet stricter standards. In any case, you will have a distinct advantage over your competitors! (See pages 224 to 225 for a step-by-step approach to handling the memory part of the exam.)

Eliminate the Last Box

If you master the memory techniques explained in the following pages, you won't need to employ this second strategy. It is believed that, with practice, you will be able to remember all 25 items. But if you have difficulty, consider skipping Box E either entirely or in part and concentrating on Boxes A, B, C, and D. *Then, when you take the test, you can mark Box E for any name or number that you don't recognize. And you'll be correct!*

Guess If You're Not Sure

What if you come across an address that you are not sure about? Should you guess? *The answer is YES.* Mathematically, even for a completely blind guess, you won't lose anything if you guess. Here's why. For each question, there are five choices, Box A, B, C, D, and E. Since one of these five has to be correct, you have one chance out of five (20 percent) of getting the correct answer, even if you guess. For example, if you took a test that had 100 questions and you guessed the answers to all of them, you would be likely to answer 20 correctly (20 percent of 100) and get the other 80 wrong. For *any* number of questions the odds are still the same. See how this fact affects your actual score. Assume you guessed the answers to five of the memory questions instead of leaving them blank. If you got only what the odds dictated, you would end up with one answer correct and four wrong.

Calculations:	Total Answered......	5
	Number right........	1
	Number wrong 4	
	$\frac{1}{4} \times 4$..............	-1
	YOUR SCORE = 1 − 1 =	0

In this case, you have not lost anything, but you have not gained anything either.

However, you won't be making a *completely* blind guess on most questions you are not sure of. More likely, you will have a glimmer of recognition and will be unsure as to which one of two or three boxes to choose. If you then guess at one of them, you are going to come out ahead in the long run. The odds are such that when you are guessing at one out of two or three choices, you will get enough questions right to more than make up for the ones you get wrong.

To summarize, you now know three vital test strategies. Decide how to use them after you have studied Chapters 5 and 6 and after you have gained some experience doing the practice tests.

IMPROVING YOUR MEMORY

Science has yet to discover exactly how the human brain works. It knows enough to tell us that the brain is an awesomely complex structure that makes the most advanced computer look crude. It is also known that it has enormous untapped potential. One commonly cited bit of knowledge has it that the average person uses only about 10 percent of his or her 30 billion brain cells. A person who could tap the unused powers of the mind might be able to accomplish wondrous things. Studies that have been made of individuals with just such extraordinary mental abilities bear out this supposition.

One famous case that was extensively documented is that of Mr. S. He was an obscure Russian who had a fantastic memory. He was able to memorize a list of 18 six-digit numbers in 3 minutes. He retained it so well that he could repeat the list in any order, even reciting each number in reverse! Amazingly, he was able to repeat these feats years later, even though he had not seen the list in the interim! Extraordinary displays of memory also are given by professional entertainers, the so-called memory experts who can recall the names and addresses of dozens of members of an audience they have never met before. In addition, you may have heard stories about famous generals, hostesses, and politicians who never forget a name or a place.

Intensive studies of people with "super memories" have helped psychologists understand how those with ordinary memories may improve them. The methods outlined below are based on such studies and on *demonstrated improvements* made by our students who have used these methods to prepare for the Postal Service exam.

The study plan that was used for these students will be followed now as you look at various memory techniques. First, the techniques applicable to remembering the names of "direct" (name) addresses will be reviewed. In the next chapter, techniques to remember "numbered" addresses will be studied. It is strongly recommended that you begin your memory improvement program with the *direct* addresses. Experience shows that the techniques for remembering direct addresses will bring you quick, encouraging results. The confidence you gain will help when you undertake the more difficult task of remembering numbered addresses.

TECHNIQUES FOR REMEMBERING DIRECT ADDRESSES

Association and Imagery

If you are like most people, you will find it easier to remember names than numbers because a name brings forth a meaningful association with something familiar. It may remind you of a place, a thing, or a word you know about. Even better, the address name may bring a vivid picture to mind. For example, take the word *ice*. As soon as you see or hear this word, you may form an association with the word *cream* or *snow*. You may also associate *ice* with ideas or feelings such as *cold* or *chilly*. In your mind's eye, the image of an *iceberg* or an *ice cube* may form without conscious effort.

When you see a name that carries a meaningful association and presents an image, the name will probably stick in your memory. Two key memorization techniques to use, therefore, are *association* and *imagery*. Here is an illustration of the power and practicality of these techniques applied to the Memory of Addresses portion of the Diagnostic Practice Test. (For the sake of clarity, only the direct addresses have been reproduced.)

A	B	C	D	E
Ceres Natoma	Cedar Foster	Niles Dexter	Cicero Pearl	Dehli Magnet

In Box A, *Ceres* looks and sounds like . . . sure, like *Cereal* or *Series*. You may also have associated Ceres with something out of a myth (Ceres happens to be the name of the ancient Roman goddess of agriculture). What about *Natoma?* It looks like the word *atom*. Remember what was discussed about associations and images? If you can form a single picture associating both names, they will stay in your memory even better. Can you picture a bowl of breakfast cereal (Ceres) with little atoms (Natoma) floating about in it? It may seem absurd, but in a way that's the point! Authorities on memory techniques say that the more vivid, colorful, and startling the image is, the better you'll remember it.

Nevertheless, you are not done yet. How about Box A? After all, on the test you are required to remember in which box each address belongs. A useful technique to employ now is to make up a little picture story to link either or both addresses to Box A. It can be weird or silly, as long as it helps to connect the box with the names. Let's assume, for example, that an *Apple* stands for *Box A*. Now the associations are complete. You have got a mental picture of little Apples (Box A) and Atoms (Natoma) floating in a bowl of Cereal (Ceres). You will never forget that.

What if you made a quick association between Ceres and Series? That brings to mind the World Series with its two opposing leagues, the *American* (Box *A*) and *National* (*Natoma*). **Remember,** the association you make does not have to fit and spell exactly right. As long as *you* make the connection, that's all that counts. You might even have imagined an *Ace* (Box *A*) pitching in the World Series (Ceres) for the *National* (*Natoma*) League. This image is vivid, and forms a good association among the two words and Box A. *You won't forget it on the test.*

Actually, Box A illustrates one of the more difficult associations you will have to make because the names Ceres and Natoma are offbeat. If you now feel confident of your ability to remember them, you will find remembering Box B even easier. Start associating the names in the box.

Cedar brings to mind . . . a tree, a storage chest, wood, shingles, and so on.

Foster brings to mind . . . a forest, a baby, the actress Jodie Foster, and so on.

That's it!

. . . see the Cedar (Cedar) tree standing in the Forest (Foster),

. . . see a Jodie Foster (Foster) baby, in her cradle, hanging from a Cedar (Cedar) tree.

How about the connection to *Box B?*

. . . Make the tree a *B*lue Cedar (which is a common type).

If you like, hang a hundred *B*ananas on it or a *B*eehive

. . . See Foster Baby *B*urping.

As you have seen, the *sound* and the *appearance* of words are especially helpful when you encounter address names such as Ceres and Natoma that do not yield good associations based on meaning.

Another technique also uses sound and appearance as aids in remembering address names in their boxes. You construct an artificial word starting with the box letter and add whatever parts of both address names you need to make the new word stick. To illustrate, for Box A you could have made "A-CER-NA." See it and sound it in your mind as one word: ACERNA. Similarly, the names in Box E could yield "E-DEH-MA" or EDEHMA. Each of these words has a pleasing, catchy lilt and would work very well to bring together, in one word, everything you need to remember. Try this method for Box D. Check on page 137 for an answer.

How about Box C? Now that you have a whole kit of memory tools at your disposal, you should have very little trouble remembering the names in Box C. Start making associations for the names in the box:

> *Niles brings to mind* . . . river, Cleopatra, Egypt.
>
> *Niles sounds like* . . . nails.
>
> *Dexter means* . . . on the right side, a boy's name.
>
> *Dexter sounds and looks like* . . . dexterity, dextrose (sugar), dexedrine.
>
> *Box C sounds like* . . . sea, see.

Undoubtedly, you may have your own associations that haven't been listed here. In any case, you now can quite readily put together some unforgettable picture-stories:

*C*leopatra (*Box C*) rowed her barge with *dexterity* (*Dexter*) down the *Nile*.

*C*leopatra ate a box of *dextrose* sugar candy (*Dexter*) while riding down the *Nile* to the *sea* (*Box C*)

Dexter said, My goodness, just *see* (*Box C*) how long your *nails* (*Niles*) are!

And so it goes. The possibilities for imagery and extended associations are great in Box C. Although everyone may use a slightly different approach, everyone *can* make helpful associations. Practice these techniques on the tests in this book, letting your imagination run free. Start now by trying your hand with the names in Boxes D and E.

The "Loci" Technique

Mr. S., the Russian with the fabulous memory, partially explained it by telling about a system of "places" he used. (*Loci* is a Greek word meaning "places.") He said that he remembered long lists of objects by mentally putting each object in a particular place that was familiar to him. By remembering the place, he could "see" the object. For example, if Mr. S. were given a list of objects to remember, such as a hat, cane, dog, and violin, he would assign each of them to a particular place in a certain scene.

A scene that he sometimes used was a street near his home. He knew every inch of it because he walked it daily. To remember the list of objects, he would merely imagine himself walking down the street. On his imaginary walk, he would place the *hat* on a lamp post, lean the *cane* against the side of a shop, see the *dog* near a tree across the road, and put the *violin* in a pawnshop window. He could recall each object by mentally retracing his path down the street. So, when he saw the tree, he would see the dog, too! Each of the other objects on his list was recalled in the same way.

Performers, politicians, students, and others from all walks of life have been using the loci system, or a variation of it, down through the ages. It will work for you, too, provided you do two things:

1. Decide on your personal systems of places, or loci. Each system will need at least five objects or features.

2. Become so familiar with your loci that you can immediately "see" every one of these places.

You might choose a street on the way to work, your shop or office, a room in your house. The objects can range from your kitchen shelf to your desk drawer. Make the scene as detailed as you wish. The more "places" it has in it, the more items you will be able to remember.

Using the Loci Technique on the Test

The system or scene that you set up needs to have only five places, each one corresponding to one of the five boxes—A, B, C, D, and E. For example, a good system to use is the layout of rooms in your home.

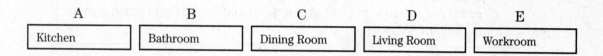

A	B	C	D	E
Kitchen	Bathroom	Dining Room	Living Room	Workroom

In your mind's eye you would be able to build the following pictures, using the boxes on page 117 as a basis.

```
┌──────────────────────────┐
│     BOX A—KITCHEN         │
│                          │
│  I'm sitting in my kitchen eating a │
│  bowl of Cereal (Ceres) with little │
│  Atoms (Natoma) floating in it.     │
└──────────────────────────┘
```

Note that you do not have to think of an association with Box A (such as Apple) because Box A is the kitchen.

```
┌──────────────────────────┐
│     BOX B—BATHROOM        │
│                          │
│  I'm giving my Foster baby a bath   │
│  and rubbing his Chest (Cedar)      │
│  with soap.                         │
└──────────────────────────┘
```

If you wish to enlarge your choice of places (rooms), you might designate two rooms (or more) for each box. For example, the system shown above could be usefully extended by picturing this layout.

A	B	C	D	E
Attic	Bathroom	Closet	Dining Room	Exercise Room
Kitchen	Basement	Company Room	Dressing Room	Empty Room

By establishing these extra "rooms," you have gained more opportunities to place more "things you want to remember" in them. *But* you now must remember most exactly which "rooms" match up with which box. We've made that task easier by giving the alternate "rooms" the same first letter as the boxes they stand for (with the exception of the kitchen).

If you like this system, see if you can use it to remember the addresses in Boxes C, D, and E. Do it now—the more you practice the art of imagery, the faster you will learn to do it. If you prefer to use your own system of places, remember to use the guidelines above.

Reduction Coding

Reduction coding, the third memory technique, has become the favorite of many students. It means that you cut down, or *reduce*, the amount you have to remember and then put what remains into a special, easy-to-remember form. Here are some simple examples:

Example

We can remember the order in which the colors of the rainbow appear (**r**ed, **o**range, **y**ellow, **g**reen, **b**lue, **i**ndigo, **v**iolet) by using their initials, ROYGBIV.

Example

If you want to remember the names of the Great Lakes, just remember the word HOMES:

> **H**uron
> **O**ntario
> **M**ichigan
> **E**rie
> **S**uperior

In each case, *one* word replaces many words.

The third example is a word frequently used by those preparing for a test to select managers. (That might be you after you enter the Postal Service.)

Example

The word is POSDCORB, and it stands for the seven basic duties of every manager:

> **P**lanning
> **O**rganizing
> **S**taffing
> **D**irecting
> **C** ⎱
> **O** ⎰ ordinating
> **R**eporting
> **B**udgeting

Seven different words made into one! Although POSDCORB, as a word, doesn't mean anything, it can be *sounded out* and seen in the mind's eye very easily. In this way, it will be remembered far longer and better than by drilling on the original seven.

You can see how this method works on another sample test question.

A	B	C	D	E
1800–2299 Peach	2400–2999 Peach	1200–1799 Peach	3000–3699 Peach	2300–2399 Peach
Frechett	Stokes	Hyberg	Graybar	Lorry
3100–3299 Kerry	4500–4999 Kerry	3600–4499 Kerry	3300–3599 Kerry	5000–5899 Kerry
Benson	Yalta	Island	Otiak	Upville
1500–1999 Martin	2000–2199 Martin	2700–3499 Martin	4100–4499 Martin	3500–4099 Martin

To remember the ten direct (name) addresses in these boxes by using *reduction coding*, you have your choice of three approaches.

Coding Method A—Work Horizontally Across the Five Boxes

STEP 1.   MAKE AN *IMAGE*.

Use the first letter of each of the five direct addresses in the second row, going from left to right, to set up your first new word.

> FSHGL . . . See it in your mind's eye.
>   Make an image.

Do the same thing with the five direct addresses in the fourth row.

> BYIOU . . . See it in your mind's eye.
>   Make an image.

STEP 2.   *SOUND* OUT THE WORD.

If your mind can retain the special sound or quality of the new "word" even though it has no meaning, then you have the battle more than half won. You will now have a fine substitute for the five original words *in the same order* in which they appear in each of the five boxes. Thereafter, whenever you see the address name Lorry, you will associate it with the last box —E, because the *l* sound comes last in the word FSHGL. Likewise, you can use the sound of FSHGL to correctly place each of the words on line 2 of each of the boxes: *F*rechett, *S*tokes, *H*yberg, *G*raybar, and *L*orry. You will be able to mentally see each of these words in its correct order.

   You now have two of your senses working for you—sound and sight. You will have no need to attempt any of the usual memorization and repetitious drilling which yield far less satisfying results.

STEP 3.   USE THE *MEANING*, IF ANY, OF THE NEW WORD.

Although it was pointed out that the new word need not have any meaning, sometimes it does. Instead, it may be associated with a word that does mean something. (It need not be an English word. A word in Spanish, German, Hindi, or any other language you know will do.) Once you have attached a meaning to the word, remembering it will become still easier.

   Now go back to FSHGL. What do these five letters sound like when you try to pronounce them? Of course! The words sounds like FISH GILL, the breathing agent of a fish. I don't think there is any chance that you will easily forget the vivid picture associated with this word. Once this picture flashes into your awareness (which should take only a brief second), you can work confidently on the rest of the addresses in the five boxes.

   What about the five remaining direct addresses on the fourth line? They formed your second new word—BYIOU. Suppose you now use these two new words to see how well you can employ the methods we've just discussed.

<!-- gray bar --> **Drill 1**

Below are 20 addresses contained in the five sample boxes on page 121. Study only the direct name addresses and their locations in these five boxes for *1 minute*, using the two new words FSHGL and BYIOU. Then, from memory, enter the correct box location (A–E) for each. (You may wish to do this exercise more than once.)

	Trials	3	2	1
Answers				
1. Frechett				
2. Lorry				
3. Benson				
4. Stokes				
5. Island				
6. Otiak				
7. Graybar				
8. Lorry				
9. Yalta				
10. Benson				

	Trials	3	2	1
Answers				
11. Hyberg				
12. Stokes				
13. Otiak				
14. Upville				
15. Frechett				
16. Otiak				
17. Island				
18. Lorry				
19. Graybar				
20. Hyberg				
Number Right				
Time				

Did you use BYIOU successfully? Did you sound it? It has a musical, easy-to-remember sound. You probably noticed immediately that BYIOU sounds exactly like the word *bayou* (as in the song "Blue Bayou"). Does it have any meaning? Indeed it does: it is a body of water, an arm of a lake or river. Now you have formed a vivid, mental image. With the triple combination of *sound*, *meaning*, and *imagery* that BYIOU conjures up, you cannot help but remember those five addresses.

STEP 4. MAKE UP A *STORY*.

Use the five letters as the initial letters of a five-word story, slogan, or phrase—the more vivid and breezy, the better.

Example

FSHGL   Feel So Happy Go Lucky.
         Few Sleepy Heads Get Lively.
         Father Saw His Green Lawn.

Example

BYIOU   Buy Yourself! IOU.
         Bananas are Yellow, Inside, Outside and Underneath.
         Baby is Young and Innocent, not Old and Ugly.

The trick is to be able to create the story freely and quickly. With a little practice, you can develop the knack. When you have it, you can remember any five-letter combination even if you cannot sound it (Step 2) or find any meaning (Step 3).

Coding Method B—Work Vertically Within Each Box

For a variety of reasons that will be discussed later, you may decide to memorize all the addresses within each of the boxes A, B, C, D, and E, separately. If so, you may still employ reduction coding using the same four steps.

MAKE AN *IMAGE*.
Select the first letter of each of the two addresses in each box plus the letter above the box itself.

Example

For Box A, you would select the letters *A*, *F* and *B*. For Box B, select letters *B*, *S* and *Y*.

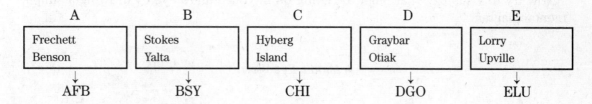

A	B	C	D	E
Frechett Benson	Stokes Yalta	Hyberg Island	Graybar Otiak	Lorry Upville
↓	↓	↓	↓	↓
AFB	BSY	CHI	DGO	ELU

SOUND OUT THE WORD.
You don't get anything too useful with AFB, but you get immediate results with Box B. When you sound BSY you get—BUSY! Notice that the *B* in "Busy" immediately gives you the box location.

USE THE *MEANING*, IF ANY, OF THE NEW WORD.
When using associations was discussed, it was said that many of the best associations are strictly personal and exist only for you. This means that one of the three-letter words may be an abbreviation of a person, place, or thing with which only *you* are familiar. If so, you will immediately make the association and store it for future use. For example, in Box A, AFB might be the initials of your best friend, <u>A</u>lfred <u>F</u>rederick <u>B</u>ates, or, in military terms, <u>A</u>ir <u>F</u>orce <u>B</u>ase. In Box C, CHI might be the letters of your old fraternity, or the <u>C</u>ity of <u>Chi</u>cago, where you once lived.

But go further. You will learn how to use the three-letter combinations in other ways, if Steps 2 and 3 don't produce immediate results.

MOVE THE LETTERS AROUND: MAKE UP A STORY
If the three letters do not produce a meaningful sound or word, play mental Scrabble. For instance, move just one letter of DGO and you've got DOG, man's best friend; DOG has the key letter *D*, which gives you the box location on which you peg the *O* and *G*. These letters stand, of course, for <u>O</u>TIAK and <u>G</u>RAYBAR. A problem arises only when you are given five boxes that contain two or more addresses with the same first letter. This problem, however, can be readily solved by Method C (see next page).

====== **Drill 2** ======

Transpose the initial letters of the direct addresses in Boxes A and C on page 123. In each case you will be able to come up with meaningful words.

1. Box A _____

2. Box C _____

MAKE UP A STORY.
Use exactly the same technique as explained on page 122. You will find this step even easier because your story needs only three words instead of five.

Coding Method C—Combine the Horizontal and Vertical Methods

Sometimes you may wish to combine Methods A and B. In our sample question you may have felt very confident about remembering BYIOU, but not about FSHGL (Method A). You might then use a few of the three-letter words developed in Method B to reinforce your memory for the remaining addresses.

Now try to visualize what might be going on in your mind's eye by drawing a simple "mental diagram."

A Mind's Eye View

A	B	C	D	E
F	S	H	G	L
B	Y	I	O	U

FAB   HIC   DOG

Here, the three-letter words, FAB, HIC, and DOG plus the word BYIOU stand out clearly. They give you eight of the ten direct addresses without any of the ordinary rote memorization on your part. They also give you cues on the two missing address names. By memorizing only *one* of them, you can ensure knowing all ten well enough to attain a perfect score!

■ EIDETIC (PHOTOGRAPHIC) MEMORY

You can form mental pictures that you are able to review whenever you want to remember something. Methods A, B, and C all employ this ability to some extent.

There are a few people who have "picture taking" ability far beyond the capabilities of most. They can reproduce a mental picture they have taken in such great detail that it is as though they literally were looking at a photograph. They can even see the picture in color and keep it stored for a long time.

Needless to say, those who were born with eidetic memories have an enormous advantage on this test. For the rest, although you cannot hope to develop photographic memories, you can learn, through practice, to intensify and retain longer the mental pictures you make.

In any case, you now have an arsenal of techniques that eliminate the need for special or hard-to-achieve powers. You can use them on some of the practice tests or wait until you have read Chapter 6, which will teach you how to deal with numbered addresses.

SPECIAL EXERCISES FOR BUILDING MEMORY FOR *DIRECT* ADDRESSES

Warm-up Drills

Do Drills 3 through 6 to get the feel of associating words and images freely and quickly. They are fun to do and you can do them by yourself or, if you prefer, with a friend.

Directions for Drills 3 through 6

Each drill consists of a list of 20 names. Cover the list with your hand or a piece of paper so that you can uncover one name at a time as you move down the list. If a friend is helping you, just hand the friend the list and ask him or her to call out each name when you are ready to begin.

As soon as you hear or see the name, call out the images and the words that come into your mind. Be free and spontaneous. Don't be concerned or embarrassed if your associations seem weird or foolish. The thing that *is* important is that the images come to you quickly and naturally. That is why there is no answer key to these drills. The only right answers are what *you* supply.

Take no more than 1 or 2 seconds per name on the average. In succeeding drills you will become able to make associations more rapidly. If you blank out on a particular name, skip over it and continue the drill until you complete all 20 names. These drills may be repeated as often as you like.

Drill 3

	Responses		
	Trials	3	2	1
1. Freund				
2. Potomac				
3. Carrie				
4. Wanda				
5. Orio				
6. Mall				
7. Kreskin				
8. Slaboff				
9. Pritchard				
10. Solomon				

	Responses		
	Trials	3	2	1
11. Miami				
12. Shearing				
13. Hudson				
14. Wynn				
15. Thatcher				
16. Choir				
17. Tile				
18. President				
19. Fuller				
20. Park				
Number Completed				
Time				

Drill 4

Trials	3	2	1
1. Anton			
2. Vechia			
3. Ithaca			
4. Reardon			
5. Exeter			
6. Thomas			
7. Helmut			
8. Newton			
9. Yuma			
10. Jackly			

Trials	3	2	1
11. Bolton			
12. Caracas			
13. Ulster			
14. X Ray			
15. Oliver			
16. Kansas			
17. Copper			
18. Quail			
19. Glen			
20. Worth			
Number Completed			
Time			

Drill 5

Trials	3	2	1
1. Barbar			
2. Quarry			
3. Dresden			
4. Unitas			
5. Lexington			
6. Gallo			
7. Zuni			
8. Amity			
9. Fairmount			
10. Volta			

Trials	3	2	1
11. Westchester			
12. Frank			
13. Tinton			
14. Charlotte			
15. Danzig			
16. Embry			
17. Pleasant			
18. Nutley			
19. Orville			
20. Juniper			
Number Completed			
Time			

Drill 6

Responses			
Trials	3	2	1
1. Kale			
2. Daly			
3. Mesmer			
4. Young			
5. Aster			
6. Robb			
7. Renfrew			
8. Grange			
9. Ponte			
10. Charles			

Responses			
Trials	3	2	1
11. Brian			
12. Mitchell			
13. Violet			
14. Indian			
15. Junction			
16. Laramie			
17. Parkridge			
18. Evansville			
19. Open			
20. Trent			
Number Completed			
Time			

Using Association and Imagery

The next two drills (7 and 8) will be especially helpful to those who intend to rely primarily on forming associations and images to remember the direct name addresses. (Numbered addresses have been left out for the sake of clarity.) For a full discussion on this method, see pages 116 to 118.

Here are some guidelines.

1. As you examine each address name, make your associations and *see* the images each brings forth.

2. Associate the images in each box with their corresponding box letter (A, B, C, D, or E) by means of a mental pricture story.

3. Drill on the names that you were not able to incorporate in your picture stories.

Drill 7

Study the ten address names and memorize in which box (A, B, C, D, or E) each belongs. *Take exactly 5 minutes to study these names and their locations.* When the study time is over, cover the boxes and answer as many of the 40 questions as you can in *2 minutes.* For each question, mark the answer space next to it to show the letter of the box in which the address belongs. (Cover the column of answers you have already completed so that they do not influence you on your second and third trials.)

A	B	C	D	E
Branch Peckham	Rail Stove	Stool Crown	Board Room	Treasure Marble

Responses					Responses					Responses			
Trials	3	2	1		Trials	3	2	1		Trials	3	2	1
1. Rail					15. Treasure					29. Rail			
2. Marble					16. Branch					30. Room			
3. Peckham					17. Crown					31. Peckham			
4. Stool					18. Stool					32. Crown			
5. Treasure					19. Room					33. Board			
6. Room					20. Peckham					34. Treasure			
7. Crown					21. Rail					35. Marble			
8. Stool					22. Stove					36. Rail			
9. Branch					23. Board					37. Stool			
10. Peckham					24. Room					38. Crown			
11. Stove					25. Stool					39. Treasure			
12. Room					26. Branch					40. Crown			
13. Board					27. Marble					**Number Completed**			
14. Marble					28. Stove					**Time**			

Drill 8

Study the ten address names and memorize in which box (A, B, C, D, or E) each belongs. *Take exactly 5 minutes to study these names and their locations.* When the study time is over, cover the boxes and answer as many of the 40 questions as you can in *2 minutes.* For each question, mark the answer space next to it to show the letter of the box in which the address belongs. (Cover the column of answers you have already completed so that they do not influence you on your second and third trials.)

A	B	C	D	E
People Mountain	Lever Daily	Bubble Shore	Ovam Grange	Cairo Fuller

Responses

Trials	3	2	1
1. Daily			
2. Lever			
3. Ovam			
4. Shore			
5. Bubble			
6. Cairo			
7. Mountain			
8. People			
9. Fuller			
10. Lever			
11. Daily			
12. Cairo			
13. Grange			
14. People			

Responses

Trials	3	2	1
15. Lever			
16. Cairo			
17. Ovam			
18. Grange			
19. People			
20. Daily			
21. Mountain			
22. Shore			
23. Grange			
24. Fuller			
25. Cairo			
26. Lever			
27. Daily			
28. People			

Responses

Trials	3	2	1
29. Mountain			
30. Shore			
31. Bubble			
32. Cairo			
33. Lever			
34. Bubble			
35. Ovam			
36. Grange			
37. Lever			
38. People			
39. Daily			
40. Ovam			
Number Completed Time			

Using the Loci System

You may have decided that you like the loci system,* in conjunction with associations and imagery, for remembering direct name addresses. If so, do Drills 9 and 10 with these guidelines in mind:

1. Make sure that your loci system is at your command. You should be able to visualize instantly which box each place in your system represents.

---

* NOTE: Those who are not using the loci system, but are relying on regular associations, may use these drills in the same way as for Drills 7 and 8.

2. Form your association with the two direct names in each box in the regular way to come up with a vivid object picture for each name.

3. Place each of these object pictures in the place representing the box in your system. Make up a little story or slogan if it helps to strengthen the association.

Drill 9

Study the ten address names and memorize in which box (A, B, C, D, or E) each belongs. *Take exactly 5 minutes to study these names and their locations.* When the study time is over, cover the boxes and answer as many of the 40 questions as you can in *2 minutes*. For each question, mark the answer space next to it to show the letter of the box in which the address belongs. (Cover the column of answers you have already completed so that they do not influence you on your second and third trials.)

A	B	C	D	E
Queen Diamond	Coop Lyman	Pitcher Bailey	Rock Trail	Nestor Greene

Responses

	Trials	3	2	1
1. Rock				
2. Nestor				
3. Greene				
4. Diamond				
5. Queen				
6. Lyman				
7. Bailey				
8. Pitcher				
9. Trail				
10. Rock				
11. Nestor				
12. Coop				
13. Lyman				
14. Pitcher				

Responses

	Trials	3	2	1
15. Queen				
16. Coop				
17. Pitcher				
18. Bailey				
19. Trail				
20. Greene				
21. Nestor				
22. Diamond				
23. Coop				
24. Bailey				
25. Pitcher				
26. Rock				
27. Trail				
28. Queen				

Responses

	Trials	3	2	1
29. Coop				
30. Nestor				
31. Greene				
32. Trail				
33. Rock				
34. Lyman				
35. Bailey				
36. Nestor				
37. Greene				
38. Pitcher				
39. Rock				
40. Queen				
Number Completed				
Time				

Drill 10

Study the ten address names and memorize in which box (A, B, C, D, or E) each belongs. *Take exactly 5 minutes to study these names and their locations.* When the study time is over, cover the boxes and answer as many of the 40 questions as you can in *2 minutes*. For each question, mark the answer space next to it to show the letter of the box in which the address belongs. (Cover the column of answers you have already completed so that they do not influence you on your second and third trials.)

A	B	C	D	E
Tablett Waxman	Oliver Abbey	Flint Ireland	Usher Track	Young Handle

Responses

Trials	3	2	1
1. Waxman			
2. Abbey			
3. Ireland			
4. Track			
5. Handle			
6. Tablett			
7. Oliver			
8. Flint			
9. Usher			
10. Young			
11. Track			
12. Oliver			
13. Flint			
14. Waxman			

Responses

Trials	3	2	1
15. Abbey			
16. Tablett			
17. Usher			
18. Young			
19. Ireland			
20. Flint			
21. Oliver			
22. Tablett			
23. Abbey			
24. Ireland			
25. Track			
26. Handle			
27. Usher			
28. Oliver			

Responses

Trials	3	2	1
29. Tablett			
30. Oliver			
31. Abbey			
32. Track			
33. Handle			
34. Young			
35. Tablett			
36. Waxman			
37. Oliver			
38. Usher			
39. Handle			
40. Waxman			
Number Completed **Time**			

Using Reduction Coding (Method A)

Drills 11 and 12 give you an opportunity to practice the reduction coding system for memorizing direct name addresses (see pages 120 to 124 for the complete discussion). Below is a summary of the steps to follow if you are going to use *horizontal* coding (Method A).

1. Use the first letter of each of the five name addresses on the top row to make a five-letter word. Visualize it.

2. Sound the word mentally. Is it catchy and easy to remember?

3. Does the word have any meaning or evoke a picture?

4. Make up a little story or slogan using the five letters. (Step 4 is optional. You need not use it if you are able to remember the new "word" after completing Steps 1 to 3.)

5. Repeat Steps 1 to 4 for the second row of five direct name addresses.

Drill 11

Study the ten address names and memorize in which box (A, B, C, D, or E) each belongs. *Take exactly 5 minutes to study these names and their locations.* When the study time is over, cover the boxes and answer as many of the 40 questions as you can in *2 minutes.* For each question, mark the answer space next to it to show the letter of the box in which the address belongs. (Cover the column of answers you have already completed so that they do not influence you on your second and third trials.)

A	B	C	D	E
Chester Danish	Raleigh Erin	Inway Leeds	Easter Yuma	Keaton Shore

Responses

Trials	3	2	1
1. Danish			
2. Erin			
3. Leeds			
4. Yuma			
5. Shore			
6. Chester			
7. Raleigh			
8. Inway			
9. Easter			
10. Keaton			
11. Inway			
12. Leeds			
13. Yuma			
14. Easter			

Responses

Trials	3	2	1
15. Erin			
16. Leeds			
17. Chester			
18. Raleigh			
19. Danish			
20. Keaton			
21. Shore			
22. Inway			
23. Easter			
24. Yuma			
25. Shore			
26. Chester			
27. Danish			
28. Shore			

Responses

Trials	3	2	1
29. Keaton			
30. Raleigh			
31. Erin			
32. Yuma			
33. Yuma			
34. Shore			
35. Easter			
36. Inway			
37. Leeds			
38. Chester			
39. Raleigh			
40. Inway			
Number Completed			
Time			

Using Reduction Coding (Method B)

In this method, you employ the same basic idea as for Method A except that you memorize the *individual* box letters as you memorize the addresses in each. Here is a summary of the steps.

1. For each individual box (A, B, C, D, and E), use the first letter of each of the two direct name addresses and the box letter itself to make up a three-letter word.

2. Sound the "word" mentally. Is it catchy and easy to remember?

3. Does the "word" have any meaning or evoke a picture?

4. Transpose the letters if it helps produce a better "word."

5. Make up a little story or slogan using the three letters. (Step 5 is optional. You need not use it if you are able to remember the new "word" after completing Step 4.)

6. Repeat Steps 1 to 5 for each box in turn.

Drill 12

Study the ten address names and memorize in which box (A, B, C, D, or E) each belongs. *Take exactly 5 minutes to study these names and their locations.* When the study time is over, cover the boxes and answer as many of the 40 questions as you can in *2 minutes.* For each question, mark the answer space next to it to show the letter of the box in which the address belongs. (Cover the column of answers you have already completed so that they do not influence you on your second and third trials.)

A	B	C	D	E
Boston Clark	Olive Darby	Aspen Perdue	Iris Drill	Spire Yard

Responses

Trials	3	2	1
1. Aspen			
2. Perdue			
3. Spire			
4. Yard			
5. Boston			
6. Clark			
7. Olive			
8. Darby			
9. Iris			
10. Drill			
11. Yard			
12. Boston			
13. Olive			
14. Darby			

Responses

Trials	3	2	1
15. Perdue			
16. Drill			
17. Iris			
18. Aspen			
19. Spire			
20. Yard			
21. Clark			
22. Boston			
23. Perdue			
24. Darby			
25. Olive			
26. Darby			
27. Spire			
28. Iris			

Responses

Trials	3	2	1
29. Drill			
30. Boston			
31. Clark			
32. Aspen			
33. Perdue			
34. Iris			
35. Drill			
36. Clark			
37. Boston			
38. Clark			
39. Aspen			
40. Perdue			
Number Completed			
Time			

Making Up Stories and Slogans

A little story or slogan that connects the address names with each other and with the box letters can be very useful for strengthening associations, particularly if you use reduction coding and want to make sure of some hard-to-remember initials (read pages 122 to 123 for a complete discussion). Here are some brief guidelines to follow.

Your task is to use five initials (Method A) or three initials (Method B) to make up the words forming a brief story or slogan. For example, if you had to deal with the initials FSTAB, you might come up with "Five Sailors Took A Boat" or "Feed Salami To A Baby." Three letters such as CTB could stand for "Cock-eyed Teddy Bears" or "Chocolate Tastes Best." Anything goes. The more humorous, colorful, and vivid the story/slogan is, the better.

Do Drills 13 to 22 to develop your facility and speed. In each of Drills 13 to 17, there are five 3-letter combinations; in each of Drills 18 to 22, two 5-letter combinations. Each drill, therefore, contains the equivalent of ten direct name addresses, the same as on the regular test.

Directions for Drills 13 through 22

Take 5 minutes to study each drill. Make up your story/slogan as you examine each group of three or five letters. When the 5 minutes are up, cover the letter groups and jot down the initials, *in the same order as originally given*, on the answer line for that group. *Take 30 seconds to do this.* (Cover the column of answers you have already completed so that they do not influence you on your second and third trials.)

Drill 13

		Responses		
	Trials	3	2	1
1. OFA				
2. GAL				
3. MMD				
4. WIZ				
5. TNT				
Number Completed				
Time				

Drill 14

		Responses		
	Trials	3	2	1
1. YEL				
2. VRO				
3. PTA				
4. NRA				
5. ELY				
Number Completed				
Time				

Drill 15

		Responses		
	Trials	3	2	1
1. PRO				
2. TSK				
3. BOD				
4. SRE				
5. CDL				
Number Completed				
Time				

Drill 16

		Responses		
	Trials	3	2	1
1. ADL				
2. FSD				
3. TVP				
4. EGO				
5. HKC				
Number Completed				
Time				

Drill 17

Trials	Responses		
	3	2	1
1. ENP			
2. RAS			
3. QPY			
4. MAR			
5. WOZ			
Number Completed			
Time			

Drill 18

Trials	Responses		
	3	2	1
1. WTHAY			
2. GMABP			
Number Completed			
Time			

Drill 19

Trials	Responses		
	3	2	1
1. ROMEL			
2. ICTLN			
Number Completed			
Time			

Drill 20

Trials	Responses		
	3	2	1
1. DYPON			
2. MLIBC			
Number Completed			
Time			

Drill 21

Trials	Responses		
	3	2	1
1. LWTEM			
2. OBWAS			
Number Completed			
Time			

Drill 22

Trials	Responses		
	3	2	1
1. BPOYI			
2. WONAT			
Number Completed			
Time			

■ ANSWER KEY FOR DRILLS

Drill 1, page 122

1. A	3. A	5. C	7. D	9. B	11. C	13. D	15. A	17. C	19. D
2. E	4. B	6. D	8. E	10. A	12. B	14. E	16. D	18. E	20. C

Drill 2, page 124

1. Box *A* plus *F* and *B* gives—*FAB*, the laundry detergent.
2. Box *C* plus *H* and *I* gives—*CHI*, slang for CHICAGO.
                                      —*HIC*, as in HICCUP.

Drills 3–6, not applicable

Drill 7, page 128

1. B	5. E	9. A	13. D	17. C	21. B	25. C	29. B	33. D	37. C
2. E	6. D	10. A	14. E	18. C	22. B	26. A	30. D	34. E	38. C
3. A	7. C	11. B	15. E	19. D	23. D	27. E	31. A	35. E	39. E
4. C	8. C	12. D	16. A	20. A	24. D	28. B	32. C	36. B	40. C

Drill 8, page 129

1. B	5. C	9. E	13. D	17. D	21. A	25. E	29. A	33. B	37. B
2. B	6. E	10. B	14. A	18. D	22. C	26. B	30. C	34. C	38. A
3. D	7. A	11. B	15. B	19. A	23. D	27. B	31. C	35. D	39. B
4. C	8. A	12. E	16. E	20. B	24. E	28. A	32. E	36. D	40. D

Drill 9, page 130

1. D	5. A	9. D	13. B	17. C	21. E	25. C	29. B	33. D	37. E
2. E	6. B	10. D	14. C	18. C	22. A	26. D	30. E	34. B	38. C
3. E	7. C	11. E	15. A	19. D	23. B	27. D	31. E	35. C	39. D
4. A	8. C	12. B	16. B	20. E	24. C	28. A	32. D	36. E	40. A

Drill 10, page 131

1. A	5. E	9. D	13. C	17. D	21. B	25. D	29. A	33. E	37. B
2. A	6. A	10. E	14. A	18. E	22. A	26. E	30. B	34. E	38. D
3. C	7. B	11. D	15. B	19. C	23. B	27. D	31. B	35. A	39. E
4. D	8. C	12. B	16. A	20. C	24. C	28. B	32. D	36. A	40. A

Drill 11, page 132

1. A	5. E	9. D	13. D	17. A	21. E	25. E	29. E	33. D	37. C
2. B	6. A	10. E	14. D	18. B	22. C	26. A	30. B	34. E	38. A
3. C	7. B	11. C	15. B	19. A	23. D	27. A	31. B	35. D	39. B
4. D	8. C	12. C	16. C	20. E	24. D	28. E	32. D	36. C	40. C

Drill 12, page 133

1. C	5. A	9. D	13. B	17. D	21. A	25. B	29. D	33. C	37. A
2. C	6. A	10. D	14. B	18. C	22. A	26. B	30. A	34. D	38. A
3. E	7. B	11. E	15. C	19. E	23. C	27. E	31. A	35. D	39. C
4. E	8. B	12. A	16. D	20. E	24. B	28. D	32. C	36. A	40. C

Drills 13–22, not applicable

Exercise from page 118, using appearance and sound to remember the Box D addresses: To remember Box D, combine D-CI-PEL to give the word DCIPEL, which looks and *sounds* like *disciple* and *decibel!*

Chapter 6

Memory for *Numbered* Addresses—How to Improve Your Score

If you have been studying and practicing as recommended, you should feel quite good about what you have accomplished. You probably are able to remember all of the direct (name) addresses in the practice tests without trouble. If you can, you must still do more to earn a respectable score. (If 40 percent of the 88 questions are direct names, and you get all of them right, your score will be 35.) Don't be satisfied with that! By pushing on and learning how to remember the numbered addresses, your score will easily rise to the sixties, seventies, and beyond.

In this chapter, solutions will be given to the problems most test takers have in remembering the numbered addresses.

■ TEST STRATEGY

In addition to the three memory strategies described in Chapter 5, pages 114 through 115, there is another strategy applicable only to the numbered addresses, which we will call "reduce the number."

Reduce the Number

The sample boxes in the Diagnostic Practice Test can serve as an illustration of this. (For the sake of clarity, only the numbered addresses have been reproduced.)

A	B	C	D	E
2100–2799 Mall	3900–4399 Mall	4400–4599 Mall	3400–3899 Mall	2800–3399 Mall
4800–4999 Cliff	4000–4299 Cliff	3300–3999 Cliff	4500–4799 Cliff	4300–4499 Cliff
1900–2299 Laurel	2300–2999 Laurel	3200–3799 Laurel	3000–3199 Laurel	1500–1899 Laurel

Original Numbered Addresses

You can reduce all of the above to a far simpler and easier-to-remember form. The boxes illustrate how few items you actually need to remember.

A	B	C	D	E
21	39	44	34	28
48	40	33	45	43
19	23	32	30	15

Simplified Numbered Addresses

Now See Why

1. *The addresses on each horizontal line follow each other in consecutive order.* This can be seen for the "Mall" line when the five addresses are rearranged:

A	E	D	B	C
2100–2799	2800–3399	3400–3899	3900–4399	4400–4599

Where one address ends, the other begins. For example, Box A covers 2100–2799 Mall; Box E begins with 2800. There are no gaps. Therefore, the last half of the address, 2799, need not be remembered. All addresses beginning with 2100 Mall must be in Box A.

2. *The questions on the text are always about the same ranges of numbers.* For example, there are no questions about single numbers in the middle of a range of numbers, such as 2345 Mall or 2697 Mall. Neither are there questions about other ranges, such as 2200–2400 Mall. You need focus only on the numbers shown, such as 2100 Mall.

3. *The last two digits of every address number are either "00" or "99."* So, why bother remembering them? It is easier to keep 21 in mind than 2100.

To sum up: Each of the address ranges is fully represented by the first two digits. Why take on the task of memorizing eight? Using this simple technique, the alert test candidate can reduce the original total of 30 four-digit numbers to 15 two-digit numbers!

An additional way to make the test easier involves the names—Mall, Cliff, Laurel. You may not have to remember them at all. That's because the two-digit numbers themselves pinpoint the box. You don't need to remember the name Mall to place the 21 in Box A except in the event that 21 is used to start *another* address on the Cliff or Laurel lines.

What would you do then? When you reach the end of this chapter, you'll find a full discussion on how to remember and place duplicate numbers.

Drill 1

Answer the questions below to get the feel of this discussion. Look only at the first two digits in each address to determine whether it would be found in Box A, B, C, D, or E of the set of boxes on page 138. (You may wish to do this exercise more than once.)

		Answers		
		Trials	3	2	1
1.	3400–3899 Mall				
2.	1900–2299 Laurel				
3.	3300–3999 Cliff				
4.	2300–2999 Laurel				
5.	2800–3399 Mall				
Number Right					
Time					

TECHNIQUES FOR REMEMBERING NUMBERED ADDRESSES

There are two principal techniques to choose from in preparing for the memory part of the posted exam: *visualization* and *association*. Both will be described fully in this chapter.

The Visualization Technique

Chunk the Number

Example

Try this experiment. Get a pencil and a blank sheet of paper. Next, study line 1 below for 5 seconds. Then look away and write, in order, the numbers you saw.

Line 1: 7 4 3 0 1 9 4 1 1 8 6 5

That was not easy. Try it once more, using line 2 below. Study the line for 5 seconds, look away, and write the numbers from memory.

Line 2: 7430   1941   1865

It was much easier to do the second time, wasn't it? Although the numbers were identical, the fact that they were organized into "chunks" made all the difference. Here is why.

The way the mind works, most people, unless they have trained themselves, cannot retain more than seven or eight pieces of information presented separately. The way the numbers were displayed on line 1, you were required to remember *12* separate items. On line 2, the same numbers were gathered into chunks of four numbers each. Each of these chunks, believe it or not, is as difficult (or easy) to remember as just *one* of the original digits. In effect, a chunk counts as a single piece of information. This is particularly true when the chunks have a meaningful association. In the example above, most people will associate 1941 with Pearl Harbor, and 1865 with the end of the Civil War or President Lincoln's assassination. The chunking technique will make it far easier to remember the numbers in the boxes. Chunk them like this:

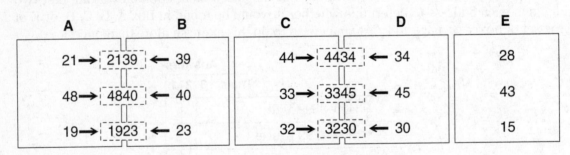

At this point, the original job of remembering 30 four-digit numbers has been cut down to remembering 6! This assumes that you are omitting Box E in accordance with "Eliminate the Last Box," the strategy discussed on page 115.

Now, use your powers of visualization. Help your memory by forming a mental screen like the one above, on which you see each four-number chunk in its place, alongside the same street. In that way, you will be able to identify in which box each part belongs. For example, when you picture 2139 between Box A and Box B on the top line (Mall) in the figure, you are automatically putting 21 in Box A and 39 in Box B. Similarly, see how 4434 can be used for Box C and Box D.

Chunking across each line in this way also has another advantage. It guarantees that you will get the right box for this address: 2800–3399 Mall—if you visualize "chunks" 2139 and 4434 "floating" on the top line of your screen (the "Mall" line). The only possible answer to an unfamiliar numbered address with "Mall" in it, *has* to be Box E.

Drill 2

Project the image below on your mental screen. It shows only what is necessary to score a perfect mark on these numbered addresses. Study it for 5 minutes.

2139	4434	28	MALL
4840	3345	43	CLIFF
1923	3230	15	LAUREL

Now cover the above boxes from view and write as many chunks as you can remember in the empty numbered boxes below. After writing each chunk, split it into 2 two-digit numbers and place each on the appropriate line below the boxes. Also enter the (3) numbers belonging in Box E.

A   **B**   **C**   **D**   **E**

1.   4.

2.   5.

3.   6.

A   B   C   D   E

1. _____ — _____   4. _____ — _____   _____

2. _____ — _____   5. _____ — _____   _____

3. _____ — _____   6. _____ — _____   _____

After using these techniques for some of the drills and practice tests, you may find that remembering 4-digit chunks comes easy to you. You may want to attempt a 6-digit chunk by combining the 3 numbers in Box E. If you are successful, there will now be only 7 separate items to remember; i.e., the (6) 4-digit chunks from Boxes A, B, C, and D, plus (1) 6-digit chunk from Box E!

In the example, Box E's numbers, written as one chunk, become 284315. *Of course, you must remember them in that order because their position determines the street name each belongs to.* (Some students are good at remembering telephone numbers and write the new number as E28-4315.)

Additional Drills Using Chunking

Drills 3 through 13 will help you to develop your ability to organize and remember four-digit number chunks (see pages 140 to 141 for a full discussion and explanation). The two-digit numbers from which the chunks are to be formed have been printed in four adjoining columns marked A, B, C, and D. The numbers representing addresses in Box E have been omitted at this point. The space between the four columns is about the same as would be between the numbers if they were in boxes. (The direct name addresses have been omitted for clarity.)

These drills proceed in stages, increasing from one line to three and thereby from two chunks to six. Each line has a street name alongside it similar to the way the questions are displayed on the test. These names are essential, of course, when there are duplicate numbers among the addresses. (Only a few of the drills in this section have such duplicates.) After you have read "Dealing With Duplicate Numbers" at the end of this chapter, you will have an opportunity to do Drills 13 to 27, which will have more and more duplicate addresses and which will include Box E addresses as well.

Directions for Drills 3 through 12

1. For each horizontal street line, combine mentally the numbers in Columns A and B on page 143 so that they become a single four-digit number. Do the same with the numbers in Columns C and D.

2. Visualize each chunk as though it were in its place between two boxes. (See the diagram on page 140.)

3. Study the numbers, using the time posted above each group as a guide. These times represent goals toward which you should be working. Because individuals vary in their experience and ability on this kind of memorization, you may find you need to increase the time allowance for particular drills. If that is the case, by all means, do so. Your starting point for all the drills is the point at which you achieve good results with a fair amount of effort. With that as a beginning, use the drills regularly to gradually develop your capacity and speed.

4. For each question on pages 144 through 148 mark the letter on the answer sheet to show the column in which each address belongs. (Cover the column of answers you have already completed so that they do not influence you on your second and third trials.) Work at a reasonable speed, gradually increasing it between trials.

Don't be discouraged if you have difficulty with these drills at first. Most people do. On the other hand, you may discover you have unsuspected capabilities. The results of a recent study on the effects of training and practice reveal that ordinary people may often achieve astounding feats. To illustrate, the standard view repeated in almost every psychology textbook, is that the ordinary limit on short-term memory is for seven or so bits of information—the length of a phone number. But in a stunning demonstration of the power of *sheer practice* to break barriers in the mind's ability to handle information . . . college students have been taught to listen to a list of as many as *102* digits and then recite it correctly. After 50 hours of *practice* with differing sets of random digits, four students were able to remember up to *20* digits after a *single hearing. One student . . . not especially talented in mathematics, was able to remember 102 digits!*

Studies of chess masters, virtuoso musicians, and star athletes show that relentless *training* routines allow them to break through ordinary limits in memory and physiology, and so perform at levels that had been thought impossible.

The old joke—"How do you get to Carnegie Hall? Practice, practice, practice" is getting a scientific spin.

Drills 3 and 4—Study 1 minute each

Drill No.	Street Name	A	B	C	D	Street Name
3.	Church	19	29	47	32	Church
4.	Browne	12	30	18	46	Browne

Drills 5 and 6—Study 3 minutes each

	Street Name	A	B	C	D	Street Name
5.	Marine	44	22	19	53	Marine
	Wright	70	65	—	—	Wright
6.	Diamont	74	91	87	78	Diamont
	Presser	52	16	—	—	Presser

Drills 7 and 8—Study 5 minutes each

	Street Name	A	B	C	D	Street Name
7.	Erasmus	14	36	28	32	Erasmus
	Klondike	57	52	38	—	Klondike
8.	Avalon	93	86	64	59	Avalon
	Schooner	49	39	19	—	Schooner

Drills 9 and 10—Study 8 minutes each

	Street Name	A	B	C	D	Street Name
9.	Orion	85	90	77	81	Orion
	Hershey	11	25	17	31	Hershey
	Pointe	63	55	—	—	Pointe
10.	Railroad	21	10	14	25	Railroad
	Vine	31	15	18	21	Vine
	Nestle	54	40	—	—	Nestle

Drills 11 and 12—Study 9 minutes each

	Street Name	A	B	C	D	Street Name
11.	Blue	66	58	73	61	Blue
	Glover	45	52	61	70	Glover
	Park	34	41	53	58	Park
12.	Creek	25	44	36	40	Creek
	Reardon	13	21	28	35	Reardon
	Mountain	20	11	33	26	Mountain

Drill 3

Trials	3	2	1
1. 19 Church			
2. 29 Church			
3. 47 Church			
4. 32 Church			
5. 19 Church			
6. 29 Church			
7. 47 Church			
8. 32 Church			
9. 47 Church			
10. 29 Church			
11. 19 Church			
12. 47 Church			
13. 32 Church			
14. 29 Church			
15. 19 Church			
16. 32 Church			

Trials	3	2	1
17. 47 Church			
18. 19 Church			
19. 32 Church			
20. 32 Church			
21. 19 Church			
22. 29 Church			
23. 47 Church			
24. 32 Church			
25. 47 Church			
26. 32 Church			
27. 19 Church			
28. 29 Church			
29. 32 Church			
30. 19 Church			
31. 47 Church			
32. 29 Church			

Trials	3	2	1
33. 47 Church			
34. 19 Church			
35. 32 Church			
36. 29 Church			
37. 19 Church			
38. 47 Church			
39. 32 Church			
40. 19 Church			
41. 19 Church			
42. 29 Church			
43. 47 Church			
44. 32 Church			
Number Right **Time**			

Drill 4

Trials	3	2	1
1. 12 Browne			
2. 30 Browne			
3. 18 Browne			
4. 46 Browne			
5. 12 Browne			
6. 30 Browne			
7. 18 Browne			
8. 46 Browne			
9. 30 Browne			
10. 12 Browne			
11. 46 Browne			
12. 18 Browne			
13. 30 Browne			
14. 46 Browne			
15. 18 Browne			
16. 12 Browne			

Trials	3	2	1
17. 12 Browne			
18. 18 Browne			
19. 46 Browne			
20. 30 Browne			
21. 18 Browne			
22. 30 Browne			
23. 12 Browne			
24. 46 Browne			
25. 12 Browne			
26. 18 Browne			
27. 30 Browne			
28. 18 Browne			
29. 46 Browne			
30. 12 Browne			
31. 12 Browne			
32. 18 Browne			

Trials	3	2	1
33. 30 Browne			
34. 18 Browne			
35. 46 Browne			
36. 12 Browne			
37. 30 Browne			
38. 46 Browne			
39. 12 Browne			
40. 18 Browne			
41. 30 Browne			
42. 12 Browne			
43. 30 Browne			
44. 18 Browne			
Number Right **Time**			

Drill 5

Answers Trials	3	2	1
1. 44 Marine			
2. 22 Marine			
3. 19 Marine			
4. 53 Marine			
5. 70 Wright			
6. 65 Wright			
7. 70 Wright			
8. 44 Marine			
9. 22 Marine			
10. 53 Marine			
11. 65 Wright			
12. 19 Marine			
13. 53 Marine			
14. 22 Marine			
15. 65 Wright			
16. 22 Marine			

Answers Trials	3	2	1
17. 19 Marine			
18. 53 Marine			
19. 70 Wright			
20. 65 Wright			
21. 65 Wright			
22. 70 Wright			
23. 53 Marine			
24. 44 Marine			
25. 19 Marine			
26. 70 Wright			
27. 19 Marine			
28. 65 Wright			
29. 22 Marine			
30. 53 Marine			
31. 22 Marine			
32. 65 Wright			

Answers Trials	3	2	1
33. 44 Marine			
34. 53 Marine			
35. 70 Wright			
36. 44 Marine			
37. 22 Marine			
38. 70 Wright			
39. 44 Marine			
40. 22 Marine			
41. 19 Marine			
42. 53 Marine			
43. 70 Wright			
44. 65 Wright			
Number Right			
Time			

Drill 6

Answers Trials	3	2	1
1. 74 Diamont			
2. 91 Diamont			
3. 87 Diamont			
4. 75 Diamont			
5. 52 Presser			
6. 16 Presser			
7. 78 Diamont			
8. 87 Diamont			
9. 78 Diamont			
10. 74 Diamont			
11. 52 Presser			
12. 16 Presser			
13. 78 Diamont			
14. 16 Presser			
15. 78 Diamont			
16. 74 Diamont			

Answers Trials	3	2	1
17. 91 Diamont			
18. 52 Presser			
19. 16 Presser			
20. 52 Presser			
21. 74 Diamont			
22. 16 Presser			
23. 91 Diamont			
24. 78 Diamont			
25. 91 Diamont			
26. 52 Presser			
27. 16 Presser			
28. 74 Diamont			
29. 91 Diamont			
30. 87 Diamont			
31. 16 Presser			
32. 74 Diamont			

Answers Trials	3	2	1
33. 91 Diamont			
34. 78 Diamont			
35. 87 Diamont			
36. 52 Presser			
37. 87 Diamont			
38. 74 Diamont			
39. 91 Diamont			
40. 87 Diamont			
41. 78 Diamont			
42. 52 Presser			
43. 16 Presser			
44. 74 Diamont			
Number Right			
Time			

Drill 7

Trials	3	2	1
1. 14 Erasmus			
2. 36 Erasmus			
3. 57 Klondike			
4. 52 Klondike			
5. 28 Erasmus			
6. 32 Erasmus			
7. 38 Klondike			
8. 57 Klondike			
9. 52 Klondike			
10. 36 Erasmus			
11. 28 Erasmus			
12. 38 Klondike			
13. 28 Erasmus			
14. 32 Erasmus			
15. 14 Erasmus			
16. 36 Erasmus			

Trials	3	2	1
17. 38 Klondike			
18. 52 Klondike			
19. 57 Klondike			
20. 14 Erasmus			
21. 28 Erasmus			
22. 57 Klondike			
23. 38 Klondike			
24. 36 Erasmus			
25. 14 Erasmus			
26. 38 Klondike			
27. 28 Erasmus			
28. 32 Erasmus			
29. 57 Klondike			
30. 52 Klondike			
31. 14 Erasmus			
32. 36 Erasmus			

Trials	3	2	1
33. 52 Klondike			
34. 36 Erasmus			
35. 14 Erasmus			
36. 32 Erasmus			
37. 38 Klondike			
38. 57 Klondike			
39. 52 Klondike			
40. 14 Erasmus			
41. 36 Erasmus			
42. 28 Erasmus			
43. 32 Erasmus			
44. 38 Klondike			
Number Right **Time**			

Drill 8

Trials	3	2	1
1. 64 Avalon			
2. 59 Avalon			
3. 49 Schooner			
4. 39 Schooner			
5. 93 Avalon			
6. 86 Avalon			
7. 64 Avalon			
8. 59 Avalon			
9. 19 Schooner			
10. 93 Avalon			
11. 86 Avalon			
12. 64 Avalon			
13. 59 Avalon			
14. 39 Schooner			
15. 19 Schooner			
16. 64 Avalon			

Trials	3	2	1
17. 59 Avalon			
18. 19 Schooner			
19. 39 Schooner			
20. 49 Schooner			
21. 64 Avalon			
22. 86 Avalon			
23. 93 Avalon			
24. 86 Avalon			
25. 59 Avalon			
26. 19 Schooner			
27. 49 Schooner			
28. 39 Schooner			
29. 59 Avalon			
30. 93 Avalon			
31. 49 Schooner			
32. 39 Schooner			

Trials	3	2	1
33. 19 Schooner			
34. 64 Avalon			
35. 59 Avalon			
36. 93 Avalon			
37. 86 Avalon			
38. 93 Avalon			
39. 86 Avalon			
40. 49 Schooner			
41. 39 Schooner			
42. 64 Avalon			
43. 59 Avalon			
44. 19 Schooner			
Number Right **Time**			

Drill 9

Trials	3	2	1
1. 11 Hershey			
2. 25 Hershey			
3. 85 Orion			
4. 90 Orion			
5. 63 Pointe			
6. 55 Pointe			
7. 77 Orion			
8. 81 Orion			
9. 17 Hershey			
10. 31 Hershey			
11. 63 Pointe			
12. 55 Pointe			
13. 77 Orion			
14. 81 Orion			
15. 85 Orion			
16. 90 Orion			

Trials	3	2	1
17. 11 Hershey			
18. 17 Hershey			
19. 31 Hershey			
20. 55 Pointe			
21. 63 Pointe			
22. 25 Hershey			
23. 25 Hershey			
24. 85 Orion			
25. 77 Orion			
26. 81 Orion			
27. 90 Orion			
28. 17 Hershey			
29. 31 Hershey			
30. 63 Pointe			
31. 55 Pointe			
32. 25 Hershey			

Trials	3	2	1
33. 17 Hershey			
34. 31 Hershey			
35. 77 Orion			
36. 81 Orion			
37. 85 Orion			
38. 90 Orion			
39. 11 Hershey			
40. 77 Orion			
41. 81 Orion			
42. 63 Pointe			
43. 55 Pointe			
44. 85 Orion			
Number Right			
Time			

Drill 10

Trials	3	2	1
1. 18 Vine			
2. 21 Vine			
3. 54 Nestle			
4. 40 Nestle			
5. 21 Railroad			
6. 10 Railroad			
7. 31 Vine			
8. 15 Vine			
9. 21 Railroad			
10. 10 Railroad			
11. 14 Railroad			
12. 25 Railroad			
13. 40 Nestle			
14. 10 Railroad			
15. 18 Vine			
16. 15 Vine			

Trials	3	2	1
17. 40 Nestle			
18. 14 Railroad			
19. 25 Railroad			
20. 21 Railroad			
21. 31 Vine			
22. 54 Nestle			
23. 18 Vine			
24. 21 Vine			
25. 15 Vine			
26. 25 Railroad			
27. 10 Railroad			
28. 18 Vine			
29. 21 Vine			
30. 54 Nestle			
31. 15 Vine			
32. 14 Railroad			

Trials	3	2	1
33. 25 Railroad			
34. 10 Railroad			
35. 15 Vine			
36. 40 Nestle			
37. 21 Vine			
38. 21 Railroad			
39. 10 Railroad			
40. 18 Vine			
41. 21 Vine			
42. 54 Nestle			
43. 40 Nestle			
44. 31 Vine			
Number Right			
Time			

Drill 11

Trials	Answers 3	2	1
1. 66 Blue			
2. 58 Blue			
3. 61 Glover			
4. 70 Glover			
5. 34 Park			
6. 41 Park			
7. 45 Glover			
8. 52 Glover			
9. 61 Glover			
10. 58 Blue			
11. 61 Blue			
12. 34 Park			
13. 45 Glover			
14. 61 Blue			
15. 73 Blue			
16. 61 Blue			

Trials	Answers 3	2	1
17. 58 Park			
18. 53 Park			
19. 45 Glover			
20. 61 Glover			
21. 61 Blue			
22. 58 Blue			
23. 66 Blue			
24. 58 Blue			
25. 53 Park			
26. 41 Park			
27. 61 Glover			
28. 52 Glover			
29. 66 Blue			
30. 58 Blue			
31. 70 Glover			
32. 66 Blue			

Trials	Answers 3	2	1
33. 58 Blue			
34. 41 Park			
35. 34 Park			
36. 45 Glover			
37. 61 Blue			
38. 53 Park			
39. 66 Blue			
40. 58 Park			
41. 34 Park			
42. 41 Park			
43. 45 Glover			
44. 52 Glover			
Number Right **Time**			

Drill 12

Trials	Answers 3	2	1
1. 25 Creek			
2. 44 Creek			
3. 28 Reardon			
4. 35 Reardon			
5. 20 Mountain			
6. 11 Mountain			
7. 33 Mountain			
8. 26 Mountain			
9. 36 Creek			
10. 40 Creek			
11. 13 Reardon			
12. 21 Reardon			
13. 28 Reardon			
14. 35 Reardon			
15. 20 Mountain			
16. 28 Reardon			

Trials	Answers 3	2	1
17. 40 Creek			
18. 26 Mountain			
19. 25 Creek			
20. 44 Creek			
21. 28 Reardon			
22. 35 Reardon			
23. 20 Mountain			
24. 20 Mountain			
25. 36 Creek			
26. 40 Creek			
27. 20 Mountain			
28. 11 Mountain			
29. 35 Reardon			
30. 21 Reardon			
31. 28 Reardon			
32. 36 Creek			

Trials	Answers 3	2	1
33. 20 Mountain			
34. 11 Mountain			
35. 33 Mountain			
36. 26 Mountain			
37. 13 Reardon			
38. 21 Reardon			
39. 33 Mountain			
40. 26 Mountain			
41. 25 Creek			
42. 44 Creek			
43. 13 Reardon			
44. 21 Reardon			
Number Right **Time**			

Hopefully, you found yourself among those capable of remembering 5 or 6 "chunks," and placing the individual addresses in the correct boxes. If so, it is suggested that you proceed directly to do the drills 13 through 27 based on the addresses on pages 161 and 162. These drills progress in difficulty by involving all five boxes and by including more and more duplicate numbers.

Those who attain high scores may very well decide to move directly on to the Memory for Addresses parts of Practice Tests 1 through 6 using the visualization skills they've perfected.

After doing these tests, you may be in a position to make the important decision as to the memory approach most suitable for you on the real test. If you have done well using visualization, you can approach the real test with confidence of attaining a perfect or nearly perfect score. But unless you are certain, read on. The association techniques furnish *another* road to a perfect score.

The Associations Technique

Using associations to remember the address names was discussed in Chapter 5. It works quickly and easily with many of the names: *Pearl*—Bailey, necklace; *Magnet*—pull, iron; *Cedar*—tree, chest, red; *Niles*—river, Cleopatra.

Numbers may be remembered in the same way.

Now See Why

THERE ARE NUMBERS THAT HOLD IMMEDIATE ASSOCIATIONS FOR ALMOST EVERYONE.

With two digits

10—Commandments, bowling pins
11—Snake eyes (two 1's)
12—Dozen eggs, noon, midnight, lunch, disciples
13—Bad luck, bar mitzvah
16—Sweet (sixteen)
18—Voting age, draft (army), amendment (drinking prohibited)
19—Women's right to vote
21—Adulthood
24—Blackbirds
25—Xmas, quarter
31—End of year (December)
40—Thieves

With four digits

1492—Columbus, Discovery of America
1773—Boston Tea Party
1776—Declaration of Independence, American Revolution
1849—California gold rush
1865—Lincoln assassinated, Civil War ends
1912—Titanic sinks
1914—World War I begins
1927—Lindbergh crosses Atlantic
1929, 1987—Stock market crashes
1941—Pearl Harbor attacked
1945—World War II ends
1963—President John F. Kennedy assassinated
1968—Martin Luther King and Robert Kennedy assassinated

1972—Watergate
1991—Desert Storm (war with Iraq)

(Only illustrations of two-digit and four-digit numbers are shown because these are the kinds of numbers you need to remember for the test.)

Now see the figure below.

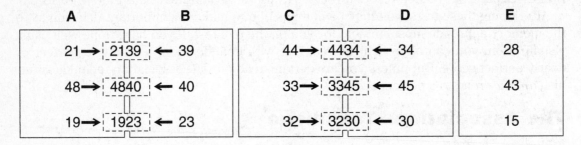

Note the number 2139. Imagine 21 as an *Adult* in Box A. What was the name of the famous comedian who always claimed he was 39 years old? Right—*Benny* in Box B.

Note the number 4840. What do you associate with 40? That's when life *Begins* (Box B).

SOME NUMBERS HOLD PERSONAL ASSOCIATIONS.

The chances are that most people can make an immediate connection with all or part of some of the following items.

address—	home, business, friend	*license plate number*—	_____
age—	yours, spouse, child	*anniversary*—	wedding, job, retirement
telephone number—	home, job, friend	*birthdate*—	yours, loved ones'
Social Security number—	_____	*credit card number*—	_____

Study for a moment the chunks and the two-digit numbers on the preceding page. Does anything connect for you? Does anyone you know have a *birthday* (Box B) in one of the years whose number is in Box B (put a 19- in front of the number, of course)? Does your home or business *address* (Box A) begin or end with 21, 48, or 19? Do you wear an undergarment sized 40B, 32C, or 34D? If any of these possibilities applies to you, then you are in luck. Keep track of these and all other numbers that have strong personal associations for you. (See page 151.)

Associate Numbers With Your "Loci"

The "loci" technique doesn't work as well with numbers as it does with direct names. Nevertheless, you may find a few good fits between some numbers and the letters of the box they are in. For example, using the place system illustrated on page 119, you might see and hear a phonograph playing old *33* rpm records in the *C*ompany room (Box C) while a stack of even older *45* rpm records is sitting on a table in the *D*INING ROOM (Box D).

Make Up a Story

Chapter 5 mentioned briefly the technique of combining address name associations in a box with each other, and with the letter of the box itself (see pages 116 to 118). The idea was to make up a picture-story that would make these names and their images vivid and easy to remember. This technique is even more important when it comes to remembering numbers. Your memory needs as much reinforcement as you can give it.

Everyone can take advantage of this method, but a lot depends on how extensively you have built your list of two-digit number-word associations. To make this clear, here are two examples based on the boxes from the Diagnostic Practice Test (see page 42).

> *For Box C:* The *c*rooks (*Box C*) used a *.32 c*aliber pistol and a *.44 c*aliber rifle to rob us of *33* silver *c*oins.
> *For Box D:* The *d*raftsmen (*Box D*) used a *d*rawing tool with a *45* degree and a *30 d*egree angle to *d*esign a *d*esk *34* inches *d*eep.

As you can see, the method really works. If you like it, you'll need to prepare thoroughly. Start off by working on Drill 13 on page 161.

Your Personal Master List

See the list of numbers from 10 to 99 below. Next to each, write the word, name, or idea that immediately comes to mind.

Example

> 10—Bowling
>
> 11—Seven Eleven food stores
>
> 12—Months in a year
>
> 13—Baker's dozen

If nothing comes to mind for a particular number, examine some of the numbers in your life (see pages 149 and 150 for suggestions). See if any of these numbers, or any part of them, evokes a word or name. Extend your list every day by ten numbers until you reach item 99. The more complete your list is, the better the odds are in your favor of making a quick number-word association on the test. Remember—these associations do not have to ring a bell with anyone else except you.

10. _____	26. _____
11. _____	27. _____
12. _____	28. _____
13. _____	29. _____
14. _____	30. _____
15. _____	31. _____
16. _____	32. _____
17. _____	33. _____
18. _____	34. _____
19. _____	35. _____
20. _____	36. _____
21. _____	37. _____
22. _____	38. _____
23. _____	39. _____
24. _____	40. _____
25. _____	41. _____

42. _____	71. _____
43. _____	72. _____
44. _____	73. _____
45. _____	74. _____
46. _____	75. _____
47. _____	76. _____
48. _____	77. _____
49. _____	78. _____
50. _____	79. _____
51. _____	80. _____
52. _____	81. _____
53. _____	82. _____
54. _____	83. _____
55. _____	84. _____
56. _____	85. _____
57. _____	86. _____
58. _____	87. _____
59. _____	88. _____
60. _____	89. _____
61. _____	90. _____
62. _____	91. _____
63. _____	92. _____
64. _____	93. _____
65. _____	94. _____
66. _____	95. _____
67. _____	96. _____
58. _____	97. _____
59. _____	98. _____
70. _____	99. _____

Use Phonetics and the Number Tree

If you worked at it, and were fortunate enough, by now you have one or more entries next to many of the 99 numbers above. On the other hand, you undoubtedly have some gaps in your list and need words to fill them in. There is a method that uses the *sounds* of words (phonetics) for that purpose. It is one of several such systems used to strengthen memory (you have already seen phonetics at work when you learned about imagery [page 116] and reduction coding [page 120]).

A Number-Language System

This is a system used to translate numbers into sounds, and then sounds into words. As you have seen, once you can replace numbers with words, you have made memorizing numbered addresses far easier. Here is how the system works:

1. *The Number Tree*—numbers into sounds (See illustration below.)
Each number, from 0 to 9, stands in a column that forms the center or "trunk" of the tree. The left side of the tree has branches that give the *beginning sound* of each number. The right side of the tree has branches that show the way each number *sounds when it ends*. For example, say the number 1 out loud. When you pronounce it, it sounds like WON or WUN (depending on your accent). The beginning sound is "w"; the ending is "on" or "un." You can see them on the top left and right branches. Similarly, the number 2 has a "t" sound to begin, and an "o͞o" sound at the

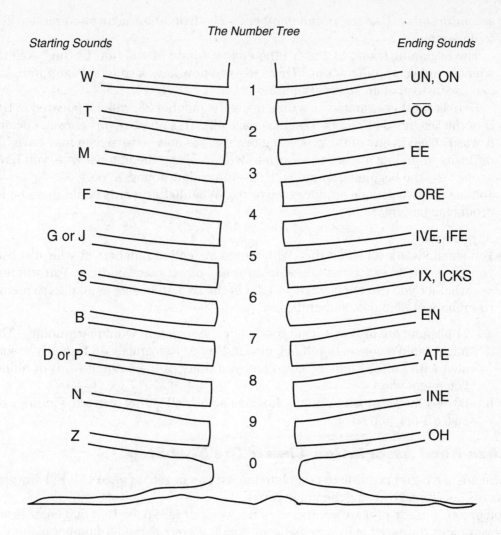

The Number Tree

Starting Sounds · Ending Sounds

Starting Sounds		Ending Sounds
W	1	UN, ON
T	2	OO
M	3	EE
F	4	ORE
G or J	5	IVE, IFE
S	6	IX, ICKS
B	7	EN
D or P	8	ATE
N	9	INE
Z	0	OH

end. As you look down the number tree, say each of the words aloud. Notice the beginning and ending sounds that compare them to the branches of the number tree, which has the phonetic breakdown for each number 0 through 9. (There are only four exceptions to this method: the beginning sounds of 3, 5, 7, and 8. These are the only parts of the number tree that you will have to memorize. Everything else follows the way you naturally pronounce the numbers.*)

2. *Sounds into Words*

The job now is to convert the two-digit address numbers into meaningful words. The *number tree* will enable you to do that since all two-digit addresses must use some combination of the numbers 0 through 9. *The way to proceed is to join the beginning sound of the first number in the address to the ending sound of the*

---

* These exceptions were made to avoid confusion between similar sounds or to provide a more useful beginning sound.
3. "m" will help build better words than "th"
5. "g" or j avoids confusion with the "f" that is used for "four"
7. "b" avoids confusion with the "s" that is used for "six"
8. "p" was chosen because "eight" (ate) doesn't have the "hard" sound useful in beginning many words.
9. Zero does not usually appear at the first digit among the addresses. If you should be given a number like 04, use the "Z" sound shown on the number tree. Think of it as an accented version of "s" and it becomes most useful. The address, (04) connects to "zore" (sore); (03) becomes zee (see), and so on.

second number. Use one of the numbers—21—from the Diagnostic Practice Test to illustrate:

The beginning sound of 2 is "t"; the ending sound of 1 is "un" or "on." Join the sounds, and you produce "ton." That's it—you now have a *concrete word, ton,* you can use instead of an *abstract number, 21.*

Here is another example, this time using the number 23, which appeared in Box B of the Diagnostic Practice Test (see page 42). This number was chosen because it wasn't used in any of the preceding discussions and because you may have had difficulty in finding a word to associate with it. Using the number tree, you have:

2—the beginning sound is "t"; 3—the ending sound is "ee."

Joining the two sounds produces *tee* or *tea.* What better words could there be for producing pictures?

3. *Application*

You should know all about this. With words instead of numbers at your disposal, you can proceed exactly as you would for any direct name address. You will now see whether you can apply what you did in the two preceding examples to memorize numbers 21 and 23 in their boxes.

a. 21 became *ton* in Box A. One good, quick association would be *amount.* (This might build a connection to 48, also in Box A. Remember *48* formerly associated with Lotto? Think of Lotto and you think of the *amount* (ton) of money you might win.)

b. 23 became *tee* or *tea* in Box B. Imagine a golf *ball* sitting on a tee. Picture a tea *bag*, a T-*bar*, and so on.

Number-Word Association Chart: The Next Step

Now you are in a better position to complete the list you began on page 151. Fill any gaps with words developed by using the number tree.

If you prefer, you can prepare another very useful chart (see page 155) that enables you to be even more thorough and systematic in building your personal number-name list. Here are some important points to keep in mind in connection with this chart.

- It is going to be *your* chart containing words useful to *you.* No one has to approve it or even understand the associations you make. Everyone has a different background and a different life experience. One person's list will probably be very different from another's.

- The best associations are the ones that come quickly and naturally. Often these come from your personal history. The most important data of your life may mean absolutely nothing to others. For example if you got married on November 28, 1967, the numbers *11 - 28 - 67* on your chart should have words like *anniversary, bride, ceremony* next to them. Your spouse's name should be there, too. If it begins with A, B, C, D, or E, so much the better.

- Even though the list is personal, others can help you build it. Perhaps you have a friend who is knowledgeable and willing to help you recall dates you learned in school, or in your reading, that you have not thought about in a long time—for example, 1776, 1789, 1812, 1914. You can match the important person or event with the date, thereby gaining additional useful associations. Similarly, your wife, parents, or an old friend can assist you in recalling important numbers in your own life: graduation dates, old addresses, the number of your public school (P.S. 28), and so on.

- It is perfectly acceptable to enter *more than one word* for any particular number—in fact, it is desirable. You will have that much more opportunity to produce images to fit different boxes. If you come up with *more than one number* that you associate with a particular word, that is also good. Just make sure that you reinforce the association between the word and the particular number you need to recall.

- If you have a choice of several words to use for a particular number, choose the one that produces the most vivid, colorful, action-filled image. Concrete nouns like *bee* and *gun* are the most effective in building picture-stories. You can see this clearly in the case of number *19*. The words produced by using the Number Tree are *wine* and *whine*. Although *whine* can be used successfully to build a connection to the boxes, *wine* is even better (see illustrations on page 157).

- If the only word you can develop for a particular number is an unfamiliar or abstract one, you must drill it until the association comes easily. Make sure that you fully understand the word's meaning and its proper use in a sentence. This is necessary if you are going to be able to incorporate it in a "picture story."

* SAMPLE NUMBER-WORD ASSOCIATION CHART FOR NUMBERS 10–19

Number	Number Tree Words	Common Associations	Personal Associations	Number
10	WOE	Commandments, decimal system, bowling pins		10
11	WON	Veterans Day, football team		11
12	WOO	Disciples, Lincoln's birthday, dozen eggs		12
13	WEE	Baker's dozen		13
14	WAR WORE	Valentine's Day Civil Rights amendment		14
15	WIFE	Tennis, Martin Luther King, Jr.'s birthday		15
16	WICKS	Sweet sixteen, pint (16 ounces)		16
17	WHEN	Magazine		17
18	WEIGHT WAIT	Vote, army		18
19	WINE WHINE	Women's suffrage amendment		19

* This is a sample of the kind of chart used to build and remember number-word associations. The format of this chart and its headings may be used as is or with any changes you desire.

The entries under "common associations" are the author's. You probably have others.

There are no entries for "personal associations" because such entries would be the author's and would mean nothing to you. It is most important that you fill in as many of yours as you can.

- Use the sounds associated with the numbers on the number tree in a *consistent* way. Unless you do so, you will have difficulty translating the number *into* a word, and even more in *reconstructing* a number *from* a word.

- Remember that you increase the odds in your favor of scoring high on the memory test each time you add another good number-word association to your chart. Try to produce some word for every number.

A Little More Insurance

At this point, you have everything you need to remember the numbers in addresses for a perfect score. You have a wide choice of association techniques to make the numbers more memorable. The illustrations and examples on the preceding pages have also shown you how to locate the numbers in their proper boxes.

Sometimes the associated word itself is used, for example, 21—*Adult*—Box A. In other cases, we employed a simple picture story—"The *crooks* (*Box C*) used a *.32 c*aliber pistol . . ." to connect the numbers to their box.

If you have prepared a good number-word chart, stories and images will make it very simple to connect any number with any box. For example, if the number 21 (Adult), instead of being in Box A, were in one of the other four boxes, how would you have made the connection? You should have had no problem. Here's how:

21—Adult—*Adult*—Box A

21—Adult—*Big*—Box B

21—Adult—*Consent, Control*—Box C

21—Adult—*Dad, Develop*—Box D

21—Adult—*Elder, End*—Box E

For that matter, if the number 21 brought you even quicker associations with the word *big* or *blackjack* than it did with *adult*, you could have made these connections:

For *Big*	For *Blackjack*
21—Big—*Apple, Ape, Adult*—Box A	21—Blackjack—*Ace*—Box A
21—Big—*Big, Bang*—Box B	21—Blackjack—*Buy, Blow*—Box B
21—Big—*Cheese, Creep*—Box C	21—Blackjack—*Cards, Cut*—Box C
21—Big—*Daddy, Deal*—Box D	21—Blackjack—*Draw*—Box D
21—Big—*Enormous*—Box E	21—Blackjack—*Enough*—Box E

All that was done was to use simple and natural *extended associations* stemming from the original number-word associations between 21 and *a*dult, *b*ig, and *b*lackjack.

See whether you can do the same thing with two of the word associations that were developed, using the number tree, for number 19—*wine, whine.* Some of the possible choices are shown on page 157.

If you do not want to rely entirely on your ability to work these extended associations at test time (the moment of truth), or if you are determined to do everything possible to insure a perfect score, then you should consider preparing the extended association *beforehand. In other words, you would do for every number from 10 through 99 what was done for number 21.* You will end up with a ready-made match connecting the original number—the original associated word—with a set of five words, each keyed to a particular box.

It is not difficult to do this, but it will take some time. Here are some guidelines to follow:

1. If you originally associated more than one word with a number (look back at your number-word chart), select the *best one* to be the original associated word. As you know, the best one is usually the most concrete and visual one. Words like *ham, cow, tree, worm,* fit the bill. Such words are the easiest to *extend* to yield additional associations.

2. In turn, try to select the four or five new *keyed* words so that each of them is concrete and as visual as possible. It is easier to visualize *eggs* than *eager.*

3. Prepare a chart specifically for the 90 key sets. (Use the examples for number 21 on page 156 and for 19 on this page as models.

4. Practice.

Number	Original Association	Extended (Keyed) Association	Box
19	Wine	Alcohol, Aroma	A
	Wine	Bottle, Bar, Burgundy	B
	Wine	Cocktail, Cellar, Chablis	C
	Wine	Drink, Dregs	D
	Wine	Elbow (bend it), Enjoy	E
19	Whine	Angry, Annoy	A
	Whine	Bother, Brat	B
	Whine	Complain	C
	Whine	Demand, Drone	D
	Whine	Engine	E

Dealing With Duplicate Numbers

At the beginning of this chapter (page 138), the possibility was raised of the number (23) appearing in more than one box. The new postal exams show that this is more than a possibility; it's certain enough so that you must be prepared. Previous tests have had as many as two or three duplicate numbers. The sample, issued by the U.S. Postal Service, reproduced on page 8, displays 15 different street addresses, with the five ranges of numbers appearing three times, each attached to a street name on a different line. This means that one can no long rely solely on the association between *one number and one particular box.* On page 154, (23) was used to illustrate a good solid connection between the number and its box that would enable you to remember it early on: (*23*) became *tea* or *tee* in Box B. Two vivid associations arose immediately; i.e., *Tea-Bag* and *T-Ball.* There was no need to remember that (23) appeared on the Laurel line. Now things are different.

What would you do if 23 appeared three times, as illustrated below? (For clarity, only the "2300" addresses are shown.)

Figure 6.1

A	B	C	D	E
	2300–2999 Laurel	2300–3999 Cliff	2300–3899 Mall	

To resolve this problem, what has been studied thus far on association will be combined with several additional memory hints. Figures 6.2 and 6.3 will illustrate how it's done.

Once again (23)'s image as *tea* or *tee* makes for good associations: In Box C, you get (23) *tea C*up; in Box D, you see (23) *tee-D*ivot. But how do you distinguish between the 23 in Box B, the 23 in Box C and the 23 in Box D, when all you are given on the test is 2300–2999 Laurel, Cliff, or Mall? The answer is, with great difficulty!

Figure 6.2

2300–2999 Laurel, becomes . . . . . . 2300 + Laurel in Box B
    Association converts to . . . . . . Tea + *Laurel* Leaves Tree in *B*ag or *B*otanical garden
        Result . . . . *Tea Leaves* in a *B*ag   *Answer B!*
        or . . . . *Tea Bush* in a *B*otanical garden *Answer B!*
    If you wished, you could
    have used *Sounds* . . . . 2300 + Laurel in Box B
        Sound . . . . *T* +   *L* +   *B*
    Combining Sounds—Result . . T + L or *Teal* (Blue) + *B* (Blue) *Answer B*

2300–2999 Cliff, becomes . . . . 2300 + Cliff in Box C
    Converts to . . . . *Tea* + *C*liff in C
    Combining Sounds . . . . *Tea* + *K* in C = *Teak* Cabinet *Answer C*
    or
    If you wished, you could . . . . . 2300 + Cliff in Box C
    have used associations . . . . *Tea* + *C*up in a *C*abinet *Answer C*

2300–2999 Mall, becomes . . . . 2300 + *M*all in Box D
    Converts to . . . . *Tea* + *Mall* + *D*
    Combining Sounds to . . . . *Team* —Dodgers—   *Answer D*
        or . . . . *Teem* (rain) + *D*(drip)— *Answer D*

No doubt you could have made your own connections as well! Now use these ideas with a numbered address as it appeared in the U.S. Postal Service Sample (see page 8). The number (47), which does *not* immediately yield as good an image or association as did (23), has been selected on purpose.

The three duplicate street addresses by themselves appear in Figures 6.2, 6.3, and 6.4.

Following the procedure described above, first try to associate (47) with an image or a meaning. Probably you can't unless (47) connects with something personal like your age, home address, Social Security number, a memorable date, and so on. If you don't come up with a quick connection, then use the number tree on page 153 to convert (47) to "fen." What is a fen? It's a bog, swamp, marsh, or Chinese coin. Given choices like these, it is usually best to pick the shortest word. It lends itself more easily to sound combinations. Now try the *4700–5599* address using *bog*. (Note, you can switch to "fen" or marsh if it *works better for you*, but you must never forget the association with *47!*)

Figure 6.3

4700–5599 Table, becomes	4700 +	Table	in Box A
	bog +	T +	A
Combining sounds	Bog-T-A or	*BOGATA*	*Answer A*
		Capital of Colombia	

"BOG-T-A" becomes *Bogota* (the capital of Colombia) when you pronounce the word and letters together as one word. Whenever you have adjoining consonants like the "g" and "T," the missing vowel sound automatically comes forth. This fact is the basis for many of the associations you may need to make in the test.

Very often, a real word is produced, and that is so much the better. But it really doesn't matter that much if you didn't recognize "Bogota" for what it is. The word has a distinctive *sound* you will hear and retain in your memory.

Figure 6.4

4700–5599 West, becomes........	4700 +	West	in Box E
Converts to.................	*Bog* +	W +	E
Combining sounds	BogWE*		*Answer E*
or, using an alternate	Swamp +	W +	E
associating initials..........	S—	W—	E
		(3 points of the compass)	

You might very well have used Box E's position and initial at the *E*nd. ... See a *Bog* at the *West End* (of your ranch).

Figure 6.5

4700–5599 Blake, becomes	4700 +	Blake	in Box D
Using associations	Bog +	Black +	Dark .... Answer D

In this case, many memory techniques were used: the *number tree* to convert (47) to Bog, the *sound* and *appearance* of Blake to derive Black, and finally the *initial* D, which rounds out the *image of a dark swamp*.

These illustrations employ almost every associative memory technique useful in dealing with duplicate numbered addresses: substituting words or images for numbers; using the numbers tree to convert numbers to words; using the sounds of words, and their appearance; and reducing names to initials. The end result is a unique, powerful tool to help the test taker. A step-by-step summary of the methods to use on the test follows.

---

* "Bogwe" doesn't mean anything but it has a good sound that leads directly to Box E. If you saw that "Bogwe" could easily become "Bogwed," you'd be using sound and appearance to form a good image. But, you'd also be running the risk of deciding that *D* was the correct box since "Bogwed" ends in a "d." Please remember that Step 3 of the procedure directs you to combine the box letter with the number and the street. *This is usually best accomplished as was seen in the various examples by using the box letter at the beginning or end of the new word or image.*

The Five Step Process

STEP 1. Scan the numbered addresses to see in which boxes and lines the *duplicate* number addresses appear. *Addresses whose numbers are not duplicated* may be remembered in the usual way, i.e., just connect the numbers to the box letters as explained on pages 150 to 157. There is no need to take the street name into account, which obviously makes matters easier.

STEP 2. If you can, establish an association between the duplicated number and some specific image. Use the list of personal associations you developed in Drill 13 on pages 150 to 152. They will be particularly helpful at this time.

STEP 3. If Step 2 does not yield a useful word or image, immediately convert the number to a word by using the number tree, e.g., (23) to tea. If *this* new word has no *meaning* for you, be prepared to use its *sound* or the sound of its *initial* letter.

STEP 4. Connect the word, image or sound you obtained for this number with its adjoining street *name* or with the *initial* of the street name, or with the *appearance* of the street name.
Example 1: (23) Tea + Laurel (leaves, tree) → tea leaves
Example 2: (23) Tea + Mall → Team
Example 3: (47) Bog + Blake (Black) → Black bog
Look at the combination or connection. Does it *mean* anything?
Sound out the combination—Does it *mean* anything? Is the sound memorable?
Step 4 is vital. It separates and places the duplicate numbers, each according to its adjoining street name. Only then can one connect the original number to its proper box.

STEP 5. Associate the result of Step 4 with its box letter.
Tea Leaves in a *B*ag   Box B
Team → *D*odgers   Box D
Black Bog → *D*ark Box D

Remember this five-step process. With practice, you will actually be able to read the answers as they arise in association, from the very numbers, words and boxes in each question.
DEVELOP YOUR IMAGINATION. WITH PRACTICE YOU WILL EASILY BE ABLE TO ATTAIN A PERFECT SCORE!
Now that you've learned the many powerful devices that may be used, it is advisable to practice and refine your memory techniques. Then you will be better able to decide on the approach or combination of approaches that works best for you.

■ DRILLS 13 Through 27

Drills 13 through 27 are displayed like Drills 3 through 12 and are to be used in much the same way. There are three important differences between the two sets.

1. Drills 13 through 27 display all five boxes, including Box E.

2. These drills contain an ever increasing number of duplicates.

3. They are designed to be answered using any or all memory tools explained in Chapters 5 and 6, not just chunking.

Directions for Drills 13 Through 27

- Study the addresses using the method(s) of your choice to remember them. Use the time indicated above each drill as a guide.

- When the study time is up, turn to the Answer Sheet. Enter the box letter for as many of the addresses as you can. Work for a reasonable amount of time but don't worry about speed as yet. Note the elapsed time to keep track of your progress. The answer sheets allow for three trials but allow a couple of weeks to pass before repeating them.

Drills 13 Through 15—Study 1 minute each

Drill No.	Street Name	A	B	C	D	E	Street Name
13	Abelson	27	20	23	16	14	Abelson
14	Mark	49	51	57	42	64	Mark
15	Larue	12	19	27	17	31	Larue

Drills 16 Through 18—Study 3 minutes each

Drill No.	Street Name	A	B	C	D	E	Street Name
16	Walnut	26	36	16	39	43	Walnut
	North	43	59	—	—	—	North
17	Merry	57	55	61	69	51	Merry
	Pinto	12	20	—	—	—	Pinto
18	Laurel	97	91	83	85	71	Laurel
	Billings	71	68	—	—	—	Billings

Drills 19 Through 21—Study 5 minutes each

Drill No.	Street Name	A	B	C	D	E	Street Name
19	Miles	38	23	33	45	40	Miles
	Grove	15	38	29	24	12	Grove
20	Clarol	21	28	37	45	19	Clarol
	Apple	19	11	21	25	30	Apple
21	Ridell	36	42	33	50	52	Ridell
	Maple	50	64	45	36	39	Maple

Drills 22 Through 23—Study 8 minutes each

Drill No.	Street Name	A	B	C	D	E	Street Name
22	Lakeview	38	63	19	48	60	Lakeview
	Wichita	91	81	83	74	70	Wichita
	Castle	41	69	74	—	—	Castle
23	Oxford	80	77	90	93	85	Oxford
	Klein	63	85	60	74	53	Klein
	Star	85	47	70	—	—	Star

Drills 24 Through 27—Study 9 minutes each

Drill No.	Street Name	A	B	C	D	E	Street Name
24	Greene	52	61	29	39	45	Greene
	Ashley	53	57	68	78	64	Ashley
	Dartmouth	57	61	75	69	—	Dartmouth
25	Fleet	39	16	23	44	10	Fleet
	Chase	40	23	39	46	19	Chase
	Ash	62	72	34	39	54	Ash
26	Race	58	73	49	54	33	Race
	Poplar	73	41	83	60	53	Poplar
	Eric	33	43	67	46	73	Eric
27	Centra	58	69	32	50	41	Centra
	Tremont	57	70	77	42	32	Tremont
	Mill	51	57	42	74	63	Mill

Drill 13

Trials	3	2	1
1. 14 Abelson			
2. 27 Abelson			
3. 16 Abelson			
4. 27 Abelson			
5. 20 Abelson			
6. 23 Abelson			
7. 20 Abelson			
8. 14 Abelson			
9. 27 Abelson			
10. 23 Abelson			
11. 20 Abelson			
12. 14 Abelson			
13. 16 Abelson			
14. 27 Abelson			
15. 20 Abelson			
16. 14 Abelson			

Trials	3	2	1
17. 16 Abelson			
18. 23 Abelson			
19. 20 Abelson			
20. 27 Abelson			
21. 20 Abelson			
22. 16 Abelson			
23. 14 Abelson			
24. 23 Abelson			
25. 20 Abelson			
26. 20 Abelson			
27. 16 Abelson			
28. 23 Abelson			
29. 20 Abelson			
30. 27 Abelson			
31. 14 Abelson			
32. 16 Abelson			

Trials	3	2	1
33. 23 Abelson			
34. 23 Abelson			
35. 20 Abelson			
36. 14 Abelson			
37. 27 Abelson			
38. 20 Abelson			
39. 14 Abelson			
40. 23 Abelson			
41. 16 Abelson			
42. 20 Abelson			
43. 23 Abelson			
44. 27 Abelson			
Number Right			
Time			

Drill 14

Trials	3	2	1
1. 49 Mark			
2. 51 Mark			
3. 57 Mark			
4. 42 Mark			
5. 64 Mark			
6. 51 Mark			
7. 49 Mark			
8. 42 Mark			
9. 64 Mark			
10. 57 Mark			
11. 42 Mark			
12. 49 Mark			
13. 51 Mark			
14. 57 Mark			
15. 64 Mark			
16. 51 Mark			

Trials	3	2	1
17. 57 Mark			
18. 64 Mark			
19. 49 Mark			
20. 64 Mark			
21. 51 Mark			
22. 57 Mark			
23. 49 Mark			
24. 51 Mark			
25. 57 Mark			
26. 42 Mark			
27. 51 Mark			
28. 49 Mark			
29. 64 Mark			
30. 42 Mark			
31. 64 Mark			
32. 51 Mark			

Trials	3	2	1
33. 57 Mark			
34. 49 Mark			
35. 64 Mark			
36. 42 Mark			
37. 57 Mark			
38. 49 Mark			
39. 57 Mark			
40. 51 Mark			
41. 42 Mark			
42. 49 Mark			
43. 51 Mark			
44. 57 Mark			
Number Right			
Time			

Drill 15

Trials	3	2	1
1. 27 Larue			
2. 17 Larue			
3. 12 Larue			
4. 19 Larue			
5. 31 Larue			
6. 12 Larue			
7. 19 Larue			
8. 31 Larue			
9. 17 Larue			
10. 27 Larue			
11. 31 Larue			
12. 19 Larue			
13. 27 Larue			
14. 17 Larue			
15. 12 Larue			
16. 27 Larue			

Trials	3	2	1
17. 17 Larue			
18. 31 Larue			
19. 27 Larue			
20. 17 Larue			
21. 12 Larue			
22. 31 Larue			
23. 19 Larue			
24. 12 Larue			
25. 27 Larue			
26. 17 Larue			
27. 31 Larue			
28. 12 Larue			
29. 19 Larue			
30. 31 Larue			
31. 17 Larue			
32. 27 Larue			

Trials	3	2	1
33. 19 Larue			
34. 12 Larue			
35. 19 Larue			
36. 27 Larue			
37. 31 Larue			
38. 12 Larue			
39. 12 Larue			
40. 17 Larue			
41. 27 Larue			
42. 17 Larue			
43. 12 Larue			
44. 19 Larue			
Number Right **Time**			

Drill 16

Trials	3	2	1
1. 16 Walnut			
2. 36 Walnut			
3. 43 North			
4. 59 North			
5. 26 Walnut			
6. 36 Walnut			
7. 59 North			
8. 16 Walnut			
9. 43 North			
10. 39 Walnut			
11. 36 Walnut			
12. 26 Walnut			
13. 43 Walnut			
14. 36 Walnut			
15. 26 Walnut			
16. 59 North			

Trials	3	2	1
17. 43 Walnut			
18. 59 North			
19. 16 Walnut			
20. 39 Walnut			
21. 26 Walnut			
22. 59 North			
23. 43 Walnut			
24. 43 North			
25. 16 Walnut			
26. 39 Walnut			
27. 26 Walnut			
28. 36 Walnut			
29. 43 North			
30. 59 North			
31. 39 Walnut			
32. 42 North			

Trials	3	2	1
33. 36 Walnut			
34. 26 Walnut			
35. 43 North			
36. 16 Walnut			
37. 39 Walnut			
38. 36 Walnut			
39. 59 North			
40. 26 Walnut			
41. 43 Walnut			
42. 39 Walnut			
43. 36 Walnut			
44. 43 Walnut			
Number Right **Time**			

Drill 17

Trials	Answers 3	2	1
1. 57 Merry			
2. 55 Merry			
3. 61 Merry			
4. 19 Merry			
5. 12 Pinto			
6. 20 Pinto			
7. 51 Merry			
8. 55 Merry			
9. 20 Pinto			
10. 12 Pinto			
11. 19 Merry			
12. 61 Merry			
13. 51 Merry			
14. 20 Pinto			
15. 12 Pinto			
16. 51 Merry			

Trials	Answers 3	2	1
17. 19 Merry			
18. 61 Merry			
19. 55 Merry			
20. 57 Merry			
21. 55 Merry			
22. 12 Pinto			
23. 20 Pinto			
24. 61 Merry			
25. 69 Merry			
26. 51 Merry			
27. 51 Merry			
28. 12 Pinto			
29. 20 Pinto			
30. 55 Merry			
31. 61 Merry			
32. 19 Merry			

Trials	Answers 3	2	1
33. 51 Merry			
34. 20 Pinto			
35. 57 Merry			
36. 12 Pinto			
37. 61 Merry			
38. 69 Merry			
39. 57 Merry			
40. 57 Merry			
41. 55 Merry			
42. 61 Merry			
43. 19 Merry			
44. 51 Merry			
Number Right			
Time			

Drill 18

Trials	Answers 3	2	1
1. 71 Billings			
2. 68 Billings			
3. 97 Laurel			
4. 91 Laurel			
5. 83 Laurel			
6. 85 Laurel			
7. 71 Laurel			
8. 71 Billings			
9. 68 Billings			
10. 85 Laurel			
11. 83 Laurel			
12. 91 Laurel			
13. 97 Laurel			
14. 71 Laurel			
15. 68 Billings			
16. 97 Laurel			

Trials	Answers 3	2	1
17. 91 Laurel			
18. 71 Laurel			
19. 83 Laurel			
20. 85 Laurel			
21. 71 Laurel			
22. 91 Laurel			
23. 83 Laurel			
24. 85 Laurel			
25. 71 Billings			
26. 97 Laurel			
27. 91 Laurel			
28. 71 Laurel			
29. 68 Billings			
30. 85 Laurel			
31. 71 Billings			
32. 68 Billings			

Trials	Answers 3	2	1
33. 83 Laurel			
34. 97 Laurel			
35. 91 Laurel			
36. 83 Laurel			
37. 85 Laurel			
38. 71 Billings			
39. 71 Laurel			
40. 68 Billings			
41. 97 Laurel			
42. 91 Laurel			
43. 71 Laurel			
44. 71 Billings			
Number Right			
Time			

Drill 19

Answers

Trials	3	2	1
1. 15 Grove			
2. 38 Grove			
3. 33 Miles			
4. 45 Miles			
5. 29 Grove			
6. 24 Grove			
7. 40 Miles			
8. 12 Grove			
9. 38 Miles			
10. 23 Miles			
11. 15 Grove			
12. 38 Grove			
13. 33 Miles			
14. 45 Miles			
15. 40 Miles			
16. 23 Miles			

Answers

Trials	3	2	1
17. 38 Miles			
18. 12 Grove			
19. 24 Grove			
20. 29 Grove			
21. 15 Grove			
22. 40 Miles			
23. 33 Miles			
24. 45 Miles			
25. 38 Miles			
26. 23 Miles			
27. 29 Grove			
28. 24 Grove			
29. 12 Grove			
30. 40 Miles			
31. 45 Miles			
32. 38 Miles			

Answers

Trials	3	2	1
33. 15 Grove			
34. 29 Grove			
35. 12 Grove			
36. 40 Miles			
37. 33 Miles			
38. 38 Grove			
39. 45 Miles			
40. 38 Grove			
41. 23 Miles			
42. 29 Grove			
43. 33 Miles			
44. 40 Miles			
Number Right			
Time			

Drill 20

Answers

Trials	3	2	1
1. 21 Clarol			
2. 28 Clarol			
3. 37 Clarol			
4. 45 Clarol			
5. 19 Clarol			
6. 11 Apple			
7. 21 Apple			
8. 25 Apple			
9. 19 Apple			
10. 30 Apple			
11. 21 Clarol			
12. 25 Apple			
13. 21 Clarol			
14. 28 Clarol			
15. 37 Clarol			
16. 21 Apple			

Answers

Trials	3	2	1
17. 19 Apple			
18. 11 Apple			
19. 30 Apple			
20. 19 Clarol			
21. 45 Clarol			
22. 37 Clarol			
23. 21 Clarol			
24. 28 Clarol			
25. 21 Apple			
26. 25 Apple			
27. 30 Apple			
28. 11 Apple			
29. 19 Apple			
30. 11 Apple			
31. 21 Clarol			
32. 28 Clarol			

Answers

Trials	3	2	1
33. 19 Clarol			
34. 30 Apple			
35. 37 Clarol			
36. 45 Clarol			
37. 21 Apple			
38. 25 Apple			
39. 28 Clarol			
40. 21 Clarol			
41. 11 Apple			
42. 19 Apple			
43. 30 Apple			
44. 19 Clarol			
Number Right			
Time			

Drill 21

Trials	3	2	1
1. 36 Ridell			
2. 42 Ridell			
3. 50 Maple			
4. 64 Maple			
5. 33 Ridell			
6. 50 Ridell			
7. 36 Maple			
8. 39 Maple			
9. 45 Maple			
10. 36 Maple			
11. 36 Ridell			
12. 42 Ridell			
13. 52 Ridell			
14. 39 Ridell			
15. 45 Maple			
16. 36 Maple			

Trials	3	2	1
17. 64 Maple			
18. 42 Ridell			
19. 33 Ridell			
20. 36 Ridell			
21. 39 Maple			
22. 33 Ridell			
23. 50 Ridell			
24. 52 Ridell			
25. 39 Maple			
26. 64 Maple			
27. 50 Maple			
28. 36 Ridell			
29. 39 Maple			
30. 36 Ridell			
31. 42 Ridell			
32. 52 Ridell			

Trials	3	2	1
33. 39 Ridell			
34. 50 Maple			
35. 64 Maple			
36. 33 Ridell			
37. 50 Ridell			
38. 45 Maple			
39. 50 Maple			
40. 36 Ridell			
41. 36 Maple			
42. 33 Ridell			
43. 50 Ridell			
44. 50 Maple			
Number Right			
Time			

Drill 22

Trials	3	2	1
1. 91 Wichita			
2. 81 Wichita			
3. 83 Wichita			
4. 74 Wichita			
5. 41 Castle			
6. 69 Castle			
7. 19 Lakeview			
8. 48 Lakeview			
9. 38 Lakeview			
10. 63 Lakeview			
11. 70 Wichita			
12. 60 Lakeview			
13. 83 Wichita			
14. 74 Wichita			
15. 70 Wichita			
16. 60 Lakeview			

Trials	3	2	1
17. 63 Lakeview			
18. 38 Lakeview			
19. 81 Wichita			
20. 91 Wichita			
21. 41 Castle			
22. 69 Castle			
23. 19 Lakeview			
24. 48 Lakeview			
25. 60 Lakeview			
26. 70 Wichita			
27. 74 Wichita			
28. 63 Lakeview			
29. 70 Wichita			
30. 19 Lakeview			
31. 48 Lakeview			
32. 60 Lakeview			

Trials	3	2	1
33. 70 Wichita			
34. 41 Castle			
35. 69 Castle			
36. 63 Lakeview			
37. 38 Lakeview			
38. 83 Wichita			
39. 74 Wichita			
40. 60 Lakeview			
41. 74 Castle			
42. 70 Wichita			
43. 19 Lakeview			
44. 48 Lakeview			
Number Right			
Time			

Drill 23

	Trials	3	2	1
1.	80 Oxford			
2.	77 Oxford			
3.	63 Klein			
4.	85 Klein			
5.	85 Star			
6.	47 Star			
7.	90 Oxford			
8.	93 Oxford			
9.	85 Oxford			
10.	53 Klein			
11.	60 Klein			
12.	74 Klein			
13.	70 Star			
14.	85 Star			
15.	47 Star			
16.	85 Oxford			

	Trials	3	2	1
17.	53 Klein			
18.	63 Klein			
19.	85 Klein			
20.	80 Oxford			
21.	77 Oxford			
22.	60 Klein			
23.	74 Klein			
24.	90 Oxford			
25.	93 Oxford			
26.	70 Star			
27.	93 Oxford			
28.	90 Oxford			
29.	85 Klein			
30.	63 Klein			
31.	80 Oxford			
32.	77 Oxford			

	Trials	3	2	1
33.	85 Star			
34.	47 Star			
35.	63 Klein			
36.	85 Klein			
37.	60 Klein			
38.	74 Klein			
39.	85 Oxford			
40.	53 Oxford			
41.	63 Klein			
42.	85 Klein			
43.	85 Star			
44.	47 Star			
Number Right				
Time				

Drill 24

	Trials	3	2	1
1.	52 Greene			
2.	61 Greene			
3.	68 Ashley			
4.	64 Ashley			
5.	39 Greene			
6.	29 Greene			
7.	78 Ashley			
8.	53 Ashley			
9.	61 Dartmouth			
10.	57 Dartmouth			
11.	57 Ashley			
12.	45 Greene			
13.	75 Dartmouth			
14.	39 Greene			
15.	29 Greene			
16.	52 Greene			

	Trials	3	2	1
17.	61 Greene			
18.	78 Ashley			
19.	53 Ashley			
20.	68 Ashley			
21.	64 Ashley			
22.	57 Ashley			
23.	45 Greene			
24.	61 Dartmouth			
25.	57 Dartmouth			
26.	75 Dartmouth			
27.	52 Greene			
28.	61 Greene			
29.	78 Ashley			
30.	53 Ashley			
31.	29 Greene			
32.	39 Greene			

	Trials	3	2	1
33.	52 Greene			
34.	61 Greene			
35.	68 Ashley			
36.	64 Ashley			
37.	57 Ashley			
38.	78 Ashley			
39.	75 Dartmouth			
40.	68 Greene			
41.	61 Greene			
42.	75 Dartmouth			
43.	57 Dartmouth			
44.	69 Dartmouth			
Number Right				
Time				

Drill 25

Trials	Answers 3	2	1
1. 62 Ash			
2. 72 Ash			
3. 39 Chase			
4. 46 Chase			
5. 39 Fleet			
6. 16 Fleet			
7. 40 Chase			
8. 23 Chase			
9. 10 Fleet			
10. 19 Chase			
11. 54 Ash			
12. 34 Ash			
13. 72 Ash			
14. 62 Ash			
15. 40 Chase			
16. 23 Chase			

Trials	Answers 3	2	1
17. 23 Fleet			
18. 44 Fleet			
19. 10 Fleet			
20. 23 Fleet			
21. 44 Fleet			
22. 54 Ash			
23. 19 Chase			
24. 10 Fleet			
25. 62 Ash			
26. 72 Ash			
27. 39 Chase			
28. 46 Chase			
29. 16 Fleet			
30. 39 Chase			
31. 34 Ash			
32. 39 Ash			

Trials	Answers 3	2	1
33. 54 Ash			
34. 40 Chase			
35. 23 Chase			
36. 39 Chase			
37. 46 Chase			
38. 23 Fleet			
39. 44 Fleet			
40. 39 Fleet			
41. 16 Fleet			
42. 16 Fleet			
43. 19 Chase			
44. 54 Ash			
Number Right			
Time			

Drill 26

Trials	Answers 3	2	1
1. 58 Race			
2. 73 Race			
3. 33 Race			
4. 60 Race			
5. 33 Race			
6. 53 Poplar			
7. 73 Eric			
8. 33 Eric			
9. 43 Eric			
10. 73 Poplar			
11. 41 Poplar			
12. 67 Eric			
13. 46 Eric			
14. 53 Poplar			
15. 73 Eric			
16. 49 Race			

Trials	Answers 3	2	1
17. 54 Race			
18. 83 Poplar			
19. 60 Poplar			
20. 33 Eric			
21. 43 Eric			
22. 58 Race			
23. 73 Race			
24. 33 Race			
25. 53 Poplar			
26. 73 Eric			
27. 73 Poplar			
28. 41 Poplar			
29. 33 Poplar			
30. 60 Poplar			
31. 53 Poplar			
32. 67 Eric			

Trials	Answers 3	2	1
33. 46 Eric			
34. 43 Eric			
35. 73 Eric			
36. 33 Race			
37. 53 Poplar			
38. 73 Eric			
39. 49 Race			
40. 54 Race			
41. 67 Eric			
42. 46 Eric			
43. 73 Poplar			
44. 41 Poplar			
Number Right			
Time			

Drill 27

Trials	3	2	1
1. 58 Centra			
2. 69 Centra			
3. 41 Centra			
4. 32 Tremont			
5. 63 Mill			
6. 51 Mill			
7. 57 Mill			
8. 77 Tremont			
9. 42 Tremont			
10. 42 Mill			
11. 74 Mill			
12. 32 Centra			
13. 50 Centra			
14. 41 Centra			
15. 32 Tremont			
16. 63 Mill			

Trials	3	2	1
17. 51 Mill			
18. 57 Mill			
19. 77 Tremont			
20. 42 Tremont			
21. 57 Tremont			
22. 70 Tremont			
23. 32 Centra			
24. 50 Centra			
25. 58 Centra			
26. 69 Centra			
27. 42 Mill			
28. 74 Mill			
29. 63 Mill			
30. 41 Centra			
31. 32 Tremont			
32. 63 Mill			

Trials	3	2	1
33. 77 Tremont			
34. 42 Tremont			
35. 57 Mill			
36. 70 Tremont			
37. 32 Centra			
38. 50 Centra			
39. 58 Centra			
40. 69 Centra			
41. 42 Mill			
42. 74 Mill			
43. 41 Centra			
44. 32 Tremont			
Number Right			
Time			

■ ANSWER KEY FOR DRILLS

Drill 1, page 139

1. D   2. A   3. C   4. B   5. E

Drill 2, not applicable

Drill 3, page 144

1. A	6. B	11. A	16. D	21. A	25. C	29. D	33. C	37. A	41. A
2. B	7. C	12. C	17. C	22. B	26. D	30. A	34. A	38. C	42. B
3. C	8. D	13. D	18. A	23. C	27. A	31. C	35. D	39. D	43. C
4. D	9. C	14. B	19. D	24. D	28. B	32. B	36. B	40. A	44. D
5. A	10. B	15. A	20. D						

Drill 4, page 144

1. A	6. B	11. D	16. A	21. C	25. A	29. D	33. B	37. B	41. B
2. B	7. C	12. C	17. A	22. B	26. C	30. A	34. C	38. D	42. A
3. C	8. D	13. B	18. C	23. A	27. B	31. A	35. D	39. A	43. B
4. D	9. B	14. D	19. D	24. D	28. C	32. C	36. A	40. C	44. C
5. A	10. A	15. C	20. B						

Drill 5, page 145

1. A	6. B	11. B	16. B	21. B	25. C	29. B	33. A	37. B	41. C
2. B	7. A	12. C	17. C	22. A	26. A	30. D	34. D	38. A	42. D
3. C	8. A	13. D	18. D	23. D	27. C	31. B	35. A	39. A	43. A
4. D	9. B	14. B	19. A	24. A	28. B	32. B	36. A	40. B	44. B
5. A	10. D	15. B	20. B						

Drill 6, page 145

1. A	6. B	11. A	16. A	21. A	25. B	29. B	33. B	37. C	41. D
2. B	7. D	12. B	17. B	22. B	26. A	30. C	34. D	38. A	42. A
3. C	8. C	13. D	18. A	23. B	27. B	31. B	35. C	39. B	43. B
4. D	9. D	14. B	19. B	24. D	28. A	32. A	36. A	40. C	44. A
5. A	10. A	15. D	20. A						

Drill 7, page 146

1. A	6. D	11. C	16. B	21. C	25. A	29. A	33. B	37. C	41. B
2. B	7. C	12. C	17. C	22. A	26. C	30. B	34. B	38. A	42. C
3. A	8. A	13. C	18. B	23. C	27. C	31. A	35. A	39. B	43. D
4. B	9. B	14. D	19. A	24. B	28. D	32. B	36. D	40. A	44. C
5. C	10. B	15. A	20. A						

Drill 8, page 146

1. C	6. B	11. B	16. C	21. C	25. D	29. D	33. C	37. B	41. B
2. D	7. C	12. C	17. D	22. B	26. C	30. A	34. C	38. A	42. C
3. A	8. D	13. D	18. C	23. A	27. A	31. A	35. D	39. B	43. D
4. B	9. C	14. B	19. B	24. B	28. B	32. B	36. A	40. A	44. C
5. A	10. A	15. C	20. A						

Drill 9, page 147

1. A	6. B	11. A	16. B	21. A	25. C	29. D	33. C	37. A	41. D
2. B	7. C	12. B	17. A	22. B	26. D	30. A	34. D	38. B	42. A
3. A	8. D	13. C	18. C	23. B	27. B	31. B	35. C	39. A	43. B
4. B	9. C	14. D	19. D	24. A	28. C	32. B	36. D	40. C	44. A
5. A	10. D	15. A	20. B						

Drill 10, page 147

1. C	6. B	11. C	16. B	21. A	25. B	29. D	33. D	37. D	41. D
2. D	7. A	12. D	17. B	22. A	26. D	30. A	34. B	38. A	42. A
3. A	8. B	13. B	18. C	23. C	27. B	31. B	35. B	39. B	43. B
4. B	9. A	14. B	19. C	24. D	28. C	32. C	36. B	40. C	44. A
5. D	10. B	15. C	20. A						

Drill 11, page 148

1. A	6. B	11. D	16. D	21. D	25. C	29. A	33. B	37. D	41. A
2. B	7. A	12. A	17. D	22. B	26. B	30. B	34. B	38. C	42. B
3. C	8. B	13. A	18. C	23. A	27. C	31. D	35. A	39. A	43. A
4. D	9. C	14. D	19. A	24. B	28. B	32. A	36. A	40. D	44. B
5. A	10. B	15. C	20. C						

Drill 12, page 148

1. A	6. B	11. A	16. C	21. C	25. D	29. D	33. A	37. A	41. A
2. B	7. C	12. B	17. D	22. D	26. D	30. B	34. B	38. B	42. B
3. C	8. D	13. C	18. D	23. A	27. A	31. C	35. C	39. C	43. A
4. D	9. C	14. D	19. A	24. A	28. B	32. C	36. D	40. D	44. B
5. A	10. D	15. A	20. B						

Drill 13, page 163

1. E	6. C	11. B	16. E	21. B	25. B	29. B	33. C	37. A	41. D
2. A	7. B	12. E	17. D	22. D	26. B	30. A	34. C	38. B	42. B
3. D	8. E	13. D	18. C	23. E	27. D	31. E	35. B	39. E	43. C
4. A	9. A	14. A	19. B	24. C	28. C	32. D	36. E	40. C	44. A
5. B	10. C	15. B	20. A						

Drill 14, page 163

1. A	6. B	11. D	16. B	21. B	25. C	29. E	33. C	37. C	41. D
2. B	7. A	12. A	17. C	22. C	26. D	30. D	34. A	38. A	42. A
3. C	8. D	13. B	18. E	23. A	27. B	31. E	35. E	39. C	43. B
4. D	9. E	14. C	19. A	24. B	28. A	32. B	36. D	40. B	44. C
5. E	10. C	15. E	20. E						

Drill 15, page 164

1. C	6. A	11. E	16. C	21. A	25. C	29. B	33. B	37. E	41. C
2. D	7. B	12. B	17. D	22. E	26. D	30. E	34. A	38. A	42. D
3. A	8. E	13. C	18. E	23. B	27. E	31. D	35. B	39. A	43. A
4. B	9. D	14. D	19. C	24. A	28. A	32. C	36. C	40. D	44. B
5. E	10. C	15. A	20. D						

Drill 16, page 164

1. C	6. B	11. B	16. B	21. A	25. C	29. A	33. B	37. D	41. E
2. B	7. B	12. A	17. E	22. B	26. D	30. B	34. A	38. B	42. D
3. A	8. C	13. E	18. B	23. E	27. A	31. D	35. A	39. B	43. B
4. B	9. A	14. B	19. C	24. A	28. B	32. A	36. C	40. A	44. E
5. A	10. D	15. A	20. D						

Drill 17, page 165

1. A	6. B	11. D	16. E	21. B	25. D	29. B	33. E	37. C	41. B
2. B	7. E	12. C	17. D	22. A	26. E	30. B	34. B	38. D	42. C
3. C	8. B	13. E	18. C	23. B	27. E	31. C	35. A	39. E	43. D
4. D	9. B	14. B	19. B	24. C	28. A	32. D	36. A	40. A	44. E
5. A	10. A	15. A	20. A						

Drill 18, page 165

1. A	6. D	11. C	16. A	21. E	25. A	29. B	33. C	37. D	41. A
2. A	7. E	12. B	17. B	22. B	26. A	30. D	34. A	38. A	42. B
3. A	8. A	13. A	18. E	23. C	27. A	31. A	35. B	39. E	43. E
4. B	9. B	14. E	19. C	24. D	28. E	32. B	36. C	40. B	44. A
5. C	10. D	15. B	20. D						

Drill 19, page 166

1. A	6. D	11. A	16. B	21. A	25. A	29. E	33. A	37. C	41. B
2. B	7. E	12. B	17. A	22. E	26. B	30. E	34. C	38. B	42. C
3. C	8. E	13. C	18. E	23. C	27. C	31. D	35. E	39. D	43. C
4. D	9. A	14. D	19. D	24. D	28. D	32. A	36. E	40. B	44. E
5. C	10. B	15. E	20. C						

Drill 20, page 166

1. A	6. B	11. A	16. C	21. D	25. C	29. A	33. A	37. C	41. B
2. B	7. C	12. D	17. A	22. C	26. D	30. B	34. E	38. D	42. A
3. C	8. D	13. A	18. B	23. A	27. E	31. A	35. C	39. B	43. E
4. D	9. A	14. B	19. E	24. B	28. B	32. B	36. D	40. A	44. E
5. E	10. E	15. C	20. E						

Drill 21, page 167

1. A	6. D	11. D	16. D	21. E	25. E	29. E	33. E	37. D	41. D
2. B	7. D	12. B	17. B	22. C	26. B	30. A	34. A	38. C	42. C
3. A	8. E	13. E	18. B	23. D	27. A	31. B	35. B	39. A	43. D
4. B	9. C	14. E	19. C	24. E	28. A	32. E	36. C	40. A	44. A
5. C	10. A	15. C	20. D						

Drill 22, page 167

1. A	6. B	11. E	16. E	21. A	25. E	29. E	33. E	37. A	41. C
2. B	7. C	12. E	17. B	22. B	26. E	30. C	34. A	38. C	42. E
3. C	8. D	13. C	18. A	23. C	27. C	31. D	35. B	39. D	43. C
4. D	9. A	14. D	19. B	24. D	28. B	32. E	36. B	40. E	44. D
5. A	10. B	15. E	20. A						

Drill 23, page 168

1. A	6. B	11. C	16. E	21. B	25. D	29. B	33. B	37. C	41. A
2. B	7. C	12. D	17. E	22. C	26. C	30. A	34. B	38. D	42. B
3. A	8. D	13. C	18. A	23. D	27. D	31. A	35. A	39. E	43. A
4. B	9. E	14. A	19. B	24. C	28. C	32. B	36. B	40. E	44. B
5. A	10. E	15. B	20. A						

Drill 24, page 168

1. A	6. C	11. B	16. A	21. E	25. A	29. D	33. A	37. B	41. B
2. B	7. D	12. E	17. B	22. B	26. C	30. A	34. B	38. D	42. C
3. C	8. A	13. C	18. D	23. E	27. A	31. C	35. C	39. C	43. A
4. E	9. B	14. D	19. A	24. B	28. B	32. D	36. E	40. C	44. D
5. D	10. A	15. C	20. C						

Drill 25, page 169

1. A	6. B	11. E	16. B	21. D	25. A	29. B	33. E	37. D	41. B
2. B	7. A	12. C	17. C	22. E	26. B	30. C	34. A	38. C	42. B
3. C	8. B	13. B	18. D	23. E	27. C	31. C	35. B	39. D	43. E
4. D	9. E	14. A	19. E	24. E	28. D	32. D	36. C	40. A	44. E
5. A	10. E	15. A	20. C						

Drill 26, page 169

1. A	6. E	11. B	16. C	21. B	25. E	29. C	33. D	37. E	41. C
2. B	7. E	12. C	17. D	22. A	26. E	30. D	34. B	38. E	42. D
3. E	8. A	13. D	18. C	23. B	27. A	31. E	35. A	39. C	43. A
4. D	9. B	14. E	19. D	24. E	28. B	32. C	36. E	40. D	44. B
5. E	10. A	15. E	20. A						

Drill 27, page 170

1. A	6. A	11. D	16. E	21. A	25. A	29. E	33. C	37. C	41. C
2. B	7. B	12. C	17. A	22. B	26. B	30. E	34. D	38. D	42. D
3. E	8. C	13. D	18. B	23. C	27. C	31. E	35. B	39. A	43. E
4. E	9. D	14. E	19. C	24. D	28. D	32. E	36. B	40. B	44. E
5. E	10. C	15. E	20. D						

Chapter 7

Number Series—How To Improve Your Score

■ TEST STRATEGY

Go in Turn

Start at question 1 and answer each question in turn. Don't be tempted to look for the easy ones to do first. You'll probably be able to do most of them without any problem. If you do get stuck and you are uncertain about the answer to a question *after a reasonable try* (see below), leave the answer space blank and move on to the next question. Be sure that you answer the new question in its correct number space.

Use Time Wisely

Without rushing, you should be able to complete all 24 questions in the 20 minutes allotted. But you can't afford to spend too long on any one question. After you've completed a few timed practice tests, you'll know how to pace yourself. Bring a watch, just for insurance.

Guess

You won't have much need for guessing if you've mastered the techniques for doing number series questions. Every once in a while, however, you may get stumped by some unusual or complex series. These are the ones alluded to above, and these are the ones you will want to return to after you've gone through all the other questions. If you have timed yourself properly, you will have a few minutes to give these a last try. If you still can't figure out the answer, then by all means, guess! Put in some answer. You are not penalized for guessing—so do it. You have nothing to lose and extra points to gain.

■ NATURE OF THIS PART OF THE EXAM

It is safe to say that most people taking the postal service test for the first time have never seen number series questions before. It is also true, unfortunately, that most people are afraid of math tests. The combination of inexperience and fear is a potent one that severely penalizes those who take this test unprepared. By the same token, you, who should be fully prepared after reading this book, have a golden opportunity to outstrip your competition.

First, to allay any fears you may have about the mathematical skill you need, *only the simplest arithmetic applications of addition, subtraction, multiplication and division are involved.* You are *not* taking a *math* test. This test is designed to measure your ability to reason and to *see patterns* (more about that later).

Another comforting thing to know about number series questions is that they are very fair to the test taker. The rules for answering them are exact and easily understood. There is only one right answer and that answer can immediately be checked out. If you find you have made an error, you will have time to change your answer.

That brings you to another plus concerning the number series part (Part C) of the test. You will not have to work at the great speed required for the address checking, questions (Part A) or memory questions (Part B). All these factors put together mean that you have a real chance for a perfect score if you absorb the techniques that follow.

The basis for all the techniques you will learn is a full understanding of the directions you are supposed to follow. So, therefore, re-read these official directions—very carefully.

"For each Number Series question there is at the left a series of numbers which follow some definite order and at the right five sets of two numbers each. You are to look at the numbers in the series at the left and find out what order they follow. Then decide what the next two numbers in that series would be if the same order were continued." There are four key phrases in these directions:

1) . . . "a series of numbers which follow some definite order. . ." In other words, they are connected in some way. They just didn't pop up at random. The person who prepared the series did so according to some *definite rule* or *pattern* that determines how you go from one number to the next. The illustrations below show three number series and the pattern each follows.

> *Series A:* 1 2 3 4 5 6 7 - - -

Pattern: as you proceed from left to right, you *add 1* to each number to get the next number in the series. That is, 1 plus 1 = 2, 2 plus 1 = 3, 3 plus 1 = 4, and so on.

> *Series B:* 21 20 19 18 17 16 15 - - -

Pattern: as you proceed from left to right, you *subtract 1* from each number to get the next number in the series.

> *Series C:* 2 4 8 16 32 64 - - -

Pattern: as you proceed from left to right you multiply each number by two to get the next number in the series. That is, $2 \times 2 = 4$, $4 \times 2 = 8$, $8 \times 2 = 16$, and so on.

2) ". . . look at the numbers - - -" Sometimes you will be able to identify the pattern in a simple series such as examples A and B above, just by looking at it. But to find the order in a more complex series such as series D, below, you will probably need the help of some special techniques. For now, try to find its pattern just by looking at it. (For the answer, see paragraph 4 below).

> *Series D:* 1 8 8 5 12 12 9 16
>   *Pattern:* ?

3) ". . . find the order - - -" There are many possible patterns for number series questions. You will learn to recognize more and more of them as you answer the questions in this book. Learning the techniques for finding patterns will make it easy to pick out new ones that you've never seen before. Here is an example of a pattern you have already seen even though, at first, it looks new:

> *Series E:* 5 10 15 20 25 30 35 - - -

Pattern: You get from one number to the next in the series by *addition*, exactly as you did in Series A. The only difference is that you add 5 each time instead of 1. What happens is, 5 plus 5 = 10, 10 plus 5 = 15, 15 plus 5 = 20, and so on.

4) ". . . what the next two numbers are - - -" This is the easiest part of all. Once you have figured out the rule, it is mostly a matter of using ordinary arithmetic to find the next two numbers, *that is—in simple series!*

Here are the next two numbers for the series completed above:

Series A—	1	2	3	4	5	6	7	8 9		(keep adding 1)
Series B—	21	20	19	18	17	16	15	14 13		(keep subtracting 1)
Series C—	2	4	8	16	32	64	128	256		(keep multiplying by 2)
Series D—	1	8	8	5	12	12	9	16	16 13	*
Series E—	5	10	15	20	25	30	35	40 45		(keep adding 5)

* This pattern cannot be explained just by a simple progression of additions or subtractions. It is one of the more complex types for which you will want the techniques explained in the next section.

TECHNIQUES FOR ANSWERING NUMBER SERIES QUESTIONS

In this section, you will learn to use a technique for answering number series questions. With it you will be able to troubleshoot a question and uncover the pattern governing the numbers. You have already seen some techniques used to explain the answers to a few of the Number Series questions in the Diagnostic Test. Because the loop technique is so important, you should take a closer look at it. On this section of the test *only*, test takers have been allowed to write in their test booklet. Obviously, this fact is of major importance when using the loop diagrams and some of the other techniques described here.

The **loop diagram** helps you to *see the connections among the numbers.* On this page there is an enlarged illustration of a typical number series question with a loop diagram and labels. Instead of your trying to keep the number connections in your mind, the loops actually form a visual record that shows which numbers follow each other to make a pattern. Sometimes, the pattern is easy to grasp and remember. In the illustration, for example, where there is a direct connection between one number and the next, you draw the loops as shown. That's easy. *But*, if the connections are *not* direct, and are supposed to skip every second or third number (as in examples 7 and 8 from the Diagnostic Test), then the pattern becomes very difficult to visualize and remember. This is where the loops are *indispensable* if you want to be sure that you are *not skipping* any number and that your pattern is *consistent* and that you will be picking out the next two numbers in the *correct order.* A very common error committed by test takers is for them to select an answer with the two correct numbers—but, *in the wrong order.* (See example 7—Choice D is incorrect because it has *14 12* instead of *12 14*.)

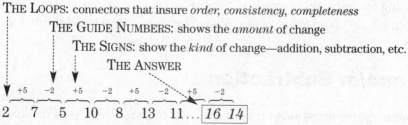

THE LOOPS: connectors that insure *order, consistency, completeness*

THE GUIDE NUMBERS: shows the *amount* of change

THE SIGNS: show the *kind* of change—addition, subtraction, etc.

THE ANSWER

+5 −2 +5 −2 +5 −2 +5 −2

2   7   5   10   8   13   11 . . . 16 14

The pattern immediately comes into view: "You proceed from one number to the next by first adding 5, and then subtracting 2."

The Guide Numbers

These are the numbers you put in to show by *how much* one number differs from the other. For many number series questions such as the example in the illustration you go from one number to another by adding or subtracting. It is suggested that the first thing you do when you begin answering a question is to test it out to see if there is a pattern of addition or subtraction. Get the difference between each number and the next. Write it down above the center of the loop as shown. That way you can't forget it. It's just another piece of insurance to help you find a *consistent* pattern. In the series: 2 4 6 8 10 12 14, it is easy to see and remember that the difference between one number and the next is always +2. But in a more complex series like Example 2 of the Diagnostic Test, the pattern of +3, +3, −4, repeated, would be most difficult to keep in mind without writing down the guide numbers above the loops.

The Signs

You have seen from various examples that sometimes the numbers in a series go up, sometimes down, and sometimes they alternate, like in the illustrated example. Unless you put a + or a − in front of each guide number, you may become hopelessly confused (it's like zigging, when you should have zagged).

Now you can appreciate the beauty and the value of the loop diagram. It allows you to *see* the pattern clearly and unmistakably. If you have used the diagram correctly, you will *know* it when you are right. You could even *hear* the pattern if you were to chant it to yourself.

This is why it is said that number series questions are fair. Now, all you have to do is to be careful about applying the techniques and you are on your way to scoring 100 percent on this test.

Applying the Loop

There are two other factors involved in using the loop diagram that can affect your mark on number series questions. One is your ability to add, subtract, multiply and divide simple numbers. The other involves your ability to draw the loops accurately when you connect the numbers. Two tables are provided at the back of this chapter to help you review and check your arithmetic. One is for addition and subtraction; the other is for multiplication and division. There is also a series of drills on arithmetic and on drawing loops. (Please note that you are allowed to mark the loops, guide numbers, and so on *on your exam booklet*, but make these notations lightly, and in pencil. You may have to change something as you test the series to see what pattern fits. Do *not*, however, make any extraneous marks on your *answer sheet*).

■ TYPES OF NUMBER SERIES QUESTIONS

Now you are going to learn about many different kinds of number series questions and how they are formed. As you do that, you will also be introduced to additional techniques for solving them.

Addition and/or Subtraction

Most of the number series questions on your test will probably be based on some pattern involving addition and/or subtraction. What you have already learned about the loop diagram is sufficient to solve all of them. Here are some of the major types:

A Constant Adder or Subtractor

Example 1

$$\underbrace{}_{+2} \underbrace{}_{+2} \underbrace{}_{+2} \underbrace{}_{+2}$$
2   4   6   8   10…

This is the simplest type. The guide number is +2 and never changes as you go from one number to the next.

Alternating Adders and/or Subtractors

Example 2

$$\underbrace{}_{+3} \underbrace{}_{+1} \underbrace{}_{+3} \underbrace{}_{+1} \underbrace{}_{+3}$$
2   5   6   9   10   13…

The guide numbers alternate between +3 and +1 as you go from one number to the next.

Example 3

$$\underbrace{}_{+6} \underbrace{}_{-2} \underbrace{}_{+6} \underbrace{}_{-2} \underbrace{}_{+6}$$
6   12   10   16   14   20…

This is exactly the same type as in Example 2 except you alternately *add* 6 and *subtract* 2.

"Complex" Rules

Example 4

$$\underbrace{}_{-2} \underbrace{}_{-2} \underbrace{}_{+6} \underbrace{}_{-2} \underbrace{}_{-2} \underbrace{}_{+6}$$
8   6   4   10   8   6   12…

This pattern goes in a cycle of three operations: −2, −2, +6 and then repeats the cycle −2, −2, +6, and so on. You can see it at a glance at the loop diagram.

The Variable Adder and/or Subtractor

Example 5

$$\underbrace{}_{+1} \underbrace{}_{+2} \underbrace{}_{+3} \underbrace{}_{+4} \underbrace{}_{+5}$$
4   5   7   10   14   19…

Here, the guide number is ever changing. It keeps increasing by 1 as you advance in the series.

Example 6

$$\underbrace{}_{-18} \underbrace{}_{-15} \underbrace{}_{-12} \underbrace{}_{-9}$$
73   55   40   28   19…

There are two ways of describing this pattern. First, you may readily notice that the difference keeps decreasing by 3 as you go from one number to the next. Second, you may see that each guide number is a multiple of 3. That is, 18 is 6 × 3; 15 is 5 × 3; 12 is 4 × 3; etc.

Repeating Elements

Sometimes an addition/subtraction series will include certain numbers as part of its pattern that cannot be accounted for by addition or subtraction. These questions usually fall into three categories:

1. REPETITIONS USING SERIES NUMBERS.
Example 7

$$\overset{+2}{10\ \ \overset{\frown}{10\ \ 12}}\ \ \overset{+2}{\overset{\frown}{12\ \ 14}}\ \ \overset{+2}{\overset{\frown}{14\ \ 16}}\ldots$$

Here, the numbers progress by adding 2. But, after each addition, the new number is repeated. Although Example 7 is fairly simple, other repetitions are not. It is suggested you add the following techniques to use with the loop diagram.

- connect the repetitions with a loop and use the *guide number* "0," or the *guide letter* "R."

$$\overset{+0}{\overset{\frown}{10\ \ 10}}\ \ \overset{+2}{\overset{\frown}{10\ \ 12}}\ \ \overset{+0}{\overset{\frown}{12\ \ 12}}\ \ \overset{+2}{\overset{\frown}{12\ \ 14}}\ \ \overset{+0}{\overset{\frown}{14\ \ 14}}\ \ \overset{+2}{\overset{\frown}{14\ \ 16}}\ldots$$

$$\overset{R}{\overset{\frown}{10\ \ 10}}\ \ \overset{+2}{\overset{\frown}{10\ \ 12}}\ \ \overset{R}{\overset{\frown}{12\ \ 12}}\ \ \overset{+2}{\overset{\frown}{12\ \ 14}}\ \ \overset{R}{\overset{\frown}{14\ \ 14}}\ \ \overset{+2}{\overset{\frown}{14\ \ 16}}\ldots$$

Either way, a consistent pattern is established that is easily seen and continued.

- Join the repetitions by *underlining* or *blocking* them.

$$\underline{10\ \ \overset{+2}{\overset{\frown}{10}\ \ 12}}\ \ \underline{\overset{+2}{\overset{\frown}{12\ \ 14}}}\ \ \underline{\overset{+2}{\overset{\frown}{14\ \ 14}}}\ \ 16\ldots$$

$$\boxed{10\ \ 10}\ \ \overset{+2}{\overset{\frown}{\boxed{12\ \ 12}}}\ \ \overset{+2}{\overset{\frown}{\boxed{14\ \ 14}}}\ \ 16\ldots$$

2. REPETITION OF AN ARBITRARY NUMBER
Occasionally, a number that is entirely unrelated by addition, subtraction, or anything else is introduced at regular intervals in the series. The result can be quite confusing.

Example 8   3   4   <u>11</u>   5   6   <u>11</u>   7...

Here the number 11 is inserted after every second number in the series. The series itself follows a simple +1 pattern.

3. REPETITIONS USING BOTH SERIES AND ARBITRARY NUMBERS
All sorts of even more complex patterns can be established in this way.

Example 9

$$\underline{3}\ \ \overset{+0}{\overset{\frown}{4\ \ 4}}\ \ \overset{+1}{\overset{\frown}{\underline{3}\ \ 5}}\ \ \overset{+0}{\overset{\frown}{5\ \ \underline{3}}}\ \ \overset{+1}{\overset{\frown}{6}}\ldots$$

Another technique to use when you want to test the pattern to see if repetition is involved is to *softly chant* the number series. You can pick up the rhythm that occurs when numbers repeat themselves.

━━━━━━━━━━ **Drill 1** ━━━━━━━━━━

It would be a good idea if you checked yourself now to see how well you understand the Addition/Subtraction series. See if you can continue the series for two more numbers in each of Examples 1 through 9 discussed above. The answers are given on page 202.

Do questions 1 through 8 below for more practice answering number series questions in the category of addition/subtraction. The answers and explanations are given at the end of this chapter on page 202.

1.   10 13 17 20 24 27 31 __ __
    A) 37 34   B) 33 35   C) 35 38   D) 34 38   E) 35 37

2.   11 5 13 7 15 9 17 __ __
    A) 11 19   B) 9 17   C) 23 15   D) 19 11   E) 12 20

3.   6 6 10 12 12 16 18 __ __
    A) 22 24   B) 24 20   C) 20 22   D) 18 24   E) 18 22

4.   37 32 29 28 23 20 19 __ __
    A) 13 10   B) 15 16   C) 18 13   D) 16 15   E) 14 11

5.   8 8 10 14 20 28 38 __ __
    A) 52 66   B) 54 64   C) 48 66   D) 50 64   E) 50 70

6.   41 41 40 42 42 41 43 __ __
    A) 43 44   B) 42 43   C) 43 42   D) 45 46   E) 42 44

7.   7 9 10 11 13 10 15 __ __
    A) 17 19   B) 17 10   C) 18 20   D) 10 18   E) 11 18

8.   4 5 6 6 7 8 8 9 __ __
    A) 9 10   B) 9 9   C) 9 11   D) 10 10   E) 10 11

Multiplication and/or Division

As mentioned previously, your first step in doing a number series question is to examine it for addition, subtraction, and repetition. If that doesn't work, one of the next things to do is to quickly check to see if multiplication and/or division was used to connect the numbers. Although this type appears less frequently than addition/subtraction series, it is worth knowing about since a few such questions probably will appear and thereby affect your score.

The loop diagram and the other techniques described for addition/subtraction apply here just as well but with two modifications. The *signs* you use in front of the guide number will be ✕ for multiplication, and ÷ for division. The other change concerns the way you determine the guide number(s). Examples 1 and 2 that follow will explain the methods.

A. A Constant Multiplier

Example 1   1   2   4   8   16   32   ...

Just by inspection, you can see that each number in the series is far greater than the one before it. That means multiplication ($\times$) may be involved. The next step is to determine what the guide number is. You do that by taking any number in the series (usually the second) and dividing it by the preceding number. In this example, this is $2 \div 1 = 2$. 2 is the guide number provided it checks out. You do this by using it to go from one number to the next as follows: $1 \times \underline{2} = 2$; $2 \times \underline{2} = 4$; $4 \times \underline{2} = 8$; $8 \times \underline{2} = 16$; $6 \times \underline{2} = 32$. The pattern is now established as $\times 2$, $\times 2$, $\times 2$, etc., which you can then enter on the loop diagram.

$$\overset{\times 2}{\frown}\;\overset{\times 2}{\frown}\;\overset{\times 2}{\frown}\;\overset{\times 2}{\frown}\;\overset{\times 2}{\frown}$$
$$1 \quad 2 \quad 4 \quad 8 \quad 16 \quad 32 \ldots$$

Example 2   800   400   200   100   50   ...

By inspection, you can see that each of the numbers decreases greatly. That means that division ($\div$) is a possibility. The guide number is determined by dividing the first number by the second. Thus, $800 \div 400 = 2$, which is the guide number, *if it checks out*. (Another way of finding the guide number is by asking yourself—"400 times ? = 800"; *Answer* $400 \times \underline{2} = 800$). In any case, you then should check out 2, to see if it really is the guide number, by using it to divide each number in turn: $800 \div \underline{2} = 400$; $400 \div \underline{2} = 200$; $200 \div \underline{2} = 100$; $100 \div \underline{2} = 50$. It fits, and the problem is solved.

$$\overset{\div 2}{\frown}\;\overset{\div 2}{\frown}\;\overset{\div 2}{\frown}\;\overset{\div 2}{\frown}$$
$$800 \quad 400 \quad 200 \quad 100 \quad 50 \ \ldots$$

B. Alternating Multipliers and/or Divisors

Example 3
$$\overset{\times 3}{\frown}\;\overset{\times 2}{\frown}\;\overset{\times 3}{\frown}\;\overset{\times 2}{\frown}\;\overset{\times 3}{\frown}$$
$$1 \quad 3 \quad 6 \quad 18 \quad 36 \quad 108 \ldots$$

The rule for this series is to alternately multiply by 3, then by 2, then by 3, and so on.

Example 4   1   4   2   8   4   16   8

The numbers in this kind of series do not steadily increase *or* decrease as the series progresses. They *alternately* increase and decrease, which means that you must find one guide number for multiplying and one for dividing. In this example, we find the multiplier and the divisor in the same way as we did in Examples 1 and 2 in Section A above.

For the Multiplier: $4 \div 1 = 4$. The guide number is written as $\times 4$.

For the Divisor: (In this series the second and the third numbers are examined since this is where the first decrease occurs.) Thus, you have: $4 \div 2 = 2$. The guide number is written as $\div 2$. Drawing in the loops completes the pattern for this question.

$$\overset{\times 4}{\frown}\;\overset{\div 2}{\frown}\;\overset{\times 4}{\frown}\;\overset{\div 2}{\frown}\;\overset{\times 4}{\frown}\;\overset{\div 2}{\frown}$$
$$1 \quad 4 \quad 2 \quad 8 \quad 4 \quad 16 \quad 8 \ldots$$

C. Complex Rules

Example 5

$$\overbrace{2\quad}^{\times2}\overbrace{4\quad}^{\times3}\overbrace{12\quad}^{\div2}\overbrace{6\quad}^{\times2}\overbrace{12\quad}^{\times3}\overbrace{36\quad}^{\div2}18\ldots$$

This pattern follows a cycle of three operations: ×2, ×3, ÷2; ×2, ×3, ÷2; and so on. The method of finding each guide number and its sign is the same as in Examples 1 and 2.

D. The Variable Multiplier and/or Divisor

Example 6

$$\overbrace{2\quad}^{\times1}\overbrace{2\quad}^{\times2}\overbrace{4\quad}^{\times3}\overbrace{12\quad}^{\times4}48\ldots$$

The multiplier keeps increasing by 1 as you progress in the series.

Repeating Numbers Included in Multiplication/Division Series

You have seen numbers that are repeated and used to form part of the pattern in the Addition/Subtraction number series. They are used in the Multiplication/Division series as well. Such numbers, whether they come from the numbers in the series itself, whether they are totally unrelated to the series, or whether some combination is used, make the pattern more complex. Any of them, however, can be identified by using the methods shown on pages 177 to 178.

Example 7

$$\overbrace{1\quad}^{\times3}\overbrace{3\quad}^{R}\overbrace{3\quad}^{\times3}\overbrace{9\quad}^{R}\overbrace{9\quad}^{\times3}\overbrace{27\quad}^{R}27\ldots$$

This series follows a pattern of × 3, repeat (R); × 3, repeat. . .

Multiplication/Division Combined With Addition/Subtraction

These combinations are among the most complex number series you might ever encounter. Nevertheless, if you use the methods already presented, you will be able to handle them. Just be extra careful about entering the guide numbers and the signs. The signs are particularly important because it is easy to confuse a + for an ×. You are in for a lot of trouble if you multiply when you should have added. This is why it is suggested that you work on the drills at the end of the chapter, especially if your entries are not as clear as they should be.

Example 8   14   10   20   16   32   28 . . .

If you start out as usually suggested, you will first check for addition/subtraction. In this series, you will find that every second number in it is 4 less than the one before it, i.e., $14 - 10 = 4$; $20 - 16 = 4$; etc. But you still must find a rule that decides how you go from 10 to 20 and from 16 to 32. Arithmetic differences do not work here, but multiplication does, i.e., $10 \times 2 = 20$; $16 \times 2 = 32$. When you combine these two rules, using the loop diagram, you arrive at a consistent pattern that accounts for every number in the series. It looks like this:

$$\overbrace{14\quad}^{-4}\overbrace{10\quad}^{\times2}\overbrace{20\quad}^{-4}\overbrace{16\quad}^{\times2}\overbrace{32\quad}^{-4}28$$

There are other combinations with even more complex rules, some of which involve repeating numbers as well. You have all the ammunition you need to solve them.

================================ **Drill 3** ================================

Continue the series in each of Examples 1 through 8 on the previous pages for two more numbers. The answers are given on page 202.

================================ **Drill 4** ================================

Do questions 1 through 8 below to practice answering number series questions in the category of multiplication/division. The answers and explanations are given at the end of this chapter on pages 202, 203.

1. 8 8 10 20 20 22 44 __ __
    A) 44 46   B) 44 88   C) 46 48   D) 46 46   E) 88 90

2. 1 2 2 4 4 4 8 8 __ __
    A) 8 12   B) 8 8   C) 8 16   D) 16 8   E) 12 12

3. 2 12 6 36 18 108 __ __
    A) 218 1296   B) 54 108   C) 216 27   D) 54 324   E) 216 36

4. 2 1 2 7 6 12 17 __ __
    A) 34 33   B) 32 31   C) 16 32   D) 22 44   E) 18 36

5. 11 12 7 11 14 9 11 18 __ __
    A) 36 13   B) 23 11   C) 16 36   D) 15 21   E) 13 11

6. 1 200 2 100 4 50 8 __ __
    A) 12 16   B) 16 25   C) 12 25   D) 40 16   E) 25 16

7. 9 6 3 12 9 6 24 __ __
    A) 21 72   B) 72 69   C) 12 48   D) 21 18   E) 18 36

8. 2 8 3 12 4 16 __ __
    A) 6 18   B) 5 20   C) 8 24   D) 24 8   E) 6 24

Alternating Series

Sometimes, the easiest way to see the pattern in a number series question is to look for *two* separate series whose numbers *alternate* with each other.

Example 1
$$\overset{-36}{}\ \overset{+34}{}\ \overset{-31}{}\ \overset{+29}{}\ \overset{-26}{}\ \overset{+24}{}$$
40   4   38   7   36   10   34...

It is perfectly possible to use a loop diagram in the usual way (see page 177) to pick out the pattern and continue the series. But it isn't easy when you are dealing with a series like Example 1. (Before you read on, try to figure out the next two numbers.) If you found it a bit difficult or if you didn't get the correct answer—(13 32)—it isn't surprising. You have to do some mental gymnastics and possibly use a pencil and paper to get the answer.

A much easier, quicker, and safer method to use in this case is shown below:

$$40 \quad 4 \quad 38 \quad 7 \quad 36 \quad 10 \quad 34 \quad 13 \quad \underline{32} \ldots$$

(top loops: -2, -2, -2, -2; bottom loops: $+3$, $+3$, $+3$)

Many series lend themselves to this approach including some you have already worked on in this book. (See Example 7 on the Diagnostic Test; Example 2, on page 179; and Examples 3 and 4 on page 179). In these cases, it really doesn't matter which approach you take as long as you feel comfortable with it and as long as it works for you. In other cases (like Example 1, above), using the alternating series approach is far superior and very often, indispensable. Typical examples of such cases follow. As you go along, you will learn some additional techniques.

Example 2

$$13 \quad 34 \quad 31 \quad 14 \quad 27 \quad 24 \quad 15 \quad 20 \quad 17 \quad 16$$

(A loops, top: -3, -4, -3, -4, -3, ending A; B loops, bottom: $+1$, $+1$, $+1$, ending B)

This is an example of two alternating series, both of the addition/subtraction type. The series labeled "A" follows the rule: -3, -4; -3, -4, etc. The other series, labeled "B" keeps increasing by $+1$. In Example 1 above, each number in both series alternates one-for-one with the other. In this example, the numbers in series "B" appear after every *two* numbers of series A.

In order to keep track of this rather complex pattern, it is suggested that you do something to differentiate between the two sets of loops. In the example the letters A and B were used. Some students prefer to make one set of loops with solid lines; the other with dashed lines. Do what is best for you.

Example 3

$$128 \quad 3 \quad 64 \quad 12 \quad 32 \quad 48 \quad 16 \ldots$$

(top solid loops: $\div 2$, $\div 2$, $\div 2$; bottom dashed loops: $\times 4$, $\times 4$)

Here is an example of a multiplication series alternating number-for-number with a division series. The first decreases by following the rule of $\div 2$, $\div 2$, $\div 2$, etc. The other increases by $\times 4$, $\times 4$, $\times 4$, and so on. This question would be impossible to answer if you didn't look for alternating series. (This time, a dashed loop was used to point up the difference between the two series.)

Example 4

$$18 \quad 20 \mid 1 \quad 2 \quad 3 \mid 22 \quad 24 \mid 4 \quad 5 \quad 6 \mid$$

(loops: A $+2$; B $+1$, $+1$; A $+2$ with $+2$ above; B $+1$, $+1$; bottom $+1$)

These might be called alternating "mini-series." One mini-series, A, increases by $+2$ and continues for two numbers before being interrupted by the other mini-series B, which increases by $+1$ and comes in bunches of three. If you should encounter a question like this where you believe there are alternating mini-series, try putting in light vertical lines (see above) to partition one group from the other. The lines highlight each group (A and B) and make it easy to keep track of their alternations.

Example 5   15 19 27 15 20 28 15 21 29...

This series contains a repeating number, 15, which is entirely unrelated to the other numbers. It just serves to make the pattern more difficult to discern. Once you have spotted it, separate it from the rest of the numbers by underlining it, circling it, or using a partition line as in Example 4 above. It is underlined so you could see how it works. Now, the remaining numbers are far easier to analyze. You can view them in two ways:

A) Following a +8, −7; rule:

$$\overset{+8}{15\ 19\ 27}\ \overset{-7}{15\ 20\ 28}\ \overset{+8}{15\ 21\ 29}$$

or,

B) As two alternating series, each following a +1 rule:

$$15\ 19\ \overset{+1}{27\ 15}\ 20\ \overset{+1}{28\ 15}\ 21\ 29$$
$$\underset{+1}{}\quad\underset{+1}{}$$

Once again, it is stressed that you can choose any of the methods above. You'll know what suits you best after you have done some of the practice exercises and drills.

Example 6
$$7\ \overset{A\ +3}{1\ 10}\ \overset{R}{10}\ \overset{+3}{2\ 13}\ \overset{R}{13}\ \overset{+3}{4\ 16}\ \overset{R}{16}\ 8...$$
$$\underset{B\ \times2}{}\quad\underset{\times2}{}\quad\underset{\times2}{}$$

Once again, there is a repeater that makes the series more difficult. In this example, you have two alternating series. One increases by 3, and repeats the number before adding 3 again (see Series A). Series B is one that follows the rule of multiplying by 2.

Drill 5

Continue the series for two more numbers in each of Examples 1 through 6 above. The answers are given on page 203.

Drill 6

Do questions 1 through 8 below, to practice answering number series questions in the category of Alternating Series. The answers and explanations are given at the end of this chapter on pages 203, 204.

1.   4 37 9 35 14 33 19 __ __

   A) 28 24   B) 24 31   C) 31 24   D) 24 28   E) 31 17

2.   1 2 3 4 6 8 4 5 6 10 __ __

   A) 11 12   B) 12 13   C) 7 8   D) 12 14   E) 10 7

3.   6 18 23 12 21 23 18 24 23 __ __
     A) 25 24   B) 27 33   C) 26 27   D) 24 25   E) 24 27

4.   64 64 34 32 32 42 16 16 50 __ __
     A) 50 12   B) 8 50   C) 58 8   D) 12 52   E) 8 8

5.   16 29 21 28 26 26 31 23 __ __
     A) 22 35   B) 23 36   C) 36 19   D) 21 28   E) 27 34

6.   31 1 27 3 23 9 19 __ __
     A) 12 17   B) 15 24   C) 27 15   D) 16 27   E) 15 27

7.   40 42 38 40 36 38 34 __ __
     A) 34 36   B) 30 34   C) 32 34   D) 38 36   E) 36 32

8.   21 8 19 11 18 14 16 17 15 __ __
     A) 13 20   B) 11 18   C) 16 17   D) 14 19   E) 20 13

Cycles/Repetitions/Combinations

You have already seen numbers repeat themselves as part of the pattern of many number series. Sometimes, the pattern of a series is based more on repeating, cycling or combining numbers than on arithmetic rules. In the section that follows, you will see examples of such series and learn the techniques of answering them.

Example 1   64   13   87 | 64   13   87 | 64...

This is a series that uses a sequence of three unrelated numbers and keeps recycling them. If you take a quick look at the series as a whole, you will easily pick up the pattern. Using *partition* lines as shown above is a quick and easy way of proving you are right and helping you continue the series. You may encounter series of this kind that use sequences of 2 or 4 numbers. It makes no difference. The principle is the same.

Example 2   9 10 11 14 9 10 11 14 9...

This series is formed by *recycling* the numbers 9 10 11. It is similar to the sequence in Example 1, except that the number 14 appears between each cycle. Incidentally, you could use an arithmetic rule +1, +1, 14; repeat +1, +1, 14; and so on... but it is easier to use the numbers themselves in sequence.

Example 3   2 3 4 5 4 3 2 3...

This series *ascends* from 2 to 5 and then *descends* in *reverse* order. Then the cycle repeats.

Example 4   1 2 12 3 4 34 5...

This example shows how number *combinations* (or placement) may be used to form series. Here, every third number is formed by combining the previous *two* and writing them as *one* number, i.e., 1→2 becomes 12; 3→4 becomes 34.

Example 5   1 1 2 1 2 3 1 2 3 4...

Here, although you could find an arithmetic rule, it is much easier to see this series as a series of sequences, each increasing in length by one number. Once again, drawing partition lines makes the rule stand out clearly:

$$1 \mid 1 \quad 2 \mid 1 \quad 2 \quad 3 \mid 1 \quad 2 \quad 3 \quad 4 \mid \ldots$$

The technique of softly *chanting* the numbers to yourself, which was mentioned before, is another way you can "see" the pattern.

Example 6
$$\overbrace{30 \quad 31 \quad 32}^{+10} \mid \overbrace{40 \quad 41 \quad 42}^{+10} \mid 50 \ldots$$

You could see this as three alternating series, or as successive *cycles* of three number sequences each beginning with a number ten higher than the one before it. Each sequence follows a +1 rule.

Example 7   1 2 2 3 3 3 4 4...

In this series, the number of *repetitions* is *directly related* to the number itself—for example, number 2 is repeated *twice*; number 3 is repeated *three* times, etc.

Example 8   68 86 82 28 24 42...

Part of the rule governing this series depends upon *reversals of numbers*. For example, 68 and 86 use the same numbers but in reverse order. Each succeeding pair does the same thing. The rule for connecting the pairs is to subtract 4. When you draw the loop diagram, the full pattern shows up more clearly:

$$\mid 68 \quad 86 \mid \overbrace{\quad}^{-4} \mid 82 \quad 28 \mid \overbrace{\quad}^{-4} \mid 24 \quad 42 \mid \ldots$$

As you have already learned, any series can be made more complex by inserting an extraneous number into it at regular intervals. With the use of the various devices we have introduced, however, such as partitions, underlining, and so on, you should be able to fit them into the pattern.

Drill 7

Continue the series for two more numbers in each of Examples 1 through 8 above. The answers are on page 204.

████████████████████████   **Drill 8**   ████████████████████████

Do questions 1 through 8 below to practice answering number series questions in the category of Cycles/Repetitions/Combinations. The answers and explanations are at the end of this chapter on page 204.

1. 47 46 45 44 43 44 45 __ __
    A) 47 48   B) 46 45   C) 46 44   D) 45 47   E) 46 47

2. 29 74 61 19 29 74 61 __ __
    A) 29 19   B) 54 41   C) 51 74   D) 19 29   E) 49 29

3. 8 7 9 7 6 8 6 5 __ __
    A) 4 3   B) 7 8   C) 7 5   D) 8 9   E) 7 7

4. 24 26 28 14 34 36 38 14 __ __
    A) 40 44   B) 44 14   C) 14 40   D) 44 46   E) 46 48

5. 38 3 8 49 4 9 60 __ __
    A) 71 5   B) 5 10   C) 7 9   D) 6 0   E) 10 71

6. 15 16 17 17 18 19 20 20 __ __
    A) 20 21   B) 22 21   C) 21 22   D) 22 23   E) 21 21

7. 30 50 70 30 50 70 30 __ __
    A) 50 70   B) 40 50   C) 50 60   D) 30 50   E) 70 50

8. 51 52 53 52 53 54 53 __ __
    A) 56 55   B) 54 55   C) 55 55   D) 53 55   E) 55 56

Miscellaneous

This is the fifth and last category of number series questions. It includes series based on other kinds of rules. Some of these types have appeared on prior Number Series tests; others have not. Since it is in your interest to be fully prepared, the following have been assembled for you to study.

Example 1 $1 + 4 \stackrel{=}{+} 5 \stackrel{+}{=} 9 \stackrel{=}{+} 14 \stackrel{+}{=} 23 = 37\ldots$

Each number in this series, beginning with 5, is obtained by adding together the two numbers preceding it: $1 + 4 = 5$; $4 + 5 = 9$; $5 + 9 = 14$; and so on. One way of diagramming this series is shown above.

Example 2   3 2 6 3 3 9 3 4 12 3...

Like Example 1 above, this series uses the numbers in the series itself to progress. Here the rule is to *multiply* the first two numbers in the series to get the third in a trio, i.e., $3 \times 2 = 6$; $3 \times 3 = 9$; $3 \times 4 = 12$. You will notice that for each new trio, you multiply *3* by an ever-increasing number.

Example 3   1 4 9 16 25 36...

Each number in this series is the *square* of consecutive numbers starting with number 1. (You square a number by multiplying it by itself.) Thus, $1 \times 1 = 1$; $2 \times 2 = 4$; $3 \times 3 = 9$; $4 \times 4 = 16$; and so on.

Example 4 $\dfrac{1}{2}$ $\dfrac{1}{3}$ $\dfrac{1}{4}$ $\dfrac{1}{5}$ $\dfrac{1}{6}$ $\dfrac{1}{7}$...

You may have forgotten how to work with fractions but that really doesn't matter. It was mentioned at the very beginning of this chapter that you are not taking a math test. You are being tested on your ability to see the pattern existing in a progression of numbers. In this example, all you need is to detect that the bottom number (the denominator) of each fraction keeps increasing by 1. It is that simple.

Example 5 10^{14} 10^{13} 10^{12} 10^{11} 10^{10} 10^{9} 10^{8}...

The moral behind this series is the same as for Example 4. You do not have to know that the little numbers are called exponents or what they do, just as long as you see that in each successive number they decrease by 1.

Example 6   +2 +2 −4 +2 +2 −4 +2...

In this series, each number has a sign before it. The numbers themselves follow a repetitive sequence of three and, of course, carry their signs with them.

Drill 9

Continue the series for two more numbers in each of Examples 1 through 6 above. The answers are on page 204.

Drill 10

Do questions 1 through 8 below to practice answering number series questions in the Miscellaneous category. The answers and explanations are given at the end of this chapter on page 204.

1. 81 9 64 8 49 7 36 __ __
    A) 25 6   B) 6 36   C) 5 25   D) 6 25   E) 25 16

2. $9\frac{1}{9}$ $10\frac{2}{10}$ $11\frac{3}{11}$ $12\frac{4}{12}$ $13\frac{5}{13}$ $14\frac{6}{14}$
    A) $14\frac{7}{16}$ $15\frac{5}{15}$ B) $15\frac{7}{14}$ $16\frac{8}{16}$ C) $15\frac{7}{15}$ $14\frac{8}{16}$
    D) $15\frac{7}{15}$ $16\frac{8}{16}$ E) $16\frac{7}{16}$ $17\frac{8}{17}$

3. 2 2 4 3 3 9 4 4 16 __ __
    A) 16 16   B) 16 4   C) 5 5   D) 5 17   E) 5 25

4. −1 +2 −3 −1 +2 −3 −1 +2 __ __
    A) +3 −1   B) −3 +2   C) +3 −2   D) −2 −3   E) −3 −1

5. .1 1.1 1.01 11.01 11.001 111.001 __ __
    A) 111.001 1111.001   B) 111.0100 111.00001   C) 101.001 111.001
    D) 110.001 1110.0001   E) 111.0001 1111.0001

6. 89 55 34 21 13 8 __ __
    A) 7 6   B) 5 6   C) 5 3   D) 9 4   E) 7 5

7. 3 8 63 80 99 __ __
    A) 109 142   B) 119 153   C) 120 143   D) 109 150   E) 131 165

8. 5 6 8 12 20 36 __ __
    A) 48 66   B) 68 132   C) 44 70   D) 56 88   E) 49 81

SPECIAL EXERCISES FOR BUILDING NUMBER SERIES SKILLS

You now have the tools. You have learned the strategies and techniques that make a high score possible. Now you must be certain that you can apply them at test time. That means practice.

Addition/Subtraction Review

You may have found by now that you are a little rusty on the arithmetic required for Number Series, even though it is very basic. This can show up in two ways. First, you may find that as you do a series and look for differences between numbers, your guide numbers keep changing, not in accordance with any rule, but because you are making errors. Second, you may be taking too long on each calculation. In either case, you are wasting time, and even worse, getting confused, and thereby having difficulty seeing the pattern.

If this is the case with you,* your problem can be easily remedied. Read and follow the following directions for improving your arithmetic.

The table below gives you a convenient way to review and drill on adding and subtracting numbers between 1 and 10.

Scale B										
Scale A	1	2	3	4	5	6	7	8	9	10
1	2	3	4	5	6	7	8	9	10	11
2	3	4	5	6	7	8	9	10	11	12
3	4	5	6	7	8	9	10	11	12	13
4	5	6	7	8	9	10	11	12	13	14
5	6	7	8	9	10	11	12	13	14	15
6	7	8	9	10	11	12	13	14	15	16
7	8	9	10	11	12	13	14	15	16	17
8	9	10	11	12	13	14	15	16	17	18
9	10	11	12	13	14	15	16	17	18	19
10	11	12	13	14	15	16	17	18	19	20

To Add

As an example, assume you wanted to check the answer to adding 9 + 8. Find the number 9 on either of the two scales of numbers on the outside of the table. If you used the horizontal scale (labeled the "A" scale), your next step is to find the other number—8—on the vertical "B" scale. The answer 17 is obtained in a moment, by following the vertical column under the 9 until it intersects with the horizontal row alongside the 8. (See Figure 6.1)

* If you have no difficulty with the arithmetic in the number series, skip directly to page 197.

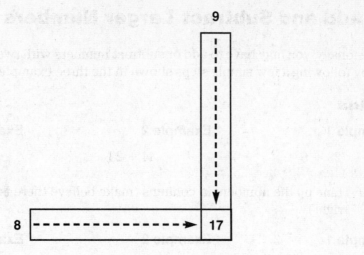

Figure 7.1 Adding: 9 + 8

To Subtract

As an example, if you were checking 16−7, you would locate the number 7 on either the A or the B scale. If you used the vertical scale, B, then you would follow the row alongside number 7 until you reached the number 16. Then, all you do is follow the vertical column from 16 up until it reaches the A scale. It shows the answer—9. (See Figure 7.2)

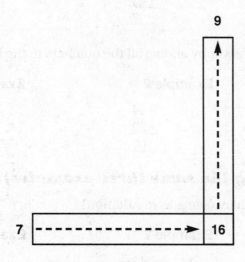

Figure 7.2 Subtracting: 16 – 7

Drills

With the table, you can drill by yourself or with the help of a friend.

For Addition: Pick any number from Scale A and any other number from Scale B. Without looking at the table and without using a paper and pencil, add the two and call out the answer.

For Subtraction: Pick out any number in the table itself and any other number on either scale. Then calculate the difference.

If necessary, check your answer against the table. Your aim is to perform each calculation mentally and with reasonable speed.

To Add and Subtract Larger Numbers

Occasionally, you may have to add or subtract numbers with two digits. You can easily do this by following a few simple steps shown in the three examples below.

To Add

Example 1   **Example 2**   **Example 3**

$28 + 6$ $44 + 23$ $33 + 18$

Step 1   Line up the numbers in columns (make believe there is an imaginary line on the right).

Example 1   **Example 2**   **Example 3**

$$\begin{array}{r} 28 \\ +\ 6 \\ \hline \end{array}$$ $$\begin{array}{r} 44 \\ +23 \\ \hline \end{array}$$ $$\begin{array}{r} 33 \\ +18 \\ \hline \end{array}$$

Step 2   Mentally, add the two numbers in the farthest column on the right and enter the answer in the same columns on the bottom. If the answer has two digits, carry the first one into the next column (see the small circled numbers).

Example 1   **Example 2**   **Example 3**

$$\begin{array}{r} 28 \\ +_{\textcircled{1}}6 \\ \hline 4 \end{array}$$ $$\begin{array}{r} 44 \\ +23 \\ \hline 7 \end{array}$$ $$\begin{array}{r} 33 \\ +_{\textcircled{1}}18 \\ \hline 1 \end{array}$$

Step 3:   Complete the answer by adding all the numbers in the left-hand column.

Example 1   **Example 2**   **Example 3**

$$\begin{array}{r} 28 \\ +_{\textcircled{1}}6 \\ \hline 34 \end{array}$$ $$\begin{array}{r} 44 \\ +23 \\ \hline 67 \end{array}$$ $$\begin{array}{r} 33 \\ +_{\textcircled{1}}18 \\ \hline 51 \end{array}$$

To Subtract (Using the same three examples):

Step 1   Line up the numbers (same as in Addition)

Example 1   **Example 2**   **Example 3**

$$\begin{array}{r} 28 \\ -\ 6 \\ \hline \end{array}$$ $$\begin{array}{r} 44 \\ -23 \\ \hline \end{array}$$ $$\begin{array}{r} 33 \\ -18 \\ \hline \end{array}$$

Step 2   Mentally, subtract the two numbers in the farthest column on the right

Example 1   **Example 2**   **Example 3**

$8-6=2$ $4-3=1$ $13-8=5$

and enter the answer on the bottom of the same column. In cases like Example 3 where the first number—3—is smaller than the second—8, a 1 has been placed in front of the 3 making it 13. When you do that you have to make up for it by putting 1 in the second column (see next page).

Example 1

```
  28
 − 6
   2
```

Example 2

```
  44
 −23
   1
```

Example 3

```
    33
 −① 18
     5
```

Step 3 Complete the answer by subtracting the bottom numbers from the top ones.

Example 1

```
  28
 − 6
  22
```

Example 2

```
  44
 −23
  21
```

Example 3

```
    33
 −① 18
    15
```

Note—Example 3, you must add both bottom numbers before subtracting, i.e., 1 + 1 = 2; 3 − 2 = 1.

Drills

If you wish to practice adding and subtracting two-digit numbers, work on Examples 1 through 60. The answers are given on page 205. Try to do as many of these questions as you can without rewriting them. You will lose time if you do; on the real test you can't afford the time. Just call out your answer if you are drilling with a friend or jot down the answer in the space provided.

Addition

	Answers		
Trials	3	2	1
1. 28 + 4 =			
2. 15 + 6 =			
3. 23 + 9 =			
4. 48 + 16 =			
5. 52 + 8 =			
6. 19 + 8 =			
7. 27 + 8 =			
8. 31 + 10 =			
9. 81 + 6 =			
10. 77 + 19 =			
11. 15 + 23 =			
12. 11 + 3 =			
13. 33 + 49 =			
14. 91 + 13 =			
15. 12 + 3 =			

	Answers		
Trials	3	2	1
16. 44 + 5 =			
17. 47 + 22 =			
18. 17 + 4 =			
19. 46 + 6 =			
20. 18 + 9 =			
21. 21 + 12 =			
22. 38 + 19 =			
23. 14 + 7 =			
24. 35 + 7 =			
25. 52 + 6 =			
26. 19 + 2 =			
27. 39 + 4 =			
28. 16 + 9 =			
29. 10 + 10 =			
30. 41 + 3 =			
Number Right			
Time			

Subtraction

		Answers						Answers		
	Trials	3	2	1			Trials	3	2	1
31. $12 - 3 =$						46. $63 - 7 =$				
32. $34 - 2 =$						47. $78 - 14 =$				
33. $16 - 9 =$						48. $50 - 16 =$				
34. $38 - 7 =$						49. $37 - 16 =$				
35. $49 - 9 =$						50. $48 - 12 =$				
36. $27 - 8 =$						51. $21 - 5 =$				
37. $14 - 6 =$						52. $57 - 7 =$				
38. $58 - 2 =$						53. $24 - 6 =$				
39. $71 - 14 =$						54. $78 - 8 =$				
40. $44 - 8 =$						55. $36 - 6 =$				
41. $12 - 9 =$						56. $42 - 4 =$				
42. $38 - 5 =$						57. $33 - 3 =$				
43. $86 - 8 =$						58. $11 - 8 =$				
44. $19 - 9 =$						59. $15 - 7 =$				
45. $14 - 8 =$						60. $26 - 7 =$				
						Number Right				
						Time				

Multiplication/Division Review

Scale A	Scale B	1	2	3	4	5	6	7	8	9	10
1			2	3	4	5	6	7	8	9	10
2			4	6	8	10	12	14	16	18	20
3			6	9	12	15	18	21	24	27	30
4			8	12	16	20	24	28	32	36	40
5			10	15	20	25	30	35	40	45	50
6			12	18	24	30	36	42	48	54	60
7			14	21	28	35	42	49	56	63	70
8			16	24	32	40	48	56	64	72	80
9			18	27	36	45	54	63	72	81	90
10			20	30	40	50	60	70	80	90	100

The table above will be helpful to those wishing to check their multiplication and division. There are relatively few questions of this type on most Number Series tests and those that do appear are of the simplest kind, involving multipliers and divisors like 2, 3, or 4. Just to be safe, however, it is suggested that you check the table and drill on any products or quotients you may have forgotten. The two illustrations below the table show how to check multiplication and division examples. (Figures 7.3 and 7.4).

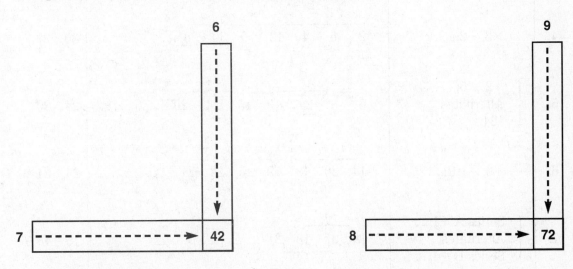

Figure 7.3 Multiplying: 6 × 7 = 42   Figure 7.4 Dividing: 72 ÷ 9 = 8

Drills Using the Loop Diagram

This series of drills is designed to give you practice on the arithmetical and mechanical operations used in making a loop diagram. They will help you avoid making careless errors on the real test. Common errors test takers make include: losing track of which numbers to connect, errors in arithmetic, writing guide numbers that do not do the job because they are too small, too large, or illegible; losing track of the proper sequence in the case of complex or alternating series.

In these drills you will be given the rule that series is to follow, together with the first sequence of numbers needed to illustrate the rule. It is your job to write in the *next six numbers* in the series according to this rule. Use connecting loops and guide numbers to do this. Check the *last two* numbers in the series you developed against the key answers given in the column on the far right side of the page. The first six questions have been worked out to illustrate what you should do.

DRILL—LOOP DIAGRAMS

No.	Rule	Number Series	Answer
1.	+4; . . .	+4 +4 +4 +4 +4 +4 5　9　13　17　21　<u>25</u>　<u>29</u>	25　29
2.	−1, +2; . . .	−1 +2 −1 +2 −1 +2 3　2　4　3　5　<u>4</u>　<u>6</u>	4　6
3.	Series A −5; . . . Alternates Series B +8; . . .	−5　　−5　　−5 45　5　40　13　35　21　<u>30</u>　29 . . . . +8　　+8　　+8	30　29
4.	×3, −2; . . .	×3 −2 ×3 −2 ×3 −2 2　6　4　12　10　<u>30</u>　<u>28</u>	30　28
5.	+2, +5; . . . Alternates 24	+2　　+5　　+2　　+5 6　8　[24]　13　15　[24]　<u>20</u>	24　20
6.	+6, −1,R; . . .	+6 −1 R +6 −1 R 14　20　19　19　25　<u>24</u>　<u>24</u>	24　24
7.	Series A +1; . . . Alternates Series B +4; . . .	A +1 12　27　13　31 _ _ _ _ _ _ B +4	16　43
8.	+3; . . .	+3 32　35 _ _ _ _ _ _	50　53
9.	−2, −3; . . .	−2 −3 29　27　24 _ _ _ _ _ _	12　9

No.	Rule	Number Series	Answer	
10.	Series A ×3; ... Alternates Series B −4; ...	$\overset{A\ \times 3}{\frown}$ 1 47 3 43 _ _ _ _ _ _ $\underset{B\ \ \ -4}{\smile}$	81	31
11.	−8, R; ...	$\overset{-8}{\frown}\ \overset{R}{\frown}$ 36 28 28 _ _ _ _ _ _	4	4
12.	Series A −1; ... Alternates Series B R, −1; ...	$\overset{-1}{\frown}$ 20 41 41 19 40 _ _ _ _ _ $\underset{R}{\smile}\ \underset{-1}{\smile}$	17	38
13.	21, 22, 23; ...	21 22 23 │ 21 _ _ _ _ _	23	21
14.	−2, +3, −4, R; ...	$\overset{-2}{\frown}\ \overset{+3}{\frown}\ \overset{-4}{\frown}\ \overset{R}{\frown}$ 25 23 26 22 22 _ _ _ _ _	17	20
15.	−3, −3,R; ...	$\overset{-3}{\frown}\ \overset{-3}{\frown}\ \overset{R}{\frown}$ 30 30 27 27 _ _ _ _ _ _	15	15
16.	R, R, +2; ...	$\overset{R}{\frown}\ \overset{R}{\frown}\ \overset{+2}{\frown}$ 9 9 9 11 _ _ _ _ _ _	13	15
17.	×2, −1, R; ...	$\overset{\times 2}{\frown}\ \overset{-1}{\frown}\ \overset{R}{\frown}$ 8 16 15 15 _ _ _ _ _ _	57	57
18.	Series A +10; ... Alternates Series B −5; ...	$\overset{A\ +10}{\frown}$ 10 45 20 40 _ _ _ _ _ _ $\underset{B\ -5}{\smile}$	50	25
19.	17, 18, 19; ...	17 18 19 │ _ _ _ _ _ _	18	19
20.	Series A −2; ... Alternates Series B +5; ...	$\overset{A\ \ -2}{\frown}$ 22 1 20 6 _ _ _ _ _ _ $\underset{B\ +5}{\smile}$	14	21
21.	Series A −3; ... Alternates 19	$\overset{A\ \ \ -3}{\frown}$ 47 [19] 44 _ _ _ _ _ _	19	35
22.	Series A ×4; ... Alternates Series B +3; ...	$\overset{A\ \times 4}{\frown}$ 1 19 4 22 _ _ _ _ _ _ $\underset{B\ \ \ +3}{\smile}$	256	31

No.	Rule	Number Series	Answer
23.	+1, R, R, −2; . . .	$\overset{+1}{\frown}$ $\overset{R}{\frown}$ $\overset{R}{\frown}$ $\overset{-2}{\frown}$ 10 11 11 11 9 _ _ _ _ _ _	9 9
24.	−9, R; . . .	$\overset{-9}{\frown}$ $\overset{R}{\frown}$ 65 56 56 _ _ _ _ _	29 29
25.	×2, ×3, ÷2; . . .	$\overset{\times 2}{\frown}$ $\overset{\times 3}{\frown}$ $\overset{\div 2}{\frown}$ 3 6 18 9 _ _ _ _ _ _	162 81
26.	{ Mini-Series A +1, +1; . . . Alternates Series B +2, +2; . . .	A A $\overset{+1}{\frown}$ $\overset{+1}{\frown}$ 1 2 3 │ 2 4 6 │ 4 _ _ _ _ _ _ $\underset{+2}{\smile}$ $\underset{+2}{\smile}$ B	12 7
27.	{ Series A ×5; . . . Alternates Series B −6; . . .	A $\overset{\times 5}{\frown}$ 2 49 10 43 _ _ _ _ _ _ $\underset{B}{\smile}$ $\underset{-6}{\smile}$	1250 25
28.	{ Series A +1; . . . Alternates Series B −2, −3; . . .	$\overset{A\quad +1}{\frown}$ 14 27 25 15 22 _ _ _ _ _ _ $\underset{B\ -2}{\smile}$ $\underset{-3}{\smile}$	17 12
29.	{ 11 Alternates Series A +6; . . . and Series B −2; . . .	$\overset{A\quad +6}{\frown}$ ⬜11 4 57 ⬜11 10 55 _ _ _ _ _ _ $\underset{B\ -2}{\smile}$	22 51
30.	−10, −9, −8, etc.; . . .	$\overset{-10}{\frown}$ $\overset{-9}{\frown}$ $\overset{-8}{\frown}$ $\overset{-7}{\frown}$ 71 61 52 44 37 _ _ _ _ _ _	16 15
31.	{ Series A −2; . . . Alternates Series B +7; . . .	A $\overset{-2}{\frown}$ $\overset{-2}{\frown}$ 50 48 1 8 15 46 _ _ _ _ _ _ $\underset{B\ \ +7}{\smile}$ $\underset{+7}{\smile}$	42 40
32.	{ Series A +1; . . . Alternates 32	$\overset{+1}{\frown}$ $\overset{+1}{\frown}$ $\overset{+1}{\frown}$ 24 25 26 ⬜32 27 _ _ _ _ _ _	31 32
33.	+3, ×2, −4, R; . . .	$\overset{+3}{\frown}$ $\overset{\times 2}{\frown}$ $\overset{-4}{\frown}$ $\overset{R}{\frown}$ 3 6 12 8 8 _ _ _ _ _ _	21 42
34.	−1, R, +2, R; . . .	$\overset{-1}{\frown}$ $\overset{R}{\frown}$ $\overset{+2}{\frown}$ $\overset{R}{\frown}$ 6 5 5 7 7 _ _ _ _ _ _	7 7
35.	−3, +9; . . .	$\overset{-3}{\frown}$ $\overset{+9}{\frown}$ 4 1 10 _ _ _ _ _ _	19 28

No.	Rule	Number Series	Answer
36.	+5, R, +5; . . .	$\overset{+5}{\overbrace{10\quad 15}}\ \overset{R}{}\ \overset{+5}{\overbrace{15\quad 20}}$ _ _ _ _ _ _	35 40

Symbols
; . . . shows a rule is complete
R   Tells you to repeat the previous
       number
2   the number in the box is
       periodically repeated

ANSWERS AND EXPLANATIONS FOR NUMBER SERIES EXERCISES

Addition and/or Subtraction

Drill 1, page 180

1. **12 14**   3. **18 24**   5. **25 32**   7. **16 18**   9. **6 3**
2. **14 17**   4. **10 8**   6. **13 10**   8. **8 11**

Drill 2, page 181

1. **D** The rule is: $+ 3, + 4, +3, + 4$; and so on.
2. **A** You may see this series in two ways. First, as following the pattern: $- 6, + 8, - 6, + 8$; and so on. Second, you may view it as two alternating series, each increasing by 2.
3. **E** A more complex rule applies here, easily seen using a loop diagram:

    $$\overbrace{\underset{6}{R} \quad \overset{+4}{\underset{6}{}} \quad \overset{+2}{\underset{10}{}}}\quad \overbrace{\underset{12}{R} \quad \overset{+4}{\underset{12}{}} \quad \overset{+2}{\underset{16}{}}} \quad \overbrace{\underset{18\ldots}{R} \quad \overset{+4}{\underset{\underline{18}}{}}} \quad \underline{22}$$

    You might also see the entire series as composed of two alternating series, one of which repeats each of its numbers. (For practice, diagram it that way.)
4. **E** The rule here is: $- 5, - 3, - 1; - 5, - 3, - 1$; and so on.
5. **D** The "adder" for the series is variable. Its keeps increasing by $+ 2$. Your guide numbers should be: $0, + 2, + 4, + 6, + 8, + 10$. Continuing the series: $38 + \underline{12} = 50; 50 + \underline{14} = 64$.
6. **C** This series is another one that follows a complex rule. Here, beginning with the first number, 41, it is: repeat the number, $- 1, + 2$; repeat the number, $- 1, + 2$; and so on.
7. **B** This is a simple $+ 2$ series, with the number 10 inserted after every two of its numbers.
8. **D** This series follows the rule: $+ 1, + 1$, repeat the number; $+ 1, + 1$, repeat the number. You might also see it as a progression of three-number mini-series, each beginning 2 higher than the previous one:

    $$4 \quad 5 \quad 6 \mid 6 \quad 7 \quad 8 \mid 8 \quad 9 \quad 10 \mid 10 \text{ and so on.}$$

Multiplication/Division

Drill 3, page 184

1. **64 128**   3. **216 648**   5. **36 108**   7. **81 81**
2. **25 12½**   4. **32 16**   6. **240 1440**   8. **56 52**

Drill 4, page 184

1. **A** This series follows a complex rule that includes repetition, addition, and multiplication. The loop diagram shows it clearly:

    $$\overbrace{\underset{8}{R} \quad \overset{+2}{\underset{8}{}} \quad \overset{\times2}{\underset{10}{}}}\quad \overbrace{\underset{20}{R} \quad \overset{+2}{\underset{20}{}} \quad \overset{\times2}{\underset{22}{}}} \quad \overbrace{\underset{44\ldots}{R} \quad \overset{+2}{\underset{\underline{44}}{}}} \quad \underline{46}$$

2. **B** This is a × 2 series that repeats each new term the same number of times as its positions in the series, e.g., 2 appears *twice*, 4 appears *three* times (it's in *third* place). Therefore 8, which is in *fourth* place, appears *four* times.

3. **D** The pattern here is: × 6, ÷ 2; × 6, ÷ 2; and so on. If you prefer, you may view it as two alternating series, each following a × 3 rule.

4. **C** Here is another complex series. It combines subtraction, multiplication and addition. The rule is: − 1, × 2, + 5; − 1, × 2, + 5; and so on.

5. **E** This series follows a pattern of × 2, − 5, × 2, − 5; and so on. It is made difficult to see because an arbitrary number, 11, is inserted as every third number in the series.

6. **E** There are two alternating series here. The first one increases by successive multiplications by 2. The other decreases by successive divisions by 2.

7. **D** The complex rule for this series is: − 3, − 3, × 4; − 3, − 3, × 4; and so on.

8. **B** Each pair of numbers beginning with 2 8 is connected by × 4, i.e. 2 × 4 = 8; 3 × 4 = 12. The first number in each successive pair increases by 1. You can also consider the pattern as composed of two alternating series—one following a + 1 rule, and the other following a + 4 rule.

Alternating Series

Drill 5, page 186

1. **16 30**	3. **192 8**	5. **15 22**
2. **13 10**	4. **26 28**	6. **19 19**

Drill 6, page 186

1. **C** There are two alternating series here, one of which increases by a + 5 rule; the other decreases by a − 2 rule.

2. **D** There are two alternating series here, each of which continues for three numbers, after which it is interrupted by the other. One increases by + 1; the other by + 2. In effect, each group of three numbers is a "mini-series." Partitions and guide numbers make it easier to see.

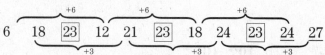

3. **E** This series of numbers is formed by two alternating series and the arbitrary number 23. Without a loop diagram like the one shown, such a complex pattern is extremely difficult to pick up.

$$6 \quad 18 \quad \boxed{23} \quad 12 \quad 21 \quad \boxed{23} \quad 18 \quad 24 \quad \boxed{23} \quad 24 \quad 27$$

4. **E** Here, one series decreases by dividing by 2. This series repeats each of its numbers. The alternating series follows a + 8 rule.

5. **C** One of the two alternating series contained in this progression increases steadily by adding 5. The other has *variable* "subtractors" starting with − 1 and continuously increasing to − 2, − 3, − 4, and so on.

6. **C** Two alternating series are present here. One follows a × 3 rule. The other decreases by a − 4 rule.

7. **E** Here is a comparatively easy one. Both alternating series decrease, each by − 2.

8. **E** In this pair of alternating series, one of them *steadily* increases by adding 3. The other series alternates its subtractors according to a − 2, − 1; − 2, − 1; pattern.

Cycles/Repetitions/Combinations

Drill 7, page 188

1. **13 87**	3. **4 5**	5. **1 2**	7. **4 4**
2. **10 11**	4. **6 56**	6. **51 52**	8. **38 83**

Drill 8, page 189

1. **E** This series of numbers *descends* from 47 to 43 and then *ascends* using the same numbers in reverse order.
2. **D** This is a sequence of four unrelated numbers (29 74 61 19) that keeps repeating itself.
3. **C** Here you have a succession of three-number "mini-series" each of whose numbers is one less than the corresponding number in the preceding series. You could also see this progression as made up of three alternating series, each following a − 1 rule. (For practice, try diagramming it that way.)
4. **D** Again, you find "mini-series." This time, each group of numbers starts 10 higher than the one before. Within each "mini-series," the numbers follow a + 2 rule. The arbitrary number 14 separates one mini-series from the next.
5. **D** Each two-digit number, starting with 38, is followed by the two numbers that combined to form it. Thus, 38 breaks down into 3 and 8, 49 into 4 and 9, and so on. The rule for going from one two-digit number to the next is to add 11.
6. **C** Each of the four-member mini-series (like 15, 16, 17, 17) that makes up the progression follows a + 1 rule and repeats the last number. Each mini-series begins three numbers higher than the last series began.
7. **A** The sequence: 30 50 70 keeps recycling.
8. **B** If you draw a partition between each group of three numbers it becomes easy to see that each group begins and ends one number higher than in the preceding group. This pattern can also be revealed by softly chanting the numbers in groups of three.

51 52 53 | 52 53 54 | 53 54 55
      +1   +1

Miscellaneous

Drill 9, page 190

1. **60 97**	3. **49 64**	5. **10^7 10^6**
2. **5 15**	4. **⅛ ⅑**	6. **+2 −4**

Drill 10, pages 190 to 191

1. **D** This is a series based on the *square* of numbers from 9 on down. The first number 81 is the square of 9, which follows it in the series. The third number 64 is the square of 8, which follows it, and so on.
2. **D** You do not need to understand fractions to do this question. You do have to see that each fraction has *three* parts: the whole number at the beginning 9, 10, 11, and so

on. These increase by 1 for each successive fraction. Then there is the number at the top of the fraction (numerator) and the number at the bottom (denominator) each of which follows the simple rule of + 1. If you're careful to track each one of those three numbers, you'll get the answer.

3. **C** This series illustrates the case where a series uses its own numbers to progress. This process works like this: $\underline{2} \times \underline{2} = 4$; $\underline{3} \times \underline{3} = 9$; and so on. For each group of three numbers, the multipliers increase by 1.

4. **E** The sequence $- 1, + 2, - 3$ keeps repeating. This series may look unusual because each number is preceded by a *sign*, but the idea of finding a pattern is the same.

5. **E** This series is difficult to keep track of because each number is so long. The pattern is a simple one nevertheless. As you proceed from left to right, you alternately add a 1 to the left of the decimal point and a 0 to the right of the decimal point.

6. **C** Like the series in example 3, this one uses its own numbers to progress. The rule is: subtract each number from its preceding number to get the number next in the series, e.g., $\underline{89} - \underline{55} = 34$; $55 - 34 = 21$; $34 - 21 = 13$; and so on.

7. **C** Again, squares are involved in a series. This time, each number in the series is the square of a number, $- 1$. Starting with 4 (which is the square of 2) $- 1 = 3$; 9 (square of 3) $- 1 = 8$; and so on.

8. **B** Unless you have seen one of this type of series before, you would find it most difficult. A *double* operation $(- 2, \times 2)$ is performed to arrive at each number. Starting with the number 5 we have $5 - 2 \times 2 = \underline{6}$; $6 - 2 \times 2 = \underline{8}$; $8 - 2 \times 2 = \underline{12}$ and so on.

Drills, pages 195 to 196

1. **32**	7. **35**	13. **82**	19. **52**	25. **58**	31. **9**	37. **8**	43. **78**	49. **21**	55. **30**
2. **21**	8. **41**	14. **104**	20. **27**	26. **21**	32. **32**	38. **56**	44. **10**	50. **36**	56. **38**
3. **32**	9. **87**	15. **15**	21. **33**	27. **43**	33. **7**	39. **57**	45. **6**	51. **16**	57. **30**
4. **64**	10. **96**	16. **49**	22. **57**	28. **25**	34. **31**	40. **36**	46. **56**	52. **50**	58. **3**
5. **60**	11. **38**	17. **69**	23. **21**	29. **20**	35. **40**	41. **3**	47. **64**	53. **18**	59. **8**
6. **27**	12. **14**	18. **21**	24. **42**	30. **44**	36. **19**	42. **33**	48. **34**	54. **70**	60. **19**

Chapter 8

Following Oral Directions—
How to Improve Your Score

NATURE OF THE TEST

This may seem like an easy test. After all, everyone has had to listen to someone giving orders, instructions, or advice. Whether your spouse, your boss, or your doctor does the talking, each of them expects you to be able to listen. Most probably *hear*, but how good are people at *listening?* Do you always understand what others tell you, and are you willing to take the actions they propose? On this test you had better prepare yourself to do both.

Other demands are made upon you in this test. As you've probably discovered after doing the sample questions in Chapter 1 and the Diagnostic Practice Test, the test instructions themselves may be difficult to follow at first. Ninety percent of students reported they had a problem concerning *where* to mark their answers because the questions and answers do not follow each other in the normal order. If you don't understand these points *exactly*, you are a "dead duck" on this exam.

On top of all this, you will find yourself in a highly competitive situation when you take the new Postal Service examination. You want the job, and you must score high to get it. This means that you have to overcome a certain amount of natural nervousness and tension.

Therefore it's important, just as for every other part of the test, that you learn every possible technique to achieve your maximum performance.

TEST STRATEGY

Almost everything about Part D of the test is different from the other parts. The test strategies and techniques discussed below take these differences into account.

Sit Close to the Examiner

Every word the examiner says is important. You will not be able to follow the directions unless you can hear them. Therefore, if you have a hearing problem, come early and request a seat close to the examiner or a loudspeaker.

Guess Cautiously

Ordinarily, guessing would be fine on a test like this. You are not penalized for wrong answers (as you are in Address Checking). If you don't make *any* choice, you earn nothing for that question. Therefore you have a point to gain and nothing to lose by guessing, *provided you observe one very important precaution. You must not end up with more than one letter space darkened for each number on your answer sheet.* If you do, you will lose all credit for your answers on that number. (At the time of your test, check this point with the oral and written instructions given by the test examiner.)

Go for 100 Percent

The standards for a "good" mark are very high (see guidelines for Part D on page 68). Strive for perfection in the way you listen and carry out the directions. The examiner will speak at a normal pace, and you need not feel time conscious or rushed. You will not have to sacrifice accuracy for speed. Your strategy is simple: you know you can make a perfect score, so go for it!

TECHNIQUES FOR INCREASING YOUR ABILITY TO FOLLOW ORAL DIRECTIONS

Become a Good Listener

Becoming a good listener is the most important part of your test preparation. It also happens to be one of the most useful skills you can acquire, since it affects every area of your life—how well you learn new things on the job or in school, how adept you are in dealing with others, how well you carry on your affairs in business, how much you get out of a play, TV program, or movie, and so on. Whole books have been written on the subject, but for your purposes you will consider some basic highlights, as they relate to this exam.

CULTIVATE AN ACCEPTING ATTITUDE.
It is important to understand that no one is trying to trick you. You need to feel confident about accepting the directions the examiner gives you without delay or hesitation. The test is fair, even though some of the directions you receive will be unfamiliar and even seem silly. For example, on the Diagnostic Practice Test the directions for line 17 began, "If the number in the left-hand circle is smaller than the number in the right-hand circle, add 2 to the number in the left-hand circle, and change the number in that circle to this number. Then write B as in *baker* next to the new number. Otherwise . . . ." Whoever gets directions like that? Certainly mail handlers on the job don't. The purpose of this test is to assess your ability and willingness to follow directions *exactly;* it is not a test of your judgment. Therefore, for the purposes of this test, make believe you're a soldier or a robot. Listen with an open mind. Do whatever you're told.

FREE YOURSELF FROM ALL PHYSICAL AND MENTAL TENSION.
Get yourself into the most relaxed and receptive state possible. You want to be calm, yet alert. If you know any effective relaxation or meditation techniques, use them. (See page 212 for a sample exercise.) Sometimes, merely stretching, taking a few slow, deep breaths, or closing your eyes for a few moments will do the trick. Make sure you work on the sample questions the examiner will give preceding the actual test. They will help you get into the proper mood.

AVOID ANY PHYSICAL DISTRACTIONS.
Wear comfortable clothing. Eat an adequate meal before you leave home so that you are not hungry or thirsty during the test.

Respond Properly

REMEMBER THAT EVERY NEW SET OF DIRECTIONS BEGINS WITH THE SAME WORDS, "LOOK AT THE LINE . . . ," OR A SLIGHT VARIATION.

The *way you look* at the line can help you later on. For example, on the Diagnostic Practice Test the instructions for line 15 began, "Look at the boxes and words in line 15 . . . ." The examiner then paused slightly and continued, "Write the second letter of the first word in the third box . . . ."

| 53___ | 79 ___ | 67 ___ | ABLE | EASY | DESK |

Listeners who had *looked properly* at line 15 during the pause would at least have picked up a picture of three boxes, each containing a number, followed by three short words. They would have been able to go directly to the word *able*, pick out the letter *B*, and place it next to 67, more quickly and smoothly than those who didn't look at line 15 in the *right* way.

Looking properly means more than an idle glance. It means getting an overall view of the *key* elements on a line and their positions relative to one another. In the example, listeners who had looked properly at line 15 knew immediately where the *first word* and the *third box* were. They didn't have to orient themselves as the instructions were being given. When you look at a line, therefore, try to take in as many of the following aspects as you can:

What the items are—circles, boxes, letters, numbers, crosses, and so on.

What differences in size exist—are some items smaller than others?

You probably will not be able to pick up any more details, but if you have the time, focus on characteristics such as these: the largest item, the smallest, how many of each, and their relative positions.

ACTIVELY RESPOND TO THE DIRECTIONS AS THEY ARE GIVEN.

Use the directions for line 13 of the Diagnostic Practice Test as an example. The examiner read, "In the second circle [you should immediately put your finger on the second circle], write the answer to this question: Which of the following numbers is smallest: 83, 71, 90, 82, 77?" As these numbers were read, you could (unless otherwise directed) be jotting them down in the margin of your worksheet. Why commit them to memory?

Here is another example, taken from line 5. While the examiner was reading, "The truck with the highest number is to be loaded first," you should be placing your finger on the third box, which contains the number 48.

WATCH OUT FOR THE TWO-PART, "IF . . . OTHERWISE" TYPE OF QUESTION.

In the preceding item, it was suggested that you respond actively. That doesn't mean you should stop listening and anticipate the answer. For this type of question many test takers make the error of selecting an answer *before* they've heard the *entire* question. The directions for line 14 of the Diagnostic Practice Test will illustrate.

"Look at line 14 on your worksheet. There are two circles and two boxes of different sizes with numbers in them. If 2 is smaller than 4 and if 7 is less than 3, write A in the larger circle." *Many test takers stopped listening after hearing "4."* If they had kept listening, they would have heard ". . . and if 7 is less than 3 . . . ," a statement that is, of course, untrue. The key word is *and*, which means that *both* parts of the condition must be true. Otherwise the *entire* choice is wrong. Remember this principle for this test and for any other civil service multiple-choice test you take.

The correct action to take for line 14 is given after the word *Otherwise:* "write B as in *baker* in the smaller box." The correct answer is 20B.

KEEP PACE.

If you miss part of the instructions for a line, continue listening to the remainder anyhow. The question may have several parts, some of which you may still be able to answer based on what you did pick up. The most important thing is to keep pace with the examiner as he/she continues to read the subsequent directions. Do not dwell on what you have missed.

Mark Your Answer in the Right Place

Previously, it was mentioned that many test takers became confused about where to enter their answers. This problem arises because, on most exams, you are directed to enter the answers to questions 1, 2, and so on, in spaces or boxes, or on lines, on an answer sheet, that are correspondingly marked Answer 1, Answer 2, and so on. For example, on the Address Checking part of this examination, you are told to darken the space for your answer, A or D, for question 1 on the line marked 1 on the answer sheet, and similarly for the answers to questions 2, 3, and so on.

Not so on this test. Do not try to match up questions and answers in that way. The Following Oral Directions part uses a system whereby you are given a worksheet or question booklet and a separate answer sheet. The lines on the worksheet are called line 1, line 2, and so on, or just 1, 2, and so on. The questions are *based* on the lines, but the *answer numbers* do not necessarily correspond to the *line numbers*. For example, on the Diagnostic Practice Test, the directions for line 1 were to draw a line under the fourth number on the line. That number was 22. You were then told to find the same number (22) on your answer sheet and darken space A. The final result, 22A, on your answer sheet bears no relationship to the fact that it is the answer to the first question. Unfortunately, many test takers darken space A on line 1 of their answer sheet because this line corresponds numerically to the first question they answer.

Another new feature you may expect is to have two, three, or even more questions based on a single line. Line 4 of the Diagnostic Test illustrates this. You were directed to place a B in the circle for the sack holding the largest number of packages. That sack contained a 29. Then you were told to darken your answer sheet space for the number-letter combination in that circle, which, of course, was 29B. Later, you were told to look at line 4 again, and this time to put an E in the circle for the sack with the smallest number of packages. The resulting number-letter combination was 16E on your answer sheet.

Be prepared, therefore, to skip around on your answer sheet, which may contain anywhere from 32 to 88 spaces. *Do not* forget, however, that, when you have entered all your answers, you should not have more than *one* space darkened for any *one* line on the answer sheet.

ADDITIONAL TIPS AND TECHNIQUES

Various questions from the Diagnostic Practice Test will illustrate some more helpful ideas.

Count From Left to Right

When you are told to "draw a line under the fourth number on the line" (see directions for line 1), you are to begin counting from the *left end of the line:*

33 49 68 22 8

Starting with the number 33, proceed until you reach the count of four. That brings you to the correct number, 22. If you had started counting from the right side of the line, you would have ended at 49, which is absolutely wrong.

Many questions on the test required you to count off a certain number of numbers, letters, circles, boxes, and so on, in the same way. Others asked you to select the *first* or the *last* item on a line. The rule is the same—begin counting from the left. (The only exception would occur if the test examiner specifically directed you to proceed from the right side. This can happen. That's why it is so important for you to really listen!)

Persons with an English-speaking background find it natural to read from left to right. Other test candidates, such as those speaking the Hebrew language, may be used to reading from right to left. The latter group needs to be particularly careful on this type of question.

Watch Out for the "More Than and Less Than" Direction

This type of direction seems to appear at least once or twice on each of these examinations. Many test takers have trouble with it. Lines 9 and 10 of the Diagnostic Practice Test can be used to show the proper way of handling these directions.

The directions for line 9 were as follows: "Draw a line under every number that is more than 40 but less than 50."

57 <u>43</u> 61 38 50 52 <u>45</u> 40 39

You should have underlined only numbers 43 and 45. Many test takers get this question wrong because they underline numbers 40 and 50 as well. They violate the directions, which specifically state "*more* than 40 and *less* than 50." The rule for this kind of question is simple: exclude whatever numbers are given as *limits.*

For line 10 you were directed to "Draw a line under every number that is more than 65 but less than 75."

65 80 <u>73</u> 64 76 <u>66</u> 78 75 <u>69</u>

Following the rule above, you would exclude 75 and 65 and underline only numbers 73, 66, and 69.

Screen Out "Extra" Information

Line 5 of the Diagnostic Practice Test contained superfluous information. The fact that the four boxes are trucks for carrying mail is not needed to answer the question. The boxes might as well have been crates containing herrings. Harm is done only if you let the extra information distract you. Remember: good listening includes the skill to screen out irrelevant materials and select what is really important.

Learn to Handle the Complex, Multiple-Part Direction

Line 17 of the Diagnostic Practice Test is different because its directions require you to do several things in less time than most of the other lines do. There is no need to feel rushed, however; this line seems more difficult than it really is, particularly if you haven't practiced as yet.

Here is a breakdown of the directions to show what you should be doing as the examiner is reading. Additionally, it will help you review some of the techniques you've already covered.

Examiner	You
"Look at line 17 . . ."	*Really look!* Notice two circles and two boxes of different size.
"If . . ."	*Go on alert!* A yes or no decision is coming.
"the number in the left-hand circle is smaller than the number in the right-hand circle . . ."	*Make an instant comparison:* 22 versus 28. The *decision* is yes (place one finger on each circle if you wish).
"add 2 to the number in the left-hand circle . . ."	*Mentally add* 22 + 2 = 24.
"change the number in that circle to this number."	*Change:* 24/22
"Then write B as in *baker* next to the new number."	*Write:* 24B/22

Some Key Words to Listen For

all	every	more	otherwise
and	first	none	same
but	if	not	than
different	last	only	
each	less		

The words above frequently are heard in this exam. Any one of them can radically change what the correct answer should be. Stay on the alert! (See the Appendix, Checklist 1, page 447, for additional important words.)

■ TWO IMPORTANT CHECKLISTS

In order to follow the directions for any line, you must be prepared in three ways. First, you must *understand the meanings* of all the words you hear. Second, you have to be able to *perform the actions* called for. Finally, you should *possess certain general knowledge*, such as the number of items that make up a dozen. You should be prepared in these three ways so well that you can respond to the directions without the slightest hesitation. There isn't time enough during the test to sit and wonder what the directions mean.

To help you on these three areas, three special checklists have been compiled, which appear on pages 447 to 448 in the Appendix. At the end of this chapter (page 219) there are suggestions for further practice.

EXERCISES FOR RELAXING, LOOKING, AND LISTENING

Relaxing

Undoubtedly, you have your own favorite way to relax. It may be reading a book, playing ball, watching TV, or playing cards. There is nothing wrong with any of these, except that you can't use them to relax yourself immediately before or during a test. The relaxation exercise described below can be done just about anytime, anywhere.

1. Sit comfortably in your seat. Rest your arms on a desk or table, and close your eyes.

2. Inhale slowly. As you do, you may wish to count to yourself: "1, 2, 3, 4." At the count of 4, say to yourself a word or nonsense sound such as *peace, rest, calm, om*. Keep that word or sound in your mind as you gently exhale. The idea of counting and using the word or sound is to help your mind (and nervous system) free itself from all thoughts and the tensions they cause.

3. Relax the muscles in your face, neck, shoulders, and arms. As you breathe gently, *visualize* these muscles progressively relaxing. A good way to help the process is to run your fingertips down your face from time to time. You will actually feel the muscles soften and smooth out.

4. Don't concentrate or strain as you are doing this exercise. If a thought or a worry about the test or anything else enters your mind, just let it drift away. Let the breaths you take, and the counting, gently wash the thought away. Keep in mind a picture of your muscles relaxing and losing their tension. A feeling of peace will take its place.

5. Keep in mind that 2 to 5 minutes should be all you need to achieve the desired state of awareness. Experienced practitioners of this method report that they can put themselves into this relaxed state in 30 seconds to 1 minute. You *do not* want to get sleepy. Remember: the effect you are after is calm, yet alert consciousness.

6. If you believe that this relaxation approach can help you, start practicing it now. Doing it twice a day for about 20 minutes at a time is recommended.

Although the chief purpose of presenting this relaxation exercise has been to help you on the test, you should know that it can also help in other ways. Studies have shown that it can produce a wide range of benefits, including lowered blood pressure, control of heart rate, and improved academic performance.

Looking

Look and Respond

The following exercises are designed to make you more effective as a "looker." One of the techniques given earlier (see page 208) suggested that test takers take full advantage of the slight pause the examiner usually allows after saying, "Look at line. . . ."

It is recommended that you secure the help of a friend when you practice these exercises. You will get a better practice session, and find it more interesting as well. You can, however, work alone and still benefit.

DIRECTIONS

Look at the figures on pages 215 and 217. They show various symbols, shapes, numbers, letters, and words similar to the items that appear on Part D of the new Postal Service examination. Paste each sheet on a piece of cardboard or some other stiff and fairly durable material (e.g., a piece of light plastic or linoleum). Then cut the sheet along the dotted line, and you will have a "deck" of 54 cards for each figure set. Mark the back of each card with an arrow, ↑, to indicate the top edge.

IF YOU ARE PRACTICING ALONE

1. Place the "cards" face down on a table, and shuffle them by moving them about for a moment or two.

2. Then select two or three cards, and align them with the arrows facing upward. *Now, look away as you turn over each card.*

3. When all the cards are right side up, allow yourself 2 seconds to scan the line of cards.

4. Immediately thereafter, look away and copy on a piece of paper whatever you remember seeing on the cards. Remember: you want to see how much registered in your mind about the shape and position of each item and what, if anything, it contained.

IF YOU ARE PRACTICING WITH A FRIEND

1. Have your friend do all the shuffling and selection of cards. *Do not look on.*

2. Instruct your friend to say, when he/she has finished setting up a line of cards, "Now look at the line."

3. Begin scanning the line as soon as you hear your friend say "now," and continue for 2 seconds.

4. Then, without looking at the line, tell your friend as much as you remember about the items on the line.

5. Continue following whatever directions your friend gives you concerning the items on the line. Your friend may wish to make up the directions as he/she is looking at the line. It is better, however, if your friend prepares them ahead of time, just after setting up the line. The directions can be modeled after those in the diagnostic and practice tests. Most of the symbols in Figure Set I were purposely left blank so your friend can insert letters, numbers, or anything else he/she wishes to select as part of the instructions. With a little imagination and practice, your friend will easily be able to make up the directions. (See the example on the next page.)

Example

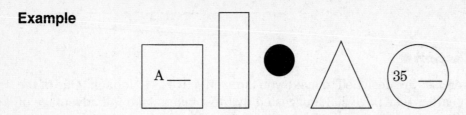

Directions: "Now look at the line. (Pause slightly.) There is a number in the circle at the right-hand end of the line. Subtract 4 from that number. (Pause slightly.) Place the new number on the line next to the letter in the box at the left end of the line. (Pause 2 seconds.) Now darken the space for the number-letter combination that is in the box you just wrote in." (Pause 5 seconds.) *Answer:* 35A

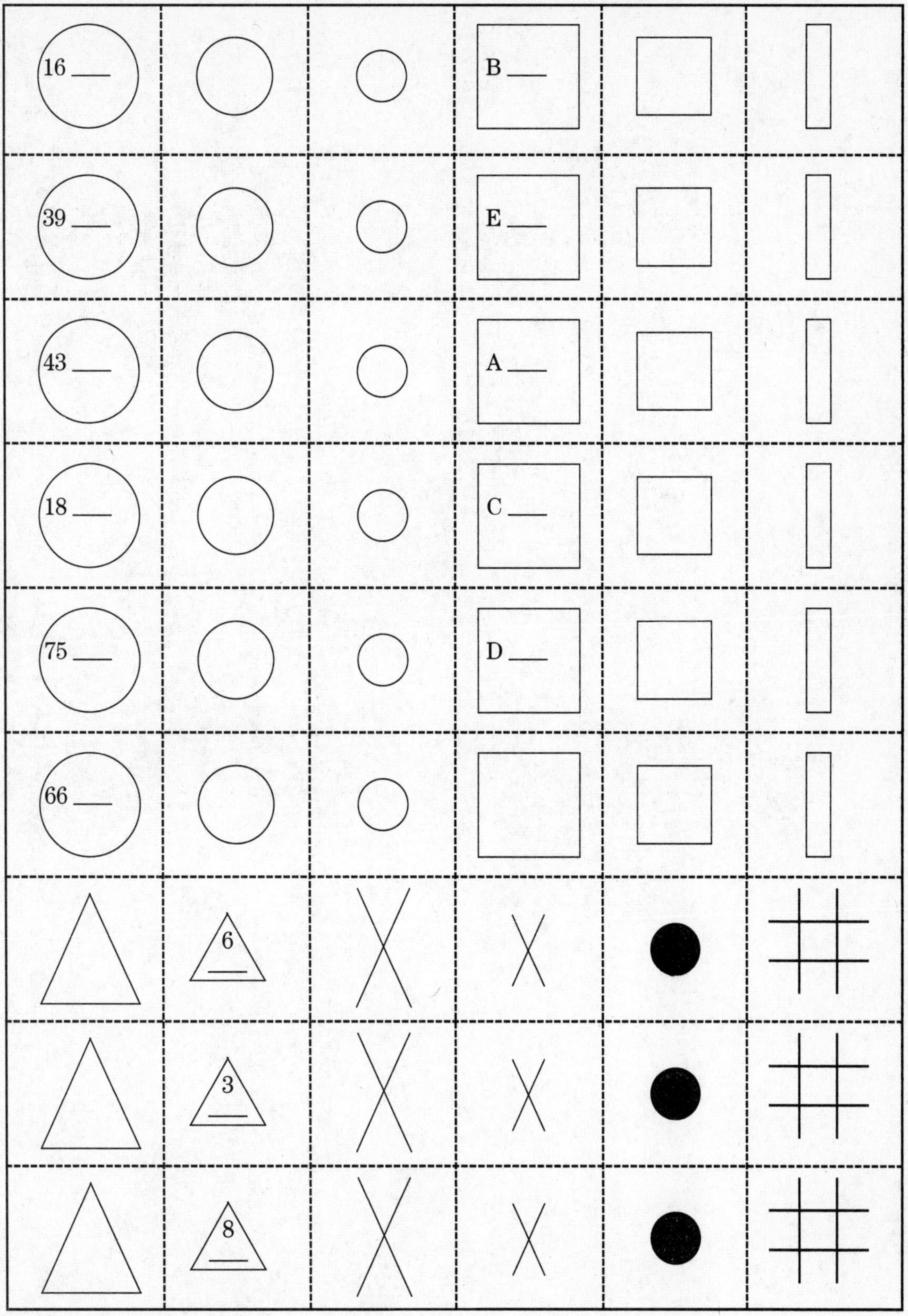

✂ Remove by cutting on dotted line.

1	2	3	4	5	6
7	8	9	10	11	12
32	33	45	46	57	58
69	70	71	83	84	97
A	B	C	D	E	F
G	H	I	J	K	L
M	N	P	R	S	T
DESK	BOLT	PEACH	CLUB	SHOE	CAR
ELSE	READ	TABLE	STAIR	NEAT	PILE

FURTHER SUGGESTIONS FOR PRACTICE

- As you keep practicing and improving, increase the number of items on a line. There can be as many as ten separate items on a line, although the average line should have no more than five or six. Remember that a line *may* contain only one or two items.

- If you discover that you have difficulty in following certain kinds of directions, such as those involving counting or arithmetic, ask your friend to include more of these types of directions.

- Although most of the time you can write your answers on a piece of scrap paper, occasionally practice entering answers the way you will on the actual test. For this purpose, use the answer sheets provided on page 221. Make photocopies if you need more. (The answer sheet you will be given on the actual test may contain only 32 or as many as 88 lines. Answer sheets with 88 lines have been supplied here to allow you to practice making entries in widely separated spaces.)

- Note that literally thousands of lines and directions can be constructed from the 108 cards that have been supplied. Use them to supplement the practice tests and to drill on areas of weakness. The "deck" of cards may be coated with a thin layer of spray-on lacquer or shellac. Once coated, they can be written on and erased many times without damaging the surface.

Listening

You can practice listening skills every day of your life. Whenever and wherever you hear human speech, there is the opportunity to practice. A brief summary of some important ideas on listening is given below. Look it over before you take each practice test. You might want to read it to yourself before you do a relaxation exercise. Incorporate its ideas into the calm and alert state of mind you are seeking to achieve.

Acceptance:

- This is a fair, not a trick, test.
- My job is to do exactly what I'm told.
- I can easily make a perfect score.

Attention:

- After the test has begun, nothing in the world exists except the examiner's voice and the worksheet.

- Outside noises or distractions and internal thoughts cannot interfere. I will let them flow through me and drift away.

Reaction:

- My mind will remain free, calm, and alert.
- I will not anticipate the examiner's words.
- I will use my fingers and my eyes to respond to the directions as I hear them.

Answer Sheets for Practice Exercises on Looking

Remove by cutting on dotted line.

Exercise 1

1 Ⓐ Ⓑ Ⓒ Ⓓ Ⓔ	19 Ⓐ Ⓑ Ⓒ Ⓓ Ⓔ	37 Ⓐ Ⓑ Ⓒ Ⓓ Ⓔ	55 Ⓐ Ⓑ Ⓒ Ⓓ Ⓔ	73 Ⓐ Ⓑ Ⓒ Ⓓ Ⓔ
2 Ⓐ Ⓑ Ⓒ Ⓓ Ⓔ	20 Ⓐ Ⓑ Ⓒ Ⓓ Ⓔ	38 Ⓐ Ⓑ Ⓒ Ⓓ Ⓔ	56 Ⓐ Ⓑ Ⓒ Ⓓ Ⓔ	74 Ⓐ Ⓑ Ⓒ Ⓓ Ⓔ
3 Ⓐ Ⓑ Ⓒ Ⓓ Ⓔ	21 Ⓐ Ⓑ Ⓒ Ⓓ Ⓔ	39 Ⓐ Ⓑ Ⓒ Ⓓ Ⓔ	57 Ⓐ Ⓑ Ⓒ Ⓓ Ⓔ	75 Ⓐ Ⓑ Ⓒ Ⓓ Ⓔ
4 Ⓐ Ⓑ Ⓒ Ⓓ Ⓔ	22 Ⓐ Ⓑ Ⓒ Ⓓ Ⓔ	40 Ⓐ Ⓑ Ⓒ Ⓓ Ⓔ	58 Ⓐ Ⓑ Ⓒ Ⓓ Ⓔ	76 Ⓐ Ⓑ Ⓒ Ⓓ Ⓔ
5 Ⓐ Ⓑ Ⓒ Ⓓ Ⓔ	23 Ⓐ Ⓑ Ⓒ Ⓓ Ⓔ	41 Ⓐ Ⓑ Ⓒ Ⓓ Ⓔ	59 Ⓐ Ⓑ Ⓒ Ⓓ Ⓔ	77 Ⓐ Ⓑ Ⓒ Ⓓ Ⓔ
6 Ⓐ Ⓑ Ⓒ Ⓓ Ⓔ	24 Ⓐ Ⓑ Ⓒ Ⓓ Ⓔ	42 Ⓐ Ⓑ Ⓒ Ⓓ Ⓔ	60 Ⓐ Ⓑ Ⓒ Ⓓ Ⓔ	78 Ⓐ Ⓑ Ⓒ Ⓓ Ⓔ
7 Ⓐ Ⓑ Ⓒ Ⓓ Ⓔ	25 Ⓐ Ⓑ Ⓒ Ⓓ Ⓔ	43 Ⓐ Ⓑ Ⓒ Ⓓ Ⓔ	61 Ⓐ Ⓑ Ⓒ Ⓓ Ⓔ	79 Ⓐ Ⓑ Ⓒ Ⓓ Ⓔ
8 Ⓐ Ⓑ Ⓒ Ⓓ Ⓔ	26 Ⓐ Ⓑ Ⓒ Ⓓ Ⓔ	44 Ⓐ Ⓑ Ⓒ Ⓓ Ⓔ	62 Ⓐ Ⓑ Ⓒ Ⓓ Ⓔ	80 Ⓐ Ⓑ Ⓒ Ⓓ Ⓔ
9 Ⓐ Ⓑ Ⓒ Ⓓ Ⓔ	27 Ⓐ Ⓑ Ⓒ Ⓓ Ⓔ	45 Ⓐ Ⓑ Ⓒ Ⓓ Ⓔ	63 Ⓐ Ⓑ Ⓒ Ⓓ Ⓔ	81 Ⓐ Ⓑ Ⓒ Ⓓ Ⓔ
10 Ⓐ Ⓑ Ⓒ Ⓓ Ⓔ	28 Ⓐ Ⓑ Ⓒ Ⓓ Ⓔ	46 Ⓐ Ⓑ Ⓒ Ⓓ Ⓔ	64 Ⓐ Ⓑ Ⓒ Ⓓ Ⓔ	82 Ⓐ Ⓑ Ⓒ Ⓓ Ⓔ
11 Ⓐ Ⓑ Ⓒ Ⓓ Ⓔ	29 Ⓐ Ⓑ Ⓒ Ⓓ Ⓔ	47 Ⓐ Ⓑ Ⓒ Ⓓ Ⓔ	65 Ⓐ Ⓑ Ⓒ Ⓓ Ⓔ	83 Ⓐ Ⓑ Ⓒ Ⓓ Ⓔ
12 Ⓐ Ⓑ Ⓒ Ⓓ Ⓔ	30 Ⓐ Ⓑ Ⓒ Ⓓ Ⓔ	48 Ⓐ Ⓑ Ⓒ Ⓓ Ⓔ	66 Ⓐ Ⓑ Ⓒ Ⓓ Ⓔ	84 Ⓐ Ⓑ Ⓒ Ⓓ Ⓔ
13 Ⓐ Ⓑ Ⓒ Ⓓ Ⓔ	31 Ⓐ Ⓑ Ⓒ Ⓓ Ⓔ	49 Ⓐ Ⓑ Ⓒ Ⓓ Ⓔ	67 Ⓐ Ⓑ Ⓒ Ⓓ Ⓔ	85 Ⓐ Ⓑ Ⓒ Ⓓ Ⓔ
14 Ⓐ Ⓑ Ⓒ Ⓓ Ⓔ	32 Ⓐ Ⓑ Ⓒ Ⓓ Ⓔ	50 Ⓐ Ⓑ Ⓒ Ⓓ Ⓔ	68 Ⓐ Ⓑ Ⓒ Ⓓ Ⓔ	86 Ⓐ Ⓑ Ⓒ Ⓓ Ⓔ
15 Ⓐ Ⓑ Ⓒ Ⓓ Ⓔ	33 Ⓐ Ⓑ Ⓒ Ⓓ Ⓔ	51 Ⓐ Ⓑ Ⓒ Ⓓ Ⓔ	69 Ⓐ Ⓑ Ⓒ Ⓓ Ⓔ	87 Ⓐ Ⓑ Ⓒ Ⓓ Ⓔ
16 Ⓐ Ⓑ Ⓒ Ⓓ Ⓔ	34 Ⓐ Ⓑ Ⓒ Ⓓ Ⓔ	52 Ⓐ Ⓑ Ⓒ Ⓓ Ⓔ	70 Ⓐ Ⓑ Ⓒ Ⓓ Ⓔ	88 Ⓐ Ⓑ Ⓒ Ⓓ Ⓔ
17 Ⓐ Ⓑ Ⓒ Ⓓ Ⓔ	35 Ⓐ Ⓑ Ⓒ Ⓓ Ⓔ	53 Ⓐ Ⓑ Ⓒ Ⓓ Ⓔ	71 Ⓐ Ⓑ Ⓒ Ⓓ Ⓔ	
18 Ⓐ Ⓑ Ⓒ Ⓓ Ⓔ	36 Ⓐ Ⓑ Ⓒ Ⓓ Ⓔ	54 Ⓐ Ⓑ Ⓒ Ⓓ Ⓔ	72 Ⓐ Ⓑ Ⓒ Ⓓ Ⓔ	

Exercise 2

1 Ⓐ Ⓑ Ⓒ Ⓓ Ⓔ	19 Ⓐ Ⓑ Ⓒ Ⓓ Ⓔ	37 Ⓐ Ⓑ Ⓒ Ⓓ Ⓔ	55 Ⓐ Ⓑ Ⓒ Ⓓ Ⓔ	73 Ⓐ Ⓑ Ⓒ Ⓓ Ⓔ
2 Ⓐ Ⓑ Ⓒ Ⓓ Ⓔ	20 Ⓐ Ⓑ Ⓒ Ⓓ Ⓔ	38 Ⓐ Ⓑ Ⓒ Ⓓ Ⓔ	56 Ⓐ Ⓑ Ⓒ Ⓓ Ⓔ	74 Ⓐ Ⓑ Ⓒ Ⓓ Ⓔ
3 Ⓐ Ⓑ Ⓒ Ⓓ Ⓔ	21 Ⓐ Ⓑ Ⓒ Ⓓ Ⓔ	39 Ⓐ Ⓑ Ⓒ Ⓓ Ⓔ	57 Ⓐ Ⓑ Ⓒ Ⓓ Ⓔ	75 Ⓐ Ⓑ Ⓒ Ⓓ Ⓔ
4 Ⓐ Ⓑ Ⓒ Ⓓ Ⓔ	22 Ⓐ Ⓑ Ⓒ Ⓓ Ⓔ	40 Ⓐ Ⓑ Ⓒ Ⓓ Ⓔ	58 Ⓐ Ⓑ Ⓒ Ⓓ Ⓔ	76 Ⓐ Ⓑ Ⓒ Ⓓ Ⓔ
5 Ⓐ Ⓑ Ⓒ Ⓓ Ⓔ	23 Ⓐ Ⓑ Ⓒ Ⓓ Ⓔ	41 Ⓐ Ⓑ Ⓒ Ⓓ Ⓔ	59 Ⓐ Ⓑ Ⓒ Ⓓ Ⓔ	77 Ⓐ Ⓑ Ⓒ Ⓓ Ⓔ
6 Ⓐ Ⓑ Ⓒ Ⓓ Ⓔ	24 Ⓐ Ⓑ Ⓒ Ⓓ Ⓔ	42 Ⓐ Ⓑ Ⓒ Ⓓ Ⓔ	60 Ⓐ Ⓑ Ⓒ Ⓓ Ⓔ	78 Ⓐ Ⓑ Ⓒ Ⓓ Ⓔ
7 Ⓐ Ⓑ Ⓒ Ⓓ Ⓔ	25 Ⓐ Ⓑ Ⓒ Ⓓ Ⓔ	43 Ⓐ Ⓑ Ⓒ Ⓓ Ⓔ	61 Ⓐ Ⓑ Ⓒ Ⓓ Ⓔ	79 Ⓐ Ⓑ Ⓒ Ⓓ Ⓔ
8 Ⓐ Ⓑ Ⓒ Ⓓ Ⓔ	26 Ⓐ Ⓑ Ⓒ Ⓓ Ⓔ	44 Ⓐ Ⓑ Ⓒ Ⓓ Ⓔ	62 Ⓐ Ⓑ Ⓒ Ⓓ Ⓔ	80 Ⓐ Ⓑ Ⓒ Ⓓ Ⓔ
9 Ⓐ Ⓑ Ⓒ Ⓓ Ⓔ	27 Ⓐ Ⓑ Ⓒ Ⓓ Ⓔ	45 Ⓐ Ⓑ Ⓒ Ⓓ Ⓔ	63 Ⓐ Ⓑ Ⓒ Ⓓ Ⓔ	81 Ⓐ Ⓑ Ⓒ Ⓓ Ⓔ
10 Ⓐ Ⓑ Ⓒ Ⓓ Ⓔ	28 Ⓐ Ⓑ Ⓒ Ⓓ Ⓔ	46 Ⓐ Ⓑ Ⓒ Ⓓ Ⓔ	64 Ⓐ Ⓑ Ⓒ Ⓓ Ⓔ	82 Ⓐ Ⓑ Ⓒ Ⓓ Ⓔ
11 Ⓐ Ⓑ Ⓒ Ⓓ Ⓔ	29 Ⓐ Ⓑ Ⓒ Ⓓ Ⓔ	47 Ⓐ Ⓑ Ⓒ Ⓓ Ⓔ	65 Ⓐ Ⓑ Ⓒ Ⓓ Ⓔ	83 Ⓐ Ⓑ Ⓒ Ⓓ Ⓔ
12 Ⓐ Ⓑ Ⓒ Ⓓ Ⓔ	30 Ⓐ Ⓑ Ⓒ Ⓓ Ⓔ	48 Ⓐ Ⓑ Ⓒ Ⓓ Ⓔ	66 Ⓐ Ⓑ Ⓒ Ⓓ Ⓔ	84 Ⓐ Ⓑ Ⓒ Ⓓ Ⓔ
13 Ⓐ Ⓑ Ⓒ Ⓓ Ⓔ	31 Ⓐ Ⓑ Ⓒ Ⓓ Ⓔ	49 Ⓐ Ⓑ Ⓒ Ⓓ Ⓔ	67 Ⓐ Ⓑ Ⓒ Ⓓ Ⓔ	85 Ⓐ Ⓑ Ⓒ Ⓓ Ⓔ
14 Ⓐ Ⓑ Ⓒ Ⓓ Ⓔ	32 Ⓐ Ⓑ Ⓒ Ⓓ Ⓔ	50 Ⓐ Ⓑ Ⓒ Ⓓ Ⓔ	68 Ⓐ Ⓑ Ⓒ Ⓓ Ⓔ	86 Ⓐ Ⓑ Ⓒ Ⓓ Ⓔ
15 Ⓐ Ⓑ Ⓒ Ⓓ Ⓔ	33 Ⓐ Ⓑ Ⓒ Ⓓ Ⓔ	51 Ⓐ Ⓑ Ⓒ Ⓓ Ⓔ	69 Ⓐ Ⓑ Ⓒ Ⓓ Ⓔ	87 Ⓐ Ⓑ Ⓒ Ⓓ Ⓔ
16 Ⓐ Ⓑ Ⓒ Ⓓ Ⓔ	34 Ⓐ Ⓑ Ⓒ Ⓓ Ⓔ	52 Ⓐ Ⓑ Ⓒ Ⓓ Ⓔ	70 Ⓐ Ⓑ Ⓒ Ⓓ Ⓔ	88 Ⓐ Ⓑ Ⓒ Ⓓ Ⓔ
17 Ⓐ Ⓑ Ⓒ Ⓓ Ⓔ	35 Ⓐ Ⓑ Ⓒ Ⓓ Ⓔ	53 Ⓐ Ⓑ Ⓒ Ⓓ Ⓔ	71 Ⓐ Ⓑ Ⓒ Ⓓ Ⓔ	
18 Ⓐ Ⓑ Ⓒ Ⓓ Ⓔ	36 Ⓐ Ⓑ Ⓒ Ⓓ Ⓔ	54 Ⓐ Ⓑ Ⓒ Ⓓ Ⓔ	72 Ⓐ Ⓑ Ⓒ Ⓓ Ⓔ	

Chapter 9

Putting It All Together

Before you take the practice tests in Chapters 10 through 15, it is suggested that you read this brief chapter. It summarizes key information on the four parts of the Test Battery 460/470 that you can review quickly and conveniently. Examine it periodically, especially a day or two before you take the actual examination. Read it now, before you take Practice Test 1.

A REVIEW OF TEST STRATEGIES AND TECHNIQUES

Address Checking

1. *Work out the optimum balance for you.* Find *your* best combination of speed and accuracy.

2. *Don't go for 100 percent.* Percentages do not count. It is okay to make some errors. Your final score—number right minus number wrong—is what counts.

3. *Do not guess wildly.* Your score will suffer in the long run.

4. *Use your hands properly.* Do not lose time or your place because of wasted motions.

5. *Prepare the point of your pencil.* Shape it to a flat, oval form.

6. *Make your mark properly.* Make it neat, dark, and *fast*—but *don't* seek perfection.

7. *Do not read for comprehension.* Your job is to perceive differences between addresses, not to study and interpret them.

8. *Do not sound out addresses.* This will waste time. No one is listening, anyway.

9. *Do not regress.* Don't reread addresses. Make your choice, and go on to the next question.

10. *Widen your eye span.* If you see more at a glance, your checking speed will increase. Never read word for word.

11. *Work with rhythm.* Maintain a smooth, even pace. You will get more done.

12. *Practice, practice, practice.*

Memory for Addresses—Final Study Plans

Up until now, the discussion on memory has separated questions on direct name addresses from questions on numbered addresses. This was done to help you become thoroughly familiar with the special techniques for each and with the techniques common to both. Now, you can put together everything you have learned so that you will achieve the highest possible score on the real test, where you must handle both direct name and numbered addresses. Consider these factors:

1. *How to divide your study time between the direct and numbered addresses on Part B?* If you, like most people, find it easier to memorize the direct name addresses, it is suggested that you start out by allocating one third of your study time (about 5 minutes) to the direct names, and two thirds of your study time (about 9 minutes) to the numbers. (It is estimated that a *total* of 14 minutes may be used for studying.)

   During the exam, if there should be *any other brief intervals between* the various exercises on Part B, use this extra time to study. Even if you don't have the boxes before you, use the time to review your imagery and associations, especially for the addresses you were weak on. See the boxes in your mind's eye, once more. Keep the memories alive.

2. *What method to use for memorization?* Use any of the memorization methods, or combination of methods, that work best for you. See the list of these methods on pages 225 to 226 for a quick review. As you do more of the practice tests, you will be in a good position to make a final decision on how to proceed on the real test. **Make this decision by the time you complete all of the practice tests in this book and, definitely, *before* you take the actual exam.** For example, if you have been getting good scores on the practice tests by the use of reduction coding, stick to it. For memorizing numbers, you may be doing very well remembering number associations. Others will have found they are good at chunking and should immediately use that technique on the test.

3. *How much to go for?* After sufficient practice, you will know more or less what your memory achievement level is. For example, you will know whether or not you can remember five or six chunks of numbers. If you find that you have no problem with six, then you have to decide whether to concentrate on those six and use visualization to remember Box E, *or* to go for all seven chunks. Keep in mind that a *perfect* score is attainable.

4. *How to make the best use of test time?* It is recommended that you take each question in order, and answer each to the best of your ability. Some people feel that they might do better on Part B by answering all of the direct names first, and then going back to work on the numbers. Do this *only* if you cannot remember any numbers at all. This is extremely unlikely. Even if you can remember only a few numbered addresses, answer every question in turn, guessing when you must. Chapters 4 through 8 contain detailed discussions about guessing on each part of the examination.

   The timing and directions for taking Practice Tests 1 through 6 are exactly the same as those for the Diagnostic Practice Test. These directions are reprinted at the beginning of each part of each test.

5. *How much time will I actually have for memorization?* As noted previously for the new exam, the time *designated* for study is 8 minutes. Test candidates who fol-

low the given suggestions and take all the time *available* for study, can increase that to 14 minutes and more. For example: Use the 3 minutes or so allotted to the pretest sample to study the addresses. In the past, they were identical to the boxes on the real test. Work on the direct (name) addresses only. If the direct names for the real test turn out to differ, nothing has been lost. But if they *are* the same, you will have gained extra time to study the more difficult numbered addresses—that is a tremendous advantage! Do not study the numbered addresses in the pretest sample. That could lead to confusion later on when you take the real exam.

Memory Checklists

DIRECT ADDRESSES

1. *Use association and imagery.* Attach a vivid, colorful, or active image to the address, and it comes alive and is easier to remember—for example, Grand with Canyon, Crescent with Moon, Carpenter with Swinging a Hammer.

2. *Make up a new word.* Start it with the letter of a box. Add whatever parts of the two address names in that box are needed to give the new "word" a distinctive sound or look. Remember ACERNA (see page 118).

3. *Use loci.* Decide on a familiar setting and imagine each of the five boxes—A, B, C, D, and E—to be parts of that scene. For example, the setting could be your office, with Box A standing for your desk; Box B, for the filing cabinet; Box C for the window; and so on. Assume that, on a test the actual address names in Box A were Gruyère and French. The picture you could come up with could show a big, smelly piece of cheese (Gruyère) between two slices of bread (French) lying on top of your desk—Box A.

4. *Apply reduction coding.* NATO is easier to remember than North Atlantic Treaty Organization. The acronyms CIA, FBI, and UNICEF are other examples of how lengthy words and phrases may be easily remembered by using their initials to form a new word. On the test you can use this principle to remember each box individually with its two direct name addresses. For example, if Box B has Newton and Fresco, reduce this to BNF. The same idea is employed if you take five names on a line that includes all the boxes.

   Check the sound. The new word may have a distinctive sound, like "BUZ" or "CRUMP."

   Check for meaning. The new word may mean something, as does the one formed by the initials of these five address names:

   GANTT   RAMAPO   OTIS   WEST   SHORE

   Make up a story/slogan. Use the initials to make up a story or slogan. For example, if the five letters are TRMAB you could think of The Red Monkey Ate Bananas. The three initials above, BNF, might be used for the slogan "broiled, not fried."

5. *Eliminate the last box.* If you have memorized all the address names in four out of the five boxes, you know automatically that an unfamiliar address belongs in the fifth box.

6. *Guess.* You have more to gain than to lose. Enter an answer for every question.

7. *Practice, practice, practice.*

NUMBERED ADDRESSES

(All references are to the addresses on page 138.)

1. *Reduce numbers.* 2100–2799 Mall can be replaced by 21.

2. *Chunking numbers.* Combine two adjoining (reduced) numbers such as 21 in box A and 39 in Box B to get 2139. Do the same for the numbers in Box C and D.

3. *Visualize* the chunks on the *same horizontal street line;* e.g., Mall. Do the same for all three lines. *Use your mental screen.*

4. *If you are able*—remember one 6-digit chunk for the reduced numbers in Box E. Otherwise, *visualize* Box E with its numbers and street name, separately.

5. *Make associations to the box letters:* use stories, images, sounds, and so on.

6. *Prepare a number-word chart.* Use the *number tree* and associations of all kinds to build your *personal* list of words to associate with each number from 10 through 99.

7. *Dealing with Duplicate Numbers*

   a. Review the five-step procedure on page 160. This is the key technique to use for combining the *street number* with the *street name* with the *box letter.*

   b. *Use every tool*—images, meanings, sounds, initials, appearances, placement, and so on *in any way that works for you.*

8. *Use your imagination.* This is the magic cement that helps to combine all your associations as need be. You can develop it by practicing.

Number Series

1. *Find the Pattern.* There is *always* a definite rule to be found in every number series question. It must account for every number. If it doesn't, look for a new rule.

2. *Use a Loop Diagram*—a most useful tool for identifying and applying the rule.

   a. The loops are connections that ensure order, consistency, and completeness.

   b. The guide numbers show the amount of change.

   c. The signs show the kind of change—addition, subtraction, multiplication, and so on.

   d. *The answer*—make sure your numbers are in the correct order.

3. *Softly chant the numbers to yourself.* Sometimes this leads directly to the next two numbers.

4. *Types of Number Series.* The most common types are a) addition/subtraction, b) alternating series, c) cycles, repetitions, and combinations, and d) multiplication/division.

5. *Check It Out.* You will know it when you've found the rule. If you're not sure, you can always check it.

▪ FOLLOWING ORAL DIRECTIONS

1. *Go for 100 percent.* The standard for a good mark on this test is very high. There is no reason why you cannot achieve a perfect score.

2. *Guess intelligently.* If you must, guess rather than miss a question altogether. Just make sure that you do not end up with two answers on the same line.

3. *Sit where you can easily hear the examiner's voice.*

4. *Become a good listener.* Accept the examiner's directions exactly as heard. Free yourself of physical and mental tension. Avoid physical distractions like uncomfortable clothing and hunger pangs.

5. *Look properly.* Get an overall view of *what kind* of items are on a line and any *differences* in size or shape among them.

6. *Actively respond.* Direct your eyes and your fingers to the proper items as they are mentioned.

7. *Keep pace.* If you should miss *part* of the instructions, keep listening to the *remainder.* You may be able to score on another part of the question.

8. *Watch out for the two-part "if . . . otherwise" question.* Don't anticipate the answer.

9. *Mark your answers in the spaces specified by the directions.* Remember that the lines on the worksheet, and the questions based on them, do *not* necessarily correspond to the numbered lines on the answer sheet.

10. Be alert to "key" words (see the lists on pages 211 and 447 to 448).

11. *Periodically, review pages 209 to 210 for some additional tips and techniques.*

TEST YOURSELF

In Chapters 10 through 15 there are six increasingly difficult complete practice tests. Each chapter also contains an answer key and information on how to compute your scores, record your personal progress, and diagnose your particular weak areas.*

The 460/470 Test Battery has four parts: Part A—Address Checking, with 95 questions; Part B—Memory for Addresses, with 88 questions; Part C—Number Series, with 24 questions; and Part D—Following Oral Directions, with 30 questions.

Suggestions for the Practice Sessions

- When you sit down to take these practice tests, select a time and place where there will be no interruptions or distractions.

- Work on a clean, well-lighted desk or table.

- Time yourself or get a friend to help you. (See page 37.)

- Tear out the appropriate answer sheet, and position it in accordance with the sketch on page 78.

---

* Before doing any of the practice tests, you may wish to make copies of the answer sheets that are at the beginning of each test. That way you will be able to retake these tests for additional practice as you see fit.

Answer Sheet—Practice Test 1

Part A—Address Checking

1 Ⓐ Ⓓ	25 Ⓐ Ⓓ	49 Ⓐ Ⓓ	73 Ⓐ Ⓓ
2 Ⓐ Ⓓ	26 Ⓐ Ⓓ	50 Ⓐ Ⓓ	74 Ⓐ Ⓓ
3 Ⓐ Ⓓ	27 Ⓐ Ⓓ	51 Ⓐ Ⓓ	75 Ⓐ Ⓓ
4 Ⓐ Ⓓ	28 Ⓐ Ⓓ	52 Ⓐ Ⓓ	76 Ⓐ Ⓓ
5 Ⓐ Ⓓ	29 Ⓐ Ⓓ	53 Ⓐ Ⓓ	77 Ⓐ Ⓓ
6 Ⓐ Ⓓ	30 Ⓐ Ⓓ	54 Ⓐ Ⓓ	78 Ⓐ Ⓓ
7 Ⓐ Ⓓ	31 Ⓐ Ⓓ	55 Ⓐ Ⓓ	79 Ⓐ Ⓓ
8 Ⓐ Ⓓ	32 Ⓐ Ⓓ	56 Ⓐ Ⓓ	80 Ⓐ Ⓓ
9 Ⓐ Ⓓ	33 Ⓐ Ⓓ	57 Ⓐ Ⓓ	81 Ⓐ Ⓓ
10 Ⓐ Ⓓ	34 Ⓐ Ⓓ	58 Ⓐ Ⓓ	82 Ⓐ Ⓓ
11 Ⓐ Ⓓ	35 Ⓐ Ⓓ	59 Ⓐ Ⓓ	83 Ⓐ Ⓓ
12 Ⓐ Ⓓ	36 Ⓐ Ⓓ	60 Ⓐ Ⓓ	84 Ⓐ Ⓓ
13 Ⓐ Ⓓ	37 Ⓐ Ⓓ	61 Ⓐ Ⓓ	85 Ⓐ Ⓓ
14 Ⓐ Ⓓ	38 Ⓐ Ⓓ	62 Ⓐ Ⓓ	86 Ⓐ Ⓓ
15 Ⓐ Ⓓ	39 Ⓐ Ⓓ	63 Ⓐ Ⓓ	87 Ⓐ Ⓓ
16 Ⓐ Ⓓ	40 Ⓐ Ⓓ	64 Ⓐ Ⓓ	88 Ⓐ Ⓓ
17 Ⓐ Ⓓ	41 Ⓐ Ⓓ	65 Ⓐ Ⓓ	89 Ⓐ Ⓓ
18 Ⓐ Ⓓ	42 Ⓐ Ⓓ	66 Ⓐ Ⓓ	90 Ⓐ Ⓓ
19 Ⓐ Ⓓ	43 Ⓐ Ⓓ	67 Ⓐ Ⓓ	91 Ⓐ Ⓓ
20 Ⓐ Ⓓ	44 Ⓐ Ⓓ	68 Ⓐ Ⓓ	92 Ⓐ Ⓓ
21 Ⓐ Ⓓ	45 Ⓐ Ⓓ	69 Ⓐ Ⓓ	93 Ⓐ Ⓓ
22 Ⓐ Ⓓ	46 Ⓐ Ⓓ	70 Ⓐ Ⓓ	94 Ⓐ Ⓓ
23 Ⓐ Ⓓ	47 Ⓐ Ⓓ	71 Ⓐ Ⓓ	95 Ⓐ Ⓓ
24 Ⓐ Ⓓ	48 Ⓐ Ⓓ	72 Ⓐ Ⓓ	

Remove by cutting on dotted line.

Part B—Memory for Addresses—List 1

1 Ⓐ Ⓑ Ⓒ Ⓓ Ⓔ	19 Ⓐ Ⓑ Ⓒ Ⓓ Ⓔ	37 Ⓐ Ⓑ Ⓒ Ⓓ Ⓔ	55 Ⓐ Ⓑ Ⓒ Ⓓ Ⓔ	73 Ⓐ Ⓑ Ⓒ Ⓓ Ⓔ
2 Ⓐ Ⓑ Ⓒ Ⓓ Ⓔ	20 Ⓐ Ⓑ Ⓒ Ⓓ Ⓔ	38 Ⓐ Ⓑ Ⓒ Ⓓ Ⓔ	56 Ⓐ Ⓑ Ⓒ Ⓓ Ⓔ	74 Ⓐ Ⓑ Ⓒ Ⓓ Ⓔ
3 Ⓐ Ⓑ Ⓒ Ⓓ Ⓔ	21 Ⓐ Ⓑ Ⓒ Ⓓ Ⓔ	39 Ⓐ Ⓑ Ⓒ Ⓓ Ⓔ	57 Ⓐ Ⓑ Ⓒ Ⓓ Ⓔ	75 Ⓐ Ⓑ Ⓒ Ⓓ Ⓔ
4 Ⓐ Ⓑ Ⓒ Ⓓ Ⓔ	22 Ⓐ Ⓑ Ⓒ Ⓓ Ⓔ	40 Ⓐ Ⓑ Ⓒ Ⓓ Ⓔ	58 Ⓐ Ⓑ Ⓒ Ⓓ Ⓔ	76 Ⓐ Ⓑ Ⓒ Ⓓ Ⓔ
5 Ⓐ Ⓑ Ⓒ Ⓓ Ⓔ	23 Ⓐ Ⓑ Ⓒ Ⓓ Ⓔ	41 Ⓐ Ⓑ Ⓒ Ⓓ Ⓔ	59 Ⓐ Ⓑ Ⓒ Ⓓ Ⓔ	77 Ⓐ Ⓑ Ⓒ Ⓓ Ⓔ
6 Ⓐ Ⓑ Ⓒ Ⓓ Ⓔ	24 Ⓐ Ⓑ Ⓒ Ⓓ Ⓔ	42 Ⓐ Ⓑ Ⓒ Ⓓ Ⓔ	60 Ⓐ Ⓑ Ⓒ Ⓓ Ⓔ	78 Ⓐ Ⓑ Ⓒ Ⓓ Ⓔ
7 Ⓐ Ⓑ Ⓒ Ⓓ Ⓔ	25 Ⓐ Ⓑ Ⓒ Ⓓ Ⓔ	43 Ⓐ Ⓑ Ⓒ Ⓓ Ⓔ	61 Ⓐ Ⓑ Ⓒ Ⓓ Ⓔ	79 Ⓐ Ⓑ Ⓒ Ⓓ Ⓔ
8 Ⓐ Ⓑ Ⓒ Ⓓ Ⓔ	26 Ⓐ Ⓑ Ⓒ Ⓓ Ⓔ	44 Ⓐ Ⓑ Ⓒ Ⓓ Ⓔ	62 Ⓐ Ⓑ Ⓒ Ⓓ Ⓔ	80 Ⓐ Ⓑ Ⓒ Ⓓ Ⓔ
9 Ⓐ Ⓑ Ⓒ Ⓓ Ⓔ	27 Ⓐ Ⓑ Ⓒ Ⓓ Ⓔ	45 Ⓐ Ⓑ Ⓒ Ⓓ Ⓔ	63 Ⓐ Ⓑ Ⓒ Ⓓ Ⓔ	81 Ⓐ Ⓑ Ⓒ Ⓓ Ⓔ
10 Ⓐ Ⓑ Ⓒ Ⓓ Ⓔ	28 Ⓐ Ⓑ Ⓒ Ⓓ Ⓔ	46 Ⓐ Ⓑ Ⓒ Ⓓ Ⓔ	64 Ⓐ Ⓑ Ⓒ Ⓓ Ⓔ	82 Ⓐ Ⓑ Ⓒ Ⓓ Ⓔ
11 Ⓐ Ⓑ Ⓒ Ⓓ Ⓔ	29 Ⓐ Ⓑ Ⓒ Ⓓ Ⓔ	47 Ⓐ Ⓑ Ⓒ Ⓓ Ⓔ	65 Ⓐ Ⓑ Ⓒ Ⓓ Ⓔ	83 Ⓐ Ⓑ Ⓒ Ⓓ Ⓔ
12 Ⓐ Ⓑ Ⓒ Ⓓ Ⓔ	30 Ⓐ Ⓑ Ⓒ Ⓓ Ⓔ	48 Ⓐ Ⓑ Ⓒ Ⓓ Ⓔ	66 Ⓐ Ⓑ Ⓒ Ⓓ Ⓔ	84 Ⓐ Ⓑ Ⓒ Ⓓ Ⓔ
13 Ⓐ Ⓑ Ⓒ Ⓓ Ⓔ	31 Ⓐ Ⓑ Ⓒ Ⓓ Ⓔ	49 Ⓐ Ⓑ Ⓒ Ⓓ Ⓔ	67 Ⓐ Ⓑ Ⓒ Ⓓ Ⓔ	85 Ⓐ Ⓑ Ⓒ Ⓓ Ⓔ
14 Ⓐ Ⓑ Ⓒ Ⓓ Ⓔ	32 Ⓐ Ⓑ Ⓒ Ⓓ Ⓔ	50 Ⓐ Ⓑ Ⓒ Ⓓ Ⓔ	68 Ⓐ Ⓑ Ⓒ Ⓓ Ⓔ	86 Ⓐ Ⓑ Ⓒ Ⓓ Ⓔ
15 Ⓐ Ⓑ Ⓒ Ⓓ Ⓔ	33 Ⓐ Ⓑ Ⓒ Ⓓ Ⓔ	51 Ⓐ Ⓑ Ⓒ Ⓓ Ⓔ	69 Ⓐ Ⓑ Ⓒ Ⓓ Ⓔ	87 Ⓐ Ⓑ Ⓒ Ⓓ Ⓔ
16 Ⓐ Ⓑ Ⓒ Ⓓ Ⓔ	34 Ⓐ Ⓑ Ⓒ Ⓓ Ⓔ	52 Ⓐ Ⓑ Ⓒ Ⓓ Ⓔ	70 Ⓐ Ⓑ Ⓒ Ⓓ Ⓔ	88 Ⓐ Ⓑ Ⓒ Ⓓ Ⓔ
17 Ⓐ Ⓑ Ⓒ Ⓓ Ⓔ	35 Ⓐ Ⓑ Ⓒ Ⓓ Ⓔ	53 Ⓐ Ⓑ Ⓒ Ⓓ Ⓔ	71 Ⓐ Ⓑ Ⓒ Ⓓ Ⓔ	
18 Ⓐ Ⓑ Ⓒ Ⓓ Ⓔ	36 Ⓐ Ⓑ Ⓒ Ⓓ Ⓔ	54 Ⓐ Ⓑ Ⓒ Ⓓ Ⓔ	72 Ⓐ Ⓑ Ⓒ Ⓓ Ⓔ	

Part B—Memory for Addresses—List 2

1 Ⓐ Ⓑ Ⓒ Ⓓ Ⓔ	19 Ⓐ Ⓑ Ⓒ Ⓓ Ⓔ	37 Ⓐ Ⓑ Ⓒ Ⓓ Ⓔ	55 Ⓐ Ⓑ Ⓒ Ⓓ Ⓔ	73 Ⓐ Ⓑ Ⓒ Ⓓ Ⓔ
2 Ⓐ Ⓑ Ⓒ Ⓓ Ⓔ	20 Ⓐ Ⓑ Ⓒ Ⓓ Ⓔ	38 Ⓐ Ⓑ Ⓒ Ⓓ Ⓔ	56 Ⓐ Ⓑ Ⓒ Ⓓ Ⓔ	74 Ⓐ Ⓑ Ⓒ Ⓓ Ⓔ
3 Ⓐ Ⓑ Ⓒ Ⓓ Ⓔ	21 Ⓐ Ⓑ Ⓒ Ⓓ Ⓔ	39 Ⓐ Ⓑ Ⓒ Ⓓ Ⓔ	57 Ⓐ Ⓑ Ⓒ Ⓓ Ⓔ	75 Ⓐ Ⓑ Ⓒ Ⓓ Ⓔ
4 Ⓐ Ⓑ Ⓒ Ⓓ Ⓔ	22 Ⓐ Ⓑ Ⓒ Ⓓ Ⓔ	40 Ⓐ Ⓑ Ⓒ Ⓓ Ⓔ	58 Ⓐ Ⓑ Ⓒ Ⓓ Ⓔ	76 Ⓐ Ⓑ Ⓒ Ⓓ Ⓔ
5 Ⓐ Ⓑ Ⓒ Ⓓ Ⓔ	23 Ⓐ Ⓑ Ⓒ Ⓓ Ⓔ	41 Ⓐ Ⓑ Ⓒ Ⓓ Ⓔ	59 Ⓐ Ⓑ Ⓒ Ⓓ Ⓔ	77 Ⓐ Ⓑ Ⓒ Ⓓ Ⓔ
6 Ⓐ Ⓑ Ⓒ Ⓓ Ⓔ	24 Ⓐ Ⓑ Ⓒ Ⓓ Ⓔ	42 Ⓐ Ⓑ Ⓒ Ⓓ Ⓔ	60 Ⓐ Ⓑ Ⓒ Ⓓ Ⓔ	78 Ⓐ Ⓑ Ⓒ Ⓓ Ⓔ
7 Ⓐ Ⓑ Ⓒ Ⓓ Ⓔ	25 Ⓐ Ⓑ Ⓒ Ⓓ Ⓔ	43 Ⓐ Ⓑ Ⓒ Ⓓ Ⓔ	61 Ⓐ Ⓑ Ⓒ Ⓓ Ⓔ	79 Ⓐ Ⓑ Ⓒ Ⓓ Ⓔ
8 Ⓐ Ⓑ Ⓒ Ⓓ Ⓔ	26 Ⓐ Ⓑ Ⓒ Ⓓ Ⓔ	44 Ⓐ Ⓑ Ⓒ Ⓓ Ⓔ	62 Ⓐ Ⓑ Ⓒ Ⓓ Ⓔ	80 Ⓐ Ⓑ Ⓒ Ⓓ Ⓔ
9 Ⓐ Ⓑ Ⓒ Ⓓ Ⓔ	27 Ⓐ Ⓑ Ⓒ Ⓓ Ⓔ	45 Ⓐ Ⓑ Ⓒ Ⓓ Ⓔ	63 Ⓐ Ⓑ Ⓒ Ⓓ Ⓔ	81 Ⓐ Ⓑ Ⓒ Ⓓ Ⓔ
10 Ⓐ Ⓑ Ⓒ Ⓓ Ⓔ	28 Ⓐ Ⓑ Ⓒ Ⓓ Ⓔ	46 Ⓐ Ⓑ Ⓒ Ⓓ Ⓔ	64 Ⓐ Ⓑ Ⓒ Ⓓ Ⓔ	82 Ⓐ Ⓑ Ⓒ Ⓓ Ⓔ
11 Ⓐ Ⓑ Ⓒ Ⓓ Ⓔ	29 Ⓐ Ⓑ Ⓒ Ⓓ Ⓔ	47 Ⓐ Ⓑ Ⓒ Ⓓ Ⓔ	65 Ⓐ Ⓑ Ⓒ Ⓓ Ⓔ	83 Ⓐ Ⓑ Ⓒ Ⓓ Ⓔ
12 Ⓐ Ⓑ Ⓒ Ⓓ Ⓔ	30 Ⓐ Ⓑ Ⓒ Ⓓ Ⓔ	48 Ⓐ Ⓑ Ⓒ Ⓓ Ⓔ	66 Ⓐ Ⓑ Ⓒ Ⓓ Ⓔ	84 Ⓐ Ⓑ Ⓒ Ⓓ Ⓔ
13 Ⓐ Ⓑ Ⓒ Ⓓ Ⓔ	31 Ⓐ Ⓑ Ⓒ Ⓓ Ⓔ	49 Ⓐ Ⓑ Ⓒ Ⓓ Ⓔ	67 Ⓐ Ⓑ Ⓒ Ⓓ Ⓔ	85 Ⓐ Ⓑ Ⓒ Ⓓ Ⓔ
14 Ⓐ Ⓑ Ⓒ Ⓓ Ⓔ	32 Ⓐ Ⓑ Ⓒ Ⓓ Ⓔ	50 Ⓐ Ⓑ Ⓒ Ⓓ Ⓔ	68 Ⓐ Ⓑ Ⓒ Ⓓ Ⓔ	86 Ⓐ Ⓑ Ⓒ Ⓓ Ⓔ
15 Ⓐ Ⓑ Ⓒ Ⓓ Ⓔ	33 Ⓐ Ⓑ Ⓒ Ⓓ Ⓔ	51 Ⓐ Ⓑ Ⓒ Ⓓ Ⓔ	69 Ⓐ Ⓑ Ⓒ Ⓓ Ⓔ	87 Ⓐ Ⓑ Ⓒ Ⓓ Ⓔ
16 Ⓐ Ⓑ Ⓒ Ⓓ Ⓔ	34 Ⓐ Ⓑ Ⓒ Ⓓ Ⓔ	52 Ⓐ Ⓑ Ⓒ Ⓓ Ⓔ	70 Ⓐ Ⓑ Ⓒ Ⓓ Ⓔ	88 Ⓐ Ⓑ Ⓒ Ⓓ Ⓔ
17 Ⓐ Ⓑ Ⓒ Ⓓ Ⓔ	35 Ⓐ Ⓑ Ⓒ Ⓓ Ⓔ	53 Ⓐ Ⓑ Ⓒ Ⓓ Ⓔ	71 Ⓐ Ⓑ Ⓒ Ⓓ Ⓔ	
18 Ⓐ Ⓑ Ⓒ Ⓓ Ⓔ	36 Ⓐ Ⓑ Ⓒ Ⓓ Ⓔ	54 Ⓐ Ⓑ Ⓒ Ⓓ Ⓔ	72 Ⓐ Ⓑ Ⓒ Ⓓ Ⓔ	

Part B—Memory for Addresses—List 3

1 Ⓐ Ⓑ Ⓒ Ⓓ Ⓔ	19 Ⓐ Ⓑ Ⓒ Ⓓ Ⓔ	37 Ⓐ Ⓑ Ⓒ Ⓓ Ⓔ	55 Ⓐ Ⓑ Ⓒ Ⓓ Ⓔ	73 Ⓐ Ⓑ Ⓒ Ⓓ Ⓔ
2 Ⓐ Ⓑ Ⓒ Ⓓ Ⓔ	20 Ⓐ Ⓑ Ⓒ Ⓓ Ⓔ	38 Ⓐ Ⓑ Ⓒ Ⓓ Ⓔ	56 Ⓐ Ⓑ Ⓒ Ⓓ Ⓔ	74 Ⓐ Ⓑ Ⓒ Ⓓ Ⓔ
3 Ⓐ Ⓑ Ⓒ Ⓓ Ⓔ	21 Ⓐ Ⓑ Ⓒ Ⓓ Ⓔ	39 Ⓐ Ⓑ Ⓒ Ⓓ Ⓔ	57 Ⓐ Ⓑ Ⓒ Ⓓ Ⓔ	75 Ⓐ Ⓑ Ⓒ Ⓓ Ⓔ
4 Ⓐ Ⓑ Ⓒ Ⓓ Ⓔ	22 Ⓐ Ⓑ Ⓒ Ⓓ Ⓔ	40 Ⓐ Ⓑ Ⓒ Ⓓ Ⓔ	58 Ⓐ Ⓑ Ⓒ Ⓓ Ⓔ	76 Ⓐ Ⓑ Ⓒ Ⓓ Ⓔ
5 Ⓐ Ⓑ Ⓒ Ⓓ Ⓔ	23 Ⓐ Ⓑ Ⓒ Ⓓ Ⓔ	41 Ⓐ Ⓑ Ⓒ Ⓓ Ⓔ	59 Ⓐ Ⓑ Ⓒ Ⓓ Ⓔ	77 Ⓐ Ⓑ Ⓒ Ⓓ Ⓔ
6 Ⓐ Ⓑ Ⓒ Ⓓ Ⓔ	24 Ⓐ Ⓑ Ⓒ Ⓓ Ⓔ	42 Ⓐ Ⓑ Ⓒ Ⓓ Ⓔ	60 Ⓐ Ⓑ Ⓒ Ⓓ Ⓔ	78 Ⓐ Ⓑ Ⓒ Ⓓ Ⓔ
7 Ⓐ Ⓑ Ⓒ Ⓓ Ⓔ	25 Ⓐ Ⓑ Ⓒ Ⓓ Ⓔ	43 Ⓐ Ⓑ Ⓒ Ⓓ Ⓔ	61 Ⓐ Ⓑ Ⓒ Ⓓ Ⓔ	79 Ⓐ Ⓑ Ⓒ Ⓓ Ⓔ
8 Ⓐ Ⓑ Ⓒ Ⓓ Ⓔ	26 Ⓐ Ⓑ Ⓒ Ⓓ Ⓔ	44 Ⓐ Ⓑ Ⓒ Ⓓ Ⓔ	62 Ⓐ Ⓑ Ⓒ Ⓓ Ⓔ	80 Ⓐ Ⓑ Ⓒ Ⓓ Ⓔ
9 Ⓐ Ⓑ Ⓒ Ⓓ Ⓔ	27 Ⓐ Ⓑ Ⓒ Ⓓ Ⓔ	45 Ⓐ Ⓑ Ⓒ Ⓓ Ⓔ	63 Ⓐ Ⓑ Ⓒ Ⓓ Ⓔ	81 Ⓐ Ⓑ Ⓒ Ⓓ Ⓔ
10 Ⓐ Ⓑ Ⓒ Ⓓ Ⓔ	28 Ⓐ Ⓑ Ⓒ Ⓓ Ⓔ	46 Ⓐ Ⓑ Ⓒ Ⓓ Ⓔ	64 Ⓐ Ⓑ Ⓒ Ⓓ Ⓔ	82 Ⓐ Ⓑ Ⓒ Ⓓ Ⓔ
11 Ⓐ Ⓑ Ⓒ Ⓓ Ⓔ	29 Ⓐ Ⓑ Ⓒ Ⓓ Ⓔ	47 Ⓐ Ⓑ Ⓒ Ⓓ Ⓔ	65 Ⓐ Ⓑ Ⓒ Ⓓ Ⓔ	83 Ⓐ Ⓑ Ⓒ Ⓓ Ⓔ
12 Ⓐ Ⓑ Ⓒ Ⓓ Ⓔ	30 Ⓐ Ⓑ Ⓒ Ⓓ Ⓔ	48 Ⓐ Ⓑ Ⓒ Ⓓ Ⓔ	66 Ⓐ Ⓑ Ⓒ Ⓓ Ⓔ	84 Ⓐ Ⓑ Ⓒ Ⓓ Ⓔ
13 Ⓐ Ⓑ Ⓒ Ⓓ Ⓔ	31 Ⓐ Ⓑ Ⓒ Ⓓ Ⓔ	49 Ⓐ Ⓑ Ⓒ Ⓓ Ⓔ	67 Ⓐ Ⓑ Ⓒ Ⓓ Ⓔ	85 Ⓐ Ⓑ Ⓒ Ⓓ Ⓔ
14 Ⓐ Ⓑ Ⓒ Ⓓ Ⓔ	32 Ⓐ Ⓑ Ⓒ Ⓓ Ⓔ	50 Ⓐ Ⓑ Ⓒ Ⓓ Ⓔ	68 Ⓐ Ⓑ Ⓒ Ⓓ Ⓔ	86 Ⓐ Ⓑ Ⓒ Ⓓ Ⓔ
15 Ⓐ Ⓑ Ⓒ Ⓓ Ⓔ	33 Ⓐ Ⓑ Ⓒ Ⓓ Ⓔ	51 Ⓐ Ⓑ Ⓒ Ⓓ Ⓔ	69 Ⓐ Ⓑ Ⓒ Ⓓ Ⓔ	87 Ⓐ Ⓑ Ⓒ Ⓓ Ⓔ
16 Ⓐ Ⓑ Ⓒ Ⓓ Ⓔ	34 Ⓐ Ⓑ Ⓒ Ⓓ Ⓔ	52 Ⓐ Ⓑ Ⓒ Ⓓ Ⓔ	70 Ⓐ Ⓑ Ⓒ Ⓓ Ⓔ	88 Ⓐ Ⓑ Ⓒ Ⓓ Ⓔ
17 Ⓐ Ⓑ Ⓒ Ⓓ Ⓔ	35 Ⓐ Ⓑ Ⓒ Ⓓ Ⓔ	53 Ⓐ Ⓑ Ⓒ Ⓓ Ⓔ	71 Ⓐ Ⓑ Ⓒ Ⓓ Ⓔ	
18 Ⓐ Ⓑ Ⓒ Ⓓ Ⓔ	36 Ⓐ Ⓑ Ⓒ Ⓓ Ⓔ	54 Ⓐ Ⓑ Ⓒ Ⓓ Ⓔ	72 Ⓐ Ⓑ Ⓒ Ⓓ Ⓔ	

Part C—Number Series

1 Ⓐ Ⓑ Ⓒ Ⓓ Ⓔ	6 Ⓐ Ⓑ Ⓒ Ⓓ Ⓔ	11 Ⓐ Ⓑ Ⓒ Ⓓ Ⓔ	16 Ⓐ Ⓑ Ⓒ Ⓓ Ⓔ	21 Ⓐ Ⓑ Ⓒ Ⓓ Ⓔ
2 Ⓐ Ⓑ Ⓒ Ⓓ Ⓔ	7 Ⓐ Ⓑ Ⓒ Ⓓ Ⓔ	12 Ⓐ Ⓑ Ⓒ Ⓓ Ⓔ	17 Ⓐ Ⓑ Ⓒ Ⓓ Ⓔ	22 Ⓐ Ⓑ Ⓒ Ⓓ Ⓔ
3 Ⓐ Ⓑ Ⓒ Ⓓ Ⓔ	8 Ⓐ Ⓑ Ⓒ Ⓓ Ⓔ	13 Ⓐ Ⓑ Ⓒ Ⓓ Ⓔ	18 Ⓐ Ⓑ Ⓒ Ⓓ Ⓔ	23 Ⓐ Ⓑ Ⓒ Ⓓ Ⓔ
4 Ⓐ Ⓑ Ⓒ Ⓓ Ⓔ	9 Ⓐ Ⓑ Ⓒ Ⓓ Ⓔ	14 Ⓐ Ⓑ Ⓒ Ⓓ Ⓔ	19 Ⓐ Ⓑ Ⓒ Ⓓ Ⓔ	24 Ⓐ Ⓑ Ⓒ Ⓓ Ⓔ
5 Ⓐ Ⓑ Ⓒ Ⓓ Ⓔ	10 Ⓐ Ⓑ Ⓒ Ⓓ Ⓔ	15 Ⓐ Ⓑ Ⓒ Ⓓ Ⓔ	20 Ⓐ Ⓑ Ⓒ Ⓓ Ⓔ	

Part D—Following Oral Directions

1 Ⓐ Ⓑ Ⓒ Ⓓ Ⓔ	19 Ⓐ Ⓑ Ⓒ Ⓓ Ⓔ	37 Ⓐ Ⓑ Ⓒ Ⓓ Ⓔ	55 Ⓐ Ⓑ Ⓒ Ⓓ Ⓔ	73 Ⓐ Ⓑ Ⓒ Ⓓ Ⓔ
2 Ⓐ Ⓑ Ⓒ Ⓓ Ⓔ	20 Ⓐ Ⓑ Ⓒ Ⓓ Ⓔ	38 Ⓐ Ⓑ Ⓒ Ⓓ Ⓔ	56 Ⓐ Ⓑ Ⓒ Ⓓ Ⓔ	74 Ⓐ Ⓑ Ⓒ Ⓓ Ⓔ
3 Ⓐ Ⓑ Ⓒ Ⓓ Ⓔ	21 Ⓐ Ⓑ Ⓒ Ⓓ Ⓔ	39 Ⓐ Ⓑ Ⓒ Ⓓ Ⓔ	57 Ⓐ Ⓑ Ⓒ Ⓓ Ⓔ	75 Ⓐ Ⓑ Ⓒ Ⓓ Ⓔ
4 Ⓐ Ⓑ Ⓒ Ⓓ Ⓔ	22 Ⓐ Ⓑ Ⓒ Ⓓ Ⓔ	40 Ⓐ Ⓑ Ⓒ Ⓓ Ⓔ	58 Ⓐ Ⓑ Ⓒ Ⓓ Ⓔ	76 Ⓐ Ⓑ Ⓒ Ⓓ Ⓔ
5 Ⓐ Ⓑ Ⓒ Ⓓ Ⓔ	23 Ⓐ Ⓑ Ⓒ Ⓓ Ⓔ	41 Ⓐ Ⓑ Ⓒ Ⓓ Ⓔ	59 Ⓐ Ⓑ Ⓒ Ⓓ Ⓔ	77 Ⓐ Ⓑ Ⓒ Ⓓ Ⓔ
6 Ⓐ Ⓑ Ⓒ Ⓓ Ⓔ	24 Ⓐ Ⓑ Ⓒ Ⓓ Ⓔ	42 Ⓐ Ⓑ Ⓒ Ⓓ Ⓔ	60 Ⓐ Ⓑ Ⓒ Ⓓ Ⓔ	78 Ⓐ Ⓑ Ⓒ Ⓓ Ⓔ
7 Ⓐ Ⓑ Ⓒ Ⓓ Ⓔ	25 Ⓐ Ⓑ Ⓒ Ⓓ Ⓔ	43 Ⓐ Ⓑ Ⓒ Ⓓ Ⓔ	61 Ⓐ Ⓑ Ⓒ Ⓓ Ⓔ	79 Ⓐ Ⓑ Ⓒ Ⓓ Ⓔ
8 Ⓐ Ⓑ Ⓒ Ⓓ Ⓔ	26 Ⓐ Ⓑ Ⓒ Ⓓ Ⓔ	44 Ⓐ Ⓑ Ⓒ Ⓓ Ⓔ	62 Ⓐ Ⓑ Ⓒ Ⓓ Ⓔ	80 Ⓐ Ⓑ Ⓒ Ⓓ Ⓔ
9 Ⓐ Ⓑ Ⓒ Ⓓ Ⓔ	27 Ⓐ Ⓑ Ⓒ Ⓓ Ⓔ	45 Ⓐ Ⓑ Ⓒ Ⓓ Ⓔ	63 Ⓐ Ⓑ Ⓒ Ⓓ Ⓔ	81 Ⓐ Ⓑ Ⓒ Ⓓ Ⓔ
10 Ⓐ Ⓑ Ⓒ Ⓓ Ⓔ	28 Ⓐ Ⓑ Ⓒ Ⓓ Ⓔ	46 Ⓐ Ⓑ Ⓒ Ⓓ Ⓔ	64 Ⓐ Ⓑ Ⓒ Ⓓ Ⓔ	82 Ⓐ Ⓑ Ⓒ Ⓓ Ⓔ
11 Ⓐ Ⓑ Ⓒ Ⓓ Ⓔ	29 Ⓐ Ⓑ Ⓒ Ⓓ Ⓔ	47 Ⓐ Ⓑ Ⓒ Ⓓ Ⓔ	65 Ⓐ Ⓑ Ⓒ Ⓓ Ⓔ	83 Ⓐ Ⓑ Ⓒ Ⓓ Ⓔ
12 Ⓐ Ⓑ Ⓒ Ⓓ Ⓔ	30 Ⓐ Ⓑ Ⓒ Ⓓ Ⓔ	48 Ⓐ Ⓑ Ⓒ Ⓓ Ⓔ	66 Ⓐ Ⓑ Ⓒ Ⓓ Ⓔ	84 Ⓐ Ⓑ Ⓒ Ⓓ Ⓔ
13 Ⓐ Ⓑ Ⓒ Ⓓ Ⓔ	31 Ⓐ Ⓑ Ⓒ Ⓓ Ⓔ	49 Ⓐ Ⓑ Ⓒ Ⓓ Ⓔ	67 Ⓐ Ⓑ Ⓒ Ⓓ Ⓔ	85 Ⓐ Ⓑ Ⓒ Ⓓ Ⓔ
14 Ⓐ Ⓑ Ⓒ Ⓓ Ⓔ	32 Ⓐ Ⓑ Ⓒ Ⓓ Ⓔ	50 Ⓐ Ⓑ Ⓒ Ⓓ Ⓔ	68 Ⓐ Ⓑ Ⓒ Ⓓ Ⓔ	86 Ⓐ Ⓑ Ⓒ Ⓓ Ⓔ
15 Ⓐ Ⓑ Ⓒ Ⓓ Ⓔ	33 Ⓐ Ⓑ Ⓒ Ⓓ Ⓔ	51 Ⓐ Ⓑ Ⓒ Ⓓ Ⓔ	69 Ⓐ Ⓑ Ⓒ Ⓓ Ⓔ	87 Ⓐ Ⓑ Ⓒ Ⓓ Ⓔ
16 Ⓐ Ⓑ Ⓒ Ⓓ Ⓔ	34 Ⓐ Ⓑ Ⓒ Ⓓ Ⓔ	52 Ⓐ Ⓑ Ⓒ Ⓓ Ⓔ	70 Ⓐ Ⓑ Ⓒ Ⓓ Ⓔ	88 Ⓐ Ⓑ Ⓒ Ⓓ Ⓔ
17 Ⓐ Ⓑ Ⓒ Ⓓ Ⓔ	35 Ⓐ Ⓑ Ⓒ Ⓓ Ⓔ	53 Ⓐ Ⓑ Ⓒ Ⓓ Ⓔ	71 Ⓐ Ⓑ Ⓒ Ⓓ Ⓔ	
18 Ⓐ Ⓑ Ⓒ Ⓓ Ⓔ	36 Ⓐ Ⓑ Ⓒ Ⓓ Ⓔ	54 Ⓐ Ⓑ Ⓒ Ⓓ Ⓔ	72 Ⓐ Ⓑ Ⓒ Ⓓ Ⓔ	

Remove by cutting on dotted line.

Chapter 10

Practice Test 1

PART A — ADDRESS CHECKING

Work — 6 minutes

In this part of the test, you are to decide whether two addresses are alike or different. If the two addresses are *exactly alike in every way*, darken space Ⓐ. If they are *different in any way*, darken space Ⓓ.

Mark your answers on the Answer Sheet on page 231. Tear it out, put today's date on it, and place it next to the questions.

Allow yourself exactly 6 minutes to do as many of the 95 questions as you can. If you finish before the time is up, check your answers.

1.	2543 Reeves Dr	2534 Reeves Dr
2.	East Thetford Vt	West Thetford Vt
3.	9453 San Ramon Ave	9458 San Ramon Ave
4.	8113 Hutton Blvd S	8113 Hutton Blvd S
5.	10234 Henninger Park NW	10234 Henninger Park NW
6.	61 Ingalls Way	61 Ingalls Way
7.	1416 Bellhaven Ct	1461 Bellhaven Ct
8.	Midland TX	Midlawn TX
9.	2604 N Jaynes Lane	2604 N Jaynes Lane
10.	470 Fremont Cir	470 Fremont Cir
11.	Abington PA 19001	Abington PA 19010
12.	2998 Columbine Cir	2998 Columbus Cir
13.	9015 Tancred Oval	9015 Trancred Oval
14.	Louisville, KY	Louisville, KS
15.	7004 Jennie Path	7004 Jennie Path
16.	133 St Johns Pl	133 St Johns St
17.	552 Clowes Ave NE	552 Clowes Ave NE
18.	Brick NJ 08724	Brick NJ 80724
19.	98 S Byron Pl	98 S Bryon Pl
20.	4400 E Bradcliff Pkwy	4400 W Bradcliff Pkwy
21.	15 W Cumberland Blvd.	51 W Cumberland Blvd.
22.	8985 Stuart St.	8985 Stewart St.
23.	Wilmington Industrial Park DE 19801	Wilmington Industrial Park DE 19801
24.	8701 Ardwick Blvd SW	8701 Ardwood Blvd SW

25.	709 E Peckhame St.	709 E Peckheim St.
26.	69 Dunster Path S	69 Dunster Path S
27.	126 Abington Dr	126 Abingdon Dr
28.	4228 Lime Orchard Way	4228 Lime Orchard Way
29.	U S Highway 9 07306	U S Highway 9 07346
30.	834 Essen Heights Ct E	834 Essen Heights Ct E
31.	6145 Hillside Mill Rd	6145 Hillside Hill Rd
32.	897 Mabry Ct	897 Mabry Ct
33.	96 Newberry Ct	96 Newberry Ct
34.	3004 Whitworth Dr	3004 Whitworth Rd
35.	Kansas City MO	Kansas City MO
36.	12 Ogden Pl	12 Ogden Pl
37.	5053 W Ely Ct	5053 W Ely Ct
38.	88 McMahon Rd W	88 MacMahon Rd W
39.	23 New Fritsche Cemetery Dr	23 New Fritze Cemetery Dr
40.	2400 SE Grosvenor Pl	2400 SE Grosvenor Pl
41.	148 E Eggleston Ln	148 W Eggleston Ln
42.	8451 Saulburg Plz	8451 Saulburg Plz
43.	98 Vicki Ln SE	93 Vicki Ln SE
44.	49 S Rockland Ave	49 S Rocklane Ave
45.	734 Ladeah St.	734 Ladeah St.
46.	6263 W 233 Ave	6263 W 234 Ave
47.	13405 1 St E	13405 1 St E
48.	7982 Richthofen Pky	7982 Richthofen Pky
49.	4776 Yoakum Rd	4776 Yoakun Rd
50.	Hammond IN 46324	Hammond IN 46324
51.	919 Agua Dulce Creek Dr	909 Agua Dulce Creek Dr
52.	Auburn ME	Auburn ME
53.	3612 Shove St N	3612 Shave St N
54.	506 Haseltone Ct	506 Hazeltone Ct
55.	654 Forest Pl W	654 Forest Pl W
56.	5707 Mary Ella Dr	5707 Mary Ella Rd
57.	676 14 Pl NW	676 14 Rd NW
58.	973 W Newton Path	973 W Newton Path
59.	222 Union St W	222 Union St E
60.	7000 W Guildford Ct	7000 W Guildford Ct

61.	702 La Louisiane Ct N	702 La Louisiane Ct N
62.	Lake Orion MI 48361	Lake Orion MI 48361
63.	9234 Amberwood Ct	9234 Amberwood Pl
64.	684 Big Cyprus Neck Trl	684 Big Cyprus Neck Trl
65.	5583 Robertson Blvd	5583 Roberson Blvd
66.	La Place LA 70069	La Place LA 70069
67.	808 Woodford Blvd W	808 Woodford Blvd W
68.	8200 Kalamath St	8200 Kalamath St
69.	Chillicothe IA 52548	Chillicothe GA 52548
70.	722 Quieto Ct	722 Quiet Ct
71.	723 Yonah Dr NE	723 Jonah Dr NE
72.	2314 Doncaster St NW	2314 Doncaster Ct SW
73.	17094 Highway 370	17094 Highway 370
74.	297 Parket Blvd	297 Parket Blvd
75.	3565 Donner Dr	3565 Danner Dr
76.	901 Flat Shoals Rd	901 Flat Shoals Rd
77.	321 S Jecks Ct	321 N Jecks Ct
78.	24 Irma Ln N	24 Irme Ln N
79.	591 E Ashlea Ter	591 E Ashlea Ter
80.	1041 Indiana Ct N	1041 Indiana Ct N
81.	7152 Chanruss Pl	7152 Chanross Pl
82.	1231 Lewin Pl E	1231 Levin Pl E
83.	Box B Denver 80209	Box B Denver 80209
84.	1616 N Oakgrove Ave	1616 N Oakgrove Ave
85.	20 Dunridge Ct N	20 Danridge Ct N
86.	Tulsa OK 74145	Tulsa OH 74145
87.	243 Prospect Park SW	243 Prospect Park NW
88.	36 Cranbourne Cir E	36 Craybourne Cir E
89.	302 Kansas Plz W	302 Kansas Plz W
90.	6409 Oakhurst Ln	6409 Oakhurst St
91.	648 Mother Gaston Blvd	648 Mother Gaston Blvd
92.	10123 49 Ave S	10123 49 Ave S
93.	1005 Trimble Lk Plz	1005 Trimble Lk Pl
94.	2404 N Berkshire Oval	2044 N Berkshire Oval
95.	14 Old Ringgold Rd S	14 Old Ringgold Rd S

STOP
If you finish before the time is up, go back and check
the questions in this section of the test only.

PART B — MEMORY FOR ADDRESSES

In this part of the test, you will have five boxes labeled A, B, C, D, and E. Each box contains five addresses. Three of the five are street addresses, such as 4000–4799 Cherry, 1300–1799 White, and 2400–2899 Cherry. Two are names of places, such as Hester and Gunhill. The addresses are different in each box.

There will be several opportunities to study the addresses and the boxes they are in. You will also be given three tests of 88 questions each, and the task of deciding where each address belongs. In some cases, you will have the list *and* the boxes in front of you at the same time; in others you will not. List 1 and List 2 are for warm-up practice. List 3 is the real one that will be scored.

Make sure you understand the format by examining the pretest samples below.

Pretest Samples

A	B	C	D	E
2400–3199 White	3200–3999 White	1300–1799 White	1800–2399 White	4000–5099 White
Beale	Rustin	Ankre	Gunhill	Church
4000–4799 Cherry	4800–5199 Cherry	1000–2399 Cherry	2900–3999 Cherry	2400–2899 Cherry
Crydon	Hester	Shore	Barile	John
3700–4199 Molloy	5800–6399 Molloy	5100–5799 Molloy	4200–4799 Molloy	4800–5099 Molloy

Questions 1 through 7 show the way the questions look. You have to decide in which lettered box (A, B, C, D, or E) the address belongs and then mark your answer by darkening the appropriate space in the answer grid.

1. Crydon   1 Ⓐ Ⓑ Ⓒ Ⓓ Ⓔ
2. 3700–4199 Molloy 2 Ⓐ Ⓑ Ⓒ Ⓓ Ⓔ
3. 1000–2399 Cherry 3 Ⓐ Ⓑ Ⓒ Ⓓ Ⓔ
4. Church   4 Ⓐ Ⓑ Ⓒ Ⓓ Ⓔ
5. 3200–3999 White   5 Ⓐ Ⓑ Ⓒ Ⓓ Ⓔ
6. Barile   6 Ⓐ Ⓑ Ⓒ Ⓓ Ⓔ
7. 2400–2899 Cherry 7 Ⓐ Ⓑ Ⓒ Ⓓ Ⓔ

Answers

1. **A**   2. **A**   3. **C**   4. **E**   5. **B**   6. **D**   7. **E**

Now that you know what to do, you may begin Part B of Practice Test 1. To get the most out of it and the other five practice tests in this book, follow the directions and timing *exactly*. Follow each phase of Part B of the test, page by page, until you've completed List 3. It is modeled on the way the Postal Service actually conducts its tests.

Turn to the next page to begin.

Study — 3 minutes

You will be given 3 minutes to spend memorizing the addresses in the boxes. *They are exactly the same ones that will be used for all three tests.* Try to memorize as many as you can. When the 3 minutes are up, turn to page 240 and read the instructions for *List 1*.

A	B	C	D	E
2400–3199 White	3200–3999 White	1300–1799 White	1800–2399 White	4000–5099 White
Beale	Rustin	Ankre	Gunhill	Church
4000–4799 Cherry	4800–5199 Cherry	1000–2399 Cherry	2900–3999 Cherry	2400–2899 Cherry
Crydon	Hester	Shore	Barile	John
3700–4199 Molloy	5800–6399 Molloy	5100–5799 Molloy	4200–4799 Molloy	4800–5099 Molloy

List 1

Work — 3 minutes

Tear out the Answer Sheet for List 1. For each question, mark the Answer Sheet on page 232 to show the letter of the box in which the address belongs. Try to remember the locations of as many addresses as you can. *You will now have 3 minutes to complete List 1.* If you are not sure of an answer, you should guess.

A	B	C	D	E
2400–3199 White	3200–3999 White	1300–1799 White	1800–2399 White	4000–5099 White
Beale	Rustin	Ankre	Gunhill	Church
4000–4799 Cherry	4800–5199 Cherry	1000–2399 Cherry	2900–3999 Cherry	2400–2899 Cherry
Crydon	Hester	Shore	Barile	John
3700–4199 Molloy	5800–6399 Molloy	5100–5799 Molloy	4200–4799 Molloy	4800–5099 Molloy

1. Gunhill
2. John
3. Ankre
4. 3200–3999 White
5. Shore
6. 4800–5099 Molloy
7. Beale
8. 5800–6399 Molloy
9. Barile
10. Ankre
11. 2400–3199 White

12. Hester
13. Crydon
14. 5800–6399 Molloy
15. Barile
16. 3200–3999 White
17. 3700–4199 Molloy
18. 1000–2399 Cherry
19. 2900-3999 Cherry
20. Crydon
21. Rustin
22. 5100–5799 Molloy

23. 1800–2399 White
24. 4800–5199 Cherry
25. 4000–4799 Cherry
26. 4000–5099 White
27. 4200–4799 Molloy
28. Church
29. Rustin
30. 1300–1799 White
31. 5100–5799 Molloy
32. Shore
33. Beale

34. 2400–2899 Cherry
35. John
36. 4800–5099 Molloy
37. Rustin
38. 1800–2399 White
39. Barile
40. 1000–2399 Cherry
41. Shore
42. 5800–6399 Molloy
43. Beale
44. 2400–2899 Cherry

45. Barile
46. Shore
47. 4800–5199 Cherry
48. Gunhill
49. 2400–3199 White
50. Church
51. 4000–5099 White
52. 1300–1799 White
53. Ankre
54. Church
55. Gunhill

56. Beale
57. 3700–4199 Molloy
58. 3700–4199 Molloy
59. 1300–1799 White
60. 4000–5099 White
61. Crydon
62. 1800–2399 White
63. 5100–5799 Molloy
64. Hester
65. John
66. Church

67. 2400–3199 White
68. Hester
69. 2900–3999 Cherry
70. Barile
71. 3200–3999 White
72. Hester
73. 4800–5199 Cherry
74. Gunhill
75. 2900–3999 Cherry
76. Ankre
77. 2400–2899 Cherry

78. Gunhill
79. John
80. 4800–5099 Molloy
81. Rustin
82. 4200–4799 Molloy
83. 4000–4799 Cherry
84. 1000–2399 Cherry
85. 4200–4799 Molloy
86. 2400–3199 White
87. Crydon
88. 4000–4799 Cherry

STOP.
If you finish before the time is up, go back and check
the questions in this section of the test only.

List 2

Work — 3 minutes

Do these questions *without* looking back at the boxes. For each question, mark your answer on the Answer Sheet for List 2 on page 232. If you are not sure of an answer, you should guess.

1. 4800–5099 Molloy
2. John
3. 2400–2899 Cherry
4. Beale
5. Shore
6. 5100–5799 Molloy
7. 1300–1799 White
8. Rustin
9. Church
10. 4200–4799 Molloy
11. 4000–5099 White

12. 4000–4799 Cherry
13. 4800–5199 Cherry
14. 1800–2399 White
15. 5100–5799 Molloy
16. Rustin
17. Crydon
18. 2900–3999 Cherry
19. 1000–2399 Cherry
20. 3700–4199 Molloy
21. 3200–3999 White
22. Barile

23. 5800–6399 Molloy
24. Crydon
25. Hester
26. 2400–3199 White
27. Ankre
28. Barile
29. 5800–6399 Molloy
30. Beale
31. 4800–5099 Molloy
32. Shore
33. 3200–3999 White

34. Ankre
35. John
36. Gunhill
37. 4000–4799 Cherry
38. Crydon
39. 2400–3199 White
40. 4200–4799 Molloy
41. 1000–2399 Cherry
42. 4000–4799 Cherry
43. 4200–4799 Molloy
44. Rustin

45. 4800–5099 Molloy
46. John
47. Gunhill
48. 2400–2899 Cherry
49. Ankre
50. 2900–3999 Cherry
51. Gunhill
52. 4800–5199 Cherry
53. Hester
54. 3200–3999 White
55. Barile

56. 2900–3999 Cherry
57. Hester
58. 2400–3199 White
59. Church
60. John
61. Hester
62. 5100–5799 Molloy
63. 1800–2309 White
64. Crydon
65. 4000–5099 White
66. 1300–1799 White

67. 3700–4199 Molloy
68. 3700–4199 Molloy
69. Beale
70. Gunhill
71. Church
72. Ankre
73. 1300–1799 White
74. 4000–5099 White
75. Church
76. 2400–3199 White
77. Gunhill

78. 4800–5199 Cherry
79. Shore
80. Barile
81. 2400–2899 Cherry
82. Beale
83. 5800–6399 Molloy
84. Shore
85. 1000–2399 Cherry
86. Barile
87. 1800–2399 White
88. Rustin

STOP.
If you finish before the time is up, go back and check
the questions in this section of the test only.

List 3

Study — 5 minutes

You are now about to take the test using List 3. *(This is the test that counts!)*

Turn back to page 239 and study the boxes again. *You have 5 minutes to restudy the addresses.*

Work — 5 minutes

For each question, mark the Answer Sheet on page 233 to show the letter of the box in which the address belongs. You have *exactly 5 minutes* to do the test. During these 5 minutes, *do not* turn to any other page.

1. 4000–4799 Cherry
2. Crydon
3. 2400–3199 White
4. 4200–4799 Molloy
5. 1000–2399 Cherry
6. 4000–4799 Cherry
7. 4200–4799 Molloy
8. Rustin
9. 4800–5099 Molloy
10. John
11. Gunhill

12. 2400–2899 Cherry
13. Ankre
14. 2900–3999 Cherry
15. Gunhill
16. 4800–5199 Cherry
17. Hester
18. 3200–3999 White
19. Barile
20. 2900–3999 Cherry
21. Hester
22. 2400–3199 White

23. Beale
24. John
25. Hester
26. 5100–5799 Molloy
27. 1800–2309 White
28. Crydon
29. 4000–5099 White
30. Ankre
31. 3700–4199 Molloy
32. 3700–4199 Molloy
33. Beale

34. Gunhill
35. Church
36. Ankre
37. 1300–1799 White
38. 4000–5099 White
39. Church
40. 2400–3199 White
41. Gunhill
42. 4800–5199 Cherry
43. Shore
44. Barile

45. 2400–2899 Cherry
46. Beale
47. 5800–6399 Molloy
48. Ankre
49. 1000–2399 Cherry
50. Barile
51. 1800–2399 White
52. Shore
53. 4800–5099 Molloy
54. John
55. 2400–2899 Cherry

56. Beale
57. Shore
58. 5100–5799 Molloy
59. 1300–1799 White
60. Rustin
61. Church
62. Beale
63. 4000–5099 White
64. 4000–4799 Cherry
65. 4800–5199 Cherry
66. 1800–2399 White

67. 5100–5799 Molloy
68. Rustin
69. Crydon
70. 2900–3999 Cherry
71. Shore
72. 3700–4199 Molloy
73. 3200–3999 White
74. Barile
75. 5800–6399 Molloy
76. Crydon
77. Hester

78. 2400–3199 White
79. Ankre
80. Barile
81. 5800–6399 Molloy
82. Beale
83. 4800–5099 Molloy
84. Shore
85. 3200–3999 White
86. Ankre
87. John
88. Gunhill

STOP.
If you finish before the time is up, go back and check
the questions in this section of the test only.

PART C — NUMBER SERIES

Work — 20 minutes

For each Number Series question, there is a series of numbers that follow some definite order, and below each are five sets of two numbers each. You are to look at the numbers in the series and find out what order they follow. Then decide what the next two numbers in that series would be if the same order were continued. Mark your answers on the Answer Sheet for Number Series on page 233.

You have 20 minutes to complete this part of the test. If you finish before the time is up, check your answers. The answers and explanations are on page 256.

1. 12 17 22 27 32 37 42 __ __
   A) 47 51   B) 52 47   C) 47 52   D) 46 50   E) 42 47

2. 55 52 52 49 49 46 46 __ __
   A) 46 43   B) 43 40   C) 43 39   D) 43 43   E) 42 39

3. 8 17 10 20 12 23 14 __ __
   A) 26 17   B) 16 25   C) 26 16   D) 17 25   E) 25 16

4. 7 8 9 11 12 13 15 __ __
   A) 16 18   B) 17 18   C) 17 19   D) 15 16   E) 16 17

5. 1 2 2 4 4 8 8 __ __
   A) 16 32   B) 8 12   C) 12 11   D) 16 16   E) 8 16

6. 7 16 9 7 16 9 7 __ __
   A) 9 7   B) 16 9   C) 9 16   D) 7 16   E) 16 7

7. 20 17 21 18 22 19 23 __ __
   A) 24 20   B) 20 24   C) 21 25   D) 24 21   E) 23 24

8. 9 19 19 19 29 29 29 __ __
   A) 29 39   B) 39 49   C) 39 29   D) 49 59   E) 39 39

9. 28 29 31 34 38 43 49 __ __
   A) 56 63   B) 57 64   C) 59 65   D) 55 62   E) 56 64

10. 36 35 35 31 30 30 26 __ __
    A) 26 25   B) 25 25   C) 26 24   D) 25 21   E) 25 26

11. 17 46 18 44 19 42 20 __ __
    A) 21 41   B) 41 18   C) 40 22   D) 22 44   E) 40 21

12. 5 7 9 6 9 12 7 __ __
   A) 10 13   B) 9 8   C) 9 10   D) 9 11   E) 11 13

13. 3 19 9 25 15 31 21 __ __
   A) 38 18   B) 37 27   C) 37 17   D) 24 40   E) 39 20

14. 9 18 10 20 12 24 16 __ __
   A) 24 12   B) 36 28   C) 32 24   D) 40 32   E) 28 20

15. 61 58 55 52 49 46 43 __ __
   A) 41 38   B) 42 39   C) 40 38   D) 39 37   E) 40 37

16. 31 18 28 26 18 23 21 18 __ __
   A) 18 16   B) 18 18   C) 15 13   D) 15 18   E) 16 18

17. 7 19 19 8 16 16 9 __ __
   A) 10 17   B) 17 10   C) 9 13   D) 13 10   E) 13 13

18. 12 14 14 10 12 14 14 __ __
   A) 10 12   B) 14 10   C) 12 10   D) 12 14   E) 16 12

19. 51 56 61 61 66 71 71 __ __
   A) 76 76   B) 71 77   C) 76 81   D) 81 81   E) 76 77

20. 18 24 22 21 27 25 24 __ __
   A) 22 21   B) 30 28   C) 23 21   D) 30 29   E) 28 30

21. 2 3 5 8 13 21 34 __ __
   A) 42 57   B) 48 63   C) 55 89   D) 65 109   E) 49 65

22. 6 7 10 8 9 11 10 __ __
   A) 12 13   B) 11 13   C) 11 10   D) 12 10   E) 11 12

23. 36 4 33 11 30 18 27 __ __
   A) 25 20   B) 26 19   C) 18 22   D) 25 24   E) 34 24

24. 11 6 13 8 15 10 17 __ __
   A) 12 19   B) 18 12   C) 19 21   D) 18 19   E) 12 18

STOP.
If you finish before the time is up, go back and check
the questions in this part of the test only.

Part D — FOLLOWING ORAL DIRECTIONS

This part of the test gauges your ability to understand and carry out spoken directions *exactly* as they are given to you.

In order to prepare to take Part D of the test, follow the steps below:

1. Enlist the help of a friend who will be the "reader." It will be his or her job to read aloud a series of directions that you are to follow *exactly*. The reader will need a watch that displays seconds, because the directions must be read at the correct speed.

2. Tear out pages 253 and 254. These are the worksheets you should have in front of you as you listen to the directions given by the reader, who will tell you to do certain things with the items on each line on the worksheets.

3. Use the Answer Sheet for Following Oral Directions on page 233 and insert today's date. You will darken the appropriate spaces in accordance with the directions given by the reader.

4. *Now hand this entire book to the reader.* Ask him/her to review the section below headed "Instructions to the Reader." It explains exactly how the reader is to proceed.

When you and the reader are ready to start this part of Practice Test 1, he/she will begin reading to you the section marked "Directions." YOU ARE NOT TO READ THESE AT ANY TIME BEFORE OR DURING THE TEST. If you do, you will lose the benefit of this part of the practice test.

Instructions to the "Reader"

These instructions should be read at about 80 words per minute. You should practice reading the material in the box until you can do it in exactly 1 minute. The number of words in the passage and the natural pauses described below will give you a good feel for the rate of speed and the way you should read the test questions.

1–MINUTE PRACTICE

> Look at line 20 on your worksheet. There are two circles and two boxes of different sizes with numbers in them. If 7 is less than 3 and if 2 is smaller than 4, write C in the larger circle. Otherwise write B as in *baker* in the smaller box. Now on your answer sheet, darken the space for the number-letter combination in the box or circle.

You should read the entire test aloud before you read it to the person taking the test, in order to thoroughly acquaint yourself with the procedure and the desired rate of reading.

Read slowly, but at a natural pace. In other words, do not space the words so that there are unnaturally long pauses between them. the instruction "Pause slightly" indicates only enough time to take a breath. The other instructions for pauses give the recommended length for each. If possible, use a watch with a second hand.

All the material that follows, except the words in parentheses, is to be read aloud. Now start reading the directions. *Do not repeat any of the directions.*

Directions: In this test, I will read instructions to you.

You are to mark your worksheets according to the instructions that I read to you. After each set of instructions, I'll give you time to record your answers on your answer sheet.

Try to understand the instructions as I read them; I cannot repeat them. Do not ask any questions from now on.

If, when you go to darken a space for a number, you find that you have already darkened another space for that number, either (1) erase the first mark and darken the space for your new choice, or (2) let the first mark stay and do not darken any other space. When you finish, you should have no more than one space darkened for each number.

Turn to Worksheet 1.

Look at the letters on line 1 on your worksheet. (Pause slightly.) Draw a line under the third letter in the line. (Pause 2 seconds.) Now, on your answer sheet, find number 47 and darken the space for the letter under which you drew a line. (Pause 5 seconds.)

Look at line 1 again. (Pause slightly.) Draw 2 lines under the fifth letter in the line. (Pause 3 seconds.) Now, on your answer sheet, find number 82 and darken the space for the letter under which you drew two lines. (Pause 5 seconds.)

Look at line 2 on your worksheet. (Pause slightly.) There are five circles on the line. Some of the circles are partially or entirely shaded. (Pause slightly.) Count the number of circles that have no shading, add 8, and write that number in the middle circle. (Pause 2 seconds.) Now, on your answer sheet, darken the space for the number-letter combination that is in the circle you just wrote in. (Pause 5 seconds.)

Look at line 2 again. (Pause slightly.) Count the number of circles that are partially or entirely shaded, subtract 2, and write that number in the first circle. (Pause 2 seconds.) Now, on your answer sheet, darken the space for the number-letter combination that is in the circle you just wrote in. (Pause 5 seconds.)

Now, look at line 3 on your worksheet. (Pause slightly.) There are four boxes with numbers inside them. Each number represents the weight of a parcel brought to a mail handling section. (Pause slightly.) Write B as in *baker* on the line in the box containing the highest weight parcel. (Pause 2 seconds.) Now, on your answer sheet, darken the space for the number-letter combination that is in the box you just wrote in. (Pause 5 seconds.)

Look at line 4 on your worksheet. There are three boxes with names and numbers in them. (Pause slightly.) Each box represents a post office in a different town. The number in each box is the area code for that town. Write the letter C on the line in the right-hand box. (Pause 2 seconds.) Now, on your answer sheet, find number 55 and darken the space for the letter that is in the box you just wrote in. (Pause 5 seconds.)

Look at line 4 again. (Pause slightly.) Multiply the first and the last digit in the left-hand box, add 3, and write the answer on the line in that box. (Pause 2 seconds.)

Now, on your answer sheet, locate the number you just wrote and darken space D as in *dog*. (Pause 5 seconds.)

Look at line 5 on your worksheet. (Pause slightly.) Draw a line under every number that is more than 41 but less than 51. (Pause 12 seconds.) Now, on your answer sheet, for every number that you drew a line under, darken space A. (Pause 25 seconds.)

Look at line 6 on your worksheet. (Pause slightly.) There are 5 triangles, each with a letter in it. In the second triangle, write the answer to this question: Which of the following numbers is largest: 29, 23, 27, 25, 28? (Pause 5 seconds.) Now, on your answer sheet, darken the space for the number-letter combination that is in the triangle you just wrote in. (Pause 5 seconds.)

In the middle triangle, do nothing. In the first triangle, write 75. (Pause 2 seconds.) Now, on your answer sheet, darken the space for the number-letter combination that is in the triangle you just wrote in. (Pause 5 seconds.)

Look at line 6 again. In the triangle that is next-to-last on the right, write the answer to this question: How many states are there in the United States of America? (Pause 2 seconds.) Now, on your answer sheet, darken the space for the number-letter combination that is in the triangle you just wrote in. (Pause 5 seconds.)

Look at line 7 on your worksheet. (Pause slightly.) There are 5 circles. Each circle, except one, has both a number and a letter inside it. (Pause slightly.) Write the letter C in the circle that does not have a number and a letter inside. (Pause 3 seconds.)

Now, on your answer sheet, darken the space for the number-letter combination in the circle you wrote in. (Pause 5 seconds.)

Look at line 8 on your worksheet. (Pause slightly.) Put a line under the middle number and write that number in the first circle at the right of the line. (Pause 2 seconds.) Now, in the second circle, write the answer to this question: What is the fourth letter of the alphabet? (Pause 2 seconds.) Now, on your answer sheet, darken the space for the number-letter combination that you just wrote. (Pause 5 seconds.)

Now turn to Worksheet 2. (Pause 5 seconds.)

Look at line 9 on your worksheet. (Pause slightly.) There are two circles and two squares of different sizes with numbers in them. (Pause slightly.) If 9 is more than 8 and if 7 is less than 6, write B as in *baker* in the larger circle. (Pause slightly.) Otherwise, write D as in *dog* in the smaller box. (Pause 2 seconds.) Now, on your answer sheet, darken the space for the number-letter combination that is in the box or circle you just wrote in. (Pause 5 seconds.)

Look at line 10 on your worksheet. (Pause slightly.) Count the number of C's in the three boxes, add 10, and write that number on the first line at the right side of the 3 boxes. (Pause 3 seconds.) On the line next to that number, write the letter B as in *baker*. (Pause 2 seconds.) Now, on your answer sheet, darken the space for the number-letter combination that is on the two lines you just wrote in. (Pause 5 seconds.)

Look at line 11 on your worksheet. (Pause slightly.) Each box has a number above it. Each box also has a different number inside it. (Pause 2 seconds.) For each box that contains fewer than four digits, write E on the line next to the number above the box. (Pause 10 seconds.) Now, on your answer sheet, darken the spaces for the number-letter combinations on the lines above the boxes. (Pause 10 seconds.)

Look at the drawing on line 12 of your worksheet. (Pause slightly.) The four boxes are *bins* used to sort mail. If an inch is shorter than a foot and a foot is shorter than a yard, write the number 36 in the box in the upper right corner of the figure. Otherwise, write the number 64 in the box in the bottom left corner of the figure. (Pause 2 seconds.) Now, on your answer sheet, find the number in the box you just wrote in and darken the space for the letter C. (Pause 5 seconds.)

Look at line 13. (Pause slightly.) On the line next to the left letter, write the answer to this question: How many days are there in a week? (Pause 2 seconds.) On the line next to the letter at the extreme right, write the answer to this question: How many months are there in a year? (Pause 2 seconds.)

Now, on your answer sheet, darken the spaces for the number-letter combinations you just wrote. (Pause 5 seconds.)

Look at line 13 again. Add together the numbers you just wrote on the lines and put the sum on the line next to the middle letter. (Pause 5 seconds.)

Look at line 14 on your worksheet. (Pause slightly.) In each circle, there is the time when a piece of express mail was sent out. In the circle for the latest time, write on the line the last two figures of the time. (Pause 2 seconds.) Now, on your answer sheet, darken the space for the number-letter combination that is in the circle you just wrote in. (Pause 5 seconds.)

Look at line 15 on your worksheet. (Pause slightly.) Draw a line under every "X" on the line. (Pause 5 seconds.) Count the number of lines you have drawn, divide by 2, and put the answer in the box at the end of the line. (Pause 4 seconds.)

Now, on your answer sheet, find the number you just wrote in the box and darken space E. (Pause 5 seconds.)

Look at line 16 on your worksheet. (Pause slightly.) Each of the boxes and circles has a letter of the alphabet in it. If, in the alphabet, the letter in the small box comes after the letter in the large circle, write 85 on the line in the small circle. (Pause 2 seconds.) Otherwise, write 58 in the large box. (Pause 2 seconds.) Now, on your answer sheet, darken the space for the number-letter combination that is in the circle or box you just wrote in. (Pause 5 seconds.)

Look at line 17 on your worksheet. (Pause slightly.) There are a number and a letter in each of the five boxes. In the box that has the highest number, write on the line the first two figures of that number. (Pause 2 seconds.) Now, on your answer sheet, darken the space for the number-letter combination that is in the box you just wrote in. (Pause 5 seconds.)

Look at line 18. Some of the numbers on the line are odd, and others are even. (Pause slightly.) Draw a circle around every one of the odd numbers. (Pause 5 seconds.) Now, on your answer sheet, find the numbers you have just encircled and darken the space in each for the letter B as in *baker*. (Pause 15 seconds.)

Look at line 19. (Pause slightly.) There is a number in the only circle on the line. Subtract 5 from that number. (Pause slightly.) Place the new number on the line in the only box that has a letter inside it. (Pause 2 seconds.) Now, darken the space on your answer sheet for the number-letter combination that is in the figure you just wrote in. (Pause 5 seconds.)

END OF EXAMINATION.
If you finish before the time is up, go back and check
the questions in this section of the test only.

Practice Test 1—Worksheet 1
Part D—Following Oral Directions

1.   D   E   B   A   E   D   E   C   B

2.   __C   __D   __B   __E   __A

3.   25 __   31 __   29 __   22 __

4.   MASSAPEQUA PARK 11762 __   GLEN COVE 11542 __   FRANKLIN SQUARE 11010 __

5.   41   40   43   52   49   51   41   44

6.   E __   B __   D __   C __   A __

7.   5E   12A   80   3B   17D

8.   72   73   66   63   78   58   59   61   56

9.   74 __   11 __   86 __   53 __

Remove by cutting on dotted line.

Practice Test 1—Worksheet 2
Part D—Following Oral Directions

10.
```
C        A        D
B        C        A        —        —
D        E        C
```

11. 20 ___   15 ___   3 ___   38 ___   71 ___

 | 10 | | 1300 | | 121 | | 19156 | | 4846 |

12.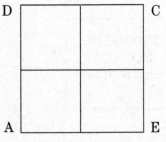

13.   ___ A   ___ B   ___ C

14.
(8:57 / ___ D)   (8:08 / ___ A)   (7:59 / ___ B)   (8:01 / ___ C)   (8:54 / ___ E)

15.   O X O O X X X O X X O O O X X X [___]

16.   [___ E]   (___ C)   (___ D)   [___ B]

17.
| 617 / ___ A | | 294 / ___ C | | 349 / ___ D | | 510 / ___ E | | 615 / ___ B |

18.   59   22   11   46   8   16   10   37

19.   [C ___]   [___]

■ ANSWER KEY

Part A—Address Checking

1. D	11. D	21. D	31. D	41. A	51. D	61. A	71. D	81. D	91. A
2. D	12. D	22. D	32. A	42. A	52. A	62. A	72. D	82. D	92. A
3. D	13. A	23. A	33. A	43. D	53. D	63. D	73. A	83. A	93. D
4. A	14. D	24. D	34. D	44. D	54. D	64. A	74. A	84. A	94. D
5. A	15. A	25. D	35. A	45. A	55. A	65. D	75. D	85. D	95. A
6. A	16. D	26. A	36. A	46. D	56. D	66. A	76. A	86. D	
7. D	17. A	27. D	37. A	47. A	57. D	67. A	77. A	87. D	
8. D	18. D	28. A	38. D	48. A	58. A	68. A	78. D	88. D	
9. A	19. D	29. D	39. D	49. D	59. D	69. D	79. A	89. A	
10. A	20. D	30. A	40. A	50. A	60. A	69. D	80. A	90. D	

Part B—Memory for Addresses

List 1

1. D	10. C	19. D	28. E	37. B	46. C	55. D	64. B	73. B	82. D
2. E	11. A	20. A	29. B	38. D	47. B	56. A	65. E	74. D	83. A
3. C	12. B	21. B	30. C	39. D	48. D	57. A	66. E	75. D	84. C
4. B	13. A	22. C	31. C	40. C	49. A	58. A	67. A	76. C	85. D
5. C	14. B	23. D	32. C	41. C	50. E	59. C	68. B	77. E	86. A
6. E	15. D	24. B	33. A	42. B	51. E	60. E	69. D	78. D	87. A
7. A	16. B	25. A	34. E	43. A	52. C	61. A	70. D	79. E	88. A
8. B	17. A	26. E	35. E	44. E	53. C	62. D	71. B	80. E	
9. D	18. C	27. D	36. E	45. D	54. E	63. C	72. B	81. B	

List 2

1. E	10. D	19. C	28. D	37. A	46. E	55. D	64. A	73. C	82. A
2. E	11. E	20. A	29. B	38. A	47. D	56. D	65. E	74. E	83. B
3. E	12. B	21. B	30. A	39. A	48. E	57. B	66. C	75. E	84. C
4. A	13. B	22. D	31. E	40. D	49. C	58. A	67. A	76. A	85. C
5. C	14. D	23. B	32. C	41. E	50. D	59. E	68. A	77. D	86. D
6. C	15. C	24. A	33. B	42. A	51. D	60. E	69. A	78. B	87. D
7. C	16. B	25. B	34. C	43. D	52. E	61. B	70. D	79. C	88. B
8. B	17. A	26. A	35. E	44. B	53. B	62. C	71. E	80. D	
9. E	18. D	27. C	36. D	45. E	54. B	63. D	72. C	81. E	

List 3

1. A	10. E	19. D	28. A	37. C	46. A	55. E	64. A	73. B	82. A
2. A	11. D	20. D	29. E	38. E	47. B	56. A	65. B	74. D	83. E
3. A	12. E	21. B	30. C	39. E	48. C	57. C	66. D	75. B	84. C
4. D	13. C	22. A	31. A	40. A	49. C	58. C	67. C	76. A	85. B
5. C	14. D	23. A	32. A	41. D	50. D	59. C	68. B	77. B	86. C
6. A	15. D	24. E	33. A	42. B	51. D	60. B	69. A	78. A	87. E
7. D	16. B	25. B	34. D	43. C	52. C	61. E	79. D	79. C	88. D
8. B	17. B	26. C	35. E	44. D	53. E	62. A	71. C	80. D	
9. E	18. B	27. D	36. C	45. E	54. E	63. E	72. A	81. B	

Part C—Number Series

1. C	4. E	7. B	10. B	13. B	16. A	19. C	22. E
2. D	5. D	8. E	11. E	14. C	17. E	20. B	23. D
3. C	6. B	9. E	12. D	15. E	18. A	21. C	24. A

Part D—Following Oral Directions

1. C	7. A	13. B	31. B	44. A	55. C	61. A	80. C
3. E	10. B	19. B	36. C	47. B	57. D	65. C	82. E
4. E	11. B	20. E	37. B	49. A	58. E	75. E	86. D
5. D	12. C	29. B	43. A	50. C	59. B	78. D	

ANSWER EXPLANATIONS FOR PART C—NUMBER SERIES

1. **C** This is a simple +5 series.
2. **D** The pattern for this series is –3, repeat the number; repeat the number; and so on.
3. **C** There are two alternating series here: one that increases by 2; the other that increases by 3.
4. **E** This series follows the complex rule: +1, +1 +2; +1, +1, +2; and so on. Or, if you wish, you could see it as a simple +1 series that omits every fourth number.
5. **D** The rule for this series is × 2, repeat the number; × 2, repeat the number; and so on. You can be thrown off at the very beginning if you do not see that $\underline{1} \times 2 = 2$.
6. **B** The sequence 7 16 9 keeps repeating.
7. **B** Here again are two alternating series: one series begins with 20 and increases by 1; the other begins with 17 and increases by 1. If you saw it as following the rule –3, +4; –3, +4; and so on, you would also get the correct answer.
8. **E** Each number in this series is repeated three times before increasing by 10.
9. **E** The numbers in this series increase according to a *variable* "adder." It keeps increasing by 1. The correct answer is calculated as follows:

$$\overset{+7}{\frown} \quad \overset{+8}{\frown}$$
$$49 \quad \underline{56} \quad \underline{64}$$

10. **B** This series follows the rule: –1, repeat the number, –4; –1, repeat the number, –4. A loop diagram makes this clear instantly.

$$\overset{-1}{\frown} \ \overset{R}{\frown} \ \overset{-4}{\frown} \ \overset{-1}{\frown} \ \overset{R}{\frown} \ \overset{-4}{\frown} \ \overset{-1}{\frown} \ \overset{R}{\frown}$$
$$36 \quad 35 \quad 35 \quad 31 \quad 30 \quad 30 \quad 26 \quad \underline{25} \quad \underline{25}$$

11. **E** In this pair of alternating series, the series starting with 17 is ascending by +1. The other series starting with 46 is descending by –2.
12. **D** Two alternating "mini-series" are present here, each of which continues for three numbers, after which it is interrupted by the other. One increases by +2. The other increases by +3. Each sequence of three numbers begins one higher than the last. Partition lines in a loop diagram show this clearly.

$$\overset{+2}{\frown}\overset{+2}{\frown} \qquad \overset{+3}{\frown}\overset{+3}{\frown} \qquad \overset{+2}{\frown}\overset{+2}{\frown}$$
$$5 \quad 7 \quad 9 \ | \ 6 \quad 9 \quad 12 \ | \ 7 \quad \underline{9} \quad \underline{11}$$
$$\underset{+1}{\smile} \qquad\qquad \underset{+1}{\smile}$$

13. **B** Two alternating series make up this group of numbers. Both follow a +6 rule.

14. **C** Multiplication and subtraction are used to form this series. The numbers follow a $\times 2, -8; \times 2, -8$; and so on rule.

15. **E** Each number in this series decreases by 3.

16. **A** This can be a difficult pattern to find because the arbitrary number 18 is periodically inserted in the series. The series itself follows a $-3, -2; -3, -2$; and so on rule.

17. **E** One of the two alternating series here increases by 1 (7, 8, 9). The other decreases by 3 after each of its numbers has been repeated once (19, 19, 16, 16).

18. **A** A sequence of *four* numbers, 12 14 14 10; keeps recycling.

19. **C** There is a complex rule used here: +5, +5, repeat the number; +5, +5, repeat the number.

20. **B** Another complex rule underlies this series, too. It is $+6, -2, -1; +6, -2, -1$; and so on. Without using a loop diagram, this and the previous example would be most difficult.

21. **C** Here is an example of a series that uses its own numbers to progress itself. Each number in this series, beginning with 5, is obtained by adding together the two numbers preceding it.

$$2 + 3 = 5 + 8 = 13 + 21 = 34 + \underline{55} = \underline{89}$$

22. **E** Because the numbers are so close together, it may have been difficult to identify the two alternating series present here. Both follow a simple +1 rule. One intrudes after every *two* numbers of the other.

23. **D** There are two alternating series here. One (starting with 36) decreases by 3; the other (starting with 4) increases by 7.

24. **A** The pattern this series follows is $-5, +7; -5, +7$; and so on. If you wish, you may see this as two alternating series, each increasing by 2.

▓ EVALUATING YOUR PROGRESS*

Part A—Address Checking

Computing Your Score

Check your answers against the Answer Key. Score yourself by using this formula:

Number right
      − Number wrong

          YOUR SCORE

---

* Please note that the scores you obtain by following the computation instructions for the various parts of this test are "raw" scores. The Postal Service combines and converts the raw scores for the various parts of the test into a scaled score obtained by using special conversion formulas that are kept confidential. This scaled score (plus any veteran's credits to which you are entitled) forms the basis for your final rating and your standing on the list. This final rating will be sent to you after the tests have been marked.

Furthermore, even though you take one test, your final score will vary depending on the title. For example, your rating on the Mail Handler register may very well be different from your rating on the Postal Clerk-Carrier register. Apparently, the relative rate given to each part of the test varies according to title. This is another argument for taking as many tests in as many titles as possible, as suggested on page 3.

You are encouraged to calculate your raw scores because they furnish a realistic and convenient way for you to keep track of your relative performance and progress as you work your way through this book.

For example, if you completed 52 questions and got 8 wrong,

$$\begin{array}{lcr} \text{Number right} & = & 44 \\ -\text{ Number wrong} & = & -\ 8 \\ \hline \text{Your score} & = & 36 \end{array}$$

Notice that you do *not* figure in the questions that you did not answer.

Guidelines

How good is the score you just made?

$$\begin{array}{ll} \text{52 or higher} \dots\dots\dots & \text{Good} \\ \text{Between 32 and 52} \dots\dots & \text{Fair} \\ \text{Below 32} \dots\dots\dots\dots & \text{You need to improve.} \end{array}$$

These are commonly accepted figures. It is believed, however, that you should not be satisfied with anything *less* than 52. Experience in training many people to prepare for this test shows that most serious test candidates who use the preparation program described in this book (Chapter 4 covers Address Checking) will be able to raise their score to the upper sixties, seventies, or eighties.

Personal Progress Record

One of the most satisfying things that can happen while you are working toward a goal is to see signs of progress. The improvement you make on Address Checking can readily be seen by examining the scores you make on the practice tests and exercises in this book. Keeping track of your growing skill is important, so a Personal Progress Record has been furnished for your use on page 439.

The following is a sample of this Personal Progress Record to familiarize you with it. The entries on this sample are based on the example above.

PERSONAL PROGRESS RECORD—SAMPLE

ADDRESS CHECKING										
Initial Tests							**Repeated Tests**			
Date	Test	Number Completed	Number Correct	−	Number Wrong	= Score	Date	Score	Date	Score
5/15	Diagnostic Practice Test	52	44	−	8	= 36				
5/16	Practice Test 1	64	54	−	10	= 44				
5/18	Practice Test 2	66	57	−	9	= 48				
5/20	Practice Test 3	70	60	−	10	= 50				
	Practice Test 4			−		=				
	Practice Test 5			−		=				
	Practice Test 6			−		=				

Now turn to page 439. In the table entitled "Personal Progress Record—Address Checking," make the proper entries on the line for Practice Test 1, which you just took. Review the special techniques in Chapter 4: Address Checking—How to Improve Your Score, before taking Practice Test 2. After taking the additional practice tests, enter the results immediately. Keep this record. It will help you record your progress.

Part B—Memory for Addresses

Computing Your Score

Check the answers on your answer sheet against the Answer Key. Calculate your score by using these four steps:

1. Enter the number of answers you got right . . . . _____

2. Enter the number of answers you got wrong . . . . _____

3. Divide the number wrong by 4 (or multiply by ¼) . . . . − _____

4. Subtract Line 3 from Line 1 . . . . YOUR SCORE = _____

Follow this example to make sure that you have figured your score correctly. It will be assumed that you completed 32 questions, of which you got 24 right and 8 wrong.

Line 1 . . . . . . Number right 24

Line 2 . . . . . . Number wrong 8

Line 3 . . . . . . ¼ of line 2 = ¼ × 8 . . . . . . − 2

Line 4 . . . . . . 24 − 2 . . YOUR SCORE = 22

Notice that, just as for Address Checking, questions that are *not* answered are not taken into account.

Guidelines

How good is the score you just made?

44 or more . . . . Good
26 to 43 . . . . Fair
25 or less . . . . You need to improve.

If your score on this test was low, don't be discouraged. Nevertheless, you may wish to review Chapters 5 and 6, which offer special techniques for handling Part B—Memory for Addresses, before taking Practice Test 2.

Personal Progress Record

Turn to page 439. Use the table entitled "Personal Progress—Memory for Addresses" to keep a permanent record of your scores on List 3 of the practice tests. A sample is printed on the next page to familiarize you with it. The first entry is based on the preceding example.

PERSONAL PROGRESS RECORD—SAMPLE

MEMORY FOR ADDRESSES												
Initial Tests									**Repeated Tests**			
Date	Test	Number Completed	Number Correct **A**	Number Wrong	× ¼ =		Points off **B**	Score **(A − B)**	Date	Score	Date	Score
5/15	Diagnostic Practice Test	32	24	8	× ¼ =		2	22				
5/16	Practice Test 1	46	38	8	× ¼ =		2	36				
5/18	Practice Test 2	58	52	6	× ¼ =		1½	50½				
5/20	Practice Test 3	64	60	4	× ¼ =		1	59				
	Practice Test 4				× ¼ =							
	Practice Test 5				× ¼ =							
	Practice Test 6				× ¼ =							

Part C—Number Series

Computing Your Score

Check the answers on your Answer Sheet against the Answer Key. Calculate your score by adding up the number of correct answers you have. You *do not* lost any credit for wrong answers or for questions you don't answer. For example, on a test having 24 questions, if you had 5 correct, 3 incorrect, and omitted 16, your score would be 5.

Guidelines

How good is the score you just made?

> 17 or higher . . . . Good
> Between 12 and 16 . . . . . . Fair
> Below 12 . . . . You need to improve.

Once you have mastered the techniques explained in this book, you should routinely be scoring 20 to 24 correct.

Personal Progress Record

The following is a sample of this Personal Progress Record to familiarize you with it. The entries on this sample are based on the example above.

PERSONAL PROGRESS RECORD—SAMPLE

NUMBER SERIES							
Initial Tests				**Repeated Tests**			
Date	Test	Number Completed	Number Correct (Your Score)	Date	Score	Date	Score
5/15	Diagnostic Practice Test	8	5				
5/16	Practice Test 1	15	11				
5/18	Practice Test 2	17	15				
5/20	Practice Test 3	20	19				
	Practice Test 4						
	Practice Test 5						
	Practice Test 6						

Now turn to page 440. Look at the table entitled "Personal Progress Record—Number Series." Make the proper entries on the line for the practice test you just took. This table will help you record your progress as you take additional practice tests.

Part D—Following Oral Directions

Computing Your Score

Check your answers against the Answer Key. Calculate your score by adding up the number of correct answers you have. You do *not* lose any credit for wrong answers or for questions you don't answer. For example, on a test having 30 questions, if you had 17 correct and 6 incorrect, and omitted 7, your score would be 17.

Guidelines

How good is the score you just made?

> 28 or higher . . . . Good
> Between 24 and 27 . . . . . . Fair
> Below 24 . . . . You need to improve.

Once you have mastered the techniques explained in this book (Chapter 8 covers Following Oral Directions), you should routinely score 28 to 30 correct.

Personal Progress Record

Now turn to page 440. In the table entitled "Personal Progress Record—Following Oral Directions," make the proper entries on the line for the practice test you just took. This table will help you record your progress as you take additional practice tests. A sample is printed on the next page to familiarize you with it. The first entry is based on the preceding example.

PERSONAL PROGRESS RECORD—SAMPLE

		FOLLOWING ORAL DIRECTIONS					
		Initial Tests			Repeated Tests		
Date	Test	Number Completed	Number Correct (Your Score)	Date	Score	Date	Score
5/15	Diagnostic Practice Test	23	17				
5/16	Practice Test 1	23	19				
5/18	Practice Test 2	27	25				
5/20	Practice Test 3	29	28				
	Practice Test 4						
	Practice Test 5						
	Practice Test 6						

DIAGNOSTIC CHARTS

The following charts will help pinpoint your weaknesses by making it easy for you to determine what particular type of question in each part of the test is most difficult for you.

Part A—Address Checking

Type of Difference	"D" Questions	Number of "D" Questions Wrong		
		Trial 1	Trial 2	Trial 3
Numbers: transposed	1, 7, 18, 21			
changed	3, 11, 29, 43, 46, 51, 94			
omitted				
Directions	2, 20, 41, 59, 72, 77, 87			
Abbreviations: streets, roads, avenues, etc.	16, 34, 56, 57, 63, 90, 93			
states	14, 69, 86			
Spelling: single letters	19, 27, 31, 38, 44, 49, 53, 54, 65, 70, 71, 75, 78, 81, 82, 85, 88			
groups of letters	8, 12, 22, 24, 25, 39			
Total Number of All Types	51			
	Use the columns on the right to enter the question numbers of "A" items you marked "D."			

This chart will help you to pinpoint the kinds of errors you made on Practice Test 1. Use it as directed below after you have taken and marked the test.

The first column on the left, "Type of Difference," contains the categories whereby addresses may differ (see page 69). On the same line across, the second column gives the numbers of the questions that fall within each category. In the third column, you are to enter the numbers of any "A" questions you answered as "D." Do not include questions that you did not do. Checking the addresses you got wrong may reveal a problem on which you will want to work.

After you have made all the entries, you will be able to see the areas in which you need to improve. Then turn to the appropriate parts of Chapter 4: Address Checking—How to Improve Your Score, read them, and practice the drills that can help. For example, if you find you have been making too many errors picking out number differences, read page 94 and do Drills 18 through 21. If you have a problem with single letters because of reversals like *b* and *d*, or if you have been overlooking the differences between *a*, *e*, and *o*, read page 91. Examine the table and work on Drills 10 and 11 if the problem persists.

Remember that this chart is designed for diagnostic purposes and guidance on further practice. It has been drawn so that you can enter the results each time you retake a practice test. In this way you will be able to see how you are progressing. It is not necessary to record your scores here. That is best done by using the Personal Progress Record Card.

Part B—Memory for Addresses

Kind of Address		Number of Questions	Number Wrong		
			Trial 1	Trial 2	Trial 3
Direct:					
	List 1	43			
	List 2	42			
	List 3	44			
Numbered:					
	List 1	45			
	List 2	46			
	List 3	44			

The purpose of this chart is to help you evaluate your performance on the two kinds of memory questions that appear in these memory tests—the questions on the direct (name) addresses and the questions on the numbered addresses. Use the chart as directed below after you have taken and marked the entire test.

The first column on the left, "Kind of Address," is divided by category into "Direct Address" versus "Numbered Address." The second column gives the number of questions in each category on List 1, List 2, and List 3. Use the third column to enter the total number of questions in each category that you answered incorrectly. There is room for you to make additional entries if you take the practice test more than once.

At a glance, you will be able to see which area you need to concentrate on and how well you are progressing as you take repeat trials. Use Chapter 5 and the drills in it to improve your memory for the direct addresses. Use Chapter 6 for the numbered addresses.

Remember to use the Personal Progress Record Card (Memory for Addresses) on page 439 to keep track of your actual scores as you keep studying and practicing.

Part C—Number Series and Part D—Following Oral Directions

Because of the nature of the questions in these tests, Diagnostic Charts are not provided for them. If you find that you made many errors on these tests, study the techniques suggested in Chapters 7 and 8.

Answer Sheet—Practice Test 2

Part A – Address Checking

1 Ⓐⓓ	25 Ⓐⓓ	49 Ⓐⓓ	73 Ⓐⓓ
2 Ⓐⓓ	26 Ⓐⓓ	50 Ⓐⓓ	74 Ⓐⓓ
3 Ⓐⓓ	27 Ⓐⓓ	51 Ⓐⓓ	75 Ⓐⓓ
4 Ⓐⓓ	28 Ⓐⓓ	52 Ⓐⓓ	76 Ⓐⓓ
5 Ⓐⓓ	29 Ⓐⓓ	53 Ⓐⓓ	77 Ⓐⓓ
6 Ⓐⓓ	30 Ⓐⓓ	54 Ⓐⓓ	78 Ⓐⓓ
7 Ⓐⓓ	31 Ⓐⓓ	55 Ⓐⓓ	79 Ⓐⓓ
8 Ⓐⓓ	32 Ⓐⓓ	56 Ⓐⓓ	80 Ⓐⓓ
9 Ⓐⓓ	33 Ⓐⓓ	57 Ⓐⓓ	81 Ⓐⓓ
10 Ⓐⓓ	34 Ⓐⓓ	58 Ⓐⓓ	82 Ⓐⓓ
11 Ⓐⓓ	35 Ⓐⓓ	59 Ⓐⓓ	83 Ⓐⓓ
12 Ⓐⓓ	36 Ⓐⓓ	60 Ⓐⓓ	84 Ⓐⓓ
13 Ⓐⓓ	37 Ⓐⓓ	61 Ⓐⓓ	85 Ⓐⓓ
14 Ⓐⓓ	38 Ⓐⓓ	62 Ⓐⓓ	86 Ⓐⓓ
15 Ⓐⓓ	39 Ⓐⓓ	63 Ⓐⓓ	87 Ⓐⓓ
16 Ⓐⓓ	40 Ⓐⓓ	64 Ⓐⓓ	88 Ⓐⓓ
17 Ⓐⓓ	41 Ⓐⓓ	65 Ⓐⓓ	89 Ⓐⓓ
18 Ⓐⓓ	42 Ⓐⓓ	66 Ⓐⓓ	90 Ⓐⓓ
19 Ⓐⓓ	43 Ⓐⓓ	67 Ⓐⓓ	91 Ⓐⓓ
20 Ⓐⓓ	44 Ⓐⓓ	68 Ⓐⓓ	92 Ⓐⓓ
21 Ⓐⓓ	45 Ⓐⓓ	69 Ⓐⓓ	93 Ⓐⓓ
22 Ⓐⓓ	46 Ⓐⓓ	70 Ⓐⓓ	94 Ⓐⓓ
23 Ⓐⓓ	47 Ⓐⓓ	71 Ⓐⓓ	95 Ⓐⓓ
24 Ⓐⓓ	48 Ⓐⓓ	72 Ⓐⓓ	

postal exam :
test battery
series 460/470
for eight top
positions

Please take to
CHECK OUT.

Thank you!

Part B—Memory for Addresses—List 1

1 Ⓐ Ⓑ Ⓒ Ⓓ Ⓔ	19 Ⓐ Ⓑ Ⓒ Ⓓ Ⓔ	37 Ⓐ Ⓑ Ⓒ Ⓓ Ⓔ	55 Ⓐ Ⓑ Ⓒ Ⓓ Ⓔ	73 Ⓐ Ⓑ Ⓒ Ⓓ Ⓔ
2 Ⓐ Ⓑ Ⓒ Ⓓ Ⓔ	20 Ⓐ Ⓑ Ⓒ Ⓓ Ⓔ	38 Ⓐ Ⓑ Ⓒ Ⓓ Ⓔ	56 Ⓐ Ⓑ Ⓒ Ⓓ Ⓔ	74 Ⓐ Ⓑ Ⓒ Ⓓ Ⓔ
3 Ⓐ Ⓑ Ⓒ Ⓓ Ⓔ	21 Ⓐ Ⓑ Ⓒ Ⓓ Ⓔ	39 Ⓐ Ⓑ Ⓒ Ⓓ Ⓔ	57 Ⓐ Ⓑ Ⓒ Ⓓ Ⓔ	75 Ⓐ Ⓑ Ⓒ Ⓓ Ⓔ
4 Ⓐ Ⓑ Ⓒ Ⓓ Ⓔ	22 Ⓐ Ⓑ Ⓒ Ⓓ Ⓔ	40 Ⓐ Ⓑ Ⓒ Ⓓ Ⓔ	58 Ⓐ Ⓑ Ⓒ Ⓓ Ⓔ	76 Ⓐ Ⓑ Ⓒ Ⓓ Ⓔ
5 Ⓐ Ⓑ Ⓒ Ⓓ Ⓔ	23 Ⓐ Ⓑ Ⓒ Ⓓ Ⓔ	41 Ⓐ Ⓑ Ⓒ Ⓓ Ⓔ	59 Ⓐ Ⓑ Ⓒ Ⓓ Ⓔ	77 Ⓐ Ⓑ Ⓒ Ⓓ Ⓔ
6 Ⓐ Ⓑ Ⓒ Ⓓ Ⓔ	24 Ⓐ Ⓑ Ⓒ Ⓓ Ⓔ	42 Ⓐ Ⓑ Ⓒ Ⓓ Ⓔ	60 Ⓐ Ⓑ Ⓒ Ⓓ Ⓔ	78 Ⓐ Ⓑ Ⓒ Ⓓ Ⓔ
7 Ⓐ Ⓑ Ⓒ Ⓓ Ⓔ	25 Ⓐ Ⓑ Ⓒ Ⓓ Ⓔ	43 Ⓐ Ⓑ Ⓒ Ⓓ Ⓔ	61 Ⓐ Ⓑ Ⓒ Ⓓ Ⓔ	79 Ⓐ Ⓑ Ⓒ Ⓓ Ⓔ
8 Ⓐ Ⓑ Ⓒ Ⓓ Ⓔ	26 Ⓐ Ⓑ Ⓒ Ⓓ Ⓔ	44 Ⓐ Ⓑ Ⓒ Ⓓ Ⓔ	62 Ⓐ Ⓑ Ⓒ Ⓓ Ⓔ	80 Ⓐ Ⓑ Ⓒ Ⓓ Ⓔ
9 Ⓐ Ⓑ Ⓒ Ⓓ Ⓔ	27 Ⓐ Ⓑ Ⓒ Ⓓ Ⓔ	45 Ⓐ Ⓑ Ⓒ Ⓓ Ⓔ	63 Ⓐ Ⓑ Ⓒ Ⓓ Ⓔ	81 Ⓐ Ⓑ Ⓒ Ⓓ Ⓔ
10 Ⓐ Ⓑ Ⓒ Ⓓ Ⓔ	28 Ⓐ Ⓑ Ⓒ Ⓓ Ⓔ	46 Ⓐ Ⓑ Ⓒ Ⓓ Ⓔ	64 Ⓐ Ⓑ Ⓒ Ⓓ Ⓔ	82 Ⓐ Ⓑ Ⓒ Ⓓ Ⓔ
11 Ⓐ Ⓑ Ⓒ Ⓓ Ⓔ	29 Ⓐ Ⓑ Ⓒ Ⓓ Ⓔ	47 Ⓐ Ⓑ Ⓒ Ⓓ Ⓔ	65 Ⓐ Ⓑ Ⓒ Ⓓ Ⓔ	83 Ⓐ Ⓑ Ⓒ Ⓓ Ⓔ
12 Ⓐ Ⓑ Ⓒ Ⓓ Ⓔ	30 Ⓐ Ⓑ Ⓒ Ⓓ Ⓔ	48 Ⓐ Ⓑ Ⓒ Ⓓ Ⓔ	66 Ⓐ Ⓑ Ⓒ Ⓓ Ⓔ	84 Ⓐ Ⓑ Ⓒ Ⓓ Ⓔ
13 Ⓐ Ⓑ Ⓒ Ⓓ Ⓔ	31 Ⓐ Ⓑ Ⓒ Ⓓ Ⓔ	49 Ⓐ Ⓑ Ⓒ Ⓓ Ⓔ	67 Ⓐ Ⓑ Ⓒ Ⓓ Ⓔ	85 Ⓐ Ⓑ Ⓒ Ⓓ Ⓔ
14 Ⓐ Ⓑ Ⓒ Ⓓ Ⓔ	32 Ⓐ Ⓑ Ⓒ Ⓓ Ⓔ	50 Ⓐ Ⓑ Ⓒ Ⓓ Ⓔ	68 Ⓐ Ⓑ Ⓒ Ⓓ Ⓔ	86 Ⓐ Ⓑ Ⓒ Ⓓ Ⓔ
15 Ⓐ Ⓑ Ⓒ Ⓓ Ⓔ	33 Ⓐ Ⓑ Ⓒ Ⓓ Ⓔ	51 Ⓐ Ⓑ Ⓒ Ⓓ Ⓔ	69 Ⓐ Ⓑ Ⓒ Ⓓ Ⓔ	87 Ⓐ Ⓑ Ⓒ Ⓓ Ⓔ
16 Ⓐ Ⓑ Ⓒ Ⓓ Ⓔ	34 Ⓐ Ⓑ Ⓒ Ⓓ Ⓔ	52 Ⓐ Ⓑ Ⓒ Ⓓ Ⓔ	70 Ⓐ Ⓑ Ⓒ Ⓓ Ⓔ	88 Ⓐ Ⓑ Ⓒ Ⓓ Ⓔ
17 Ⓐ Ⓑ Ⓒ Ⓓ Ⓔ	35 Ⓐ Ⓑ Ⓒ Ⓓ Ⓔ	53 Ⓐ Ⓑ Ⓒ Ⓓ Ⓔ	71 Ⓐ Ⓑ Ⓒ Ⓓ Ⓔ	
18 Ⓐ Ⓑ Ⓒ Ⓓ Ⓔ	36 Ⓐ Ⓑ Ⓒ Ⓓ Ⓔ	54 Ⓐ Ⓑ Ⓒ Ⓓ Ⓔ	72 Ⓐ Ⓑ Ⓒ Ⓓ Ⓔ	

Part B—Memory for Addresses—List 2

1 Ⓐ Ⓑ Ⓒ Ⓓ Ⓔ	19 Ⓐ Ⓑ Ⓒ Ⓓ Ⓔ	37 Ⓐ Ⓑ Ⓒ Ⓓ Ⓔ	55 Ⓐ Ⓑ Ⓒ Ⓓ Ⓔ	73 Ⓐ Ⓑ Ⓒ Ⓓ Ⓔ
2 Ⓐ Ⓑ Ⓒ Ⓓ Ⓔ	20 Ⓐ Ⓑ Ⓒ Ⓓ Ⓔ	38 Ⓐ Ⓑ Ⓒ Ⓓ Ⓔ	56 Ⓐ Ⓑ Ⓒ Ⓓ Ⓔ	74 Ⓐ Ⓑ Ⓒ Ⓓ Ⓔ
3 Ⓐ Ⓑ Ⓒ Ⓓ Ⓔ	21 Ⓐ Ⓑ Ⓒ Ⓓ Ⓔ	39 Ⓐ Ⓑ Ⓒ Ⓓ Ⓔ	57 Ⓐ Ⓑ Ⓒ Ⓓ Ⓔ	75 Ⓐ Ⓑ Ⓒ Ⓓ Ⓔ
4 Ⓐ Ⓑ Ⓒ Ⓓ Ⓔ	22 Ⓐ Ⓑ Ⓒ Ⓓ Ⓔ	40 Ⓐ Ⓑ Ⓒ Ⓓ Ⓔ	58 Ⓐ Ⓑ Ⓒ Ⓓ Ⓔ	76 Ⓐ Ⓑ Ⓒ Ⓓ Ⓔ
5 Ⓐ Ⓑ Ⓒ Ⓓ Ⓔ	23 Ⓐ Ⓑ Ⓒ Ⓓ Ⓔ	41 Ⓐ Ⓑ Ⓒ Ⓓ Ⓔ	59 Ⓐ Ⓑ Ⓒ Ⓓ Ⓔ	77 Ⓐ Ⓑ Ⓒ Ⓓ Ⓔ
6 Ⓐ Ⓑ Ⓒ Ⓓ Ⓔ	24 Ⓐ Ⓑ Ⓒ Ⓓ Ⓔ	42 Ⓐ Ⓑ Ⓒ Ⓓ Ⓔ	60 Ⓐ Ⓑ Ⓒ Ⓓ Ⓔ	78 Ⓐ Ⓑ Ⓒ Ⓓ Ⓔ
7 Ⓐ Ⓑ Ⓒ Ⓓ Ⓔ	25 Ⓐ Ⓑ Ⓒ Ⓓ Ⓔ	43 Ⓐ Ⓑ Ⓒ Ⓓ Ⓔ	61 Ⓐ Ⓑ Ⓒ Ⓓ Ⓔ	79 Ⓐ Ⓑ Ⓒ Ⓓ Ⓔ
8 Ⓐ Ⓑ Ⓒ Ⓓ Ⓔ	26 Ⓐ Ⓑ Ⓒ Ⓓ Ⓔ	44 Ⓐ Ⓑ Ⓒ Ⓓ Ⓔ	62 Ⓐ Ⓑ Ⓒ Ⓓ Ⓔ	80 Ⓐ Ⓑ Ⓒ Ⓓ Ⓔ
9 Ⓐ Ⓑ Ⓒ Ⓓ Ⓔ	27 Ⓐ Ⓑ Ⓒ Ⓓ Ⓔ	45 Ⓐ Ⓑ Ⓒ Ⓓ Ⓔ	63 Ⓐ Ⓑ Ⓒ Ⓓ Ⓔ	81 Ⓐ Ⓑ Ⓒ Ⓓ Ⓔ
10 Ⓐ Ⓑ Ⓒ Ⓓ Ⓔ	28 Ⓐ Ⓑ Ⓒ Ⓓ Ⓔ	46 Ⓐ Ⓑ Ⓒ Ⓓ Ⓔ	64 Ⓐ Ⓑ Ⓒ Ⓓ Ⓔ	82 Ⓐ Ⓑ Ⓒ Ⓓ Ⓔ
11 Ⓐ Ⓑ Ⓒ Ⓓ Ⓔ	29 Ⓐ Ⓑ Ⓒ Ⓓ Ⓔ	47 Ⓐ Ⓑ Ⓒ Ⓓ Ⓔ	65 Ⓐ Ⓑ Ⓒ Ⓓ Ⓔ	83 Ⓐ Ⓑ Ⓒ Ⓓ Ⓔ
12 Ⓐ Ⓑ Ⓒ Ⓓ Ⓔ	30 Ⓐ Ⓑ Ⓒ Ⓓ Ⓔ	48 Ⓐ Ⓑ Ⓒ Ⓓ Ⓔ	66 Ⓐ Ⓑ Ⓒ Ⓓ Ⓔ	84 Ⓐ Ⓑ Ⓒ Ⓓ Ⓔ
13 Ⓐ Ⓑ Ⓒ Ⓓ Ⓔ	31 Ⓐ Ⓑ Ⓒ Ⓓ Ⓔ	49 Ⓐ Ⓑ Ⓒ Ⓓ Ⓔ	67 Ⓐ Ⓑ Ⓒ Ⓓ Ⓔ	85 Ⓐ Ⓑ Ⓒ Ⓓ Ⓔ
14 Ⓐ Ⓑ Ⓒ Ⓓ Ⓔ	32 Ⓐ Ⓑ Ⓒ Ⓓ Ⓔ	50 Ⓐ Ⓑ Ⓒ Ⓓ Ⓔ	68 Ⓐ Ⓑ Ⓒ Ⓓ Ⓔ	86 Ⓐ Ⓑ Ⓒ Ⓓ Ⓔ
15 Ⓐ Ⓑ Ⓒ Ⓓ Ⓔ	33 Ⓐ Ⓑ Ⓒ Ⓓ Ⓔ	51 Ⓐ Ⓑ Ⓒ Ⓓ Ⓔ	69 Ⓐ Ⓑ Ⓒ Ⓓ Ⓔ	87 Ⓐ Ⓑ Ⓒ Ⓓ Ⓔ
16 Ⓐ Ⓑ Ⓒ Ⓓ Ⓔ	34 Ⓐ Ⓑ Ⓒ Ⓓ Ⓔ	52 Ⓐ Ⓑ Ⓒ Ⓓ Ⓔ	70 Ⓐ Ⓑ Ⓒ Ⓓ Ⓔ	88 Ⓐ Ⓑ Ⓒ Ⓓ Ⓔ
17 Ⓐ Ⓑ Ⓒ Ⓓ Ⓔ	35 Ⓐ Ⓑ Ⓒ Ⓓ Ⓔ	53 Ⓐ Ⓑ Ⓒ Ⓓ Ⓔ	71 Ⓐ Ⓑ Ⓒ Ⓓ Ⓔ	
18 Ⓐ Ⓑ Ⓒ Ⓓ Ⓔ	36 Ⓐ Ⓑ Ⓒ Ⓓ Ⓔ	54 Ⓐ Ⓑ Ⓒ Ⓓ Ⓔ	72 Ⓐ Ⓑ Ⓒ Ⓓ Ⓔ	

Remove by cutting on dotted line.

Part B—Memory for Addresses—List 3

1 Ⓐ Ⓑ Ⓒ Ⓓ Ⓔ	19 Ⓐ Ⓑ Ⓒ Ⓓ Ⓔ	37 Ⓐ Ⓑ Ⓒ Ⓓ Ⓔ	55 Ⓐ Ⓑ Ⓒ Ⓓ Ⓔ	73 Ⓐ Ⓑ Ⓒ Ⓓ Ⓔ
2 Ⓐ Ⓑ Ⓒ Ⓓ Ⓔ	20 Ⓐ Ⓑ Ⓒ Ⓓ Ⓔ	38 Ⓐ Ⓑ Ⓒ Ⓓ Ⓔ	56 Ⓐ Ⓑ Ⓒ Ⓓ Ⓔ	74 Ⓐ Ⓑ Ⓒ Ⓓ Ⓔ
3 Ⓐ Ⓑ Ⓒ Ⓓ Ⓔ	21 Ⓐ Ⓑ Ⓒ Ⓓ Ⓔ	39 Ⓐ Ⓑ Ⓒ Ⓓ Ⓔ	57 Ⓐ Ⓑ Ⓒ Ⓓ Ⓔ	75 Ⓐ Ⓑ Ⓒ Ⓓ Ⓔ
4 Ⓐ Ⓑ Ⓒ Ⓓ Ⓔ	22 Ⓐ Ⓑ Ⓒ Ⓓ Ⓔ	40 Ⓐ Ⓑ Ⓒ Ⓓ Ⓔ	58 Ⓐ Ⓑ Ⓒ Ⓓ Ⓔ	76 Ⓐ Ⓑ Ⓒ Ⓓ Ⓔ
5 Ⓐ Ⓑ Ⓒ Ⓓ Ⓔ	23 Ⓐ Ⓑ Ⓒ Ⓓ Ⓔ	41 Ⓐ Ⓑ Ⓒ Ⓓ Ⓔ	59 Ⓐ Ⓑ Ⓒ Ⓓ Ⓔ	77 Ⓐ Ⓑ Ⓒ Ⓓ Ⓔ
6 Ⓐ Ⓑ Ⓒ Ⓓ Ⓔ	24 Ⓐ Ⓑ Ⓒ Ⓓ Ⓔ	42 Ⓐ Ⓑ Ⓒ Ⓓ Ⓔ	60 Ⓐ Ⓑ Ⓒ Ⓓ Ⓔ	78 Ⓐ Ⓑ Ⓒ Ⓓ Ⓔ
7 Ⓐ Ⓑ Ⓒ Ⓓ Ⓔ	25 Ⓐ Ⓑ Ⓒ Ⓓ Ⓔ	43 Ⓐ Ⓑ Ⓒ Ⓓ Ⓔ	61 Ⓐ Ⓑ Ⓒ Ⓓ Ⓔ	79 Ⓐ Ⓑ Ⓒ Ⓓ Ⓔ
8 Ⓐ Ⓑ Ⓒ Ⓓ Ⓔ	26 Ⓐ Ⓑ Ⓒ Ⓓ Ⓔ	44 Ⓐ Ⓑ Ⓒ Ⓓ Ⓔ	62 Ⓐ Ⓑ Ⓒ Ⓓ Ⓔ	80 Ⓐ Ⓑ Ⓒ Ⓓ Ⓔ
9 Ⓐ Ⓑ Ⓒ Ⓓ Ⓔ	27 Ⓐ Ⓑ Ⓒ Ⓓ Ⓔ	45 Ⓐ Ⓑ Ⓒ Ⓓ Ⓔ	63 Ⓐ Ⓑ Ⓒ Ⓓ Ⓔ	81 Ⓐ Ⓑ Ⓒ Ⓓ Ⓔ
10 Ⓐ Ⓑ Ⓒ Ⓓ Ⓔ	28 Ⓐ Ⓑ Ⓒ Ⓓ Ⓔ	46 Ⓐ Ⓑ Ⓒ Ⓓ Ⓔ	64 Ⓐ Ⓑ Ⓒ Ⓓ Ⓔ	82 Ⓐ Ⓑ Ⓒ Ⓓ Ⓔ
11 Ⓐ Ⓑ Ⓒ Ⓓ Ⓔ	29 Ⓐ Ⓑ Ⓒ Ⓓ Ⓔ	47 Ⓐ Ⓑ Ⓒ Ⓓ Ⓔ	65 Ⓐ Ⓑ Ⓒ Ⓓ Ⓔ	83 Ⓐ Ⓑ Ⓒ Ⓓ Ⓔ
12 Ⓐ Ⓑ Ⓒ Ⓓ Ⓔ	30 Ⓐ Ⓑ Ⓒ Ⓓ Ⓔ	48 Ⓐ Ⓑ Ⓒ Ⓓ Ⓔ	66 Ⓐ Ⓑ Ⓒ Ⓓ Ⓔ	84 Ⓐ Ⓑ Ⓒ Ⓓ Ⓔ
13 Ⓐ Ⓑ Ⓒ Ⓓ Ⓔ	31 Ⓐ Ⓑ Ⓒ Ⓓ Ⓔ	49 Ⓐ Ⓑ Ⓒ Ⓓ Ⓔ	67 Ⓐ Ⓑ Ⓒ Ⓓ Ⓔ	85 Ⓐ Ⓑ Ⓒ Ⓓ Ⓔ
14 Ⓐ Ⓑ Ⓒ Ⓓ Ⓔ	32 Ⓐ Ⓑ Ⓒ Ⓓ Ⓔ	50 Ⓐ Ⓑ Ⓒ Ⓓ Ⓔ	68 Ⓐ Ⓑ Ⓒ Ⓓ Ⓔ	86 Ⓐ Ⓑ Ⓒ Ⓓ Ⓔ
15 Ⓐ Ⓑ Ⓒ Ⓓ Ⓔ	33 Ⓐ Ⓑ Ⓒ Ⓓ Ⓔ	51 Ⓐ Ⓑ Ⓒ Ⓓ Ⓔ	69 Ⓐ Ⓑ Ⓒ Ⓓ Ⓔ	87 Ⓐ Ⓑ Ⓒ Ⓓ Ⓔ
16 Ⓐ Ⓑ Ⓒ Ⓓ Ⓔ	34 Ⓐ Ⓑ Ⓒ Ⓓ Ⓔ	52 Ⓐ Ⓑ Ⓒ Ⓓ Ⓔ	70 Ⓐ Ⓑ Ⓒ Ⓓ Ⓔ	88 Ⓐ Ⓑ Ⓒ Ⓓ Ⓔ
17 Ⓐ Ⓑ Ⓒ Ⓓ Ⓔ	35 Ⓐ Ⓑ Ⓒ Ⓓ Ⓔ	53 Ⓐ Ⓑ Ⓒ Ⓓ Ⓔ	71 Ⓐ Ⓑ Ⓒ Ⓓ Ⓔ	
18 Ⓐ Ⓑ Ⓒ Ⓓ Ⓔ	36 Ⓐ Ⓑ Ⓒ Ⓓ Ⓔ	54 Ⓐ Ⓑ Ⓒ Ⓓ Ⓔ	72 Ⓐ Ⓑ Ⓒ Ⓓ Ⓔ	

Part C—Number Series

1 Ⓐ Ⓑ Ⓒ Ⓓ Ⓔ	6 Ⓐ Ⓑ Ⓒ Ⓓ Ⓔ	11 Ⓐ Ⓑ Ⓒ Ⓓ Ⓔ	16 Ⓐ Ⓑ Ⓒ Ⓓ Ⓔ	21 Ⓐ Ⓑ Ⓒ Ⓓ Ⓔ
2 Ⓐ Ⓑ Ⓒ Ⓓ Ⓔ	7 Ⓐ Ⓑ Ⓒ Ⓓ Ⓔ	12 Ⓐ Ⓑ Ⓒ Ⓓ Ⓔ	17 Ⓐ Ⓑ Ⓒ Ⓓ Ⓔ	22 Ⓐ Ⓑ Ⓒ Ⓓ Ⓔ
3 Ⓐ Ⓑ Ⓒ Ⓓ Ⓔ	8 Ⓐ Ⓑ Ⓒ Ⓓ Ⓔ	13 Ⓐ Ⓑ Ⓒ Ⓓ Ⓔ	18 Ⓐ Ⓑ Ⓒ Ⓓ Ⓔ	23 Ⓐ Ⓑ Ⓒ Ⓓ Ⓔ
4 Ⓐ Ⓑ Ⓒ Ⓓ Ⓔ	9 Ⓐ Ⓑ Ⓒ Ⓓ Ⓔ	14 Ⓐ Ⓑ Ⓒ Ⓓ Ⓔ	19 Ⓐ Ⓑ Ⓒ Ⓓ Ⓔ	24 Ⓐ Ⓑ Ⓒ Ⓓ Ⓔ
5 Ⓐ Ⓑ Ⓒ Ⓓ Ⓔ	10 Ⓐ Ⓑ Ⓒ Ⓓ Ⓔ	15 Ⓐ Ⓑ Ⓒ Ⓓ Ⓔ	20 Ⓐ Ⓑ Ⓒ Ⓓ Ⓔ	

Part D—Following Oral Directions

1 Ⓐ Ⓑ Ⓒ Ⓓ Ⓔ	19 Ⓐ Ⓑ Ⓒ Ⓓ Ⓔ	37 Ⓐ Ⓑ Ⓒ Ⓓ Ⓔ	55 Ⓐ Ⓑ Ⓒ Ⓓ Ⓔ	73 Ⓐ Ⓑ Ⓒ Ⓓ Ⓔ
2 Ⓐ Ⓑ Ⓒ Ⓓ Ⓔ	20 Ⓐ Ⓑ Ⓒ Ⓓ Ⓔ	38 Ⓐ Ⓑ Ⓒ Ⓓ Ⓔ	56 Ⓐ Ⓑ Ⓒ Ⓓ Ⓔ	74 Ⓐ Ⓑ Ⓒ Ⓓ Ⓔ
3 Ⓐ Ⓑ Ⓒ Ⓓ Ⓔ	21 Ⓐ Ⓑ Ⓒ Ⓓ Ⓔ	39 Ⓐ Ⓑ Ⓒ Ⓓ Ⓔ	57 Ⓐ Ⓑ Ⓒ Ⓓ Ⓔ	75 Ⓐ Ⓑ Ⓒ Ⓓ Ⓔ
4 Ⓐ Ⓑ Ⓒ Ⓓ Ⓔ	22 Ⓐ Ⓑ Ⓒ Ⓓ Ⓔ	40 Ⓐ Ⓑ Ⓒ Ⓓ Ⓔ	58 Ⓐ Ⓑ Ⓒ Ⓓ Ⓔ	76 Ⓐ Ⓑ Ⓒ Ⓓ Ⓔ
5 Ⓐ Ⓑ Ⓒ Ⓓ Ⓔ	23 Ⓐ Ⓑ Ⓒ Ⓓ Ⓔ	41 Ⓐ Ⓑ Ⓒ Ⓓ Ⓔ	59 Ⓐ Ⓑ Ⓒ Ⓓ Ⓔ	77 Ⓐ Ⓑ Ⓒ Ⓓ Ⓔ
6 Ⓐ Ⓑ Ⓒ Ⓓ Ⓔ	24 Ⓐ Ⓑ Ⓒ Ⓓ Ⓔ	42 Ⓐ Ⓑ Ⓒ Ⓓ Ⓔ	60 Ⓐ Ⓑ Ⓒ Ⓓ Ⓔ	78 Ⓐ Ⓑ Ⓒ Ⓓ Ⓔ
7 Ⓐ Ⓑ Ⓒ Ⓓ Ⓔ	25 Ⓐ Ⓑ Ⓒ Ⓓ Ⓔ	43 Ⓐ Ⓑ Ⓒ Ⓓ Ⓔ	61 Ⓐ Ⓑ Ⓒ Ⓓ Ⓔ	79 Ⓐ Ⓑ Ⓒ Ⓓ Ⓔ
8 Ⓐ Ⓑ Ⓒ Ⓓ Ⓔ	26 Ⓐ Ⓑ Ⓒ Ⓓ Ⓔ	44 Ⓐ Ⓑ Ⓒ Ⓓ Ⓔ	62 Ⓐ Ⓑ Ⓒ Ⓓ Ⓔ	80 Ⓐ Ⓑ Ⓒ Ⓓ Ⓔ
9 Ⓐ Ⓑ Ⓒ Ⓓ Ⓔ	27 Ⓐ Ⓑ Ⓒ Ⓓ Ⓔ	45 Ⓐ Ⓑ Ⓒ Ⓓ Ⓔ	63 Ⓐ Ⓑ Ⓒ Ⓓ Ⓔ	81 Ⓐ Ⓑ Ⓒ Ⓓ Ⓔ
10 Ⓐ Ⓑ Ⓒ Ⓓ Ⓔ	28 Ⓐ Ⓑ Ⓒ Ⓓ Ⓔ	46 Ⓐ Ⓑ Ⓒ Ⓓ Ⓔ	64 Ⓐ Ⓑ Ⓒ Ⓓ Ⓔ	82 Ⓐ Ⓑ Ⓒ Ⓓ Ⓔ
11 Ⓐ Ⓑ Ⓒ Ⓓ Ⓔ	29 Ⓐ Ⓑ Ⓒ Ⓓ Ⓔ	47 Ⓐ Ⓑ Ⓒ Ⓓ Ⓔ	65 Ⓐ Ⓑ Ⓒ Ⓓ Ⓔ	83 Ⓐ Ⓑ Ⓒ Ⓓ Ⓔ
12 Ⓐ Ⓑ Ⓒ Ⓓ Ⓔ	30 Ⓐ Ⓑ Ⓒ Ⓓ Ⓔ	48 Ⓐ Ⓑ Ⓒ Ⓓ Ⓔ	66 Ⓐ Ⓑ Ⓒ Ⓓ Ⓔ	84 Ⓐ Ⓑ Ⓒ Ⓓ Ⓔ
13 Ⓐ Ⓑ Ⓒ Ⓓ Ⓔ	31 Ⓐ Ⓑ Ⓒ Ⓓ Ⓔ	49 Ⓐ Ⓑ Ⓒ Ⓓ Ⓔ	67 Ⓐ Ⓑ Ⓒ Ⓓ Ⓔ	85 Ⓐ Ⓑ Ⓒ Ⓓ Ⓔ
14 Ⓐ Ⓑ Ⓒ Ⓓ Ⓔ	32 Ⓐ Ⓑ Ⓒ Ⓓ Ⓔ	50 Ⓐ Ⓑ Ⓒ Ⓓ Ⓔ	68 Ⓐ Ⓑ Ⓒ Ⓓ Ⓔ	86 Ⓐ Ⓑ Ⓒ Ⓓ Ⓔ
15 Ⓐ Ⓑ Ⓒ Ⓓ Ⓔ	33 Ⓐ Ⓑ Ⓒ Ⓓ Ⓔ	51 Ⓐ Ⓑ Ⓒ Ⓓ Ⓔ	69 Ⓐ Ⓑ Ⓒ Ⓓ Ⓔ	87 Ⓐ Ⓑ Ⓒ Ⓓ Ⓔ
16 Ⓐ Ⓑ Ⓒ Ⓓ Ⓔ	34 Ⓐ Ⓑ Ⓒ Ⓓ Ⓔ	52 Ⓐ Ⓑ Ⓒ Ⓓ Ⓔ	70 Ⓐ Ⓑ Ⓒ Ⓓ Ⓔ	88 Ⓐ Ⓑ Ⓒ Ⓓ Ⓔ
17 Ⓐ Ⓑ Ⓒ Ⓓ Ⓔ	35 Ⓐ Ⓑ Ⓒ Ⓓ Ⓔ	53 Ⓐ Ⓑ Ⓒ Ⓓ Ⓔ	71 Ⓐ Ⓑ Ⓒ Ⓓ Ⓔ	
18 Ⓐ Ⓑ Ⓒ Ⓓ Ⓔ	36 Ⓐ Ⓑ Ⓒ Ⓓ Ⓔ	54 Ⓐ Ⓑ Ⓒ Ⓓ Ⓔ	72 Ⓐ Ⓑ Ⓒ Ⓓ Ⓔ	

Chapter 11

Practice Test 2

PART A — ADDRESS CHECKING

Work — 6 minutes

In this part of the test you are to decide whether two addresses are alike or different. If the two addresses are *exactly alike in every way*, darken space Ⓐ. If they are different in any way, darken space Ⓓ.

Mark your answers on the Answer Sheet on page 265. Tear it out, put today's date on it, and place it next to the questions.

Allow yourself *exactly 6 minutes* to do as many of the 95 questions as you can. If you finish before the time is up, check your answers.

1.	7004 W 214 St	7004 W 241 St
2.	8996 Harthlodge Dr W	8996 Harthlodge Dr W
3.	3064 10th Ave NE	3064 10th Ave SE
4.	9606 Itaska Dr SE	9606 Itaska Dr SE
5.	216 West Anawanda Dr	217 West Anawanda Dr
6.	Evensville TN	Evansville TN
7.	16049 E 229 St	19049 E 229 St
8.	6256 Wachusett Ave	6256 Wachusett St
9.	2884 Cavvy Rd	2884 Cavvy Rd
10.	Toledo OH 44483	Toledo OK 44483
11.	5690 Vespa Ln	5690 Vesda Ln
12.	9777 64th St E	9777 64th Rd E
13.	9412 Ingham Ave W	9412 Ingram Ave W
14.	5209 S Emilie Pl	5209 S Emilie Pl
15.	Provo UT	Provo UT
16.	5851 Marionette Ave	5815 Marionette Ave
17.	Cherry Hill NJ 07013	Cherry Hill NJ 07103
18.	75 Grosvenor Rd	75 Grosvenor Rd
19.	Warren MI	Warren MT
20.	5237 Vandaveer Ave SE	2537 Vandaveer Ave SE
21.	2408 W Bernath Dr	2408 W Bernath Dr
22.	9073 Hacienda Ave E	9078 Hacienda Ave E
23.	6130 Florister Dr N	6130 Florister Dr N
24.	Green Bay WI	Green Bay WI

25. 1316 Jachurst St SE	1316 Jachurst St SE
26. 4893 West Haven Ct	4893 West Haven Ct
27. 7692 Woodbine Ave	7629 Woodbine Ave
28. 383 Armijo Pl SW	383 Armija Pl SW
29. Farmington GA	Farmington GU
30. 3047 E Charlotte Ave	3047 E Charlotte Ave
31. 3782 SE Kassabian Ave	3782 SE Kassabian Ave
32. Glendale CA	Glendale CO
33. 1213 Provencher St	1231 Provencher St
34. 2704 S Winchester St	2704 S Westchester St
35. 3764 Disbrow Ct	3763 Disbrow Ct
36. 3006 Le Brun Ln	3006 Le Brun Ln
37. 8034 Hudson River Rd	8034 Hudson River Rd
38. 1981 E Rickman Way	1981 E Rickman Way
39. 9700 Alamosa Dr	9700 Amalosa Dr
40. 6883 E Wyandanch Ave	6883 W Wyandanch Ave
41. 601 Orange Blvd	601 Orange Blvd
42. 5723 Emaline Ave NW	5723 Evaline Ave NW
43. 2867 Kingshighway Blvd N	2867 Kingshighway Blvd N
44. 1390 E Dean St	1390 E Dean St
45. 2417 W Townsend Ave	2417 W Townsend Ter
46. 1103 W Sindelar Rd	1103 W Sindelar Rd
47. 8090 W Zeamer St	8090 W Zoamer St
48. 6083 Oso Grande Ct	6803 Oso Grande Ct
49. 3841 Tanglewood Cir W	3841 Tanglewood Cir W
50. 8004 Quimera Trl SE	8004 Guimera Trl SE
51. 4723 McDougal Dr	4723 McDougal Dr
52. 9170 Worthen Pl	9170 Worthen Pl
53. 7481 Prince Charles Ct	7481 Prince Charles St
54. Arlington VA	Arlington WA
55. 1401 Abbott Dr	1401 Abbott Dr
56. 152 Nez Perce Lookout	152 Nez Perce Lookout
57. Homestead FL 33034	Homestead FL 33034
58. 7470 Oakleigh St	7470 Oakland St
59. 94 Quimby Rd E	94 Quimby Rd E
60. 89140 Palmyra Ave	89104 Palmyra Ave

61. 8182 Stream Ct NW	8182 Stream Pl NW
62. 10 Burlington Ave	10 Burlingham Ave
63. Gadsden AL 39503	Gapsdan AL 39503
64. 2647 E Pearsonville Rd	2647 E Pearsonville Rd
65. 6083 Featherstone Dr	6083 Featherstone Dr
66. Wilkes-Barre, PA 17402	Wilkes-Barre, PE 17402
67. 714 Gapsch Ln	714 Gapsch Ln
68. 1033 Remillard Rd	1033 Remillard Rd
69. Pawtucket RI 02861	Pawtucket RI 02851
70. 5148 Nemesia Pl NE	5148 Nemesia Pl NE
71. 1114 S Sycamore St	1114 E Sycamore St
72. 9276 Interpol Blvd NE	9276 Interpol Blvd NE
73. 4342 E Upstone St	4234 E Upstone St
74. 4101 Ludington St	4101 Ludington St
75. 8270 S Homestead Ave	8270 S Homestead Ave
76. 6398 S Oquendo Rd	6398 S Oquendo Rd
77. 141 Aberfeldy Ter	141 Abernathy Ter
78. 505 Fairfax St	505 Fairfax St
79. 3381 Claymont Path	3381 Claymont Path
80. 6814 Havelock Blvd	6814 Havelock Blvd
81. 7 Paso Del Puma NW	7 Paso Del Puma NE
82. Corpus Christi TX 78410	Corpus Christi TX 78410
83. 5504 Wilmore Dr E	5504 Wilmont Dr E
84. Fort Smith AR 72903	Forth Smith AR 72903
85. Los Alamos CA 93440	Los Alamos CA 93440
86. 801 Xenia St	801 Xenia St
87. 8430 Quanta Ln SW	8430 Quanta Ln SW
88. 83 Grass Valley St	83 Green Valley St
89. 4799 SW Eastgate Cir	4789 SW Eastgate Cir
90. 3994 Vista Campo Blvd	3994 Vista Campo Blvd
91. 1809 N 236th Ave	1809 S 236th Ave
92. 2908 Sagamore Ave	2908 Sagamore Ter
93. 2403 Jamestown Way	2403 Jameston Way
94. 462 Los Poblanos Ranch Ln	462 Los Poblanos Ranch Pl
95. 4871 Dadebridge Ct	4871 Dadebridge Ct

STOP.
If you finish before the time is up, go back and check
the questions in this section of the test only.

PART B — MEMORY FOR ADDRESSES

In this part of the test you will have five boxes labeled A, B, C, D, and E. Each box contains five addresses. Three of the five are groups of street addresses, such as 8100–8899 Tremont, 6100–6999 Caleb, and 4500–5799 Broad; and two are names of places. The addresses are different in each box.

There will be several opportunities to study the addresses and the boxes they are in. You will also be given three tests of 88 questions each, and the task of deciding where each address belongs. In some cases, you will have the list *and* the boxes in front of you at the same time; in others you will not. List 1 and List 2 are for warm-up practice. List 3 is the real one that will be scored.

Make sure you understand the format by examining the pretest samples below.

Pretest Samples

A	B	C	D	E
7300–7799 Tremont	6900–7299 Tremont	6300–6899 Tremont	7800–8099 Tremont	8100–8899 Tremont
Pierce	Rockport	April	Desert	Zane
5800–6099 Caleb	7000–7299 Caleb	6100–6999 Caleb	7300–7999 Caleb	4900–5799 Caleb
Veil	Indian	Pullman	Crystal	Eva
6300–6899 Broad	7200–7599 Broad	5800–6299 Broad	4500–5799 Broad	6900–7199 Broad

Questions 1 through 7 show the way the questions look. You have to decide in which lettered box (A, B, C, D, or E) the address belongs and then mark your answer by darkening the appropriate space in the answer grid.

1. 5800–6099 Caleb   1 Ⓐ Ⓑ Ⓒ Ⓓ Ⓔ
2. Indian   2 Ⓐ Ⓑ Ⓒ Ⓓ Ⓔ
3. Pullman   3 Ⓐ Ⓑ Ⓒ Ⓓ Ⓔ
4. 8100–8899 Tremont   4 Ⓐ Ⓑ Ⓒ Ⓓ Ⓔ
5. 7200–7599 Broad   5 Ⓐ Ⓑ Ⓒ Ⓓ Ⓔ
6. Veil   6 Ⓐ Ⓑ Ⓒ Ⓓ Ⓔ
7. Desert   7 Ⓐ Ⓑ Ⓒ Ⓓ Ⓔ

Answers

1. **A**   2. **B**   3. **C**   4. **E**   5. **B**   6. **A**   7. **D**

Now that you know what to do, you may begin Part B of Practice Test 2. To get the most out of it and the remaining four practice tests in this book, follow the directions and timing *exactly*. Follow each phase of Part B of the test, page by page, until you've completed List 3. It is modeled on the way the Postal Service actually conducts its tests.

Turn to the next page to begin.

Study — 3 minutes

You will be given 3 minutes to spend memorizing the addresses in the boxes. *They are exactly the same ones that will be used for all three tests.* Try to memorize as many as you can. When the 3 minutes are up, turn to page 274 and read the instructions for *List 1.*

A	B	C	D	E
7300–7799 Tremont	6900–7299 Tremont	6300–6899 Tremont	7800–8099 Tremont	8100–8899 Tremont
Pierce	Rockport	April	Desert	Zane
5800–6099 Caleb	7000–7299 Caleb	6100–6999 Caleb	7300–7999 Caleb	4900–5799 Caleb
Veil	Indian	Pullman	Crystal	Eva
6300–6899 Broad	7200–7599 Broad	5800–6299 Broad	4500–5799 Broad	6900–7199 Broad

List 1

Work — 3 minutes

Tear out the Answer Sheet for List 1. For each question, mark the Answer Sheet on page 266 to show the letter of the box in which the address belongs. Try to remember the locations of as many addresses as you can. *You will now have 3 minutes to complete List 1.* If you are not sure of an answer, you should guess.

A	B	C	D	E
7300–7799 Tremont Pierce 5800–6099 Caleb Veil 6300–6899 Broad	6900–7299 Tremont Rockport 7000–7299 Caleb Indian 7200–7599 Broad	6300–6899 Tremont April 6100–6999 Caleb Pullman 5800–6299 Broad	7800–8099 Tremont Desert 7300–7999 Caleb Crystal 4500–5799 Broad	8100–8899 Tremont Zane 4900–5799 Caleb Eva 6900–7199 Broad

1. 6300–6899 Broad
2. 7200–7599 Broad
3. Pierce
4. Rockport
5. 7300–7799 Tremont
6. 8100–8899 Tremont
7. 5800–6699 Caleb
8. Veil
9. April
10. Desert
11. 6900–7299 Tremont
12. Pierce
13. Zane
14. 6300–6899 Tremont
15. Zane
16. 6900–7199 Broad
17. Indian
18. 6300–6899 Broad
19. Pullman
20. Eva
21. Rockport
22. 4900–5799 Caleb
23. Crystal
24. 6900–7199 Broad
25. 7800–8099 Tremont
26. Indian
27. 5800–6299 Broad
28. Eva
29. 7000–7299 Caleb
30. 4500–5799 Broad
31. 7300–7999 Caleb
32. 6100–6999 Caleb
33. Veil
34. 4500–5799 Broad
35. Rockport
36. Pierce
37. 6900–7199 Broad
38. Zane
39. 4900–5799 Caleb
40. 7300–7999 Caleb
41. Crystal
42. 7000–7299 Caleb
43. Veil
44. 5800–6299 Broad

45. Crystal
46. 8100–8899 Tremont
47. Pullman
48. 7800–8099 Tremont
49. 7000–7299 Caleb
50. Pullman
51. April
52. 7300–7999 Caleb
53. Desert
54. 7200–7599 Broad
55. Pierce

56. Eva
57. Zane
58. 7300–7799 Tremont
59. 6900–7199 Broad
60. 5800–6099 Caleb
61. Pierce
62. Desert
63. Crystal
64. 6300–6899 Tremont
65. 6300–6899 Broad
66. 7300–7799 Tremont

67. 4900–5799 Tremont
68. April
69. 7800–8099 Tremont
70. 6300–6899 Tremont
71. 8100–8899 Tremont
72. Rockport
73. Eva
74. 5800–6099 Caleb
75. Indian
76. Pullman
77. Indian

78. April
79. 4500–5799 Broad
80. 6100–6999 Caleb
81. Eva
82. 7200–7599 Broad
83. 6300–6899 Broad
84. Veil
85. Desert
86. 6100–6999 Caleb
87. 5800–6299 Broad
88. Pullman

STOP.
If you finish before the time is up, go back and check
the questions in this section of the test only.

List 2

Work — 3 minutes

Do these questions *without* looking back at the boxes. For each question, mark your answer on the Answer Sheet for List 2 on page 266. If you are not sure of an answer, you should guess.

1. 7200–7599 Broad
2. Rockport
3. 8100–8899 Tremont
4. Veil
5. Desert
6. Pierce
7. 6300–6899 Tremont
8. 6900–7199 Broad
9. 6300–6899 Broad
10. Eva
11. 4900–5799 Caleb

12. 6900–7199 Broad
13. Indian
14. Eva
15. 4500–5799 Broad
16. 6100–6999 Caleb
17. 4500–5799 Broad
18. Pierce
19. Zane
20. 7300–7999 Caleb
21. 7000–7299 Caleb
22. 5800–6299 Broad

23. 8100–8899 Tremont
24. 7800–8099 Tremont
25. Pullman
26. 7300–7999 Caleb
27. 7200–7599 Broad
28. Eva
29. 7300–7799 Tremont
30. 5800–6099 Caleb
31. Desert
32. 6300–6899 Tremont
33. 7300–7799 Tremont

34. April
35. 6300–6899 Tremont
36. Rockport
37. 5800–6099 Caleb
38. Pullman
39. April
40. 6100–6999 Caleb
41. 7200–7599 Broad
42. Veil
43. 6100–6999 Caleb
44. Pullman

45. 6300–6899 Broad

46. Pierce

47. 7300–7799 Tremont

48. 5800–6699 Caleb

49. April

50. 6900–7299 Tremont

51. Zane

52. 6100–6999 Caleb

53. Indian

54. Pullman

55. Rockport

56. Crystal

57. 7800–8099 Tremont

58. 5800–6299 Broad

59. 7000–7299 Caleb

60. 7300–7999 Caleb

61. Veil

62. Rockport

63. 6900–7199 Broad

64. 4900–5799 Caleb

65. Crystal

66. Veil

67. Crystal

68. Pullman

69. 7000–7299 Caleb

70. April

71. Desert

72. Pierce

73. Zane

74. 6900–7199 Broad

75. Pierce

76. Crystal

77. 6300–6899 Broad

78. 4900–5799 Caleb

79. 7800–8099 Tremont

80. 8100–8899 Tremont

81. Eva

82. Indian

83. 7000–7299 Caleb

84. 4500–5799 Broad

85. Eva

86. 6300–6899 Broad

87. Desert

88. 5800–6299 Broad

STOP.
If you finish before the time is up, go back and check
the questions in this section of the test only.

List 3

You are now about to take the test using List 3. *(This is the test that counts!)*

Turn back to page 273 and study the boxes again. *You have 5 minutes to restudy the addresses.*

Work — 5 minutes

For each question, mark the Answer Sheet on page 267 to show the letter of the box in which the address belongs. You have *exactly 5 minutes* to do the test. During these 5 minutes, *do not* turn to any other page.

1. 5800–6299 Broad
2. Veil
3. 7000–7299 Caleb
4. Crystal
5. 7300–7999 Caleb
6. 4900–5799 Caleb
7. Zane
8. 6900–7199 Broad
9. Pierce
10. Rockport
11. 4500–5799 Broad
12. Veil
13. 6100–6999 Caleb
14. 7300–7999 Caleb
15. 4500–5799 Broad
16. 7000–7299 Caleb
17. Eva
18. 5800–6299 Broad
19. Indian
20. 7800–8099 Tremont
21. 6900–7199 Broad
22. Crystal
23. 4900–5799 Caleb
24. Rockport
25. Eva
26. Pullman
27. 6300–6899 Broad
28. Indian
29. 6900–7199 Broad
30. Zane
31. 6300–6899 Tremont
32. Zane
33. Pierce
34. 6900–7299 Tremont
35. Desert
36. April
37. Veil
38. 5800–6699 Caleb
39. 8100–8899 Tremont
40. 7300–7799 Tremont
41. Rockport
42. Pierce
43. 7200–7599 Broad
44. 6300–6899 Broad

45. Pullman
46. 5800–6299 Broad
47. 6100–6999 Caleb
48. Desert
49. Veil
50. 6300–6899 Broad
51. 7200–7599 Broad
52. Eva
53. 6100–6999 Caleb
54. 4500–5799 Broad
55. April

56. Indian
57. Pullman
58. 7000–7299 Caleb
59. 5800–6099 Caleb
60. Eva
61. Rockport
62. 8100–8899 Tremont
63. 6300–6899 Tremont
64. 7800–8099 Tremont
65. April
66. 4900–5799 Caleb

67. 7300–7799 Tremont
68. 6300–6899 Broad
69. 6300–6899 Tremont
70. Crystal
71. Desert
72. Pierce
73. 5800–6099 Caleb
74. 6900–7199 Broad
75. 7300–7799 Tremont
76. Zane
77. Eva

78. Pierce
79. 7200–7599 Broad
80. Desert
81. 7300–7999 Caleb
82. April
83. Pullman
84. 7000–7299 Caleb
85. 7800–8099 Tremont
86. Pullman
87. 8100–8899 Tremont
88. Crystal

STOP.
If you finish before the time is up, go back and check
the questions in this section of the test only.

PART C — NUMBER SERIES

Work — 20 minutes

For each Number Series question, there is a series of numbers that follow some definite order, and below each are five sets of two numbers each. You are to look at the numbers in the series and find out what order they follow. Then decide what the next two numbers in that series would be if the same order were continued. Mark your answers on the Answer Sheet for Number Series on page 267.

You have 20 minutes to complete this part of the test. If you finish before the time is up, check your answers. The answers and explanations are on page 290.

1. 80 70 65 60 50 65 40 __ __
   A) 30 20   B) 55 45   C) 30 65   D) 65 55   E) 65 30

2. 17 14 18 15 19 16 20 __ __
   A) 21 17   B) 18 19   C) 17 15   D) 17 21   E) 19 16

3. 36 37 38 39 38 37 36 __ __
   A) 35 34   B) 36 37   C) 37 38   D) 38 39   E) 35 33

4. 2 2 2 3 6 6 4 12 __ __
   A) 12 5   B) 12 12   C) 5 12   D) 7 14   E) 12 7

5. 28 18 31 21 34 24 37 __ __
   A) 26 36   B) 27 38   C) 38 25   D) 28 38   E) 27 40

6. 41 36 31 26 21 16 11 __ __
   A) 10 5   B) 11 6   C) 6 5   D) 6 1   E) 7 2

7. 6 38 18 31 30 24 42 __ __
   A) 34 48   B) 30 54   C) 17 54   D) 35 36   E) 52 18

8. $\frac{1}{3}$ $\frac{2}{6}$ $\frac{3}{9}$ $\frac{4}{12}$ $\frac{5}{15}$ $\frac{6}{18}$ $\frac{7}{21}$ __ __
   A) $\frac{8}{22}$ $\frac{9}{23}$ B) $\frac{9}{24}$ $\frac{9}{25}$ C) $\frac{9}{24}$ $\frac{10}{26}$ D) $\frac{6}{23}$ $\frac{7}{23}$ E) $\frac{8}{24}$ $\frac{9}{27}$

9. 11 13 8 15 17 12 19 __ __
   A) 20 21   B) 14 21   C) 13 18   D) 23 11   E) 21 16

10. 18 20 21 21 23 24 24 __ __
    A) 25 27   B) 24 25   C) 28 27   D) 26 27   E) 25 26

11. 1 4 2 8 3 12 4 __ __
    A) 5 13   B) 14 5   C) 16 5   D) 8 20   E) 6 18

12. 5 6 3 12 13 10 40 __ __

   A) 20 50   B) 39 50   C) 11 8   D) 15 60   E) 41 38

13. 15 12 89 15 12 89 15 __ __

   A) 12 89   B) 15 12   C) 89 15   D) 12 15   E) 89 12

14. 11 53 22 42 33 31 44 __ __

   A) 30 22   B) 20 55   C) 32 53   D) 29 40   E) 56 36

15. 20 17 8 9 14 11 8 9 8 __ __

   A) 5 8   B) 9 9   C) 8 9   D) 10 5   E) 12 4

16. 81 27 27 27 9 9 9 __ __

   A) 6 6   B) 3 3   C) 6 3   D) 3 6   E) 3 1

17. 18 14 14 24 12 12 30 __ __

   A) 14 36   B) 16 22   C) 10 10   D) 7 15   E) 5 15

18. 13 21 11 19 9 17 7 __ __

   A) 15 9   B) 18 8   C) 5 19   D) 7 15   E) 15 5

19. 12 3 10 3 8 3 6 __ __

   A) 3 6   B) 4 3   C) 3 3   D) 3 4   E) 2 3

20. 3 4 4 3 3 4 4 __ __

   A) 4 3   B) 5 3   C) 3 3   D) 4 4   E) 3 4

21. 18 26 24 19 18 16 20 __ __

   A) 21 19   B) 12 10   C) 14 8   D) 10 8   E) 18 10

22. 10 14 12 6 10 8 4 __ __

   A) 4 10   B) 6 10   C) 8 6   D) 8 10   E) 4 2

23. 5 6 7 10 8 9 10 9 __ __

   A) 10 11   B) 11 10   C) 9 8   D) 11 12   E) 7 10

24. 2 11 11 3 12 12 4 __ __

   A) 5 12   B) 13 5   C) 5 13   D) 13 14   E) 13 13

STOP.
If you finish before the time is up, go back and check
the questions in this section of the test only.

PART D — FOLLOWING ORAL DIRECTIONS

This part of the test gauges your ability to understand and carry out spoken directions *exactly* as they are given to you.

In order to prepare to take Part D of the test, follow the steps below:

1. Enlist the help of a friend who will be the "reader." It will be his or her job to read aloud a series of directions that you are to follow *exactly*. The reader will need a watch that displays seconds, because the directions must be read at the correct speed.

2. Tear out pages 287 and 288. These are the worksheets you should have in front of you as you listen to the directions given by the reader, who will tell you to do certain things with the items on each line on the worksheets.

3. Use the Answer Sheet for Following Oral Directions on page 267, and insert today's date. You will darken the appropriate spaces in accordance with the directions given by the reader.

4. *Now hand this entire book to the reader.* Ask him/her to review the section below headed "Instructions to the Reader." It explains exactly how the reader is to proceed.

When you and the reader are ready to start this part of Practice Test 2, he/she will begin reading to you the section marked "Directions." YOU ARE NOT TO READ THESE AT ANY TIME BEFORE OR DURING THE TEST. If you do, you will lose the benefit of this part of the practice test.

Instructions to the "Reader"

These instructions should be read at about 80 words per minute. You should practice reading the material in the box until you can do it in exactly 1 minute. The number of words in the passage and the natural pauses described below will give you a good feel for the rate of speed and the way you should read the test questions.

1-MINUTE PRACTICE

> Look at line 20 on your worksheet. There are two circles and two boxes of different sizes with numbers in them. If 7 is less than 3 and if 2 is smaller than 4, write C in the larger circle. Otherwise write B as in *baker* in the smaller box. Now, on your answer sheet, darken the space for the number-letter combination in the box or circle.

You should read the entire test aloud before you read it to the person taking the test, in order to thoroughly acquaint yourself with the procedure and the desired rate of reading.

Read slowly but at a natural pace. In other words, do not space the words so that there are unnaturally long pauses between them. The instruction "Pause slightly" indicates only enough time to take a breath. The other instructions for pauses give the recommended length for each. If possible, use a watch with a second hand.

All the material that follows, except the words in parentheses, is to be read aloud. Now start reading the directions. *Do not repeat any of the directions.*

Directions: In the test, I will read instructions to you. You are to mark your worksheets according to the instructions that I read to you. After each set of instructions, I'll give you time to record your answers on your answer sheet.

Try to understand the instructions as I read them; I cannot repeat them. Do not ask any questions from now on.

If, when you go to darken a space for a number, you find that you have already darkened another space for that number, either (1) erase the first mark and darken the space for your new choice, or (2) let the first mark stay and do not darken any other space. When you finish, you should have no more than one space darkened for each number.

Turn to Worksheet 1.

Look at line 1 on your worksheet. (Pause slightly.) Write A next to the middle number. (Pause 2 seconds.) Now, on your answer sheet, find the number beside which you wrote and darken space A for that number. (Pause 5 seconds.)

Look at line 2 on your worksheet. (Pause slightly.) There are 5 circles. Each circle has a number in it. (Pause slightly.) Write an E in the circle that has the highest number in it. (Pause 2 seconds.) Now, on your answer sheet, darken the space for the number-letter combination that is in the circle you just wrote in. (Pause 5 seconds.)

Look at line 2 again. (Pause slightly.) In the circle with the lowest number write B as in *baker.* (Pause 2 seconds.) Now, on your answer sheet, darken the space for the number-letter combination that is in the circle you just wrote in. (Pause 5 seconds.)

Look at line 3 on your worksheet. (Pause slightly.) There are 5 boxes. Each box has a letter in it. In the fourth box write the answer to this question: Which of the following numbers is largest: 17, 21, 23, 15, 19? (Pause 5 seconds.) Now, on your answer sheet, darken the space for the number-letter combination that is in the box you just wrote in. (Pause 5 seconds.)

In the second box do nothing. In the first box write 46. (Pause 2 seconds.) Now, on your answer sheet, darken the space for the number-letter combination that is in the box you just wrote in. (Pause 5 seconds.)

Look at line 3 again. (Pause slightly.) In the fifth box, write the answer to this question: At what number do the hands of a clock point when it is midnight? (Pause 2 seconds.) Now, on your answer sheet, darken the space for the number-letter combination that is in the box you just wrote in. (Pause 5 seconds.)

Look at line 4 on your worksheet. (Pause slightly.) Draw a line under every number that is more than 25 but less than 35. (Pause 12 seconds.) Now, on your answer sheet, for every number that you drew a line under, darken space C. (Pause 25 seconds.)

Look at line 5 on your worksheet. There are three boxes with letters and words in them. (Pause slightly.) Each box represents a post office in a different area of the city. Post Office E delivers mail in the Westchester Square area, Post Office D delivers mail in the Corley Circle area, and Post Office C delivers mail in the Union Junction area. (Pause slightly.) Write the number 68 on the line inside the box which represents the post office that delivers mail in the Corley Circle area. (Pause 2 seconds.) Now, on your answer sheet, find number 68 and darken the space for the letter that is in the box you just wrote in. (Pause 5 seconds.)

Now look at line 6 on your worksheet. (Pause slightly.) There are four boxes with numbers on them. Each number represents the age of one of the four workers in a local post office. (Pause slightly.) Write B as in *baker* on the line in the box containing the age of the youngest worker in that post office. (Pause 2 seconds.) Now, on your answer sheet, darken the space for the number-letter combination that is in the box you just wrote in. (Pause 5 seconds.)

Look at line 7 on your worksheet. (Pause slightly.) There are five circles on the line. Some of the circles are partially or entirely shaded. (Pause slightly.) Count the number of circles that are partially or entirely shaded, add 3, and write that number in the middle circle. (Pause 2 seconds.) Now, on your answer sheet, darken the space for the number-letter combination that is in the circle you just wrote in.

Look at line 7 again. (Pause slightly.) Count the number of circles that do not have any shading, subtract 1, and write that number in the first circle. (Pause 2 seconds.) Now, on your answer sheet, darken the space for the number-letter combination that is in the circle you just wrote in. (Pause 5 seconds.)

Look at the letters on line 8 on your worksheet. (Pause slightly.) Draw a line under the second letter in the line. (Pause 2 seconds.) Now, on your answer sheet, find number 53 and darken the space for the letter under which you drew a line. (Pause 5 seconds.)

Look at line 8 again. (Pause slightly.) Draw two lines under the sixth letter in the line. (Pause 3 seconds.) Now, on your answer sheet, find number 63 and darken the space for the letter under which you drew two lines. (Pause 5 seconds.)

Look at line 9 on your worksheet. (Pause slightly.) There are two circles and two boxes of different sizes with numbers in them. (Pause slightly.) If 8 is more than 5 and if 7 is less than 4, write E in the larger circle. (Pause slightly.) Otherwise, write D as in *dog* in the smaller box. (Pause 2 seconds.) Now, on your answer sheet, darken the space for the number-letter combination that is in the box or circle you just wrote in. (Pause 5 seconds.)

Look at line 10 on your worksheet. (Pause slightly.) Draw a line under every "O" in the line. (Pause 5 seconds.) Count the number of lines you have drawn, and write that number at the end of the line. (Pause 5 seconds.) Now, write an E next to the number you just wrote. (Pause 2 seconds.) Now, on your answer sheet, darken the space for the number-letter combination you just wrote at the end of the line. (Pause 5 seconds.)

Look at the numbers on line 11 on your worksheet. (Pause slightly.) Draw a circle around every number that is more than 35 but less than 45. (Pause 12 seconds.) Now, on your answer sheet, for each number around which you drew a circle, darken box E. (Pause 25 seconds.)

Now turn to Worksheet 2. (Pause 5 seconds.)

Look at line 12 on your worksheet. (Pause slightly.) There are a number and a letter in each of the five boxes. In the box that has the highest number write on the line the last two figures of that number. (Pause 2 seconds.) Now, on your answer sheet, darken the space for the number-letter combination that is in the box you just wrote in. (Pause 5 seconds.)

Look at line 13 on your worksheet. (Pause slightly.) Each of the boxes and circles has a letter of the alphabet in it. If, in the alphabet, the letter in the small box comes after the letter in the large circle, write 84 on the line in the small circle. (Pause 2 seconds.) Otherwise, write 71 in the large box. (Pause 2 seconds.) Now, on your answer sheet, darken the space for the number-letter combination that is in the circle or box you just wrote in. (Pause 5 seconds.)

Look at the boxes and words on line 14 on your worksheet. (Pause slightly.) Write the second letter of the first word in the third box. (Pause 2 seconds.) Write the first letter of the second word in the first box. (Pause 2 seconds.) Write the fourth letter of the third word in the second box. (Pause 2 seconds.) Now, on your answer sheet, darken the spaces for the number-letter combinations that are in the three boxes you just wrote in. (Pause 25 seconds.)

Look at line 15 on your worksheet. (Pause slightly.) In each circle there is the time when a piece of express mail was received. In the circle for the earliest time, write on the line the last two figures of the time. (Pause 2 seconds.) Now, on your answer sheet, darken the space for the number-letter combination that is in the circle you just wrote in. (Pause 5 seconds.)

Look at line 16. (Pause slightly.) On the line next to the left-hand letter write the answer to this question: how many weeks are there in a year? (Pause 2 seconds.) Now, on your answer sheet, find the number you just wrote and darken the space for the letter you wrote it next to. (Pause 5 seconds.)

Look at the drawing on line 17 on your worksheet. (Pause slightly.) The four boxes are bins used to sort mail. If 6 is smaller than 9, and 7 is more than 5, write C in the lower right-hand bin. Otherwise, write D as in *dog* in the upper left-hand bin. (Pause 2 seconds.) Now, on your answer sheet, darken the space for the number-letter combination that is in the bin you just wrote in. (Pause 5 seconds.)

Now look at line 18 on your worksheet. (Pause slightly.) Each box has a number in it. Write C in any box which has a number that does not have three digits in it. (Pause 2 seconds.) Now, on your answer sheet, darken the space for the number-letter combination in each box you just wrote in. (Pause 5 seconds.)

Look at line 19 on your worksheet. (Pause slightly.) Count the number of A's in the three boxes, add 5, and write that number on the first line to the right of the three boxes. (Pause 2 seconds.) On the line next to that number, write B as in *boy*. (Pause 2 seconds.) Now, on your answer sheet, darken the space for the number-letter combination that is on the two lines you just wrote on. (Pause 5 seconds.)

END OF EXAMINATION.
**If you finish before the time is up, go back and check
the questions in this section of the test only.**

Practice Test 2—Worksheet 1
Part D—Following Oral Directions

1. 68 ___   13 ___   37 ___

2. (19 ___)   (65 ___)   (49 ___)   (72 ___)   (74 ___)

3. [C ___]   [A ___]   [E ___]   [B ___]   [D ___]

4. 29   11   16   33   20   9   15   35   26

5. [E / WESTCHESTER SQUARE / ___]   [D / CORLEY CIRCLE / ___]   [C / UNION JUNCTION / ___]

6. [41 ___]   [62 ___]   [47 ___]   [53 ___]

7. (___B)   (___D)   (___A)   ( )   (___E)

8. B   C   E   D   E   A   B   E   D

9. (57 ___)   (18 ___)   [39 ___]   [13 ___]

10. X O O O X O X X X O O X O X X

11. 44   35   57   38   46   30   40   45

Practice Test 2—Worksheet 2
Part D—Following Oral Directions

12.

| 285 ___D | 361 ___A | 455 ___C | 371 ___B | 514 E ___ |

13.

___A   ___C   ___D   ___B

14.

5 ___   17 ___   56 ___   CAMP   BEND   RIPE

15.

10:12 ___E   10:51 ___D   10:11 ___C   10:32 ___B   10:45 ___A

16.

___B   ___E

17.

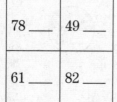

| 78 ___ | 49 ___ |
| 61 ___ | 82 ___ |

18.

| 741 ___ | 580 ___ | 194 ___ | 692 ___ | 85 ___ | 304 ___ |

19.

A	A	D
D	E	A
A	C	B

■ ANSWER KEY

Part A—Address Checking

1. D	11. D	21. A	31. A	41. A	51. A	61. D	71. D	81. D	91. D
2. A	12. D	22. D	32. D	42. D	52. A	62. D	72. A	82. A	92. D
3. D	13. D	23. A	33. D	43. A	53. D	63. D	73. D	83. D	93. D
4. A	14. A	24. A	34. D	44. D	54. D	64. A	74. A	84. A	94. D
5. D	15. A	25. A	35. D	45. D	55. A	65. A	75. A	85. A	95. A
6. D	16. D	26. A	36. A	46. A	56. A	66. D	76. A	86. A	
7. D	17. D	27. D	37. A	47. D	57. A	67. A	77. D	87. A	
8. D	18. A	28. D	38. A	48. D	58. D	68. A	78. A	88. D	
9. A	19. D	29. D	39. D	49. A	59. A	69. D	79. A	89. D	
10. D	20. A	30. A	40. D	50. D	60. D	70. A	80. A	90. A	

Part B—Memory for Addresses

List 1

1. A	10. D	19. C	28. E	37. E	46. E	55. A	64. C	73. E	82. B
2. B	11. B	20. E	29. B	38. E	47. C	56. E	65. B	74. A	83. A
3. A	12. A	21. B	30. E	39. E	48. D	57. E	66. A	75. B	84. A
4. B	13. E	22. E	31. D	40. D	49. B	58. A	67. E	76. C	85. D
5. A	14. C	23. D	32. C	41. D	50. C	59. E	68. C	77. B	86. C
6. E	15. E	24. E	33. A	42. B	51. C	60. A	69. D	78. C	87. C
7. A	16. E	25. D	34. D	43. A	52. A	61. A	70. C	79. D	88. C
8. A	17. B	26. B	35. B	44. C	53. D	62. D	71. E	80. C	
9. C	18. E	27. C	36. A	45. D	54. B	63. D	72. B	81. E	

List 2

1. B	10. E	19. E	28. E	37. A	46. A	55. B	64. E	73. E	82. B
2. B	11. E	20. D	29. A	38. C	47. A	56. D	65. D	74. E	83. B
3. E	12. E	21. B	30. A	39. C	48. A	57. D	66. A	75. A	84. D
4. A	13. B	22. A	31. D	40. C	49. C	58. C	67. D	76. D	85. E
5. D	14. E	23. E	32. C	41. B	50. B	59. B	68. C	77. A	86. A
6. A	15. D	24. D	33. A	42. A	51. E	60. D	69. B	78. E	87. D
7. C	16. C	25. C	34. C	43. C	52. C	61. A	70. C	79. D	88. C
8. E	17. D	26. D	35. C	44. C	53. B	62. B	71. D	80. E	
9. A	18. A	27. B	36. B	45. A	54. C	63. E	72. A	81. E	

List 3

1. C	10. B	19. B	28. B	37. A	46. C	55. C	64. D	73. A	82. C
2. A	11. D	20. D	29. E	38. A	47. C	56. B	65. C	74. E	83. C
3. B	12. A	21. E	30. E	39. E	48. D	57. C	66. E	75. A	84. B
4. D	13. C	22. D	31. C	40. A	49. A	58. B	67. A	76. E	85. D
5. D	14. D	23. E	32. E	41. B	50. A	59. A	68. A	77. E	86. C
6. E	15. D	24. B	33. A	42. A	51. B	60. E	69. C	78. A	87. E
7. E	16. B	25. E	34. B	43. B	52. E	61. B	70. D	79. B	88. D
8. E	17. E	26. C	35. D	44. A	53. C	62. E	71. D	80. D	
9. A	18. C	27. A	36. C	45. C	54. D	63. C	72. A	81. D	

Part C—Number Series

1. C	4. A	7. C	10. D	13. A	16. B	19. D	22. C
2. D	5. E	8. E	11. C	14. B	17. C	20. C	23. D
3. C	6. D	9. E	12. E	15. A	18. E	21. D	24. E

Part D—Following Oral Directions

1. B	7. E	12. D	17. E	26. C	38. E	41. B	52. B	63. A	74. E
5. B	9. B	13. A	19. B	29. C	39. D	44. E	53. C	68. D	82. C
6. A	11. C	14. E	23. B	33. C	40. E	46. C	56. A	71. A	85. C

ANSWER EXPLANATIONS FOR PART C—NUMBER SERIES

1. **C** The numbers in this series decrease by 10. 65 is inserted after every two numbers of the series.
2. **D** This series follows a − 3, + 4; and so on rule.
3. **C** These numbers follow an ascending-descending pattern, from 36 to 39 and back down again; repeating the same cycle again and again.
4. **A** Each group of three numbers, beginning with 2 2 2 may be considered to be a mini-series. Each mini-series begins one number higher than the first number in the preceding series. Each beginning number is multiplied and the result is repeated. The multipliers keep increasing by one. It is a lot easier to see what is happening if you use a loop diagram.

5. **E** Here you have a pair of alternating series, each increasing by 3. If you wish, you could consider these numbers as following a − 10, + 13; rule, but the arithmetic can be a little tricky.
6. **D** This series is absolutely simple compared to the series in Examples 4 and 5 above. It merely follows a − 5 rule.
7. **C** Here again is a case of two alternating series. One ascends by + 12. The other descends by − 7.
8. **E** The top number of each fraction keeps increasing by 1. The bottom number increases by 3.
9. **E** One of these two alternating series follows a + 2 rule. The other one, which increases by 4, appears after every *two* numbers of the first.
10. **D** There is a complex rule that governs these numbers: + 2, + 1, repeat; + 2, + 1, repeat; and so on.
11. **C** You can see this series in two ways. First, as a pair of alternating series, one increasing by 1; the other increasing by 4. Or, you could see each pair of numbers as connected by × 4. For example:

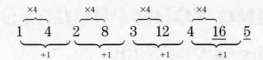

12. **E** A complex rule that includes addition, subtraction and multiplication is at work here: $+1$, -3, $\times 4$; and so on.

13. **A** A sequence of three unrelated numbers: 15, 12, 89 keeps repeating.

14. **B** These are two alternating series. One follows a $+11$ rule; the other a -11 rule.

15. **A** This series appears confusing. It is a -3 series that continues for two numbers and is then interrupted by the arbitrary numbers, 8 9. This pattern keeps repeating. You have to be extremely careful in selecting the next two numbers.

16. **B** After a number has been *divided* by 3, the answer repeats three times.

17. **C** Here you have two alternating series. One (starting with 18) increases by 6. The other decreases by 2 and repeats the number.

18. **E** You may consider these numbers either as following a $+8$, -10 pattern, or as two alternating series, each following a -2 rule.

19. **D** The number 3 appears between every two numbers in this -2 series.

20. **C** Here you have the numbers 3 and 4 continually reversing their order. You might also see a pattern that consists of the sequence 3 4 4 3 continually recycling.

21. **D** There are two alternating series here. The loop diagram shown makes this very difficult question easy to answer.

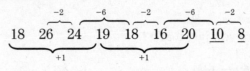

22. **C** The complex rule: $+4$, -2, $\div 2$ connects members of this series. Here, too, a loop diagram is most important.

23. **D** One of the two alternating series in this group of numbers increases by 1. It continues for *three* numbers and is then interrupted by *one* member of a descending series that follows a -1 rule.

24. **E** Both alternating series follow a $+1$ rule. One series repeats each number before being interrupted by a member of the other series.

EVALUATING YOUR PROGRESS*

Part A—Address Checking

Computing Your Score

Check your answers against the Answer Key. Score yourself by using this formula:

$$\frac{\text{Number right}}{- \text{Number wrong}}$$

YOUR SCORE

For example, if you completed 52 questions and got 8 wrong,

Number right	=	44
− Number wrong	=	− 8
Your score	=	36

Notice that you do *not* figure in the questions that you did not answer.

Guidelines

How good is the score you just made?

52 or higher . . . . Good
Between 32 and 52 . . . . . . Fair
Below 32 . . . . You need to improve.

These are commonly accepted figures. It is believed, however, that you should not be satisfied with anything *less* than 52. Experience in training many people to prepare for this test shows that most serious test candidates who use the preparation program described in this book (Chapter 4 covers Address Checking) will be able to raise their score to the upper sixties, seventies, or eighties.

Personal Progress Record

One of the most satisfying things that can happen while you are working toward a goal is to see signs of progress. The improvement you make on Address Checking can readily be seen by examining the scores you make on the practice tests and exercises in this book. Keeping track of your growing skill is important so a Personal Progress Record has been furnished for your use on page 439.

---

* Please note that the scores you obtain by following the computation instructions for the various parts of this test are "raw" scores. The Postal Service combines and converts the raw scores for the various parts of the test into a scaled score obtained by using special conversion formulas that are kept confidential. This scaled score (plus any veteran's credits to which you are entitled) forms the basis for your final rating and your standing on the list. This final rating will be sent to you after the tests have been marked.

Furthermore, even though you take one test, your final score will vary depending on the title. For example, your rating on the Mail Handler register may very well be different from your rating on the Postal Clerk-Carrier register. Apparently, the relative rating given to each part of the test varies according to title. This is another argument for taking as many tests in as many titles as possible, as suggested on page 3.

You are encouraged to calculate your raw scores because they furnish a realistic and convenient way for you to keep track of your relative performance and progress as you work your way through this book.

The following is a sample of this Personal Progress Record to familiarize you with it. The entries on this sample are based on the example above.

PERSONAL PROGRESS RECORD—SAMPLE

ADDRESS CHECKING										
Initial Tests							**Repeated Tests**			
Date	Test	Number Completed	Number Correct	− Number Wrong	= Score		Date	Score	Date	Score
5/15	Diagnostic Practice Test	52	44	− 8	= 36					
5/16	Practice Test 1	64	54	− 10	= 44					
5/18	Practice Test 2	66	57	− 9	= 48					
5/20	Practice Test 3	70	60	− 10	= 50					
	Practice Test 4			−	=					
	Practice Test 5			−	=					
	Practice Test 6			−	=					

Now turn to page 439. In the table entitled "Personal Progress Record—Address Checking," make the proper entries on the line for Practice Test 2, which you just took. Review the special techniques in Chapter 4: Address Checking—How to Improve Your Score, before taking Practice Test 3. After taking the additional practice tests, enter the results immediately. Keep this record. It will help you record your progress.

Part B—Memory for Addresses

Computing Your Score

Check the answers on your answer sheet against the Answer Key. Calculate your score by using these four steps:

1. Enter the number of answers you got right . . . .   _____

2. Enter the number of answers you got wrong . . . . _____

3. Divide the number wrong by 4 (or multiply by ¼) . . . . − _____

4. Subtract Line 3 from Line 1 . . . . YOUR SCORE =   _____

Follow this example to make sure that you have figured your score correctly. It will be assumed that you completed 32 questions, of which you got 24 right and 8 wrong.

Line 1 . . . . Number right   24

Line 2 . . . . Number wrong 8

Line 3 . . . . ¼ of line 2 = ¼ × 8 . . . . . .   − 2

Line 4 . . . . 24 − 2 . . YOUR SCORE =   22

Notice that, just as for Address Checking, questions that are not answered are *not* taken into account.

Guidelines

How good is the score you just made?

> 52 or higher . . . . Good
> Between 32 and 52 . . . . . . Fair
> Below 32 . . . . You need to improve.

If your score on this test was low, don't be discouraged. Nevertheless, you may wish to review Chapters 5 and 6, which offer special techniques for handling Part B—Memory for Addresses, before taking Practice Test 3.

Personal Progress Record

Turn to page 439. Use the table entitled "Personal Progress—Memory for Addresses" to keep a permanent record of your scores on List 3 of the practice tests. A sample is printed below to familiarize you with it. The first entry is based on the preceding example.

PERSONAL PROGRESS RECORD—SAMPLE

MEMORY FOR ADDRESSES												
Initial Tests									**Repeated Tests**			
Date	Test	Number Completed	Number Correct A	Number Wrong	$\times \frac{1}{4} =$		Points off B	Score (A − B)	Date	Score	Date	Score
5/15	Diagnostic Practice Test	32	24	8	$\times \frac{1}{4} =$		2	22				
5/16	Practice Test 1	46	38	8	$\times \frac{1}{4} =$		2	36				
5/18	Practice Test 2	58	52	6	$\times \frac{1}{4} =$		$1\frac{1}{2}$	$50\frac{1}{2}$				
5/20	Practice Test 3	64	60	4	$\times \frac{1}{4} =$		1	59				
	Practice Test 4				$\times \frac{1}{4} =$							
	Practice Test 5				$\times \frac{1}{4} =$							
	Practice Test 6				$\times \frac{1}{4} =$							

Part C—Number Series

Computing Your Score

Check the answers on your Answer Sheet against the Answer Key. Calculate your score by adding up the number of correct answers you have. You *do not* lose any credit for wrong answers or for questions you don't answer. For example, on a test having 24 questions, if you had 5 correct, 3 incorrect, and omitted 16, your score would be 5.

Guidelines

How good is the score you just made?

> 17 or higher . . . . Good
> Between 12 and 16 . . . . . . Fair
> Below 12 . . . . You need to improve.

Once you have mastered the techniques explained in this book, you should routinely be scoring 20 to 24 correct.

Personal Progress Record

The following is a sample of this Personal Progress Record to familiarize you with it. The entries on this sample are based on the example above.

PERSONAL PROGRESS RECORD—SAMPLE

NUMBER SERIES							
Initial Tests				Repeated Tests			
Date	Test	Number Completed	Number Correct (Your Score)	Date	Score	Date	Score
5/15	Diagnostic Practice Test	8	5				
5/16	Practice Test 1	15	11				
5/18	Practice Test 2	17	15				
5/20	Practice Test 3	20	19				
	Practice Test 4						
	Practice Test 5						
	Practice Test 6						

Now turn to page 440. Look at the table entitled "Personal Progress Record—Number Series." Make the proper entries on the line for the practice test you just took. This table will help you record your progress as you take additional practice tests.

Part D—Following Oral Directions

Computing Your Score

Check your answers against the Answer Key. Calculate your score by adding up the number of correct answers you have. You do *not* lose any credit for wrong answers or for questions you don't answer. For example, on a test having 30 questions, if you had 17 correct and 6 incorrect, and omitted 7, your score would be 17.

Guidelines

How good is the score you just made?

> 28 or higher . . . . Good
> Between 24 and 27 . . . . . . Fair
> Below 24 . . . . You need to improve.

Once you have mastered the techniques explained in this book (Chapter 8 covers Following Oral Directions), you should routinely score 28 to 30 correct.

Personal Progress Record

Now turn to page 440. In the table entitled "Personal Progress Record—Following Oral Directions," make the proper entries on the line for the practice test you just took. This table will help you record your progress as you take additional practice tests. A sample is printed below to familiarize you with it. The first entry is based on the preceding example.

PERSONAL PROGRESS RECORD—SAMPLE

FOLLOWING ORAL DIRECTIONS							
Initial Tests				Repeated Tests			
Date	Test	Number Completed	Number Correct (Your Score)	Date	Score	Date	Score
5/15	Diagnostic Practice Test	23	17				
5/16	Practice Test 1	23	19				
5/18	Practice Test 2	27	25				
5/20	Practice Test 3	29	28				
	Practice Test 4						
	Practice Test 5						
	Practice Test 6						

■ DIAGNOSTIC CHARTS

The following charts will help pinpoint your weaknesses by making it easy for you to determine what particular type of question in each part of the test is most difficult for you.

Part A—Address Checking

Type of Difference	"D" Questions	Number of "D" Questions Wrong		
		Trial 1	Trial 2	Trial 3
Numbers: transposed	1, 16, 17, 27, 33, 48, 60			
changed	5, 7, 22, 35, 69, 73, 89			
omitted				
Directions	3, 40, 71, 81, 91			
Abbreviations: streets, roads, avenues, etc.	8, 12, 45, 53, 61, 92 95			
states	10, 19, 29, 32, 54, 66			
Spelling: single letters	6, 11, 13, 28, 42, 47, 50 63			
groups of letters	34, 39, 58, 62, 77, 83, 88 93			
Total Number of All Types	48			
	Use the columns on the right to enter the question numbers of "A" items you marked "D."			

This chart will help you to pinpoint the kinds of errors you made on Practice Test 2. Use it as directed below after you have taken and marked the test.

The first column on the left, "Type of Difference," contains the categories whereby addresses may differ (see page 69). On the same line across, the second column gives the numbers of the questions that fall within each category. In the third column, you are to enter the numbers of any "A" questions you answered as "D." Do not include questions that you did not do. Checking the addresses you got wrong may reveal a problem on which you will want to work.

After you have made all the entries, you will be able to see the areas in which you need to improve. Then turn to the appropriate parts of Chapter 4: Address Checking—How to Improve Your Score, read them, and practice the drills that can help. For example, if you find you have been making too many errors picking out number differences, read page 94 and do Drills 18 through 21. If you have a problem with single letters because of reversals like *b* and *d*, or if you have been overlooking the differences between *a*, *e*, and *o*, read page 91. Examine the table and work on Drills 10 and 11 if the problem persists.

Remember that this chart is designed for diagnostic purposes and guidance on further practice. It has been drawn so that you can enter the results each time you retake a practice test. In this way you will be able to see how you are progressing. It is not necessary to record your scores here. That is best done by using the Personal Progress Record Card.

Part B—Memory for Addresses

Kind of Address		Number of Questions	Number Wrong		
			Trial 1	Trial 2	Trial 3
Direct:					
	List 1	43			
	List 2	41			
	List 3	42			
Numbered:					
	List 1	45			
	List 2	47			
	List 3	46			

The purpose of this chart is to help you evaluate your performance on the two kinds of memory questions that appear in these memory tests—the questions on the direct (name) addresses and the questions on the numbered addresses. Use the chart as directed below after you have taken and marked the entire test.

The first column on the left, "Kind of Address," is divided by category into "Direct Address" versus "Numbered Address." The second column gives the number of questions in each category on List 1, List 2, and List 3. Use the third column to enter the total number of questions in each category that you answered incorrectly. There is room for you to make additional entries if you take the practice test more than once.

At a glance, you will be able to see which area you need to concentrate on and how well you are progressing as you take repeat trials. Use Chapter 5 and the drills in it to improve your memory for the direct addresses. Use Chapter 6 for the numbered addresses.

Remember to use the Personal Progress Record Card (Memory for Addresses) on page 439 to keep track of your actual scores as you keep studying and practicing.

Part C—Number Series and Part D—Following Oral Directions

Because of the nature of the questions in these tests, Diagnostic Charts are not provided for them. If you find that you made many errors on these tests, study the techniques suggested in Chapters 7 and 8.

Answer Sheet—Practice Test 3

Part A—Address Checking

1 Ⓐⓓ	25 Ⓐⓓ	49 Ⓐⓓ	73 Ⓐⓓ
2 Ⓐⓓ	26 Ⓐⓓ	50 Ⓐⓓ	74 Ⓐⓓ
3 Ⓐⓓ	27 Ⓐⓓ	51 Ⓐⓓ	75 Ⓐⓓ
4 Ⓐⓓ	28 Ⓐⓓ	52 Ⓐⓓ	76 Ⓐⓓ
5 Ⓐⓓ	29 Ⓐⓓ	53 Ⓐⓓ	77 Ⓐⓓ
6 Ⓐⓓ	30 Ⓐⓓ	54 Ⓐⓓ	78 Ⓐⓓ
7 Ⓐⓓ	31 Ⓐⓓ	55 Ⓐⓓ	79 Ⓐⓓ
8 Ⓐⓓ	32 Ⓐⓓ	56 Ⓐⓓ	80 Ⓐⓓ
9 Ⓐⓓ	33 Ⓐⓓ	57 Ⓐⓓ	81 Ⓐⓓ
10 Ⓐⓓ	34 Ⓐⓓ	58 Ⓐⓓ	82 Ⓐⓓ
11 Ⓐⓓ	35 Ⓐⓓ	59 Ⓐⓓ	83 Ⓐⓓ
12 Ⓐⓓ	36 Ⓐⓓ	60 Ⓐⓓ	84 Ⓐⓓ
13 Ⓐⓓ	37 Ⓐⓓ	61 Ⓐⓓ	85 Ⓐⓓ
14 Ⓐⓓ	38 Ⓐⓓ	62 Ⓐⓓ	86 Ⓐⓓ
15 Ⓐⓓ	39 Ⓐⓓ	63 Ⓐⓓ	87 Ⓐⓓ
16 Ⓐⓓ	40 Ⓐⓓ	64 Ⓐⓓ	88 Ⓐⓓ
17 Ⓐⓓ	41 Ⓐⓓ	65 Ⓐⓓ	89 Ⓐⓓ
18 Ⓐⓓ	42 Ⓐⓓ	66 Ⓐⓓ	90 Ⓐⓓ
19 Ⓐⓓ	43 Ⓐⓓ	67 Ⓐⓓ	91 Ⓐⓓ
20 Ⓐⓓ	44 Ⓐⓓ	68 Ⓐⓓ	92 Ⓐⓓ
21 Ⓐⓓ	45 Ⓐⓓ	69 Ⓐⓓ	93 Ⓐⓓ
22 Ⓐⓓ	46 Ⓐⓓ	70 Ⓐⓓ	94 Ⓐⓓ
23 Ⓐⓓ	47 Ⓐⓓ	71 Ⓐⓓ	95 Ⓐⓓ
24 Ⓐⓓ	48 Ⓐⓓ	72 Ⓐⓓ	

Remove by cutting on dotted line.

Part B—Memory for Addresses—List 1

1 Ⓐ Ⓑ Ⓒ Ⓓ Ⓔ	19 Ⓐ Ⓑ Ⓒ Ⓓ Ⓔ	37 Ⓐ Ⓑ Ⓒ Ⓓ Ⓔ	55 Ⓐ Ⓑ Ⓒ Ⓓ Ⓔ	73 Ⓐ Ⓑ Ⓒ Ⓓ Ⓔ
2 Ⓐ Ⓑ Ⓒ Ⓓ Ⓔ	20 Ⓐ Ⓑ Ⓒ Ⓓ Ⓔ	38 Ⓐ Ⓑ Ⓒ Ⓓ Ⓔ	56 Ⓐ Ⓑ Ⓒ Ⓓ Ⓔ	74 Ⓐ Ⓑ Ⓒ Ⓓ Ⓔ
3 Ⓐ Ⓑ Ⓒ Ⓓ Ⓔ	21 Ⓐ Ⓑ Ⓒ Ⓓ Ⓔ	39 Ⓐ Ⓑ Ⓒ Ⓓ Ⓔ	57 Ⓐ Ⓑ Ⓒ Ⓓ Ⓔ	75 Ⓐ Ⓑ Ⓒ Ⓓ Ⓔ
4 Ⓐ Ⓑ Ⓒ Ⓓ Ⓔ	22 Ⓐ Ⓑ Ⓒ Ⓓ Ⓔ	40 Ⓐ Ⓑ Ⓒ Ⓓ Ⓔ	58 Ⓐ Ⓑ Ⓒ Ⓓ Ⓔ	76 Ⓐ Ⓑ Ⓒ Ⓓ Ⓔ
5 Ⓐ Ⓑ Ⓒ Ⓓ Ⓔ	23 Ⓐ Ⓑ Ⓒ Ⓓ Ⓔ	41 Ⓐ Ⓑ Ⓒ Ⓓ Ⓔ	59 Ⓐ Ⓑ Ⓒ Ⓓ Ⓔ	77 Ⓐ Ⓑ Ⓒ Ⓓ Ⓔ
6 Ⓐ Ⓑ Ⓒ Ⓓ Ⓔ	24 Ⓐ Ⓑ Ⓒ Ⓓ Ⓔ	42 Ⓐ Ⓑ Ⓒ Ⓓ Ⓔ	60 Ⓐ Ⓑ Ⓒ Ⓓ Ⓔ	78 Ⓐ Ⓑ Ⓒ Ⓓ Ⓔ
7 Ⓐ Ⓑ Ⓒ Ⓓ Ⓔ	25 Ⓐ Ⓑ Ⓒ Ⓓ Ⓔ	43 Ⓐ Ⓑ Ⓒ Ⓓ Ⓔ	61 Ⓐ Ⓑ Ⓒ Ⓓ Ⓔ	79 Ⓐ Ⓑ Ⓒ Ⓓ Ⓔ
8 Ⓐ Ⓑ Ⓒ Ⓓ Ⓔ	26 Ⓐ Ⓑ Ⓒ Ⓓ Ⓔ	44 Ⓐ Ⓑ Ⓒ Ⓓ Ⓔ	62 Ⓐ Ⓑ Ⓒ Ⓓ Ⓔ	80 Ⓐ Ⓑ Ⓒ Ⓓ Ⓔ
9 Ⓐ Ⓑ Ⓒ Ⓓ Ⓔ	27 Ⓐ Ⓑ Ⓒ Ⓓ Ⓔ	45 Ⓐ Ⓑ Ⓒ Ⓓ Ⓔ	63 Ⓐ Ⓑ Ⓒ Ⓓ Ⓔ	81 Ⓐ Ⓑ Ⓒ Ⓓ Ⓔ
10 Ⓐ Ⓑ Ⓒ Ⓓ Ⓔ	28 Ⓐ Ⓑ Ⓒ Ⓓ Ⓔ	46 Ⓐ Ⓑ Ⓒ Ⓓ Ⓔ	64 Ⓐ Ⓑ Ⓒ Ⓓ Ⓔ	82 Ⓐ Ⓑ Ⓒ Ⓓ Ⓔ
11 Ⓐ Ⓑ Ⓒ Ⓓ Ⓔ	29 Ⓐ Ⓑ Ⓒ Ⓓ Ⓔ	47 Ⓐ Ⓑ Ⓒ Ⓓ Ⓔ	65 Ⓐ Ⓑ Ⓒ Ⓓ Ⓔ	83 Ⓐ Ⓑ Ⓒ Ⓓ Ⓔ
12 Ⓐ Ⓑ Ⓒ Ⓓ Ⓔ	30 Ⓐ Ⓑ Ⓒ Ⓓ Ⓔ	48 Ⓐ Ⓑ Ⓒ Ⓓ Ⓔ	66 Ⓐ Ⓑ Ⓒ Ⓓ Ⓔ	84 Ⓐ Ⓑ Ⓒ Ⓓ Ⓔ
13 Ⓐ Ⓑ Ⓒ Ⓓ Ⓔ	31 Ⓐ Ⓑ Ⓒ Ⓓ Ⓔ	49 Ⓐ Ⓑ Ⓒ Ⓓ Ⓔ	67 Ⓐ Ⓑ Ⓒ Ⓓ Ⓔ	85 Ⓐ Ⓑ Ⓒ Ⓓ Ⓔ
14 Ⓐ Ⓑ Ⓒ Ⓓ Ⓔ	32 Ⓐ Ⓑ Ⓒ Ⓓ Ⓔ	50 Ⓐ Ⓑ Ⓒ Ⓓ Ⓔ	68 Ⓐ Ⓑ Ⓒ Ⓓ Ⓔ	86 Ⓐ Ⓑ Ⓒ Ⓓ Ⓔ
15 Ⓐ Ⓑ Ⓒ Ⓓ Ⓔ	33 Ⓐ Ⓑ Ⓒ Ⓓ Ⓔ	51 Ⓐ Ⓑ Ⓒ Ⓓ Ⓔ	69 Ⓐ Ⓑ Ⓒ Ⓓ Ⓔ	87 Ⓐ Ⓑ Ⓒ Ⓓ Ⓔ
16 Ⓐ Ⓑ Ⓒ Ⓓ Ⓔ	34 Ⓐ Ⓑ Ⓒ Ⓓ Ⓔ	52 Ⓐ Ⓑ Ⓒ Ⓓ Ⓔ	70 Ⓐ Ⓑ Ⓒ Ⓓ Ⓔ	88 Ⓐ Ⓑ Ⓒ Ⓓ Ⓔ
17 Ⓐ Ⓑ Ⓒ Ⓓ Ⓔ	35 Ⓐ Ⓑ Ⓒ Ⓓ Ⓔ	53 Ⓐ Ⓑ Ⓒ Ⓓ Ⓔ	71 Ⓐ Ⓑ Ⓒ Ⓓ Ⓔ	
18 Ⓐ Ⓑ Ⓒ Ⓓ Ⓔ	36 Ⓐ Ⓑ Ⓒ Ⓓ Ⓔ	54 Ⓐ Ⓑ Ⓒ Ⓓ Ⓔ	72 Ⓐ Ⓑ Ⓒ Ⓓ Ⓔ	

Part B—Memory for Addresses—List 2

1 Ⓐ Ⓑ Ⓒ Ⓓ Ⓔ	19 Ⓐ Ⓑ Ⓒ Ⓓ Ⓔ	37 Ⓐ Ⓑ Ⓒ Ⓓ Ⓔ	55 Ⓐ Ⓑ Ⓒ Ⓓ Ⓔ	73 Ⓐ Ⓑ Ⓒ Ⓓ Ⓔ
2 Ⓐ Ⓑ Ⓒ Ⓓ Ⓔ	20 Ⓐ Ⓑ Ⓒ Ⓓ Ⓔ	38 Ⓐ Ⓑ Ⓒ Ⓓ Ⓔ	56 Ⓐ Ⓑ Ⓒ Ⓓ Ⓔ	74 Ⓐ Ⓑ Ⓒ Ⓓ Ⓔ
3 Ⓐ Ⓑ Ⓒ Ⓓ Ⓔ	21 Ⓐ Ⓑ Ⓒ Ⓓ Ⓔ	39 Ⓐ Ⓑ Ⓒ Ⓓ Ⓔ	57 Ⓐ Ⓑ Ⓒ Ⓓ Ⓔ	75 Ⓐ Ⓑ Ⓒ Ⓓ Ⓔ
4 Ⓐ Ⓑ Ⓒ Ⓓ Ⓔ	22 Ⓐ Ⓑ Ⓒ Ⓓ Ⓔ	40 Ⓐ Ⓑ Ⓒ Ⓓ Ⓔ	58 Ⓐ Ⓑ Ⓒ Ⓓ Ⓔ	76 Ⓐ Ⓑ Ⓒ Ⓓ Ⓔ
5 Ⓐ Ⓑ Ⓒ Ⓓ Ⓔ	23 Ⓐ Ⓑ Ⓒ Ⓓ Ⓔ	41 Ⓐ Ⓑ Ⓒ Ⓓ Ⓔ	59 Ⓐ Ⓑ Ⓒ Ⓓ Ⓔ	77 Ⓐ Ⓑ Ⓒ Ⓓ Ⓔ
6 Ⓐ Ⓑ Ⓒ Ⓓ Ⓔ	24 Ⓐ Ⓑ Ⓒ Ⓓ Ⓔ	42 Ⓐ Ⓑ Ⓒ Ⓓ Ⓔ	60 Ⓐ Ⓑ Ⓒ Ⓓ Ⓔ	78 Ⓐ Ⓑ Ⓒ Ⓓ Ⓔ
7 Ⓐ Ⓑ Ⓒ Ⓓ Ⓔ	25 Ⓐ Ⓑ Ⓒ Ⓓ Ⓔ	43 Ⓐ Ⓑ Ⓒ Ⓓ Ⓔ	61 Ⓐ Ⓑ Ⓒ Ⓓ Ⓔ	79 Ⓐ Ⓑ Ⓒ Ⓓ Ⓔ
8 Ⓐ Ⓑ Ⓒ Ⓓ Ⓔ	26 Ⓐ Ⓑ Ⓒ Ⓓ Ⓔ	44 Ⓐ Ⓑ Ⓒ Ⓓ Ⓔ	62 Ⓐ Ⓑ Ⓒ Ⓓ Ⓔ	80 Ⓐ Ⓑ Ⓒ Ⓓ Ⓔ
9 Ⓐ Ⓑ Ⓒ Ⓓ Ⓔ	27 Ⓐ Ⓑ Ⓒ Ⓓ Ⓔ	45 Ⓐ Ⓑ Ⓒ Ⓓ Ⓔ	63 Ⓐ Ⓑ Ⓒ Ⓓ Ⓔ	81 Ⓐ Ⓑ Ⓒ Ⓓ Ⓔ
10 Ⓐ Ⓑ Ⓒ Ⓓ Ⓔ	28 Ⓐ Ⓑ Ⓒ Ⓓ Ⓔ	46 Ⓐ Ⓑ Ⓒ Ⓓ Ⓔ	64 Ⓐ Ⓑ Ⓒ Ⓓ Ⓔ	82 Ⓐ Ⓑ Ⓒ Ⓓ Ⓔ
11 Ⓐ Ⓑ Ⓒ Ⓓ Ⓔ	29 Ⓐ Ⓑ Ⓒ Ⓓ Ⓔ	47 Ⓐ Ⓑ Ⓒ Ⓓ Ⓔ	65 Ⓐ Ⓑ Ⓒ Ⓓ Ⓔ	83 Ⓐ Ⓑ Ⓒ Ⓓ Ⓔ
12 Ⓐ Ⓑ Ⓒ Ⓓ Ⓔ	30 Ⓐ Ⓑ Ⓒ Ⓓ Ⓔ	48 Ⓐ Ⓑ Ⓒ Ⓓ Ⓔ	66 Ⓐ Ⓑ Ⓒ Ⓓ Ⓔ	84 Ⓐ Ⓑ Ⓒ Ⓓ Ⓔ
13 Ⓐ Ⓑ Ⓒ Ⓓ Ⓔ	31 Ⓐ Ⓑ Ⓒ Ⓓ Ⓔ	49 Ⓐ Ⓑ Ⓒ Ⓓ Ⓔ	67 Ⓐ Ⓑ Ⓒ Ⓓ Ⓔ	85 Ⓐ Ⓑ Ⓒ Ⓓ Ⓔ
14 Ⓐ Ⓑ Ⓒ Ⓓ Ⓔ	32 Ⓐ Ⓑ Ⓒ Ⓓ Ⓔ	50 Ⓐ Ⓑ Ⓒ Ⓓ Ⓔ	68 Ⓐ Ⓑ Ⓒ Ⓓ Ⓔ	86 Ⓐ Ⓑ Ⓒ Ⓓ Ⓔ
15 Ⓐ Ⓑ Ⓒ Ⓓ Ⓔ	33 Ⓐ Ⓑ Ⓒ Ⓓ Ⓔ	51 Ⓐ Ⓑ Ⓒ Ⓓ Ⓔ	69 Ⓐ Ⓑ Ⓒ Ⓓ Ⓔ	87 Ⓐ Ⓑ Ⓒ Ⓓ Ⓔ
16 Ⓐ Ⓑ Ⓒ Ⓓ Ⓔ	34 Ⓐ Ⓑ Ⓒ Ⓓ Ⓔ	52 Ⓐ Ⓑ Ⓒ Ⓓ Ⓔ	70 Ⓐ Ⓑ Ⓒ Ⓓ Ⓔ	88 Ⓐ Ⓑ Ⓒ Ⓓ Ⓔ
17 Ⓐ Ⓑ Ⓒ Ⓓ Ⓔ	35 Ⓐ Ⓑ Ⓒ Ⓓ Ⓔ	53 Ⓐ Ⓑ Ⓒ Ⓓ Ⓔ	71 Ⓐ Ⓑ Ⓒ Ⓓ Ⓔ	
18 Ⓐ Ⓑ Ⓒ Ⓓ Ⓔ	36 Ⓐ Ⓑ Ⓒ Ⓓ Ⓔ	54 Ⓐ Ⓑ Ⓒ Ⓓ Ⓔ	72 Ⓐ Ⓑ Ⓒ Ⓓ Ⓔ	

Remove by cutting on dotted line.

Part B—Memory for Addresses—List 3

1 Ⓐ Ⓑ Ⓒ Ⓓ Ⓔ	19 Ⓐ Ⓑ Ⓒ Ⓓ Ⓔ	37 Ⓐ Ⓑ Ⓒ Ⓓ Ⓔ	55 Ⓐ Ⓑ Ⓒ Ⓓ Ⓔ	73 Ⓐ Ⓑ Ⓒ Ⓓ Ⓔ
2 Ⓐ Ⓑ Ⓒ Ⓓ Ⓔ	20 Ⓐ Ⓑ Ⓒ Ⓓ Ⓔ	38 Ⓐ Ⓑ Ⓒ Ⓓ Ⓔ	56 Ⓐ Ⓑ Ⓒ Ⓓ Ⓔ	74 Ⓐ Ⓑ Ⓒ Ⓓ Ⓔ
3 Ⓐ Ⓑ Ⓒ Ⓓ Ⓔ	21 Ⓐ Ⓑ Ⓒ Ⓓ Ⓔ	39 Ⓐ Ⓑ Ⓒ Ⓓ Ⓔ	57 Ⓐ Ⓑ Ⓒ Ⓓ Ⓔ	75 Ⓐ Ⓑ Ⓒ Ⓓ Ⓔ
4 Ⓐ Ⓑ Ⓒ Ⓓ Ⓔ	22 Ⓐ Ⓑ Ⓒ Ⓓ Ⓔ	40 Ⓐ Ⓑ Ⓒ Ⓓ Ⓔ	58 Ⓐ Ⓑ Ⓒ Ⓓ Ⓔ	76 Ⓐ Ⓑ Ⓒ Ⓓ Ⓔ
5 Ⓐ Ⓑ Ⓒ Ⓓ Ⓔ	23 Ⓐ Ⓑ Ⓒ Ⓓ Ⓔ	41 Ⓐ Ⓑ Ⓒ Ⓓ Ⓔ	59 Ⓐ Ⓑ Ⓒ Ⓓ Ⓔ	77 Ⓐ Ⓑ Ⓒ Ⓓ Ⓔ
6 Ⓐ Ⓑ Ⓒ Ⓓ Ⓔ	24 Ⓐ Ⓑ Ⓒ Ⓓ Ⓔ	42 Ⓐ Ⓑ Ⓒ Ⓓ Ⓔ	60 Ⓐ Ⓑ Ⓒ Ⓓ Ⓔ	78 Ⓐ Ⓑ Ⓒ Ⓓ Ⓔ
7 Ⓐ Ⓑ Ⓒ Ⓓ Ⓔ	25 Ⓐ Ⓑ Ⓒ Ⓓ Ⓔ	43 Ⓐ Ⓑ Ⓒ Ⓓ Ⓔ	61 Ⓐ Ⓑ Ⓒ Ⓓ Ⓔ	79 Ⓐ Ⓑ Ⓒ Ⓓ Ⓔ
8 Ⓐ Ⓑ Ⓒ Ⓓ Ⓔ	26 Ⓐ Ⓑ Ⓒ Ⓓ Ⓔ	44 Ⓐ Ⓑ Ⓒ Ⓓ Ⓔ	62 Ⓐ Ⓑ Ⓒ Ⓓ Ⓔ	80 Ⓐ Ⓑ Ⓒ Ⓓ Ⓔ
9 Ⓐ Ⓑ Ⓒ Ⓓ Ⓔ	27 Ⓐ Ⓑ Ⓒ Ⓓ Ⓔ	45 Ⓐ Ⓑ Ⓒ Ⓓ Ⓔ	63 Ⓐ Ⓑ Ⓒ Ⓓ Ⓔ	81 Ⓐ Ⓑ Ⓒ Ⓓ Ⓔ
10 Ⓐ Ⓑ Ⓒ Ⓓ Ⓔ	28 Ⓐ Ⓑ Ⓒ Ⓓ Ⓔ	46 Ⓐ Ⓑ Ⓒ Ⓓ Ⓔ	64 Ⓐ Ⓑ Ⓒ Ⓓ Ⓔ	82 Ⓐ Ⓑ Ⓒ Ⓓ Ⓔ
11 Ⓐ Ⓑ Ⓒ Ⓓ Ⓔ	29 Ⓐ Ⓑ Ⓒ Ⓓ Ⓔ	47 Ⓐ Ⓑ Ⓒ Ⓓ Ⓔ	65 Ⓐ Ⓑ Ⓒ Ⓓ Ⓔ	83 Ⓐ Ⓑ Ⓒ Ⓓ Ⓔ
12 Ⓐ Ⓑ Ⓒ Ⓓ Ⓔ	30 Ⓐ Ⓑ Ⓒ Ⓓ Ⓔ	48 Ⓐ Ⓑ Ⓒ Ⓓ Ⓔ	66 Ⓐ Ⓑ Ⓒ Ⓓ Ⓔ	84 Ⓐ Ⓑ Ⓒ Ⓓ Ⓔ
13 Ⓐ Ⓑ Ⓒ Ⓓ Ⓔ	31 Ⓐ Ⓑ Ⓒ Ⓓ Ⓔ	49 Ⓐ Ⓑ Ⓒ Ⓓ Ⓔ	67 Ⓐ Ⓑ Ⓒ Ⓓ Ⓔ	85 Ⓐ Ⓑ Ⓒ Ⓓ Ⓔ
14 Ⓐ Ⓑ Ⓒ Ⓓ Ⓔ	32 Ⓐ Ⓑ Ⓒ Ⓓ Ⓔ	50 Ⓐ Ⓑ Ⓒ Ⓓ Ⓔ	68 Ⓐ Ⓑ Ⓒ Ⓓ Ⓔ	86 Ⓐ Ⓑ Ⓒ Ⓓ Ⓔ
15 Ⓐ Ⓑ Ⓒ Ⓓ Ⓔ	33 Ⓐ Ⓑ Ⓒ Ⓓ Ⓔ	51 Ⓐ Ⓑ Ⓒ Ⓓ Ⓔ	69 Ⓐ Ⓑ Ⓒ Ⓓ Ⓔ	87 Ⓐ Ⓑ Ⓒ Ⓓ Ⓔ
16 Ⓐ Ⓑ Ⓒ Ⓓ Ⓔ	34 Ⓐ Ⓑ Ⓒ Ⓓ Ⓔ	52 Ⓐ Ⓑ Ⓒ Ⓓ Ⓔ	70 Ⓐ Ⓑ Ⓒ Ⓓ Ⓔ	88 Ⓐ Ⓑ Ⓒ Ⓓ Ⓔ
17 Ⓐ Ⓑ Ⓒ Ⓓ Ⓔ	35 Ⓐ Ⓑ Ⓒ Ⓓ Ⓔ	53 Ⓐ Ⓑ Ⓒ Ⓓ Ⓔ	71 Ⓐ Ⓑ Ⓒ Ⓓ Ⓔ	
18 Ⓐ Ⓑ Ⓒ Ⓓ Ⓔ	36 Ⓐ Ⓑ Ⓒ Ⓓ Ⓔ	54 Ⓐ Ⓑ Ⓒ Ⓓ Ⓔ	72 Ⓐ Ⓑ Ⓒ Ⓓ Ⓔ	

Part C—Number Series

1 Ⓐ Ⓑ Ⓒ Ⓓ Ⓔ	6 Ⓐ Ⓑ Ⓒ Ⓓ Ⓔ	11 Ⓐ Ⓑ Ⓒ Ⓓ Ⓔ	16 Ⓐ Ⓑ Ⓒ Ⓓ Ⓔ	21 Ⓐ Ⓑ Ⓒ Ⓓ Ⓔ
2 Ⓐ Ⓑ Ⓒ Ⓓ Ⓔ	7 Ⓐ Ⓑ Ⓒ Ⓓ Ⓔ	12 Ⓐ Ⓑ Ⓒ Ⓓ Ⓔ	17 Ⓐ Ⓑ Ⓒ Ⓓ Ⓔ	22 Ⓐ Ⓑ Ⓒ Ⓓ Ⓔ
3 Ⓐ Ⓑ Ⓒ Ⓓ Ⓔ	8 Ⓐ Ⓑ Ⓒ Ⓓ Ⓔ	13 Ⓐ Ⓑ Ⓒ Ⓓ Ⓔ	18 Ⓐ Ⓑ Ⓒ Ⓓ Ⓔ	23 Ⓐ Ⓑ Ⓒ Ⓓ Ⓔ
4 Ⓐ Ⓑ Ⓒ Ⓓ Ⓔ	9 Ⓐ Ⓑ Ⓒ Ⓓ Ⓔ	14 Ⓐ Ⓑ Ⓒ Ⓓ Ⓔ	19 Ⓐ Ⓑ Ⓒ Ⓓ Ⓔ	24 Ⓐ Ⓑ Ⓒ Ⓓ Ⓔ
5 Ⓐ Ⓑ Ⓒ Ⓓ Ⓔ	10 Ⓐ Ⓑ Ⓒ Ⓓ Ⓔ	15 Ⓐ Ⓑ Ⓒ Ⓓ Ⓔ	20 Ⓐ Ⓑ Ⓒ Ⓓ Ⓔ	

Part D—Following Oral Directions

1 Ⓐ Ⓑ Ⓒ Ⓓ Ⓔ	19 Ⓐ Ⓑ Ⓒ Ⓓ Ⓔ	37 Ⓐ Ⓑ Ⓒ Ⓓ Ⓔ	55 Ⓐ Ⓑ Ⓒ Ⓓ Ⓔ	73 Ⓐ Ⓑ Ⓒ Ⓓ Ⓔ
2 Ⓐ Ⓑ Ⓒ Ⓓ Ⓔ	20 Ⓐ Ⓑ Ⓒ Ⓓ Ⓔ	38 Ⓐ Ⓑ Ⓒ Ⓓ Ⓔ	56 Ⓐ Ⓑ Ⓒ Ⓓ Ⓔ	74 Ⓐ Ⓑ Ⓒ Ⓓ Ⓔ
3 Ⓐ Ⓑ Ⓒ Ⓓ Ⓔ	21 Ⓐ Ⓑ Ⓒ Ⓓ Ⓔ	39 Ⓐ Ⓑ Ⓒ Ⓓ Ⓔ	57 Ⓐ Ⓑ Ⓒ Ⓓ Ⓔ	75 Ⓐ Ⓑ Ⓒ Ⓓ Ⓔ
4 Ⓐ Ⓑ Ⓒ Ⓓ Ⓔ	22 Ⓐ Ⓑ Ⓒ Ⓓ Ⓔ	40 Ⓐ Ⓑ Ⓒ Ⓓ Ⓔ	58 Ⓐ Ⓑ Ⓒ Ⓓ Ⓔ	76 Ⓐ Ⓑ Ⓒ Ⓓ Ⓔ
5 Ⓐ Ⓑ Ⓒ Ⓓ Ⓔ	23 Ⓐ Ⓑ Ⓒ Ⓓ Ⓔ	41 Ⓐ Ⓑ Ⓒ Ⓓ Ⓔ	59 Ⓐ Ⓑ Ⓒ Ⓓ Ⓔ	77 Ⓐ Ⓑ Ⓒ Ⓓ Ⓔ
6 Ⓐ Ⓑ Ⓒ Ⓓ Ⓔ	24 Ⓐ Ⓑ Ⓒ Ⓓ Ⓔ	42 Ⓐ Ⓑ Ⓒ Ⓓ Ⓔ	60 Ⓐ Ⓑ Ⓒ Ⓓ Ⓔ	78 Ⓐ Ⓑ Ⓒ Ⓓ Ⓔ
7 Ⓐ Ⓑ Ⓒ Ⓓ Ⓔ	25 Ⓐ Ⓑ Ⓒ Ⓓ Ⓔ	43 Ⓐ Ⓑ Ⓒ Ⓓ Ⓔ	61 Ⓐ Ⓑ Ⓒ Ⓓ Ⓔ	79 Ⓐ Ⓑ Ⓒ Ⓓ Ⓔ
8 Ⓐ Ⓑ Ⓒ Ⓓ Ⓔ	26 Ⓐ Ⓑ Ⓒ Ⓓ Ⓔ	44 Ⓐ Ⓑ Ⓒ Ⓓ Ⓔ	62 Ⓐ Ⓑ Ⓒ Ⓓ Ⓔ	80 Ⓐ Ⓑ Ⓒ Ⓓ Ⓔ
9 Ⓐ Ⓑ Ⓒ Ⓓ Ⓔ	27 Ⓐ Ⓑ Ⓒ Ⓓ Ⓔ	45 Ⓐ Ⓑ Ⓒ Ⓓ Ⓔ	63 Ⓐ Ⓑ Ⓒ Ⓓ Ⓔ	81 Ⓐ Ⓑ Ⓒ Ⓓ Ⓔ
10 Ⓐ Ⓑ Ⓒ Ⓓ Ⓔ	28 Ⓐ Ⓑ Ⓒ Ⓓ Ⓔ	46 Ⓐ Ⓑ Ⓒ Ⓓ Ⓔ	64 Ⓐ Ⓑ Ⓒ Ⓓ Ⓔ	82 Ⓐ Ⓑ Ⓒ Ⓓ Ⓔ
11 Ⓐ Ⓑ Ⓒ Ⓓ Ⓔ	29 Ⓐ Ⓑ Ⓒ Ⓓ Ⓔ	47 Ⓐ Ⓑ Ⓒ Ⓓ Ⓔ	65 Ⓐ Ⓑ Ⓒ Ⓓ Ⓔ	83 Ⓐ Ⓑ Ⓒ Ⓓ Ⓔ
12 Ⓐ Ⓑ Ⓒ Ⓓ Ⓔ	30 Ⓐ Ⓑ Ⓒ Ⓓ Ⓔ	48 Ⓐ Ⓑ Ⓒ Ⓓ Ⓔ	66 Ⓐ Ⓑ Ⓒ Ⓓ Ⓔ	84 Ⓐ Ⓑ Ⓒ Ⓓ Ⓔ
13 Ⓐ Ⓑ Ⓒ Ⓓ Ⓔ	31 Ⓐ Ⓑ Ⓒ Ⓓ Ⓔ	49 Ⓐ Ⓑ Ⓒ Ⓓ Ⓔ	67 Ⓐ Ⓑ Ⓒ Ⓓ Ⓔ	85 Ⓐ Ⓑ Ⓒ Ⓓ Ⓔ
14 Ⓐ Ⓑ Ⓒ Ⓓ Ⓔ	32 Ⓐ Ⓑ Ⓒ Ⓓ Ⓔ	50 Ⓐ Ⓑ Ⓒ Ⓓ Ⓔ	68 Ⓐ Ⓑ Ⓒ Ⓓ Ⓔ	86 Ⓐ Ⓑ Ⓒ Ⓓ Ⓔ
15 Ⓐ Ⓑ Ⓒ Ⓓ Ⓔ	33 Ⓐ Ⓑ Ⓒ Ⓓ Ⓔ	51 Ⓐ Ⓑ Ⓒ Ⓓ Ⓔ	69 Ⓐ Ⓑ Ⓒ Ⓓ Ⓔ	87 Ⓐ Ⓑ Ⓒ Ⓓ Ⓔ
16 Ⓐ Ⓑ Ⓒ Ⓓ Ⓔ	34 Ⓐ Ⓑ Ⓒ Ⓓ Ⓔ	52 Ⓐ Ⓑ Ⓒ Ⓓ Ⓔ	70 Ⓐ Ⓑ Ⓒ Ⓓ Ⓔ	88 Ⓐ Ⓑ Ⓒ Ⓓ Ⓔ
17 Ⓐ Ⓑ Ⓒ Ⓓ Ⓔ	35 Ⓐ Ⓑ Ⓒ Ⓓ Ⓔ	53 Ⓐ Ⓑ Ⓒ Ⓓ Ⓔ	71 Ⓐ Ⓑ Ⓒ Ⓓ Ⓔ	
18 Ⓐ Ⓑ Ⓒ Ⓓ Ⓔ	36 Ⓐ Ⓑ Ⓒ Ⓓ Ⓔ	54 Ⓐ Ⓑ Ⓒ Ⓓ Ⓔ	72 Ⓐ Ⓑ Ⓒ Ⓓ Ⓔ	

Practice Test 3

■ THE LAST WORD

You now know that score improvements are possible and that the means to attain them lie in your hands. The study techniques for all four parts of the test are yours. You know they work. You have completed drills and practice tests to sharpen your skills. You have also completed special drills and practice tests to help correct any areas of weakness, such as narrow eye span, regression, and perception problems. The strategies to use to make the most of your technique and skill have been prepared for you.

Also, by now you should be on your way to answering the test-taking questions posed in this book that are strictly personal:

- How fast should you go on the Address Checking questions to strike the balance between speed and accuracy that will yield the highest score?

- How should you divide your study time between the names and numbers on the Memory for Addresses questions?

- What method or combination of methods should you use to memorize the addresses in the boxes?

- How many addresses is it realistic for you to try to remember? Should you go for all 25, or are you better off concentrating on 16, 18, or 20?

As was noted before, it is important to come to the real test with your mind made up on these points.

There are four more full-scale practice tests to help you continue your exam preparation program. You may take them each more than once if you choose. Don't forget to make copies of the three blank Answer Sheets preceding each test chapter before you take the test itself. Remember that the keys to skills improvement are knowledge and practice. Use the tests in this book to forge ahead. There is a good Postal Service job waiting.

Practice Test 3

Part A — ADDRESS CHECKING

Work — 6 minutes

In this part of the test, you are to decide whether two addresses are alike or different. If the two addresses are *exactly alike in every way*, darken space Ⓐ. If they are *different in any way*, darken space Ⓓ.

Mark your answers on the Answer Sheet on page 299. Tear it out, put today's date on it, and place it next to the questions.

Allow yourself *exactly 6 minutes* to do as many of the 95 questions as you can. If you finish before the time is up, check your answers.

1.	Riverside CA	Riverside CO
2.	9006 Gage Center Cir	9060 Cage Center Cir
3.	3403 Lakeside Rd NW	3403 Lakeside Rd NW
4.	1734 E Alexandrine St	1734 E Alexandrine St
5.	2607 Maple Rd SE	2607 Mable Rd SE
6.	2323 18th St NE	2323 13th St NE
7.	7074 North Western Pky	7047 North Western Pky
8.	970 Harvard Sq	970 Harvard Ct
9.	6980 Montwood Ln	6890 Montwood Ln
10.	Sunflower MS 38778	Sunflower MS 38778
11.	515 Edmar Rd	515 Admar Rd
12.	3727 Imperial Woods Dr SW	3727 Imperial Woods Rd SW
13.	941 Rolf Ave	941 Rolf Ct
14.	3905 Renate Rd	3905 Renate Rd
15.	4600 Oak Lawn Rd	4600 Oak Lawn Rd
16.	Portland ME 04108	Portland ME 04018
17.	8612 Old Shepherdsville Rd	8612 Old Shepherdsville Rd
18.	95 Prentice St E	95 Prentice St E
19.	7432 Caffin Ave S	7432 Coffin Ave S
20.	2002 Grand Bayou Ln	2002 Grand Bayou Ln
21.	3715 Adams St SE	3715 Adams St NE
22.	6963 Fullerdale Ave	6963 Fullerdale Ave
23.	5837 White Oak Dr	5837 White Oak Dr
24.	10289 Hammond St	10289 Hammond St

25. Whitesboro OK   Whitesboro OH
26. 4883 Bloomsbury St   4883 Bloomsburg St
27. Wichita KS 67203   Wichita KS 67203
28. 57 Sheila Dr   57 Skeila Dr
29. 8409 Deckbar Ave NE   8409 Deckrab Ave NE
30. 4942 Woodward Hts E   4924 Woodward Hts E
31. 209 Valley Fair Way   209 Varley Fair Way
32. 7314 Edgewood Dr NE   7314 Edgeworth Dr NE
33. 3506 N Claireview St   3506 N Claireville St
34. Rushsylvania OH 43347   Rushsylvania OH 43847
35. 8023 Sea Cove Rd   8023 Sea Cove Rd
36. 948 Washington St SE   948 Washington St SE

37. 42 Maplebrook Pky N   42 Maplebrook Pky N
38. Saint Paul MN 55113   Saint Paul NM 55113
39. 5675 Zircon St   5765 Zircon St
40. 5998 Lakecrest Path N   5998 Lakecrest Path N
41. 8264 Queen Ct   8264 Queen St
42. 1412 Ingleside Ave SW   1412 Ingleside Ave SW
43. 7409 Parkdale Dr   7409 Parkdale Dr
44. 565 Zender Ln   565 Zender Ln
45. 3662 Westview St   3662 Westwood St
46. Baton Rouge LA 70807   Baton Rouge LA 70870
47. 2794 Beacon Hill Rd   2794 Beacon Hill Rd
48. 98 Wainwright Cir E   98 Wainwright Cir W

49. 5999 Nevada Ave N   5999 Nevada Ave N
50. Marquette NE   Marquette NH
51. 2401 Knollwood Dr NE   2401 Knollwood Dr NE
52. 174 W Lee St   174 W Lee Dr
53. 3019 Wentworth Dr   3109 Wentworth Dr
54. Louisville KY 40504   Louisville KY 40504
55. 3039 Kearney Rd W   3039 Kearney Rd W
56. 9038 N Kossuth St   9038 E Kossuth St
57. Forestdale PA   Forestdale PA
58. Champaign IL   Champaign IN
59. 4417 Daniels Ave   4417 Daniels Ave
60. 15299 Highway K4 SW   15299 Highway P4 SW

61.	Litchfield Ct	Litchfield Ct
62.	7610 Russell St	7610 Russett St
63.	8768 E Ormond Ct	8768 E Ormont Ct
64.	5100 E Madeline St	5100 E Madeline St
65.	Gathersburg MD 20879	Gathersburg MD 20879
66.	4001 Virginia Ave	4001 Virginia Ave
67.	2104 Illinois Ave	2014 Illinois Ave
68.	1899 7 Mile Rd W	1899 7 Mile Rd W
69.	5713 Eastlawn St	5713 Eastland St
70.	16473 Fiarfield St	16493 Fairfield St
71.	7465 Navarre Pl	7465 Navarro Pl
72.	4817 W Yupon St	4817 W Yupon St
73.	4010 Saint Charles Ln	4010 Saint Charles Rd
74.	2908 Jane Rd	2908 Janet Rd
75.	6453 Twin Hill Rd	6543 Twin Hill Rd
76.	642 Quebec Pl	642 Quebec Pl
77.	5927 Carnahan Pl	5927 Caravan Pl
78.	1447 James Ave S	1474 James Ave S
79.	6203 North Riverview Ln	6203 North Riverview Ln
80.	6686 Dancaster Rd SW	6686 Dancaster Rd SW
81.	4019 King Oak Ter	4019 King Oak Ter
82.	17046 U.S. Highway 60	17046 U.S. Highway 60
83.	9431 Elysian Fields Ave	9431 Elysian Fields Ave
84.	6213 E Barrington Dr	6213 W Barrington Dr
85.	3491 New Island Ave	3491 New Island Ave
86.	94 N 9th Ave W	94 N 9th Ave W
87.	1740 Gray Haven Ct	1749 Gray Haven Ct
88.	4427 Normandale Highlands Dr	4427 Normandale Highlands Dr
89.	8904 N Hampson St	8904 N Hampton St
90.	3008 S Catherine St	3080 S Catherine St
91.	Venetia PA 15481	Vanetia PA 15481
92.	Lowell MA 01850	Lowell MO 01850
93.	5294 Pamela Ter	5294 Pamela Trl
94.	3734 Upper Darby Rd	3734 Upper Darby Rd
95.	1043 N Abington Ave	1043 N Apington Ave

STOP.
If you finish before the time is up, go back and check
the questions in this section of the test only.

PART B — MEMORY FOR ADDRESSES

In this part of the test, you will have five boxes labeled A, B, C, D, and E. Each box contains five addresses. Three of the five are groups of street addresses, such as 8000–8399 Orange, 8500–8899 Dellwood, and 6800–7599 Newman; and two are names of places. The addresses are different in each box.

There will be several opportunities to study the addresses and the boxes they are in. You will also be given three tests of 88 questions each, and the task of deciding where each address belongs. In some cases, you will have the list *and* the boxes in front of you at the same time; in others you will not. List 1 and List 2 are for warm-up practice. List 3 is the real one that will be scored.

Make sure you understand the format by examining the pretest samples below.

Pretest Samples

A	B	C	D	E
8900–9099 Orange	7400–7999 Orange	8000–8399 Orange	8400–8899 Orange	6900–7399 Orange
Tarmount	Railroad	Juniper	Alden	Sealey
8500–8899 Dellwood	8000–8499 Dellwood	8900–9499 Dellwood	7400–7999 Dellwood	7200–7399 Dellwood
Wheeling	Yule	Cantor	Hart	King
8400–8999 Newman	6800–7599 Newman	7600–7999 Newman	8000–8399 Newman	8900–9699 Newman

Questions 1 through 7 show the way the questions look. You have to decide in which lettered box (A, B, C, D, or E) the address belongs and then mark your answer by darkening the appropriate space in the answer grid.

1. Juniper   1 Ⓐ Ⓑ Ⓒ Ⓓ Ⓔ
2. 7400–7999 Dellwood   2 Ⓐ Ⓑ Ⓒ Ⓓ Ⓔ
3. 6900–7399 Orange   3 Ⓐ Ⓑ Ⓒ Ⓓ Ⓔ
4. Yule   4 Ⓐ Ⓑ Ⓒ Ⓓ Ⓔ
5. Sealey   5 Ⓐ Ⓑ Ⓒ Ⓓ Ⓔ
6. 8400–8999 Newman   6 Ⓐ Ⓑ Ⓒ Ⓓ Ⓔ
7. Cantor   7 Ⓐ Ⓑ Ⓒ Ⓓ Ⓔ

Answers

1. **C**   2. **D**   3. **E**   4. **B**   5. **E**   6. **A**   7. **C**

Now that you know what to do, you may begin Part B of Practice Test 3. To get the most out of it and the remaining three practice tests in this book, follow the directions and timing *exactly*. Follow each phase of Part B of the test, page by page, until you've completed List 3. It is modeled on the way the Postal Service actually conducts its tests.

Turn to the next page to begin.

Study — 3 minutes

You will be given 3 minutes to spend memorizing the addresses in the boxes. *They are exactly the same ones that will be used for all three tests.* Try to memorize as many as you can. When the 3 minutes are up, turn to page 309 and read the instructions for *List 1*.

A	B	C	D	E
8900–9099 Orange	7400–7999 Orange	8000–8399 Orange	8400–8899 Orange	6900–7399 Orange
Tarmount	Railroad	Juniper	Alden	Sealey
8500–8899 Dellwood	8000–8499 Dellwood	8900–9499 Dellwood	7400–7999 Dellwood	7200–7399 Dellwood
Wheeling	Yule	Cantor	Hart	King
8400–8999 Newman	6800–7599 Newman	7600–7999 Newman	8000–8399 Newman	8900–9699 Newman

List 1

Work — 3 minutes

Tear out the Answer Sheet for List 1. For each question, mark the Answer Sheet on page 300 to show the letter of the box in which the address belongs. Try to remember the locations of as many addresses as you can. *You will now have 3 minutes to complete List 1.* If you are not sure of an answer, you should guess.

A	B	C	D	E
8900–9099 Orange	7400–7999 Orange	8000–8399 Orange	8400–8899 Orange	6900–7399 Orange
Tarmount	Railroad	Juniper	Alden	Sealey
8500–8899 Dellwood	8000–8499 Dellwood	8900–9499 Dellwood	7400–7999 Dellwood	7200–7399 Dellwood
Wheeling	Yule	Canter	Hart	King
8400–8999 Newman	6800–7599 Newman	7600–7999 Newman	8000–8399 Newman	8900–9699 Newman

1. Hart
2. 8400–8899 Orange
3. Tarmount
4. 7200–7399 Dellwood
5. Alden
6. 8000–8399 Orange
7. 8400–8999 Newman
8. Railroad
9. Hart
10. 7400–7999 Orange
11. 8500–8899 Dellwood

12. Cantor
13. 8900–9099 Orange
14. 6800–7599 Newman
15. Yule
16. 8900–9699 Newman
17. 6900–7399 Orange
18. King
19. 8900–9499 Dellwood
20. 8000–8399 Newman
21. Tarmount
22. 7400–7999 Dellwood

23. 7600–7999 Newman
24. Juniper
25. Railroad
26. 8000–8499 Dellwood
27. Wheeling
28. 8000–8399 Newman
29. 8400–8899 Orange
30. Railroad
31. 7400–7999 Dellwood
32. King
33. Tarmount
34. 8400–8999 Newman
35. 8000–8499 Dellwood
36. Wheeling
37. 8500–8899 Dellwood
38. Sealey
39. 7200–7399 Dellwood
40. Wheeling
41. 8900–9499 Dellwood
42. Yule
43. 8900–9099 Orange
44. 8000–8499 Dellwood

45. Alden
46. 8000–8399 Newman
47. Hart
48. Juniper
49. 6800–7599 Newman
50. Sealey
51. 6900–7399 Orange
52. 6800–7599 Newman
53. Juniper
54. 8000–8399 Orange
55. Tarmount

56. Juniper
57. 8900–9699 Newman
58. Wheeling
59. Cantor
60. 8500–8899 Dellwood
61. 7200–7399 Dellwood
62. Yule
63. King
64. 7400–7999 Orange
65. Tarmount
66. Alden

67. 7400–7999 Orange
68. 6900–7399 Orange
69. 7600–7999 Newman
70. Yule
71. 7400–7999 Dellwood
72. Cantor
73. 8900–9099 Orange
74. King
75. 8900–9699 Newman
76. Cantor
77. 8900–9499 Dellwood

78. Alden
79. Railroad
80. 8400–8899 Orange
81. Hart
82. Sealey
83. 8000–8399 Orange
84. 7600–7999 Newman
85. Hart
86. Sealey
87. 8400–8899 Newman
88. King

STOP.
If you finish before the time is up, go back and check
the questions in this section of the test only.

List 2

Work — 3 minutes

Do these questions *without* looking back at the boxes. For each question, mark your answer on the Answer Sheet for List 2 on page 300. If you are not sure of an answer, you should guess.

1. 7400–7999 Orange
2. 7200–7399 Dellwood
3. 8000–8499 Dellwood
4. Alden
5. Sealey
6. 7200–7399 Dellwood
7. Juniper
8. 7400–7999 Dellwood
9. Alden
10. 7200–7399 Dellwood
11. 8900–9699 Newman

12. 6900–7399 Orange
13. 8500–8899 Dellwood
14. Alden
15. 8000–8399 Newman
16. Tarmount
17. 8000–8399 Newman
18. 6900–7399 Orange
19. Tarmount
20. Sealey
21. 8000–8399 Orange
22. King

23. Cantor
24. 7400–7999 Orange
25. 8000–8399 Orange
26. Wheeling
27. Hart
28. 8900–9499 Dellwood
29. King
30. 6800–7599 Newman
31. Railroad
32. Hart
33. 7600–7999 Newman

34. Wheeling
35. 8000–8399 Orange
36. Yule
37. 7400–7999 Dellwood
38. 6800–7599 Newman
39. 8900–9699 Newman
40. 8400–8899 Orange
41. Hart
42. Cantor
43. 8900–9499 Dellwood
44. Railroad

45. Juniper
46. Sealey
47. Wheeling
48. 7600–7999 Newman
49. 8900–9699 Newman
50. 8000–8499 Dellwood
51. King
52. 7400–7999 Orange
53. 8400–8999 Newman
54. Yule
55. 8900–9499 Dellwood

56. 8900–9099 Orange
57. Wheeling
58. 8400–8899 Orange
59. Tarmount
60. King
61. 8500–8899 Dellwood
62. Hart
63. Railroad
64. 6800–7599 Newman
65. 7600–7999 Newman
66. Tarmount

67. Hart
68. Cantor
69. Alden
70. 8900–9099 Orange
71. 8400–8999 Newman
72. Juniper
73. 8400–8899 Orange
74. 8000–8399 Newman
75. Railroad
76. Tarmount
77. Cantor

78. King
79. 8900–9699 Newman
80. Yule
81. 8400–8999 Newman
82. 6900–7399 Orange
83. 7400–7999 Dellwood
84. 8000–8499 Dellwood
85. Yule
86. 8500–8899 Dellwood
87. Juniper
88. 8900–9099 Orange

STOP.
If you finish before the time is up, go back and check
the questions in this section of the test only.

List 3

Study — 5 minutes

You are now about to take the test using List 3. *(This is the test that counts!)*
    Turn back to page 308 and study the boxes again. *You have 5 minutes to restudy the addresses.*

Work — 5 minutes

For each question, mark the Answer Sheet on page 301 to show the letter of the box in which the address belongs. You have *exactly 5 minutes* to do the test. During these 5 minutes, *do not* turn to any other page.

1. Railroad
2. 8900–9499 Dellwood
3. Cantor
4. Hart
5. 8400–8899 Orange
6. 8900–9699 Newman
7. 6800–7599 Newman
8. 7400–7999 Dellwood
9. Yule
10. 8000–8399 Orange
11. Wheeling

12. 7600–7999 Newman
13. Hart
14. Railroad
15. 6800–7599 Newman
16. King
17. 8900–9499 Dellwood
18. Hart
19. Wheeling
20. 8000–8399 Orange
21. 7400–7999 Orange
22. Cantor

23. King
24. 8000–8399 Orange
25. Sealey
26. Tarmount
27. 6900–7399 Orange
28. 8000–8399 Newman
29. Tarmount
30. 8000–8399 Newman
31. Alden
32. 8500–8899 Dellwood
33. 6900–7399 Orange

34. 6800–7599 Newman
35. 7200–7399 Dellwood
36. Alden
37. 7400–7999 Dellwood
38. Juniper
39. 7200–7399 Dellwood
40. Sealey
41. Alden
42. 8000–8499 Dellwood
43. 7200–7399 Dellwood
44. 7400–7999 Orange

45. 8900–9099 Orange

46. Juniper

47. 8500–8899 Dellwood

48. Yule

49. 8000–8499 Dellwood

50. 7400–7999 Dellwood

51. 6900–7399 Orange

52. 8400–8999 Newman

53. Yule

54. 8900–9699 Newman

55. King

56. Cantor

57. Tarmount

58. Railroad

59. 8000–8399 Newman

60. 8400–8899 Orange

61. Juniper

62. 8400–8999 Newman

63. 8900–9099 Orange

64. Alden

65. Cantor

66. Hart

67. Tarmount

68. 7600–7999 Newman

69. 6800–7599 Newman

70. Railroad

71. Hart

72. 8500–8899 Dellwood

73. King

74. Tarmount

75. 8400–8899 Orange

76. Wheeling

77. 8900–9099 Orange

78. 8900–9499 Dellwood

79. Yule

80. 8400–8999 Newman

81. 7400–7999 Orange

82. King

83. 8000–8499 Dellwood

84. 8900–9699 Newman

85. 7600–7999 Newman

86. Wheeling

87. Sealey

88. 6900–7399 Orange

STOP.
If you finish before the time is up, go back and check
the questions in this section of the test only.

PART C — NUMBER SERIES

Work — 20 minutes

For each Number Series question, there is a series of numbers that follow some definite order, and below each are five sets of two numbers each. You are to look at the numbers in the series and find out what order they follow. Then decide what the next two numbers in that series would be if the same order were continued. Mark your answers on the Answer Sheet on page 301.

You have 20 minutes to complete this part of the test. If you finish before the time is up, check your answers. The answers and explanations are on page 324.

1. 17 41 13 17 41 13 17 __ __
   A) 13 41   B) 17 13   C) 41 13   D) 41 17   E) 17 41

2. 81 72 72 63 63 54 54 __ __
   A) 45 38   B) 54 45   C) 45 45   D) 46 46   E) 46 38

3. 5 4 6 6 7 8 8 __ __
   A) 9 8   B) 10 9   C) 8 9   D) 10 11   E) 9 10

4. 15 10 20 15 25 20 30 __ __
   A) 25 35   B) 30 25   C) 25 20   D) 35 20   E) 35 25

5. 18 16 14 19 17 15 20 __ __
   A) 17 18   B) 16 17   C) 18 17   D) 18 16   E) 19 17

6. 24 21 23 20 22 19 21 __ __
   A) 20 18   B) 19 21   C) 19 16   D) 18 20   E) 20 22

7. 29 26 32 23 20 26 17 __ __
   A) 14 20   B) 23 29   C) 20 11   D) 8 3   E) 8 14

8. 100 10 81 9 64 8 49 __ __
   A) 7 34   B) 34 8   C) 36 6   D) 7 25   E) 7 36

9. 36 33 43 30 27 40 24 21 37 __ __
   A) 34 31   B) 20 34   C) 18 34   D) 15 19   E) 18 15

10. 4 8 4 12 4 16 4 __ __
    A) 4 20   B) 18 4   C) 18 22   D) 14 20   E) 20 4

11. 128 2 64 4 32 8 16 __ __
    A) 32 10   B) 16 8   C) 12 8   D) 8 12   E) 12 16

12. 6 5 7 6 8 7 9 __ __

A) 8 10   B) 9 10   C) 7 9   D) 10 9   E) 8 9

13. 1 1 2 2 3 3 2 2 1 __ __

A) 2 3   B) 1 2   C) 1 1   D) 2 2   E) 2 3

14. 3 6 11 8 11 10 13 16 9 __ __

A) 19 17   B) 19 18   C) 18 20   D) 18 21   E) 17 20

15. 70 60 20 50 40 20 30 __ __

A) 20 10   B) 10 10   C) 20 30   D) 20 20   E) 10 0

16. 1 2 6 2 4 12 3 6 __ __

A) 7 18   B) 7 10   C) 4 18   D) 18 4   E) 8 10

17. 42 21 38 25 34 29 30 __ __

A) 31 35   B) 32 31   C) 33 26   D) 39 30   E) 28 35

18. +17 −18 +19 −20 +21 −22 +23 __ __

A) −25 +26   B) +24 +25   C) +24 −25   D) −24 −25   E) −24 +25

19. 6 6 6 7 8 8 8 10 10 9 __ __

A) 9 9   B) 11 12   C) 12 12   D) 10 11   E) 11 11

20. 16 15 14 12 11 10 8 __ __

A) 7 6   B) 6 7   C) 9 10   D) 9 11   E) 10 11

21. 0 1 1 2 4 7 13 24 __ __

A) 35 47   B) 44 81   C) 48 96   D) 54 83   E) 37 61

22. 24 25 26 12 27 28 29 13 30 31 __ __

A) 32 14   B) 15 33   C) 32 16   D) 14 32   E) 16 33

23. 8 6 4 12 10 8 24 22 __ __

A) 18 54   B) 22 20   C) 20 60   D) 18 36   E) 20 40

24. 16 18 22 21 20 20 22 19 __ __

A) 18 17   B) 19 21   C) 24 18   D) 22 24   E) 17 19

STOP.
If you finish before the time is up, go back and check
the questions in this section of the test only.

PART D — FOLLOWING ORAL DIRECTIONS

This part of the test gauges your ability to understand and carry out spoken directions *exactly* as they are given to you.

In order to prepare to take Part D of the test, follow the steps below:

1. Enlist the help of a friend who will be the "reader." His or her job will be to read aloud a series of directions that you are to follow *exactly*. The reader will need a watch that displays seconds, because the directions must be read at the correct speed.

2. Tear out pages 321 and 322. These are the worksheets you should have in front of you as you listen to the directions given by the reader, who will tell you to do certain things with the items on each line on the worksheets.

3. Use the Answer Sheet for Following Oral Directions on page 301, and insert today's date. You will darken the appropriate spaces in accordance with the directions given by the reader.

4. *Now hand this entire book to the reader.* Ask him/her to review the section below headed "Instructions to the Reader." It explains exactly how the reader is to proceed.

When you and the reader are ready to start this part of Practice Test 3, he/she will begin reading to you the section marked "Directions." YOU ARE NOT TO READ THESE AT ANY TIME BEFORE OR DURING THE TEST. If you do, you will lose the benefit of this part of the practice test.

Instructions to the "Reader"

These instructions should be read at about 80 words per minute. You should practice reading the material in the box until you can do it in exactly 1 minute. The number of words in the passage and the natural pauses described below will give you a good feel for the rate of speed and the way you should read the test scores.

1-MINUTE PRACTICE

> Look at line 20 on your worksheet. There are two circles and two boxes of different sizes with numbers in them. If 7 is less than 3 and if 2 is smaller than 4, write C in the larger circle. Otherwise write B as in *baker* in the smaller box. Now, on your answer sheet, darken the space for the number-letter combination in the box or circle.

You should read the entire test aloud before you read it to the person taking the test, in order to thoroughly acquaint yourself with the procedure and the desired rate of reading.

Read slowly but at a natural pace. In other words, do not space the words so that there are unnaturally long pauses between them. The instruction "Pause slightly" indicates only enough time to take a breath. The other instructions for pauses give the recommended length for each. If possible, use a watch with a second hand.

All the material that follows, except the words in parentheses, is to be read aloud. Now start reading the directions. *Do not repeat any of the directions.*

Directions: In this test, I will read instructions to you. You are to mark your worksheets according to the instructions that I read to you. After each set of instructions, I'll give you time to record your answers on your answer sheet.

Try to understand the instructions as I read them; I cannot repeat them. Do not ask any questions from now on.

If, when you go to darken a space for a number, you find that you have already darkened another space for that number, either (1) erase the first mark and darken the space for your new choice, or (2) let the first mark stay and do not darken any other space. When you finish, you should have no more than one space darkened for each number.

Turn to Worksheet 1.

Look at line 1 on your worksheet. (Pause slightly.) Draw a line under the second letter in the line. (Pause 2 seconds.) Now, on your answer sheet, find number 16 and darken space E for the letter under which you drew a line. (Pause 5 seconds.)

Look at line 2 on your worksheet. (Pause slightly.) Draw a line under every "X" in the line. (Pause 5 seconds.) Count the number of lines you have drawn, add 4, and write that number at the end of the line. (Pause 5 seconds.) Now, on your answer sheet, find that number and darken space D as in *dog*. (Pause 5 seconds.)

Look at line 3 on your worksheet. (Pause slightly.) Write B as in *boy* in the last circle. (Pause 2 seconds.) Now, on your answer sheet, find the number in that circle and darken space B as in *boy* for that number. (Pause 5 seconds.)

Now, look at line 3 again. (Pause slightly.) Write a C in the third circle. (Pause 2 seconds.) Now, on your answer sheet, find the number in that circle and darken space C for that number. (Pause 5 seconds.)

Look at line 4 on your worksheet. (Pause slightly.) Draw a line under every number that is more than 15 but less than 30. (Pause 12 seconds.) Now, on your answer sheet, for each number that you drew a line under, darken space A. (Pause 25 seconds.)

Look at line 5 on your worksheet. (Pause slightly.) The four boxes are bins for storing mail. The bin with the lowest number is to be emptied last. Write a C on the line beside the lowest number. (Pause 2 seconds.) Now, on your answer sheet, darken the space for the number-letter combination that is in the bin you just wrote in. (Pause 5 seconds.)

Look at the five boxes in line 6 on your worksheet. (Pause slightly.) Write 74 on the blank in the middle box. (Pause 2 seconds.) Now, on your answer sheet, darken the space for the number-letter combination that is in the box you just wrote in. (Pause 5 seconds.)

Now look at line 6 again. (Pause slightly.) Write 31 on the blank in the fourth box. (Pause 2 seconds.) Now, on your answer sheet, darken the space for the number-letter combination that is in the box you just wrote in. (Pause 5 seconds.)

Look at the circle and words in line 7 on your worksheet. (Pause slightly.) Write the last letter of the first word in the last circle. (Pause 2 seconds.) Write the second letter of the last word in the second circle. (Pause 2 seconds.) Write the first letter of the second word in the first circle. (Pause 2 seconds.) Now, on your answer sheet, darken the spaces for the number-letter combinations that are in the three circles you just wrote in. (Pause 12 seconds.)

Look at the figures in line 8 on your worksheet. (Pause slightly.) In every figure that has more than four sides, write the letter A on the line in the figure. (Pause 5 seconds.) Now, on your answer sheet, darken the spaces for the number-letter combinations that are in the figures you just wrote in. (Pause 10 seconds.)

Look at line 9 on your worksheet. (Pause slightly.) Draw a line under every number that is more than 55 but less than 70. (Pause 12 seconds.) Now, on your answer sheet, for each number you drew a line under, darken space B as in *baker*. (Pause 25 seconds.)

Now look at line 10 on your worksheet. (Pause slightly.) There are five boxes on the line. Each box has a letter in it. (Pause slightly.) In the first box write the answer to this question: How many pennies are there in a half dollar? (Pause 2 seconds.) Now, on your answer sheet, darken the space for the number-letter combination that is in the box you just wrote in. (Pause 5 seconds.)

Look at line 10 again. In the second box write the number 87. (Pause 2 seconds.) Now, on your answer sheet, darken the space for the number-letter combination that is in the box you just wrote in. (Pause 5 seconds.) In the fourth box do nothing. In the last box write the answer to this question: Which of the following numbers is largest: 28, 56, 34, 52, 48? (Pause 2 seconds.) Now, on your answer sheet, darken the space for the number-letter combination that is in the box you just wrote in. (Pause 5 seconds.)

Look at line 11 on your worksheet. (Pause slightly.) In each circle there is a time when the mail is checked in. In the circle for the latest time, write on the line the last two figures of the time. (Pause 2 seconds.) Now, on your answer sheet, darken the space for the number-letter combination that is in the circle you just wrote in. (Pause 5 seconds.)

Now turn to Worksheet 2. (Pause 5 seconds.)

Look at the six boxes in line 12 on your worksheet. (Pause slightly.) If 6 is more than 7, write A in the fifth box. (Pause 2 seconds.) If 6 is not more than 7, write B as in *baker* in the second box. (Pause 2 seconds.) Now, on your answer sheet, darken the space for the number-letter combination that is in the box you just wrote in. (Pause 5 seconds.)

Look at line 13 on your worksheet. (Pause slightly.) Next to the left-hand number write the letter A. (Pause 2 seconds.) Now, on your answer sheet, find the number beside which you wrote and darken space E for that number. (Pause 5 seconds.)

Look at the letters in line 14 on your worksheet. (Pause slightly.) Draw a line under the fourth letter in the line. (Pause 2 seconds.) Now, on your answer sheet, find number 73 and darken the space for the letter under which you drew a line. (Pause 5 seconds.)

Look at line 14 again. Draw two lines under the second letter in the line. (Pause 2 seconds.) Now, on your answer sheet, find number 58 and darken the space for the letter under which you drew two lines. (Pause 5 seconds.)

Look at line 15 on your worksheet. There are two circles and two boxes of different sizes with numbers in them. (Pause slightly.) If 7 is more than 3 and if 5 is less than 4, write C in the larger circle. (Pause 2 seconds.) Otherwise, write E in the smaller box. (Pause 2 seconds.) Now, on your answer sheet, darken the space for the number-letter combination that is in the box or circle you just wrote in. (Pause 5 seconds.)

Look at line 16 on your worksheet. (Pause slightly.) If, in a year, August comes before July, write D as in *dog* in the box with the smallest number. (Pause 2 seconds.) If it does not, write A in the second box. (Pause 2 seconds.) Now, on your answer sheet, darken the space for the number-letter combination that is in the box you just wrote in. (Pause 5 seconds.)

Now look at line 17 on your worksheet. (Pause slightly.) Write the number 3 on the line next to the middle letter. (Pause 2 seconds.) Now, on your answer sheet, find the number that you just wrote and darken the space for the letter beside which you just wrote it. (Pause 5 seconds.)

Look at line 18 on your worksheet. (Pause slightly.) Mail for Coral Gables and Gainesville is to be put in box 64. Mail for Atlanta and Buford is to be put in box 84. (Pause slightly.) Write A on the line in the box in which you would put mail for Gainesville. (Pause 2 seconds.) Now, on your answer sheet, darken the space for the number-letter combination that is in the box you just wrote in. (Pause 5 seconds.)

Look at line 19 on your worksheet. (Pause slightly.) If the number in the left-hand box is smaller than the number in the right-hand circle, add 2 to the number in the left-hand box, and change the number in that box to this number. (Pause 2 seconds.) Then write D as in *dog* next to the new number. (Pause 2 seconds.) Otherwise, write E next to the number in the larger box. (Pause 2 seconds.) Now, on your answer sheet, darken the space for the number-letter combination in the box or circle you just wrote in. (Pause 5 seconds.)

END OF EXAMINATION.
If you finish before the time is up, go back and check
the questions in this section of the test only.

Practice Test 3—Worksheet 1
Part D—Following Oral Directions

1.   D   E   A   C   B

2.   X O X O O X X X O O X X O O X

3.   (48 ___)   (17 ___)   (76 ___)   (29 ___)   (81 ___)

4.   19   29   32   30   21   15   14

5.   [82 ___]   [40 ___]   [38 ___]   [59 ___]

6.   [D ___]   [A ___]   [C ___]   [B ___]   [E ___]

7.   (63 ___)   (44 ___)   (23 ___)   REED   AUNT   BALL

8.   [10 ___]   △59 ___   ⬡51 ___   ▱49 ___   ⌂71 ___

9.   75   60   55   77   53   49   51   69   71

10.   [___ C]   [___ E]   [___ A]   [___ B]   [___ D]

11.   (3:45 ___ A)   (3:30 ___ D)   (3:09 ___ C)   (3:57 ___ E)   (3:54 ___ B)

Practice Test 3—Worksheet 2
Part D—Following Oral Directions

12. 32 ___   79 ___   29 ___   11 ___   49 ___   43 ___

13. 48 ___   63 ___

14. C   E   D   A   E   B   C

15. 25 ___   9 ___   4 ___   77 ___

16. 2 ___   8 ___   13 ___   1 ___

17. ___ D   ___ B   ___ A

18.
64
CORAL GABLES
GAINESVILLE
___

84
ATLANTA
BUFORD
___

19. 26 ___   45 ___   53 ___   38 ___

ANSWER KEY

Part A—Address Checking

1. D	11. D	21. D	31. D	41. D	51. A	61. A	71. D	81. A	91. D
2. D	12. D	22. A	32. D	42. A	52. D	62. D	72. A	82. A	92. D
3. A	13. D	23. A	33. D	43. A	53. D	63. D	73. D	83. A	93. D
4. A	14. A	24. A	34. D	44. A	54. A	64. A	74. D	84. D	94. A
5. D	15. A	25. D	35. A	45. A	55. A	65. A	75. D	85. A	95. D
6. D	16. D	26. D	36. A	46. D	56. D	66. A	76. A	86. A	
7. D	17. A	27. A	37. A	47. A	57. A	67. D	77. D	87. D	
8. D	18. A	28. D	38. D	48. D	58. D	68. A	78. D	88. A	
9. D	19. D	29. D	39. D	49. A	59. A	69. D	79. A	89. D	
10. A	20. A	30. D	40. A	50. D	60. D	70. D	80. A	90. D	

Part B—Memory for Addresses

List 1

1. D	10. B	19. C	28. D	37. A	46. D	55. A	64. B	73. A	82. E
2. D	11. A	20. D	29. D	38. E	47. D	56. C	65. A	74. E	83. C
3. A	12. C	21. A	30. B	39. E	48. C	57. E	66. D	75. E	84. C
4. E	13. A	22. D	31. D	40. A	49. B	58. A	67. B	76. C	85. D
5. D	14. B	23. C	32. E	41. C	50. E	59. C	68. E	77. C	86. E
6. C	15. B	24. C	33. A	42. B	51. E	60. A	69. C	78. D	87. A
7. A	16. E	25. B	34. A	43. A	52. B	61. E	70. B	79. B	88. E
8. B	17. E	26. B	35. B	44. B	53. C	62. B	71. D	80. D	
9. D	18. E	27. A	36. A	45. D	54. C	63. E	72. C	81. D	

List 2

1. B	10. E	19. A	28. C	37. D	46. E	55. C	64. B	73. D	82. E
2. E	11. E	20. E	29. E	38. B	47. A	56. A	65. C	74. D	83. D
3. B	12. E	21. C	30. B	39. E	48. C	57. A	66. A	75. B	84. B
4. D	13. A	22. E	31. B	40. D	49. E	58. D	67. D	76. A	85. B
5. E	14. D	23. C	32. D	41. D	50. B	59. A	68. C	77. C	86. A
6. E	15. D	24. B	33. C	42. C	51. E	60. E	69. D	78. E	87. C
7. C	16. A	25. C	34. A	43. C	52. B	61. A	70. A	79. E	88. A
8. D	17. D	26. A	35. C	44. B	53. A	62. D	71. A	80. B	
9. D	18. E	27. D	36. B	45. C	54. B	63. B	72. C	81. A	

List 3

1. B	10. C	19. A	28. D	37. D	46. C	55. E	64. D	73. E	82. E
2. C	11. A	20. C	29. A	38. C	47. A	56. C	65. C	74. A	83. B
3. C	12. C	21. B	30. D	39. E	48. B	57. A	66. D	75. D	84. E
4. D	13. D	22. C	31. D	40. E	49. B	58. B	67. A	76. A	85. C
5. D	14. B	23. E	32. A	41. D	50. D	59. D	68. C	77. A	86. A
6. E	15. B	24. C	33. E	42. D	51. E	60. D	69. B	78. C	87. E
7. B	16. E	25. E	34. B	43. E	52. A	61. C	70. B	79. B	88. E
8. D	17. C	26. A	35. E	44. B	53. B	62. A	71. D	80. A	
9. B	18. D	27. E	36. D	45. A	54. E	63. A	72. A	81. B	

Part C—Number Series

1. C	4. A	7. A	10. E	13. B	16. D	19. C	22. A
2. C	5. D	8. E	11. B	14. D	17. C	20. A	23. C
3. B	6. D	9. E	12. A	15. D	18. E	21. B	24. A

Part D—Following Oral Directions

3. B	12. D	21. A	29. A	44. A	51. A	58. E	64. A	73. A	79. B
4. E	16. E	23. D	31. B	48. E	56. D	60. B	69. B	74. C	81. B
8. A	19. A	28. D	38. C	50. C	57. E	63. A	71. A	76. C	87. E

ANSWER EXPLANATIONS FOR PART C— NUMBER SERIES

1. **C** The three-number sequence, 17 41 13 keeps repeating.
2. **C** This series keeps decreasing by 9. Each number is repeated.
3. **B** Two alternating series make up this group of numbers. One, starting with 5, follows a + 1 rule; the other, starting with 4, a + 2 rule.
4. **A** You could progress from one number to the other by following a − 5, + 10, rule. Or you could see two alternating series here—each increasing by 5.
5. **D** Three-member mini-series make up this progression of numbers. Each series begins one number higher than the starting number of the preceding one. Within each series, a − 2 rule is used.
6. **D** The rule here is: −3, + 2; −3, + 2; and so on.
7. **A** A more complex pattern governs this series. It has three steps: − 3, + 6, − 9; which keep repeating.
8. **E** The first number in this series, 100, is the square of 10, which follows it. This pattern is used for each number descending from 10, i.e., 81 9; 64 8; and so on.
9. **E** Both of the two alternating series here follow a −3 rule. The first series continues for two numbers before it is interrupted by one number of the second series.
10. **E** The fixed number, 4, appears between each term in this simple + 4 series.
11. **B** Here you have an alternating series that uses *division* by 2 (128 ÷ 2, 64 ÷ 2, and so on), alternating with a series that uses *multiplication* by 2. (2 × 2, 4 × 2).
12. **A** You may view this either as a series following a −1, + 2; and so on rule, or as two alternating series each increasing by 1.
13. **B** This series follows an ascending-descending wave pattern. Each number is repeated after adding 1 to it. The series ascends from 1 1 until it reaches 3 3, after which it descends back to 1 1. This pattern keeps repeating.
14. **D** A series that follows a + 3, + 2; rule is interrupted after every two of its members by one member of a second series that keeps decreasing by 1.
15. **D** You have a − 10 series here, with the number *20* appearing after every second term.
16. **D** You can view these numbers in two ways. Either as *three* alternating series or as a collection of mini-series. One alternating series begins with 1 and increases by 1; the second begins with 2 and increases by 2; the third begins with 6 and increases by 6. The diagram below shows how they may be viewed as "mini-series," each using a × 2, × 3; rule.

$$\overset{\times2}{\frown}\ \overset{\times3}{\frown}\qquad \overset{\times2}{\frown}\ \overset{\times3}{\frown}\qquad \overset{\times2}{\frown}\ \overset{\times3}{\frown}$$
$$1\quad 2\quad 6\ \bigg|\ 2\quad 4\quad 12\ \bigg|\ 3\quad 6\quad 18\ \bigg|\ 4$$
$$\underbrace{}_{+1}\qquad\underbrace{}_{+1}\qquad\underbrace{}_{+1}$$

17. **C** A −4 series is alternating with a + 4 series.
18. **E** Even though these numbers follow a simple + 1 pattern, you must be careful to keep track of the alternating + and −*signs* that precede each number.
19. **C** Here again, are two alternating series. One follows a pattern of + 2, repeat the number; + 2, repeat the number; etc. After each repetition, it is interrupted by one member of a + 1 series. The proximity of the numbers makes this question quite tricky.
20. **A** You can see these numbers as following the complex rule: −1, −1, −2; −1, −1, −2; and so on. If you wish, you can consider them as three-member "mini-series." (For practice, see if you can diagram them this way.)
21. **B** The series progresses by *internal* addition of its members. Each number is obtained by adding the *three* preceding numbers together, e.g.; 0 + 1 + 1 = 2; 1 + 1 + 2 = 4; 1 + 2 + 4 = 7; and so on.
22. **A** The first of the two alternating series begins with 24, increases by 1 and continues for *three* numbers before being interrupted by the second series. This series begins with the number 12 and keeps increasing by 1.
23. **C** The rule here uses subtraction *and* multiplication according to this complex rule: −2, −2, × 3; and so on.
24. **A** One series beginning with 16 increases by 2. It is interrupted after every two of its members by three members of a second series. This series beginning with 22 decreases by 1.

EVALUATING YOUR PROGRESS*

Part A—Address Checking

Computing Your Score

Check your answers against the Answer Key. Score yourself by using this formula:

$$\begin{array}{r} \text{Number right} \\ - \text{ Number wrong} \\ \hline \text{YOUR SCORE} \end{array}$$

For example, if you completed 52 questions and got 8 wrong,

$$\begin{array}{rcr} \text{Number right} & = & 44 \\ - \text{ Number wrong} & = & - \ 8 \\ \hline \text{Your score} & = & 36 \end{array}$$

Notice that you do *not* figure in the questions that you did not answer.

Guidelines

How good is the score you just made?

52 or higher . . . . Good
Between 32 and 52 . . . . . . Fair
Below 32 . . . . You need to improve.

These are commonly accepted figures. It is believed, however, that you should not be satisfied with anything *less* than 52. Experience in training many people to prepare for this test shows that most serious test candidates who use the preparation program described in this book (Chapter 4 covers Address Checking) will be able to raise their score to the upper sixties, seventies, or eighties.

Personal Progress Record

One of the most satisfying things that can happen while you are working toward a goal is to see signs of progress. The improvement you make on Address Checking can readily be seen by examining the scores you make on the practice tests and exercises in this book. Keeping track of your growing skill is important, so a Personal Progress Record has been furnished for your use on page 439.

---

* Please note that the scores you obtain by following the computation instructions for the various parts of this test are "raw" scores. The Postal Service combines and converts the raw scores for the various parts of the test into a scaled score obtained by using special conversion formulas that are kept confidential. This scaled score (plus any veteran's credits to which you are entitled) forms the basis for your final rating and your standing on the list. This final rating will be sent to you after the tests have been marked.

Furthermore, even though you take one test, your final score will vary depending on the title. For example, your rate on the Mail Handler register may very well be different from your rating on the Postal Clerk-Carrier register. Apparently, the relative rate given to each part of the test varies according to title. This is another argument for taking as many tests in as many titles as possible, as suggested on page 3.

You are encouraged to calculate your raw scores because they furnish a realistic and convenient way for you to keep track of your relative performance and progress as you work your way through this book.

The following is a sample of this Personal Progress Record to familiarize you with it. The entries on this sample are based on the preceding example.

PERSONAL PROGRESS RECORD—SAMPLE

ADDRESS CHECKING										
Initial Tests							Repeated Tests			
Date	Test	Number Completed	Number Correct	− Number Wrong	= Score		Date	Score	Date	Score
5/15	Diagnostic Practice Test	52	44	− 8	= 36					
5/16	Practice Test 1	64	54	− 10	= 44					
5/18	Practice Test 2	66	57	− 9	= 48					
5/20	Practice Test 3	70	60	− 10	= 50					
	Practice Test 4			−	=					
	Practice Test 5			−	=					
	Practice Test 6			−	=					

Now turn to page 439. In the table entitled "Personal Progress Record—Address Checking," make the proper entries on the line for Practice Test 3, which you just took. Review the special techniques in Chapter 3: Address Checking—How to Improve Your Score, before taking Practice Test 4. After taking the additional practice tests, enter the results immediately. Keep this record. It will help you record your progress.

Part B—Memory for Addresses

Computing Your Score

Check the answers on your answer sheet against the Answer Key. Calculate your score by using these four steps:

1. Enter the number of answers you got right . . . .   _____

2. Enter the number of answers you got wrong . . . . _____

3. Divide the number wrong by 4 (or multiply by ¼) . . . . −   _____

4. Subtract Line 3 from Line 1. . . . . YOUR SCORE =   _____

Follow this example to make sure that you have figured your score correctly. It will be assumed that you completed 32 questions, of which you got 24 right and 8 wrong.

Line 1 . . . . Number right   24

Line 2 . . . . Number wrong 8

Line 3 . . . . ¼ of line 2 = ¼ × 8 . . . . . .   − 2

Line 4 . . . . 24 − 2 . . YOUR SCORE =   22

Notice that, just as for Address Checking, questions that are not answered are *not* taken into account.

Guidelines

How good is the score you just made?

> 52 or higher . . . . Good
> Between 32 and 52 . . . . . . Fair
> Below 32 . . . . You need to improve.

If your score on this test was low, don't be discouraged. Nevertheless, you may wish to review Chapters 5 and 6, which offer special techniques for handling Part B—Memory for Addresses, before taking Practice Test 4.

Personal Progress Record

Turn to page 439. Use the table entitled "Personal Progress—Memory for Addresses" to keep a permanent record of your scores on List 3 of the practice tests. A sample is printed below to familiarize you with it. The first entry is based on the preceding example.

PERSONAL PROGRESS RECORD—SAMPLE

MEMORY FOR ADDRESSES											
Initial Tests									**Repeated Tests**		
Date	Test	Number Completed	Number Correct *A*	Number Wrong	$\times$ ¼ =		Points off *B*	Score *(A − B)*	Date	Score	Date	Score
5/15	Diagnostic Practice Test	32	24	8	$\times$ ¼ =		2	22				
5/16	Practice Test 1	46	38	8	$\times$ ¼ =		2	36				
5/18	Practice Test 2	58	52	6	$\times$ ¼ =		1½	50½				
5/20	Practice Test 3	64	60	4	$\times$ ¼ =		1	59				
	Practice Test 4				$\times$ ¼ =							
	Practice Test 5				$\times$ ¼ =							
	Practice Test 6				$\times$ ¼ =							

Part C—Number Series

Computing Your Score

Check the answers on your Answer Sheet against the Answer Key. Calculate your score by adding up the number of correct answers you have. You *do not* lose any credit for wrong answers or for questions you don't answer. For example, on a test having 24 questions, if you had 5 correct, 3 incorrect, and omitted 16, your score would be 5.

Guidelines

How good is the score you just made?

17 or higher . . . . Good
Between 12 and 16 . . . . . . Fair
Below 12 . . . . You need to improve.

Once you have mastered the techniques explained in this book, you should routinely be scoring 20 to 24 correct.

Personal Progress Record

The following is a sample of this Personal Progress Record to familiarize you with it. The entries on this sample are based on the example above.

PERSONAL PROGRESS RECORD—SAMPLE

NUMBER SERIES							
Initial Tests				Repeated Tests			
Date	Test	Number Completed	Number Correct (Your Score)	Date	Score	Date	Score
5/15	Diagnostic Practice Test	8	5				
5/16	Practice Test 1	15	11				
5/18	Practice Test 2	17	15				
5/20	Practice Test 3	20	19				
	Practice Test 4						
	Practice Test 5						
	Practice Test 6						

Now turn to page 440. Look at the table entitled "Personal Progress Record—Number Series." Make the proper entries on the line for the practice test you just took. This table will help you record your progress as you take additional practice tests.

Part D—Following Oral Directions

Computing Your Score

Check your answers against the Answer Key. Calculate your score by adding up the number of correct answers you have. You do *not* lose any credit for wrong answers or for questions you don't answer. For example, on a test having 30 questions, if you had 17 correct and 6 incorrect, and omitted 7, your score would be 17.

Guidelines

How good is the score you just made?

> 28 or higher . . . . Good
> Between 24 and 27 . . . . . . Fair
> Below 24 . . . . You need to improve.

Once you have mastered the techniques explained in this book (Chapter 8 covers Following Oral Directions), you should routinely score 28 to 30 correct.

Personal Progress Record

Now turn to page 440. In the table entitled "Personal Progress Record—Following Oral Directions," make the proper entries on the line for the practice test you just took. This table will help you record your progress as you take additional practice tests. A sample is printed below to familiarize you with it. The first entry is based on the preceding example.

PERSONAL PROGRESS RECORD—SAMPLE

		FOLLOWING ORAL DIRECTIONS					
	Initial Tests			Repeated Tests			
Date	Test	Number Completed	Number Correct (Your Score)	Date	Score	Date	Score
5/15	Diagnostic Practice Test	23	17				
5/16	Practice Test 1	23	19				
5/18	Practice Test 2	27	25				
5/20	Practice Test 3	29	28				
	Practice Test 4						
	Practice Test 5						
	Practice Test 6						

▬ DIAGNOSTIC CHARTS

The following charts will help pinpoint your weaknesses by making it easy for you to determine what particular type of question in each part of the test is most difficult for you.

Part A—Address Checking

Type of Difference	"D" Questions	Number of "D" Questions Wrong		
		Trial 1	Trial 2	Trial 3
Numbers: transposed	7, 9, 16, 30, 39, 46, 53, 67, 75, 78, 90			
changed	6, 34, 70, 87			
omitted	2			
Directions	21, 48, 56, 84			
Abbreviations: streets, roads, avenues, etc.	8, 12, 13, 41, 52, 73 93			
states	1, 25, 38, 50, 58, 92			
Spelling: single letters	5, 11, 19, 28, 60, 63, 71, 74, 77, 89, 91, 95			
groups of letters	26, 29, 31, 32, 33, 45, 62, 69			
Total Number of All Types	53			
	Use the columns on the right to enter the question numbers of "A" items you marked "D."			

This chart will help you to pinpoint the kinds of errors you made on Practice Test 3. Use it as directed below after you have taken and marked the test.

The first column on the left, "Type of Difference," contains the categories whereby addresses may differ (see page 69). On the same line across, the second column gives the numbers of the questions that fall within each category. In the third column, you are to enter the numbers of any "A" questions you answered as "D." Do not include questions that you did not do. Checking the addresses you got wrong may reveal a problem on which you will want to work.

After you have made all the entries, you will be able to see the areas in which you need to improve. Then turn to the appropriate parts of Chapter 4: Address Checking—How to Improve Your Score, read them, and practice the drills that can help. For example, if you find you have been making too many errors picking out number differences, read page 94 and do Drills 18 through 21. If you have a problem with single letters because of reversals like *b* and *d*, or if you have been overlooking the differences between *a*, *e*, and *o*, read page 91. Examine the table and work on Drills 10 and 11 if the problem persists.

Remember that this chart is designed for diagnostic purposes and guidance on further practice. It has been drawn so that you can enter the results each time you retake a practice test. In this way you will be able to see how you are progressing. It is not necessary to record your scores here. That is best done by using the Personal Progress Record Card.

Part B—Memory for Addresses

Kind of Address		Number of Questions	Number Wrong		
			Trial 1	Trial 2	Trial 3
Direct:					
	List 1	43			
	List 2	42			
	List 3	41			
Numbered:					
	List 1	45			
	List 2	46			
	List 3	47			

The purpose of this chart is to help you evaluate your performance on the two kinds of memory questions that appear in these memory tests—the questions on the direct (name) addresses and the questions on the numbered addresses. Use the chart as directed below after you have taken and marked the entire test.

The first column on the left, "Kind of Address," is divided by category into "Direct Address" versus "Numbered Address." The second column gives the number of questions in each category on List 1, List 2, and List 3. Use the third column to enter the total number of questions in each category that you answered incorrectly. There is room for you to make additional entries if you take the practice test more than once.

At a glance, you will be able to see which area you need to concentrate on and how well you are progressing as you take repeat trials. Use Chapter 5 and the drills in it to improve your memory for the direct addresses. Use Chapter 6 for the numbered addresses.

Remember to use the Personal Progress Record Card (Memory for Addresses) on page 439 to keep track of your actual scores as you keep studying and practicing.

Part C—Number Series and Part D—Following Oral Directions

Because of the nature of the questions in these tests, Diagnostic Charts are not provided for them. If you find that you made many errors on these tests, study the techniques suggested in Chapters 7 and 8.

Answer Sheet—Practice Test 4

Part A—Address Checking

1 Ⓐⓓ	25 Ⓐⓓ	49 Ⓐⓓ	73 Ⓐⓓ
2 Ⓐⓓ	26 Ⓐⓓ	50 Ⓐⓓ	74 Ⓐⓓ
3 Ⓐⓓ	27 Ⓐⓓ	51 Ⓐⓓ	75 Ⓐⓓ
4 Ⓐⓓ	28 Ⓐⓓ	52 Ⓐⓓ	76 Ⓐⓓ
5 Ⓐⓓ	29 Ⓐⓓ	53 Ⓐⓓ	77 Ⓐⓓ
6 Ⓐⓓ	30 Ⓐⓓ	54 Ⓐⓓ	78 Ⓐⓓ
7 Ⓐⓓ	31 Ⓐⓓ	55 Ⓐⓓ	79 Ⓐⓓ
8 Ⓐⓓ	32 Ⓐⓓ	56 Ⓐⓓ	80 Ⓐⓓ
9 Ⓐⓓ	33 Ⓐⓓ	57 Ⓐⓓ	81 Ⓐⓓ
10 Ⓐⓓ	34 Ⓐⓓ	58 Ⓐⓓ	82 Ⓐⓓ
11 Ⓐⓓ	35 Ⓐⓓ	59 Ⓐⓓ	83 Ⓐⓓ
12 Ⓐⓓ	36 Ⓐⓓ	60 Ⓐⓓ	84 Ⓐⓓ
13 Ⓐⓓ	37 Ⓐⓓ	61 Ⓐⓓ	85 Ⓐⓓ
14 Ⓐⓓ	38 Ⓐⓓ	62 Ⓐⓓ	86 Ⓐⓓ
15 Ⓐⓓ	39 Ⓐⓓ	63 Ⓐⓓ	87 Ⓐⓓ
16 Ⓐⓓ	40 Ⓐⓓ	64 Ⓐⓓ	88 Ⓐⓓ
17 Ⓐⓓ	41 Ⓐⓓ	65 Ⓐⓓ	89 Ⓐⓓ
18 Ⓐⓓ	42 Ⓐⓓ	66 Ⓐⓓ	90 Ⓐⓓ
19 Ⓐⓓ	43 Ⓐⓓ	67 Ⓐⓓ	91 Ⓐⓓ
20 Ⓐⓓ	44 Ⓐⓓ	68 Ⓐⓓ	92 Ⓐⓓ
21 Ⓐⓓ	45 Ⓐⓓ	69 Ⓐⓓ	93 Ⓐⓓ
22 Ⓐⓓ	46 Ⓐⓓ	70 Ⓐⓓ	94 Ⓐⓓ
23 Ⓐⓓ	47 Ⓐⓓ	71 Ⓐⓓ	95 Ⓐⓓ
24 Ⓐⓓ	48 Ⓐⓓ	72 Ⓐⓓ	

Part B—Memory for Addresses—List 1

1 Ⓐ Ⓑ Ⓒ Ⓓ Ⓔ	19 Ⓐ Ⓑ Ⓒ Ⓓ Ⓔ	37 Ⓐ Ⓑ Ⓒ Ⓓ Ⓔ	55 Ⓐ Ⓑ Ⓒ Ⓓ Ⓔ	73 Ⓐ Ⓑ Ⓒ Ⓓ Ⓔ
2 Ⓐ Ⓑ Ⓒ Ⓓ Ⓔ	20 Ⓐ Ⓑ Ⓒ Ⓓ Ⓔ	38 Ⓐ Ⓑ Ⓒ Ⓓ Ⓔ	56 Ⓐ Ⓑ Ⓒ Ⓓ Ⓔ	74 Ⓐ Ⓑ Ⓒ Ⓓ Ⓔ
3 Ⓐ Ⓑ Ⓒ Ⓓ Ⓔ	21 Ⓐ Ⓑ Ⓒ Ⓓ Ⓔ	39 Ⓐ Ⓑ Ⓒ Ⓓ Ⓔ	57 Ⓐ Ⓑ Ⓒ Ⓓ Ⓔ	75 Ⓐ Ⓑ Ⓒ Ⓓ Ⓔ
4 Ⓐ Ⓑ Ⓒ Ⓓ Ⓔ	22 Ⓐ Ⓑ Ⓒ Ⓓ Ⓔ	40 Ⓐ Ⓑ Ⓒ Ⓓ Ⓔ	58 Ⓐ Ⓑ Ⓒ Ⓓ Ⓔ	76 Ⓐ Ⓑ Ⓒ Ⓓ Ⓔ
5 Ⓐ Ⓑ Ⓒ Ⓓ Ⓔ	23 Ⓐ Ⓑ Ⓒ Ⓓ Ⓔ	41 Ⓐ Ⓑ Ⓒ Ⓓ Ⓔ	59 Ⓐ Ⓑ Ⓒ Ⓓ Ⓔ	77 Ⓐ Ⓑ Ⓒ Ⓓ Ⓔ
6 Ⓐ Ⓑ Ⓒ Ⓓ Ⓔ	24 Ⓐ Ⓑ Ⓒ Ⓓ Ⓔ	42 Ⓐ Ⓑ Ⓒ Ⓓ Ⓔ	60 Ⓐ Ⓑ Ⓒ Ⓓ Ⓔ	78 Ⓐ Ⓑ Ⓒ Ⓓ Ⓔ
7 Ⓐ Ⓑ Ⓒ Ⓓ Ⓔ	25 Ⓐ Ⓑ Ⓒ Ⓓ Ⓔ	43 Ⓐ Ⓑ Ⓒ Ⓓ Ⓔ	61 Ⓐ Ⓑ Ⓒ Ⓓ Ⓔ	79 Ⓐ Ⓑ Ⓒ Ⓓ Ⓔ
8 Ⓐ Ⓑ Ⓒ Ⓓ Ⓔ	26 Ⓐ Ⓑ Ⓒ Ⓓ Ⓔ	44 Ⓐ Ⓑ Ⓒ Ⓓ Ⓔ	62 Ⓐ Ⓑ Ⓒ Ⓓ Ⓔ	80 Ⓐ Ⓑ Ⓒ Ⓓ Ⓔ
9 Ⓐ Ⓑ Ⓒ Ⓓ Ⓔ	27 Ⓐ Ⓑ Ⓒ Ⓓ Ⓔ	45 Ⓐ Ⓑ Ⓒ Ⓓ Ⓔ	63 Ⓐ Ⓑ Ⓒ Ⓓ Ⓔ	81 Ⓐ Ⓑ Ⓒ Ⓓ Ⓔ
10 Ⓐ Ⓑ Ⓒ Ⓓ Ⓔ	28 Ⓐ Ⓑ Ⓒ Ⓓ Ⓔ	46 Ⓐ Ⓑ Ⓒ Ⓓ Ⓔ	64 Ⓐ Ⓑ Ⓒ Ⓓ Ⓔ	82 Ⓐ Ⓑ Ⓒ Ⓓ Ⓔ
11 Ⓐ Ⓑ Ⓒ Ⓓ Ⓔ	29 Ⓐ Ⓑ Ⓒ Ⓓ Ⓔ	47 Ⓐ Ⓑ Ⓒ Ⓓ Ⓔ	65 Ⓐ Ⓑ Ⓒ Ⓓ Ⓔ	83 Ⓐ Ⓑ Ⓒ Ⓓ Ⓔ
12 Ⓐ Ⓑ Ⓒ Ⓓ Ⓔ	30 Ⓐ Ⓑ Ⓒ Ⓓ Ⓔ	48 Ⓐ Ⓑ Ⓒ Ⓓ Ⓔ	66 Ⓐ Ⓑ Ⓒ Ⓓ Ⓔ	84 Ⓐ Ⓑ Ⓒ Ⓓ Ⓔ
13 Ⓐ Ⓑ Ⓒ Ⓓ Ⓔ	31 Ⓐ Ⓑ Ⓒ Ⓓ Ⓔ	49 Ⓐ Ⓑ Ⓒ Ⓓ Ⓔ	67 Ⓐ Ⓑ Ⓒ Ⓓ Ⓔ	85 Ⓐ Ⓑ Ⓒ Ⓓ Ⓔ
14 Ⓐ Ⓑ Ⓒ Ⓓ Ⓔ	32 Ⓐ Ⓑ Ⓒ Ⓓ Ⓔ	50 Ⓐ Ⓑ Ⓒ Ⓓ Ⓔ	68 Ⓐ Ⓑ Ⓒ Ⓓ Ⓔ	86 Ⓐ Ⓑ Ⓒ Ⓓ Ⓔ
15 Ⓐ Ⓑ Ⓒ Ⓓ Ⓔ	33 Ⓐ Ⓑ Ⓒ Ⓓ Ⓔ	51 Ⓐ Ⓑ Ⓒ Ⓓ Ⓔ	69 Ⓐ Ⓑ Ⓒ Ⓓ Ⓔ	87 Ⓐ Ⓑ Ⓒ Ⓓ Ⓔ
16 Ⓐ Ⓑ Ⓒ Ⓓ Ⓔ	34 Ⓐ Ⓑ Ⓒ Ⓓ Ⓔ	52 Ⓐ Ⓑ Ⓒ Ⓓ Ⓔ	70 Ⓐ Ⓑ Ⓒ Ⓓ Ⓔ	88 Ⓐ Ⓑ Ⓒ Ⓓ Ⓔ
17 Ⓐ Ⓑ Ⓒ Ⓓ Ⓔ	35 Ⓐ Ⓑ Ⓒ Ⓓ Ⓔ	53 Ⓐ Ⓑ Ⓒ Ⓓ Ⓔ	71 Ⓐ Ⓑ Ⓒ Ⓓ Ⓔ	
18 Ⓐ Ⓑ Ⓒ Ⓓ Ⓔ	36 Ⓐ Ⓑ Ⓒ Ⓓ Ⓔ	54 Ⓐ Ⓑ Ⓒ Ⓓ Ⓔ	72 Ⓐ Ⓑ Ⓒ Ⓓ Ⓔ	

Part B—Memory for Addresses—List 2

1 Ⓐ Ⓑ Ⓒ Ⓓ Ⓔ	19 Ⓐ Ⓑ Ⓒ Ⓓ Ⓔ	37 Ⓐ Ⓑ Ⓒ Ⓓ Ⓔ	55 Ⓐ Ⓑ Ⓒ Ⓓ Ⓔ	73 Ⓐ Ⓑ Ⓒ Ⓓ Ⓔ
2 Ⓐ Ⓑ Ⓒ Ⓓ Ⓔ	20 Ⓐ Ⓑ Ⓒ Ⓓ Ⓔ	38 Ⓐ Ⓑ Ⓒ Ⓓ Ⓔ	56 Ⓐ Ⓑ Ⓒ Ⓓ Ⓔ	74 Ⓐ Ⓑ Ⓒ Ⓓ Ⓔ
3 Ⓐ Ⓑ Ⓒ Ⓓ Ⓔ	21 Ⓐ Ⓑ Ⓒ Ⓓ Ⓔ	39 Ⓐ Ⓑ Ⓒ Ⓓ Ⓔ	57 Ⓐ Ⓑ Ⓒ Ⓓ Ⓔ	75 Ⓐ Ⓑ Ⓒ Ⓓ Ⓔ
4 Ⓐ Ⓑ Ⓒ Ⓓ Ⓔ	22 Ⓐ Ⓑ Ⓒ Ⓓ Ⓔ	40 Ⓐ Ⓑ Ⓒ Ⓓ Ⓔ	58 Ⓐ Ⓑ Ⓒ Ⓓ Ⓔ	76 Ⓐ Ⓑ Ⓒ Ⓓ Ⓔ
5 Ⓐ Ⓑ Ⓒ Ⓓ Ⓔ	23 Ⓐ Ⓑ Ⓒ Ⓓ Ⓔ	41 Ⓐ Ⓑ Ⓒ Ⓓ Ⓔ	59 Ⓐ Ⓑ Ⓒ Ⓓ Ⓔ	77 Ⓐ Ⓑ Ⓒ Ⓓ Ⓔ
6 Ⓐ Ⓑ Ⓒ Ⓓ Ⓔ	24 Ⓐ Ⓑ Ⓒ Ⓓ Ⓔ	42 Ⓐ Ⓑ Ⓒ Ⓓ Ⓔ	60 Ⓐ Ⓑ Ⓒ Ⓓ Ⓔ	78 Ⓐ Ⓑ Ⓒ Ⓓ Ⓔ
7 Ⓐ Ⓑ Ⓒ Ⓓ Ⓔ	25 Ⓐ Ⓑ Ⓒ Ⓓ Ⓔ	43 Ⓐ Ⓑ Ⓒ Ⓓ Ⓔ	61 Ⓐ Ⓑ Ⓒ Ⓓ Ⓔ	79 Ⓐ Ⓑ Ⓒ Ⓓ Ⓔ
8 Ⓐ Ⓑ Ⓒ Ⓓ Ⓔ	26 Ⓐ Ⓑ Ⓒ Ⓓ Ⓔ	44 Ⓐ Ⓑ Ⓒ Ⓓ Ⓔ	62 Ⓐ Ⓑ Ⓒ Ⓓ Ⓔ	80 Ⓐ Ⓑ Ⓒ Ⓓ Ⓔ
9 Ⓐ Ⓑ Ⓒ Ⓓ Ⓔ	27 Ⓐ Ⓑ Ⓒ Ⓓ Ⓔ	45 Ⓐ Ⓑ Ⓒ Ⓓ Ⓔ	63 Ⓐ Ⓑ Ⓒ Ⓓ Ⓔ	81 Ⓐ Ⓑ Ⓒ Ⓓ Ⓔ
10 Ⓐ Ⓑ Ⓒ Ⓓ Ⓔ	28 Ⓐ Ⓑ Ⓒ Ⓓ Ⓔ	46 Ⓐ Ⓑ Ⓒ Ⓓ Ⓔ	64 Ⓐ Ⓑ Ⓒ Ⓓ Ⓔ	82 Ⓐ Ⓑ Ⓒ Ⓓ Ⓔ
11 Ⓐ Ⓑ Ⓒ Ⓓ Ⓔ	29 Ⓐ Ⓑ Ⓒ Ⓓ Ⓔ	47 Ⓐ Ⓑ Ⓒ Ⓓ Ⓔ	65 Ⓐ Ⓑ Ⓒ Ⓓ Ⓔ	83 Ⓐ Ⓑ Ⓒ Ⓓ Ⓔ
12 Ⓐ Ⓑ Ⓒ Ⓓ Ⓔ	30 Ⓐ Ⓑ Ⓒ Ⓓ Ⓔ	48 Ⓐ Ⓑ Ⓒ Ⓓ Ⓔ	66 Ⓐ Ⓑ Ⓒ Ⓓ Ⓔ	84 Ⓐ Ⓑ Ⓒ Ⓓ Ⓔ
13 Ⓐ Ⓑ Ⓒ Ⓓ Ⓔ	31 Ⓐ Ⓑ Ⓒ Ⓓ Ⓔ	49 Ⓐ Ⓑ Ⓒ Ⓓ Ⓔ	67 Ⓐ Ⓑ Ⓒ Ⓓ Ⓔ	85 Ⓐ Ⓑ Ⓒ Ⓓ Ⓔ
14 Ⓐ Ⓑ Ⓒ Ⓓ Ⓔ	32 Ⓐ Ⓑ Ⓒ Ⓓ Ⓔ	50 Ⓐ Ⓑ Ⓒ Ⓓ Ⓔ	68 Ⓐ Ⓑ Ⓒ Ⓓ Ⓔ	86 Ⓐ Ⓑ Ⓒ Ⓓ Ⓔ
15 Ⓐ Ⓑ Ⓒ Ⓓ Ⓔ	33 Ⓐ Ⓑ Ⓒ Ⓓ Ⓔ	51 Ⓐ Ⓑ Ⓒ Ⓓ Ⓔ	69 Ⓐ Ⓑ Ⓒ Ⓓ Ⓔ	87 Ⓐ Ⓑ Ⓒ Ⓓ Ⓔ
16 Ⓐ Ⓑ Ⓒ Ⓓ Ⓔ	34 Ⓐ Ⓑ Ⓒ Ⓓ Ⓔ	52 Ⓐ Ⓑ Ⓒ Ⓓ Ⓔ	70 Ⓐ Ⓑ Ⓒ Ⓓ Ⓔ	88 Ⓐ Ⓑ Ⓒ Ⓓ Ⓔ
17 Ⓐ Ⓑ Ⓒ Ⓓ Ⓔ	35 Ⓐ Ⓑ Ⓒ Ⓓ Ⓔ	53 Ⓐ Ⓑ Ⓒ Ⓓ Ⓔ	71 Ⓐ Ⓑ Ⓒ Ⓓ Ⓔ	
18 Ⓐ Ⓑ Ⓒ Ⓓ Ⓔ	36 Ⓐ Ⓑ Ⓒ Ⓓ Ⓔ	54 Ⓐ Ⓑ Ⓒ Ⓓ Ⓔ	72 Ⓐ Ⓑ Ⓒ Ⓓ Ⓔ	

Part B—Memory for Addresses—List 3

1 Ⓐ Ⓑ Ⓒ Ⓓ Ⓔ	19 Ⓐ Ⓑ Ⓒ Ⓓ Ⓔ	37 Ⓐ Ⓑ Ⓒ Ⓓ Ⓔ	55 Ⓐ Ⓑ Ⓒ Ⓓ Ⓔ	73 Ⓐ Ⓑ Ⓒ Ⓓ Ⓔ
2 Ⓐ Ⓑ Ⓒ Ⓓ Ⓔ	20 Ⓐ Ⓑ Ⓒ Ⓓ Ⓔ	38 Ⓐ Ⓑ Ⓒ Ⓓ Ⓔ	56 Ⓐ Ⓑ Ⓒ Ⓓ Ⓔ	74 Ⓐ Ⓑ Ⓒ Ⓓ Ⓔ
3 Ⓐ Ⓑ Ⓒ Ⓓ Ⓔ	21 Ⓐ Ⓑ Ⓒ Ⓓ Ⓔ	39 Ⓐ Ⓑ Ⓒ Ⓓ Ⓔ	57 Ⓐ Ⓑ Ⓒ Ⓓ Ⓔ	75 Ⓐ Ⓑ Ⓒ Ⓓ Ⓔ
4 Ⓐ Ⓑ Ⓒ Ⓓ Ⓔ	22 Ⓐ Ⓑ Ⓒ Ⓓ Ⓔ	40 Ⓐ Ⓑ Ⓒ Ⓓ Ⓔ	58 Ⓐ Ⓑ Ⓒ Ⓓ Ⓔ	76 Ⓐ Ⓑ Ⓒ Ⓓ Ⓔ
5 Ⓐ Ⓑ Ⓒ Ⓓ Ⓔ	23 Ⓐ Ⓑ Ⓒ Ⓓ Ⓔ	41 Ⓐ Ⓑ Ⓒ Ⓓ Ⓔ	59 Ⓐ Ⓑ Ⓒ Ⓓ Ⓔ	77 Ⓐ Ⓑ Ⓒ Ⓓ Ⓔ
6 Ⓐ Ⓑ Ⓒ Ⓓ Ⓔ	24 Ⓐ Ⓑ Ⓒ Ⓓ Ⓔ	42 Ⓐ Ⓑ Ⓒ Ⓓ Ⓔ	60 Ⓐ Ⓑ Ⓒ Ⓓ Ⓔ	78 Ⓐ Ⓑ Ⓒ Ⓓ Ⓔ
7 Ⓐ Ⓑ Ⓒ Ⓓ Ⓔ	25 Ⓐ Ⓑ Ⓒ Ⓓ Ⓔ	43 Ⓐ Ⓑ Ⓒ Ⓓ Ⓔ	61 Ⓐ Ⓑ Ⓒ Ⓓ Ⓔ	79 Ⓐ Ⓑ Ⓒ Ⓓ Ⓔ
8 Ⓐ Ⓑ Ⓒ Ⓓ Ⓔ	26 Ⓐ Ⓑ Ⓒ Ⓓ Ⓔ	44 Ⓐ Ⓑ Ⓒ Ⓓ Ⓔ	62 Ⓐ Ⓑ Ⓒ Ⓓ Ⓔ	80 Ⓐ Ⓑ Ⓒ Ⓓ Ⓔ
9 Ⓐ Ⓑ Ⓒ Ⓓ Ⓔ	27 Ⓐ Ⓑ Ⓒ Ⓓ Ⓔ	45 Ⓐ Ⓑ Ⓒ Ⓓ Ⓔ	63 Ⓐ Ⓑ Ⓒ Ⓓ Ⓔ	81 Ⓐ Ⓑ Ⓒ Ⓓ Ⓔ
10 Ⓐ Ⓑ Ⓒ Ⓓ Ⓔ	28 Ⓐ Ⓑ Ⓒ Ⓓ Ⓔ	46 Ⓐ Ⓑ Ⓒ Ⓓ Ⓔ	64 Ⓐ Ⓑ Ⓒ Ⓓ Ⓔ	82 Ⓐ Ⓑ Ⓒ Ⓓ Ⓔ
11 Ⓐ Ⓑ Ⓒ Ⓓ Ⓔ	29 Ⓐ Ⓑ Ⓒ Ⓓ Ⓔ	47 Ⓐ Ⓑ Ⓒ Ⓓ Ⓔ	65 Ⓐ Ⓑ Ⓒ Ⓓ Ⓔ	83 Ⓐ Ⓑ Ⓒ Ⓓ Ⓔ
12 Ⓐ Ⓑ Ⓒ Ⓓ Ⓔ	30 Ⓐ Ⓑ Ⓒ Ⓓ Ⓔ	48 Ⓐ Ⓑ Ⓒ Ⓓ Ⓔ	66 Ⓐ Ⓑ Ⓒ Ⓓ Ⓔ	84 Ⓐ Ⓑ Ⓒ Ⓓ Ⓔ
13 Ⓐ Ⓑ Ⓒ Ⓓ Ⓔ	31 Ⓐ Ⓑ Ⓒ Ⓓ Ⓔ	49 Ⓐ Ⓑ Ⓒ Ⓓ Ⓔ	67 Ⓐ Ⓑ Ⓒ Ⓓ Ⓔ	85 Ⓐ Ⓑ Ⓒ Ⓓ Ⓔ
14 Ⓐ Ⓑ Ⓒ Ⓓ Ⓔ	32 Ⓐ Ⓑ Ⓒ Ⓓ Ⓔ	50 Ⓐ Ⓑ Ⓒ Ⓓ Ⓔ	68 Ⓐ Ⓑ Ⓒ Ⓓ Ⓔ	86 Ⓐ Ⓑ Ⓒ Ⓓ Ⓔ
15 Ⓐ Ⓑ Ⓒ Ⓓ Ⓔ	33 Ⓐ Ⓑ Ⓒ Ⓓ Ⓔ	51 Ⓐ Ⓑ Ⓒ Ⓓ Ⓔ	69 Ⓐ Ⓑ Ⓒ Ⓓ Ⓔ	87 Ⓐ Ⓑ Ⓒ Ⓓ Ⓔ
16 Ⓐ Ⓑ Ⓒ Ⓓ Ⓔ	34 Ⓐ Ⓑ Ⓒ Ⓓ Ⓔ	52 Ⓐ Ⓑ Ⓒ Ⓓ Ⓔ	70 Ⓐ Ⓑ Ⓒ Ⓓ Ⓔ	88 Ⓐ Ⓑ Ⓒ Ⓓ Ⓔ
17 Ⓐ Ⓑ Ⓒ Ⓓ Ⓔ	35 Ⓐ Ⓑ Ⓒ Ⓓ Ⓔ	53 Ⓐ Ⓑ Ⓒ Ⓓ Ⓔ	71 Ⓐ Ⓑ Ⓒ Ⓓ Ⓔ	
18 Ⓐ Ⓑ Ⓒ Ⓓ Ⓔ	36 Ⓐ Ⓑ Ⓒ Ⓓ Ⓔ	54 Ⓐ Ⓑ Ⓒ Ⓓ Ⓔ	72 Ⓐ Ⓑ Ⓒ Ⓓ Ⓔ	

Part C—Number Series

1 Ⓐ Ⓑ Ⓒ Ⓓ Ⓔ	6 Ⓐ Ⓑ Ⓒ Ⓓ Ⓔ	11 Ⓐ Ⓑ Ⓒ Ⓓ Ⓔ	16 Ⓐ Ⓑ Ⓒ Ⓓ Ⓔ	21 Ⓐ Ⓑ Ⓒ Ⓓ Ⓔ
2 Ⓐ Ⓑ Ⓒ Ⓓ Ⓔ	7 Ⓐ Ⓑ Ⓒ Ⓓ Ⓔ	12 Ⓐ Ⓑ Ⓒ Ⓓ Ⓔ	17 Ⓐ Ⓑ Ⓒ Ⓓ Ⓔ	22 Ⓐ Ⓑ Ⓒ Ⓓ Ⓔ
3 Ⓐ Ⓑ Ⓒ Ⓓ Ⓔ	8 Ⓐ Ⓑ Ⓒ Ⓓ Ⓔ	13 Ⓐ Ⓑ Ⓒ Ⓓ Ⓔ	18 Ⓐ Ⓑ Ⓒ Ⓓ Ⓔ	23 Ⓐ Ⓑ Ⓒ Ⓓ Ⓔ
4 Ⓐ Ⓑ Ⓒ Ⓓ Ⓔ	9 Ⓐ Ⓑ Ⓒ Ⓓ Ⓔ	14 Ⓐ Ⓑ Ⓒ Ⓓ Ⓔ	19 Ⓐ Ⓑ Ⓒ Ⓓ Ⓔ	24 Ⓐ Ⓑ Ⓒ Ⓓ Ⓔ
5 Ⓐ Ⓑ Ⓒ Ⓓ Ⓔ	10 Ⓐ Ⓑ Ⓒ Ⓓ Ⓔ	15 Ⓐ Ⓑ Ⓒ Ⓓ Ⓔ	20 Ⓐ Ⓑ Ⓒ Ⓓ Ⓔ	

Part D—Following Oral Directions

1 Ⓐ Ⓑ Ⓒ Ⓓ Ⓔ	19 Ⓐ Ⓑ Ⓒ Ⓓ Ⓔ	37 Ⓐ Ⓑ Ⓒ Ⓓ Ⓔ	55 Ⓐ Ⓑ Ⓒ Ⓓ Ⓔ	73 Ⓐ Ⓑ Ⓒ Ⓓ Ⓔ
2 Ⓐ Ⓑ Ⓒ Ⓓ Ⓔ	20 Ⓐ Ⓑ Ⓒ Ⓓ Ⓔ	38 Ⓐ Ⓑ Ⓒ Ⓓ Ⓔ	56 Ⓐ Ⓑ Ⓒ Ⓓ Ⓔ	74 Ⓐ Ⓑ Ⓒ Ⓓ Ⓔ
3 Ⓐ Ⓑ Ⓒ Ⓓ Ⓔ	21 Ⓐ Ⓑ Ⓒ Ⓓ Ⓔ	39 Ⓐ Ⓑ Ⓒ Ⓓ Ⓔ	57 Ⓐ Ⓑ Ⓒ Ⓓ Ⓔ	75 Ⓐ Ⓑ Ⓒ Ⓓ Ⓔ
4 Ⓐ Ⓑ Ⓒ Ⓓ Ⓔ	22 Ⓐ Ⓑ Ⓒ Ⓓ Ⓔ	40 Ⓐ Ⓑ Ⓒ Ⓓ Ⓔ	58 Ⓐ Ⓑ Ⓒ Ⓓ Ⓔ	76 Ⓐ Ⓑ Ⓒ Ⓓ Ⓔ
5 Ⓐ Ⓑ Ⓒ Ⓓ Ⓔ	23 Ⓐ Ⓑ Ⓒ Ⓓ Ⓔ	41 Ⓐ Ⓑ Ⓒ Ⓓ Ⓔ	59 Ⓐ Ⓑ Ⓒ Ⓓ Ⓔ	77 Ⓐ Ⓑ Ⓒ Ⓓ Ⓔ
6 Ⓐ Ⓑ Ⓒ Ⓓ Ⓔ	24 Ⓐ Ⓑ Ⓒ Ⓓ Ⓔ	42 Ⓐ Ⓑ Ⓒ Ⓓ Ⓔ	60 Ⓐ Ⓑ Ⓒ Ⓓ Ⓔ	78 Ⓐ Ⓑ Ⓒ Ⓓ Ⓔ
7 Ⓐ Ⓑ Ⓒ Ⓓ Ⓔ	25 Ⓐ Ⓑ Ⓒ Ⓓ Ⓔ	43 Ⓐ Ⓑ Ⓒ Ⓓ Ⓔ	61 Ⓐ Ⓑ Ⓒ Ⓓ Ⓔ	79 Ⓐ Ⓑ Ⓒ Ⓓ Ⓔ
8 Ⓐ Ⓑ Ⓒ Ⓓ Ⓔ	26 Ⓐ Ⓑ Ⓒ Ⓓ Ⓔ	44 Ⓐ Ⓑ Ⓒ Ⓓ Ⓔ	62 Ⓐ Ⓑ Ⓒ Ⓓ Ⓔ	80 Ⓐ Ⓑ Ⓒ Ⓓ Ⓔ
9 Ⓐ Ⓑ Ⓒ Ⓓ Ⓔ	27 Ⓐ Ⓑ Ⓒ Ⓓ Ⓔ	45 Ⓐ Ⓑ Ⓒ Ⓓ Ⓔ	63 Ⓐ Ⓑ Ⓒ Ⓓ Ⓔ	81 Ⓐ Ⓑ Ⓒ Ⓓ Ⓔ
10 Ⓐ Ⓑ Ⓒ Ⓓ Ⓔ	28 Ⓐ Ⓑ Ⓒ Ⓓ Ⓔ	46 Ⓐ Ⓑ Ⓒ Ⓓ Ⓔ	64 Ⓐ Ⓑ Ⓒ Ⓓ Ⓔ	82 Ⓐ Ⓑ Ⓒ Ⓓ Ⓔ
11 Ⓐ Ⓑ Ⓒ Ⓓ Ⓔ	29 Ⓐ Ⓑ Ⓒ Ⓓ Ⓔ	47 Ⓐ Ⓑ Ⓒ Ⓓ Ⓔ	65 Ⓐ Ⓑ Ⓒ Ⓓ Ⓔ	83 Ⓐ Ⓑ Ⓒ Ⓓ Ⓔ
12 Ⓐ Ⓑ Ⓒ Ⓓ Ⓔ	30 Ⓐ Ⓑ Ⓒ Ⓓ Ⓔ	48 Ⓐ Ⓑ Ⓒ Ⓓ Ⓔ	66 Ⓐ Ⓑ Ⓒ Ⓓ Ⓔ	84 Ⓐ Ⓑ Ⓒ Ⓓ Ⓔ
13 Ⓐ Ⓑ Ⓒ Ⓓ Ⓔ	31 Ⓐ Ⓑ Ⓒ Ⓓ Ⓔ	49 Ⓐ Ⓑ Ⓒ Ⓓ Ⓔ	67 Ⓐ Ⓑ Ⓒ Ⓓ Ⓔ	85 Ⓐ Ⓑ Ⓒ Ⓓ Ⓔ
14 Ⓐ Ⓑ Ⓒ Ⓓ Ⓔ	32 Ⓐ Ⓑ Ⓒ Ⓓ Ⓔ	50 Ⓐ Ⓑ Ⓒ Ⓓ Ⓔ	68 Ⓐ Ⓑ Ⓒ Ⓓ Ⓔ	86 Ⓐ Ⓑ Ⓒ Ⓓ Ⓔ
15 Ⓐ Ⓑ Ⓒ Ⓓ Ⓔ	33 Ⓐ Ⓑ Ⓒ Ⓓ Ⓔ	51 Ⓐ Ⓑ Ⓒ Ⓓ Ⓔ	69 Ⓐ Ⓑ Ⓒ Ⓓ Ⓔ	87 Ⓐ Ⓑ Ⓒ Ⓓ Ⓔ
16 Ⓐ Ⓑ Ⓒ Ⓓ Ⓔ	34 Ⓐ Ⓑ Ⓒ Ⓓ Ⓔ	52 Ⓐ Ⓑ Ⓒ Ⓓ Ⓔ	70 Ⓐ Ⓑ Ⓒ Ⓓ Ⓔ	88 Ⓐ Ⓑ Ⓒ Ⓓ Ⓔ
17 Ⓐ Ⓑ Ⓒ Ⓓ Ⓔ	35 Ⓐ Ⓑ Ⓒ Ⓓ Ⓔ	53 Ⓐ Ⓑ Ⓒ Ⓓ Ⓔ	71 Ⓐ Ⓑ Ⓒ Ⓓ Ⓔ	
18 Ⓐ Ⓑ Ⓒ Ⓓ Ⓔ	36 Ⓐ Ⓑ Ⓒ Ⓓ Ⓔ	54 Ⓐ Ⓑ Ⓒ Ⓓ Ⓔ	72 Ⓐ Ⓑ Ⓒ Ⓓ Ⓔ	

Remove by cutting on dotted line.

Chapter 13

Practice Test 4

PART A — ADDRESS CHECKING

Work — 6 minutes

In this part of the test, you are to decide whether two addresses are alike or different. If the two addresses are *exactly alike in every way*, darken space Ⓐ. If they are *different in any way*, darken space Ⓓ.

Mark your answers on the Answer Sheet on page 333. Tear it out, put today's date on it, and place it next to the questions.

Allow yourself exactly 6 minutes to do as many of the 95 questions as you can. If you finish before the time is up, check your answers.

1. Columbine Hills CO 80123   Columbine Hills CO 80123
2. Ponce PR   Ponce PA
3. 492 Iolantha Lane   492 Iolantha Lane
4. 110 Hambiton Ave   110 Hamilton Ave
5. 53 S Dockerry Lane   53 S Bockerry Lane
6. 3776 E Yoakum St   3776 E Yoakum Sq
7. 910 Jumel Ter   910 Jumel Ter
8. 3992 Aristotle Dr   3992 Aristotel Dr
9. 4704 Clavier St   4740 Clavier St
10. 438 Hamakawai Court   438 Hamakawai Court
11. 3404 N Barrymore Ct   3404 N Barrymore Ct
12. 6381 W Blumberg Ave   6318 W Blumberg Ave

13. 58 SE Kramden Pl   58 SE Kramden Pl
14. 8940 N Dunkirk St   8940 N Dunkirk St
15. 9120 Martin Marietto Sq   9210 Martin Marietto Sq
16. 5038 Farley Granger Woods Walk   5038 Farley Granger Woods Walk
17. 3048 Damon Farms Ln   3048 Damon Farms Ln
18. 2401 Knight Blvd   2401 Knight Blvd
19. 8864 N Cheshire Pl   8864 S Cheshire Pl
20. 789 Iago Dr   789 Iaga Dr
21. 501 Wheelwood Blvd E   501 Wheelwood Blvd E
22. Denham Springs 71232   Denham Springs 72132
23. 683 N Quebec Tpke   683 N Quebec Tpke
24. Plainfield NH 03781   Plainfield NV 03781

25.	6234 S Drummond Dr	6234 W Drummond Dr
26.	7576 Goldwater Ter	7576 Goldwater Trl
27.	2341 Carmine Blvd	2341 Carmine Blvd
28.	49 Westlake Ave	49 Westlake Ave
29.	823 W Palmetto St	823 E Palmetto St
30.	119 Albermarle Rd N	119 Alpermarle Rd N
31.	959 NE Polakalua Pl	959 NE Polakalua Pl
32.	984 Classenfuls Ave NE	984 Clasenfuls Ave NE
33.	1382 Grindel Rock Blvd	1382 Glindel Rock Blvd
34.	2219 Altamount Canyon Tpke	2219 Altamount Canyon Tpke
35.	9412 Young Pl	9412 Youth Pl
36.	2800 Regalos el Modina	2800 Regaldos el Modina
37.	7383 Tremont West Dr	7383 Tremont East Dr
38.	2764 Partridge Ct	2764 Partridge Ct
39.	1005 W San Obispa Cir	1005 W San Obispa Cir
40.	1045 Chekea Ct SE	1045 Chekea Ct NE
41.	8000 Coronado de Bolivar Trail	8000 Coronado de Bolivar Trail
42.	3528 Virginia Park Pkwy	3528 Virginia Park Cswy
43.	6223 Farmingdale Park W	6223 Farmingdale Park W
44.	50 Iverness Pl	50 Iverness Pl
45.	1002 W 7 St	1002 W 7 St
46.	Teton ID 83451	Teton DC 83451
47.	116 Evermonde Rd SW	116 Evermonde Dr SW
48.	North Underwood City OH	North Underwood City OH
49.	1683 S Roanoke Ave	1685 S Roanoke Ave
50.	424 W Vernier Ave	424 W Vernier Ave
51.	308 Quentin Rd	308 Quentin Dr
52.	7721 Jerseyside Via	7721 Jerseyside Via
53.	875 Castle Hill Ave	875 Castel Hill Ave
54.	7904 Herricks Place	7904 Herricks Place
55.	1040 Davenport St	1040 Davenport Sq
56.	Riverale MD 20737	Riverale MO 20737
57.	489 Esterwood Ln	489 Westerwood Ln
58.	5055 NW 264th Ave	5055 NW 26th Ave
59.	5005 Slatterside Loop E	5006 Slatterside Loop E
60.	Bay City MI 48707	Boy City MI 48707

61.	3704 Eldano St	3704 Eldamo St
62.	4488 W Merryweather Ave	4488 W Merryweather Ave
63.	North Attleboro MA	North Attleberg MA
64.	7803 S Uster Rd	7803 S Ulster Rd
65.	East Meadow NY 11554	East Meadow NJ 11554
66.	707 E Wallington St	707 E Wallington St
67.	6016 Broadwatter Rd S	6016 Broadwatter Rd S
68.	8103 E. Shannon St	8103 E Shannon Ct
69.	1023 Fleissig St	1032 Fleissig St
70.	298 Hialeah St	298 Hialeah St
71.	9101 En Pacada Sq	9101 En Pacado Sq
72.	62 Old Woods Drive West	62 Old Woods Drive West
73.	2460 Nortondale Blvd	2460 Nortondell Blvd
74.	255 Ingersoll Pkwy NE	255 Ingersoll Pky SE
75.	31 E Greeley Sq	31 E Greeley Sq
76.	6515 Weathersfield Ct N	6515 Weathersford Ct N
77.	347 N 104th St	347 N 104th St
78.	15510 Jesper Blvd	15510 Jasper Blvd
79.	610 South Handy Ln NW	610 South Candy Ln NW
80.	San Jose PR 00924	San Juan PR 00924
81.	403 Yuletide Tree Road	403 Yuletide Tree Road
82.	7704 NE 20th St	7704 NE 20th St
83.	Glenham SD 57631	Glenham SD 57621
84.	2008 Steinway St	2008 Steinway St
85.	971 Larch Lake Road	917 Larch Lake Road
86.	6994 Kristofferson Blvd S	6994 Kristofferson Blvd S
87.	Moorehead MN 56501	Moosehead MN 56501
88.	8138 S Ettiger Rd	8183 S Ettinger Rd
89.	88 E Garinow Dr	88 E Garinow Dr
90.	928 N 11th Rd	928 N 111th Rd
91.	43 Riverdale Cir S	43 Riverside Cir S
92.	846 Fremont Pl	846 Fremount Pl
93.	5912 E 213 St	5912 E 213 St
94.	1136 Simpson St	1136 Simpson St
95.	4106 East Country Hill Path	4106 East Country Hill Path

STOP.
If you finish before the time is up, go back and check
the questions in this section of the test only.

PART B — MEMORY FOR ADDRESSES

In this part of the test, you will have five boxes labeled A, B, C, D, and E. Each box contains five addresses. Three of the five are groups of street addresses, such as 5400–5699 Garden, 6400–6699 Sunset, and 6000–6399 Ulster; and two are names of places. The addresses are different in each box.

There will be several opportunities to study the addresses and the boxes they are in. You will also be given three tests of 88 questions each, and the task of deciding where each address belongs. In some cases, you will have the list *and* the boxes in front of you at the same time; in others you will not. List 1 and List 2 are for warm-up practice. List 3 is the real one that will be scored.

Make sure you understand the format by examining the pretest samples below.

Pretest Samples

A	B	C	D	E
4100–4599 Garden	5400–5699 Garden	5700–6399 Garden	4600–5399 Garden	6400–6999 Garden
Raimes	Emory	Clarke	Sargeant	Violet
6400–6699 Sunset	5700–6399 Sunset	5400–5699 Sunset	4100–5399 Sunset	6700–7199 Sunset
Temple	Pearle	Atlantic	Bliss	Illinois
4600–5399 Ulster	6400–6899 Ulster	6000–6399 Ulster	5400–5999 Ulster	4100–4599 Ulster

Questions 1 through 7 show the way the questions look. You have to decide in which lettered box (A, B, C, D, or E) the address belongs and then mark your answer by darkening the appropriate space in the answer grid.

1. Sargeant   1 Ⓐ Ⓑ Ⓒ Ⓓ Ⓔ
2. Pearle   2 Ⓐ Ⓑ Ⓒ Ⓓ Ⓔ
3. Illinois   3 Ⓐ Ⓑ Ⓒ Ⓓ Ⓔ
4. 4100–4599 Garden   4 Ⓐ Ⓑ Ⓒ Ⓓ Ⓔ
5. Emory   5 Ⓐ Ⓑ Ⓒ Ⓓ Ⓔ
6. 6400–6899 Ulster   6 Ⓐ Ⓑ Ⓒ Ⓓ Ⓔ
7. 5700–6399 Sunset   7 Ⓐ Ⓑ Ⓒ Ⓓ Ⓔ

Answers

1. **D**   2. **B**   3. **E**   4. **A**   5. **B**   6. **B**   7. **B**

Now that you know what to do, you may begin Part B of Practice Test 4. To get the most out of it and the remaining two practice tests in this book, follow the directions and timing *exactly*. Follow each phase of Part B of the test, page by page, until you've completed List 3. It is modeled on the way the Postal Service actually conducts its tests.

Turn to the next page to begin.

Study — 3 minutes

You will be given 3 minutes to spend memorizing the addresses in the boxes. *They are exactly the same ones that will be used for all three tests.* Try to memorize as many as you can. When the 3 minutes are up, turn to page 342 and read the instructions for *List 1*.

A	B	C	D	E
4100–4599 Garden	5400–5699 Garden	5700–6399 Garden	4600–5399 Garden	6400–6999 Garden
Raimes	Emory	Clarke	Sargeant	Violet
6400–6699 Sunset	5700–6399 Sunset	5400–5699 Sunset	4100–5399 Sunset	6700–7199 Sunset
Temple	Pearle	Atlantic	Bliss	Illinois
4600–5399 Ulster	6400–6899 Ulster	6000–6399 Ulster	5400–5999 Ulster	4100–4599 Ulster

List 1

Work — 3 minutes

For each question, mark the Answer Sheet on page 334 to show the letter of the box in which the address belongs. Try to remember the locations of as many addresses as you can. *You will now have 3 minutes to complete List 1.* If you are not sure of an answer, you should guess.

A	B	C	D	E
4100–4599 Garden	5400–5699 Garden	5700–6399 Garden	4600–5399 Garden	6400–6999 Garden
Raimes	Emory	Clarke	Sargeant	Violet
6400–6699 Sunset	5700–6399 Sunset	5400–5699 Sunset	4100–5399 Sunset	6700–7199 Sunset
Temple	Pearle	Atlantic	Bliss	Illinois
4600–5399 Ulster	6400–6899 Ulster	6000–6399 Ulster	5400–5999 Ulster	4100–4599 Ulster

1. Bliss
2. 5700–6399 Garden
3. Violet
4. Atlantic
5. 4100–5399 Sunset
6. Raines
7. 6700–7199 Sunset
8. 4600–5399 Ulster
9. 5400–5999 Ulster
10. Illinois
11. Temple

12. 4600–5399 Garden
13. 6000–6399 Ulster
14. Atlantic
15. Clarke
16. 6400–6899 Ulster
17. 5700–6399 Sunset
18. Raines
19. 5400–5699 Sunset
20. 5400–5999 Ulster
21. 5700–6399 Garden
22. Pearle

23. Emory
24. 6400–6999 Garden
25. Violet
26. 4100–4599 Ulster
27. 4100–4599 Garden
28. 5400–5699 Garden
29. Sargeant
30. 5700–6399 Sunset
31. 5400–5699 Sunset
32. Clarke
33. 6700–7199 Sunset

34. Sargeant
35. 5400–5699 Garden
36. Raines
37. 5400–5699 Sunset
38. Sargeant
39. 4600–5399 Ulster
40. Temple
41. 6400–6699 Sunset
42. Pearle
43. Violet
44. 4100–4599 Garden

45. 5400–5999 Ulster
46. 6000–6399 Ulster
47. 6400–6699 Sunset
48. 5700–6399 Garden
49. Emory
50. Temple
51. 6400–6699 Sunset
52. 5700–6399 Sunset
53. Atlantic
54. 4100–4599 Ulster
55. Pearle

56. 6000–6399 Ulster
57. 4600–5399 Garden
58. Emory
59. 4100–4599 Ulster
60. Bliss
61. Clarke
62. 4600–5399 Garden
63. Pearle
64. 6700–7199 Sunset
65. Violet
66. 4600–5399 Ulster

67. Temple
68. Atlantic
69. 4100–5399 Sunset
70. Bliss
71. Clarke
72. 6400–6999 Garden
73. Sargeant
74. Atlantic
75. Illinois
76. 6400–6899 Ulster
77. 4100–4599 Garden

78. 4100–5399 Sunset
79. 6400–6899 Ulster
80. Emory
81. 5400–5699 Garden
82. Bliss
83. Raines
84. 6400–6699 Sunset
85. Sargeant
86. Raines
87. 6400–6999 Garden
88. Illinois

STOP.
If you finish before the time is up, go back and check
the questions in this section of the test only.

List 2

Do these questions *without* looking back at the boxes. For each question, mark your answer on the Answer Sheet for List 2 on page 334. If you are not sure of an answer, you should guess.

1. Atlantic
2. Sargeant
3. Violet
4. 5700–6399 Sunset
5. 6400–6699 Sunset
6. Emory
7. 4100–4599 Garden
8. Bliss
9. 4100–4599 Garden
10. 4600–5399 Ulster
11. 4100–5399 Sunset

12. 4100–4599 Garden
13. Illinois
14. 4600–5399 Garden
15. 5400–5699 Sunset
16. Temple
17. Atlantic
18. Emory
19. 5400–5699 Sunset
20. Sargeant
21. 4100–4599 Ulster
22. Raines

23. Temple
24. 6700–7199 Sunset
25. Raines
26. Atlantic
27. 5700–6399 Sunset
28. 5400–5999 Ulster
29. 4100–4599 Ulster
30. 5700–6399 Garden
31. Bliss
32. 6000–6399 Ulster
33. Sargeant

34. 5400–5999 Ulster
35. Emory
36. Bliss
37. 4600–5399 Ulster
38. Emory
39. Illinois
40. Temple
41. 4600–5399 Garden
42. 6400–6699 Sunset
43. 5700–6399 Sunset
44. 5400–5699 Garden

45. Clarke

46. Pearle

47. 4100–5399 Sunset

48. 5400–5699 Garden

49. 6400–6899 Ulster

50. Raines

51. Atlantic

52. Illinois

53. 6400–6699 Sunset

54. 6400–6999 Garden

55. Temple

56. 6400–6999 Garden

57. 4600–5399 Ulster

58. 5400–5699 Sunset

59. Pearle

60. 6000–6399 Ulster

61. Raines

62. Clarke

63. 4100–5399 Sunset

64. Raines

65. 5700–6399 Garden

66. 6000–6399 Ulster

67. 6400–6899 Ulster

68. Violet

69. Atlantic

70. 4100–4599 Ulster

71. Clarke

72. Violet

73. 6400–6999 Garden

74. 6700–7199 Sunset

75. Sargeant

76. Bliss

77. 6400–6899 Ulster

78. Violet

79. 4600–5399 Garden

80. 6700–7199 Sunset

81. 5400–5999 Ulster

82. 4100–4599 Ulster

83. Clarke

84. 5400–5699 Garden

85. 5700–6399 Garden

86. Pearle

87. Sargeant

88. 4600–5399 Ulster

STOP.
If you finish before the time is up, go back and check
the questions in this section of the test only.

List 3

Study — 5 minutes

You are now about to take the test using List 3. *(This is the test that counts!)*

Turn back to page 341 and study the boxes again. *You have 5 minutes to restudy the addresses.*

Work — 5 minutes

For each question, mark the Answer Sheet on page 335 to show the letter of the box in which the address belongs. You have *exactly 5 minutes* to do the test. During these 5 minutes, *do not* turn to any other page.

1. 5400–5699 Garden
2. 5700–6399 Sunset
3. 6400–6699 Sunset
4. 4600–5399 Garden
5. Temple
6. Illinois
7. Emory
8. 4600–5399 Ulster
9. Bliss
10. Emory
11. 5400–5999 Ulster

12. Sargeant
13. 6000–6399 Ulster
14. Bliss
15. 5700–6399 Garden
16. 4100–4599 Ulster
17. 5400–5999 Ulster
18. 5700–6399 Sunset
19. Atlantic
20. Raines
21. 6700–7199 Sunset
22. Temple

23. 6400–6999 Garden
24. Pearle
25. Sargeant
26. 5400–5699 Sunset
27. Emory
28. Atlantic
29. Temple
30. 5400–5699 Sunset
31. 4600–5399 Garden
32. Illinois
33. 4100–4599 Garden

34. 4100–5399 Sunset
35. 4600–5399 Ulster
36. 4100–4599 Garden
37. Bliss
38. 4100–4599 Garden
39. Emory
40. 6400–6699 Sunset
41. 5700–6399 Sunset
42. Violet
43. Sargeant
44. Atlantic

45. Illinois
46. Sargeant
47. Pearle
48. 5700–6399 Garden
49. 5400–5699 Garden
50. Clarke
51. 4100–4599 Ulster
52. 5400–5999 Ulster
53. 6700–7199 Sunset
54. 4600–5399 Garden
55. Violet

56. 6400–6899 Ulster
57. Bliss
58. Sargeant
59. 6700–7199 Sunset
60. 6400–6999 Garden
61. Violet
62. Clarke
63. 4100–4599 Ulster
64. Atlantic
65. Violet
66. 6400–6899 Ulster

67. 6000–6399 Ulster
68. 5700–6399 Garden
69. Raines
70. 4100–5399 Sunset
71. 5700–6399 Sunset
72. Raines
73. 6000–6399 Ulster
74. Pearle
75. 5400–5699 Sunset
76. 4600–5399 Ulster
77. 6400–6999 Garden

78. Temple
79. 6400–6999 Garden
80. 6400–6699 Sunset
81. Illinois
82. 4600–5399 Ulster
83. Raines
84. 6400–6899 Ulster
85. 5400–5699 Garden
86. 4100–5399 Sunset
87. Pearle
88. Clarke

STOP.
If you finish before the time is up, go back and check
the questions in this section of the test only.

PART C — NUMBER SERIES

Work — 20 minutes

For each Number Series question, there is a series of numbers that follow some definite order, and below each are five sets of two numbers each. You are to look at the numbers in the series and find out what order they follow. Then decide what the next two numbers in that series would be if the same order were continued. Mark your answers on the Answer Sheet for Number Series on page 335.

You have 20 minutes to complete this part of the test. If you finish before the time is up, check your answers. The answers and explanations are on pages 358 to 359.

1. 40 50 60 40 50 60 40 __ __
   A) 40 50   B) 50 60   C) 60 70   D) 50 40   E) 60 40

2. 31 40 28 37 25 34 22 __ __
   A) 18 21   B) 32 10   C) 19 31   D) 31 19   E) 30 18

3. 57 53 53 49 49 45 45 __ __
   A) 45 41   B) 41 37   C) 39 39   D) 41 41   E) 37 41

4. 16 21 19 18 23 21 20 __ __
   A) 24 22   B) 19 18   C) 18 17   D) 21 26   E) 25 23

5. 68 67 67 50 49 49 32 __ __
   A) 40 18   B) 32 15   C) 32 14   D) 29 19   E) 31 31

6. 36 30 30 32 23 23 28 16 __ __
   A) 24 24   B) 24 26   C) 16 24   D) 9 16   E) 21 24

7. 9 12 15 30 25 20 18 21 24 15 __ __
   A) 10 5   B) 18 21   C) 20 25   D) 18 10   E) 15 20

8. 15 35 20 28 25 21 30 __ __
   A) 14 35   B) 40 18   C) 14 40   D) 35 24   E) 23 24

9. 43 17 36 28 16 21 13 __ __
   A) 17 9   B) 5 17   C) 15 6   D) 12 14   E) 17 7

10. 32 30 38 28 26 36 24 __ __
    A) 22 32   B) 26 36   C) 22 34   D) 28 36   E) 24 34

11. 4 6 8 8 5 7 7 7 6 8 6 __ __
    A) 7 9   B) 8 9   C) 8 7   D) 7 8   E) 6 7

12. 1 2 4 5 7 8 10 __ __
   A) 10 11   B) 11 13   C) 11 12   D) 9 10   E) 12 13

13. 5 7 10 10 12 15 10 __ __
   A) 18 10   B) 10 10   C) 17 20   D) 10 13   E) 13 10

14. 4 10 8 14 12 18 16 __ __
   A) 22 20   B) 14 20   C) 18 22   D) 22 26   E) 20 24

15. 3 6 2 5 10 6 9 __ __
   A) 14 8   B) 10 12   C) 18 14   D) 12 24   E) 5 10

16. 27 72 62 26 16 61 51 __ __
   A) 71 17   B) 16 6   C) 41 14   D) 17 71   E) 15 5

17. 1 13 8 8 13 15 15 13 __ __
   A) 20 22   B) 22 25   C) 25 20   D) 22 22   E) 20 20

18. 56 56 48 48 41 41 35 __ __
   A) 35 35   B) 35 30   C) 35 29   D) 29 29   E) 30 30

19. 16 17 18 12 14 19 20 21 16 18 22 __ __
   A) 24 23   B) 19 23   C) 20 22   D) 23 24   E) 24 25

20. 26 24 16 23 21 17 20 18 18 17 __ __
   A) 15 14   B) 17 19   C) 14 20   D) 15 19   E) 19 14

21. 31 32 33 32 33 34 33 __ __
   A) 35 35   B) 32 33   C) 33 34   D) 33 33   E) 34 35

22. 1 20 2 18 4 16 8 __ __
   A) 10 12   B) 12 10   C) 14 18   D) 32 10   E) 14 16

23. 5 10 11 6 12 13 7 __ __
   A) 8 9   B) 14 8   C) 10 15   D) 14 15   E) 8 14

24. 2 3 5 9 17 33 65 __ __
   A) 82 104   B) 120 162   C) 129 257   D) 165 330   E) 189 377

STOP.
If you finish before the time is up, go back and check
the questions in this section of the test only.

PART D — FOLLOWING ORAL DIRECTIONS

This part of the test gauges your ability to understand and carry out spoken directions *exactly* as they are given to you.

In order to prepare to take Part D of the test, follow the steps below:

1. Enlist the help of a friend who will be the "reader." His or her job will be to read aloud a series of directions that you are to follow *exactly*. The reader will need a watch that displays seconds, because the directions must be read at the correct speed.

2. Tear out pages 355 and 356. These are the worksheets you should have in front of you as you listen to the directions given by the reader, who will tell you to do certain things with the items on each line on the worksheets.

3. Use the Answer Sheet for Following Oral Directions on page 335, and insert today's date. You will darken the appropriate spaces in accordance with the directions given by the reader.

4. *Now hand this entire book to the reader.* Ask him/her to review the section below headed "Instructions to the Reader." It explains exactly how the reader is to proceed.

When you and the reader are ready to start this part of Practice Test 4, he/she will begin reading to you the section marked "Directions." YOU ARE NOT TO READ THESE AT ANY TIME BEFORE OR DURING THE TEST. If you do, you will lose the benefit of this part of the practice test.

Instructions to the "Reader"

These instructions should be read at about 80 words per minute. You should practice reading the material in the box until you can do it in exactly 1 minute. The number of words in the passage and the natural pauses described below will give you a good feel for the rate of speed and the way you should read the test questions.

1-MINUTE PRACTICE

> Look at line 20 on your worksheet. There are two circles and two boxes of different sizes with numbers in them. If 7 is less than 3 and if 2 is smaller than 4, write C in the larger circle. Otherwise write B as in *baker* in the smaller box. Now, on your answer sheet, darken the space for the number-letter combination in the box or circle.

You should read the entire test aloud before you read it to the person taking the test, in order to thoroughly acquaint yourself with the procedure and the desired rate of reading.

Read slowly but at a natural pace. In other words, do not space the words so that there are unnaturally long pauses between them. The instruction "Pause slightly" indicates only enough time to take a breath. The other instructions for pauses give the recommended length for each. If possible, use a watch with a second hand.

All the material that follows, except the words in parentheses, is to be read aloud. Now start reading the directions. *Do not repeat any of the directions.*

Directions: In this test, I will read instructions to you. You are to mark your worksheets according to the instructions that I read to you. After each set of instructions, I'll give you time to record your answers on your answer sheet.

Try to understand the instructions as I read them; I cannot repeat them. Do not ask any questions from now on.

If, when you go to darken a space for a number, you find that you have already darkened another space for that number, either (1) erase the first mark and darken the space for your new choice, or (2) let the first mark stay and do not darken any other space. When you finish, you should have no more than one space darkened for each number.

Turn to Worksheet 1.

Look at line 1 on your worksheet. (Pause slightly.) Write an E in the last box. (Pause 2 seconds.) Now, on your answer sheet, find the number in that box and darken space E for that number. (Pause 5 seconds.)

Now look at the numbers in line 2 on your worksheet. (Pause slightly.) Draw a line under the second number in the line. (Pause 2 seconds.) Now, on your answer sheet, find the number under which you drew a line and darken space C for that number. (Pause 5 seconds.)

Look at line 2 again. (Pause slightly.) Draw two lines under the first number in the line. (Pause 2 seconds.) Now, on your answer sheet, find the number under which you drew two lines and darken space D as in *dog*. (Pause 5 seconds.)

Look at the letters in line 3 on your worksheet. (Pause slightly.) Draw a circle around the fifth letter in the line. (Pause 2 seconds.) Now, on your answer sheet, find the number 19 and darken the space for the letter around which you drew a circle. (Pause 5 seconds.)

Look at line 3 again. (Pause slightly.) Draw a line under the middle letter in the line. (Pause 2 seconds.) Now, on your answer sheet, find the number 12 and darken the space for the letter under which you drew a line. (Pause 5 seconds.)

Look at the five circles in line 4 on your worksheet. (Pause slightly.) Each circle has a letter of the alphabet inside it. Write the number 2 in the circle that has the third letter of the alphabet inside it. (Pause 3 seconds.) Now, on your answer sheet, darken the space for the number-letter combination that is in the circle you just wrote in. (Pause 5 seconds.)

Look at line 5 on your worksheet. (Pause slightly.) Draw a line under every number that is more than 50 but less than 60. (Pause 10 seconds.) Now, on your answer sheet, for every number that you drew a line under, darken space A. (Pause 5 seconds.)

Look at the figures in line 6. (Pause slightly.) Each figure is made up of two triangles with a number or a letter in each triangle. (Pause slightly.) Add the number in the upper triangle of the first figure to the number in the lower triangle of the middle figure, and write that number in the upper triangle of the last figure. (Pause 5 seconds.) Now, on your answer sheet, darken the space for the number-letter combination that is in the triangle you just wrote in. (Pause 5 seconds.)

Look at line 7 on your worksheet. The number in each box is the number of customers visiting a certain post office in 1 hour. (Pause slightly.) In the box for the post office having the fewest number of visitors write on the line the first two figures of that number. (Pause 5 seconds.) Now, on your answer sheet, darken the space for the number-letter combination that is in the box you just wrote in. (Pause 5 seconds.)

Look at line 8 on your worksheet. (Pause slightly.) On the line next to the left-hand letter write the answer to this question: How many feet are there in 1 yard? (Pause 2 seconds.) Now, on your answer sheet, find the number you just wrote and darken space D as in *dog* for that number. (Pause 5 seconds.)

Look at the circles in line 9 on your worksheet. (Pause slightly.) Some circles on the line are fully shaded, some circles are partly shaded, and some circles have no shading. (Pause slightly.) Count the number of circles that have no shading, add 4, and write that number at the end of the line. (Pause 5 seconds.) Now, on your answer sheet, find the number you just wrote and darken space A for that number. (Pause 5 seconds.)

Look at line 9 again. (Pause slightly.) Count the number of circles that are fully or partly shaded, and put that number in the last circle. (Pause 4 seconds.) Now, on your answer sheet, find the number you just wrote and darken space D as in *dog* for that number. (Pause 5 seconds.)

Now look at line 10 on your worksheet. (Pause slightly.) There are two boxes and two circles of different sizes with numbers in them. (Pause slightly.) If 5 is smaller than 8 and 4 is larger than 6, write A in the smaller box. (Pause slightly.) Otherwise, write B as in *baker* in the larger circle. (Pause 2 seconds.) Now, on your answer sheet, darken the space for the number-letter combination in the box or circle you just wrote in. (Pause 5 seconds.)

Look at line 11 on your worksheet. (Pause slightly.) In each circle there is a time when a mail truck is dispatched. In the circle for the latest time, write on the line the last two figures of the time. (Pause 5 seconds.) Now, on your answer sheet, darken the space for the number-letter combination that is in the circle you just wrote in. (Pause 5 seconds.)

Now turn to Worksheet 2. (Pause 5 seconds.)

Look at line 12 on your worksheet. (Pause slightly.) If, in a minute, there are 60 seconds, write the letter A in the box with the largest number. (Pause slightly.) Otherwise, write the letter C in the box with the smallest number. (Pause 2 seconds.) Now, on your answer sheet, darken the space for the number-letter combination that is in the box you just wrote in. (Pause 5 seconds.)

Look at line 13 on your worksheet. (Pause slightly.) There are three boxes and three words on the line. (Pause slightly.) Write the second letter of the third word in the first box. (Pause 2 seconds.) Write the first letter of the second word in the third box. (Pause 2 seconds.) Write the third letter of the first word in the second box. (Pause 2 seconds.) Now, on your answer sheet, darken the spaces for the number-letter combinations that are in the three boxes you just wrote in. (Pause 10 seconds.)

Look at line 14 on your worksheet. (Pause slightly.) Draw a line under every "X" in the line. (Pause 5 seconds.) Count the number of lines that you have drawn, and write that number at the end of the line. (Pause 5 seconds.) If the number you just wrote is an even number, write an A next to it. (Pause slightly.) Otherwise, write a B next to the number. (Pause slightly.) Now, on your answer sheet, darken the space for the number-letter combination you just wrote at the end of the line. (Pause 5 seconds.)

Now, look at line 15 on your worksheet. (Pause slightly.) There are five circles, each with a letter inside it. (Pause slightly.) In the fourth circle write the answer to this question: Which of the following numbers is largest: 28, 47, 36, 42, 39? (Pause 5 seconds.) In the first circle write 86. (Pause 2 seconds.) In the middle circle do nothing. In the last circle, write the answer to this question: How many hours are there in a day? (Pause 2 seconds.) Now, on your answer sheet, darken the spaces for the number-letter combinations that are in the circles you just wrote in. (Pause 10 seconds.)

Look at the numbers in line 16 on your worksheet. (Pause slightly.) Draw a line under every number that is more than 25 but less than 40. (Pause 10 seconds.) Now, on your answer sheet, darken space C for every number under which you drew a line. (Pause 20 seconds.)

Look at line 17 on your worksheet. (Pause slightly.) The number in each circle is the number of parcels in a mail sack. The three boxes with letters in them are bins to collect these parcels. (Pause slightly.) In the middle bin, write the number of parcels in the sack holding the smallest number of parcels. (Pause 2 seconds.) Now, on your answer sheet, darken the space for the number-letter combination that is in the bin you just wrote in. (Pause 5 seconds.)

Look at line 17 again. In the third bin, write the number of parcels in the sack holding the largest number of parcels. (Pause 2 seconds.) Now, on your answer sheet, darken the space for the number-letter combination that is in the bin you just wrote in. (Pause 5 seconds.)

Look at line 18 on your worksheet. (Pause slightly.) Mail for Nyack and Hudson is to be put in Box 40. Mail for Albany and Groton is to be put in box 79. (Pause slightly.) Write A on the line in the box in which you would put mail for Hudson. (Pause 2 seconds.) Now, on your answer sheet, darken the space for the number-letter combination that is in the box you just wrote in. (Pause 5 seconds.)

Now look at the letters and boxes in line 19 on your worksheet. (Pause slightly.) Write the right-hand letter below the number in the third box. (Pause 2 seconds.) Subtract 2 from the number in the box you just wrote in, and change the number in that box to this number. (Pause 3 seconds.) Now, on your answer sheet, darken the space for the number-letter combination that is in the box you just wrote in. (Pause 5 seconds.)

END OF EXAMINATION.
**If you finish before the time is up, go back and check
the questions in this section of the test only.**

Practice Test 4—Worksheet 1
Part D—Following Oral Directions

1. [64 __]   [15 __]   [49 __]

2. 43   61   57   29

3. C   E   D   B   B   A   E

4. (__ C)   (__ B)   (__ A)   (__ D)   (__ E)

5. 49   50   66   57   61   53   48   39

6. 3/6   2/7   __ B / __ C

7. [B __]   [E __]   [A __]   [C __]   [D __]
    151   311   298   140   532

8. ___ D   ___ B

9.

10. [76 __]   (69 __)   [16 __]   (84 __)

11. (12:51 __ D)   (12:15 __ E)   (12:41 __ A)   (12:02 __ C)   (12:34 __ B)

Practice Test 4—Worksheet 2
Part D—Following Oral Directions

12. | 43 __ | | 19 __ | | 36 __ | | 68 __ |

13. | 75 __ | | 62 __ | | 27 __ | MICE   ARM   MEAT

14. O X X X O O X O O O X O X O X X

15. (__ E)   (__ D)   (__ C)   (__ B)   (__ A)

16. 25   15   39   14   32   55   40   28   35

17. (76)   (82)   (67) | C __ | | D __ | | B __ |

18. | 40 __
NYACK
HUDSON | | 79 __
ALBANY
GROTON |

19. __ E   __ C | 37 __ | | 76 __ | | 83 __ |

■ ANSWER KEY

Part A—Address Checking

1. A	11. A	21. A	31. A	41. A	51. D	61. D	71. D	81. A	91. D
2. D	12. D	22. D	32. D	42. D	52. A	62. A	72. A	82. A	92. D
3. A	13. A	23. A	33. D	43. A	53. D	63. D	73. D	83. D	93. A
4. D	14. A	24. D	34. A	44. A	54. D	64. D	74. D	84. A	94. A
5. D	15. D	25. D	35. D	45. A	55. D	65. D	75. A	85. D	95. A
6. D	16. A	26. D	36. D	46. D	56. D	66. A	76. D	86. A	
7. A	17. A	27. A	37. D	47. D	57. D	67. A	77. A	87. D	
8. D	18. A	28. A	38. A	48. A	58. D	68. D	78. D	88. D	
9. D	19. D	29. D	39. A	49. D	59. D	69. D	79. D	89. A	
10. A	20. D	30. D	40. D	50. A	60. D	70. A	80. D	90. D	

Part B—Memory for Addresses

List 1

1. D	10. E	19. C	28. B	37. C	46. C	55. B	64. E	73. D	82. D
2. C	11. A	20. D	29. D	38. D	47. A	56. C	65. E	74. C	83. A
3. E	12. D	21. C	30. B	39. A	48. C	57. D	66. A	75. E	84. A
4. C	13. C	22. B	31. C	40. A	49. B	58. B	67. A	76. B	85. D
5. D	14. C	23. B	32. C	41. A	50. A	59. E	68. C	77. A	86. A
6. A	15. C	24. E	33. E	42. B	51. A	60. D	69. D	78. D	87. E
7. E	16. B	25. E	34. D	43. E	52. B	61. C	70. D	79. B	88. E
8. A	17. B	26. E	35. B	44. A	53. A	62. D	71. C	80. B	
9. D	18. A	27. A	36. A	45. D	54. E	63. B	72. E	81. B	

List 2

1. C	10. A	19. C	28. D	37. A	46. B	55. A	64. A	73. E	82. E
2. D	11. D	20. D	29. E	38. B	47. D	56. E	65. C	74. E	83. C
3. E	12. A	21. E	30. C	39. E	48. B	57. A	66. C	75. D	84. B
4. B	13. E	22. A	31. A	40. A	49. B	58. C	67. B	76. D	85. C
5. A	14. D	23. A	32. C	41. D	50. A	59. B	68. E	77. B	86. B
6. B	15. C	24. E	33. D	42. A	51. C	60. C	69. C	78. E	87. D
7. A	16. A	25. A	34. D	43. B	52. E	61. A	70. E	79. D	88. A
8. D	17. C	26. C	35. B	44. B	53. A	62. C	71. C	80. E	
9. A	18. B	27. B	36. D	45. C	54. E	63. D	72. E	81. D	

List 3

1. B	10. B	19. C	28. C	37. D	46. D	55. E	64. C	73. C	82. A
2. B	11. D	20. A	29. A	38. A	47. B	56. B	65. E	74. B	83. A
3. A	12. D	21. E	30. C	39. B	48. C	57. D	66. B	75. C	84. B
4. D	13. C	22. A	31. D	40. A	49. B	58. D	67. C	76. A	85. B
5. A	14. D	23. E	32. E	41. B	50. C	59. E	68. C	77. E	86. D
6. E	15. C	24. B	33. A	42. E	51. E	60. E	69. A	78. A	87. B
7. B	16. E	25. D	34. D	43. D	52. D	61. E	70. D	79. E	88. C
8. A	17. D	26. C	35. A	44. C	53. E	62. C	71. B	80. A	
9. D	18. B	27. B	36. A	45. E	54. D	63. E	72. A	81. E	

Part C—Number Series

1. **B**	4. **E**	7. **A**	10. **C**	13. **C**	16. **E**	19. **D**	22. **E**
2. **D**	5. **E**	8. **A**	11. **E**	14. **A**	17. **D**	20. **D**	23. **D**
3. **D**	6. **C**	9. **C**	12. **B**	15. **C**	18. **B**	21. **E**	24. **C**

Part D—Following Oral Directions

2. **C**	7. **A**	12. **B**	24. **A**	32. **C**	43. **D**	51. **D**	61. **C**	68. **A**	81. **C**
3. **D**	8. **A**	14. **C**	27. **A**	39. **C**	47. **B**	53. **A**	62. **C**	69. **B**	82. **B**
6. **D**	10. **B**	19. **B**	28. **C**	40. **A**	49. **E**	57. **A**	67. **D**	75. **E**	86. **E**

ANSWER EXPLANATIONS FOR PART C—NUMBER SERIES

1. **B** The three numbers 40 50 60 keep repeating in the same sequence.
2. **D** Each of these two alternating series keeps decreasing by 3.
3. **D** The pattern is: – 4, repeat the number; – 4, repeat the number.
4. **E** This series follows the complex rule: + 5, – 2, – 1.
5. **E** The rule for this series is: – 1, repeat the number, – 17; and so on.
6. **C** There are two alternating series here. One decreases by 7 and repeats the number. The other decreases by 4 and appears after every second number of the first series.
7. **A** These two alternating series appear as triads. One increases by 3. The other, starting with <u>30</u>, decreases by 5.
8. **A** Again, you have two alternating series but this time they appear in regular fashion, one number of each in turn. One ascends by 5; the other descends by 7.
9. **C** One of these two series follows the complex rule – 7, – 8; – 7, – 8; and so on. The other is a simple – 1 series. This pattern is very difficult to see unless you use a loop diagram (see below):

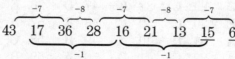

10. **C** Both series decrease by 2. One appears after every two numbers of the first.
11. **E** In effect, there are *three* alternating series here. The easiest way to visualize this most complex pattern is with a loop diagram:

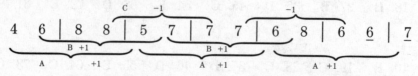

12. **B** The numbers in this series follow a + 1, + 2; + 1, + 2; and so on rule.
13. **C** The rule for this series is: + 2, + 3; + 2, + 3. The number <u>10</u> is inserted after every two numbers in the series.
14. **A** You may view this as a series that follows a + 6, – 2; + 6, – 2; rule or as two alternating series, each increasing by 4.
15. **C** Multiplication, subtraction, *and* addition are included in this rule: × 2, – 4, + 3; repeated.

16. **E** A key element in this pattern is *reversal*. A number reverses its digits to produce the next number, which is then reduced by 10. For example, <u>27</u> reversed is <u>72</u>; 72 − 10 = <u>62</u>, and so on.

17. **D** There is a + 7 series, which repeats each number. The arbitrary number <u>13</u> interrupts the series.

18. **B** The "subtractors" keep getting *smaller* as the series progresses. In addition, the numbers repeat. (See the diagram below.)

$$\overbrace{56 \quad 56}^{R} \overbrace{\quad 48}^{-8} \overbrace{48 \quad 41}^{R \quad -7} \overbrace{41 \quad 35}^{R \quad -6} \overbrace{\underline{35} \quad 30}^{R \quad -5}$$

19. **D** There is a + 1 series here (16, 17, 18, 19, 20, and so on) that is interrupted after every *three* numbers by two members of a + 2 series (12 14 16 18, and so on).

20. **D** One of these two alternating series follows a − 2, − 1; rule. The other series increases by 1 and appears after every *two* numbers of the first. (If you tried to do this question without the aid of a loop diagram, you probably got the wrong answer. If so, do it over—this time, with a diagram.)

21. **E** You could see this as a + 1, + 1, − 1; series. You could also see the pattern by *chanting* the numbers in groups of three:

$$\underline{31} \quad 32 \quad 33 \quad \underline{32} \quad 33 \quad 34 \quad \underline{33} \quad \underline{34} \quad 35$$

22. **E** One pair of these two alternating series *increases* by × <u>2</u>; the other *decreases* by − <u>2</u>.

23. **D** Both alternating series increase by 1. (One begins with <u>5</u>; the other with <u>10</u>.) One proceeds for two numbers before being interrupted by a member of the other series.

24. **C** The rule used to go from one number to the next involves *two* operations—multiplication by 2 and then subtraction by 1—in order to advance to the next number. For example, the first number in this series 2 × 2 = 4; 4 − 1 = <u>3</u>. Similarly, to go from <u>3</u> to 5, you proceed as follows: 3 × 2 = 6; 6 − 1 = 5; and so on.

■ EVALUATING YOUR PROGRESS

Throughout this book, the importance of evaluating and recording your progress has been stressed, as you study and practice for the 460/470 Test Battery. At this point, if you have completed Practice Tests 1 through 3 and have made all the entries on your Personal Progress Record, you are quite familiar with the discussion on Computing Your Score, Guidelines, and the Personal Progress Record. If you wish to review the details of these subjects, refer to pages 58 through 68 or pages 326 through 332.

You have probably seen great improvement in your test scores, but don't stop now. Take the remaining practice tests and record the results on your Personal Progress Record. Go for a perfect score!

■ DIAGNOSTIC CHARTS

The following charts will help pinpoint your weaknesses by making it easy for you to determine what particular type of question in each part of the test is most difficult for you.

Part A—Address Checking

Type of Difference	"D" Questions	Number of "D" Questions Wrong		
		Trial 1	Trial 2	Trial 3
Numbers: transposed	9, 12, 15, 69, 85, 88			
changed	22, 49, 59, 83			
omitted	58, 90			
Directions	19, 25, 29, 40, 74			

Abbreviations:
    streets, roads,
        avenues, etc.
	6, 26, 42, 47, 51, 55, 68			

states	2, 24, 46, 56, 65			
Spelling: single letters	5, 8, 20, 30, 32, 33, 36, 53, 57, 60, 61, 64, 71, 78, 79, 87, 92			
groups of letters	4, 35, 37, 63, 73, 76, 80, 91			
Total Number of All Types	54			
	Use the columns on the right to enter the question numbers of "A" items you marked "D."			

This chart will help you to pinpoint the kinds of errors you made on Practice Test 4. Use it as directed below after you have taken and marked the test.

The first column on the left, "Type of Difference," contains the categories whereby addresses may differ (see page 69). On the same line across, the second column gives the numbers of the questions that fall within each category. In the third column, you are to enter the numbers of any "A" questions you answered as "D." Do not include questions that you did not do. Checking the addresses you got wrong may reveal a problem on which you will want to work.

After you have made all the entries, you will be able to see the areas in which you need to improve. Then turn to the appropriate parts of Chapter 4: Address Checking—How to Improve Your Score, read them, and practice the drills that can help. For example, if you find you have been making too many errors picking out number differences, read page 94 and do Drills 18 through 21. If you have a problem with single letters because of reversals like *b* and *d*, or if you have been overlooking the differences between *a*, *e*, and *o*, read page 91. Examine the table and work on Drills 10 and 11 if the problem persists.

Remember that this chart is designed for diagnostic purposes and guidance on further practice. It has been drawn so that you can enter the results each time you retake a practice test. In this way you will be able to see how you are progressing. It is not necessary to record your scores here. That is best done by using the Personal Progress Record Card.

Part B—Memory for Addresses

Kind of Address		Number of Questions	Number Wrong		
			Trial 1	Trial 2	Trial 3
Direct:					
	List 1	42			
	List 2	41			
	List 3	40			
Numbered:					
	List 1	46			
	List 2	47			
	List 3	48			

The purpose of this chart is to help you evaluate your performance on the two kinds of memory questions that appear in these memory tests—the questions on the direct (name) addresses and the questions on the numbered addresses. Use the chart as directed below after you have taken and marked the entire test.

The first column on the left, "Kind of Address," is divided by category into "Direct Address" versus "Numbered Address." The second column gives the number of questions in each category on List 1, List 2, and List 3. Use the third column to enter the total number of questions in each category that you answered incorrectly. There is room for you to make additional entries if you take the practice test more than once.

At a glance, you will be able to see which area you need to concentrate on and how well you are progressing as you take repeat trials. Use Chapter 5 and the drills in it to improve your memory for the direct addresses. Use Chapter 6 for the numbered addresses.

Remember to use the Personal Progress Record Card (Memory for Addresses) on page 439 to keep track of your actual scores as you keep studying and practicing.

Part C—Number Series and Part D—Following Oral Directions

Because of the nature of the questions in these tests, Diagnostic Charts are not provided for them. If you find that you made many errors on these tests, study the techniques suggested in Chapters 7 and 8.

Answer Sheet—Practice Test 5

Part A—Address Checking

1 Ⓐⓓ	25 Ⓐⓓ	49 Ⓐⓓ	73 Ⓐⓓ
2 Ⓐⓓ	26 Ⓐⓓ	50 Ⓐⓓ	74 Ⓐⓓ
3 Ⓐⓓ	27 Ⓐⓓ	51 Ⓐⓓ	75 Ⓐⓓ
4 Ⓐⓓ	28 Ⓐⓓ	52 Ⓐⓓ	76 Ⓐⓓ
5 Ⓐⓓ	29 Ⓐⓓ	53 Ⓐⓓ	77 Ⓐⓓ
6 Ⓐⓓ	30 Ⓐⓓ	54 Ⓐⓓ	78 Ⓐⓓ
7 Ⓐⓓ	31 Ⓐⓓ	55 Ⓐⓓ	79 Ⓐⓓ
8 Ⓐⓓ	32 Ⓐⓓ	56 Ⓐⓓ	80 Ⓐⓓ
9 Ⓐⓓ	33 Ⓐⓓ	57 Ⓐⓓ	81 Ⓐⓓ
10 Ⓐⓓ	34 Ⓐⓓ	58 Ⓐⓓ	82 Ⓐⓓ
11 Ⓐⓓ	35 Ⓐⓓ	59 Ⓐⓓ	83 Ⓐⓓ
12 Ⓐⓓ	36 Ⓐⓓ	60 Ⓐⓓ	84 Ⓐⓓ
13 Ⓐⓓ	37 Ⓐⓓ	61 Ⓐⓓ	85 Ⓐⓓ
14 Ⓐⓓ	38 Ⓐⓓ	62 Ⓐⓓ	86 Ⓐⓓ
15 Ⓐⓓ	39 Ⓐⓓ	63 Ⓐⓓ	87 Ⓐⓓ
16 Ⓐⓓ	40 Ⓐⓓ	64 Ⓐⓓ	88 Ⓐⓓ
17 Ⓐⓓ	41 Ⓐⓓ	65 Ⓐⓓ	89 Ⓐⓓ
18 Ⓐⓓ	42 Ⓐⓓ	66 Ⓐⓓ	90 Ⓐⓓ
19 Ⓐⓓ	43 Ⓐⓓ	67 Ⓐⓓ	91 Ⓐⓓ
20 Ⓐⓓ	44 Ⓐⓓ	68 Ⓐⓓ	92 Ⓐⓓ
21 Ⓐⓓ	45 Ⓐⓓ	69 Ⓐⓓ	93 Ⓐⓓ
22 Ⓐⓓ	46 Ⓐⓓ	70 Ⓐⓓ	94 Ⓐⓓ
23 Ⓐⓓ	47 Ⓐⓓ	71 Ⓐⓓ	95 Ⓐⓓ
24 Ⓐⓓ	48 Ⓐⓓ	72 Ⓐⓓ	

Remove by cutting on dotted line.

Part B—Memory for Addresses—List 1

1 Ⓐ Ⓑ Ⓒ Ⓓ Ⓔ 19 Ⓐ Ⓑ Ⓒ Ⓓ Ⓔ 37 Ⓐ Ⓑ Ⓒ Ⓓ Ⓔ 55 Ⓐ Ⓑ Ⓒ Ⓓ Ⓔ 73 Ⓐ Ⓑ Ⓒ Ⓓ Ⓔ
2 Ⓐ Ⓑ Ⓒ Ⓓ Ⓔ 20 Ⓐ Ⓑ Ⓒ Ⓓ Ⓔ 38 Ⓐ Ⓑ Ⓒ Ⓓ Ⓔ 56 Ⓐ Ⓑ Ⓒ Ⓓ Ⓔ 74 Ⓐ Ⓑ Ⓒ Ⓓ Ⓔ
3 Ⓐ Ⓑ Ⓒ Ⓓ Ⓔ 21 Ⓐ Ⓑ Ⓒ Ⓓ Ⓔ 39 Ⓐ Ⓑ Ⓒ Ⓓ Ⓔ 57 Ⓐ Ⓑ Ⓒ Ⓓ Ⓔ 75 Ⓐ Ⓑ Ⓒ Ⓓ Ⓔ
4 Ⓐ Ⓑ Ⓒ Ⓓ Ⓔ 22 Ⓐ Ⓑ Ⓒ Ⓓ Ⓔ 40 Ⓐ Ⓑ Ⓒ Ⓓ Ⓔ 58 Ⓐ Ⓑ Ⓒ Ⓓ Ⓔ 76 Ⓐ Ⓑ Ⓒ Ⓓ Ⓔ
5 Ⓐ Ⓑ Ⓒ Ⓓ Ⓔ 23 Ⓐ Ⓑ Ⓒ Ⓓ Ⓔ 41 Ⓐ Ⓑ Ⓒ Ⓓ Ⓔ 59 Ⓐ Ⓑ Ⓒ Ⓓ Ⓔ 77 Ⓐ Ⓑ Ⓒ Ⓓ Ⓔ
6 Ⓐ Ⓑ Ⓒ Ⓓ Ⓔ 24 Ⓐ Ⓑ Ⓒ Ⓓ Ⓔ 42 Ⓐ Ⓑ Ⓒ Ⓓ Ⓔ 60 Ⓐ Ⓑ Ⓒ Ⓓ Ⓔ 78 Ⓐ Ⓑ Ⓒ Ⓓ Ⓔ
7 Ⓐ Ⓑ Ⓒ Ⓓ Ⓔ 25 Ⓐ Ⓑ Ⓒ Ⓓ Ⓔ 43 Ⓐ Ⓑ Ⓒ Ⓓ Ⓔ 61 Ⓐ Ⓑ Ⓒ Ⓓ Ⓔ 79 Ⓐ Ⓑ Ⓒ Ⓓ Ⓔ
8 Ⓐ Ⓑ Ⓒ Ⓓ Ⓔ 26 Ⓐ Ⓑ Ⓒ Ⓓ Ⓔ 44 Ⓐ Ⓑ Ⓒ Ⓓ Ⓔ 62 Ⓐ Ⓑ Ⓒ Ⓓ Ⓔ 80 Ⓐ Ⓑ Ⓒ Ⓓ Ⓔ
9 Ⓐ Ⓑ Ⓒ Ⓓ Ⓔ 27 Ⓐ Ⓑ Ⓒ Ⓓ Ⓔ 45 Ⓐ Ⓑ Ⓒ Ⓓ Ⓔ 63 Ⓐ Ⓑ Ⓒ Ⓓ Ⓔ 81 Ⓐ Ⓑ Ⓒ Ⓓ Ⓔ
10 Ⓐ Ⓑ Ⓒ Ⓓ Ⓔ 28 Ⓐ Ⓑ Ⓒ Ⓓ Ⓔ 46 Ⓐ Ⓑ Ⓒ Ⓓ Ⓔ 64 Ⓐ Ⓑ Ⓒ Ⓓ Ⓔ 82 Ⓐ Ⓑ Ⓒ Ⓓ Ⓔ
11 Ⓐ Ⓑ Ⓒ Ⓓ Ⓔ 29 Ⓐ Ⓑ Ⓒ Ⓓ Ⓔ 47 Ⓐ Ⓑ Ⓒ Ⓓ Ⓔ 65 Ⓐ Ⓑ Ⓒ Ⓓ Ⓔ 83 Ⓐ Ⓑ Ⓒ Ⓓ Ⓔ
12 Ⓐ Ⓑ Ⓒ Ⓓ Ⓔ 30 Ⓐ Ⓑ Ⓒ Ⓓ Ⓔ 48 Ⓐ Ⓑ Ⓒ Ⓓ Ⓔ 66 Ⓐ Ⓑ Ⓒ Ⓓ Ⓔ 84 Ⓐ Ⓑ Ⓒ Ⓓ Ⓔ
13 Ⓐ Ⓑ Ⓒ Ⓓ Ⓔ 31 Ⓐ Ⓑ Ⓒ Ⓓ Ⓔ 49 Ⓐ Ⓑ Ⓒ Ⓓ Ⓔ 67 Ⓐ Ⓑ Ⓒ Ⓓ Ⓔ 85 Ⓐ Ⓑ Ⓒ Ⓓ Ⓔ
14 Ⓐ Ⓑ Ⓒ Ⓓ Ⓔ 32 Ⓐ Ⓑ Ⓒ Ⓓ Ⓔ 50 Ⓐ Ⓑ Ⓒ Ⓓ Ⓔ 68 Ⓐ Ⓑ Ⓒ Ⓓ Ⓔ 86 Ⓐ Ⓑ Ⓒ Ⓓ Ⓔ
15 Ⓐ Ⓑ Ⓒ Ⓓ Ⓔ 33 Ⓐ Ⓑ Ⓒ Ⓓ Ⓔ 51 Ⓐ Ⓑ Ⓒ Ⓓ Ⓔ 69 Ⓐ Ⓑ Ⓒ Ⓓ Ⓔ 87 Ⓐ Ⓑ Ⓒ Ⓓ Ⓔ
16 Ⓐ Ⓑ Ⓒ Ⓓ Ⓔ 34 Ⓐ Ⓑ Ⓒ Ⓓ Ⓔ 52 Ⓐ Ⓑ Ⓒ Ⓓ Ⓔ 70 Ⓐ Ⓑ Ⓒ Ⓓ Ⓔ 88 Ⓐ Ⓑ Ⓒ Ⓓ Ⓔ
17 Ⓐ Ⓑ Ⓒ Ⓓ Ⓔ 35 Ⓐ Ⓑ Ⓒ Ⓓ Ⓔ 53 Ⓐ Ⓑ Ⓒ Ⓓ Ⓔ 71 Ⓐ Ⓑ Ⓒ Ⓓ Ⓔ
18 Ⓐ Ⓑ Ⓒ Ⓓ Ⓔ 36 Ⓐ Ⓑ Ⓒ Ⓓ Ⓔ 54 Ⓐ Ⓑ Ⓒ Ⓓ Ⓔ 72 Ⓐ Ⓑ Ⓒ Ⓓ Ⓔ

Part B—Memory for Addresses—List 2

1 Ⓐ Ⓑ Ⓒ Ⓓ Ⓔ 19 Ⓐ Ⓑ Ⓒ Ⓓ Ⓔ 37 Ⓐ Ⓑ Ⓒ Ⓓ Ⓔ 55 Ⓐ Ⓑ Ⓒ Ⓓ Ⓔ 73 Ⓐ Ⓑ Ⓒ Ⓓ Ⓔ
2 Ⓐ Ⓑ Ⓒ Ⓓ Ⓔ 20 Ⓐ Ⓑ Ⓒ Ⓓ Ⓔ 38 Ⓐ Ⓑ Ⓒ Ⓓ Ⓔ 56 Ⓐ Ⓑ Ⓒ Ⓓ Ⓔ 74 Ⓐ Ⓑ Ⓒ Ⓓ Ⓔ
3 Ⓐ Ⓑ Ⓒ Ⓓ Ⓔ 21 Ⓐ Ⓑ Ⓒ Ⓓ Ⓔ 39 Ⓐ Ⓑ Ⓒ Ⓓ Ⓔ 57 Ⓐ Ⓑ Ⓒ Ⓓ Ⓔ 75 Ⓐ Ⓑ Ⓒ Ⓓ Ⓔ
4 Ⓐ Ⓑ Ⓒ Ⓓ Ⓔ 22 Ⓐ Ⓑ Ⓒ Ⓓ Ⓔ 40 Ⓐ Ⓑ Ⓒ Ⓓ Ⓔ 58 Ⓐ Ⓑ Ⓒ Ⓓ Ⓔ 76 Ⓐ Ⓑ Ⓒ Ⓓ Ⓔ
5 Ⓐ Ⓑ Ⓒ Ⓓ Ⓔ 23 Ⓐ Ⓑ Ⓒ Ⓓ Ⓔ 41 Ⓐ Ⓑ Ⓒ Ⓓ Ⓔ 59 Ⓐ Ⓑ Ⓒ Ⓓ Ⓔ 77 Ⓐ Ⓑ Ⓒ Ⓓ Ⓔ
6 Ⓐ Ⓑ Ⓒ Ⓓ Ⓔ 24 Ⓐ Ⓑ Ⓒ Ⓓ Ⓔ 42 Ⓐ Ⓑ Ⓒ Ⓓ Ⓔ 60 Ⓐ Ⓑ Ⓒ Ⓓ Ⓔ 78 Ⓐ Ⓑ Ⓒ Ⓓ Ⓔ
7 Ⓐ Ⓑ Ⓒ Ⓓ Ⓔ 25 Ⓐ Ⓑ Ⓒ Ⓓ Ⓔ 43 Ⓐ Ⓑ Ⓒ Ⓓ Ⓔ 61 Ⓐ Ⓑ Ⓒ Ⓓ Ⓔ 79 Ⓐ Ⓑ Ⓒ Ⓓ Ⓔ
8 Ⓐ Ⓑ Ⓒ Ⓓ Ⓔ 26 Ⓐ Ⓑ Ⓒ Ⓓ Ⓔ 44 Ⓐ Ⓑ Ⓒ Ⓓ Ⓔ 62 Ⓐ Ⓑ Ⓒ Ⓓ Ⓔ 80 Ⓐ Ⓑ Ⓒ Ⓓ Ⓔ
9 Ⓐ Ⓑ Ⓒ Ⓓ Ⓔ 27 Ⓐ Ⓑ Ⓒ Ⓓ Ⓔ 45 Ⓐ Ⓑ Ⓒ Ⓓ Ⓔ 63 Ⓐ Ⓑ Ⓒ Ⓓ Ⓔ 81 Ⓐ Ⓑ Ⓒ Ⓓ Ⓔ
10 Ⓐ Ⓑ Ⓒ Ⓓ Ⓔ 28 Ⓐ Ⓑ Ⓒ Ⓓ Ⓔ 46 Ⓐ Ⓑ Ⓒ Ⓓ Ⓔ 64 Ⓐ Ⓑ Ⓒ Ⓓ Ⓔ 82 Ⓐ Ⓑ Ⓒ Ⓓ Ⓔ
11 Ⓐ Ⓑ Ⓒ Ⓓ Ⓔ 29 Ⓐ Ⓑ Ⓒ Ⓓ Ⓔ 47 Ⓐ Ⓑ Ⓒ Ⓓ Ⓔ 65 Ⓐ Ⓑ Ⓒ Ⓓ Ⓔ 83 Ⓐ Ⓑ Ⓒ Ⓓ Ⓔ
12 Ⓐ Ⓑ Ⓒ Ⓓ Ⓔ 30 Ⓐ Ⓑ Ⓒ Ⓓ Ⓔ 48 Ⓐ Ⓑ Ⓒ Ⓓ Ⓔ 66 Ⓐ Ⓑ Ⓒ Ⓓ Ⓔ 84 Ⓐ Ⓑ Ⓒ Ⓓ Ⓔ
13 Ⓐ Ⓑ Ⓒ Ⓓ Ⓔ 31 Ⓐ Ⓑ Ⓒ Ⓓ Ⓔ 49 Ⓐ Ⓑ Ⓒ Ⓓ Ⓔ 67 Ⓐ Ⓑ Ⓒ Ⓓ Ⓔ 85 Ⓐ Ⓑ Ⓒ Ⓓ Ⓔ
14 Ⓐ Ⓑ Ⓒ Ⓓ Ⓔ 32 Ⓐ Ⓑ Ⓒ Ⓓ Ⓔ 50 Ⓐ Ⓑ Ⓒ Ⓓ Ⓔ 68 Ⓐ Ⓑ Ⓒ Ⓓ Ⓔ 86 Ⓐ Ⓑ Ⓒ Ⓓ Ⓔ
15 Ⓐ Ⓑ Ⓒ Ⓓ Ⓔ 33 Ⓐ Ⓑ Ⓒ Ⓓ Ⓔ 51 Ⓐ Ⓑ Ⓒ Ⓓ Ⓔ 69 Ⓐ Ⓑ Ⓒ Ⓓ Ⓔ 87 Ⓐ Ⓑ Ⓒ Ⓓ Ⓔ
16 Ⓐ Ⓑ Ⓒ Ⓓ Ⓔ 34 Ⓐ Ⓑ Ⓒ Ⓓ Ⓔ 52 Ⓐ Ⓑ Ⓒ Ⓓ Ⓔ 70 Ⓐ Ⓑ Ⓒ Ⓓ Ⓔ 88 Ⓐ Ⓑ Ⓒ Ⓓ Ⓔ
17 Ⓐ Ⓑ Ⓒ Ⓓ Ⓔ 35 Ⓐ Ⓑ Ⓒ Ⓓ Ⓔ 53 Ⓐ Ⓑ Ⓒ Ⓓ Ⓔ 71 Ⓐ Ⓑ Ⓒ Ⓓ Ⓔ
18 Ⓐ Ⓑ Ⓒ Ⓓ Ⓔ 36 Ⓐ Ⓑ Ⓒ Ⓓ Ⓔ 54 Ⓐ Ⓑ Ⓒ Ⓓ Ⓔ 72 Ⓐ Ⓑ Ⓒ Ⓓ Ⓔ

Part B—Memory for Addresses—List 3

1 Ⓐ Ⓑ Ⓒ Ⓓ Ⓔ	19 Ⓐ Ⓑ Ⓒ Ⓓ Ⓔ	37 Ⓐ Ⓑ Ⓒ Ⓓ Ⓔ	55 Ⓐ Ⓑ Ⓒ Ⓓ Ⓔ	73 Ⓐ Ⓑ Ⓒ Ⓓ Ⓔ
2 Ⓐ Ⓑ Ⓒ Ⓓ Ⓔ	20 Ⓐ Ⓑ Ⓒ Ⓓ Ⓔ	38 Ⓐ Ⓑ Ⓒ Ⓓ Ⓔ	56 Ⓐ Ⓑ Ⓒ Ⓓ Ⓔ	74 Ⓐ Ⓑ Ⓒ Ⓓ Ⓔ
3 Ⓐ Ⓑ Ⓒ Ⓓ Ⓔ	21 Ⓐ Ⓑ Ⓒ Ⓓ Ⓔ	39 Ⓐ Ⓑ Ⓒ Ⓓ Ⓔ	57 Ⓐ Ⓑ Ⓒ Ⓓ Ⓔ	75 Ⓐ Ⓑ Ⓒ Ⓓ Ⓔ
4 Ⓐ Ⓑ Ⓒ Ⓓ Ⓔ	22 Ⓐ Ⓑ Ⓒ Ⓓ Ⓔ	40 Ⓐ Ⓑ Ⓒ Ⓓ Ⓔ	58 Ⓐ Ⓑ Ⓒ Ⓓ Ⓔ	76 Ⓐ Ⓑ Ⓒ Ⓓ Ⓔ
5 Ⓐ Ⓑ Ⓒ Ⓓ Ⓔ	23 Ⓐ Ⓑ Ⓒ Ⓓ Ⓔ	41 Ⓐ Ⓑ Ⓒ Ⓓ Ⓔ	59 Ⓐ Ⓑ Ⓒ Ⓓ Ⓔ	77 Ⓐ Ⓑ Ⓒ Ⓓ Ⓔ
6 Ⓐ Ⓑ Ⓒ Ⓓ Ⓔ	24 Ⓐ Ⓑ Ⓒ Ⓓ Ⓔ	42 Ⓐ Ⓑ Ⓒ Ⓓ Ⓔ	60 Ⓐ Ⓑ Ⓒ Ⓓ Ⓔ	78 Ⓐ Ⓑ Ⓒ Ⓓ Ⓔ
7 Ⓐ Ⓑ Ⓒ Ⓓ Ⓔ	25 Ⓐ Ⓑ Ⓒ Ⓓ Ⓔ	43 Ⓐ Ⓑ Ⓒ Ⓓ Ⓔ	61 Ⓐ Ⓑ Ⓒ Ⓓ Ⓔ	79 Ⓐ Ⓑ Ⓒ Ⓓ Ⓔ
8 Ⓐ Ⓑ Ⓒ Ⓓ Ⓔ	26 Ⓐ Ⓑ Ⓒ Ⓓ Ⓔ	44 Ⓐ Ⓑ Ⓒ Ⓓ Ⓔ	62 Ⓐ Ⓑ Ⓒ Ⓓ Ⓔ	80 Ⓐ Ⓑ Ⓒ Ⓓ Ⓔ
9 Ⓐ Ⓑ Ⓒ Ⓓ Ⓔ	27 Ⓐ Ⓑ Ⓒ Ⓓ Ⓔ	45 Ⓐ Ⓑ Ⓒ Ⓓ Ⓔ	63 Ⓐ Ⓑ Ⓒ Ⓓ Ⓔ	81 Ⓐ Ⓑ Ⓒ Ⓓ Ⓔ
10 Ⓐ Ⓑ Ⓒ Ⓓ Ⓔ	28 Ⓐ Ⓑ Ⓒ Ⓓ Ⓔ	46 Ⓐ Ⓑ Ⓒ Ⓓ Ⓔ	64 Ⓐ Ⓑ Ⓒ Ⓓ Ⓔ	82 Ⓐ Ⓑ Ⓒ Ⓓ Ⓔ
11 Ⓐ Ⓑ Ⓒ Ⓓ Ⓔ	29 Ⓐ Ⓑ Ⓒ Ⓓ Ⓔ	47 Ⓐ Ⓑ Ⓒ Ⓓ Ⓔ	65 Ⓐ Ⓑ Ⓒ Ⓓ Ⓔ	83 Ⓐ Ⓑ Ⓒ Ⓓ Ⓔ
12 Ⓐ Ⓑ Ⓒ Ⓓ Ⓔ	30 Ⓐ Ⓑ Ⓒ Ⓓ Ⓔ	48 Ⓐ Ⓑ Ⓒ Ⓓ Ⓔ	66 Ⓐ Ⓑ Ⓒ Ⓓ Ⓔ	84 Ⓐ Ⓑ Ⓒ Ⓓ Ⓔ
13 Ⓐ Ⓑ Ⓒ Ⓓ Ⓔ	31 Ⓐ Ⓑ Ⓒ Ⓓ Ⓔ	49 Ⓐ Ⓑ Ⓒ Ⓓ Ⓔ	67 Ⓐ Ⓑ Ⓒ Ⓓ Ⓔ	85 Ⓐ Ⓑ Ⓒ Ⓓ Ⓔ
14 Ⓐ Ⓑ Ⓒ Ⓓ Ⓔ	32 Ⓐ Ⓑ Ⓒ Ⓓ Ⓔ	50 Ⓐ Ⓑ Ⓒ Ⓓ Ⓔ	68 Ⓐ Ⓑ Ⓒ Ⓓ Ⓔ	86 Ⓐ Ⓑ Ⓒ Ⓓ Ⓔ
15 Ⓐ Ⓑ Ⓒ Ⓓ Ⓔ	33 Ⓐ Ⓑ Ⓒ Ⓓ Ⓔ	51 Ⓐ Ⓑ Ⓒ Ⓓ Ⓔ	69 Ⓐ Ⓑ Ⓒ Ⓓ Ⓔ	87 Ⓐ Ⓑ Ⓒ Ⓓ Ⓔ
16 Ⓐ Ⓑ Ⓒ Ⓓ Ⓔ	34 Ⓐ Ⓑ Ⓒ Ⓓ Ⓔ	52 Ⓐ Ⓑ Ⓒ Ⓓ Ⓔ	70 Ⓐ Ⓑ Ⓒ Ⓓ Ⓔ	88 Ⓐ Ⓑ Ⓒ Ⓓ Ⓔ
17 Ⓐ Ⓑ Ⓒ Ⓓ Ⓔ	35 Ⓐ Ⓑ Ⓒ Ⓓ Ⓔ	53 Ⓐ Ⓑ Ⓒ Ⓓ Ⓔ	71 Ⓐ Ⓑ Ⓒ Ⓓ Ⓔ	
18 Ⓐ Ⓑ Ⓒ Ⓓ Ⓔ	36 Ⓐ Ⓑ Ⓒ Ⓓ Ⓔ	54 Ⓐ Ⓑ Ⓒ Ⓓ Ⓔ	72 Ⓐ Ⓑ Ⓒ Ⓓ Ⓔ	

Part C—Number Series

1 Ⓐ Ⓑ Ⓒ Ⓓ Ⓔ	6 Ⓐ Ⓑ Ⓒ Ⓓ Ⓔ	11 Ⓐ Ⓑ Ⓒ Ⓓ Ⓔ	16 Ⓐ Ⓑ Ⓒ Ⓓ Ⓔ	21 Ⓐ Ⓑ Ⓒ Ⓓ Ⓔ
2 Ⓐ Ⓑ Ⓒ Ⓓ Ⓔ	7 Ⓐ Ⓑ Ⓒ Ⓓ Ⓔ	12 Ⓐ Ⓑ Ⓒ Ⓓ Ⓔ	17 Ⓐ Ⓑ Ⓒ Ⓓ Ⓔ	22 Ⓐ Ⓑ Ⓒ Ⓓ Ⓔ
3 Ⓐ Ⓑ Ⓒ Ⓓ Ⓔ	8 Ⓐ Ⓑ Ⓒ Ⓓ Ⓔ	13 Ⓐ Ⓑ Ⓒ Ⓓ Ⓔ	18 Ⓐ Ⓑ Ⓒ Ⓓ Ⓔ	23 Ⓐ Ⓑ Ⓒ Ⓓ Ⓔ
4 Ⓐ Ⓑ Ⓒ Ⓓ Ⓔ	9 Ⓐ Ⓑ Ⓒ Ⓓ Ⓔ	14 Ⓐ Ⓑ Ⓒ Ⓓ Ⓔ	19 Ⓐ Ⓑ Ⓒ Ⓓ Ⓔ	24 Ⓐ Ⓑ Ⓒ Ⓓ Ⓔ
5 Ⓐ Ⓑ Ⓒ Ⓓ Ⓔ	10 Ⓐ Ⓑ Ⓒ Ⓓ Ⓔ	15 Ⓐ Ⓑ Ⓒ Ⓓ Ⓔ	20 Ⓐ Ⓑ Ⓒ Ⓓ Ⓔ	

Part D—Following Oral Directions

1 Ⓐ Ⓑ Ⓒ Ⓓ Ⓔ	19 Ⓐ Ⓑ Ⓒ Ⓓ Ⓔ	37 Ⓐ Ⓑ Ⓒ Ⓓ Ⓔ	55 Ⓐ Ⓑ Ⓒ Ⓓ Ⓔ	73 Ⓐ Ⓑ Ⓒ Ⓓ Ⓔ
2 Ⓐ Ⓑ Ⓒ Ⓓ Ⓔ	20 Ⓐ Ⓑ Ⓒ Ⓓ Ⓔ	38 Ⓐ Ⓑ Ⓒ Ⓓ Ⓔ	56 Ⓐ Ⓑ Ⓒ Ⓓ Ⓔ	74 Ⓐ Ⓑ Ⓒ Ⓓ Ⓔ
3 Ⓐ Ⓑ Ⓒ Ⓓ Ⓔ	21 Ⓐ Ⓑ Ⓒ Ⓓ Ⓔ	39 Ⓐ Ⓑ Ⓒ Ⓓ Ⓔ	57 Ⓐ Ⓑ Ⓒ Ⓓ Ⓔ	75 Ⓐ Ⓑ Ⓒ Ⓓ Ⓔ
4 Ⓐ Ⓑ Ⓒ Ⓓ Ⓔ	22 Ⓐ Ⓑ Ⓒ Ⓓ Ⓔ	40 Ⓐ Ⓑ Ⓒ Ⓓ Ⓔ	58 Ⓐ Ⓑ Ⓒ Ⓓ Ⓔ	76 Ⓐ Ⓑ Ⓒ Ⓓ Ⓔ
5 Ⓐ Ⓑ Ⓒ Ⓓ Ⓔ	23 Ⓐ Ⓑ Ⓒ Ⓓ Ⓔ	41 Ⓐ Ⓑ Ⓒ Ⓓ Ⓔ	59 Ⓐ Ⓑ Ⓒ Ⓓ Ⓔ	77 Ⓐ Ⓑ Ⓒ Ⓓ Ⓔ
6 Ⓐ Ⓑ Ⓒ Ⓓ Ⓔ	24 Ⓐ Ⓑ Ⓒ Ⓓ Ⓔ	42 Ⓐ Ⓑ Ⓒ Ⓓ Ⓔ	60 Ⓐ Ⓑ Ⓒ Ⓓ Ⓔ	78 Ⓐ Ⓑ Ⓒ Ⓓ Ⓔ
7 Ⓐ Ⓑ Ⓒ Ⓓ Ⓔ	25 Ⓐ Ⓑ Ⓒ Ⓓ Ⓔ	43 Ⓐ Ⓑ Ⓒ Ⓓ Ⓔ	61 Ⓐ Ⓑ Ⓒ Ⓓ Ⓔ	79 Ⓐ Ⓑ Ⓒ Ⓓ Ⓔ
8 Ⓐ Ⓑ Ⓒ Ⓓ Ⓔ	26 Ⓐ Ⓑ Ⓒ Ⓓ Ⓔ	44 Ⓐ Ⓑ Ⓒ Ⓓ Ⓔ	62 Ⓐ Ⓑ Ⓒ Ⓓ Ⓔ	80 Ⓐ Ⓑ Ⓒ Ⓓ Ⓔ
9 Ⓐ Ⓑ Ⓒ Ⓓ Ⓔ	27 Ⓐ Ⓑ Ⓒ Ⓓ Ⓔ	45 Ⓐ Ⓑ Ⓒ Ⓓ Ⓔ	63 Ⓐ Ⓑ Ⓒ Ⓓ Ⓔ	81 Ⓐ Ⓑ Ⓒ Ⓓ Ⓔ
10 Ⓐ Ⓑ Ⓒ Ⓓ Ⓔ	28 Ⓐ Ⓑ Ⓒ Ⓓ Ⓔ	46 Ⓐ Ⓑ Ⓒ Ⓓ Ⓔ	64 Ⓐ Ⓑ Ⓒ Ⓓ Ⓔ	82 Ⓐ Ⓑ Ⓒ Ⓓ Ⓔ
11 Ⓐ Ⓑ Ⓒ Ⓓ Ⓔ	29 Ⓐ Ⓑ Ⓒ Ⓓ Ⓔ	47 Ⓐ Ⓑ Ⓒ Ⓓ Ⓔ	65 Ⓐ Ⓑ Ⓒ Ⓓ Ⓔ	83 Ⓐ Ⓑ Ⓒ Ⓓ Ⓔ
12 Ⓐ Ⓑ Ⓒ Ⓓ Ⓔ	30 Ⓐ Ⓑ Ⓒ Ⓓ Ⓔ	48 Ⓐ Ⓑ Ⓒ Ⓓ Ⓔ	66 Ⓐ Ⓑ Ⓒ Ⓓ Ⓔ	84 Ⓐ Ⓑ Ⓒ Ⓓ Ⓔ
13 Ⓐ Ⓑ Ⓒ Ⓓ Ⓔ	31 Ⓐ Ⓑ Ⓒ Ⓓ Ⓔ	49 Ⓐ Ⓑ Ⓒ Ⓓ Ⓔ	67 Ⓐ Ⓑ Ⓒ Ⓓ Ⓔ	85 Ⓐ Ⓑ Ⓒ Ⓓ Ⓔ
14 Ⓐ Ⓑ Ⓒ Ⓓ Ⓔ	32 Ⓐ Ⓑ Ⓒ Ⓓ Ⓔ	50 Ⓐ Ⓑ Ⓒ Ⓓ Ⓔ	68 Ⓐ Ⓑ Ⓒ Ⓓ Ⓔ	86 Ⓐ Ⓑ Ⓒ Ⓓ Ⓔ
15 Ⓐ Ⓑ Ⓒ Ⓓ Ⓔ	33 Ⓐ Ⓑ Ⓒ Ⓓ Ⓔ	51 Ⓐ Ⓑ Ⓒ Ⓓ Ⓔ	69 Ⓐ Ⓑ Ⓒ Ⓓ Ⓔ	87 Ⓐ Ⓑ Ⓒ Ⓓ Ⓔ
16 Ⓐ Ⓑ Ⓒ Ⓓ Ⓔ	34 Ⓐ Ⓑ Ⓒ Ⓓ Ⓔ	52 Ⓐ Ⓑ Ⓒ Ⓓ Ⓔ	70 Ⓐ Ⓑ Ⓒ Ⓓ Ⓔ	88 Ⓐ Ⓑ Ⓒ Ⓓ Ⓔ
17 Ⓐ Ⓑ Ⓒ Ⓓ Ⓔ	35 Ⓐ Ⓑ Ⓒ Ⓓ Ⓔ	53 Ⓐ Ⓑ Ⓒ Ⓓ Ⓔ	71 Ⓐ Ⓑ Ⓒ Ⓓ Ⓔ	
18 Ⓐ Ⓑ Ⓒ Ⓓ Ⓔ	36 Ⓐ Ⓑ Ⓒ Ⓓ Ⓔ	54 Ⓐ Ⓑ Ⓒ Ⓓ Ⓔ	72 Ⓐ Ⓑ Ⓒ Ⓓ Ⓔ	

Remove by cutting on dotted line.

Chapter 14

Practice Test 5

PART A — ADDRESS CHECKING

Work — 6 minutes

In this part of the test, you are to decide whether two addresses are alike or different. If the two addresses are *exactly alike in every way*, darken space Ⓐ. If they are *different in any way*, darken space Ⓓ for the question.

Mark your answers on the Answer Sheet on page 363. Tear it out, put today's date on it, and place it next to the questions.

Allow yourself *exactly 6 minutes* to do as many of the 95 questions as you can. If you finish before the time is up, check your answers.

1.	8728 South Chelmsford Ave	8729 South Chelmsford Ave
2.	Wolcott IN 47995	Walcott IN 47995
3.	454 E Delgado Rd	454 E Delgado Rd
4.	4812 S Holmesburg Ave	4812 S Holmesbury Ave
5.	Colwich KS 67030	Colwich KS 67030
6.	4700 Mahopac Ln	4700 Mahopac Ln
7.	6304 Avalun Rd	6304 Avalun Rd
8.	5606 Quail Hollow Rd	5660 Quail Hollow Rd
9.	10472 Rolens Ave W	10472 Rolens Ave W
10.	8341 Quail Roost Rd N	8341 Quail Roost Rd N
11.	4811 E Yates St	4811 E Gates St
12.	5178 Indian Queen Ln	5178 Indian Queen Ln
13.	6118 Brushmore Ave NW	6118 Brushmore Ave NW
14.	3689 S Oxlow Ct	3689 S Oslow Ct
15.	2486 Zanfagna St NE	2486 Zanfagna St NE
16.	2001 Gorsten St	2001 Gorsten St
17.	362 Ortega Ct	362 Ortega Ct
18.	2037 Williamette Blvd	2037 Williamette Blvd
19.	Roselle IL 60172	Rosette IL 60172
20.	4401 Pickford Blvd N	4401 Pickford Ave N
21.	2140 S Magdalena Dr	1240 S Magdalena Dr
22.	4172 Ponagansett St	4172 Ponagansett St
23.	1012 Northwood Rd	1012 Northwalk Rd
24.	5116 Newell St	5116 Newall St

25.	2771 Onondago Trl	2771 Onondaga Trl
26.	Independence MO	Independence MO
27.	1501 SW 2nd Ave	1501 SW 2nd Ave
28.	178 El Camino Way	178 El Camino Way
29.	4401 11th Ave E	4401 11th Ave W
30.	Beaconsfield NY	Bakersfield NY
31.	4056 Yoncalla Ct	4056 Yoncalla Ct
32.	8630 Tim Dr	8630 Tin Dr
33.	290 Davisville River Rd	209 Davisville River Rd
34.	72 Peranna Path	72 Peranna Path
35.	3740 E Ellsworth Ave	3741 E Ellsworth Ave
36.	Norfolk VA 23505	Norwalk VA 23505
37.	6198 Juniata Cir	6198 Juniata Cir
38.	3008 N Graham St	3008 N Graham Ct
39.	9134 McTaggard Dr	9134 McTaggard Dr
40.	3431 W 65th Cir	3431 W 64th Cir
41.	7260 Aldawood Hill Dr	7260 Aldawood Mill Dr
42.	5836 S Inverness Rd	5836 S Inverness Rd
43.	6405 Worcester Blvd N	6405 Worcester Blvd N
44.	Medomak ME	Medomak MD
45.	923 Violet Memorial Pl	923 Violet Memorial Pl
46.	1045 East View Dr	1045 East View Dr
47.	Rochester NY 14625	Rochester NY 14625
48.	913 Manayunk Hill St	913 Manayunk Hill Ct
49.	1908 West Van Cortland Ave	1908 East Van Cortland Ave
50.	Tamassee SC 29686	Tamassee SC 29686
51.	1172 Jacobus St SE	1172 Jacobine St SE
52.	1137 N Woodstock Ave	1137 N Woodstock Ave
53.	14081 32 St NE	14081 32 St NE
54.	6962 Rolling Stone Rd	6632 Rolling Stone Rd
55.	1992 Verde Vista Ter NW	1992 Verde Vista Ter NW
56.	Davanport IA 52807	Davanport LA 52807
57.	431 Coddington Ave	431 Coddingtown Ave
58.	Kingshill VI	Kingshill VA
59.	Bowlus MN	Bowlus MN
60.	1415 Ave X S	1415 Ave Y S

61.	2445 Nemesio Canales Rd	2444 Nemesio Canales Rd
62.	8232 La Burnum Dr	8232 La Barnum Dr
63.	3400 Aspen St	3400 Aspen St
64.	2976 Barrington Square Ext	2976 Barrington Square Ext
65.	8456 W Lancaster Pike	845 W Lancaster Pike
66.	7149 E Berghammer Ln	7149 E Bernhander Ln
67.	617 Owen Blvd	617 Owen Blvd
68.	7405 Kennebec Ln	7405 Kennebec Ln
69.	Salkum WA	Saltum WA
70.	4713 Hurlburt Ave	4713 Hurlburt Ave
71.	2638 Kingsbridge Ter W	2683 Kingsbridge Ter W
72.	1046 N Wynmill Rd	1046 N Windmill Rd
73.	7048 Kingsessing St	7048 Kingsessing St
74.	3810 University Commercial Place	3810 University Commercial Place
75.	398 N Laurel Ave	398 N Laurel St
76.	9081 Dogwood Ter	9181 Dogwood Ter
77.	1808 Armand Pl	1808 Armond Pl
78.	164 E Firestone Blvd	164 E Firestone Blvd
79.	619 Fairmount Pl S	619 Fairmount Pl N
80.	718 Schofield View Cir	718 Schofield View Ter
81.	5054 Digney Ln	5504 Digney Ln
82.	91 Whispering Oak Canyon Trl	91 Whispering Oak Canyon Trl
83.	5968 Ziggarut Cir	5968 Ziggarut Cir
84.	2066 Timrod St NE	2066 Timrod St SE
85.	9789 E Rhone Ct	9789 E Rhine Ct
86.	984 Derry Dell Ct	984 Derry Dell Ct
87.	Springfield MA 01104	Springfield MA 01104
88.	8560 Tanglewood St	8506 Tanglewood St
89.	6809 Jenkintown Rd	6809 Jenkintown Rd
90.	Frametown WV 26623	Frametown WV 26623
91.	Warwick RI	Warwick RI
92.	2803 Flowering Tree Cir	2803 Flowering Tree Cir
93.	2709 Bailey Ave	2709 Baisley Ave
94.	8452 Caroline Ct	8452 Caroline St
95.	5054 W Quapah Pl	5054 W Quapah Pl

STOP.
If you finish before the time is up, go back and check
the questions in this section of the test only.

PART B — MEMORY FOR ADDRESSES

In this part of the test, you will have five boxes labeled A, B, C, D, and E. Each box contains five addresses. Three of the five are groups of street addresses, such as 5400–5699 Clocks, 3800–3999 Harmony, and 2600–3599 Parker; and two are names of places. The addresses are different in each box.

There will be several opportunities to study the addresses and the boxes they are in. You will also be given three tests of 88 questions each, and the task of deciding where each address belongs. In some cases, you will have the list *and* the boxes in front of you at the same time; in others you will not. List 1 and List 2 are for warm-up practice. List 3 is the real one that will be scored.

Make sure you understand the format by examining the pretest samples below.

Pretest Samples

A	B	C	D	E
4000–5099 Clocks	2600–3799 Clocks	5400–5699 Clocks	3800–3999 Clocks	5100–5399 Clocks
Hunt	Mason	Placid	Oakland	Carmel
5100–5399 Harmony	3800–3999 Harmony	2600–3799 Harmony	5400–6599 Harmony	4000–5099 Harmony
Victor	Wyatt	Dreier	Arkansas	McDonald
3600–3799 Parker	5400–6299 Parker	4000–5399 Parker	2600–3599 Parker	3800–3999 Parker

Questions 1 through 7 show the way the questions look. You have to decide in which lettered box (A, B, C, D, or E) the address belongs and then mark your answer by darkening the appropriate space in the answer grid.

1. Carmel   1 Ⓐ Ⓑ Ⓒ Ⓓ Ⓔ
2. 4000–5399 Parker   2 Ⓐ Ⓑ Ⓒ Ⓓ Ⓔ
3. 5100–5399 Clocks   3 Ⓐ Ⓑ Ⓒ Ⓓ Ⓔ
4. Wyatt   4 Ⓐ Ⓑ Ⓒ Ⓓ Ⓔ
5. Hunt   5 Ⓐ Ⓑ Ⓒ Ⓓ Ⓔ
6. 5100–5399 Harmony   6 Ⓐ Ⓑ Ⓒ Ⓓ Ⓔ
7. Placid   7 Ⓐ Ⓑ Ⓒ Ⓓ Ⓔ

Answers

1. **E** 2. **C** 3. **E** 4. **B** 5. **A** 6. **A** 7. **C**

Now that you know what to do, you may begin Part B of Practice Test 5. To get the most out of it and the final practice test in this book, follow the directions and timing *exactly*. Follow each phase of Part B of the test, page by page, until you've completed List 3. It is modeled on the way the Postal Service actually conducts its tests.

Turn to the next page to begin.

Study — 3 minutes

You will be given 3 minutes to spend memorizing the addresses in the boxes. *They are exactly the same ones that will be used for all three tests.* Try to memorize as many as you can. When the 3 minutes are up, turn to page 372 and read the instructions for *List 1*.

A	B	C	D	E
4000–5099 Clocks	2600–3799 Clocks	5400–5699 Clocks	3800–3999 Clocks	5100–5399 Clocks
Hunt	Mason	Placid	Oakland	Carmel
5100–5399 Harmony	3800–3999 Harmony	2600–3799 Harmony	5400–6599 Harmony	4000–5099 Harmony
Victor	Wyatt	Dreier	Arkansas	McDonald
3600–3799 Parker	5400–6299 Parker	4000–5399 Parker	2600–3599 Parker	3800–3999 Parker

List 1

Work — 3 minutes

Tear out the Answer Sheet for List 1. For each question, mark the answer sheet on page 364 to show the letter of the box in which the address belongs. Try to remember the locations of as many addresses as you can. *You will now have 3 minutes to complete List 1.* If you are not sure of an answer, you should guess.

A	B	C	D	E
4000–5099 Clocks	2600–3799 Clocks	5400–5699 Clocks	3800–3999 Clocks	5100–5399 Clocks
Hunt	Mason	Placid	Oakland	Carmel
5100–5399 Harmony	3800–3999 Harmony	2600–3799 Harmony	5400–6599 Harmony	4000–5099 Harmony
Victor	Wyatt	Dreier	Arkansas	McDonald
3600–3799 Parker	5400–6299 Parker	4000–5399 Parker	2600–3599 Parker	3800–3999 Parker

1. 2600–3799 Clocks
2. 4000–5099 Clocks
3. Dreier
4. 5100–5399 Harmony
5. 3800–3999 Parker
6. 5400–5699 Clocks
7. Victor
8. Arkansas
9. 3600–3799 Parker
10. 4000–5099 Harmony
11. Mason

12. 3800–3900 Clocks
13. 3800–3999 Harmony
14. 2600–3599 Parker
15. Oakland
16. 5100–5399 Clocks
17. 2600–3799 Harmony
18. Carmel
19. 5400–6299 Parker
20. Hunt
21. Placid
22. McDonald

23. Wyatt
24. 4000–5399 Parker
25. 5400–6599 Harmony
26. Victor
27. 3600–3799 Parker
28. 2600–3599 Parker
29. McDonald
30. 5100–5399 Clocks
31. 4000–5099 Harmony
32. 3800–3999 Parker
33. Wyatt

34. Carmel
35. Dreier
36. 5400–5699 Clocks
37. Placid
38. 5400–6299 Parker
39. 5100–5399 Harmony
40. 5400–6299 Parker
41. Hunt
42. 4000–5399 Parker
43. Arkansas
44. 3800–3999 Harmony

45. Victor
46. 4000–5099 Clocks
47. Carmel
48. Dreier
49. McDonald
50. Placid
51. 5400–5699 Clocks
52. 2600–3799 Clocks
53. 4000–5099 Harmony
54. McDonald
55. Arkansas

56. Hunt
57. 5400–6599 Harmony
58. 2600–3599 Parker
59. Mason
60. 3600–3799 Parker
61. Oakland
62. Mason
63. 3800–3999 Clocks
64. Oakland
65. 4000–5399 Parker
66. 5100–5399 Clocks

67. 4000–5099 Clocks
68. Mason
69. 2600–3799 Clocks
70. 5400–6599 Harmony
71. 3800–3999 Harmony
72. Hunt
73. 2600–3799 Harmony
74. Arkansas
75. Oakland
76. Wyatt
77. Victor

78. 3800–3999 Parker
79. Dreier
80. Wyatt
81. 3800–3999 Clocks
82. 5100–5399 Harmony
83. 2600–3799 Harmony
84. Placid
85. Carmel
86. 2600–3599 Parker
87. McDonald
88. 4000–5099 Harmony

STOP.
If you finish before the time is up, go back and check
the questions in this section of the test only.

List 2

Work — 3 minutes

Do these questions *without* looking back at the boxes. For each question, mark your answer on the Answer Sheet for List 2 on page 364. If you are not sure of an answer, you should guess.

1. Hunt
2. 4000–5099 Harmony
3. 3800–3999 Harmony
4. Arkansas
5. Dreier
6. Carmel
7. 3800–3999 Parker
8. Mason
9. 2600–3799 Harmony
10. 2600–3599 Parker
11. McDonald

12. 5400–5699 Clocks
13. 2600–3799 Clocks
14. Wyatt
15. Placid
16. 4000–5399 Parker
17. 4000–5099 Harmony
18. 5400–6599 Harmony
19. Carmel
20. 2600–3599 Parker
21. 5100–5399 Harmony
22. McDonald

23. 5100–5399 Harmony
24. Hunt
25. Arkansas
26. 3800–3999 Clocks
27. Arkansas
28. 4000–5099 Clocks
29. 4000–5099 Harmony
30. 3800–3999 Clocks
31. Dreier
32. 2600–3799 Harmony
33. Oakland

34. 5400–5699 Clocks
35. Victor
36. McDonald
37. 5100–5399 Clocks
38. 3800–3999 Parker
39. 3800–3999 Harmony
40. 4000–5099 Harmony
41. Oakland
42. 2600–3799 Clocks
43. 4000–5399 Parker
44. Wyatt

45. 5100–5399 Clocks
46. Placid
47. McDonald
48. 5400–5699 Clocks
49. 3600–3799 Parker
50. 5400–6299 Parker
51. 5100–5399 Clocks
52. 4000–5099 Clocks
53. Carmel
54. 5400–6599 Harmony
55. 3600–3799 Parker

56. Arkansas
57. 5100–5399 Harmony
58. Victor
59. 4000–5099 Clocks
60. 2600–3599 Parker
61. 3600–3799 Parker
62. Oakland
63. Victor
64. Hunt
65. Carmel
66. Mason

67. 3800–3999 Harmony
68. Oakland
69. Wyatt
70. Oakland
71. 2600–3799 Clocks
72. Dreier
73. Mason
74. McDonald
75. 2600–3799 Clocks
76. 3800–3999 Clocks
77. 3800–3999 Parker

78. Wyatt
79. 5400–6599 Harmony
80. 2600–3799 Harmony
81. Placid
82. 5400–5699 Clocks
83. Placid
84. Hunt
85. 4000–5399 Parker
86. 5400–6299 Parker
87. Mason
88. 5400–6299 Parker

STOP.
If you finish before the time is up, go back and check
the questions in this section of the test only.

List 3

Study — 5 minutes

You are now about to take the test using List 3. *(This is the test that counts!)*

Turn back to page 371 and study the boxes again. *You have 5 minutes to restudy the addresses.*

Work — 5 minutes

For each question, mark the Answer Sheet on page 365 to show the letter of the box in which the address belongs. You have *exactly 5 minutes* to do the test. During these 5 minutes, *do not* turn to any other page.

1. Wyatt
2. 4000–5399 Parker
3. Victor
4. Oakland
5. 4000–5099 Harmony
6. 3800–3999 Harmony
7. 3800–3999 Harmony
8. 5100–5399 Clocks
9. McDonald
10. Victor
11. 5400–5699 Clocks

12. Oakland
13. 2600–3799 Harmony
14. Dreier
15. 3800–3999 Clocks
16. 4000–5099 Harmony
17. 4000–5099 Clocks
18. Arkansas
19. 3800–3999 Clocks
20. Hunt
21. 5100–5399 Harmony
22. McDonald

23. 5100–5399 Harmony
24. 2600–3599 Parker
25. Carmel
26. 5400–6599 Harmony
27. 4000–5099 Harmony
28. 4000–5399 Parker
29. Victor
30. Placid
31. Wyatt
32. 2600–3799 Clocks
33. 5400–5699 Clocks

34. McDonald
35. 2600–3599 Parker
36. 2600–3799 Harmony
37. Mason
38. 3800–3999 Parker
39. Carmel
40. Dreier
41. Arkansas
42. 3800–3999 Harmony
43. 4000–5099 Harmony
44. Hunt

45. 5400–6299 Parker
46. Mason
47. 5400–6299 Parker
48. 4000–5399 Parker
49. Hunt
50. Placid
51. Dreier
52. Placid
53. 2600–3799 Harmony
54. 5400–6599 Harmony
55. Wyatt

56. 3800–3999 Parker
57. 3800–3999 Clocks
58. 2600–3799 Clocks
59. McDonald
60. Mason
61. Dreier
62. 2600–3799 Clocks
63. Oakland
64. Wyatt
65. Oakland
66. 3800–3999 Harmony

67. 5100–5399 Clocks
68. Carmel
69. Hunt
70. Victor
71. Oakland
72. 3600–3799 Parker
73. 2600–3599 Parker
74. 4000–5099 Clocks
75. Victor
76. 5100–5399 Harmony
77. Arkansas

78. 3600–3799 Parker
79. 5400–6599 Harmony
80. Carmel
81. 4000–5099 Clocks
82. 5100–5399 Clocks
83. 5400–6299 Parker
84. 3600–3799 Parker
85. 5400–5699 Clocks
86. McDonald
87. Placid
88. 5100–5399 Clocks

STOP.
If you finish before the time is up, go back and check
the questions in this section of the test only.

PART C — NUMBER SERIES

Work — 20 minutes

For each Number Series question, there is a series of numbers that follow some definite order, and below each are five sets of two numbers each. You are to look at the numbers in the series and find out what order they follow. Then decide what the next two numbers in that series would be if the same order were continued. Mark your answers on the Answer Sheet on page 365.

You have 20 minutes to complete this part of the test. If you finish before the time is up, check your answers. The answers and explanations are on pages 368 to 369.

1. 50 45 45 40 35 35 30 __ __
   A) 30 25   B) 25 25   C) 25 30   D) 30 30   E) 25 20

2. 4 6 6 6 7 7 8 8 __ __
   A) 8 10   B) 9 8   C) 9 9   D) 8 9   E) 9 10

3. 27 22 28 24 29 26 30 __ __
   A) 31 27   B) 28 31   C) 32 28   D) 28 30   E) 27 28

4. 10 1 15 20 10 1 15 20 __ __
   A) 15 1   B) 10 20   C) 10 15   D) 10 1   E) 20 15

5. 6 15 9 5 15 8 4 __ __
   A) 8 5   B) 5 11   C) 8 10   D) 3 9   E) 15 7

6. 18 22 17 21 16 20 15 __ __
   A) 17 18   B) 14 17   C) 18 19   D) 14 20   E) 19 14

7. $10^{3/12}$ $11^{4/11}$ $12^{5/10}$ $13^{6/9}$ $14^{7/8}$ $15^{8/7}$ $16^{9/6}$ __ __
   A) $17^{9/6}$ $18^{10/7}$ B) $16^{10/5}$ $16^{11/6}$ C) $17^{10/5}$ $18^{11/4}$ D) $18^{9/7}$ $19^{10/6}$ E) $17^{8/5}$ $18^{7/6}$

8. 26 2 6 38 3 8 40 __ __
   A) 9 50   B) 4 9   C) 4 0   D) 40 10   E) 9 10

9. 9 2 8 14 14 20 19 __ __
   A) 15 18   B) 24 30   C) 25 31   D) 30 24   E) 26 32

10. 2 4 6 12 11 8 10 12 10 __ __
    A) 9 14   B) 14 16   C) 11 13   D) 14 15   E) 13 10

11. 2 3 2 3 3 2 4 3 __ __
    A) 3 4   B) 2 3   C) 2 5   D) 3 5   E) 3 3

12. 9 7 5 11 9 7 13 __ __
    A) 11 9   B) 12 11   C) 14 8   D) 12 8   E) 10 12

13. 9 10 17 11 12 16 13 __ __
    A) 15 16   B) 12 13   C) 14 15   D) 13 14   E) 12 15

14. 37 44 45 51 58 45 65 __ __
    A) 75 45   B) 72 79   C) 65 45   D) 45 75   E) 72 45

15. 9 18 16 11 22 20 15 30 __ __
    A) 25 23   B) 28 26   C) 60 58   D) 28 23   E) 23 25

16. 32 30 28 16 26 24 22 20 __ __
    A) 18 20   B) 20 18   C) 16 18   D) 20 20   E) 18 16

17. 39 38 38 36 35 35 33 __ __
    A) 31 31   B) 32 31   C) 32 32   D) 33 32   E) 31 30

18. 17 14 11 16 13 10 15 __ __
    A) 20 17   B) 10 7   C) 12 9   D) 7 10   E) 13 10

19. 15 10 15 20 10 20 25 __ __
    A) 20 25   B) 15 20   C) 20 20   D) 10 25   E) 25 25

20. 16 18 16 22 24 20 28 30 __ __
    A) 32 18   B) 22 26   C) 30 32   D) 24 34   E) 32 38

21. 2 3 3 5 5 8 8 __ __
    A) 12 12   B) 11 12   C) 8 11   D) 8 8   E) 11 11

22. 45 35 40 30 35 25 30 __ __
    A) 25 35   B) 20 25   C) 40 45   D) 35 40   E) 35 30

23. 8 11 10 9 13 10 10 15 __ __
    A) 16 10   B) 10 11   C) 12 14   D) 12 10   E) 11 10

24. 19 18 16 15 15 14 12 11 11 __ __
    A) 10 9   B) 11 10   C) 10 10   D) 10 9   E) 10 8

STOP.
If you finish before the time is up, go back and check
the questions in this section of the test only.

PART D — FOLLOWING ORAL DIRECTIONS

This part of the test gauges your ability to understand and carry out spoken directions *exactly* as they are given to you.

In order to prepare to take Part D of the test, follow the steps below:

1. Enlist the help of a friend who will be the "reader." His or her job will be to read aloud a series of directions that you are to follow *exactly*. The reader will need a watch that displays seconds, because the directions must be read at the correct speed.

2. Tear out pages 385 to 386. These are the worksheets you should have in front of you as you listen to the directions given by the reader, who will tell you to do certain things with the items on each line on the worksheets.

3. Use the Answer Sheet for Following Oral Directions on page 365, and insert today's date. You will darken the appropriate spaces in accordance with the directions given by the reader.

4. *Now hand this entire book to the reader.* Ask him/her to review the section below headed "Instructions to the Reader." It explains exactly how the reader is to proceed.

When you and the reader are ready to start this part of Practice Test 5, he/she will begin reading to you the section marked "Directions." YOU ARE NOT TO READ THESE AT ANY TIME BEFORE OR DURING THE TEST. If you do, you will lose the benefit of this part of the practice test.

Instructions to the "Reader"

These instructions should be read at about 80 words per minute. You should practice reading the material in the box until you can do it in exactly 1 minute. The number of words in the passage and the natural pauses described below will give you a good feel for the rate of speed and the way you should read the test questions.

1-MINUTE PRACTICE

> Look at line 20 in your worksheet. There are two circles and two boxes of different sizes with numbers in them. If 7 is less than 3 and if 2 is smaller than 4, write C in the larger circle. Otherwise write B as in *baker* in the smaller box. Now, on your answer sheet, darken the space for the number-letter combination in the box or circle.

You should read the entire test aloud before you read it to the person taking the test, in order to thoroughly acquaint yourself with the procedure and the desired rate of reading.

Read slowly but at a natural pace. In other words, do not space the words so that there are unnaturally long pauses between them. The instruction "Pause slightly" indicates only enough time to take a breath. The other instructions for pauses give the recommended length for each. If possible, use a watch with a second hand.

All the material that follows, except the words in parentheses, is to be read aloud. Now start reading the directions. *Do not repeat any of the directions.*

Directions: In this test, I will read instructions to you.

You are to mark your worksheets according to the instructions that I read to you. After each set of instructions, I'll give you time to record your answers on your answer sheet.

Try to understand the instructions as I read them; I cannot repeat them. Do not ask any questions from now on.

If, when you go to darken a space for a number, you find that you have already darkened another space for that number, either (1) erase the first mark and darken the space for your new choice, or (2) let the first mark stay and do not darken any other space. When you finish, you should have no more than one space darkened for each number.

Turn to Worksheet 1.

Look at line 1 on your worksheet. (Pause slightly.) Draw a line under the first number in the line. (Pause 2 seconds.) Now, on your answer sheet, find the number under which you drew a line and darken space D as in *dog*. (Pause 5 seconds.)

Look at the circles in line 2 on your worksheet. (Pause slightly.) In the last circle, write the answer to this question: How many days are there in a week? (Pause 2 seconds.) Now, on your answer sheet, darken the space for the number-letter combination that is in the circle you just wrote in. (Pause 5 seconds.)

Look at line 2 again. In the third circle, write the number 18. (Pause 2 seconds.) Now, on your answer sheet, darken the space for the number-letter combination that is in the circle you just wrote in. (Pause 5 seconds.)

Look at the boxes in line 3 on your worksheet. (Pause slightly.) If the largest number is in the smallest box, write C on the line in the first box. (Pause slightly.) Otherwise, write D as in *dog* on the line in the largest box. (Pause 2 seconds.) Now, on your answer sheet, darken the space for the number-letter combination that is in the box you just wrote in. (Pause 5 seconds.)

Look at the letters in line 4 on your worksheet. (Pause slightly.) Draw a line under the letter that is the third letter in the alphabet. (Pause 2 seconds.) Now, on your answer sheet, find number 76 and darken the space for the letter under which you just drew a line. (Pause 5 seconds.)

Look at line 5 on your worksheet. (Pause slightly.) Mail for Liberty and Munsey is to be put in box 50. Mail for St. Clair and Reading is to be put in box 72. (Pause slightly.) Write A in the box in which you would put mail for Munsey. (Pause 2 seconds.) Now, on your answer sheet, darken the space for the number-letter combination that is in the box you just wrote in. (Pause 5 seconds.)

Look at the numbers in line 6 on your worksheet. (Pause slightly.) Draw a line under the fourth number in the line. (Pause 2 seconds.) Now, on your answer sheet, find the number under which you drew a line and darken space E for that number. (Pause 5 seconds.)

Look at line 6 again. Draw two lines under the second number in the line. (Pause 2 seconds.) Now, on your answer sheet, find the number under which you drew two lines and darken space B as in *baker*. (Pause 5 seconds.)

Now look at line 7 on your worksheet. (Pause slightly.) Each box has a number and a letter in it. In the box that has the highest number write on the line the middle figure of that number. (Pause 2 seconds.) Now, on your answer sheet, darken the space for the number-letter combination that is in the box you just wrote in. (Pause 5 seconds.)

Look at line 8 on your worksheet. (Pause slightly.) There are two boxes and two circles of different sizes with numbers in them. (Pause slightly.) If 4 is smaller than 6, and if 8 is less than 5, write E in the larger box. (Pause 2 seconds.) Otherwise, write A in the smaller circle. (Pause 2 seconds.) Now, on your answer sheet, darken the space for the number-letter combination that is in the box or circle you just wrote in. (Pause 5 seconds.)

Look at line 9 on your worksheet. (Pause slightly.) Draw a line under every "O" in the line. (Pause 5 seconds.) Count the number of lines you have drawn, subtract 3, and write that number at the end of the line. (Pause 5 seconds.) Now, on your answer sheet, find that number and darken space E. (Pause 5 seconds.)

Now look at line 10 on your worksheet. (Pause slightly.) Draw a line under every number in the line that is more than 50 but less than 65. (Pause 12 seconds.) Now, on your answer sheet, darken space B as in *baker* for every number under which you drew a line. (Pause 25 seconds.)

Look at line 11 on your worksheet. (Pause slightly.) There are 5 boxes, each with a letter in it. In the fifth box, write the answer to this question: Which of the following numbers is smallest: 28, 12, 23, 19, 14? (Pause 5 seconds.) Now, on your answer sheet, darken the space for the number-letter combination that is in the box you just wrote in. (Pause 5 seconds.)

In the middle box on line 11, write the number 35. (Pause 5 seconds.) Now, on your answer sheet, darken the space for the number-letter combination that is in the box you just wrote in. (Pause 5 seconds.) In the second box, do nothing. In the fourth box write the answer to this question: How many pennies are there in a dime? (Pause 2 seconds.) Now, on your answer sheet, darken the space for the number-letter combination that is in the box you just wrote in. (Pause 5 seconds.)

Now turn to Worksheet 2. (Pause 5 seconds.)

Look at line 12 on your worksheet. (Pause slightly.) There are two boxes and two circles of different sizes with numbers in them. If the number in the left-hand box is larger than the number in the right-hand box, subtract 3 from the number in the left-hand box and change the number in that box to this number. (Pause 6 seconds.) Then write D as in *dog* next to the new number. (Pause 2 seconds.) Otherwise, write C next to the number in the left-hand circle. (Pause 2 seconds.) Now, on your answer sheet, darken the space for the number-letter combination that is in the box or circle you just wrote in. (Pause 5 seconds.)

Look at the boxes and words in line 13 on your worksheet. (Pause slightly.) Write the fourth letter of the first word in the last box. (Pause 2 seconds.) Write the third letter of the second word in the first box. (Pause 2 seconds.) Write the second letter of the third word in the second box. (Pause 2 seconds.) Now, on your answer sheet, darken the spaces for the number-letter combinations that are in the boxes you just wrote in. (Pause 12 seconds.)

Look at line 14 on your answer sheet. (Pause slightly.) In each circle there is a time when the mail must leave. In the circle for the latest time, write on the line the last two figures of the time. (Pause 2 seconds.) Now, on your answer sheet, darken the space for the number-letter combination that is in the circle you just wrote in. (Pause 5 seconds.)

Now look at line 15 on your worksheet. (Pause slightly.) If, in a year, Independence Day comes after Labor Day, write the number 70 on the line next to the first letter. (Pause 2 seconds.) If it does not, write 40 on the line next to the last letter. (Pause 2 seconds.) Now, on your answer sheet, find the number you just wrote and darken the space for the letter next to which you wrote it. (Pause 5 seconds.)

Look at the numbers in line 16 on your worksheet. (Pause slightly.) Draw a line under every number that is more than 25 but less than 45. (Pause 12 seconds.) Now, on your answer sheet, for each number you drew a line under, darken space A. (Pause 25 seconds.)

Look at the circles in line 17 on your worksheet. (Pause slightly.) The number in each circle is the number of packages in a mail sack. In each of the circles holding an even number of packages write the letter C. (Pause 10 seconds.) Now, on your answer sheet, darken the spaces for the number-letter combinations in the circles you just wrote in. (Pause 25 seconds.)

Look at the boxes and circles in line 18 on your worksheet. (Pause slightly.) If the number in the first box is greater than the number in the last box, write B as in *baker* in the first circle. (Pause 2 seconds.) If it is not, write D as in *dog* in the last circle. (Pause 2 seconds.) Now, on your answer sheet, darken the space for the number-letter combination that is in the circle you just wrote in. (Pause 5 seconds.)

Look at the two rows of numbers and the single row of circles in line 19 on your worksheet. (Pause slightly.) Draw a line under the second number in the upper row of numbers. (Pause slightly.) Draw a line under the third number in the lower row of numbers. (Pause slightly.) Now, add up the numbers under which you have drawn lines and write the total in the last circle in the row. (Pause 5 seconds.) Now, on your answer sheet, darken the space for the number-letter combination that is in the circle you just wrote in. (Pause 5 seconds.)

END OF EXAMINATION.
If you finish before the time is up, go back and check
the questions in this section of the test only.

Practice Test 5—Worksheet 1
Part D—Following Oral Directions

1.   84   57   16

2. ___ D   ___ E   ___ A   ___ C

3.
64	39	72
___	___	___

4. B   C   E   A   D   A   B

5.

50		72
LIBERTY MUNSEY		ST. CLAIR READING
___		___

6. 13   29   27   23   9   38

7.
398 ___ B	422 ___ D	276 ___ A	349 ___ C	432 ___ E

8. 57 ___   79 ___   33 ___   19 ___

9. O X O O X O X X O O O X O X

10. 67   45   49   51   72   58   43   50   64

11.
D	A	B	C	E
___	___	___	___	___

Practice Test 5—Worksheet 2
Part D—Following Oral Directions

12. 64 ___   13 ___   51 ___   48 ___

13. JUNE   SCAR   ABOVE   86 ___   17 ___   45 ___

14. 5:05 ___ D   5:15 ___ E   5:46 ___ C   5:32 ___ B   5:12 ___ A

15. ___ C   ___ A   ___ E

16. 47   25   43   22   15   48   27   50

17. 73 ___   68 ___   59 ___   81 ___   32 ___   80 ___

18. 11 ___   23 ___   61 ___   29 ___   77 ___

19. 2 1   4 3   8 2   6 5

___ D   ___ E   ___ A   ___ C

ANSWER KEY

Part A—Address Checking

1. D	11. D	21. D	31. A	41. D	51. D	61. D	71. D	81. D	91. A
2. D	12. A	22. A	32. D	42. A	52. A	62. D	72. D	82. A	92. A
3. A	13. A	23. D	33. D	43. A	53. A	63. A	73. A	83. A	93. D
4. D	14. D	24. D	34. A	44. D	54. D	64. A	74. A	84. D	94. D
5. A	15. A	25. D	35. D	45. A	55. A	65. D	75. D	85. D	95. A
6. A	16. A	26. A	36. D	46. A	56. D	66. D	76. D	86. A	
7. A	17. A	27. A	37. A	47. A	57. D	67. A	77. D	87. A	
8. D	18. A	28. A	38. D	48. D	58. D	68. A	78. A	88. D	
9. A	19. D	29. D	39. A	49. D	59. A	69. D	79. D	89. A	
10. A	20. D	30. D	40. D	50. A	60. D	70. A	80. D	90. A	

Part B—Memory for Addresses

List 1

1. B	10. E	19. B	28. D	37. C	46. A	55. D	64. D	73. C	82. A
2. A	11. B	20. A	29. E	38. B	47. E	56. A	65. C	74. D	83. C
3. C	12. D	21. C	30. E	39. A	48. C	57. D	66. E	75. D	84. C
4. A	13. B	22. E	31. E	40. B	49. E	58. D	67. A	76. B	85. E
5. E	14. D	23. B	32. E	41. A	50. C	59. B	68. B	77. A	86. D
6. C	15. D	24. C	33. B	42. C	51. C	60. A	69. B	78. E	87. E
7. A	16. E	25. D	34. E	43. D	52. B	61. D	70. D	79. C	88. E
8. D	17. C	26. A	35. C	44. B	53. E	62. B	71. B	80. B	
9. A	18. E	27. A	36. C	45. A	54. E	63. D	72. A	81. D	

List 2

1. A	10. D	19. E	28. A	37. E	46. C	55. A	64. A	73. B	82. C
2. E	11. E	20. D	29. E	38. E	47. E	56. D	65. E	74. E	83. C
3. B	12. C	21. A	30. D	39. B	48. C	57. A	66. B	75. B	84. A
4. D	13. B	22. E	31. C	40. E	49. A	58. A	67. B	76. D	85. C
5. C	14. B	23. A	32. C	41. D	50. B	59. A	68. D	77. E	86. B
6. E	15. C	24. A	33. D	42. B	51. A	60. D	69. B	78. B	87. B
7. E	16. C	25. D	34. C	43. C	52. A	61. A	70. D	79. D	88. B
8. B	17. E	26. D	35. A	44. B	53. E	62. D	71. B	80. C	
9. C	18. D	27. D	36. E	45. E	54. D	63. A	72. C	81. C	

List 3

1. B	10. A	19. D	28. C	37. B	46. B	55. B	64. B	73. D	82. E
2. C	11. C	20. A	29. A	38. E	47. B	56. E	65. D	74. A	83. B
3. A	12. D	21. A	30. C	39. E	48. C	57. D	66. B	75. A	84. A
4. D	13. C	22. E	31. B	40. C	49. A	58. B	67. E	76. A	85. C
5. E	14. C	23. A	32. B	41. D	50. C	59. E	68. E	77. D	86. E
6. B	15. D	24. D	33. C	42. B	51. C	60. B	69. A	78. A	87. C
7. B	16. E	25. E	34. E	43. B	52. C	61. C	70. A	79. D	88. E
8. E	17. A	26. D	35. D	44. A	53. C	62. B	71. D	80. E	
9. E	18. D	27. E	36. C	45. B	54. D	63. D	72. A	81. A	

Part C—Number Series

1. **B**	4. **D**	7. **C**	10. **A**	13. **C**	16. **B**	19. **D**	22. **B**		
2. **A**	5. **E**	8. **C**	11. **C**	14. **E**	17. **C**	20. **D**	23. **B**		
3. **B**	6. **E**	9. **E**	12. **A**	15. **D**	18. **C**	21. **A**	24. **E**		

Part D—Following Oral Directions

3. **E**	7. **C**	17. **B**	27. **A**	35. **B**	45. **E**	51. **B**	61. **D**	72. **D**	80. **C**
5. **E**	10. **C**	18. **A**	29. **B**	40. **E**	46. **C**	57. **A**	64. **B**	76. **C**	84. **D**
6. **C**	12. **E**	23. **E**	32. **C**	43. **A**	50. **A**	58. **B**	68. **C**	77. **D**	86. **A**

■ ANSWER EXPLANATIONS FOR PART C—NUMBER SERIES

1. **B** This is a series that descends by 5. The new number is repeated after every second subtraction.

2. **A** The numbers of the two alternating series coincide in a way that makes the pattern in this question difficult to pick out. One series increases by 2. The other increases by 1 after repeating the number.

3. **B** There are two alternating series here, one increasing by 1; the other increasing by 2.

4. **D** The sequence 10 1 15 20 keeps recycling.

5. **E** The rule here is: + 3, − 4; with the arbitrary number 15 inserted after every second member of the series.

6. **E** You may consider these numbers as following the rule: + 4, − 5; or as belonging to two alternating series, each of which decreases by 1.

7. **C** There are *three* changes occurring among these fractions as they progress. The whole number at the beginning keeps increasing by 1. So does the numerator (top) of each fraction. The denominator (bottom) on the other hand keeps decreasing by 1. It's very easy to lose track of things unless you are really careful.

8. **C** Here is a series that uses *addition and position* to determine its pattern. Each two-digit number appears once and is followed by each of the *separate* digits that make it up. Thus, 26 leads to 2 and 6, 38 leads to 3 and 8, and so on. You must add 12 to go from one two-digit number to the next.

9. **E** Here are two series that alternate in a little more complex fashion than usual. The series that begins with the number 9 increases by 5 (9, 14, 19). It interrupts the + 6 series that starts with 2 after every second number.

10. **A** The two series in this question alternate in an even more complex manner than in question 9. As it progresses, every *three* members of the + 2 series (2, 4, 6) alternate with two members of the − 1 series, which begins with the number 12.

11. **C** This is merely a + 1 series made difficult because the arbitrary numbers *3* and *2* are periodically inserted.

12. **A** Here is a group of mini-series each of which descends by 2. Each three-member mini-series begins 2 higher than the one before. You could also see the numbers in this progression following a − 2, − 2, + 6; − 2, − 2, + 6; rule.

13. **C** One member of a −1 series (17, 16) appears after every two members of a + 1 series (9, 10, 11, 12, and so on)

14. **E** This is a + 7 series with the arbitrary number 45 appearing as every third number in the progression.

15. **D** There is a complex rule here using multiplication and subtraction: × 2, − 2, − 5; × 2, − 2, − 5; and so on.

16. **B** A descending series following a −2 rule is interrupted after every three members by one member of an ascending series starting with 16 and following a + 4 rule.

17. **C** The rule here is − 1, repeat the number, − 2; − 1, repeat the number, − 2; and so on.

18. **C** Here again we see a three-member mini-series. Each of these descends by 3. Each mini-series begins one number lower than the preceding series. You could also see a − 3, − 3, + 5 rule governing these numbers.

19. **D** There is a series here that follows the rule + 5, repeat the number; etc. The number 10 separates each repetition.

20. **D** Here the loop diagram is used to identify the complex pattern (three alternating series) for this series.

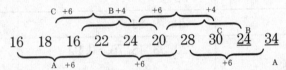

21. **A** This series uses a *variable* adder starting with + 1 and then repeats the number before going on.

$$\underbrace{2 \quad 3}_{+1} \; \overbrace{3}^{R} \; \underbrace{\quad 5}_{+2} \; \overbrace{5}^{R} \; \underbrace{\quad 8}_{+3} \; \overbrace{8}^{R} \; \underbrace{\quad \underline{12}}_{+4} \; \overbrace{\underline{12}}^{R}$$

22. **B** You can see this as following a − 10, + 5; − 10, + 5; rule, or as two alternating series each decreasing by 5.

23. **B** There are two alternating series here, one (8, 9, and so on) increasing by a + 1 rule; the other by a + 2 rule (11, 3, and so on). The arbitrary number 10 appears as every third number in the series.

24. **E** The rule here is a complex one: − 1, − 2, − 1, repeat the number; − 1, − 2, − 1, repeat the number; and so on.

■ EVALUATING YOUR PROGRESS

Throughout this book, the importance of evaluating and recording your progress has been stressed, as you study and practice for the 460/470 Test Battery. At this point, if you have completed Practice Tests 1 through 4 and have made all the entries on your Personal Progress Record, you are quite familiar with the discussion on Computing Your Score, Guidelines, and the Personal Progress Record. If you wish to review the details of these subjects, refer to pages 58 through 68 or pages 326 through 332.

You have probably seen great improvement in your test scores, but don't stop now. Take the remaining practice test and record the results on your Personal Progress Record. Go for a perfect score!

DIAGNOSTIC CHARTS

The following charts will help pinpoint your weaknesses by making it easy for you to determine what particular type of question in each part of the test is most difficult for you.

Part A—Address Checking

Type of Difference	"D" Questions	Number of "D" Questions Wrong		
		Trial 1	Trial 2	Trial 3
Numbers: transposed	8, 21, 33, 71, 78			
changed	1, 35, 40, 54, 61, 76, 81			
omitted	65			
Directions	29, 79, 84			
Abbreviations: streets, roads, avenues, etc.	20, 38, 48, 75, 80, 94			
states	44, 56, 58			
Spelling: single letters	2, 4, 11, 14, 24, 25, 32, 41, 60, 62, 69, 77, 85, 93			
groups of letters	19, 23, 30, 36, 49, 51, 57, 66, 72			
Total Number of All Types	48			
	Use the columns on the right to enter the question numbers of "A" items you marked "D."			

This chart will help you to pinpoint the kinds of errors you made on Practice Test 5. Use it as directed below after you have taken and marked the test.

The first column on the left, "Type of Difference," contains the categories whereby addresses may differ (see page 69). On the same line across, the second column gives the numbers of the questions that fall within each category. In the third column, you are to enter the numbers of any "A" questions you answered as "D." Do not include questions that you did not do. Checking the addresses you got wrong may reveal a problem on which you will want to work.

After you have made all the entries, you will be able to see the areas in which you need to improve. Then turn to the appropriate parts of Chapter 4: Address Checking—How to Improve Your Score, read them, and practice the drills that can help. For example, if you find you have been making too many errors picking out number differences, read page 94 and do Drills 18 through 21. If you have a problem with single letters because of reversals like *b* and *d*, or if you have been overlooking the differences between *a*, *e*, and *o*, read page 91. Examine the table and work on Drills 10 and 11 if the problem persists.

Remember that this chart is designed for diagnostic purposes and guidance on further practice. It has been drawn so that you can enter the results each time you retake a practice test. In this way you will be able to see how you are progressing. It is not necessary to record your scores here. That is best done by using the Personal Progress Record Card.

Part B—Memory for Addresses

Kind of Address		Number of Questions	Number Wrong		
			Trial 1	Trial 2	Trial 3
Direct:	List 1	41			
	List 2	40			
	List 3	41			
Numbered:	List 1	47			
	List 2	48			
	List 3	47			

The purpose of this chart is to help you evaluate your performance on the two kinds of memory questions that appear in these memory tests—the questions on the direct (name) addresses and the questions on the numbered addresses. Use the chart as directed below after you have taken and marked the entire test.

The first column on the left, "Kind of Address," is divided by category into "Direct Address" versus "Numbered Address." The second column gives the number of questions in each category on List 1, List 2, and List 3. Use the third column to enter the total number of questions in each category that you answered incorrectly. There is room for you to make additional entries if you take the practice tests more than once.

At a glance, you will be able to see which area you need to concentrate on and how well you are progressing as you take repeat trials. Use Chapter 5 and the drills in it to improve your memory for the direct addresses. Use Chapter 6 for the numbered addresses.

Remember to use the Personal Progress Record Card (Memory for Addresses) on page 439 to keep track of your actual scores as you keep studying and practicing.

Part C—Number Series and Part D—Following Oral Directions

Because of the nature of the questions in these tests, Diagnostic Charts are not provided for them. If you find that you made many errors on these tests, study the techniques suggested in Chapters 7 and 8.

Answer Sheet—Practice Test 6

Part A—Address Checking

1 Ⓐ Ⓓ	25 Ⓐ Ⓓ	49 Ⓐ Ⓓ	73 Ⓐ Ⓓ
2 Ⓐ Ⓓ	26 Ⓐ Ⓓ	50 Ⓐ Ⓓ	74 Ⓐ Ⓓ
3 Ⓐ Ⓓ	27 Ⓐ Ⓓ	51 Ⓐ Ⓓ	75 Ⓐ Ⓓ
4 Ⓐ Ⓓ	28 Ⓐ Ⓓ	52 Ⓐ Ⓓ	76 Ⓐ Ⓓ
5 Ⓐ Ⓓ	29 Ⓐ Ⓓ	53 Ⓐ Ⓓ	77 Ⓐ Ⓓ
6 Ⓐ Ⓓ	30 Ⓐ Ⓓ	54 Ⓐ Ⓓ	78 Ⓐ Ⓓ
7 Ⓐ Ⓓ	31 Ⓐ Ⓓ	55 Ⓐ Ⓓ	79 Ⓐ Ⓓ
8 Ⓐ Ⓓ	32 Ⓐ Ⓓ	56 Ⓐ Ⓓ	80 Ⓐ Ⓓ
9 Ⓐ Ⓓ	33 Ⓐ Ⓓ	57 Ⓐ Ⓓ	81 Ⓐ Ⓓ
10 Ⓐ Ⓓ	34 Ⓐ Ⓓ	58 Ⓐ Ⓓ	82 Ⓐ Ⓓ
11 Ⓐ Ⓓ	35 Ⓐ Ⓓ	59 Ⓐ Ⓓ	83 Ⓐ Ⓓ
12 Ⓐ Ⓓ	36 Ⓐ Ⓓ	60 Ⓐ Ⓓ	84 Ⓐ Ⓓ
13 Ⓐ Ⓓ	37 Ⓐ Ⓓ	61 Ⓐ Ⓓ	85 Ⓐ Ⓓ
14 Ⓐ Ⓓ	38 Ⓐ Ⓓ	62 Ⓐ Ⓓ	86 Ⓐ Ⓓ
15 Ⓐ Ⓓ	39 Ⓐ Ⓓ	63 Ⓐ Ⓓ	87 Ⓐ Ⓓ
16 Ⓐ Ⓓ	40 Ⓐ Ⓓ	64 Ⓐ Ⓓ	88 Ⓐ Ⓓ
17 Ⓐ Ⓓ	41 Ⓐ Ⓓ	65 Ⓐ Ⓓ	89 Ⓐ Ⓓ
18 Ⓐ Ⓓ	42 Ⓐ Ⓓ	66 Ⓐ Ⓓ	90 Ⓐ Ⓓ
19 Ⓐ Ⓓ	43 Ⓐ Ⓓ	67 Ⓐ Ⓓ	91 Ⓐ Ⓓ
20 Ⓐ Ⓓ	44 Ⓐ Ⓓ	68 Ⓐ Ⓓ	92 Ⓐ Ⓓ
21 Ⓐ Ⓓ	45 Ⓐ Ⓓ	69 Ⓐ Ⓓ	93 Ⓐ Ⓓ
22 Ⓐ Ⓓ	46 Ⓐ Ⓓ	70 Ⓐ Ⓓ	94 Ⓐ Ⓓ
23 Ⓐ Ⓓ	47 Ⓐ Ⓓ	71 Ⓐ Ⓓ	95 Ⓐ Ⓓ
24 Ⓐ Ⓓ	48 Ⓐ Ⓓ	72 Ⓐ Ⓓ	

✂ Remove by cutting on dotted line.

Part B—Memory for Addresses—List 1

1 Ⓐ Ⓑ Ⓒ Ⓓ Ⓔ   19 Ⓐ Ⓑ Ⓒ Ⓓ Ⓔ   37 Ⓐ Ⓑ Ⓒ Ⓓ Ⓔ   55 Ⓐ Ⓑ Ⓒ Ⓓ Ⓔ   73 Ⓐ Ⓑ Ⓒ Ⓓ Ⓔ
2 Ⓐ Ⓑ Ⓒ Ⓓ Ⓔ   20 Ⓐ Ⓑ Ⓒ Ⓓ Ⓔ   38 Ⓐ Ⓑ Ⓒ Ⓓ Ⓔ   56 Ⓐ Ⓑ Ⓒ Ⓓ Ⓔ   74 Ⓐ Ⓑ Ⓒ Ⓓ Ⓔ
3 Ⓐ Ⓑ Ⓒ Ⓓ Ⓔ   21 Ⓐ Ⓑ Ⓒ Ⓓ Ⓔ   39 Ⓐ Ⓑ Ⓒ Ⓓ Ⓔ   57 Ⓐ Ⓑ Ⓒ Ⓓ Ⓔ   75 Ⓐ Ⓑ Ⓒ Ⓓ Ⓔ
4 Ⓐ Ⓑ Ⓒ Ⓓ Ⓔ   22 Ⓐ Ⓑ Ⓒ Ⓓ Ⓔ   40 Ⓐ Ⓑ Ⓒ Ⓓ Ⓔ   58 Ⓐ Ⓑ Ⓒ Ⓓ Ⓔ   76 Ⓐ Ⓑ Ⓒ Ⓓ Ⓔ
5 Ⓐ Ⓑ Ⓒ Ⓓ Ⓔ   23 Ⓐ Ⓑ Ⓒ Ⓓ Ⓔ   41 Ⓐ Ⓑ Ⓒ Ⓓ Ⓔ   59 Ⓐ Ⓑ Ⓒ Ⓓ Ⓔ   77 Ⓐ Ⓑ Ⓒ Ⓓ Ⓔ
6 Ⓐ Ⓑ Ⓒ Ⓓ Ⓔ   24 Ⓐ Ⓑ Ⓒ Ⓓ Ⓔ   42 Ⓐ Ⓑ Ⓒ Ⓓ Ⓔ   60 Ⓐ Ⓑ Ⓒ Ⓓ Ⓔ   78 Ⓐ Ⓑ Ⓒ Ⓓ Ⓔ
7 Ⓐ Ⓑ Ⓒ Ⓓ Ⓔ   25 Ⓐ Ⓑ Ⓒ Ⓓ Ⓔ   43 Ⓐ Ⓑ Ⓒ Ⓓ Ⓔ   61 Ⓐ Ⓑ Ⓒ Ⓓ Ⓔ   79 Ⓐ Ⓑ Ⓒ Ⓓ Ⓔ
8 Ⓐ Ⓑ Ⓒ Ⓓ Ⓔ   26 Ⓐ Ⓑ Ⓒ Ⓓ Ⓔ   44 Ⓐ Ⓑ Ⓒ Ⓓ Ⓔ   62 Ⓐ Ⓑ Ⓒ Ⓓ Ⓔ   80 Ⓐ Ⓑ Ⓒ Ⓓ Ⓔ
9 Ⓐ Ⓑ Ⓒ Ⓓ Ⓔ   27 Ⓐ Ⓑ Ⓒ Ⓓ Ⓔ   45 Ⓐ Ⓑ Ⓒ Ⓓ Ⓔ   63 Ⓐ Ⓑ Ⓒ Ⓓ Ⓔ   81 Ⓐ Ⓑ Ⓒ Ⓓ Ⓔ
10 Ⓐ Ⓑ Ⓒ Ⓓ Ⓔ   28 Ⓐ Ⓑ Ⓒ Ⓓ Ⓔ   46 Ⓐ Ⓑ Ⓒ Ⓓ Ⓔ   64 Ⓐ Ⓑ Ⓒ Ⓓ Ⓔ   82 Ⓐ Ⓑ Ⓒ Ⓓ Ⓔ
11 Ⓐ Ⓑ Ⓒ Ⓓ Ⓔ   29 Ⓐ Ⓑ Ⓒ Ⓓ Ⓔ   47 Ⓐ Ⓑ Ⓒ Ⓓ Ⓔ   65 Ⓐ Ⓑ Ⓒ Ⓓ Ⓔ   83 Ⓐ Ⓑ Ⓒ Ⓓ Ⓔ
12 Ⓐ Ⓑ Ⓒ Ⓓ Ⓔ   30 Ⓐ Ⓑ Ⓒ Ⓓ Ⓔ   48 Ⓐ Ⓑ Ⓒ Ⓓ Ⓔ   66 Ⓐ Ⓑ Ⓒ Ⓓ Ⓔ   84 Ⓐ Ⓑ Ⓒ Ⓓ Ⓔ
13 Ⓐ Ⓑ Ⓒ Ⓓ Ⓔ   31 Ⓐ Ⓑ Ⓒ Ⓓ Ⓔ   49 Ⓐ Ⓑ Ⓒ Ⓓ Ⓔ   67 Ⓐ Ⓑ Ⓒ Ⓓ Ⓔ   85 Ⓐ Ⓑ Ⓒ Ⓓ Ⓔ
14 Ⓐ Ⓑ Ⓒ Ⓓ Ⓔ   32 Ⓐ Ⓑ Ⓒ Ⓓ Ⓔ   50 Ⓐ Ⓑ Ⓒ Ⓓ Ⓔ   68 Ⓐ Ⓑ Ⓒ Ⓓ Ⓔ   86 Ⓐ Ⓑ Ⓒ Ⓓ Ⓔ
15 Ⓐ Ⓑ Ⓒ Ⓓ Ⓔ   33 Ⓐ Ⓑ Ⓒ Ⓓ Ⓔ   51 Ⓐ Ⓑ Ⓒ Ⓓ Ⓔ   69 Ⓐ Ⓑ Ⓒ Ⓓ Ⓔ   87 Ⓐ Ⓑ Ⓒ Ⓓ Ⓔ
16 Ⓐ Ⓑ Ⓒ Ⓓ Ⓔ   34 Ⓐ Ⓑ Ⓒ Ⓓ Ⓔ   52 Ⓐ Ⓑ Ⓒ Ⓓ Ⓔ   70 Ⓐ Ⓑ Ⓒ Ⓓ Ⓔ   88 Ⓐ Ⓑ Ⓒ Ⓓ Ⓔ
17 Ⓐ Ⓑ Ⓒ Ⓓ Ⓔ   35 Ⓐ Ⓑ Ⓒ Ⓓ Ⓔ   53 Ⓐ Ⓑ Ⓒ Ⓓ Ⓔ   71 Ⓐ Ⓑ Ⓒ Ⓓ Ⓔ
18 Ⓐ Ⓑ Ⓒ Ⓓ Ⓔ   36 Ⓐ Ⓑ Ⓒ Ⓓ Ⓔ   54 Ⓐ Ⓑ Ⓒ Ⓓ Ⓔ   72 Ⓐ Ⓑ Ⓒ Ⓓ Ⓔ

Part B—Memory for Addresses—List 2

1 Ⓐ Ⓑ Ⓒ Ⓓ Ⓔ   19 Ⓐ Ⓑ Ⓒ Ⓓ Ⓔ   37 Ⓐ Ⓑ Ⓒ Ⓓ Ⓔ   55 Ⓐ Ⓑ Ⓒ Ⓓ Ⓔ   73 Ⓐ Ⓑ Ⓒ Ⓓ Ⓔ
2 Ⓐ Ⓑ Ⓒ Ⓓ Ⓔ   20 Ⓐ Ⓑ Ⓒ Ⓓ Ⓔ   38 Ⓐ Ⓑ Ⓒ Ⓓ Ⓔ   56 Ⓐ Ⓑ Ⓒ Ⓓ Ⓔ   74 Ⓐ Ⓑ Ⓒ Ⓓ Ⓔ
3 Ⓐ Ⓑ Ⓒ Ⓓ Ⓔ   21 Ⓐ Ⓑ Ⓒ Ⓓ Ⓔ   39 Ⓐ Ⓑ Ⓒ Ⓓ Ⓔ   57 Ⓐ Ⓑ Ⓒ Ⓓ Ⓔ   75 Ⓐ Ⓑ Ⓒ Ⓓ Ⓔ
4 Ⓐ Ⓑ Ⓒ Ⓓ Ⓔ   22 Ⓐ Ⓑ Ⓒ Ⓓ Ⓔ   40 Ⓐ Ⓑ Ⓒ Ⓓ Ⓔ   58 Ⓐ Ⓑ Ⓒ Ⓓ Ⓔ   76 Ⓐ Ⓑ Ⓒ Ⓓ Ⓔ
5 Ⓐ Ⓑ Ⓒ Ⓓ Ⓔ   23 Ⓐ Ⓑ Ⓒ Ⓓ Ⓔ   41 Ⓐ Ⓑ Ⓒ Ⓓ Ⓔ   59 Ⓐ Ⓑ Ⓒ Ⓓ Ⓔ   77 Ⓐ Ⓑ Ⓒ Ⓓ Ⓔ
6 Ⓐ Ⓑ Ⓒ Ⓓ Ⓔ   24 Ⓐ Ⓑ Ⓒ Ⓓ Ⓔ   42 Ⓐ Ⓑ Ⓒ Ⓓ Ⓔ   60 Ⓐ Ⓑ Ⓒ Ⓓ Ⓔ   78 Ⓐ Ⓑ Ⓒ Ⓓ Ⓔ
7 Ⓐ Ⓑ Ⓒ Ⓓ Ⓔ   25 Ⓐ Ⓑ Ⓒ Ⓓ Ⓔ   43 Ⓐ Ⓑ Ⓒ Ⓓ Ⓔ   61 Ⓐ Ⓑ Ⓒ Ⓓ Ⓔ   79 Ⓐ Ⓑ Ⓒ Ⓓ Ⓔ
8 Ⓐ Ⓑ Ⓒ Ⓓ Ⓔ   26 Ⓐ Ⓑ Ⓒ Ⓓ Ⓔ   44 Ⓐ Ⓑ Ⓒ Ⓓ Ⓔ   62 Ⓐ Ⓑ Ⓒ Ⓓ Ⓔ   80 Ⓐ Ⓑ Ⓒ Ⓓ Ⓔ
9 Ⓐ Ⓑ Ⓒ Ⓓ Ⓔ   27 Ⓐ Ⓑ Ⓒ Ⓓ Ⓔ   45 Ⓐ Ⓑ Ⓒ Ⓓ Ⓔ   63 Ⓐ Ⓑ Ⓒ Ⓓ Ⓔ   81 Ⓐ Ⓑ Ⓒ Ⓓ Ⓔ
10 Ⓐ Ⓑ Ⓒ Ⓓ Ⓔ   28 Ⓐ Ⓑ Ⓒ Ⓓ Ⓔ   46 Ⓐ Ⓑ Ⓒ Ⓓ Ⓔ   64 Ⓐ Ⓑ Ⓒ Ⓓ Ⓔ   82 Ⓐ Ⓑ Ⓒ Ⓓ Ⓔ
11 Ⓐ Ⓑ Ⓒ Ⓓ Ⓔ   29 Ⓐ Ⓑ Ⓒ Ⓓ Ⓔ   47 Ⓐ Ⓑ Ⓒ Ⓓ Ⓔ   65 Ⓐ Ⓑ Ⓒ Ⓓ Ⓔ   83 Ⓐ Ⓑ Ⓒ Ⓓ Ⓔ
12 Ⓐ Ⓑ Ⓒ Ⓓ Ⓔ   30 Ⓐ Ⓑ Ⓒ Ⓓ Ⓔ   48 Ⓐ Ⓑ Ⓒ Ⓓ Ⓔ   66 Ⓐ Ⓑ Ⓒ Ⓓ Ⓔ   84 Ⓐ Ⓑ Ⓒ Ⓓ Ⓔ
13 Ⓐ Ⓑ Ⓒ Ⓓ Ⓔ   31 Ⓐ Ⓑ Ⓒ Ⓓ Ⓔ   49 Ⓐ Ⓑ Ⓒ Ⓓ Ⓔ   67 Ⓐ Ⓑ Ⓒ Ⓓ Ⓔ   85 Ⓐ Ⓑ Ⓒ Ⓓ Ⓔ
14 Ⓐ Ⓑ Ⓒ Ⓓ Ⓔ   32 Ⓐ Ⓑ Ⓒ Ⓓ Ⓔ   50 Ⓐ Ⓑ Ⓒ Ⓓ Ⓔ   68 Ⓐ Ⓑ Ⓒ Ⓓ Ⓔ   86 Ⓐ Ⓑ Ⓒ Ⓓ Ⓔ
15 Ⓐ Ⓑ Ⓒ Ⓓ Ⓔ   33 Ⓐ Ⓑ Ⓒ Ⓓ Ⓔ   51 Ⓐ Ⓑ Ⓒ Ⓓ Ⓔ   69 Ⓐ Ⓑ Ⓒ Ⓓ Ⓔ   87 Ⓐ Ⓑ Ⓒ Ⓓ Ⓔ
16 Ⓐ Ⓑ Ⓒ Ⓓ Ⓔ   34 Ⓐ Ⓑ Ⓒ Ⓓ Ⓔ   52 Ⓐ Ⓑ Ⓒ Ⓓ Ⓔ   70 Ⓐ Ⓑ Ⓒ Ⓓ Ⓔ   88 Ⓐ Ⓑ Ⓒ Ⓓ Ⓔ
17 Ⓐ Ⓑ Ⓒ Ⓓ Ⓔ   35 Ⓐ Ⓑ Ⓒ Ⓓ Ⓔ   53 Ⓐ Ⓑ Ⓒ Ⓓ Ⓔ   71 Ⓐ Ⓑ Ⓒ Ⓓ Ⓔ
18 Ⓐ Ⓑ Ⓒ Ⓓ Ⓔ   36 Ⓐ Ⓑ Ⓒ Ⓓ Ⓔ   54 Ⓐ Ⓑ Ⓒ Ⓓ Ⓔ   72 Ⓐ Ⓑ Ⓒ Ⓓ Ⓔ

Part B—Memory for Addresses—List 3

1 Ⓐ Ⓑ Ⓒ Ⓓ Ⓔ	19 Ⓐ Ⓑ Ⓒ Ⓓ Ⓔ	37 Ⓐ Ⓑ Ⓒ Ⓓ Ⓔ	55 Ⓐ Ⓑ Ⓒ Ⓓ Ⓔ	73 Ⓐ Ⓑ Ⓒ Ⓓ Ⓔ
2 Ⓐ Ⓑ Ⓒ Ⓓ Ⓔ	20 Ⓐ Ⓑ Ⓒ Ⓓ Ⓔ	38 Ⓐ Ⓑ Ⓒ Ⓓ Ⓔ	56 Ⓐ Ⓑ Ⓒ Ⓓ Ⓔ	74 Ⓐ Ⓑ Ⓒ Ⓓ Ⓔ
3 Ⓐ Ⓑ Ⓒ Ⓓ Ⓔ	21 Ⓐ Ⓑ Ⓒ Ⓓ Ⓔ	39 Ⓐ Ⓑ Ⓒ Ⓓ Ⓔ	57 Ⓐ Ⓑ Ⓒ Ⓓ Ⓔ	75 Ⓐ Ⓑ Ⓒ Ⓓ Ⓔ
4 Ⓐ Ⓑ Ⓒ Ⓓ Ⓔ	22 Ⓐ Ⓑ Ⓒ Ⓓ Ⓔ	40 Ⓐ Ⓑ Ⓒ Ⓓ Ⓔ	58 Ⓐ Ⓑ Ⓒ Ⓓ Ⓔ	76 Ⓐ Ⓑ Ⓒ Ⓓ Ⓔ
5 Ⓐ Ⓑ Ⓒ Ⓓ Ⓔ	23 Ⓐ Ⓑ Ⓒ Ⓓ Ⓔ	41 Ⓐ Ⓑ Ⓒ Ⓓ Ⓔ	59 Ⓐ Ⓑ Ⓒ Ⓓ Ⓔ	77 Ⓐ Ⓑ Ⓒ Ⓓ Ⓔ
6 Ⓐ Ⓑ Ⓒ Ⓓ Ⓔ	24 Ⓐ Ⓑ Ⓒ Ⓓ Ⓔ	42 Ⓐ Ⓑ Ⓒ Ⓓ Ⓔ	60 Ⓐ Ⓑ Ⓒ Ⓓ Ⓔ	78 Ⓐ Ⓑ Ⓒ Ⓓ Ⓔ
7 Ⓐ Ⓑ Ⓒ Ⓓ Ⓔ	25 Ⓐ Ⓑ Ⓒ Ⓓ Ⓔ	43 Ⓐ Ⓑ Ⓒ Ⓓ Ⓔ	61 Ⓐ Ⓑ Ⓒ Ⓓ Ⓔ	79 Ⓐ Ⓑ Ⓒ Ⓓ Ⓔ
8 Ⓐ Ⓑ Ⓒ Ⓓ Ⓔ	26 Ⓐ Ⓑ Ⓒ Ⓓ Ⓔ	44 Ⓐ Ⓑ Ⓒ Ⓓ Ⓔ	62 Ⓐ Ⓑ Ⓒ Ⓓ Ⓔ	80 Ⓐ Ⓑ Ⓒ Ⓓ Ⓔ
9 Ⓐ Ⓑ Ⓒ Ⓓ Ⓔ	27 Ⓐ Ⓑ Ⓒ Ⓓ Ⓔ	45 Ⓐ Ⓑ Ⓒ Ⓓ Ⓔ	63 Ⓐ Ⓑ Ⓒ Ⓓ Ⓔ	81 Ⓐ Ⓑ Ⓒ Ⓓ Ⓔ
10 Ⓐ Ⓑ Ⓒ Ⓓ Ⓔ	28 Ⓐ Ⓑ Ⓒ Ⓓ Ⓔ	46 Ⓐ Ⓑ Ⓒ Ⓓ Ⓔ	64 Ⓐ Ⓑ Ⓒ Ⓓ Ⓔ	82 Ⓐ Ⓑ Ⓒ Ⓓ Ⓔ
11 Ⓐ Ⓑ Ⓒ Ⓓ Ⓔ	29 Ⓐ Ⓑ Ⓒ Ⓓ Ⓔ	47 Ⓐ Ⓑ Ⓒ Ⓓ Ⓔ	65 Ⓐ Ⓑ Ⓒ Ⓓ Ⓔ	83 Ⓐ Ⓑ Ⓒ Ⓓ Ⓔ
12 Ⓐ Ⓑ Ⓒ Ⓓ Ⓔ	30 Ⓐ Ⓑ Ⓒ Ⓓ Ⓔ	48 Ⓐ Ⓑ Ⓒ Ⓓ Ⓔ	66 Ⓐ Ⓑ Ⓒ Ⓓ Ⓔ	84 Ⓐ Ⓑ Ⓒ Ⓓ Ⓔ
13 Ⓐ Ⓑ Ⓒ Ⓓ Ⓔ	31 Ⓐ Ⓑ Ⓒ Ⓓ Ⓔ	49 Ⓐ Ⓑ Ⓒ Ⓓ Ⓔ	67 Ⓐ Ⓑ Ⓒ Ⓓ Ⓔ	85 Ⓐ Ⓑ Ⓒ Ⓓ Ⓔ
14 Ⓐ Ⓑ Ⓒ Ⓓ Ⓔ	32 Ⓐ Ⓑ Ⓒ Ⓓ Ⓔ	50 Ⓐ Ⓑ Ⓒ Ⓓ Ⓔ	68 Ⓐ Ⓑ Ⓒ Ⓓ Ⓔ	86 Ⓐ Ⓑ Ⓒ Ⓓ Ⓔ
15 Ⓐ Ⓑ Ⓒ Ⓓ Ⓔ	33 Ⓐ Ⓑ Ⓒ Ⓓ Ⓔ	51 Ⓐ Ⓑ Ⓒ Ⓓ Ⓔ	69 Ⓐ Ⓑ Ⓒ Ⓓ Ⓔ	87 Ⓐ Ⓑ Ⓒ Ⓓ Ⓔ
16 Ⓐ Ⓑ Ⓒ Ⓓ Ⓔ	34 Ⓐ Ⓑ Ⓒ Ⓓ Ⓔ	52 Ⓐ Ⓑ Ⓒ Ⓓ Ⓔ	70 Ⓐ Ⓑ Ⓒ Ⓓ Ⓔ	88 Ⓐ Ⓑ Ⓒ Ⓓ Ⓔ
17 Ⓐ Ⓑ Ⓒ Ⓓ Ⓔ	35 Ⓐ Ⓑ Ⓒ Ⓓ Ⓔ	53 Ⓐ Ⓑ Ⓒ Ⓓ Ⓔ	71 Ⓐ Ⓑ Ⓒ Ⓓ Ⓔ	
18 Ⓐ Ⓑ Ⓒ Ⓓ Ⓔ	36 Ⓐ Ⓑ Ⓒ Ⓓ Ⓔ	54 Ⓐ Ⓑ Ⓒ Ⓓ Ⓔ	72 Ⓐ Ⓑ Ⓒ Ⓓ Ⓔ	

Part C—Number Series

1 Ⓐ Ⓑ Ⓒ Ⓓ Ⓔ	6 Ⓐ Ⓑ Ⓒ Ⓓ Ⓔ	11 Ⓐ Ⓑ Ⓒ Ⓓ Ⓔ	16 Ⓐ Ⓑ Ⓒ Ⓓ Ⓔ	21 Ⓐ Ⓑ Ⓒ Ⓓ Ⓔ
2 Ⓐ Ⓑ Ⓒ Ⓓ Ⓔ	7 Ⓐ Ⓑ Ⓒ Ⓓ Ⓔ	12 Ⓐ Ⓑ Ⓒ Ⓓ Ⓔ	17 Ⓐ Ⓑ Ⓒ Ⓓ Ⓔ	22 Ⓐ Ⓑ Ⓒ Ⓓ Ⓔ
3 Ⓐ Ⓑ Ⓒ Ⓓ Ⓔ	8 Ⓐ Ⓑ Ⓒ Ⓓ Ⓔ	13 Ⓐ Ⓑ Ⓒ Ⓓ Ⓔ	18 Ⓐ Ⓑ Ⓒ Ⓓ Ⓔ	23 Ⓐ Ⓑ Ⓒ Ⓓ Ⓔ
4 Ⓐ Ⓑ Ⓒ Ⓓ Ⓔ	9 Ⓐ Ⓑ Ⓒ Ⓓ Ⓔ	14 Ⓐ Ⓑ Ⓒ Ⓓ Ⓔ	19 Ⓐ Ⓑ Ⓒ Ⓓ Ⓔ	24 Ⓐ Ⓑ Ⓒ Ⓓ Ⓔ
5 Ⓐ Ⓑ Ⓒ Ⓓ Ⓔ	10 Ⓐ Ⓑ Ⓒ Ⓓ Ⓔ	15 Ⓐ Ⓑ Ⓒ Ⓓ Ⓔ	20 Ⓐ Ⓑ Ⓒ Ⓓ Ⓔ	

Part D—Following Oral Directions

1 Ⓐ Ⓑ Ⓒ Ⓓ Ⓔ	19 Ⓐ Ⓑ Ⓒ Ⓓ Ⓔ	37 Ⓐ Ⓑ Ⓒ Ⓓ Ⓔ	55 Ⓐ Ⓑ Ⓒ Ⓓ Ⓔ	73 Ⓐ Ⓑ Ⓒ Ⓓ Ⓔ
2 Ⓐ Ⓑ Ⓒ Ⓓ Ⓔ	20 Ⓐ Ⓑ Ⓒ Ⓓ Ⓔ	38 Ⓐ Ⓑ Ⓒ Ⓓ Ⓔ	56 Ⓐ Ⓑ Ⓒ Ⓓ Ⓔ	74 Ⓐ Ⓑ Ⓒ Ⓓ Ⓔ
3 Ⓐ Ⓑ Ⓒ Ⓓ Ⓔ	21 Ⓐ Ⓑ Ⓒ Ⓓ Ⓔ	39 Ⓐ Ⓑ Ⓒ Ⓓ Ⓔ	57 Ⓐ Ⓑ Ⓒ Ⓓ Ⓔ	75 Ⓐ Ⓑ Ⓒ Ⓓ Ⓔ
4 Ⓐ Ⓑ Ⓒ Ⓓ Ⓔ	22 Ⓐ Ⓑ Ⓒ Ⓓ Ⓔ	40 Ⓐ Ⓑ Ⓒ Ⓓ Ⓔ	58 Ⓐ Ⓑ Ⓒ Ⓓ Ⓔ	76 Ⓐ Ⓑ Ⓒ Ⓓ Ⓔ
5 Ⓐ Ⓑ Ⓒ Ⓓ Ⓔ	23 Ⓐ Ⓑ Ⓒ Ⓓ Ⓔ	41 Ⓐ Ⓑ Ⓒ Ⓓ Ⓔ	59 Ⓐ Ⓑ Ⓒ Ⓓ Ⓔ	77 Ⓐ Ⓑ Ⓒ Ⓓ Ⓔ
6 Ⓐ Ⓑ Ⓒ Ⓓ Ⓔ	24 Ⓐ Ⓑ Ⓒ Ⓓ Ⓔ	42 Ⓐ Ⓑ Ⓒ Ⓓ Ⓔ	60 Ⓐ Ⓑ Ⓒ Ⓓ Ⓔ	78 Ⓐ Ⓑ Ⓒ Ⓓ Ⓔ
7 Ⓐ Ⓑ Ⓒ Ⓓ Ⓔ	25 Ⓐ Ⓑ Ⓒ Ⓓ Ⓔ	43 Ⓐ Ⓑ Ⓒ Ⓓ Ⓔ	61 Ⓐ Ⓑ Ⓒ Ⓓ Ⓔ	79 Ⓐ Ⓑ Ⓒ Ⓓ Ⓔ
8 Ⓐ Ⓑ Ⓒ Ⓓ Ⓔ	26 Ⓐ Ⓑ Ⓒ Ⓓ Ⓔ	44 Ⓐ Ⓑ Ⓒ Ⓓ Ⓔ	62 Ⓐ Ⓑ Ⓒ Ⓓ Ⓔ	80 Ⓐ Ⓑ Ⓒ Ⓓ Ⓔ
9 Ⓐ Ⓑ Ⓒ Ⓓ Ⓔ	27 Ⓐ Ⓑ Ⓒ Ⓓ Ⓔ	45 Ⓐ Ⓑ Ⓒ Ⓓ Ⓔ	63 Ⓐ Ⓑ Ⓒ Ⓓ Ⓔ	81 Ⓐ Ⓑ Ⓒ Ⓓ Ⓔ
10 Ⓐ Ⓑ Ⓒ Ⓓ Ⓔ	28 Ⓐ Ⓑ Ⓒ Ⓓ Ⓔ	46 Ⓐ Ⓑ Ⓒ Ⓓ Ⓔ	64 Ⓐ Ⓑ Ⓒ Ⓓ Ⓔ	82 Ⓐ Ⓑ Ⓒ Ⓓ Ⓔ
11 Ⓐ Ⓑ Ⓒ Ⓓ Ⓔ	29 Ⓐ Ⓑ Ⓒ Ⓓ Ⓔ	47 Ⓐ Ⓑ Ⓒ Ⓓ Ⓔ	65 Ⓐ Ⓑ Ⓒ Ⓓ Ⓔ	83 Ⓐ Ⓑ Ⓒ Ⓓ Ⓔ
12 Ⓐ Ⓑ Ⓒ Ⓓ Ⓔ	30 Ⓐ Ⓑ Ⓒ Ⓓ Ⓔ	48 Ⓐ Ⓑ Ⓒ Ⓓ Ⓔ	66 Ⓐ Ⓑ Ⓒ Ⓓ Ⓔ	84 Ⓐ Ⓑ Ⓒ Ⓓ Ⓔ
13 Ⓐ Ⓑ Ⓒ Ⓓ Ⓔ	31 Ⓐ Ⓑ Ⓒ Ⓓ Ⓔ	49 Ⓐ Ⓑ Ⓒ Ⓓ Ⓔ	67 Ⓐ Ⓑ Ⓒ Ⓓ Ⓔ	85 Ⓐ Ⓑ Ⓒ Ⓓ Ⓔ
14 Ⓐ Ⓑ Ⓒ Ⓓ Ⓔ	32 Ⓐ Ⓑ Ⓒ Ⓓ Ⓔ	50 Ⓐ Ⓑ Ⓒ Ⓓ Ⓔ	68 Ⓐ Ⓑ Ⓒ Ⓓ Ⓔ	86 Ⓐ Ⓑ Ⓒ Ⓓ Ⓔ
15 Ⓐ Ⓑ Ⓒ Ⓓ Ⓔ	33 Ⓐ Ⓑ Ⓒ Ⓓ Ⓔ	51 Ⓐ Ⓑ Ⓒ Ⓓ Ⓔ	69 Ⓐ Ⓑ Ⓒ Ⓓ Ⓔ	87 Ⓐ Ⓑ Ⓒ Ⓓ Ⓔ
16 Ⓐ Ⓑ Ⓒ Ⓓ Ⓔ	34 Ⓐ Ⓑ Ⓒ Ⓓ Ⓔ	52 Ⓐ Ⓑ Ⓒ Ⓓ Ⓔ	70 Ⓐ Ⓑ Ⓒ Ⓓ Ⓔ	88 Ⓐ Ⓑ Ⓒ Ⓓ Ⓔ
17 Ⓐ Ⓑ Ⓒ Ⓓ Ⓔ	35 Ⓐ Ⓑ Ⓒ Ⓓ Ⓔ	53 Ⓐ Ⓑ Ⓒ Ⓓ Ⓔ	71 Ⓐ Ⓑ Ⓒ Ⓓ Ⓔ	
18 Ⓐ Ⓑ Ⓒ Ⓓ Ⓔ	36 Ⓐ Ⓑ Ⓒ Ⓓ Ⓔ	54 Ⓐ Ⓑ Ⓒ Ⓓ Ⓔ	72 Ⓐ Ⓑ Ⓒ Ⓓ Ⓔ	

Chapter 15

Practice Test 6

PART A — ADDRESS CHECKING
Work — 6 minutes

In this part of the test, you are to decide whether two addresses are alike or different. If the two addresses are *exactly alike* in every way, darken space Ⓐ. If they are *different in any way*, darken space Ⓓ.

Mark your answers on the Answer Sheet on page 393. Tear it out, put today's date on it, and place it next to the questions.

Allow yourself *exactly 6 minutes* to do as many of the 95 questions as you can. If you finish before the time is up, check your answers.

1.	Le Droit Park DC 20370	Le Droit Park DC 20370
2.	Salisbury NC 28146	Salisbury NC 28146
3.	8 Overlook Dr	8 Overlook Dr
4.	7112 Lawton Ct S	7112 Lomgton Ct S
5.	Riverside CA 92507	Riverside PA 92507
6.	104 E Rigby Rd	104 E Rigby Rd
7.	East Blue Hill ME 04629	East Blue Hill ME 04629
8.	8381 Pollock Ln	8831 Pollock Ln
9.	Sample Square FL	Sample Square FL
10.	474 Cherry Hill Pl	474 Cherry Hill Pl
11.	742 McDougall Dr	742 McDougall Rd
12.	8119 Sumpter Ave	8119 Sumpter Ave
13.	443 Breamwood Ln S	443 Brentwood Ln S
14.	West Palm Beach FL 33401	West Palm Beach FL 33401
15.	309 Horace Harding Blvd	309 Horace Harding Blvd
16.	377 S Crichton Dr	377 S Crichson Dr
17.	36 Terry Marie Way	36 Terry Marie Way
18.	2003 N Persall Way	2003 N Persall Way
19.	9413 Tonnelle Path	9513 Tonnelle Path
20.	112 Noble St	112 Moble St
21.	Tuscaloosa AL 35405	Tusacaloosa LA 35405
22.	86 W Norland Trl	86 W Norland Trl
23.	190 E Washington Walk	190 W Washington Walk
24.	Wolbach NE 68882	Welbach NE 68882

25.	5850 Greenpoint Ave	5850 Greenpoint Ave
26.	Paerdegat 7 St	Paerdegat 7 St
27.	4009 Zuni Ct	4009 Suni Ct
28.	9004 Naudain Ct	9004 Naudain Ct
29.	34 S Bertram Plz	34 S Bertram Pl
30.	2804 S Eckford St	2804 S Eckfore St
31.	1819 Dorchester Ct S	1819 Dorchester Pl S
32.	2348 Karen St W	2348 Laren St W
33.	Box 2341 Bridgeport 06601	Box 2341 Bridgeport 60601
34.	861 W Frances Pl	861 W Frances Pl
35.	41 Espejo Ave SW	41 Espejo Ave SW
36.	3702 Irving Pl	3702 Irvin Pl
37.	6119 Rothbury Dr	6119 Rothbury Dr
38.	9245 Vincennes Way S	9254 Vincennes Way S
39.	Easley SC	Eastley SC
40.	2741 Utica Ave S	2741 Utica Ave N
41.	Longmont CO 80537	Longmont CO 80857
42.	1441 S Gardner Ter	1441 N Gardner Ter
43.	7104 Querida St E	7104 Querida St E
44.	Bartlesville OK 74005	Battlesville OK 74005
45.	Reno NV 89509	Reno NV 89509
46.	643 Convey Rd SE	643 Convey Rd NE
47.	802 Trumbull Ave NE	802 Trumbull Ave NE
48.	5593 Ege Ave	5593 Edge Ave
49.	5010 Kimbrough Pkwy S	5030 Kimbrough Pkwy S
50.	Big Stone Gap VA 24219	Big Stone Gap VA 42219
51.	Laconia TN 38045	Laconia TN 38045
52.	64912 Eloy St	64192 Eloy St
53.	1624 Laidlaw Blvd	1624 Laidlow Blvd
54.	575 N Intervale Ave	575 N Intervale Ave
55.	899 W Alexander Ave	899 W Alexandre Ave
56.	3004 E Ishee Way	3004 W Ishee Way
57.	7294 Pembrey Oval	7294 Pembrey Oval
58.	Gainsville GA	Gainsville GA
59.	7135 Roebling Cir	7135 Roabling Cir
60.	1300 Holmes St	1300 Holmes Ct

61.	723 S Verona Dr	723 S Varona Dr
62.	333 Eldert Ln	333 Eldert Ln
63.	4531 Cates Ridge Way	4531 Gates Ridge Way
64.	Liverpool NY	Liverpool NJ
65.	6033 Hallock St SW	6033 Hallock St SW
66.	74 Marsdale Blvd W	74 Marsdale Blvd W
67.	6301 E 119 Rd	6301 E 219 Rd
68.	52 Summerset Rd	52 Summerset Rd
69.	943 Taylor Dr W	943 Taylor Dr W
70.	3800 Greenspring Blvd S	3800 Greensping Blvd S
71.	5062 Wilmont Dr W	5062 Wilmont Rd W
72.	6061 Forrest Street	606 Forrest Street
73.	1311 N 345 Hwy	1311 N 354 Hwy
74.	Cranston RI 02920	Cranston HI 02920
75.	641 Xenon Ct NW	641 Xenon Ct SW
76.	12 Ascot Hill Ln	12 Ascot Hill Ln
77.	Lumberton MI 39455	Lumberton MI 93455
78.	157 Uvalda St	157 Uvalda St
79.	88 S Sampson St	88 S Sampson St
80.	2402 Washburn Ave	2402 Wishburn Ave
81.	52 Oman Pl S	52 Oman Pl S
82.	2320 Fraser St SE	2320 Fraser St SE
83.	4600 Wazee St SE	4600 Wazea St SE
84.	3751 Worchaster Blvd	3751 Rochester Blvd
85.	4740 Gatlink Pl	4740 Gatlink Pl
86.	81 E Lindley Ct	81 E Lindsey Ct
87.	Grosse Pointe MI 48357	Grosse Pointe MI 48357
88.	1212 Rio Vista Ter	1212 Rio Vista Ter
89.	8798 W 292 Pkwy	8798 W 293 Pkwy
90.	9113 E Fishers Aly	9113 E Fishers Aly
91.	2420 Luquer St	2420 Laquer St
92.	New Pine Creek OR 97635	New Pine Creek OR 07635
93.	403 Turnstone Dr	403 Turnstein Dr
94.	313 Jordan Pl W	313 Jorgan Pl W
95.	289 Inwood Plz	289 Inwood Plz

STOP.
If you finish before the time is up, go back and check
the questions in this section of the test only.

PART B — MEMORY FOR ADDRESSES

In this part of the test, you will have five boxes labeled A, B, C, D, and E. Each box contains five addresses. Three of the five are street addresses, such as 6100–6799 Otto, 4900–6099 Trail, and 2000–3799 Beach. Two are names of places such as Lennon and Webster. The addresses are different in each box.

There will be several opportunities to study the addresses and the boxes they are in. You will also be given three tests of 88 questions each, and the task of deciding where each address belongs. In some cases, you will have the list *and* the boxes in front of you at the same time; in others you will not. List 1 and List 2 are for warm-up practice. List 3 is the real one that will be scored.

Make sure you understand the format by examining the pretest samples below.

Pretest Samples

A	B	C	D	E
6100–6799 Otto	2000–3799 Otto	1400–1999 Otto	4900–6099 Otto	3800–4899 Otto
Mallet	Ashley	Skelton	Thatcher	Easter
1400–1999 Trail	6100–6799 Trail	4900–6099 Trail	3800–4899 Trail	2000–3799 Trail
Park	Lennon	Oliver	Driggs	Webster
3700–4899 Beach	1400–1999 Beach	6100–6799 Beach	2000–3799 Beach	4900–6099 Beach

Questions 1 through 7 show the way the questions look. You have to decide in which lettered box (A, B, C, D, or E) the address belongs and then mark your answer by darkening the appropriate space in the answer grid.

1. 1400–1999 Trail   1 Ⓐ Ⓑ Ⓒ Ⓓ Ⓔ
2. Ashley   2 Ⓐ Ⓑ Ⓒ Ⓓ Ⓔ
3. 6100–6799 Otto   3 Ⓐ Ⓑ Ⓒ Ⓓ Ⓔ
4. 3800–4899 Otto   4 Ⓐ Ⓑ Ⓒ Ⓓ Ⓔ
5. Lennon   5 Ⓐ Ⓑ Ⓒ Ⓓ Ⓔ
6. 2000–3799 Beach   6 Ⓐ Ⓑ Ⓒ Ⓓ Ⓔ
7. Webster   7 Ⓐ Ⓑ Ⓒ Ⓓ Ⓔ

Answers

1. **A**   2. **B**   3. **A**   4. **E**   5. **B**   6. **D**   7. **E**

Now that you know what to do, you may begin Part B of Practice Test 6. To get the most out of this test, follow the directions and timing *exactly*. Follow each phase of Part B of this test, page by page, until you've completed List 3. It is modeled on the way the Postal Service actually conducts its tests.

Turn to the next page to begin.

Study — 3 minutes

You will be given 3 minutes to spend memorizing the addresses in the boxes. *They are exactly the same ones that will be used for all three tests.* Try to memorize as many as you can. When the 3 minutes are up, turn to page 402 and read the instructions for *List 1*.

A	B	C	D	E
6100–6799 Otto	2000–3799 Otto	1400–1999 Otto	4900–6099 Otto	3800–4899 Otto
Mallet	Ashley	Skelton	Thatcher	Easter
1400–1999 Trail	6100–6799 Trail	4900–6099 Trail	3800–4899 Trail	2000–3799 Trail
Park	Lennon	Oliver	Driggs	Webster
3700–4899 Beach	1400–1999 Beach	6100–6799 Beach	2000–3799 Beach	4900–6099 Beach

List 1

Work — 3 minutes

Tear out the Answer Sheet for List 1. For each question, mark the answer sheet on page 394 to show the letter of the box in which the address belongs. Try to remember the locations of as many addresses as you can. *You will now have 3 minutes to complete List 1.* If you are not sure of an answer, you should guess.

A	B	C	D	E
6100–6799 Otto Mallet 1400–1999 Trail Park 3700–4899 Beach	2000–3799 Otto Ashley 6100–6799 Trail Lennon 1400–1999 Beach	1400–1999 Otto Skelton 4900–6099 Trail Oliver 6100–6799 Beach	4900–6099 Otto Thatcher 3800–4899 Trail Driggs 2000–3799 Beach	3800–4899 Otto Easter 2000–3799 Trail Webster 4900–6099 Beach

1. 1400–1999 Beach
2. 4900–6099 Otto
3. Driggs
4. Mallet
5. 3800–4899 Otto
6. 2000–3799 Beach
7. Lennon
8. 2000–3799 Otto
9. Ashley
10. 4900–6099 Beach
11. 6100–6799 Otto

12. Driggs
13. 6100–6799 Trail
14. Driggs
15. 1400–1999 Trail
16. Thatcher
17. Webster
18. Easter
19. 2000–3799 Trail
20. 6100–6799 Trail
21. Park

23. 1400–1999 Otto
24. 3800–4899 Trail
25. Ashley
26. 3700–4899 Beach
27. Oliver
28. 4900–6099 Trail
29. Ashley
30. 4900–6099 Otto
31. Webster
32. 3700–4899 Beach
33. 3800–4899 Trail

34. Skelton
35. 6100–6799 Beach
36. Webster
37. 3800–4899 Otto
38. Mallet
39. 4900–6099 Trail
40. 2000–3799 Trail
41. 2000–3799 Otto
42. Mallet
43. Oliver

22. Skelton
45. 4900–6099 Otto
46. 2000–3799 Otto
47. Driggs
48. Park
49. Thatcher
50. 1400–1999 Beach
51. Mallet
52. 1400–1999 Trail
53. Easter
54. Lennon
55. Park

56. Mallet
57. 2000–3799 Trail
58. 1400–1999 Trail
59. Easter
60. Skelton
61. Ashley
62. Thatcher
63. Oliver
64. 6100–6799 Otto
65. Ashley
66. 4900–6099 Beach

44. Skelton
67. 2000–3799 Beach
68. 1400–1999 Beach
69. 6100–6799 Otto
70. 6100–6799 Beach
71. Lennon
72. 1400–1999 Otto
73. 4900–6099 Beach
74. 6100–6799 Beach
75. 3800–4899 Trail
76. Webster
77. Skelton

78. Lennon
79. 2000–3799 Beach
80. Park
81. 6100–6799 Trail
82. 1400–1999 Otto
83. 3800–4899 Beach
84. 4900–6099 Trail
85. Thatcher
86. Easter
87. Oliver
88. 3800–4899 Otto

STOP.
If you finish before the time is up, go back and check
the questions in this section of the test only.

List 2

Work — 3 minutes

Do these questions *without* looking back at the boxes. For each question, mark your answer on the Answer Sheet for List 2 on page 394. If you are not sure of an answer, you should guess.

1. 2000–3799 Otto
2. 4900–6099 Otto
3. Skelton
4. Oliver
5. Mallet
6. 2000–3799 Otto
7. 2000–3799 Trail
8. 4900–6099 Trail
9. Mallet
10. 3800–4899 Otto
11. Webster

12. 6100–6799 Beach
13. Skelton
14. 3800–4899 Trail
15. 3700–4899 Beach
16. Webster
17. 4900–6099 Otto
18. Ashley
19. 4900–6099 Trail
20. Oliver
21. 3700–4899 Beach
22. Ashley

23. 3800–4899 Trail
24. 1400–1999 Otto
25. Skelton
26. Park
27. 6100–6799 Trail
28. 2000–3799 Trail
29. Easter
30. Webster
31. Thatcher
32. 1400–1999 Trail
33. Driggs

34. 6100–6799 Trail
35. Driggs
36. 6100–6799 Otto
37. 4900–6099 Beach
38. Ashley
39. 2000–3799 Otto
40. Lennon
41. 2000–3799 Beach
42. 3800–4899 Otto
43. Mallet
44. Driggs

45. 4900–6099 Otto
46. 1400–1999 Beach
47. 3800–4899 Otto
48. Oliver
49. Easter
50. Thatcher
51. 4900–6099 Trail
52. 3700–4899 Beach
53. 1400–1999 Otto
54. 6100–6799 Trail
55. Park

56. 2000–3799 Beach
57. Lennon
58. Skelton
59. Webster
60. 3800–4899 Trail
61. 6100–6799 Beach
62. 4900–6099 Beach
63. 1400–1999 Otto
64. Lennon
65. 6100–6799 Beach
66. 6100–6799 Otto

67. 1400–1999 Beach
68. 2000–3799 Beach
69. 4900–6099 Beach
70. Ashley
71. 6100–6799 Otto
72. Oliver
73. Thatcher
74. 4900–6099 Otto
75. Skelton
76. Easter
77. 1400–1999 Trail

78. 2000–3799 Trail
79. Mallet
80. Park
81. Lennon
82. Easter
83. 1400–1999 Trail
84. Mallet
85. 1400–1999 Beach
86. Thatcher
87. 2000–3799 Otto
88. Driggs

STOP.
If you finish before the time is up, go back and check the questions in this section of the test only.

List 3

Study — 5 minutes

You are now about to take the test using List 3. *(This is the test that counts!)*

Turn back to page 401 and study the boxes again. *You have 5 minutes to restudy the addresses.*

Work — 5 minutes

For each question, mark the Answer Sheet on page 395 to show the letter of the box in which the address belongs. You have exactly 5 minutes to do the test. During these 5 minutes, *do not* turn to any other page.

1.	3800–4899 Otto	23.	4900–6099 Beach
2.	Oliver	24.	Ashley
3.	Easter	25.	6100–6799 Otto
4.	Thatcher	26.	Oliver
5.	4900–6099 Trail	27.	Thatcher
6.	3700–4899 Beach	28.	Ashley
7.	1400–1999 Otto	29.	Skelton
8.	6100–6799 Trail	30.	Easter
9.	Park	31.	1400–1999 Trail
10.	2000–3799 Beach	32.	2000–3799 Trail
11.	Lennon	33.	Mallet
12.	Skelton	34.	Park
13.	Webster	35.	Lennon
14.	3800–4899 Trail	36.	Easter
15.	6100–6799 Beach	37.	1400–1999 Trail
16.	4900–6099 Beach	38.	Mallet
17.	1400–1999 Otto	39.	1400–1999 Beach
18.	Lennon	40.	Thatcher
19.	6100–6799 Beach	41.	Park
20.	Oliver	42.	Driggs
21.	1400–1999 Beach	43.	2000–3799 Otto
22.	2000–3799 Beach	44.	4900–6099 Otto

45. Skelton
46. Oliver
47. Mallet
48. 2000–3799 Otto
49. 2000–3799 Trail
50. 4900–6099 Trail
51. Mallet
52. 3800–4899 Otto
53. Webster
54. 6100–6799 Beach
55. Skelton

56. 3800–4899 Trail
57. 3700–4899 Beach
58. Webster
59. 4900–6099 Otto
60. Ashley
61. 4900–6099 Trail
62. Oliver
63. 3700–4899 Beach
64. Ashley
65. 3800–4899 Trail
66. 1400–1999 Otto

67. Skelton
68. Park
69. 6100–6799 Trail
70. 2000–3799 Trail
71. Easter
72. Webster
73. Thatcher
74. 1400–1999 Trail
75. Driggs
76. 6100–6799 Trail
77. Driggs

78. 6100–6799 Otto
79. 4900–6099 Beach
80. Ashley
81. 2000–3799 Otto
82. Lennon
83. 2000–3799 Beach
84. 3800–4899 Otto
85. Mallet
86. Driggs
87. 4900–6099 Otto
88. 1400–1999 Beach

STOP.
If you finish before the time is up, go back and check
the questions in this section of the test only.

PART C — NUMBER SERIES

Work — 20 minutes

For each Number Series question, there is a series of numbers that follow some definite order, and below each are five sets of two numbers each. You are to look at the numbers in the series and find out what order they follow. Then decide what the next two numbers in that series would be if the same order were continued. Mark your answers on the Answer Sheet for Number Series on page 395.

You have 20 minutes to complete this part of the test. If you finish before the time is up, check your answers. The answers and explanations are on pages 418 to 419.

1. 16 11 17 12 18 13 19 __ __
    A) 20 14   B) 19 20   C) 15 18   D) 14 20   E) 15 14

2. 90 80 55 70 60 55 50 40 __ __
    A) 30 20   B) 55 30   C) 35 55   D) 35 45   E) 40 55

3. 2 2 2 3 6 6 4 12 __ __
    A) 12 5   B) 12 12   C) 5 12   D) 7 14   E) 20 20

4. 36 37 38 39 38 37 36 __ __
    A) 35 34   B) 36 37   C) 37 38   D) 38 39   E) 35 33

5. 28 18 31 21 34 24 37 __ __
    A) 26 36   B) 27 38   C) 38 25   D) 28 38   E) 27 40

6. 41 36 31 26 21 16 11 __ __
    A) 10 5   B) 11 6   C) 6 5   D) 6 1   E) 7 2

7. 6 38 18 31 30 24 42 __ __
    A) 34 48   B) 30 54   C) 17 54   D) 35 36   E) 52 18

8. $\frac{1}{3}$ $\frac{2}{6}$ $\frac{3}{9}$ $\frac{4}{12}$ $\frac{5}{15}$ $\frac{6}{18}$ $\frac{7}{21}$ __ __
    A) $\frac{8}{22}$ $\frac{9}{23}$ B) $\frac{9}{24}$ $\frac{9}{25}$ C) $\frac{9}{24}$ $\frac{10}{26}$ D) $\frac{6}{23}$ $\frac{7}{23}$ E) $\frac{8}{24}$ $\frac{9}{27}$

9. 11 13 8 15 17 12 19 __ __
    A) 20 21   B) 14 21   C) 13 18   D) 23 11   E) 21 16

10. 18 20 21 21 23 24 24 __ __
    A) 25 27   B) 24 25   C) 28 27   D) 26 27   E) 25 26

11. 1 4 2 8 3 12 4 __ __
    A) 5 13   B) 14 5   C) 16 5   D) 8 20   E) 6 18

12. 5 6 3 12 13 10 40 __ __
    A) 20 50   B) 39 50   C) 11 8   D) 15 60   E) 41 38

13. 15 12 89 15 12 89 15 __ __
    A) 12 89   B) 15 12   C) 89 15   D) 12 15   E) 89 12

14. 11 53 22 42 33 31 44 __ __
    A) 30 22   B) 20 55   C) 32 53   D) 29 40   E) 56 36

15. 20 17 8 9 14 11 8 9 8 __ __
    A) 5 8   B) 9 9   C) 8 9   D) 10 5   E) 12 4

16. 81 27 27 27 9 9 9 __ __
    A) 6 6   B) 3 3   C) 6 3   D) 3 6   E) 3 1

17. 18 14 14 24 12 12 30 __ __
    A) 14 36   B) 16 22   C) 10 10   D) 7 15   E) 5 15

18. 13 21 11 19 9 17 7 __ __
    A) 15 9   B) 18 8   C) 5 19   D) 7 15   E) 15 5

19. 12 3 10 3 8 3 6 __ __
    A) 3 6   B) 4 3   C) 3 3   D) 3 4   E) 2 3

20. 3 4 4 3 3 4 4 __ __
    A) 4 3   B) 5 3   C) 3 3   D) 4 4   E) 3 4

21. 18 26 24 19 18 16 20 __ __
    A) 21 19   B) 12 10   C) 14 8   D) 10 8   E) 18 10

22. 10 14 12 6 10 8 4 __ __
    A) 4 10   B) 6 10   C) 8 6   D) 8 10   E) 4 2

23. 2 11 11 3 12 12 4 __ __
    A) 5 12   B) 13 5   C) 5 13   D) 13 14   E) 13 13

24. 5 6 7 10 8 9 10 9 __ __
    A) 10 11   B) 11 10   C) 9 8   D) 11 12   E) 7 10

STOP.
If you finish before the time is up, go back and check
the questions in this section of the test only.

PART D — FOLLOWING ORAL DIRECTIONS

This part of the test gauges your ability to understand and carry out spoken directions *exactly* as they are given to you.

In order to prepare to take Part D of the test, follow the steps below:

1. Enlist the help of a friend who will be the "reader." It will be his or her job to read aloud a series of directions that you are to follow *exactly*. The reader will need a watch that displays seconds, because the directions must be read at the correct speed.

2. Tear out pages 415 and 416. These are the worksheets you should have in front of you as you listen to the directions given by the reader, who will tell you to do certain things with the items on each line on the worksheets.

3. Use the Answer Sheet for Following Oral Directions on page 395 and insert today's date. You will darken the appropriate spaces in accordance with the directions given by the reader.

4. *Now hand this entire book to the reader.* Ask him/her to review the section below headed "Instructions to the Reader." It explains exactly how the reader is to proceed.

When you and the reader are ready to start this part of Practice Test 1, he/she will begin reading to you the section marked "Directions." YOU ARE NOT TO READ THESE AT ANY TIME BEFORE OR DURING THE TEST. If you do, you will lose the benefit of this part of the practice test.

Instructions to the "Reader"

These instructions should be read at about 80 words per minute. You should practice reading the material in the box until you can do it in exactly 1 minute. The number of words in the passage and the natural pauses described below will give you a good feel for the rate of speed and the way you should read the test questions.

1-MINUTE PRACTICE

> Look at line 20 on your worksheet. There are two circles and two boxes of different sizes with numbers in them. If 7 is less than 3 and if 2 is smaller than 4, write C in the larger circle. Otherwise write B as in *baker* in the smaller box. Now, on your answer sheet, darken the space for the number-letter combination in the box or circle.

You should read the entire test aloud before you read it to the person taking the test, in order to thoroughly acquaint yourself with the procedure and the desired rate of reading.

Read slowly but at a natural pace. In other words, do not space the words so that there are unnaturally long pauses between them. The instruction "Pause slightly" indicates only enough time to take a breath. The other instructions for pauses give the recommended length for each. If possible, use a watch with a second hand.

All the material that follows, except the words in parentheses, is to be read aloud. Now start reading the directions. *Do not repeat any of the directions.*

Directions: In this test, I will read instructions to you.

You are to mark your worksheets according to the instructions that I read to you. After each set of instructions, I'll give you time to record your answers on your answer sheet.

Try to understand the instructions as I read them; I cannot repeat them. Do not ask any questions from now on.

If, when you go to darken a space for a number, you find that you have already darkened another space for that number, either (1) erase the first mark and darken the space for your new choice, or (2) let the first mark stay and do not darken any other space. When you finish, you should have no more than one space darkened for each number.

Turn to Worksheet 1.

Look at the four circles in line 1 on your worksheet. (Pause slightly.) Each circle has a number inside it. If the largest number is in the smallest circle, write the letter C on the line in the largest circle. (Pause slightly.) Otherwise, write A in the smallest circle. (Pause 2 seconds.)

Look at line 1 again. (Pause slightly.) Write the letter B as in *baker* on the line in the third circle. (Pause 2 seconds.) Now, on your answer sheet, darken the spaces for the number-letter combinations that are in the circles you just wrote in. (Pause 10 seconds.)

Look at line 3 on your worksheet. (Pause slightly.) Parcels for Miami and Dade are to be put in box 30. (Pause slightly.) Parcels for the Bronx and Queens are to be put in box 80. (Pause slightly.) Write C in the box in which you put parcels for Queens. Now, on your answer sheet, darken the space for the number-letter combination that is in the box you just wrote in. (Pause 5 seconds.)

Look at the figures in line 3 on your worksheet. (Pause slightly.) Each figure has a number inside it. Write the letter D as in *dog* inside any figure that does not have four sides. (Pause 5 seconds.) Now, on your answer sheet, darken the space for each of the number-letter combinations that are in the figures you just wrote in. (Pause 8 seconds.)

Look at line 4 on your worksheet. (Pause slightly.) Draw a line under the third letter in the line. (Pause 2 seconds.) Now, on your answer sheet, find number 36 and darken the space for the letter under which you drew the line. (Pause 5 seconds.)

Look at the number on line 5 on your worksheet. (Pause slightly.) Draw 2 lines under the last number in the line. (Pause 2 seconds.) Now, on your answer sheet, find the number under which you just drew two lines and darken space A for that number. (Pause 5 seconds.)

Now look at line 6 in your worksheet. (Pause slightly.) In each circle, there is a time when mail is dispatched. In the circle for the latest time, write on the line the last two figures of the time. (Pause 5 seconds.) Now, on your answer sheet, darken the space for the number-letter combination that is in the circle you just wrote in. (Pause 5 seconds.)

Look at the boxes and the words in line 7 on your worksheet. (Pause slightly.) Write the second letter of the third word in the first box. (Pause 2 seconds.) Write the first letter of the second word in the third box. (Pause 2 seconds.) Write the fourth letter of the first word in the second box. (Pause 2 seconds.) Now, on your answer sheet, darken the spaces for the number-letter combinations that are in the three boxes you just wrote in. (Pause 20 seconds.)

Look at line 8 on your worksheet. (Pause slightly.) On the line next to the right-hand letter, write the answer to this question. How many inches are there in a foot? (Pause 2 seconds.) Now, on your answer sheet, darken the space for the number-letter combination you have just written. (Pause 5 seconds.)

Look at line 9 on your worksheet. (Pause slightly.) Draw a line under every "O" in the line. (Pause 5 seconds.) Count the number of lines that you have drawn, subtract 3, and write that number at the end of the line. (Pause 5 seconds.) Now, on your answer sheet, find that number and darken space D as in *dog*. (Pause 6 seconds.)

Now turn to Worksheet 2. (Pause 5 seconds.)

Look at line 10 on your worksheet. (Pause slightly.) There are two circles and two triangles of different sizes with numbers in them. (Pause slightly.) If 9 is more than 6 and 11 is less than 8, write C in the larger circle. (Pause 2 seconds.) Otherwise, write D as *dog* in the smaller triangle.

Look at line 11 on your worksheet. (Pause slightly.) There are two circles and two boxes of different sizes with numbers in them. (Pause slightly.) Subtract 3 from the number in the larger box and change the number in that box to this new number. (Pause 6 seconds.) Then write A next to the number. (Pause slightly.) In the smaller circle, do nothing. In the larger circle, write the letter B as in *baker*. (Pause 2 seconds.) Now, on your answer sheet, darken the spaces for the number-letter combinations that are in the box and circle you just wrote in. (Pause 15 seconds.)

Look at line 12 on your worksheet. (Pause slightly.) Put a circle around the letter that is among the first five letters of the alphabet. (Pause 5 seconds.) Now, on your answer sheet, find the numbers 48 and 71 and for each darken the spaces for the letter around which you put a circle. (Pause 8 seconds.)

Look at line 13 on your worksheet. (Pause slightly.) Draw a line under each number that is more than 36 but less than 46. (Pause 12 seconds.) Now, on your answer sheet, for every number under which you draw a line, darken space D as in *dog*. (Pause 20 seconds.)

Look at the figure on line 14. (Pause slightly.) Each figure is made up of two boxes with a number or a letter in each box. (Pause slightly.) Multiply the number in the upper box in the first figure by the number in the lower box in the middle figure, and write the answer on the line in the upper box of the last figure. (Pause 6 seconds.) Now, on your answer sheet, darken the space for the number-letter combination that is in the box you just wrote in. (Pause 5 seconds.)

Look at line 15 on your worksheet. (Pause slightly.) Each box has a number in it. Write A on the line in any box that doesn't have three digits in it. (Pause 2 seconds.) Now, on your answer sheet, darken the space for the number-letter combination in each box you wrote in. (Pause 8 seconds.)

Look at line 16 on your worksheet. (Pause slightly.) The number in each box represents one particular month of the year. On the line in the box containing the number of the month in which New Year's Day falls, write the letter B as in *baker*. (Pause 2 seconds.) Now, on your answer sheet, darken the space for the number-letter combination that is in the box you just wrote in. (Pause 5 seconds.)

Look at line 16 again. (Pause slightly.) On the line in the box containing the number of the month in which Election Day falls, write the letter C. (Pause 2 seconds.) Now, on your answer sheet, darken the space for the number-letter combination that is in the box you just wrote in. (Pause 5 seconds.)

Now, look at the five circles in line 17 on your worksheet. (Pause slightly.) Write the letter D as in *dog* on the line in the middle circle. (Pause 2 seconds.) Now, on your answer sheet, darken the space for the number-letter combination that is in the circle you just wrote in. (Pause 5 seconds.)

Look at line 18 on your worksheet. (Pause slightly.) Draw a line under the sixth letter on the line. (Pause 2 seconds.) Now, on your answer sheet, find the number 53, and darken the space for the letter under which you drew the line. (Pause 5 seconds.)

Look at line 19 on your worksheet. (Pause slightly.) Count the number of crosses on that line and enter the total on the first blank line on the right. (Pause 5 seconds.) Now, count the number of O's on the line and enter that total on the second blank line. (Pause 2 seconds.) Now, add the two numbers you just wrote and enter the sum total on the third blank line. (Pause 2 seconds.)

Now, find the number on your answer sheet that represents the sum total and darken space E. (Pause 5 seconds.)

END OF EXAMINATION.
If you finish before the time is up, go back and check
the questions in this section of the test only.

Practice Test 6—Worksheet 1
Part D–Following Oral Directions

1.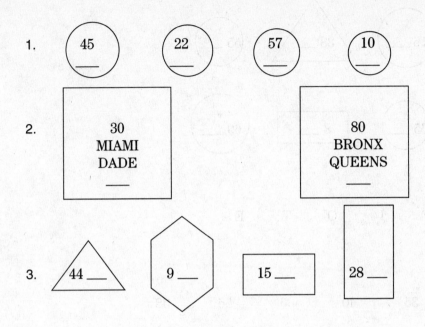
   (45 __) (22 __) (57 __) (10 __)

2.
   | 30 MIAMI DADE __ | | 80 BRONX QUEENS __ |

3. △ 44 __   ⬡ 9 __   ▭ 15 __   ▯ 28 __

4.   B   A   C   E   D

5.   18   11   55   23   72   39   64

6. (12:12 B __) (2:51 A __) (5:13 D __) (4:23 C __) (5:10 E __)

7. | 73 __ | | 84 __ | | 16 __ | HITCH   AUNT   BERRY

8. __ E   __ A

9. O O X X X O X O O X O O __

Practice Test 6—Worksheet 2
Part D—Following Oral Directions

10.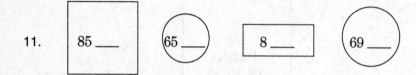

68 ___   16 ___   38 ___   55 ___

11.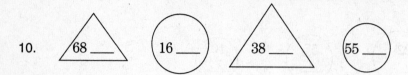

85 ___   65 ___   8 ___   69 ___

12.   R   I   F   L   O   T   E

13.   34   46   35   40   36   56   38

14.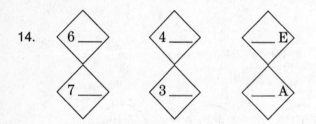

6 ___   4 ___   ___ E

7 ___   3 ___   ___ A

15.   110 ___   654 ___   33 ___   81 ___   398 ___

16.   11 ___   12 ___   1 ___   8 ___   9 ___

17.   47 ___   53 ___   31 ___   17 ___   62 ___

18.   N   A   T   E   R   C   P   W   M

19.   X X O O O O O X X X O X O X X ___   ___   ___

ANSWER KEY

Part A—Address Checking

1. A	11. D	21. D	31. D	41. D	51. A	61. D	71. D	81. A	91. D
2. A	12. A	22. A	32. D	42. D	52. D	62. A	72. D	82. A	92. D
3. A	13. D	23. D	33. D	43. A	53. D	63. D	73. D	83. D	93. D
4. D	14. A	24. D	34. A	44. D	54. A	64. D	74. D	84. D	94. D
5. D	15. A	25. A	35. A	45. A	55. D	65. A	75. D	85. A	95. A
6. A	16. D	26. A	36. D	46. D	56. D	66. A	76. A	86. D	
7. A	17. A	27. D	37. A	47. A	57. A	67. D	77. D	87. A	
8. D	18. A	28. A	38. D	48. D	58. A	68. A	78. D	88. A	
9. A	19. D	29. D	39. D	49. D	59. D	69. A	79. A	89. D	
10. A	20. D	30. D	40. D	50. D	60. D	70. D	80. D	90. A	

Part B—Memory for Addresses

List 1

1. B	10. E	19. E	28. C	37. E	46. B	55. A	64. A	73. E	82. C
2. D	11. A	20. B	29. B	38. A	47. D	56. A	65. B	74. C	83. A
3. D	12. D	21. A	30. D	39. C	48. A	57. E	66. E	75. D	84. C
4. A	13. B	22. C	31. E	40. E	49. D	58. A	67. D	76. E	85. D
5. E	14. D	23. C	32. A	41. B	50. B	59. E	68. B	77. C	86. E
6. D	15. A	24. D	33. D	42. A	51. A	60. C	69. A	78. B	87. C
7. B	16. D	25. B	34. C	43. C	52. A	61. B	70. C	79. D	88. E
8. B	17. E	26. A	35. C	44. C	53. E	62. D	71. B	80. A	
9. B	18. E	27. C	36. E	45. D	54. B	63. C	72. C	81. B	

List 2

1. B	10. E	19. C	28. E	37. E	46. B	55. A	64. B	73. D	82. E
2. D	11. E	20. C	29. E	38. B	47. E	56. D	65. C	74. D	83. A
3. C	12. C	21. A	30. E	39. B	48. C	57. B	66. A	75. C	84. A
4. C	13. C	22. B	31. D	40. B	49. E	58. C	67. B	76. E	85. B
5. A	14. C	23. D	32. A	41. D	50. D	59. E	68. D	77. A	86. D
6. B	15. A	24. C	33. D	42. E	51. C	60. E	69. E	78. E	87. B
7. E	16. E	25. C	34. B	43. A	52. A	61. C	70. B	79. A	88. D
8. C	17. D	26. A	35. D	44. D	53. C	62. E	71. A	80. A	
9. A	18. B	27. B	36. A	45. D	54. B	63. C	72. C	81. B	

List 3

1. E	10. D	19. C	28. B	37. A	46. C	55. C	64. B	73. D	82. B
2. C	11. B	20. C	29. C	38. A	47. A	56. D	65. D	74. A	83. D
3. E	12. C	21. B	30. E	39. B	48. B	57. A	66. C	75. D	84. E
4. D	13. E	22. D	31. A	40. D	49. E	58. E	67. C	76. B	85. A
5. C	14. D	23. E	32. E	41. A	50. C	59. D	68. A	77. D	86. D
6. A	15. C	24. B	33. A	42. D	51. A	60. B	69. B	78. A	87. D
7. C	16. E	25. A	34. A	43. B	52. E	61. C	70. E	79. E	88. B
8. B	17. C	26. C	35. B	44. D	53. E	62. C	71. E	80. B	
9. A	18. B	27. D	36. E	45. C	54. C	63. A	72. E	81. B	

Part C—Number Series

1. **D**	4. **C**	7. **C**	10. **D**	13. **A**	16. **B**	19. **D**	22. **C**
2. **B**	5. **E**	8. **E**	11. **C**	14. **B**	17. **C**	20. **C**	23. **E**
3. **A**	6. **D**	9. **E**	12. **E**	15. **A**	18. **E**	21. **D**	24. **D**

Part D—Following Oral Directions

1. **B**	10. **A**	13. **D**	18. **E**	36. **C**	48. **E**	64. **A**	71. **E**	81. **A**
4. **D**	11. **C**	15. **E**	31. **D**	38. **D**	53. **C**	67. **D**	73. **E**	82. **A**
9. **D**	12. **A**	16. **A**	33. **A**	40. **D**	57. **B**	69. **B**	80. **C**	84. **C**

ANSWER EXPLANATIONS FOR PART C—NUMBER SERIES

1. **D** This series follows a – 5, + 6; and so on rule.
2. **B** The numbers in this series decrease by 10. 55 is inserted after every two numbers of the series.
3. **A** Each group of three numbers, beginning with 2 2 2 may be considered to be a mini-series. Each mini-series begins one number higher than the first number in the preceding series. Each beginning number is multiplied and the result is repeated. The multipliers keep increasing by one. It is a lot easier to see what is happening if you use a loop diagram.

$$
2 \quad \underbrace{2 \quad 2}_{+1} \mid \underbrace{3 \quad 6 \quad 6}_{+1} \mid \underbrace{4 \quad 12 \quad 12}_{+1} \mid 5
$$

X1 r   X2 r   X3 r

4. **C** These numbers follow an ascending-descending pattern, from 36 to 39 and back down again; repeating the same cycle again and again.
5. **E** Here we have a pair of alternating series, each increasing by 3. If you wish, you could consider these numbers as following a – 10, + 13; rule, but the arithmetic can be a little tricky.
6. **D** This series is absolutely simple compared to the series in Examples 4 and 5 above. It merely follows a – 5 rule.
7. **C** Here again is a case of two alternating series. One ascends by + 12. The other descends by – 7.
8. **E** The top number of each fraction keeps increasing by 1. The bottom number increases by 3.
9. **E** One of these two alternating series follows a + 2 rule. The other one, which increases by 4, appears after every two numbers of the first.
10. **D** There is a complex rule that governs these numbers:
   + 2, + 1, repeat; + 2, + 1, repeat; and so on.

11. **C** You can see this series in two ways. First, as a pair of alternating series, one increasing by 1; the other increasing by 4. Or, you could see each pair of numbers as connected by × 4. For example:

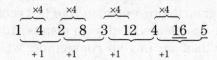

12. **E** A complex rule that includes addition, subtraction, and multiplication is at work here: + 1, – 3, × 4; and so on.
13. **A** A sequence of three unrelated numbers: 15, 12, 89 keeps repeating.
14. **B** These are two alternating series. One follows a + 11 rule; the other a – 11 rule.
15. **A** This series appears confusing. It is a – 3 series that continues for two numbers and is then interrupted by the arbitrary numbers 8 9. This pattern keeps repeating. You have to be extremely careful in selecting the next two numbers.
16. **B** After a number has been *divided* by 3, the answer repeats three times.
17. **C** Here we have two alternating series. One (starting with 18) increases by 6. The other decreases by 2 and repeats the number.
18. **E** You may consider these numbers either as following a + 8, – 10 pattern, or as two alternating series, each following a – 2 rule.
19. **D** The number 3 appears after every number in this – 2 series.
20. **C** Here we have the numbers 3 and 4 continually reversing their order. You might also see a pattern that consists of the sequence 3 4 4 3 continually recycling.
21. **D** There are two alternating series here. The loop diagram shown makes this very difficult question easy to answer.

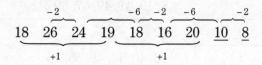

22. **C** The complex rule: = 4, – 2, ÷ 2 connects members of this series. Here, too, a loop diagram is most important.
23. **E** Both alternating series follow a + 1 rule. One series repeats each number before being interrupted by a member of the other series.
24. **D** One of the two alternating series in this group of numbers increases by 1. It continues for *three* numbers and is then interrupted by *one* member of a descending series that follows a – 1 rule.

■ EVALUATING YOUR PROGRESS

Throughout this book, the importance of evaluating and recording your progress has been stressed, as you study and practice for the Test Battery 460/470. At this point, if you have completed Practice Tests 1 through 5 and have made all the entries on your Personal Progress Record, you are quite familiar with the discussion on Computing Your Score, Guidelines, and the Personal Progress Record. If you wish to review the details of these subjects, refer to pages 58 through 68 or pages 326 through 332.

You have probably seen great improvement in your test scores as indicated on your Personal Progress Record. Are you pleased with your results? You can be certain that you are in a far, far better position than any of your competitors who have not prepared for this test. Good luck!

▄ DIAGNOSTIC CHARTS

The following charts will help pinpoint your weaknesses by making it easy for you to determine what particular type of question in each part of the test is most difficult for you.

Part A—Address Checking

Type of Difference	"D" Questions	Number of "D" Questions Wrong		
		Trial 1	Trial 2	Trial 3
Numbers: transposed	33, 38, 50, 52, 73, 77			
changed	8, 19, 41, 49, 67, 89, 92			
omitted	72			
Directions	23, 40, 44, 46, 56, 75			

Abbreviations:
    streets, roads,
        avenues, etc.
	11, 29, 31, 60, 71			

states	5, 21, 64, 74			
Spelling: single letters	16, 20, 24, 27, 30, 32, 36, 39, 48, 53, 55, 59, 60, 61, 63, 70, 78, 80, 83, 86, 91, 94			
groups of letters	4, 13, 44, 84, 93			
Total Number of All Types	56			
	Use the columns on the right to enter the question numbers of "A" items you marked "D."			

This chart will help you to pinpoint the kinds of errors you made on Practice Test 6. Use it as directed below after you have taken and marked the test.

The first column on the left, "Type of Difference," contains the categories whereby addresses may differ (see page 69). On the same line across, the second column gives the numbers of the questions that fall within each category. In the third column, you are to enter the numbers of any "A" questions you answered as "D." Do not include questions that you did not do. Checking the addresses you got wrong may reveal a problem on which you will want to work.

After you have made all the entries, you will be able to see the areas in which you need to improve. Then turn to the appropriate parts of Chapter 4: Address Checking—How to Improve Your Score, read them, and practice the drills that can help. For example, if you find you have been making too many errors picking out number differences, read page 94 and do Drills 18 through 21. If you have a problem with single letters because of reversals like *b* and *d*, or if you have been overlooking the differences between *a*, *e*, and *o*, read page 91. Examine the table and work on Drills 10 and 11 if the problem persists.

Remember that this chart is designed for diagnostic purposes and guidance on further practice. It has been drawn so that you can enter the results each time you retake a practice test. In this way you will be able to see how you are progressing. It is not necessary to record your scores here. That is best done by using the Personal Progress Record Card.

Part B—Memory for Addresses

Kind of Address		Number of Questions	Number Wrong		
			Trial 1	Trial 2	Trial 3
Direct:					
	List 1	43			
	List 2	41			
	List 3	44			
Numbered:					
	List 1	45			
	List 2	47			
	List 3	44			

The purpose of this chart is to help you evaluate your performance on the two kinds of memory questions that appear in these memory tests—the questions on the direct (name) addresses and the questions on the numbered addresses. Use the chart as directed below after you have taken and marked the entire test.

The first column on the left, "Kind of Address," is divided by category into "Direct Address" versus "Numbered Address." The second column gives the number of questions in each category on List 1, List 2, and List 3. Use the third column to enter the total number of questions in each category that you answered incorrectly. There is room for you to make additional entries if you take the practice tests more than once.

At a glance, you will be able to see which area you need to concentrate on and how well you are progressing as you take repeat trials. Use Chapter 5 and the drills in it to improve your memory for the direct addresses. Use Chapter 6 for the numbered addresses.

Remember to use the Personal Progress Record Card (Memory for Addresses) on page 439 to keep track of your actual scores as you keep studying and practicing.

Part C—Number Series and Part D—Following Oral Directions

Because of the nature of the questions in these tests, Diagnostic Charts are not provided for them. If you find that you made many errors on these tests, study the techniques suggested in Chapters 7 and 8.

APPENDIX

STATE AND TERRITORY ABBREVIATIONS

Look over the list. It is not necessary to memorize it. Rather, practice your speed and accuracy of perception by looking at two or more adjoining abbreviations at a glance. Then, look away and jot down what you saw. Because many of the abbreviations begin with the same letter, you will be getting good practice in avoiding confusion should they appear on the test.

State	Abbreviation	State	Abbreviation
Alabama	AL	Nebraska	NE
Alaska	AK	Nevada	NV
Arizona	AZ	New Hampshire	NH
Arkansas	AR	New Jersey	NJ
American Samoa	AS	New Mexico	NM
California	CA	New York	NY
Colorado	CO	North Carolina	NC
Connecticut	CT	North Dakota	ND
Delaware	DE	Northern Mariana Islands	CM
District of Columbia	DC	Ohio	OH
Florida	FL	Oklahoma	OK
Georgia	GA	Oregon	OR
Guam	GU	Pennsylvania	PA
Hawaii	HI	Puerto Rico	PR
Idaho	ID	Rhode Island	RI
Illinois	IL	South Carolina	SC
Indiana	IN	South Dakota	SD
Iowa	IA	Tennessee	TN
Kansas	KS	Trust Territory	TT
Kentucky	KY	Texas	TX
Louisiana	LA	Utah	UT
Maine	ME	Vermont	VT
Maryland	MD	Virginia	VA
Massachusetts	MA	Virgin Islands	VI
Michigan	MI	Washington	WA
Minnesota	MN	West Virginia	WV
Mississippi	MS	Wisconsin	WI
Missouri	MO	Wyoming	WY
Montana	MT		

THOROUGHFARE ABBREVIATIONS*

Almost every street address appearing in Part A—Address Checking contains one of the kinds of thoroughfares in the following list. It has been included in this book just so that you may recognize these abbreviations more rapidly when taking the test; don't try to memorize them.

Familiarizing yourself with the abbreviations is especially worthwhile because some of them are quite similar. For example, it is easy to confuse "Rd" and "Dr," or "Ter" and "Trl." Many others begin with the same letter (see the "C's") or have the same number of characters (the "A's").

Merely look the abbreviations over from time to time. Practice your speed and accuracy of perception as suggested for States and Territory Abbreviations.

Thoroughfare	Abbreviation	Thoroughfare	Abbreviation
Alley	Aly	Loop	—
Arcade	Arc	Oval	—
Avenue	Ave	Parkway	Pkwy
Boulevard	Blvd	Pass	—
Branch	Br	Path	—
Bypass	Byp	Pike	—
Campus	—	Place	Pl
Causeway	Cswy	Plaza	Plz
Center	Ctr	Point	Pt
Chase	—	Road	Rd
Circle	Cir	Square	Sq
Concourse	—	Street	St
Court	Ct	Terrace	Ter
Crescent	Cres	Trail	Trl
Curve	—	Turnpike	Tpke
Drive	Dr	Viaduct	Via
Expressway	Expwy	Vista	Vis
Extension	Ext	Walk	—
Freeway	Fwy	Way	—
Highway	Hwy	Wharf	—
Lane	Ln		

---

* These abbreviations are approved by the U.S. Postal Service for use in addressing mail. That does not mean they are the only ones you will see on the job. People often invent their own versions, such as "Str" instead of "St." It really doesn't matter on the test as long as you can spot whether the abbreviations are "A" or "D" in any particular address line.

APPLICANT INSTRUCTIONS FOR TEST 470

A copy of the actual Applicant Instructions for Test 470 that was sent to applicants for a recent examination has been reproduced on the following pages. The sample questions that were part of these instructions can be found in Chapter 1 of this book.

TEST 470
APPLICANT INSTRUCTIONS

YOU MUST BRING THE FOLLOWING TO BE ADMITTED:

Completed Sample Answer Sheet,
Admission Card/Notice,
Photo ID and
2 Sharpened No. 2 Pencils

LATECOMERS WILL NOT BE ADMITTED.

UNITED STATES POSTAL SERVICE™

These instructions will prepare you for the exam. Please take time to carefully read ALL of the instructions. THIS IS YOUR RESPONSIBILITY. You should read all of the instructions and complete the required items even if you have taken a Postal exam before. We are providing you with:

1. *A SAMPLE ANSWER SHEET TO FILL OUT AT HOME.* This will enable you to complete the Answer Sheet in the exam room.

2. *WHAT YOU CAN EXPECT DURING THE ACTUAL TEST PART OF THE EXAM SESSION.*

3. *SAMPLE QUESTIONS FOR PRACTICE.* So that you will be familiar with the type of questions on the test, sample questions are included for practice.

4. *HOW THE FOUR PARTS OF THE TEST WILL BE SCORED.*

To fill out the Sample Answer Sheet, you will need:

This booklet,

Sample Answer Sheet,

Your Admission Card/Notice,

No. 2 pencil,

Social Security card,

ZIP Code for current address and

ZIP+4 Code for current address.

In the exam room, you will be given 15 minutes to copy your work from the Sample Answer Sheet to the Answer Sheet. The test will begin soon thereafter. You will not have time in the exam room to become familiar with these instructions.

The Answer Sheet will be given to you in the exam room. It is processed by a high-speed scanner. It is important that you precisely complete the grids on the Sample Answer Sheet. This is so you will know exactly how to fill out the Answer Sheet in the exam room.

You are responsible for correctly completing the Sample Answer Sheet. When you report to take the test, you must bring it with you.

Your Sample Answer Sheet will be checked for accurate and total completion. You may not have time to fix any errors or complete items not filled out before the session starts. Only those who have a properly completed Sample Answer Sheet will be admitted. Those who still have an incomplete Sample Answer Sheet by the time the exam starts will NOT be admitted.

EFFECTIVE SEPTEMBER 1994

*THE FOLLOWING INSTRUCTIONS EXPLAIN
HOW TO FILL OUT EACH GRID ON THE SAMPLE
ANSWER SHEET.*

Examples of correct and incorrect marks are:

CORRECT
MARKS

INCORRECT
MARKS

● ● ● ●   ∅ ⊗ ⊖ ⊜

1 NAME. Use your full, legal name when completing
this grid. Use the same name every time you take a
postal exam. Use of a nickname could result in a delay
in processing the result.

GRID 1 is divided into three parts: **Last Name, First
Name** and **MI** (Middle Initial). Each part is
surrounded by a border. Each part of your name must
be entered ONLY in the place for that part.

Last Name. Enter your last name one letter to a box.
You must start with the first square box to the left.

If you are a JR, SR, III or IV, this should be included
as a part of your last name. After entering your last
name, skip a box and enter the correct letters.

To help you complete the grids correctly, you will use
the EDGE of the Admission Card/Notice or the
envelope as a guide. Place the Admission
Card/Notice or envelope on top of GRID 1 so that the
edge is to the LEFT of the first column. For example,
when the last name is "HALL III":

Last Name

EDGE

(If you are left handed, place the edge to the RIGHT
of the first column.)

For the letter in the box, find the matching circle in
the column below and darken that circle.

Next, move the edge with one hand so that it is

against the next column. Darken the circle with the
other hand for that letter.

Last Name

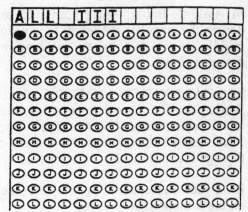

EDGE

Then proceed until you have darkened the circle for
each letter you have entered in a box.

If your name has the letter "O" in it, make sure to
darken the circle that comes after "N". Do not
mistake the letter "Q" for the letter "O".

When you come to a blank box, do nothing.

The following is an example of a completed grid
when the last name is "HALL III":

Last Name

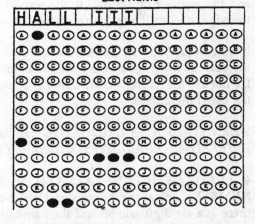

First Name. Enter your first name one letter to a box.
You must start with the first box after the border line.

As you did for Last Name, take the edge and place it
on top of this grid against the first column.

Find the matching circle below and darken that
circle. Next, move the edge so it is against the next
column. Darken the circle for that letter. Then
proceed until you have darkened the circle for each
letter you have entered in a box.

Do not mistake the letter "Q" for the letter "O".

When you come to a blank box, do nothing.

MI (Middle Initial). Enter your middle initial and darken the circle for the letter. **If you do not have a middle initial, do not enter anything in the box or darken a circle.**

2 SOCIAL SECURITY NUMBER. Look at your Social Security card. Compare the number with the one on the Admission Card/Notice. If the number on the Admission Card/Notice is not correct, draw a line through it and make the correction.

Enter your correct Social Security Number in GRID 2 on the Sample Answer Sheet.

Using the edge, darken the matching numerical circles.

3 BIRTH DATE. For GRID 3, in the box labeled "MM", enter the two numbers for your birth month, one number to a box. If you were born in January through September, you would enter a "0" in the first box and the number for the month in the second box. Using the edge, darken the matching circles.

In the box labeled "DD", enter the two numbers for your day of birth, one number to a box. If your day of birth is from one to nine, enter a "0" in the first box and the number for the day in the second box. Using the edge, darken the matching circles.

In the box labeled "YY", enter the last two numbers of the year in which you were born, one number to a box. Do not use the current year. Using the edge, darken the matching circles.

WHEN YOU FINISH GRID 3, YOU SHOULD HAVE ENTERED AND GRIDDED SIX NUMBERS.

4 LEAD OFFICE/INSTALLATION FINANCE NUMBER. Look at the Admission Card/Notice. On it there is a six digit number and the name of the office for which you have applied. With your pencil, enter this number in GRID 4, one number to a box. Using the edge, darken the matching numerical circles.

5 JOB CHOICE. Refer to the Choice Sheet for instructions.

6 TEST SERIES. Do nothing with GRID 6.

7 EXAM DATE. Look at the Admission Card/Notice for the date you are scheduled to take this exam. For GRID 7, in the box labeled "MM", enter the two numbers for the exam month, one number to a box. If the exam is in January through September, you would enter a "0" in the first box and the number for the month in the second box. Using the edge, darken the matching circles.

In the box labeled "DD", enter the two numbers for your day of exam, one number to a box. If your day of exam is from one to nine, enter a "0" in the first box and the number for the day in the second box. Using the edge, darken the matching circles.

In the box labeled "YY", enter the last two numbers of the year of the exam, one number to a box. Using the edge, darken the matching circles.

WHEN YOU FINISH GRID 7, YOU SHOULD HAVE ENTERED AND GRIDDED SIX NUMBERS.

IMPORTANT NOTE. If you are a current career Postal employee OR your Admission Card/Notice is stamped "INSERVICE", DO NOT COMPLETE GRIDS 8, 9, 17, 18 AND 19.

8 YOUR CHOICE OF INSTALLATIONS. Refer to the Choice Sheet for instructions.

9 VETERAN PREFERENCE. If you are not eligible to claim Veteran Preference, do nothing with GRID 9. The following is an explanation of the different types of Veteran Preference:

5 Points (tentative). This preference is usually given to honorably separated veterans who served on active duty in the Armed Forces of the United States under one of the following conditions:

a. During a declared war (the last one was World War II); or

b. During the period April 28, 1952 to July 1, 1955; or

c. During the period February 1, 1955 through October 14, 1976 for which any part of more than 180 consecutive days was served. (An initial period of active duty for training under the 6-month Reserve or National Guard Program does not count.)

d. In any campaign or expedition for which a campaign badge was authorized.

Veterans who served in Southwest Asia or in the surrounding contiguous waters or air space on or after August 2, 1990 AND who were awarded the Southwest Asia Service Medal can claim five points.

10 Points - Compensable (Less than 30%). This preference is given to honorably separated veterans who served on active duty in the Armed Forces at any time and have a service-connected disability for which compensation is provided at 10% or more, but less than 30%.

10 Points - Compensable (30% or more). This preference is given to honorably separated veterans who served on active duty in the Armed Forces at any time and have a service-connected disability for which compensation is provided at 30% or more.

10 Points (other). This preference is claimed by a variety of people:

a. Veterans who were awarded the Purple Heart; or

b. Veterans who have a recognized service connected disability for which no compensation is received; or

c. Until remarried, the widow or widower of an honorably separated veteran, provided the deceased veteran served in active duty during a war, or the veteran died while in the Armed Forces; or

d. Spouses of certain veterans with a service-connected disability; or

e. Mothers of certain deceased or disabled veterans.

Darken only one circle in GRID 9 if you wish to claim Veteran Preference. Do not darken more than one circle. Points claimed will be added to your score ONLY if you pass the exam with a score of 70 or better.

10 EXAM TYPE. In GRID 10, for:

Entrance, darken this circle if you applied for this exam in response to a public announcement or are taking the test for other reasons (see 11 below). Current career Postal employees do NOT darken this circle.

Inservice, darken this circle if you are a current career Postal employee. Also, darken this circle if you are taking this exam on a noncompetitive basis -- your Admission Card/Notice will be stamped "INSERVICE."

11 SPECIAL INSTRUCTIONS. If you do not have "DELAYED" or "REOPENED" stamped on your Admission Card/Notice, do nothing with GRID 11. This grid is only for people who are taking this exam because they either:

a. missed an opportunity to take the exam when last opened to the public because they were on active military duty, "DELAYED" status OR

b. entitled to 10 point Veteran Preference, "REOPENED" status.

Grid the circle labeled "3" for "DELAYED", or the circle labeled "4" for "REOPENED."

12 LEAD OFFICE (Name). Look at the right side of the Admission Card/Notice for the name of the installation for which you are applying. Print the name in the block labeled: "Lead Office/Installation (Please Print)". Print the two-letter abbreviation for the state in the block labeled "State."

Sign your name in the block labeled "Signature."

13 PRINT YOUR CITY AND STATE. Turn to Page 2 of the Sample Answer Sheet. Print the city and state of your current mailing address.

14 STREET ADDRESS. This is for the one line address that will be used to deliver your test result. If you pass and later your score is reached for consideration, the address you grid will be used to notify you. The address you grid must meet Postal standards. Study the following examples:

1234 MAIN ST APT 999

45678 MADISON BLVD S

33 1/2 IVY DR SW

4329-02 MONTGOMERY PL

2342 NW SMITH RD

RR 2 BOX 50

PO BOX 4502

You must use the correct shortened format for your one line address. Also, such an address will be easier and quicker to grid.

This grid is different from the other ones because it contains numbers, special symbols and letters. Enter your one line address in the boxes. You must start with the first box to the left. Skip a blank box where there needs to be a space. By using the edge and starting with the first column to the left, darken the circles.

Do not mistake the letter "Q" for the letter "O".

When you come to a blank box, do nothing.

15 ZIP (Code). You must have your correct ZIP Code to complete this grid. An incorrect ZIP Code will result in a delay in sending your rating to you. Your ZIP Code is found on magazines, utility bills and other business mail you receive at home. Enter your correct five digit ZIP Code in the boxes. Then use the edge to darken the matching numerical circles.

16 +4 (Code). You must have your correct ZIP+4 Code to complete this grid. Your ZIP+4 is usually found on mail you receive at home. This four digit number appears after the five digit ZIP Code. Enter this number in GRID 16. Use the edge and darken the numerical circles.

FOR GRIDS 17, 18 AND 19, read the General Instructions for the RESEARCH QUESTIONNAIRE on Page 2 of the Sample Answer Sheet.

17 SEX. Darken the appropriate circle in GRID 17.

18 DISABILITY CODE. If you do not have a disability, enter 0 in the first box and 5 in the second box in GRID 18. Code "05" indicates "No Disability." Using the edge, darken the numerical circles.

A disability refers to a physical or mental disability or history of such disability which is likely to cause difficulty in obtaining, maintaining, or advancing in employment. On Page 4, you will find a list of various disabilities. Each of the disabilities has a number. If you have a disability, read the list carefully and select the code that best describes your disability. If you have multiple disabilities, choose the code for the one that is most disabling. Enter the two numbers of the disability code in the boxes at the top of GRID 18. If your disability is not listed, enter zero in the first column and six in the second column. Using the edge, darken the numerical circles.

19 RACIAL AND NATIONAL ORIGIN. This grid is for the collection of your racial and national origin. Darken the circle for the category that applies to you. If you are of mixed racial and/or national origin, you should identify yourself by the one category for which you most closely associate yourself by darkening the appropriate circle in GRID 19.

Checking your work. After you have finished, go back and check your work. For a letter or number in a box, you should have only one circle darkened in the column found directly below. Make sure that you have completed all items as requested.

After checking your work, go back to Page 1 of the Sample Answer Sheet. In the upper left corner is the United States Postal Service eagle. Draw a circle around the eagle.

Get someone else to check your work. Since the scanner that reads the Answer Sheet only picks up what is gridded, you should have someone else check your work. Let them tell you if you made a mistake so that you can correct it. This will help make sure that you do the best job you possibly can on the Answer Sheet in the exam room.

TEST INSTRUCTIONS

During the test session, it will be your responsibility to pay close attention to what the examiner has to say and to follow all instructions. One of the purposes of the test is to see how quickly and accurately you can work. Therefore, each part of the test will be carefully timed. You will not START until being told to do so. Also, when you are told to STOP, you must immediately STOP answering the questions. When you are told to work on a particular part of the examination, regardless of which part, you are to work on that part ONLY. If you finish a part before time is called, you may review your answers for that part, but you will not go on or back to any other part. Failure to follow ANY directions given to you by the examiner may be grounds for disqualification. Instructions read by the examiner are intended to ensure that each applicant has the same fair and objective opportunity to compete in the examination.

SAMPLE QUESTIONS*

Study carefully before the examination.

The following questions are like the ones that will be on the test. Study these carefully. This will give you practice with the different kinds of questions and show you how to mark your answers.

*These have been reproduced in Chapter 1.

INSTRUCTIONS FOR COMPLETING PS FORM 2591, APPLICATION FOR EMPLOYMENT

Please read all the information on this page thoroughly. An incomplete application could have an adverse effect on your employment consideration. Bring the enclosed information including the completed application to the interview.

If your name has changed, please submit a copy of your legal paperwork, marriage license, or divorce papers.

Section A

Items 1 through 11 are self-explanatory.

Section B

ITEM 2 If you are a high school graduate, enter the graduation date. If you possess a high school equivalency diploma, enter the date you received it. If you did not graduate, enter the highest grade completed.

ITEM 5 List any additional training, for example, trade or vocational schools.

Section C

Start with your present employment/unemployment and recall back. Account for all periods in separate blocks. Go back as far as ten years or to your sixteenth birthday, whichever is later. Please given reasons for leaving, i.e., Resignation/Termination. List complete addresses, including zip code.

Section D

If you are claiming veteran preference, please submit a copy of your DD 214.

Sections E and F

These questions are self-explanatory and must be answered. If additional space is needed for your responses, please use the space provided in Section F.

Section G

Read, sign, and date.

Application for Employment
The US Postal Service is an Equal Opportunity Employer
(Shaded Areas for Postal Service Use Only)

Rated Application			Veteran preference has been verified through proof that the separation was under honorable conditions, and other proof as required. *(See Section D below.)*	Check One:
Rated For	**Rating**	**Date Rcvd.**		☐ 10 pts. CPS
		Time Rcvd.	**Type of Proof Submitted & Date Issued**	☐ 10 pts. CP
Signature & Date			**Verifier's Signature, Title & Date**	☐ 10 pts. XP
				☐ 5 pts. TP

A. General Information

1. Name *(First, MI, Last)*

2. Social Security No. (SSN)

3. Home Telephone ( )

4. Mailing Address *(No., Street, City, State, ZIP Code)*

5. Date of Birth

6. Work Telephone ( )

7. Place of Birth *(City & State or City & Country)*

8. Kind of Job Applied for and Postal Facility Name & Location *(City & State)*

9. Will You Accept: Temporary/Casual (Noncareer) Work? ☐ Yes ☐ No

10. When Will You Be Available?

11. Are You Willing to Travel? *(Complete only if you are applying for an executive or professional position.)* ☐ Yes ☐ No

B. Educational History

1. Name and Location *(City & State)* of Last High School Attended

2. Are You a High School Graduate? Answer "Yes" if you expect to graduate within the next 9 months, or you have an official equivalency certificate of graduation.
   ☐ Yes - Month & Year:
   ☐ No - Highest Grade Completed:

3a. Name and Location of College or University *(City, State, and ZIP Code if known. If you expect to graduate within 9 months, give month and year you expect degree.)*	Dates Attended		No. of Credits Completed		Type Degree (BA, etc.)	Year of Degree
	From	To	Semester Hrs.	Quarter Hrs.		

3b. Chief Undergraduate College Subjects	Semester Hrs. Completed	Quarter Hrs. Completed	3c. Chief Graduate College Subjects	Semester Hrs. Completed	Quarter Hrs. Completed

4. Major Field of Study at Highest Level of College Work

5. Other Schools or Training *(For example, trade, vocational, armed forces, or business. Give for each: Name, City, State, and ZIP Code, if known, of school; dates attended; subjects studied; number of classroom hours of instruction per week; certificates; and any other pertinent information.)*

6. Honors, Awards, and Fellowships Received

7. Special Qualifications and Skills *(Licenses; skills with machines, patents or inventions; publications - do not submit copies unless requested; public speaking; memberships in professional or scientific societies; typing or shorthand speed, etc.)*

PS Form **2591**, March 1999 *(Page 1 of 4)*

Name *(First, MI, Last)*	Social Security No.	Date

C. Work History

(Start with your present position and go back for 10 years or to your 16th birthday, whichever is later. You may include volunteer work. Account for periods of unemployment in separate blocks in order. Include military service. Use blank sheets if you need more space. Include your name, SSN, and date on each sheet.)

May the US Postal Service ask your present employer about your character, qualifications, and employment record? A "No" will not affect your consideration for employment opportunities.

☐ Yes   ☐ No

1.

Dates of Employment *(Month & Year)* From To **Present**	Grade If Postal, Federal Service or Military	Starting Salary/Earnings $ per
Exact Position Title Average Hours per Week	Number and Kind of Employees Supervised	Present Salary/Earnings $ per
Name of Employer and Complete Mailing Address	Kind of Business *(Manufacturing, etc.)*	Place of Employment *(City & State)*
	Name of Supervisor	Telephone No. *(If known)* ( )

Reason for Wanting to Leave

Description of Duties, Responsibilities, and Accomplishments

2.

Dates of Employment *(Month & Year)* From To	Grade If Postal, Federal Service or Military	Starting Salary/Earnings $ per
Exact Position Title Average Hours per Week	Number and Kind of Employees Supervised	Present Salary/Earnings $ per
Name of Employer and Complete Mailing Address	Kind of Business *(Manufacturing, etc.)*	Place of Employment *(City & State)*
	Name of Supervisor	Telephone No. *(If known)* ( )

Reason for Leaving

Description of Duties, Responsibilities, and Accomplishments

3.

Dates of Employment *(Month & Year)* From To	Grade If Postal, Federal Service or Military	Starting Salary/Earnings $ per
Exact Position Title Average Hours per Week	Number and Kind of Employees Supervised	Present Salary/Earnings $ per
Name of Employer and Complete Mailing Address	Kind of Business *(Manufacturing, etc.)*	Place of Employment *(City & State)*
	Name of Supervisor	Telephone No. *(If known)* ( )

Reason for Leaving

Description of Duties, Responsibilities, and Accomplishments

Name *(First, MI, Last)*	Social Security No.	Date

4.

Dates of Employment *(Month & Year)* From To	Grade If Postal, Federal Service or Military	Starting Salary/Earnings $ per
Exact Position Title Average Hours per Week	Number and Kind of Employees Supervised	Present Salary/Earnings $ per

Name of Employer and Complete Mailing Address	Kind of Business *(Manufacturing, etc.)*	Place of Employment *(City & State)*
	Name of Supervisor	Telephone No. *(If known)* ( )

Reason for Leaving

Description of Duties, Responsibilities, and Accomplishments

D. Veteran Preference *(Answer all parts. If a part does not apply, answer "No".)*

	Yes	No
1. Have you ever served on active duty in the US military service? *(Exclude tours of active duty for training as a reservist or guardsman.)*		
2. Have you ever been discharged from the armed service under other than honorable conditions? You may omit any such discharge changed to honorable by a Discharge Review Board or similar authority. *(If "Yes," give details in Section F.)*		
3. Do you claim 5-point preference based on active duty in the armed forces? *(If "Yes," you will be required to furnish records to support your claim.)*		
4. Do you claim a 10-point preference? If "Yes," check type of preference claimed and attach Standard Form 15, *Claim for 10-Point Veteran Preference*, together with proof called for in that form.		

☐ Compensable Disability *(Less than 30%)*   ☐ Compensable Disability *(30% or more)*   ☐ Non-Compensable Disability *(includes Receipt of the Purple Heart)*   ☐ Wife/Husband

☐ Widow/Widower   ☐ Mother   ☐ Other:

5. List for All Military Service: *(Enter N/A if not applicable)*

Date (From - To)	Serial/Service Number	Branch of Service	Type of Discharge

---

THE LAW (39 U.S. CODE 1002) PROHIBITS POLITICAL AND CERTAIN OTHER RECOMMENDATIONS FOR APPOINTMENTS, PROMOTIONS, ASSIGNMENTS, TRANSFERS, OR DESIGNATIONS OF PERSONS IN THE POSTAL SERVICE. Statements relating solely to character and residence are permitted, but every other kind of statement or recommendation is prohibited unless it either is requested by the Postal Service and consists solely of an evaluation of the work performance, ability, aptitude, and general qualifications of an individual or is requested by a government representative investigating the individual's loyalty, suitability, and character. Anyone who requests or solicits a prohibited statement or recommendation is subject to disqualification from the Postal Service and anyone in the Postal Service who accepts such a statement may be suspended or removed from office.

Privacy Act Statement: The collection of this information is authorized by 39 USC 401 and 1001. This information will be used to determine your qualifications and suitability for USPS employment. As a routine use, the information may be disclosed to an appropriate government agency, domestic or foreign, for law enforcement purposes; where pertinent, in a legal proceeding to which the USPS is a party or has an interest; to a government agency in order to obtain information relevant to a USPS decision concerning employment, security clearances, contracts, licenses, grants, permits or other benefits; to a government agency upon its request when relevant to its decision concerning employment, security clearances, security or suitability investigations, contracts, licenses, grants or other benefits; to a congressional office at your request; to an expert, consultant, or other person under contract with the USPS to fulfill an agency function; to the Federal Records Center for storage; to the Office of Management and Budget for review of private relief legislation; to an independent certified public accountant during an official audit of USPS finances; to an investigator, administrative judge or complaints examiner appointed by the Equal Employment Opportunity Commission for investigation of a formal EEO complaint under 29 CFR 1613; to the Merit Systems Protection Board or Office of Special Counsel for proceedings or investigations involving personnel practices and other matters within their jurisdiction; and to a labor organization as required by the National Labor Relations Act. Completion of this form is voluntary; however, if this information is not provided, you may not receive full consideration for a position.

COMPUTER MATCHING: Limited information may be disclosed to a federal, state, or local government administering benefits or other programs pursuant to statute for the purpose of conducting computer matching programs under the Act. These programs include, but are not limited to, matches performed to verify an individual's initial or continuing eligibility for, indebtedness to, or compliance with requirements of a benefit program.

Name *(First, MI, Last)*	Social Security No.	Date		

E. Other Information

		Yes	**No**
1.	Are you one of the following: a United States citizen, a permanent resident alien, a citizen of American Samoa or any other territory owing allegiance to the United States?		
2.	**RESERVED FOR OFFICIAL USE**		
3.	**RESERVED FOR OFFICIAL USE**		

If you answer "Yes" to question 4 and/or 5, give details in Section F below. Give the name, address (including ZIP Code) of employer, approximate date, and reasons in each case. ▶	4. Have you ever been fired from any job for any reason?		
	5. Have you ever quit a job after being notified that you would be fired?		

6.	Do you receive or have you applied for retirement pay, pension, or other compensation based upon military, postal, or federal civilian service? *(If you answer "Yes," give details in Section F.)*		
7a.	Have you ever been convicted of a crime or are you now under charges for any offense against the Law? You may omit: (1) any charges that were dismissed or resulted in acquittal; (2) any conviction that has been set aside, vacated, annulled, expunged, or sealed; (3) any offense that was finally adjudicated in a juvenile court or juvenile delinquency proceeding; and (4) any charges that resulted only in a conviction of a non-criminal offense. **All felony and misdemeanor convictions and all convictions in state and federal courts are criminal convictions and must be disclosed. Disclosure of such convictions is required even if you did not spend any time in jail and/or were not required to pay a fine.**		
7b.	While in the military service were you ever convicted by special or general court martial? **If you answer "Yes" to question 7a and/or 7b, give details in Section F. Show for each offense: (1) Date of conviction; (2) Charge convicted of; (3) Court and location; (4) Action taken. Note: A conviction does not automatically mean that you cannot be appointed. What you were convicted of, and how long ago, are important. Give all of the facts so that a decision can be made.**		
8.	Are you a former Postal Service or Federal Employee not now employed by the US Government? If you answer "Yes," give in Section F, name of employing agency(ies), position title(s), and date(s) employed.		
9.	Does the US Postal Service employ any relative of yours by blood or marriage? Postal officials may not appoint any of their relatives or recommend them for appointment in the Postal Service. Any relative who is appointed in violation of this restriction can not be paid. Thus it is necessary to have information about your relatives who are working for the USPS. These include: mother, father, daughter, son, sister, brother, aunt, uncle, first cousin, niece, nephew, wife, husband, mother-in-law, father-in-law, daughter-in-law, son-in-law, sister-in-law, brother-in-law, stepfather, stepmother, stepdaughter, stepson, stepsister, stepbrother, half sister, and half brother. If you answer "Yes" to question 9, give in section F for such relatives: (1) Full name; (2) Present address and ZIP Code; (3) Relationship; (4) Position title; (5) Name and location of postal installation where employed.		
10.	Are you now dependent on or a user of ANY addictive or hallucinogenic drug, including amphetamines, barbiturates, heroin, morphine, cocaine, mescaline, LSD, STP, hashish, marijuana, or methadone, other than for medical treatment under the supervision of a doctor?		

F. Use This Space for Detailed Answers *(Use blank sheets if you need more space. Include your name. SSN. and date on each sheet.)*

G. Certification

	Enter number of additional sheets you have attached as part of this application:	
I certify that all of the statements made in this application are true, complete, and correct to the best of my knowledge and belief and are in good faith.	Signature of Applicant	Date Signed

Disclosure by you of your Social Security Number (SSN) is mandatory to obtain the services, benefits, or processes that you are seeking. Solicitation of the SSN by the USPS is authorized under provisions of Executive Order 9397, dated November 22, 1943. The information gathered through the use of the number will be used only as necessary in authorized personnel administration processes.

A false or dishonest answer to any question in this application may be grounds for not employing you or for dismissing you after you begin work, and may be punishable by fine or imprisonment. (US Code, Title 18, Sec. 1001). All information you give will be considered in reviewing your application and is subject to investigation.

PS Form **2591**, March 1999 *(Page 4 of 4)*

PERSONAL PROGRESS RECORD

Part A

ADDRESS CHECKING									
Initial Tests						**Repeated Tests**			
Date	Test	Number Completed	Number Correct	− Number Wrong	= Score	Date	Score	Date	Score
Diagnostic Practice Test				−	=				
	Practice Test 1			−	=				
	Practice Test 2			−	=				
	Practice Test 3			−	=				
	Practice Test 4			−	=				
	Practice Test 5			−	=				
	Practice Test 6			−	=				

Part B

MEMORY FOR ADDRESSES										
Initial Tests							**Repeated Tests**			
Date	Test	Number Completed	Number Correct A	Number Wrong	$\times \frac{1}{4} =$	Points off B	Score $(A - B)$	Date	Score	Date	Score
Diagnostic Practice Test					$\times \frac{1}{4} =$					
	Practice Test 1				$\times \frac{1}{4} =$					
	Practice Test 2				$\times \frac{1}{4} =$					
	Practice Test 3				$\times \frac{1}{4} =$					
	Practice Test 4				$\times \frac{1}{4} =$					
	Practice Test 5				$\times \frac{1}{4} =$					
	Practice Test 6				$\times \frac{1}{4} =$					

Part C

				NUMBER SERIES				
	Initial Tests				Repeated Tests			
Date	Test	Number Completed	Number Correct (Your Score)		Date	Score	Date	Score
	Diagnostic Practice Test							
	Practice Test 1							
	Practice Test 2							
	Practice Test 3							
	Practice Test 4							
	Practice Test 5							
	Practice Test 6							

Part D

				FOLLOWING ORAL DIRECTIONS				
	Initial Tests				Repeated Tests			
Date	Test	Number Completed	Number Correct (Your Score)		Date	Score	Date	Score
	Diagnostic Practice Test							
	Practice Test 1							
	Practice Test 2							
	Practice Test 3							
	Practice Test 4							
	Practice Test 5							
	Practice Test 6							

■ DRILL RECORD CHARTS*

Keeping a record of your drill scores is important. Below are guidelines, with examples, to help you enter and interpret your drill scores. Each example is also shown on the actual Drill Record Chart.

		ADDRESS CHECKING										
		Initial Drills							**Repeated Drills**			
Date	Drill Number	Number Done	Number Correct	Number Incorrect	Raw Score	Time Taken	Calcu-lation	Final Score	Date	Score	Date	Score
	SAMPLE	—	80	—	—	—	—	80				
	Drill 1											
	Drill 2											
	Drill 3											
	Drill 4											
	Drill 5											
	Drill 6											
	Drill 7											
	Drill 8											
	▼Drill 9											
	SAMPLE	No entries needed										
	Drill 10											
	Drill 11											
	▼Drill 12											
	SAMPLE	10	8	—	—	30 sec.	$8 \times \frac{60}{30} = 16$					
	Drill 13											
	Drill 14											
	Drill 15											
	Drill 16											
	Drill 17											
	Drill 18											
	Drill 19											
	Drill 20											
	▼Drill 21											
	SAMPLE	No entries needed										
	Drill 22											
	▼Drill 23											

---

* NOTE: If you do not wish to go through the arithmetic, you can get an approximate, but useful, idea of your progress as follows: Merely check the Drill Record Charts to see how many answers you finally get correct (Raw Score) against "Time Taken." If the number of correct answers increases (or even if it stays the same) while the time taken decreases, you know that you are making progress.

ADDRESS CHECKING

		Initial Drills							Repeated Drills			
Date	Drill Number	Number Done	Number Correct	Number Incorrect	Raw Score	Time Taken	Calcu-lation	Final Score	Date	Score	Date	Score
	SAMPLE	20	18	2	16	80 sec.	$16 \times \frac{60}{80} = 12$					
	Drill 24											
	Drill 25											
	Drill 26											
	Drill 27											
	Drill 28											
	Drill 29											
	Drill 30											
	Drill 31											

MEMORY FOR *DIRECT* ADDRESSES

		Initial Drills							Repeated Drills			
Date	Drill Number	Number Done	Number Correct	Number Incorrect	Raw Score	Time Taken	Calcu-lation	Final Score	Date	Score	Date	Score
	SAMPLE	No entries needed										
	Drill 1											
	Drill 2											
	Drill 3											
	Drill 4											
	Drill 5											
	Drill 6											
	SAMPLE	40	28	12			$28 - \frac{1}{4}(12) = 25$					
	Drill 7											
	Drill 8											
	Drill 9											
	Drill 10											
	Drill 11											

MEMORY FOR *DIRECT* ADDRESSES

		Initial Drills							Repeated Drills			
Date	Drill Number	Number Done	Number Correct	Number Incorrect	Raw Score	Time Taken	Calcu-lation	Final Score	Date	Score	Date	Score
	Drill 12											
	Drill 13											
	Drill 14											
	Drill 15											
	Drill 16											
	Drill 17											
	Drill 18											
	Drill 19											
	Drill 20											
	Drill 21											
	▼Drill 22											

MEMORY FOR *NUMBERED* ADDRESSES

		Initial Drills							Repeated Drills			
Date	Drill Number	Number Done	Number Correct	Number Incorrect	Raw Score	Time Taken	Calcu-lation	Final Score	Date	Score	Date	Score
SAMPLE		No entries needed										
	Drill 1											
	▼Drill 2											
SAMPLE		44	35	9	—	—	$35 - \frac{1}{3} \times 9 = 32$					
	Drill 3											
	Drill 4											
	Drill 5											
	Drill 6											
	Drill 7											
	Drill 8											
	Drill 9											
	Drill 10											
	Drill 11											
	▼Drill 12											

		Initial Drills							Repeated Drills			
									MEMORY FOR *NUMBERED* ADDRESSES			

Date	Drill Number	Number Done	Number Correct	Number Incorrect	Raw Score	Time Taken	Calcu- lation	Final Score	Date	Score	Date	Score
	SAMPLE	44	36	8	—	—	$36 - \frac{1}{4} \times 8 = 34$					
	Drill 13											
	Drill 14											
	Drill 15											
	Drill 16											
	Drill 17											
	Drill 18											
	Drill 19											
	Drill 20											
	Drill 21											
	Drill 22											
	Drill 23											
	Drill 24											
	Drill 25											
	Drill 26											
	Drill 27											

Address Checking

The drills in Chapter 4 are designed to help you develop skills in different categories. Although all of them contribute to your progress and are relevant to how well you do on the address checking part of the exam, do not try to compare the results of one drill to another. That would be like judging a ballplayer's batting average by examining his fielding average. Both skills are important to his overall ability as a ballplayer, but they are, of course, entirely different. Rather, compare your results from one trial of a drill to another trial of the same drill.

Drills 1–9: Pencil Markings. Enter in the column marked Number Correct the number of satisfactory marks you make during 1 minute. Because the timing is constant (1 minute), your Final Score will be the same.

Sample: Assume that you made 80 satisfactory marks in 1 minute on Drill 1. Your score would be 80.

Drills 10–12: No entries are needed.

Drills 13–17: Word Differentiation. The time you need to complete each of these drills will keep decreasing as you build speed. Use the formula below to adjust your score so that it comes out in terms of correct answers per minute. In this way, the scores you make on Drills 13 to 17 can be compared with each other more accurately.

Formula: *Your Final Score*

$$= \text{Number of Correct Answers} \times \frac{60 \text{ (seconds)}}{\text{Time Taken (seconds)}}$$

Sample: On Drill 13, assume you had 8 correct answers in a 30-second trial test.

$$\textit{Your Final Score} = 8 \times \frac{60}{30} = 16$$

Drills 18–21: Number Differentiation. Use the same instructions as for Drills 13 to 17 above.

Drills 22 and 23. No entries are needed.

Drills 24–29: Eye Span. On these drills, you are checking complete addresses, the same as you do on the practice tests. They are rated like Drills 13 to 17 and Drills 18 to 21, but with one additional step:

Step 1: Number Right – Number Wrong = Raw Score

$$\text{Step 2: Raw Score} \times \frac{60 \text{ (seconds)}}{\text{Time Taken (seconds)}} = \text{Final Score}$$

Sample: Assume you had 18 correct answers and 2 wrong ones when you did Drill 24, and that it took you 80 seconds to do it.

Step 1: $18 - 2 = 16$ (Raw Score)

$$\text{Step 2: } 16 \times \frac{60}{80} = 12 \text{ (Final Score)}$$

Drills 30 and 31: Regression. Use the same instructions as for Drills 24 to 29 above.

Memory for Addresses

Although the drills in Chapters 5 and 6 (like the address checking drills) are arranged by category, the results on most of them can be compared to each other.

Direct Name Addresses

Drills 1–6: Association. No entries are needed.

Drills 7–12: Association and Imagery, Loci, Reduction Coding.

Formula: *Your Final Score* = Number Correct – ¼ of the Number Wrong

Sample: Assume you got 28 questions correct and 12 incorrect. Take ¼ of the number incorrect, ¼ (12) = 3, and subtract this from the number correct, 28. The answer is 25.

Drills 13–22: Making Up Stories and Slogans. Use the same scoring method as for Drills 7 through 12, but make sure that only the letters that are placed in the *original* positions shown in the questions are counted as correct.

Numbered Addresses

Drills 1 and 2. No entries are needed.

Drills 3–12: Using Four-Digit Chunks. The ability to remember four-digit chunks is common to all categories of these drills. However, because the number of chunks and other conditions vary, compare your scores only within the *same* category: Drills 3 to 5, Drills 6 to 8, and so on.

    The scoring formula is the same for all Drills 3 to 17. It reflects the fact that you have four choices instead of five. The formula to use is:

Formula: *Your Final Score* = Number Right − ⅓ of the Number Wrong

Sample: Assume that you answered 35 of the 44 questions in Drill 3 correctly.
Your Score = 35 − ⅓ × 9 = 32

Drills 13–27: simulates all five boxes. These drills are designed to be answered using any or all of the memory techniques explained in Chapters 5 and 6, not just chunking. The regular formula for scoring is applied.

Formula: *Your Final Score* = Number Right − ¼ of the Number Wrong

Sample: Assume that you answered 36 of the 44 questions in Drill 23 correctly.
Your Score = 36 − ¼ × 8 = 32

■ FINAL CHECKLISTS

Checklist 1—Directions and Important Vocabulary

The following list includes directions that have appeared frequently on past Examinations, and also directions that may appear on future tests. The directions have been arranged according to type, together with the words that may appear in each. (Words separated by a dash are opposites; a word in parentheses has the same meaning as the one it follows.)

Type of Direction	*Words Used*
1. Position	up—down; above—below; inside—outside; left—right; beginning—end; before—after (following); first—last; right-hand—middle (center)—left-hand; low—high; next to (alongside) (beside) (adjoining); under—over; vertical—horizontal
2. Counting	first, second, third, fourth, fifth, sixth, seventh, eighth, ninth, tenth; few—many; more—less; highest—lowest
3. Shapes	□ ▭ △ ◯ X — square (box); rectangle; triangle; circle; cross; dash; straight—curved; open—closed; thin—thick; figure
4. Size	small; medium; large
5. General comparison	same (identical)—different (opposite)
6. Arithmetic	add, subtract, multiply, divide; remainder (difference); total (sum); odd—even

Miscellaneous words (arranged alphabetically): blank, bracket, change, combination, draw, each, encircle, every, except, figure, indicated (shown), instruction, letter, locate (find), next, nothing, otherwise, package, parentheses, previous, represents, results, sample, space, underline, write. (See also the key words on page 211, Chapter 8.)

Checklist 2—Knowledge of Common Measures

First of all, let us again make it clear that the test on Following Oral Directions does *not* require you to possess any *special* knowledge. Such a requirement would defeat the very purpose of this exam, which is to see how well you can follow orders that *most of us* should be able to understand. The persons preparing this test do not want to confuse the issue by making special knowledge a requirement. Nevertheless, the directions occasionally include a concrete fact you do have to know, for example, the number of feet in a yard or the sequence of months in a year (see the directions for line 18 of the Diagnostic Practice Test).

Even though you will probably know most of the "common knowledge" items that may come up on the test, this section has been prepared to give you some extra insurance for a perfect score. The checklist will allow you to quickly review some measures and other items we use continually in everyday life.

Time

60 seconds = 1 minute
60 minutes = 1 hour
24 hours = 1 day
 A.M. is the period from 12 midnight to 12 noon.
 P.M. is the period from 12 noon to 12 midnight.
 7 days = 1 week
52 weeks = 1 year
12 months = 1 year

Distance	*Dry Weight*	*Liquid Measure*
12 inches = 1 foot	16 ounces = 1 pound	16 ounces = 1 pint
3 feet = 1 yard	2,000 pounds = 1 ton	2 pints = 1 quart
5,280 feet = 1 mile		4 quarts = 1 gallon

Checklist 3—Miscellaneous Facts

Important holidays

New Year's Day—January
Martin Luther King Jr.'s Birthday—January
Lincoln's Birthday—February
Washington's Birthday—February
Presidents' Day—February
Memorial Day—May
Independence Day—July

Labor Day—September
Columbus Day—October
Election Day—November
Veterans' Day—November
Thanksgiving—November
Christmas—December

Facts about the United States

Has 50 states.
Declared independence from England in 1776.
Boundaries: North—Canada
                South—Mexico
                East—Atlantic Ocean
                West—Pacific Ocean